INTERNATIONAL CONFLICT *and* COOPERATION

Current World Political Boundaries

Scale: 1 to 125,000,000

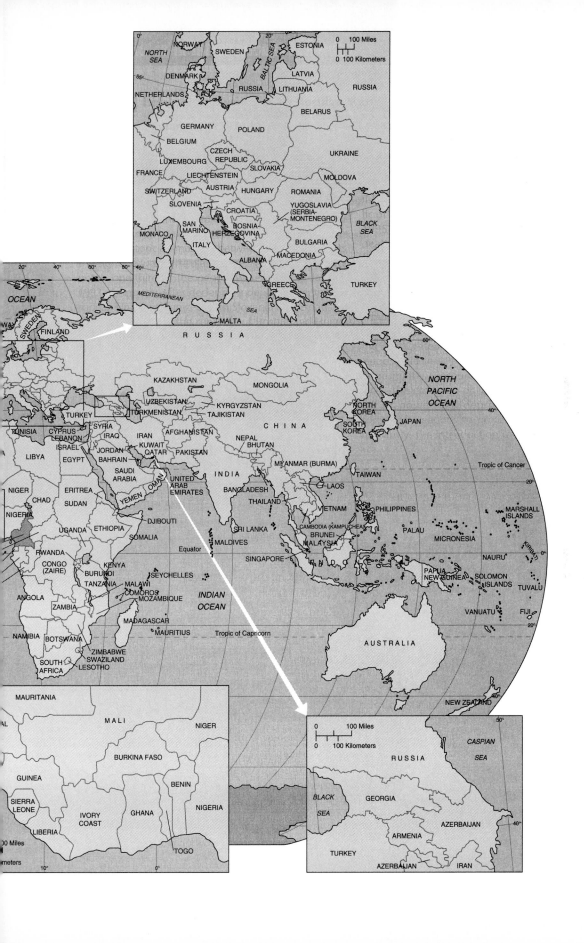

FOR
DONNA

SECOND EDITION

INTERNATIONAL CONFLICT *and* COOPERATION

An Introduction to World Politics

Mark R. Amstutz
Wheaton College

McGraw-Hill College

Boston   Burr Ridge, IL   Dubuque, IA   Madison, WI   New York   San Francisco   St. Louis
Bangkok   Bogotá   Caracas   Lisbon   London   Madrid
Mexico City   Milan   New Delhi   Seoul   Singapore   Sydney   Taipei   Toronto

McGraw-Hill College

A Division of The McGraw·Hill Companies

INTERNATIONAL CONFLICT AND COOPERATION: AN INTRODUCTION TO WORLD POLITICS, SECOND EDITION

This book is printed on acid-free paper.

2 3 4 5 6 7 8 9 0 QPD/QPD 9 3 2 1 0 9

ISBN 0–697–37014–3

Editorial director: *Jane E. Vaicunas*
Sponsoring editor: *Monica Freedman*
Senior marketing manager: *Suzanne Daghlian*
Project manager: *Sheila M. Frank*
Production supervisor: *Deborah Donner*
Freelance design coordinator: *Mary L. Christianson*
Photo research coordinator: *Lori Hancock*
Supplement coordinator: *Stacy A. Patch*
Compositor: *Shepherd, Inc.*
Typeface: *10/12 Garamond Light*
Printer: *Quebecor Printing Book Group/Dubuque, IA*

Freelance designer: *Elise Lansdon*
Cover/interior image by: *PhotoDisc*

The credits section for this book begins on page 499 and is considered an extension of the copyright page.

Library of Congress Cataloging-in Publication Data

Amstutz, Mark R.
    International conflict and cooperation : an introduction to world
politics / Mark R. Amstutz. — 2nd ed.
       p.   cm.
    Includes bibliographical references and index.
     ISBN 0–697–37014–3
     1. International relations. 2. World politics. 3. International
cooperation. 4. Conflict management. I. Title.
JZ1305.A48   1999
327.1'01—dc21   98–20212
                                    CIP

www.mhhe.com

Brief Contents

Contents

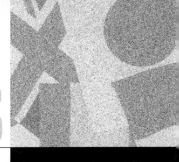

Boxed Features

*The entire chapter is a case study

ABBREVIATIONS

ABM	antiballistic missile
ACDA	U.S. Arms Control and Disarmament Agency
AID	U.S. Agency for International Development
BMD	ballistic missile defense
BWC	Biological Weapons Convention
CBW	chemical and biological weapons
CFC	chlorofluorocarbons
CFE	conventional armed forces in Europe
CIA	Central Intelligence Agency
CIS	Commonwealth of Independent States
CITES	Convention on the International Trade of Endangered Species
COMECON	Council for Mutual Economic Assistance
CSCE	Conference on Security and Cooperation in Europe (Helsinki Act)
CTBT	Comprehensive Test Ban Treaty
CWC	Chemical Weapons Convention
DMZ	demilitarized zone
EC	European Community
ECOSOC	Economic and Social Council (UN)
ECSC	European Coal and Steel Community
EEC	European Economic Community
EEZ	exclusive economic zone
EFTA	European Free Trade Association
EMS	European Monetary System
EMU	Economic and Monetary Union
EU	European Union
FAO	Food and Agriculture Organization
G-7	Group of Seven
G-8	Group of Eight
G-77	Group of Seventy-seven
GATT	General Agreement on Tariffs and Trade
GDP	gross domestic product
GNP	gross national product
HDI	human development index
IAEA	International Atomic Energy Agency
IBRD	International Bank for Reconstruction and Development
ICBM	intercontinental ballistic missile
ICJ	International Court of Justice
IDA	International Development Association
IFC	International Finance Corporation
IFOR	NATO Implementation Force (Bosnia)
IGO	international governmental organization
ILO	International Labor Organization
IMF	International Monetary Fund
INF	intermediate nuclear forces
IPE	international political economy
IR	international relations
ISA	International Seabed Authority
LDC	less developed country

LIC	low-intensity conflict
MAD	mutual assured destruction
MAS	mutual assured security
MBFR	mutual balanced force reductions
MFN	most favored nation
MIRV	multiple independently-targeted reentry vehicle
MNC	multinational corporation
NAFTA	North American Free Trade Agreement
NAM	nonaligned movement
NATO	North Atlantic Treaty Organization
NGO	nongovernmental organization
NIC	newly industrialized country
NIE	national intelligence estimates (CIA)
NIEO	new international economic order
NPT	Nonproliferation Treaty
OAS	Organization of American States
OAU	Organization of African Unity
ODA	official development assistance
OECD	Organization for Economic Cooperation and Development
OPEC	Organization of Petroleum Exporting Countries
PLO	Palestinian Liberation Organization
SALT	strategic arms limitations talks
SDI	strategic defense initiative
SDR	special drawing rights
SEA	Single European Act
SFOR	NATO Stabilization Force
SLBM	submarine-launched ballistic missile
SOP	standard operating procedures
START	strategic arms reduction talks
UN	United Nations
UNCED	United Nations Conference on Environment and Development
UNCLOS	United Nations Conference on the Law of the Sea
UNCTAD	United Nations Conference on Trade and Development
UNDP	United Nations Development Programme
UNEP	United Nations Environment Program
UNESCO	United Nations Educational, Scientific, and Cultural Organization
UNHCR	United Nations High Commission for Refugees
UNICEF	United Nations Children's Fund
UNPROFOR	United Nations Protection Force (Bosnia)
USIA	United States Information Agency
WHO	World Health Organization
WST	world system theory
WTO	World Trade Organization
WTO	Warsaw Treaty Organization

PREFACE

Preface

Knowledge of world politics is increasingly important in the modern world. As countries become more interdependent economically, socially, politically, and technologically, globalization is increasingly affecting interpersonal, intergroup, and interstate relations. While the state remains the dominant political community for most people, the explosion of cross border transactions has greatly increased the effect of foreign developments on domestic affairs and reduced the political, economic, cultural, and social independence of states. As a result of globalization, people are increasingly accepting the truism that "no state is an island."

Goals

This text introduces college students to world politics, a field commonly called international relations (IR). In examining the major elements of the field of IR, the text emphasizes five major aims. First, it *seeks to stimulate interest in foreign affairs*. If students are to develop an understanding of IR, they must have an interest in the foreign policies of states and a concern for the problems and issues of global society. Interest and imagination must precede knowledge. As a result, a major aim of this study is to excite interest in global affairs. One of the ways that the text seeks to accomplish this objective is through case studies, especially those involving significant international conflict. We emphasize political conflict not only because it is an indispensable element of politics, but also because it evokes human interest. To a significant degree, the drama of world politics lies in the expression, management, and resolution of social and political conflict.

Second, the text provides a *comprehensive introduction to the principal elements of international relations*. IR consists of numerous subfields, including theories of IR, comparative foreign policy, foreign policy decision making, international law, international organization, national security policy, and international political economy. Although the text does not examine every IR subfield, it seeks to provide a comprehensive introduction to the major concepts, theories and issues in world politics.

Third, the text presents IR as *a coherent field of knowledge by emphasizing the themes of conflict and cooperation*. Conflict is an inevitable result of all communal life, whether at the local, national, or international levels. In seeking to develop stable communities, political leaders must seek to manage and resolve conflict as well as to foster cooperation. In examining the major dynamics of IR, the text emphasizes processes and institutions that contribute to conflict management and conflict resolution and those that facilitate international cooperation. Thus, the theme of conflict and cooperation are used to present the disparate elements of IR as a coherent field of knowledge.

Fourth, the text *seeks to present core concepts and theories with clarity and simplicity*. Concepts are tools used for simplifying social reality. In IR they include such notions as levels of analysis, national interest, power, balance of power, deterrence, integration, coercive diplomacy, and international system. Theories are explanations of reality based upon recurring patterns of behavior. IR theories range from general systemic theories rooted in historical analogies to empirical theories that can be either confirmed or rejected through verification. Both concepts and theories are essential in examining world politics since they provide the tools necessary for analyzing foreign policy behavior and assessing the underlying structures and processes of global society. In addition, the text describes and compares the major approaches that scholars have used in analyzing IR.

Fifth, the text *emphasizes the role of ethics and moral analysis.* Following Aristotle, this study assumes that politics is rooted in political morality and ethical judgments. As a result, it emphasizes the role of moral norms in foreign policy and the role of alternative ethical traditions in assessing both the foreign policy behavior of states as well as the institutions and structures of global society. While personal and political morality are not the same, the conduct of statecraft is based partly on moral judgments of citizens and political leaders. A comprehensive approach to IR must therefore take into account the role of political morality and ethical judgment in international affairs.

Organization

The text has six major sections. Part I (ch. 1) defines the nature of IR, comparing the politics of domestic society with the politics of the international community. In addition, it describes the role of individuals, states, and global society in assessing foreign affairs and then presents alternative approaches to the analysis of international relations.

Part II (chs. 2–5) examines the context of world politics, focusing on the nature of global actors, essential features of the international community, and conflict and cooperation within that community. Chapter 5 examines the dominant systemic conflict of the post–World War II era—namely, the conflict between the United States and the Soviet Union. (The other major systemic conflict of the last half of the twentieth century is the North-South Conflict examined in chapter 15.)

Part III (chs. 6–11) examines key elements of global politics, focusing on the nature and implementation of foreign policy, the nature and role of power, ethics, force, and the problem of war.

Part IV (chs. 12–14) assesses the processes and institutions that facilitate global order. The key topics addressed in this section include the nature and role of diplomacy, international law, and international organizations in promoting global order.

Part V (chs. 15–17) examines the increasingly important role of international political economy in international relations, focusing on the evolution of north-south relations, the nature of international economic relations, and the problem of the Third World development.

Finally, part VI (chs. 18–19) explores two major global issues in the contemporary international community—weapons proliferation and the management of global resources. The epilogue identifies a variety of alternative future scenarios using optimistic and pessimistic versions of each of the different perspectives examined in chapter 1.

Approach

An introductory text must be more than a collection of relevant facts, definitions, and concepts. Rather, it must provide a simplified, but not simplistic, vision of a particular field of study. In order to integrate successfully the different theoretical and substantive elements of a discipline, an author must begin with an approach or perspective based on key organizing assumptions. The approach used here defines politics as the quest for community cooperation and conflict management.

According to the *conflict management perspective,* politics is the process by which stable and just political communities are created and maintained. A fundamental challenge in politics is to establish communities that allow its members—whether individuals, groups, or states—to maximize their particular interests without harming the interests of others. Since freedom inevitably results in discord and conflict, the establishment of stable, just communities is not an automatic byproduct of individual, group, and state actions. Humane communities must be created and maintained, and this is the task of politics.

A pervasive feature of all political communities is discord and conflict. Such conflicts derive from many different sources, including disagreements over the allocation of tangible resources or the quest for such intangible goods as prestige, honor, and influence. This is why E. E. Schattschneider observed that "all politics begins with billions of conflicts."[1] But the existence of conflict is not sufficient to bring about political activity. Rather, politics requires the management and resolution of major communal conflicts. Indeed, according to Carl J. Friedrich, the primordial function of politics is the "settling of disputes."[2]

In applying the conflict management approach to global politics, the text builds on the traditions of realism, idealism, and interdependence. Such an approach emphasizes the institutions and processes that facilitate transnational cooperation as well as the management and resolution of international conflicts. The conflict management perspective is thus distinguished by its emphasis on cooperation and conflict management and its focus on the role of power, law, institutions, and morality in promoting community order. The conflict management framework used in this study has five distinctive emphases:

- it gives *priority to the behavior of states*. Although international relations involve a variety of actors, states are viewed as the dominant units in global society.
- it emphasizes *the quest for national security*. Because no authoritative structures of conflict resolution exist in global society, national security is ultimately the responsibility of each state. In Susan Strange's words, national security "takes priority over all other claims on state policy."[3]
- it stresses *the role of power* in global politics. The concern with power is rooted in the conviction that politics, whether domestic or international, involves competition for both scarce resources as well as for political influence.
- it emphasizes *the role of law and institutions* in fostering cooperation and facilitating conflict resolution. The concern with international law and global organizations and institutions is rooted in the belief that communities, including the international community, can only exist in a context of order—an environment where decision making and conflict management are carried out with efficiency and predictability.
- emphasizes *the role of moral norms and ethics* in the conduct of international affairs. The emphasis on political morality and ethical judgment derives from the fact that political conflicts are partly rooted in different ways of defining and implementing the good life. The fact that humans argue about the moral ends of community life is evidence that politics is rooted in ethics.

It is, of course, much easier to imagine a better world than to understand existing global realities. Since the contemporary international system is characterized by problems such as war, hunger, international economic inequalities, and global pollution, some may be tempted to dream of a better world without comprehending present structures and existing conditions. While imagining a more just global society is relatively easy, knowledge of the major political, economic, social, and cultural forces and structures operating in the contemporary international system is indispensable in developing a more stable and humane world.

This text is both descriptive and prescriptive, empirical and normative. From the realist perspective it describes the role of power and force in global society; from the perspective of idealism, it calls attention to ethical judgments in the quest for greater peace and justice. While knowledge of the former is essential to an understanding of global society, idealism is equally important, for as the bible admonishes us, "Where there is no vision, the people perish."[4]

Changes in the Second Edition

Numerous changes have been undertaken in this edition in order to strengthen both the scholarship and organization of the text. The major revisions include:

- *significant expansion in the number of case studies*—the text includes 36 case studies on a variety of issues and topics. These cases, such as "Making Foreign Policy: The Case of NAFTA" and "Levels of Analysis and the Bosnian War," are important because they illustrate and dramatize important features of international affairs and illuminate significant conceptual and theoretical topics in the IR discipline;
- *reorganization*—the chapters covering international political economy have been placed together (chs. 15, 16, and 17), and the chapters on power and ethics have been placed earlier in the text (chs. 6 and 7);
- *increased coverage of current IR scholarship*—numerous scholarly issues and debates are presented in the narrative as well as in boxed issues; some of these 16 boxed issues include "IR from a Postmodern Perspective," "The Democratic Peace Thesis," and "Post–Cold War Conflict: Civilizations or States."

In addition to these general changes, the author has significantly revised all chapters in light of new scholarship, important international developments, and the growing impact of globalization. Some of the most significant changes are:

- chapter 1, "The Analysis of International Politics," has greatly expanded coverage of tridimensional "levels of analysis," illustrating the framework's utility with a case study on the Bosnian War;
- chapter 2, "Nation-States and Other Actors," develops further the analysis of nationalism

and describes the nature of strong and weak states;

- chapter 3, "The International Community," describes core norms of the classical, Westphalian system and compares them with the emerging norms of the post-Westphalian system;
- chapter 5, "Superpower Conflict and Cooperation," explores the prospects for world order in the post–Cold War era;
- chapter 7, "Ethics in World Politics," includes analysis of the role of human rights in global politics, focusing on the problem of cultural pluralism and rights claims. Case studies on caning and female genital mutilation illustrate the tension between the distinctive cultures found in global society and the universalistic claims of international human rights;
- chapter 8, "Foreign Policy: Defining and Pursuing National Interests," has been greatly revised to expand the analysis of major determinants of foreign policy. The nature and role of public opinion is emphasized and illustrated with a case study on NAFTA;
- chapter 10, "Force: The Use of Military Power," includes an analysis of the nature and role of coercive diplomacy and an assessment of the future role of nuclear arms;
- chapter 11, "War and Its Causes," includes a new section on three types of war— classical, total, and postmodern, with case studies illustrating each type;
- chapter 13, "International Law and Conflict Resolution," includes a new section on "other international courts" as well as a case study on the Bosnia War Crimes Tribunal that illustrates the growing significance of international criminal courts in contemporary global society;
- chapter 14, "The Role of International Organizations," includes an expanded analysis of international peacekeeping and international peacemaking. Two peacekeeping operations are examined—Bosnia and Cambodia;
- chapter 15, "North-South Conflict and Cooperation," includes a brief analysis of colonialism and its impact on the origins of the Third World;
- chapter 16, "International Economic Relations," gives greater emphasis to trade policy by comparing alternative strategies and illuminating the instruments that states use to manipulate trade;
- chapter 17, "Promoting Third World Development," greatly expands the analysis of foreign

capital and transnational flows in fomenting economic growth.

Learning Aids

To facilitate student learning, several learning aids are included in this text. For example, each chapter includes a listing of key terms and an annotated bibliography (Recommended Readings). A comprehensive glossary appears at the end of the text. Additional pedagogical aids developed for this edition include:

- definitions of key terms in the margins
- inclusion of relevant web sites in each chapter
- a listing of (27) foundational principles of the field of international relations is included at the end of the text. (Students may want to examine this list of principles at the beginning and conclusion of the IR course.)

Acknowledgments

In preparing this text, I have benefited from the ideas, suggestions, encouragement, and inspiration of many scholars, colleagues, and friends.

First, I want to thank the students in my International Relations course for helping to inspire and sustain this project.

Second, I am grateful to Wheaton College, the institution where I serve, for the priority it places on teaching and moral analysis and for providing an environment conducive to scholarly reflection. My interest in and commitment to the moral analysis of foreign affairs is due in part to the type of college where I work.

Third, I want to thank my teaching assistants Megan Holst, Jana Morgan, and Janet Rosenblad for their invaluable research and editorial assistance.

Fourth, I am grateful to the many external reviewers whose comments and suggestions have helped to improve the two editions of this book. These reviewers include the following scholars:

Stephen R. Bowers	James Madison University
Glen Chafetz	University of Memphis
Ken Conca	University of Maryland
Paul F. Diehl	University of Illinois
Larry Elowitz	Georgia College and State University
William Felice	Eckerd College
Vincent Ferraro	Mount Holyoke College
Clyde Frazier	Meredith College

Marc Genest	University of Rhode Island
Emily O. Goldman	University of California—Davis
Heidi H. Hobbs	Florida International University
William Jackson	Miami University
Howard P. Lehman	University of Utah
Timothy J. Lomperis	United States Military Academy
Richard W. Mansbach	Iowa State University
Eric Mlyn	University of North Carolina—Chapel Hill
Benjamin N. Muego	Bowling Green State University
John O'Rorke	Frostburg State University
Gregory A. Raymond	Boise State University
Mark Simon	Bowling Green State University
Roger Whitcomb	Kutztown University
Donald Will	Chapman University
Pia Christina Wood	Old Dominion University
Sandra J. Wurth-Hough	East Carolina University
Michele Zebich-Knos	Kennesaw State College
Voytek Zubek	University of Alabama at Birmingham

Fifth, I am grateful for the outstanding editorial and production support from the WCB/McGraw-Hill staff. Scott Spoolman helped to get the second edition underway, and Leslye Jackson provided invaluable inspiration and guidance in preparing the text. Sheila Frank, production editor, along with her support staff provided indispensable editorial assistance by increasing the consistency and clarity of writing, coordinating layout, and ensuring that deadlines were met in a timely manner.

Finally, I thank my wife for supporting the writing of this book and for being understanding of the heavy time commitments that such a project makes on the life of a professor. Because she has been steadfast in her support and understanding of my work, while still holding me accountable to other family commitments, I affectionately dedicate this book to her.

[1]E. E. Schattschneider, "Intensity, Visibility, Direction, and Scope," *The American Political Science Review,* 51 (December 1957), p. 936.

[2]Carl J. Friedrich, *Man and His Government* (New York: McGraw-Hill, 1963), p. 423.

[3]Susan Strange, "What About International Relations?" in Susan Strange, ed., *Paths to International Political Economy* (London: George Allen & Unwin, 1984), pp. 184–85.

[4]Proverbs 29:18.

CHAPTER

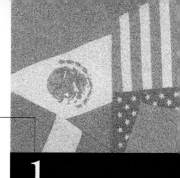

The Analysis of International Relations   1

Intellectual relations is concerned with the transnational interactions among countries. Although the field of **international relations (IR)** examines a wide variety of cross-border relationships among subnational groups, international organizations, transnational movements, private organizations, and even individuals, the chief focus in IR is on the interactions among the world's governments. Historically, states have been the major actors in the international community. But as the world has become more interdependent, nonstate actors, such as multinational corporations and nongovernmental organizations, have become more influential. As a result, contemporary IR is increasingly concerned with the growing role of movements, organizations, groups, business corporations, and transnational networks in global society.

The goal of this text is to introduce the field of IR. The aim is to illuminate some of the key issues and problems in contemporary global politics and to present the major methods, concepts, and theories that scholars have developed in seeking to understand and explain the phenomena of foreign affairs. More specifically, the text seeks both to describe significant elements of international relations and to explain how scholars seek to understand important events and developments in this discipline. The goal is thus to present foundational knowledge about contemporary foreign affairs, as well as to show how scholars study and explain IR.

This introductory chapter has four parts: First, it explores the nature and significance of the field of IR; second, the chapter contrasts the politics of domestic societies with the politics of the international community, illustrating the latter with a classic case study—the Peloponnesian War; third, it describes different elements and conceptual tools used in analyzing IR, and illustrates the role of "levels of analysis" with a case study on the Bosnian War; and finally, the chapter compares four major approaches that scholars have used in understanding IR.

The art of politics teaches men to live in peace, with collectivities, while it teaches collectivities to live in either peace or war. States have not emerged, in their mutual relations, from the State of Nature. There would be no further theory of international relations if they had.[1]

Raymond Aron, *French social scientist*

The crucial truth is that man as such does not grow better. He is free. He remains the beast/angel Pascal called him, a chaos, contradiction, prodigy. He progresses only by recognizing his nature, his misery with his sublime possibility. A politics has to be built on that.[2]

William Pfaff, *distinguished international affairs columnist*

International relations (IR)
The totality of transnational interactions among state and nonstate actors. As a field of study, IR is concerned with the analysis of the politics of global society.

THE NATURE AND SIGNIFICANCE OF IR

The Nature of IR

The study of IR is characterized by three features. First, as noted previously, IR is concerned primarily with the relations *between* and *among* the approximately 190 states of the world. To be sure, nonstate actors also influence global affairs; indeed, nongovernmental organizations and groups have become increasingly influential as the modern world has become more interdependent technologically, economically, socially, and politically. But because states remain the ultimate authority over people, the study of IR emphasizes relations among states and between states and other important nonstate actors, such as international governmental organizations (e.g., the UN and NATO) and nongovernmental organizations (e.g., International Red Cross and the International Olympic Committee).

Second, IR is concerned with the external behaviors of states—that is, with the *foreign policies* of countries. Scholars define foreign policy as the actions taken by governmental officials in order to promote national interests beyond the territorial boundaries of states. In the discipline of IR scholars analyze and compare states' foreign policies in order to understand the goals and motivations of states and the instruments by which they seek to advance their goals in global society. Although a significant portion of IR focuses on the official relations between states, foreign policies also concern countries' relations toward nonstate actors.

Finally, the study of IR is concerned with the global context in which foreign relations occur. Although there is no governing authority in the world, international affairs are not random events but actions undertaken in accordance with widely accepted principles, rules, and decision-making procedures. Because IR is carried out within a global society that is informally regulated by norms, rules, and institutions, scholars refer to the global environment as an *international system*. An important goal of this study is to describe the nature and evolution of contemporary global structures, contrasting major features of the classical international system with those of the modern or post-Westphalian order.

Although the study of IR relies on several academic disciplines, including history, economics, sociology, and psychology, most IR scholarship and teaching are from a political science perspective. Because political science is concerned with the establishment of stable and humane communities through the legitimate use of power and authority, a political science perspective on IR emphasizes political, institutional, and governmental dimensions of the global relations. It is important to stress that other disciplines are vitally important in developing an understanding of IR. For example, historical knowledge is important in developing an appreciation of the origins and evolution of the nation-state, the nature and causes of war, the evolution of diplomacy, the causes and effects of nineteenth-century imperialism, the causes and effects of World War I and World War II, and so on. Similarly, IR scholars need to be familiar with economic theory, international economics, and developmental economics if they are to understand the extraordinary expansion of national wealth in the modern world and to appreciate the role of trade in fomenting or impeding national job creation. But unlike other social scientists, IR scholars use knowledge from other disciplines to focus on the *politics* of the relevant subject matter. Thus, whether examining the history of war, international economic relations, or global ecology, IR emphasizes the political dimensions of topics. The priority of political analysis is captured in the name of one of the most important new areas of IR—international political economy (IPE).

The Significance of IR

The Impact of IR on People   International relations are important. Indeed, because of increasing global interdependence, international relations are becoming more significant to human beings worldwide. Foreign affairs are exerting increasing influence on people's economic, social, and political well-being, whereas domestic events—such as currency devaluation, civil strife, or terrorism—are similarly having a growing effect on foreign countries. The following examples illustrate the significant impact of IR in contemporary society:

1. On December 25, 1991, the Soviet Union ceased to exist, bringing to an end the long and bitter ideological conflict between communism and democracy. Because the Cold War between the United States and the Soviet Union had involved an expensive arms race, the disintegration of the Soviet empire provided the U.S. government with a "peace dividend," allowing it to reduce the size of its armed forces, to carry out significant reductions in conventional and nuclear armaments, and to shift resources from military defense to other areas of national need. The end of the Cold War has thus provided each U.S. citizen not only with tangible benefits but a far more secure global order, much less prone to major war.

2. In November 1993, the U.S. House of Representatives, after a long and bitter debate, adopted the North American Free Trade Agreement (NAFTA). The goal of NAFTA is to stimulate job creation in Canada, Mexico, and the United States through increased trade. Because the accord reduces trade barriers, some U.S. groups—especially labor unions, small business groups, and environmental lobbies—were opposed to NAFTA, believing that the accord would lead to job loses in the United States and to adverse environmental conditions in Mexico.

3. In December 1994, the Mexican government devalued its currency by some 15 percent in order to make its exports more competitive and thereby reduce the continuing balance of payments deficits. The decision to allow the exchange rate to "float" (to be set by market forces) exposed underlying weaknesses in the Mexican economy and resulted in speculators selling Mexican pesos—a development that led to a precipitous (40 percent) decline against the dollar. The impact of the peso's dramatic fall had repercussions throughout the Western Hemisphere, as stock prices declined not only in Mexico but also in other major Latin American countries. In addition, because the crisis threatened foreign investor confidence in Mexico and jeopardized the newly established NAFTA accord, the United States, in cooperation with the International Monetary Fund, provided a short-term loan guarantee of some $12 billion in order to keep the Mexican economy from collapsing. For many U.S. citizens, the immediate impact of the crisis was a loss of value in foreign investments in Mexico, lower costs to travel in Mexico, and lower prices for Mexican fruit.

4. In March 1996, the United Kingdom announced that persons consuming beef contaminated with bovine spongiform encephalopathy (BSE), or more commonly called "mad cow disease," could possibly acquire a fatal degenerative brain illness known as Creutzfeldt-Jakob disease. The British government admitted that at least ten persons had died in the previous year from this neurological disease. In order to limit its proliferation to other countries, the European Union (EU) imposed a worldwide ban on the export of British beef products and called on Britain to slaughter a significant portion of its 11 million head of cattle. Although the EU promised financial aid to

British farmers, these stringent actions placed major strains on Britain's relationship with its western European partners, precipitating what some journalists dubbed "the great beef war." Although the crisis abated somewhat after Britain slaughtered tens of thousands of head of cattle, tensions continued in 1997 between Britain and the EU over the status of beef trade. The BSE crisis illustrates how a relatively small domestic development can have significant international effects.

Why IR Is Becoming More Important   Since the end of World War II, international relations have increased in scope and significance. One reason for the growing impact of international events on states is the increasing logistical interdependence of global society. Because of the revolution in transportation, international travel and movement of goods and services can now be undertaken with speed and efficiency. Whereas in the nineteenth century travel between the United States and Europe would require more than a week, now a flight via the supersonic Concord jet requires less than four hours. The efficiency of air travel allows Colombia and the Netherlands to export large quantities of fresh flowers to the United States, and seafood merchants from the state of Louisiana to export fresh crayfish to France.

Second, because of improved transnational communication networks, global communication is rapid and efficient. For example, citizens with cable television in Tegucigalpa, Honduras, might learn about important events in their country through a U.S. cable news station before the local media report them. Similarly, because of global diffusion of sports events through satellite television, international athletic stars (such as basketball star Michael Jordan) are recognized not only in their own countries but throughout the world. Moreover, the expansion of electronic mail and computer communications has resulted in a global communications network over which governments have little control. When the Chinese government imposed controls on television reporting following the June 1989 Tiananmen Square massacre, for example, students turned to fax machines to get their reports out.

Third, the global economy is becoming more interdependent as trade among states rises and global financial markets become more integrated. A large portion of the goods sold in the United States, for example, are either made or assembled in foreign countries. An IBM personal computer is an American product, but a majority of its elements are produced in other countries. Some automobiles are manufactured with components from ten or more countries. Grocery stores in affluent states carry increasing variety of produce from foreign lands. Moreover, foreign exchange markets can significantly affect the economic stability of Third World countries. Because important imports, such as oil, are purchased with dollars, a rise in the value of the dollar can have disastrous consequences on the economy of a poor nation. At the same time, a significant decline in the value of a key export can also damage a country's economy. Following the drop in oil prices in the 1980s, Venezuela was unable to meet its foreign financial obligations and was forced, partly by the International Monetary Fund, to impose austerity measures that resulted in massive riots.

In short, international developments can and do have important consequences on the well-being of individuals. Whether a war, a drop in the value of exports, a rise in the value of foreign currencies, or a threat of terrorism, everyday life is increasingly influenced by developments in foreign lands.

DOMESTIC VERSUS INTERNATIONAL POLITICS

To illuminate distinctive features of global politics, this section compares the politics of a typical, well-developed state with the politics of the international community.

Many territorial borders are peaceful and undefended. Some—like the border between North Korea and South Korea—are heavily armed and dangerous. Here South Korean soldiers patrol the demilitarized zone (DMZ) between the two countries.

Although this comparison is based on "ideal-type" classifications, it is important to stress that some states, because of significant cultural heterogeneity, major social cleavages, large income inequalities, and limited functional integration, have more in common with the international community than with typical nation-states. Indeed, in the post–Cold War era a number of states, some of which have collapsed and disintegrated, have experienced less order than the international system itself.

Kenneth Waltz, an influential IR scholar, observes that domestic and international politics can be differentiated on the basis of the level of order and the means by which such order is achieved.[3] Fundamentally, domestic society is characterized by a high level of stability, made possible through a highly consensual domestic culture and developed governmental institutions, backed by the coercive power of the state. International society, by contrast, has a comparatively lower level of order and underdeveloped governmental institutions. The underdeveloped nature of government stems from a variety of sources, including the heterogeneous nature of global society and the absence of centralized coercive power.

Fundamental differences in domestic and international politics are rooted in different modes of organization and alternative values and cultural norms on which the structures are based. The first refers to the governmental institutions that manage and resolve political conflict; the second, to the common culture of society. Although both elements are important, culture is more basic, because governmental structures are rooted in shared values and common practices. In other words, the underlying foundation of a political community is not its governmental institutions, but its values, norms, and orientations—that is, the idea of political community itself. This is as true in the international system as it is in domestic society.

Domestic communities are often characterized by a relatively homogeneous culture, a common language, complementary patterns of communication and interaction, and widely shared political and economic values.[4] These elements contribute to the development of national cohesion, which in turn provides a stable foundation for government decision making. The international community, by contrast, is much more heterogeneous ethnically, linguistically, religiously, and socially. Essentially, the international community is a *society of societies,* comprising

TABLE 1.1 Comparison of Domestic and International Politics

	Domestic Politics	**International Politics**
Nature of culture	Homogeneous	Heterogenous
Nature of society	Consensual	Conflictual
Nature of political system	Developed	Underdeveloped
Role of government	Significant	Insignificant
Government authority	Based on monopoly of force	Based on state voluntarism
Political authority	Centralized	Decentralized

some 190 states, each with its own cultural, linguistic, and political attributes and distinct social and political institutions. Because the authority of government is based partly on the degree of community consensus, the level of cultural, social, economic, religious, and political homogeneity will affect not only the capacity of government to make and enforce its decisions, but the development of governmental institutions.

Generally, political processes and governmental institutions in domestic societies are more developed that those in the international community. Although the global society has, like all human communities, governmental institutions and processes, these are weak and underdeveloped—especially when compared with those in a modern, stable, and economically prosperous nation-state. Whereas domestic society has developed procedures and governmental institutions, international society has underdeveloped governmental structures. As a result, domestic society is characterized by authority, law, and administration; international politics, by contrast, is chiefly a realm of competition, power, and struggle. If domestic society is a domain of government, international society is a domain of politics.

Former Secretary of State John Foster Dulles once sought to explain why domestic society was more peaceful and orderly than international society. According to him, the absence of order within the international system was directly attributed to the weaknesses of the transnational governmental institutions. Dulles identified six instruments that were responsible for the peace and tranquility of domestic society: (1) laws reflecting a broad moral consensus within society; (2) political machinery to change laws; (3) an executive to enforce and apply the law; (4) courts to resolve legal disputes; (5) superior public force by which to apprehend and punish those who violate laws; and (6) economic well-being so that people are sufficiently satisfied and do not resort to violence. In his view, all these elements were absent or undeveloped in international society.[5]

A comparison of domestic and international structures suggests that the former are much more developed and institutionalized that the latter (see table 1.1). For example, in domestic society legislatures normally make and change laws. As a result, the laws of domestic society are generally specific, clearly defined, and widely accepted. In the international community, by contrast, there is no comparable legislature to make and amend international law. To be sure, the United Nations General Assembly periodically votes on global issues, whereas plenary conferences are occasionally convened to coordinate international actions and establish common policies. But these meetings are regarded as diplomatic forums, not as authoritative rule-making institutions.

Executive institutions are similarly undeveloped in global society. Although the UN Security Council has the responsibility for keeping peace among states, its ability to do so rests largely on the willingness of major powers to support common action and to make available military and economic resources to implement its resolutions. Unlike domestic executives, the UN does not have military and economic resources of its own. Its actions are those supported by its member states. The only military forces available for UN peacekeeping tasks are those of the states themselves. For example, in the Gulf War of 1991, the military forces that liberated Kuwait, in compliance with UN Security Council resolutions, were drawn from more than twenty states, especially the United States, Britain, France, Kuwait, and Saudi Arabia.

Finally, whereas domestic courts provide an authoritative method of settling legal disputes, international courts rarely resolve interstate conflicts. This is so in part because states are reluctant to give authority to regional or international courts. For example, the International Court of Justice (ICJ), the world's leading court, does not have automatic jurisdiction over international legal disputes among UN member-states. The only way that the ICJ can try a case is for the relevant parties to voluntarily consent to the court's jurisdiction.[6] Moreover, even when the court tries a case, a state may disregard the court's judgment, as was the case when Iran failed to fulfill the court's decision to free hostages at the U.S. embassy in Tehran.

Because international institutions are comparatively undeveloped, interstate conflict tends to be more intense. When vital interests are at stake, states do not hesitate to use military force to protect, and even maximize, their national interests. Not surprisingly, the ultimate means for settling disputes is war. Because each member-state in the world community is independent and sovereign, the only way to resolve conflict in the global society is either through the voluntary cooperation of member-states, or through the imposition of decisions by states with superior power.

In summary, international politics, like domestic politics, involves the quest for justice, the development and maintenance of community order, the creation of common policies to promote shared interests, and the development of conflict management procedures to settle disputes. These tasks are more difficult in international society due to the relatively low level of social and cultural consensus and the absence of authoritative international organizations. To illuminate some of the distinctive features of global politics, we examine the Peloponnesian War (see case 1.1), an ancient conflict between two famous Greek city-states, based on Thucydides' classic account.

THE ANALYSIS OF IR

Empirical and Theoretical Knowledge

In order to develop an understanding of IR, it is necessary to acquire both empirical and conceptual knowledge about global politics. **Empirical knowledge** refers to important factual information about states, governments, international organizations, and transnational issues that are essential in explaining international affairs. Although scholars stress many different types of empirical knowledge, most introductory IR texts, including this one, emphasize the following types of data: (1) *major historical developments* (e.g., the rise and evolution of the nation-state, the evolution of global institutions, the rise and fall of regimes and alliances); (2) *the nature of states and their foreign policies* (e.g., the impact of domestic politics on foreign policy, different instruments used by states to promote their foreign policy goals); (3) *major international disputes and wars* (e.g., World War I and II, the Cuban Missile Crisis, the Vietnam War, the Persian Gulf War); (4) *important areas of transnational cooperation* (e.g., arms control, trade, environmental protection, human rights, Third World development); (5) *the nature and role of interna-*

Empirical knowledge
Knowledge based on objective, observable phenomena.

Case 1.1 The Peloponnesian War

The Peloponnesian War is significant because it provides important insights about the challenge of pursuing security and economic well-being in a decentralized political system. Although the system of Greek city-states in the fifth century B.C. differs in important respects from the modern international system of nation-states, both ancient and modern states faced the dilemma of pursuing security without threatening other states. Because no governmental institutions existed in the Aegean peninsula to resolve conflicts among city-states, each state was responsible for its own security and well-being. This condition is similar to the modern international system in which each state remains ultimately responsible for its security and well-being. Thucydides's penetrating account of the Peloponnesian War is important because it illuminates the risks and challenges states face in interpreting the motivations of other actors, in reconciling competing and conflicting state interests, in using allies to deter aggression, and in resorting to force.

Background

In the fifth century B.C., Greece comprised numerous independent and largely self-sufficient city-states. Two states dominated the region—**Athens,** a democratic, commercial, and outward-looking state, and **Sparta,** an oligarchic, agricultural, and inward-looking state. Throughout the fifth century these two states dominated the foreign relations of Greece as they sought to extend their influence with other city-states in the region. Because each city-state ultimately depended upon its own resources for its security and economic welfare, ancient Greece was, to a significant degree, similar to the modern international system. In Greece no central power existed to resolve disputes or to protect states from foreign aggression. Security and economic expansion depended upon each state's capabilities and its ability and willingness to cooperate with others in promoting shared interests through military alliances and commercial trade.

Early in the fifth century, the Persians tried to extend their empire into Greece but were successfully repulsed in two major wars. The Greek success against the powerful Persians was due in great part to the military collaboration between Sparta and Athens. After defeating the Persians, the Spartans retreated to the Greek peninsula south of Athens—an area known as the Peloponnese—and through-

out much of the century confined their power to this region. The Athenians, by contrast, after defeating the Persians, sought to deter future Persian attacks by increasing their military power and economic influence throughout the Aegean Sea, including the coastal cities of Asia Minor (present-day Turkey). To increase and institutionalize its influence throughout the region, Athens established the **Delian League,** a defensive alliance of some 200 city-states. Although the Delian League involved mutual military commitments among its member-states, the basis of the alliance was Athens' growing military and economic power. By 450 B.C., Athens had become the unrivaled naval power of the region, effectively thwarting Persian naval attacks and regulating most Aegean Sea commerce.

In the mid-fifth century, relations between Athens and Sparta deteriorated, leading to the *First Peloponnesian War* (460–445 B.C.). This conflict ended with a negotiated truce based on Sparta's recognition of Athens' regional influence, while also permitting a number of reluctant city-states to withdraw from the Delian League. Although the truce was supposed to last for thirty years, within ten years tensions had developed again, eventually resulting in the second or *Great Peloponnesian War* (431–404 B.C.).

The War

Three major developments contributed to the outbreak of the second war. First, a conflict developed between Corinth, a Spartan-aligned city-state at the mouth of the Peloponnesian Peninsula and Athens. The dispute began when a civil war broke out in Epidamnus, a former colony of Corcyra (modern-day Corfu) located on the northwestern coast of Greece. The democratic forces of Epidamnus appealed to Corcyra for help, but after being rebuffed, appealed to Corinth, which decided to assist them. The pledge of Corinthian assistance, however, angered Corcyra, which then dispatched a naval force to regain control of its former colony. En route to Epidamnus, the Corcyrans fought Corinthian naval forces and defeated them. But fearing a counterattack from Corinth, Corcyra asked Athens for help. After carefully deliberating the pros and cons of its involvement, Athens decided to assist Corcyra, because its occupation by Corinthian forces would inevitably result in an imbalance of power between the two leading regional city-states, Athens and Sparta.

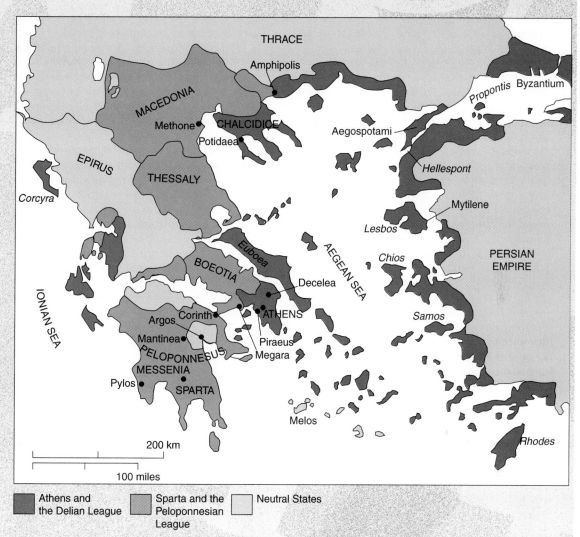

MAP 1-1
Ancient Greece

Second, Athens passed a decree imposing an economic embargo on Megara, a nearby city-state aligned with the Peloponnesian League. Athens imposed economic sanctions on Megara as punishment for its military support of Corinth, Athens' enemy. As with modern trade sanctions, the aim of the embargo was to increase diplomatic pressure on Megara (the target state), and thereby deter it and other city-states from giving further assistance to Corinth.

A third development precipitating the great war was the revolt at Potidaea, a former Corinthian colony along the northeastern coast of Greece. Because Potidaea was under Athenian economic domination, Athens feared that Potidaea, in response to Corinthian prodding, would revolt against Athenian control. It therefore demanded that Potidaea tear down its fortifications. In response to a joint Corinthian-Potidaean request, Sparta pledged to

continued

Case 1.1 The Peloponnesian War—*concluded*

assist Potidaea if attacked. When a revolt developed in Potidaea, Athens intervened to reestablish order, leading Sparta to declare war on Athens.

Donald Kagan argues that the second war was not inevitable. However, once the developments at Corcyra, Megara, and Potidaea had taken place, the Corinthians were eager to punish Athens whereas the Spartans were concerned that their security was being imperiled by the growth of Athenian power. "Individually, the affairs of Corcyra, Potidaea, and Megara were not decisive," writes Kagan, "but, taken all together with a selective choice of the history of the last fifty years, they seemed to confirm the Corinthian picture of the arrogance of the Athenians and the danger presented by their growing power."[7]

The first ten years of the great war (431–421 B.C.) resulted in a stalemate between the two contesting states. After a temporary truce of six years, military power began to tilt in Sparta's favor, in great measure because of Athens' overextension. In 416 B.C., Athens decided to invade the large Italian island of Sicily, a majority of whose city-states were aligned with Sparta. The plan backfired, and resulted in the near total defeat of its expeditionary forces in the Sicilian city-state of Syracuse—a disaster that broke Athenian morale and marked the eclipse of the Athenian empire. Despite Athens' economic and political decline, the Athenians and Spartans continued fighting for another decade until Athens was compelled to level its city walls in 404 B.C.

Significant Lessons

The continuing interest in the Peloponnesian War is due in great measure to Thucydides' penetrating account of this conflict (*History of the Peloponnesian War*) and the insights it reveals about the nature of interstate relations. Some important lessons illuminated by the conflict include:

1. The war demonstrates the important role of power in international relations. Because there is no central authority to protect communities from foreign aggression or to resolve disputes among member-states, states seek to maximize their political and economic power. One of the ways states do this is by building up their military forces, as illustrated by both Sparta and Athens. States can also establish loose coalitions or enforced alliances, such as the Delian League.

2. Increases in the power by a rival state must be challenged, lest an imbalance of power encourage aggression. Thucydides argues that the underlying cause of the war was the growing imbalance of power between Sparta and Athens. In his view, because of the growth in Athenian power, Sparta perceived a decline in its regional influence and national security and eventually felt compelled to go to war. In Thucydides' words: "what made the war inevitable was the growth of Athenian power and the fear which this caused in Sparta."[8]

3. In a decentralized system of states, such as that in ancient Greece, alliances can foster a balance of power and thereby contribute to the promotion of world order. But alliances can also serve as entangling instruments and contribute to the intensification of conflict. Sparta and Athens did not want war, but they were drawn into a general war when their allies were challenged. Each of the three precipitating developments noted concerned shifts in the regional equilibrium of power between Sparta and Athens as a result of military action among allies.

4. The history of Athens and Sparta calls attention to the priority of cooperation in a decentralized global society. Although the Greek city-states were independent political communities, none were economically or militarily self-sufficient. To defend themselves, they established coalitions with other city-states, exemplified by the Spartan and Athenian cooperation in defeating the Persians and the informal alliance systems used by both Sparta and Athens in challenging each other's power. Moreover, Athenian economic welfare was based on trade among Aegean city-states. The failure of Athens and Sparta to cooperate in promoting common interests ultimately proved the undoing of ancient Greece.

5. The war suggests that because human beings are never fully satisfied with the status quo, states are continuously seeking to maximize their interests. But such ambition can result in harmful consequences. As described by Thucydides, the Athenian quest for more power eventually brought about the collapse of the Athenian regime, for the decision to carry out a war in Sicily proved to be its undoing.

tional law and international organizations (e.g., law of the sea, outer space law, the European Union, the United Nations); and (6) *the nature and role of international economic relations* (e.g., trade policies, the World Trade Organization, the International Monetary Fund).

Conceptual and theoretical knowledge is also essential. Concepts involve abstract ideas of important elements of reality; theories, by contrast, involve the formulation of general principles designed to explain reality. Concepts and theories are necessary in developing an understanding of IR because they provide the intellectual constructs that facilitate the simplification of reality, without which fundamental knowledge is impossible. Moreover, theories and analytical models are important because they facilitate the ordering of knowledge and the development of principles that help to explain reality. In particular, they provide the cognitive structures, or intellectual maps, that guide investigation and the learning process. As William James once observed, without concepts, theories, models, and worldviews there is only "a bloomin', buzzin' confusion."[9] Just as maps are important in guiding our travel from one geographical location to another, so too intellectual maps are important in guiding our analysis of international political reality. Historian John Lewis Gaddis has observed: "Finding one's way through unfamiliar terrain generally requires a map of some sort. Cartography, like cognition itself, is a necessary simplification that allows us to see where we are, and where we may be going."[10]

This text emphasizes the following conceptual elements: (1) *core concepts* (such as power, ethics, anarchy, interdependence, international regimes); (2) *alternative worldviews or paradigms* (such as realism, idealism, liberal institutionalism); and (3) *major theories* (such as balance of power, collective security, dependency). Because the drama of international politics is best illustrated through concrete problems and conflicts, the text uses many case studies to illuminate important themes and issues.

Levels of Analysis

In analyzing global politics, scholars use different **levels of analysis,** or conceptual categories, to guide systematic investigation. Although scholars have developed a variety of different conceptual levels of analysis, the most widely used system involves a three-dimensional scheme focusing on (1) individuals, (2) states and other actors, and (3) the international system itself.[11] According to this tri-partite framework, a comprehensive analysis of international relations requires that, at a minimum, investigation of factors in each of these three levels be included.

The *individual level of analysis* focuses on the role of persons in global politics. Such analysis examines the role of political leaders and government officials in defining and pursuing the foreign policy goals of states. It also includes an assessment of the role of citizens in domestic politics and in transnational activities that influence, directly or indirectly, the international behaviors of states and other actors. This type of analysis also explores how different individual backgrounds, alternative historical experiences, and distinct leadership styles can influence foreign policy decisions. Moreover, this level of analysis examines the impact of ideologies (belief systems) on individuals' perceptions and actions and assesses the role of different decision-making contexts (e.g., routine versus crises). Finally, the individual level of analysis calls attention to the role of normative assumptions of human nature and political morality on the interpretation and analysis of IR.

The *national level of analysis* focuses on the nature and role of the state (as well as major nonstate actors) in the international community. Because states are the principal actors in global society, one of the important themes in the modern international community is the process by which subnational groups become states. Moreover, because foreign policy is the principal means by which states

Conceptual knowledge
Knowledge based on concepts—that is, abstract ideas that correspond to observable phenomena.

Theoretical knowledge
Knowledge based on explanatory or causal theories.

Levels of analysis
A tri-partite framework that explains international affairs by focusing on the role of decision makers, the attributes of states and the structures of the international system.

carry out their international relations, the analysis of the nature, sources, implementation procedures, and effects of foreign policy are a primary concern of this level of analysis. In addition, this type of analysis examines the role of domestic attributes that influence foreign policy, focusing on such factors as power, wealth, political structure, ideology, and morality. One of the important themes in this level of investigation is the potential effect of domestic structures on the conduct of foreign policy.

The *global level of analysis* focuses on the impact of the international system on the behavior of states and other actors. Because states are the ultimate source of authority in global society, the structure of the international community is anarchic—that is, without any central governmental institutions. As a result, the systemic level of analysis explores the impact of international anarchy on the priorities and behavior of states. It also examines the nature and impact of different configurations of power (e.g., unipolar, bipolar, or multipolar distributions) on global order and assesses the forces that contribute to transnational cooperation and international conflict. Finally, this type of analysis focuses on the nature, role, and impact of international law and international organizations.

Because most international issues and disputes are rooted in the ambitions and personalities of leaders, the character and political dynamics of states, and the formal and informal ties among actors in the international community, the tripartite framework is essential in explaining IR. To illustrate the important role of each of these three levels, case 1.2 examines the conflict that arose in Bosnia-Herzegovina in the early 1990s.

APPROACHES TO INTERNATIONAL RELATIONS

When scholars begin studying a subject matter, they do so with many preconceived notions and assumptions. This is especially the case with the analysis of world politics—a subject that has been influenced by widely varying political perspectives and approaches. These approaches, or **paradigms,** are significant because they guide the nature of inquiry and provide boundaries and frameworks by which inquiry is carried out. Moreover, by establishing an *intellectual framework, or cognitive map,* they illuminate important areas of study and contribute to the classification of phenomena. Sir Arthur Eddington, a British scientist, once remarked that fishing with a net of one-inch openings could lead one to conclude that there were no fish smaller than one inch! Similarly, assumptions and methodologies used in analyzing international relations are likely to influence one's views and conclusions. For example, intellectual traditions, such as post-modernism, can influence how scholarship is undertaken (see issue 1.2). Moreover, as recent studies have shown, gender can similarly influence the ideas and actions of scholars and public officials (see issue 1.3).

In the postwar era four major perspectives have dominated the study of international relations: *realism, idealism, interdependence,* and *dependency.* In the following sections we briefly examine key features of each perspective.

Realism

The approach of **realism,** the most influential postwar school of international relations in the United States, is identified with twentieth-century scholars such E.H. Carr, Hans Morgenthau, George F. Kennan, and Reinhold Niebuhr. Contemporary realists, following ancient and modern thinkers such as Thucydides, St. Augustine, Niccolò Machiavelli, and Thomas Hobbes, emphasize five key elements: a pessimistic view of human nature, a belief in the conflictual nature of politics, the

Paradigm
An intellectual framework, such as dependency theory or political realism, that structures analysis.

Realism
A political approach that emphasizes the conflictual nature of global politics, the priority of national security, a pessimistic assessment of human nature, and a consequentialist moral perspective.

Case 1.2 Levels of Analysis and the Bosnian War

The Origins of War

In the aftermath of the Cold War, Yugoslavia, a multi-ethnic state of Croats, Muslims, and Serbs, began to disintegrate when some of its republics sought to secede from the Serbian-dominated central government.[12] In June 1991 Slovenia and Croatia declared independence, leading the Serb-controlled Yugoslavian army to use force to prevent secession. Because of historic animosities between Serbs and Croats, the fighting was particularly bitter in Croatia, in which nearly one-third of the people were Serbs. In January 1992, six months after declaring independence, the European Union recognized both Slovenia and Croatia.

Subsequently, the republic of Bosnia and Herzegovina, a political entity wedged between the Croatian and Serbian belligerents, also declared its political independence. Because Bosnia was itself a multi-ethnic state of roughly equal numbers of Croat, Muslim, and Serb peoples, the demand for political autonomy led to a bitter war among the three groups. Because Bosnian Serbs were militarily supported by the Serb federal government, their superior armaments gave them the power to greatly extend their territorial control to over two-thirds of the new state, encircling numerous Muslim enclaves, such as Sarajevo, the capital of Bosnia. The ostensible aim of this campaign of aggression was to establish a "Greater Serbia" by affiliating with the republic of Serbia. It has been estimated that from 1992 to 1995 the Bosnian war resulted in some 200,000 deaths and more than a million refugees, as people fled their villages and towns in response to "ethnic cleansing" by Serbian nationalists.

After the Serbs consolidated their power over much of Bosnia, they refused to withdraw, even when faced by international pressures, including sanctions and military threats. To discourage fighting, the United Nations placed an arms embargo on Yugoslavia in 1991. Because Serbia controlled the large military resources of the Yugoslav armed services, the embargo only reinforced the Serb monopoly of power and deprived Croatian and Muslim forces of weapons to protect themselves. More significantly, the introduction in 1992 of a 20,000 mem-

(continued)

MAP 1-2
Bosnia-Herzegovina and Other Territories of the Former Yugoslavia

Case 1.2 Levels of Analysis and the Bosnian War—*continued*

International relations often involve violence. One of the most destructive post-Cold War conflicts has been the war in Bosnia. Here the historic Sarajevo library burns after being hit by Serb mortars and rockets.

ber UN peacekeeping force (known as *UNPROFOR, or UN Protection Force*) was not effective in either keeping the peace or in protecting urban centers from Serbian attacks. Because UNPROFOR was a peacekeeping force, not a peacemaking force, its forces were poorly armed and ill-equipped to counter Serb aggression. In November 1995, the United States successfully brokered a peace agreement (known as the Dayton Accords) that brought the fighting to a halt. At Dayton, the Muslim, Croat, and Serb leaders agreed to divide Bosnia into two parastates (a Muslim-Croat Federation with 51 percent of the land and a Serb Republic with 49 percent of the land), and still keep Bosnia as a single nation-state. To maintain peace among the warring factions, a 30,000-member NATO force was introduced, with one-third of the troops from the United States. Although the NATO Stabilization Force (SFOR) has prevented fighting, deep animosities remained among the three peoples two years after the signing of the Dayton Accords.

Tri-partite Analysis

How can this conflict be explained? From the individual level of analysis, it is clear that the outbreak and evolution of the fighting was a direct result of manipulative, parochial, and evil actions of political officials. Leaders, such as Serbian president Slobodan

priority of power and national security, the priority of the state, and morality rooted in consequences.

1. *Pessimism:* Realists hold a pessimistic view of human nature and social life. Because individuals are assumed to be motivated chiefly by self-interest, realists—like Edmund Burke, the famous British parliamentarian, and James Madison, a leading founding father of the United States—believe that disorder and injustice are natural by-products of all communal life, whether at the local, national, or international levels. Moreover, because communal injustice is rooted in the selfish and morally imperfect nature of persons, realists are pessimistic about the establishment of a just political order.

2. *Conflictual relations:* Realists also believe that political relations are fundamentally conflictual. The conflictual nature of global relations derives from the intense competition for scarce resources, but more importantly, from the quest for security. Because there is no common authority in the world, each state must use its own resources and capabilities to ensure its own protection from foreign aggression. Moreover, the only effective protection from one state's misuse of power is the countervailing power of another.

3. *The priority of power:* Realism places a premium on power and force. It assumes that the most important issues in world politics concern national security—often

Milosevic and Franjo Tudjman, the president of Croatia, used ethnonationalistic rhetoric to consolidate their own political power, to foster distrust among different groups, and to foment racial hatred. According to Warren Zimmermann, U.S. ambassador to Yugoslavia from 1989 to 1992, Milosevic is a man "almost totally dominated by his dark side," whereas Tudjman is a leader "obsessed by nationalism."[13] Two other leaders greatly responsible for the siege of Sarajevo and the deaths of thousands of Croats and Muslims are Bosnian Serb leader Radovan Karadzic and Serb military commander Ratko Mladic. Because of their role in Serb aggression, both have been indicted by the War Crimes Tribunal in The Hague.

The second level of analysis emphasizes the role domestic political and social developments—both within the disintegrating state of Yugoslavia, as well as in each of the seceding republics. Whereas the communist ideology provided the basis for the Yugoslavian regime's legitimacy during the Cold War, the discrediting of communism resulted in a new ethnonationalism based on ethnic claims. Although the old communism and the new nationalism differ in content, they are similar in that the media is a means for transmitting the regime's beliefs through indoctrination, manipulation, and intimidation. Moreover, whereas the old message rarely incited the people to hate other Yugoslavs, the new ideology encourages hatred among different ethnic and religious groups.[14]

Finally, from an international perspective, the origin and evolution of the Bosnian conflict is a result of several transnational developments. First, with the ending of the Cold War and the discrediting of communism in the late 1980s, the forces of disintegration quickly swept through former Soviet republics and other central European states, including Yugoslavia. The old ideology of communism was replaced by the new ideology of ethnonationalism. Second, the UN arms embargo had the ironic effect of freezing power relations, thereby protecting the dominance of the militarily powerful Serbs. Third, the introduction of a UN peacekeeping force was ineffective in protecting urban areas and in keeping the peace because there had been no agreement among the warring parties. Peace-enforcement was needed, not peacekeeping.

defined as **high politics** to differentiate it with the **low politics** of such nonsecurity issues as economic welfare, health care, and functional interdependence. Because Morgenthau defines politics as a struggle for power, he also defines the fundamental goals of a state—the national interest—in power terms. "We assume," writes Morgenthau, "that statesmen think and act in terms of interest defined as power."[15] Because of the insecurity associated with the anarchic international order, the immediate goal of states is always the same—the maximization of power, which is the method of realizing all other goals.

Realism assumes that survival is the most fundamental interest of states. Because of the anarchic nature of the global system, territorial integrity and political sovereignty are not assured. Moreover, because there is no common sovereign to defend the legitimate interests of states and to punish aggression, each state is ultimately responsible for protecting itself and for promoting its own interests in the world community. Although there are a variety of means by which states promote their interests, realists assume that military force is the most important. Because a nation's interests are best protected through force or the threat of force, states continually seek to expand their political and economic capabilities and to increase their military power. Moreover, because no state can effectively promote its interests alone, nations seek to acquire allies that can help deter aggression.

High Politics
The global politics concerned with national security and international peacekeeping.

Low politics
The global politics involving the promotion of socio-economic welfare.

4. *The priority of the state:* Realism is a state-centric approach. It assumes that the chief actor in the global system is the state. While recognizing the growing role of nonstate actors—especially multinational corporations, and international governmental organizations such as the United Nations and the European Community—the realistic perspective assumes that states are, and will continue to be in the foreseeable future, the dominant actors in world affairs.

5. *Consequential ethics:* Realists assume that foreign policy should be judged by its consequences, not its motives or goals. Realism has often been critiqued as being an amoral approach because of its emphasis on ends. But realists do not deny morality. They do not believe that any end can justify the use of any means. Indeed, Morgenthau argues that "realism is aware of the moral significance of political action."[16] What distinguishes the realist approach from others is not its immorality, but the priority given to outcomes. Realists do not apply abstract moral norms rigidly and universally but, instead, weigh alternative courses of action in the light of competing moral norms. This is why Morgenthau, following Aristotle, argues that **prudence**—the weighing of competing alternative courses of action—is the supreme moral virtue.

Prudence
The virtue of selecting and implementing policies in the light of alternative moral actions

Idealism
This approach to politics assumes that law, institutions, and morality can contribute to the development of peaceful, just international relations. An optimistic perspective towards world politics.

Idealism

Although the tradition of political **idealism** is rooted in ancient thought, its application to international relations is more recent. One of the first thinkers to apply idealism to international affairs was Dante, the fourteenth-century Italian author, who argued in his essay *Of Monarchy* for a unified world government as the best way to promote peace. In the nineteenth century, German philosopher Immanuel Kant repeated the call for world government in *On Perpetual Peace* by suggesting international peace and justice could be most effectively promoted by the creation of a world federal state. In the twentieth century, President Woodrow Wilson, the founder of the League of Nations at the end of World War I, is generally considered a leading exponent of the idealist approach to world affairs. Wilson believed that peace and justice could best be promoted internationally by strengthening the role of public opinion and reducing the power of national political elites. And in the late 1970s, President Jimmy Carter's emphasis on human rights renewed the idealistic vision of international justice.

The idealistic approach to international relations has four key features: optimism about human nature and community life, a belief that global relations are fundamentally harmonious, the priority of law and institutions in building a peaceful world, and a belief that ethics should inspire and illuminate decision making.

1. *Optimism:* The tradition of political idealism is rooted in an optimistic view of people and community life. According to idealists, human beings are motivated not only by self-interest, but also by moral aspirations, including the pursuit of the common good. One of the key tenets of idealism is that people are good, but that political structures based on power and authority are contrary to the common good. President Woodrow Wilson, for example, believed that power politics and the balance of power system were morally unacceptable and needed to be replaced by more humane global structures. This could best be achieved by building a world order based on international law, international organizations, and democratic regimes. The development of democracies was viewed as essential, because only a constitutional, representative government would reflect the goodness of people as expressed through global public opinion. Indeed, idealists had so much faith in the general public that secret diplomacy was thought to be contrary to the well-

being of the world. Indeed, one of the rallying cries of the post-World War I era was "open covenants, openly arrived at."

2. *Harmonious international relations:* International relations are regarded as fundamentally peaceful, rather than conflictual. The fundamental condition of the global society is not anarchy, but imperfect harmony and insufficient cooperation. The challenge in global society is to strengthen international cooperation. Given their optimistic assumptions about the nature of global society, idealists assume that rational dialog and peaceful negotiation are the most effective tools for resolving international tensions. Moreover, idealists believe that global cohesion can be further strengthened through increased functional interdependence. Specifically they assume that the promotion of international economic and social cooperation can strengthen transnational bonds. During the last half of the nineteenth century, British idealists, for example, advocated "peace through trade" in the belief that unregulated international commerce would promote peaceful international relations.[17]

3. *The priority of law and institutions:* Another key feature of idealism is its faith in law and government to build and maintain a peaceful and cooperative global community. Whereas realists believe that international peace and the promotion of global cooperation are by-products of interstate power relations, idealists assume that international organizations and international law can contribute greatly to global order and the resolution of transnational disputes. They also believe that international organizations like the United Nations, the Organization of American States, and the European Community can contribute significantly to global economic prosperity by facilitating coordination and cooperation.

4. *The priority of moral purposes:* According to idealism, the major function of international morality is to provide a vision of a better world, to identify ethically desirable foreign policy goals, and to illuminate relevant moral values for judging the implementation of policies. For idealists, the chief role of ethics is to inspire and guide human actions. Whereas realists emphasize the moral consequences of political action, idealists focus primarily on the morality of goals and intentions. Thus, although idealists emphasize the morality of means and ends, realists focus chiefly on the ethics of ends.

Interdependence

During the 1970s American scholars began to call attention to the increasing international economic and social interdependence. In their pioneering study *Power and Interdependence: World Politics in Transition,* Robert O. Keohane and Joseph S. Nye, Jr., argue that the global community has become increasingly interrelated in many different areas, resulting in a condition of "complex interdependence." This condition is characterized by a growing influence of "low" politics, coupled with a relative decline of national security issues.[18] Three features characterize the **interdependence** paradigm: the growing influence of nonstate actors, the priority of functional interdependence, and the declining role of force in world politics.

1. *The rise of nonstate actors:* Interdependence, or transnationalism, assumes that the state is not the only actor in international relations. The growth of nonstate actors, such as international organizations, multinational corporations (MNCs), and religious movements, has decreased the influence of the state in the world. To be sure, the state remains the most important actor, but governments are no longer the only determinants of international relations.

A corollary of this first proposition is that states do not always act as coherent, rational actors. One of the reasons for this is that modern

Interdependence
An approach to politics that emphasizes the growing influence of transnational socioeconomic cooperation and the role of nonstate actors.

Issue 1.1 Comparison of Neorealism and Neoliberal Institutionalism

In the post–Cold War world, two paradigms have dominated the analysis of IR—neorealism and neoliberal institutionalism. **Neorealism** (also called structural realism) is similar to realism in its emphasis on state actors, national power, and the quest for national security. Rather than emphasizing the moral dimensions of human and collective action, neorealism gives priority to global institutions and the impact of anarchy on the behavior of states. Because international structures are assumed to determine behavior, neorealism assumes that the world's decentralized, anarchic environment establishes structural priorities and constraints on all global actors. Indeed, because the survival and development of states cannot be guaranteed, neorealists assume that states will seek to maximize national power in order to reduce their vulnerability and increase national capabilities to advance foreign policy interests.[19]

In the 1980s, **neoliberal institutionalism** (also called neoliberalism) became the major version of the idealist approach. Like idealism, neoliberal institutionalism is optimistic about the possibility of peace and

global cooperation. This faith in peace and cooperation is not rooted simply in the goodwill of states, but in the efficacy of global institutions. Specifically neoliberalism assumes that global cooperation is a direct by-product of the work of international law, international governmental organizations, and informal global regimes that help to promote and sustain world order and peaceful conflict resolution.[20] Neoliberals are confident in the contribution of global institutions because they assume that such structures are not simply aggregations of state interests, but independent actors that influence the behavior of states. Moreover, neoliberalism, like classical idealism, emphasizes the role of international institutions in promoting global cooperation. Indeed, a major contribution of contemporary neoliberal research has been to illuminate the factors and conditions that facilitate international cooperation without the guidance of a central governmental authority.

Table 1.2 compares some of the major features of neorealism and neoliberal institutionalism.

TABLE 1.2   Major Features of Neorealism and Neoliberal Institutionalism

Major Features	Neorealism	Neoliberal Institutionalism
Nature of global society	Anarchic	Anarchic
Role of states in global society	States are the major actors	States are the major actors
Role of international institutions	Relatively insignificant	Significant; they exert independent influence on global relations
Primary state interests	Security	Security and welfare
Prospects for international cooperation	Minimal	Significant
Perspective about peace	Pessimistic	Optimistic

governments are complex organizations in which numerous offices share decision making. Moreover, issues themselves are multidimensional, so that many nongovernmental elites participate in making and implementing foreign policies. In a pioneering study analyzing the Cuban missile crisis of 1962, Graham Allison suggests that the behavior of the U.S. government during that crisis is best explained not as a coherent, rational response to events (the traditional explanation for foreign policy) but as the by-product of the different interests and perspectives of relevant political leaders and government agencies.[21] Decision making during the crisis was influenced, in other words, by bureaucratic politics and the interests and personalities of the key military and political advisors of the Kennedy administration.

2. *The priority of functional cooperation:* Keohane and Nye argue that there is no consistent hierarchy of issues in the international system. National security is not always the most important concern. As the world becomes more complex and interdependent, foreign policy issues become larger and more diverse, blurring traditional distinctions between domestic and international politics. As a result, the interdependence paradigm assumes that states are often as concerned with international cooperation and coordination as with the state autonomy. For example, the growing global economic, telecommunications, and transportation networks contributed to the fall of communism in Eastern Europe by fueling expectations about freedom and improvements in economic welfare and providing informational sources that the communist state could no longer effectively regulate. Modern technology had made state boundaries increasingly porous, including those ruled by authoritarian communist governments.

3. *The declining role of force:* Finally, the interdependence approach assumes that military force is no longer the sole, or even most important, means of exercising influence in the world community. Given the increasing social, cultural, and economic ties among states, governments can rely on instruments other than force to influence foreign states. By the same token, because the world is more interdependent, militarily powerful states are increasingly vulnerable to important nongovernmental, nonmilitary developments in foreign countries. For example, significant economic developments in one country, such as the U.S. stock market crash of October 1987, can have profound effects in other countries. Moreover, environmental crises, such as the 1986 Chernobyl nuclear power plant failure in the Soviet Union or the massive Kuwait petroleum fires, deliberately begun in February 1991 by Iraqi soldiers shortly before their withdrawal from that country, can affect environmental and social conditions in other countries as well.

To be sure, all states are vulnerable in some measure to foreign nonmilitary developments. But the degree of national vulnerability to such developments will depend greatly on the character of the states themselves. Factors that are likely to influence the impact of international developments include the level of penetration by global transportation and telecommunications networks, the level of international trade, the degree of dependence on raw materials, the level of economic development, and the nature and strength of alliances.

Dependency

Unlike the other three approaches, **dependency theory** is not a comprehensive approach to international politics. Rather, it attempts to provide an explanation for the significant economic disparities between the developed industrial states and the poor nations of the Third World. Based partly on the political economy of Marxism, the paradigm attributes the weakness and poverty of developing nations to external conditions, including exploitation by the developed nations and by the inequities of existing rules and institutions of the international economic system. This perspective is especially popular in the developing nations of the Third World because their poverty and vulnerability are attributed to the developed industrial states. According to the theory, the wealth of the *North* (the rich, industrial states) is a direct by-product of the poverty of the *South* (the developing nations).

Neorealism
Unlike realism, which bases the universality and constancy of conflict on human nature, this perspective attributes the priority of power and security on the decentralized, anarchic structure of global society.

Neoliberal institutionalism
The belief that international organizations and other nonstate actors can contribute significantly to international cooperation.

Dependency theory
A neo-Marxist theory attributing the wealth of the industrial states and the poverty of the Third World to global capitalist structures. According to the theory, international economic structures foster income inequalities among states, thereby increasing Third World dependency.

Issue 1.2 IR From a Postmodern Perspective

Postmodernism (also known as critical theory or contructivism) is not a political theory but a general approach to knowledge. It is significant because contemporary Western scholarship, including international relations, has been influenced by this intellectual tradition. According to postmodernists, the major determinants of reality are concepts that are the driving force of history. Ideas matter because they determine how people behave. Moreover, because concepts and theories are developed by human beings, individuals ultimately bear responsibility for shaping the world they inhabit. The postmodern perspective thus challenges traditional political approaches (such as realism and idealism) that assume that the primary determinants of world politics are legal, political, economic, and security structures. Postmodernists allege that, because reality is "socially constructed," the major determinants of international relations are the ideas and concepts that influence how people think. As one scholar observes, "[h]ow individuals think about and talk about the world matters greatly for determining how states act in the international system."[22]

Postmodernist IR theorists are deeply concerned with the development of a more just and peaceful world. They believe that the anarchic structures that have governed the international system since the fourteenth century have been a source of great injustice and suffering and need to be replaced. Although they acknowledge that realism has been the prevailing international relations paradigm in modern history, they believe that the post–Cold War era provides a unique opportunity to reconceptualize international politics by replacing the institutionalized practices of distrust, competition, and conflict with norms based on trust and sharing. Only by institutionalizing such alternative concepts and ideas can the world move towards a more humane and peaceful system.[23]

According to the theory, the poverty and powerlessness of the developing nations is due to their dependent status, caused in great measure by global economic and political structures. Such structures not only favor the rich, industrial states, but inhibit development in Third World states and impede their political and economic independence. Dependency is assumed to be a harmful condition because it stunts the indigenous development of a people. What the poor nations need to do, according to the theory, is to break away from the yoke of bondage and become more politically and economically independent. Only then can they carry out authentic development.

Four key elements characterize the dependency paradigm: a deep cleavage between rich and poor states, the priority of economic relationships, the priority of independence, and the importance of nonstate actors.

1. *Conflict between rich and poor states:* The dependency paradigm views the world system as deeply divided between rich, powerful states and weak, developing nations—a cleavage that derives directly from the expansion of world capitalism. Because capitalist expansion involves the exploitation of workers by the owners, the inevitable consequence of capitalism is the growth of domestic and international economic inequalities. According to Andre Gunder Frank, one of the founders of the dependency perspective, before the introduction of capitalism, Third World nations were *undeveloped,* but after they were integrated into the world capitalistic economy, they became *underdeveloped,* with wealth passing from colonies to imperial states, from poor nations to rich, industrial states. Frank writes: "It is capitalism, both world and national, which produced underdevelopment in the past and which still generates underdevelopment in the present."[29] In short, underdevelopment is not a natural condition but a direct by-product of the expansion of capitalism.

TABLE 1.3 Comparison of Perspectives on International Politics

	Realism	Idealism	Interdependence	Dependency
Major actors	States	States	Nonstates	States, MNCs
Nature of relations	Conflictual	Harmonious	Competitive and complementary	Conflictual and harmonious
Key issue	National security	Peace, prosperity	Global coordination	Vulnerability, dependence
Key symbol	Soldier	Diplomat	MNCs	Diplomat and businessman
Type of politics	High	High	Low	High and low
Role of force	High	Low	Low	Low
Role of world organizations	Limited	Significant	Significant	Moderate
Policy implications	Maximize power	Promote world community through law	Promote international cooperation	Decrease economic vulnerability

2. *The priority of economic relationships:* According to Marxism, the most important elements in society are its underlying economic structures and practices. Politics rests on these socioeconomic foundations. Following Marxism, dependency theory assumes that economics determines politics and more particularly that international economics determine international politics. Related to this, dependency theory also assumes that the road to national well-being is through wealth creation and the establishment of economic structures that assure an equitable international distribution of resources. Unlike idealism and realism, which assume that global order is achieved through the management of power, dependency theory assumes that global stability and international peace are rooted in domestic and international economic structures and the distribution of resources.

3. *The priority of independence:* Dependency theory holds that dependence is harmful to nations because it compromises political sovereignty and limits control over a nation's economic resources.[30] According to the theory, a major goal of all nations—rich or poor, large or small—is to maintain full control over its political and economic resources. Although dependency theory ostensibly is concerned with Third World poverty, the focus is not on poverty per se but economic inequalities. The crime of the international economic order is not that many people live in conditions of abject poverty in the developing nations, but that a large and growing economic gap exists between nations. This gap is harmful because it decreases the freedom of action of poor states, making them vulnerable to developed, industrial states.

Dependency theorists believe that Third World nations need to break the yoke of international bondage by encouraging greater political and economic independence. In the early manifestations of the theory, dependency was assumed to promote poverty in the developing nations. More recent elaborations, however, have suggested that participation in the world economy need not result in poverty, but may actually promote economic growth. However, a nation's participation in the world capitalistic economy is costly because it fosters economic dependence. Participation in the world economy can therefore result in the paradoxical state of **dependent**

Dependent development
Economic development that is conditioned and controlled by foreign actors.

Issue 1.3 IR from a Feminist Perspective

In recent years, scholarship on women and gender has emerged as a significant area of study within the field of international relations.[24] Although feminist scholars would agree with J. Ann Tickner that IR is a "gendered" activity,[25] they hold different viewpoints about the nature and implication of gender differences. One scholar has identified three distinct strands of feminist scholarship: essentialist, liberal, and postmodern.[26] *Essentialist feminism* assumes that differences between men and women are real and significant, rooted in biology, not in social constructions or cultural indoctrination. Because of women's unique feminine attributes, this feminist stand emphasizes the important role of women as caregivers. *Liberal feminism,* by contrast, emphasizes the fundamental equality of men and women, deploring the underrepresentation of women in foreign policy and national security affairs. Its aim is to increase the role and influence of women in international affairs. *Postmodern feminism* challenges the assumptions of both essentialists and liberals. It assumes that because gender roles are social constructions, IR should be cleansed ("deconstructed") of its harmful masculine norms so that a more humane, just world can be established.

Feminist scholars have suggested that a "gender bias" afflicts both the study of IR and the work of international affairs officials, especially soldiers, diplomats, and political leaders. This bias is based not so much on biological differences between men and women, but on the "culturally shaped and defined characteristics associated with masculinity and femininity."[27] According to feminists, this bias was clearly evident in the masculine-oriented, power-driven, state-centric realist paradigm governing Cold War IR. And because of realism's dominance, feminists have alleged that traditional IR scholarship has overemphasized masculine norms, such as hierarchy, conflict, war, collective defense, and national security, and neglected more feminine themes, such as belonging, cooperation, equality, and trust. Although most feminists believe that women have been underrepresented in global society, they do not seek to replace male dominance with feminist norms, but to reformulate the analysis of IR by transcending existing gender categories. According to Tickner, this information will require, as a first step, the integration of a feminist perspective into the discipline so that women's experiences are included in the analysis of IR on an equal basis with men's experiences. It will also require the elimination of "oppressive gender hierarchies."[28] Only then, Tickner believes, will the transcendence of gender be possible in international relations.

development,[31] in which economic growth is conditioned by foreign interests and institutions.

Because a major goal of dependency theory is to lessen dependence, countries must choose whether to participate in economic growth programs that reduce their freedom of action or whether to seek political and economic independence, even if it means continued low living standards for citizens.

4. *The importance of nonstate actors:* Like interdependence, dependency theory assumes that nonstate actors play an important role in global society. This is especially the case for multinational corporations (MNCs), which serve as major international actors in the contemporary world. Marxists writers have suggested that during the late nineteenth and early twentieth centuries, colonies served as the principle instrument by which imperial powers maintained economic and political control over foreign resources and people. With the demise of colonialism, a new form of control has replaced colonies, according to neo-Marxists. The new instrument of control is the MNC—a nonstate actor that provides almost as much economic penetration as a colony without the political control of the imperial power. Table 1.3 summarizes the major differences among the four international relations perspectives.

In Conclusion

Politics is the process by which communities promote shared interests and settle conflicts. Because domestic societies normally have authoritative governmental institutions to make, apply, and interpret rules, the promotion of shared interests and the resolution of disputes in nation-states is achieved with comparative efficiency. In global society, by contrast, there are no authoritative institutions responsible for making policies and settling disputes. As a result, the pursuit of shared interests and resolution of conflict is ultimately dependent on the individual and collective actions of member-states. Thus, whereas domestic decision making is entrusted to government, decision making in a global society is carried out informally and voluntarily by state and nonstate actors.

Although this study integrates concerns from each of the four major perspectives, the text emphasizes the realist themes of power and conflict, the idealist themes of justice and institution building, and the interdependence theme of functional cooperation.

SUMMARY

1. Politics in domestic and international societies differ in a number of significant respects. First, domestic societies are more homogenous than global society, and therefore better able to develop and maintain social order. Second, domestic societies have government institutions that are more developed than those in the international community. As a result, domestic societies normally have a higher level of stability than the international community.

2. The Peloponnesian War of the fifth century B.C. provides an insightful case study because it illuminates problems and challenges facing contemporary countries. These challenges are rooted in the decentralized, anarchic global community in which security and well-being are ultimately dependent on each state's resources.

3. The analysis of IR requires intellectual constructs that facilitate the simplification of reality and guide intellectual investigation. The most important tools include concepts, theories, and paradigms.

4. Scholars also use different conceptual tools and methods to analyze IR. The most important conceptual categories, or levels of analysis, applied in IR investigation focus on the impact of individuals, states, and the international system on the foreign relations of states.

5. During the postwar era scholars have approached international relations from a number of perspectives. The most important of these are realism, idealism, interdependence, and dependency theory. The realist orientation emphasizes the interaction of states, the role of power, and the regularity of conflict. Idealism, by contrast, emphasizes the harmonious nature of global relations and the role of law and institutions in improving international peace. Interdependence emphasizes nonstate actors, the priority of socioeconomic cooperation, and the declining role of force. Finally, dependency theory emphasizes the economic inequalities fostered by global capitalism and the vulnerability of developing nations to the developed, industrial states.

KEY TERMS

international relations (IR)	Sparta	realism	interdependence
empirical knowledge	Delian League	high politics	neorealism
conceptual knowledge	Peloponnesian War	low politics	neoliberal institutionalism
theoretical knowledge	levels of analysis	prudence	dependency theory
Athens	paradigms	idealism	dependent development

RECOMMENDED READINGS

Carr, E.H. *The Twenty Years' Crisis, 1919–1939: An Introduction to the Study of International Relations*. New York: Harper & Row, 1964. Although written just before World War II, this study remains a classic, offering a penetrating assessment of realism and idealism. The study focuses on the role of power, morality, law, and global organizations in building international order.

Dougherty, James E., and Robert L. Pfaltzgraff, Jr. *Contending Theories of International Relations: A Comprehensive Survey*. 4th ed. New York: Longman, 1997. A superior review of leading theories of international relations, including realism, geopolitics, systems, economic imperialism, decision making, and theories of conflict. A useful comparative assessment of competing theories of global politics.

Doyle, Michael W. *Ways of War and Peace: Realism, Liberalism, and Socialism*. New York: W. W. Norton, 1997. Using classical political theorists, Doyle defines three distinct worldviews that have influenced the analysis of IR—realism, liberalism, and socialism. He then illuminates how each tradition has contributed to the analysis of issues of war and peace. This penetrating study is essential reading for anyone concerned with the contribution of classical thought to the analysis of foundational IR issues.

Kennedy, Paul. *Preparing for the Twenty-First Century*. New York: Random House, 1993. Explores how increasing resource-scarcity, the population explosion, instant communications, and modern technology are likely to affect the world. Includes insightful chapters on Japan, the United States, and the developing nations.

Keohane, Robert O., ed. *Neorealism and Its Critics*. New York: Columbia University Press, 1986. A penetrating collection of essays that describe and critique the central elements of realism and neorealism, its contemporary adaptation by Kenneth Waltz. Chapter 1 by Keohane provides an especially lucid overview of realism and neorealism and its critics. In chapters 10 and 11 Robert Gilpin and Kenneth Waltz provide a spirited defense of the realist tradition.

Keohane, Robert O., and Joseph S. Nye, Jr. *Power and Interdependence: World Politics in Transition,* 2nd ed. Glenview: Scott Foresman/Little, Brown, 1989. A path-breaking study challenging the realist paradigm and offering complex interdependence as an alternative model. Study provides case studies on the growth of functional interdependence in ocean and money regimes, as well as U.S. bilateral relations with Canada and Australia.

Miller, Lynn H. *Global Order: Values and Power in International Politics*. Boulder: Westview Press, 1985. A short, readable introduction to global politics from a normative perspective. The study focuses on the problems of war, global economic inequality, human rights, and environmental degradation.

Morgenthau, Hans J., and Kenneth W. Thompson. *Politics Among Nations: The Struggle for Power and Peace*. 6th ed. New York: Alfred A. Knopf, 1985. This is an updated and revised version of the most influential American text of international politics during the postwar era. Presents a realist perspective on global politics.

Thucydides. *The Peloponnesian War*. Translated by Rex Warner. New York: Penguin Books, 1972. Written 400 years before the birth of Christ, this is a penetrating account, from a realist perspective, of the twenty-year war between Athens and Sparta. A classic.

Tickner, J. Ann. *Gender in International Relations: Feminist Perspectives on Achieving Global Security*. New York: Columbia University Press, 1992. Applying feminist scholarship to international relations phenomena, this study shows how gender sensitivity can contribute to alternative conceptions of international security.

RELEVANT WEB SITES

Central Intelligence Agency Factbook	www.odci.gov/cia/publications/ nsolo/wfb-all.htm
Foreign Policy Association See domestic and foreign newspaper links	www.fpa.org/links.html
International Affairs Network (IAN) International affairs resources	www.pitt.edu/~ian/ianres.html
International Relations and Security Network (ISN) Data on Major IR topics	www.isn.ethz.ch/
NATO Operations in Bosnia	www.nato.int/ifor
U.S. Department of Defense Bosnia activities	www.dtic.mil/bosnia/index.html
U.S. Department of State See Current Issues	www.state.gov/index.html
The Watson Institute for International Studies (Brown University)	www.brown.edu/Departments/ Watson_Institute/

CHAPTER

Nation-States and Other Actors

2

Although international relations are carried out by many different types of organizations and political communities, the chief actors in the global community are nation-states—generally referred to simply as states, nations, or countries. For more than 300 years the nation-state has remained the dominant political actor in world politics. No other political institution has greater authority over people. The state, not the world community, maintains the ultimate political claims on human beings.

This chapter sketches the rise of the nation-state and examines its nature and role in the contemporary world system. It also examines the nature and role of nonstate actors, including international organizations, multinational corporations, and international political and religious movements. In addition, the chapter describes and assesses the impact of nationalism on nation-states and, in particular, on the global order itself.

THE RISE OF THE NATION-STATE

The state, which is the political organization responsible for maintaining and sustaining community life, is as old as civilization itself. Because community life is impossible without some formal or informal patterns of community decision making, social existence is possible only within the context of the state. Throughout history there have been a variety of political communities, such as city-states, empires, kingdoms, and feudal estates. During the second and third centuries, for example, the Roman Empire was the dominant political community, while in the Middle Ages feudal kingdoms became the chief form of government and community. During this latter period, when popes exerted significant influence on the affairs of states, conflicts often emerged between spiritual and temporal rulers.

Though the state originated in ancient times, the nation-state did not begin until the mid-seventeenth century. Throughout the medieval era, Europe was governed by a multiplicity of disjointed feudal fiefdoms, but in the fifteenth and sixteenth centuries political authority was increasingly

We have made Italy; now we have to make Italians.[1]

Massimo d'Azeglio, *member of Italy's first parliament, 1861*

The urge to have a state, to create a state, and to belong to a state is one of the most fundamental political-psychological values of an era obsessed with questions of community and identity.[2]

Kalevi J. Holsti, *IR scholar*

If we give importance to other things, like religion, our [regional] state, our language or our caste, and forget our country, we shall be destroyed. All these have their proper place, but if we place [them] above the country, the nation will be destroyed.[3]

Jawaharlal Nehru, *Indian nationalist and India's first prime minister*

There may have been a certain erosion of the powers of the nation-state in recent decades, but the nation-state remains the primary locus of identity of most people. . . . even if the autonomy and functions of the state have been eroded by transnational trends, no adequate substitute has emerged to replace it as the key unit in responding to global change.[4]

Paul Kennedy, *noted historian*

TABLE 2.1 Growth of Nation-States, 1800–1995

Area	Pre-1801	1801–1917	1918–1945	1946–1985	1986–1995	Total
Europe/N. America	13	9	6	1	13	42
Latin America	0	20	0	13	0	33
Asia	6	0	3	16	9	34
Africa	1	2	0	46	2	51
Middle East	2	0	6	10	0	18
Oceania	0	2	0	4	3	9
Total New States		33	15	90	27	
Total States	22	55	70	160	187	187

Source: Data to 1945 from C. Taylor and M. Hudson, *World Handbook of Political and Social Indicators,* 2nd ed. (New Haven: Yale University Press, 1972), pp. 26-28; 1945-1990 data from John Paxton, ed., *The Statesman's Yearbook, 1991-1992,* (New York: St Martin's Press, 1991); 1991-1995 data from UN Press Release, ORG/1190 (15 December 1994).

centralized and consolidated among larger, more contiguous regions through the growing power of kings, princes, and other secular rulers. One of the major contributors to this state-building process was war—a process that encouraged rulers to consolidate and extend their authority in order to maximize their political and economic power.[5] Although the development of modern, integrated states has continued through the present century, the rise of nation-states is normally dated from the *Treaty of Westphalia* (1648), which ended the Thirty Years' War in Europe. This event marks the beginning of the modern nation-state system because it recognized the unqualified right of secular rulers to govern territories in which they had a monopoly of force. Features of the so-called "Westphalian system" of nation-states are described in the next chapter.

During the eighteenth century there were fewer than twenty active nation-states, and not until the early twentieth century did the number rise above fifty. Since the end of World War II, the number of states has increased nearly two and a half times—from 70 to more than 180—with most of the growth taking place in Asia and Africa as former colonies achieved political independence. During the 1960s more than thirty-five states received political independence in Africa alone, while the ending of the Cold War and the disintegration of the Soviet Union has spawned close to twenty new states. Table 2.1 shows the growth of nation-states.

During the 1970s and 1980s the growth of states came to a virtual halt because few former colonial territories remained without political independence. Indeed, of the remaining non-self-governing territories, most were small, underpopulated territories that preferred to remain under the protection of a larger, more powerful state. Until the late 1980s, Namibia was the largest non-self-governing territory in Africa, but it, too, received its independence from the Republic of South Africa in early 1990.

The ending of the Cold War precipitated another sudden expansion in the number of nation-states. With the weakening of Soviet communism and the growing influence of nationalism, the Soviet Union began to rapidly disintegrate and by the beginning of 1992 the Soviet empire had ceased to exist. The three Baltic republics (Estonia, Latvia, and Lithuania), which had been forcefully incorporated into the Soviet Union in 1939 as a result of a secret diplomatic accord between Germany and the USSR, were the first nations to break away from the Soviet state. After pressing for political independence for nearly two years, the Baltic states were granted independence in September 1991. A failed coup against Soviet President Mikhail Gorbachev accelerated the transfer of authority from the Soviet central government to its member republics. On December 8, the three leading republics of the Soviet Union—Russia, Ukraine, and Belarus—implicitly declared their political independence by establishing the *Commonwealth of Independent States (CIS)*. Subsequently all remaining nine republics declared their political independence. Since then, ethnic groups in many of the former Soviet republics—including Chechens in Russia, Armenians in Azerbaijan, and Abkhazians in Georgia—have continued to demand increasing self-rule from the state. Undoubtedly, the most bitter fighting has been within the former Yugoslavia, where the secession of four republics—Slovenia, Croatia, Bosnia-Herzegovina, and Macedonia—resulted in brief wars of independence and a long, bitter civil war in Bosnia among Croats, Muslims, and Serbs. In addition, in 1993 Czechoslovakia broke up into two distinct states—the Czech Republic and the Slovak Republic.

THE NATURE OF NATION-STATES

The major features of states are population, territory, government, and sovereignty. We can distinguish the contemporary state from other previous political communities by identifying the essential elements of a state and nation. Although these two terms are used interchangeably, technically they have distinct meanings. The term state refers to the governmental and political dimensions of human organization, whereas nation refers to the social and cultural aspects of community. The modern nation-state is simply the fusion of one or more nations with a state.

What Is a State?

A **state** is a legal and political concept referring to a well-defined territory controlled by a government and inhabited by a permanent population. From a rudimentary perspective, a state is a legal entity based on land, people, and government. From a more comprehensive approach, a state involves three different elements: (1) an *idea,* represented by the affective sentiments of people represented in culture, history, and ideology; (2) *physical elements,* including population, territory, and economic resources; and (3) *institutions,* including a regime constitution, laws, and governmental decision-making structures and procedures.[6]

State
A political community with people, territory, and sovereign government.

A key feature of the state is a government able to make and enforce binding rules within a defined territory without external interference. When a state is free and independent from others, and effectively commands obedience from its subjects, then it is regarded as sovereign. During the sixteenth century Jean Bodin, a French political historian, coined the concept **sovereignty** to symbolize a ruler's unqualified political power over people within a defined territory. Sovereignty, as defined by Bodin, was the "supreme power over citizens and subjects unrestrained by law."[7] Although Bodin identified sovereignty with the monarch, subsequent political theorists, such as Thomas Hobbes, John Locke, and Jean Jacques Rousseau, associated it with either the government or the people themselves.

Sovereignty
Supreme authority to make binding decisions within states, from an international perspective, state sovereignty implies states' legal equality and political independence.

Sovereignty has two important dimensions—one domestic and the other international. Domestically, sovereignty means that government has the unqualified authority to make and enforce decisions and laws within specified territorial boundaries. Internationally, it means that a state is recognized as the ultimate decision-making authority within global society. No other state or nonstate actor has the right to impose its will on a nation-state.[8]

From a perspective of interstate relations, sovereignty provides the basis for two key international norms—the juridical equality of states and the political independence of states. The notion of legal equality assumes that nation-states have a fundamental right to exist and to enjoy the rights associated with state sovereignty. Although states are obviously unequal in terms of size, population, and military power, the legal fiction of equality, explicitly affirmed in the UN Charter (art. 2), is a basic principle of the contemporary world system. Of course, in view of the international system's disparities in power, a number of important inequalities have been institutionalized in the global society. One of the most important of these is the veto, which gives the major powers the right to block substantive actions by the UN Security Council. Another illustration of institutionalized inequalities is the Nonproliferation Treaty (NPT)—an accord that prohibits the expansion of nuclear states, while allowing current nuclear states to keep their weapons.

Sovereignty is also important because it reinforces the idea of political independence. Fundamentally, aggression occurs when one state seeks to interfere in the internal affairs of another by resorting to military force. If states are equal, free, and independent, then using force to interfere in the decision-making authority of another state is a violation of a basic state right and justifies the use of force to repulse this illegal and criminal act.

What Is a Nation?

Nation
A people sharing a common culture, language, history, and desire for political self-rule.

A **nation** is a social and cultural conglomeration of people. When people share a common language, culture, economic system, and history, they develop common affinities, values, attitudes, and patterns of behavior. These common ties are the basis of a nation. Although political power may influence the evolution of a nation, governments do not create nations. Rather, they grow and evolve from shared interests, values, and habits. Most importantly, the development and evolution of nations is rooted in a *myth of common ancestry*. Whether such a myth is historically true is not important; what is significant is that a myth is regarded as true, thereby providing a shared vision for a people.[9] The basis of a nation, in short, is not the power of government, but a high degree of community interdependence based on mutual aspirations and shared values, and a belief in a common heritage. Fundamentally, a nation is a people—a group of individuals who understand each other and share a sense of "belonging."

Three factors have been especially important in the development of modern nations. First, modernization has contributed to nation building by creating and expanding transportation and communications networks. The development of railroads, highways, and telecommunications systems, for example, has helped to break down social, cultural, and economic barriers within political communities and to increase social interaction and economic interdependence among groups within defined geographical boundaries. In effect, modernization has fostered community cohesion and increased personal and group affinities within national boundaries.

A second key element in the development of nations is a common culture. Karl Deutsch defines a people as "a group with complementary communication habits whose members usually share the same language, and always share a similar culture so that all members of the group attach the same meaning to words."[10] Although a common language is important in developing a strong nation, even more important are the common cultural patterns on which trust and predictability are based. The absence of predictability of human behaviors and attitudes means no trust; and without trust there can be no community. Aliens do not feel part of the nations precisely because they do not share the common cultural norms holding nations together.

A third characteristic of a modern nation is the desire for self-rule. John Stuart Mill defined a nationality as a people who "are united among themselves by common sympathies, which do not exist between them and any others—which make them cooperate with each other more willingly than with other people, desire to be under the same government and desire that it should be government by themselves or a portion of themselves, exclusively."[11] Although a self-conscious awareness of a common heritage and culture is important, even more significant is the desire and determination to promote and protect the nation's distinctive features. Hans Kohn writes: "Although objective factors are of great importance for the formation of nationalities, the most essential element is a living and active corporate will."[12] A central requirement for a nation is, thus, the identity and will to remain a people. Nations, in short, are social organizations that become politically organized in order to ensure their survival and development.

Despite these features noted above, it is important to stress that nations are not fixed entities but are continuously being defined and redefined. As Alain Touraine has observed, nations are organic in nature, constantly redefining themselves in the light of historical challenges they confront. In his view the end of communism in Poland, for example, dates from the rise of the Solidarity Movement in 1980–1981—a movement that set forth "an alternative agenda of historical action"[13] and thereby displaced communism's leading role in Polish society.

Strength of Nation-States

Nation-states differ in their capacity to meet human needs domestically and to fulfill interstate obligations internationally. Normally, nation-states that are effective in fulfilling domestic and international obligations have a strong national identity, significant physical resources, and well-developed governmental institutions; ineffective states, by contrast, do not generally have these attributes. Although attitudes, resources, and institutions are essential in ensuring strong states, Kalevi Holsti has argued that these objective features do not themselves assure effectiveness. In his view, if states are to govern effectively and fulfill international obligations, they must be viewed as legitimate, enjoying communal approval based on domestic political cohesion and social solidarity. According to Holsti, legitimacy involves two dimensions: (1) *horizontal legitimacy,* which refers to the nature and character of political community and who is included in the "we" of the nation-states; and (2) *vertical legitimacy,* which represents the level of governmental authority and the level of loyalty between people and rulers.[14] The first dimension, based on the affective political disposition of people, establishes criteria for membership in the state. The second dimension defines who has the right to rule and on what basis. Because political systems have been based increasingly on the notion of popular sovereignty, vertical legitimacy depends heavily on political participation and consent expressed in periodic elections.

In the light of these notions, nation-states can be classified along a continuum of strong and weak states. **Strong states** are those political systems with high levels of horizontal and vertical legitimacy. Such states are characterized by, among other things, effective governmental institutions, domestic tranquillity, strong political parties and interest groups, limited corruption, and widespread support for the political system's rules. Examples of such states include Australia, Denmark, Norway, and Switzerland. By contrast, **weak states**—sometimes called *quasi-states*—are those political systems with limited domestic political and economic capabilities and limited vertical and horizontal legitimacy. As Robert Jackson has noted, such states frequently survive only through significant external support.[15] Examples of weak states include Afghanistan, Albania, Bosnia, Democratic Republic of Congo (formerly Zaire), Haiti, and Sierra Leone. In such systems, government is corrupt and ineffective, rulers command little authority, the political system is unstable, the regime provides few benefits, and crime and random violence are widespread.

Strong state
A coherent and stable nation-state with authoritative governmental institutions.

Weak state
A divided and unstable nation-state ruled by a weak government. A regime with limited legitimacy.

TABLE 2.2 Comparison of Strong and Weak States

Features	Strong States	Weak States
Legitimacy of government	Based on performance	Based on coercive power
Scope of inclusiveness within community	Inclusive of all groups	Some groups excluded
Decision-making style	Bureaucratic, impersonal	Personalistic
Type of politics	Instrumental, emphasis on process	Fundamentalist, emphasis on ends
Development of political institutions (political institutionalization)	High	Low
Level of corruption	Low	High
Capabilities to protect human rights, especially personal security	High	Low
Civilian control of the military	Yes	No
International recognition of state	Widely recognized	Not widely recognized

Because strong states and weak states represent ideal-type concepts, most states are found in between these extremes. Moreover, because states' physical capabilities and levels of political legitimacy vary in response to domestic and international developments, the strength and effectiveness of nation-states can rise or decline over time. Table 2.2 identifies a number of key features of strong and weak states.

In the post–Cold War era, the growing disintegration of existing nation-states has given rise to the phenomenon of failed or collapsed states. Fundamentally, **failed states** are those political systems that have lost their capacity to function. Unlike weak states, which provide rudimentary services and minimal governmental functions, failed states are characterized by little or no civic order, no governmental authority to make and enforce laws, and widespread violence by groups and factions competing for control of territorial regions of states. Two developments have been especially important in the breakdown of states in the 1990s: first, the collapse of the Soviet Union and the decline of communism resulted in a vacuum of domestic political authority in countries and political entities formerly controlled by communists, such as Armenia, Georgia, Tajikistan, and the former Yugoslavia; and second, the rising influence of cultural, ethnic, and religious loyalties has increased domestic political strife in a growing number of Third World states, including Burundi, Liberia, Rwanda, Sierra Leone, and Somalia. Benjamin Barber, who calls these religious and tribal affinities the forces of "Jihad," argues that the growth of local and particularistic loyalties has developed as local peoples have struggled "to sustain solidarity and tradition against the nation-state's legalistic and pluralistic abstractions."[16] In sum, although the number of states has more than tripled in the last half of the twentieth century, many of these new states have been characterized by weakness and ineffectiveness. And the rise of domestic strife and civil wars among some Third World states has compromised their ability to fulfill domestic obligations to citizens and international obligations to other states.

Patterns of Nation-States

As a general rule, nations have achieved their greatest level of cohesion and development when they are governed by a separate state. In the modern international

Failed state
A state that has lost its ability to perform the rudimentary tasks of governing.

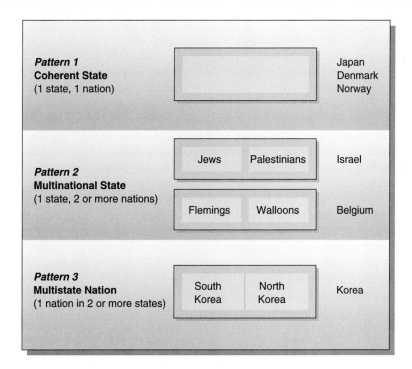

FIGURE 2.1
Comparison of
Three Nation-State
Patterns

political system, states and nations have been related in three distinct ways. (See fig. 2.1.) The first pattern, represented by the **coherent state,** involves a near congruent relationship between a nation and a state. In such countries there is a close correspondence between a people and the territorial boundaries of a state. Countries characterized by this monolithic fusion of nation and state include Denmark, the Netherlands, Japan, and Norway. Because the contemporary world system has only some 180 states but thousands of nations, only a small portion of the world's countries are coherent states. It has been estimated that less than 10 percent of the world's countries are based on a nearly perfect symmetrical relationship between nation and state.

Coherent state
A country characterized by a close fusion of nation and state.

The second pattern is the **multinational state,** in which one state includes two or more major national groupings. Nearly 90 percent of the countries in the world are based on a political union of two or more nationalities. Some countries like Belgium are based on two distinct peoples, whereas others are based on many different cultural groups. Unlike the coherent, unitary state, multinational states are held together either by strong political leadership or by negotiated settlements. As a result, such states tend to be more fragile, especially if there is an absence of strong central government.

Multinational state
A state comprising two or more nations.

Multinational states can also be differentiated in terms of their patterns of government. One type of multinational state is ruled by one dominant national group. This dominance may derive from its size or from its political and military power. For example, the Russian people comprise nearly two-thirds of the Russian Federation's population, giving them nearly absolute control over the country's politics. On the other hand, although the Tutsi people constitute only about 15 percent of Rwanda's population, they have historically dominated the Hutus, who constitute the bulk of the country's people. Similarly, although whites constitute less than 20 percent of South Africa's population, the white minority has historically dominated South Africa's government. With the establishment of democratic rule based on universal suffrage, the black majority, led by Nelson Mandela, gained political control in 1994 for the first time in the country's history.

The second type of authority pattern is one in which the different nationalities share in governing the state. Canada, with its French-speaking nation in the province of Quebec, illustrates this pattern. Although some radical Quebec nationalists have demanded secession from the English-speaking state, the Canadian government has sought to accommodate the ethnic wishes of the people from Quebec, allowing a great deal of self-government under a federal system. Switzerland, a multinational state of German-, French-, and Italian-speaking peoples, is another example. Despite the distinct ethnic differences among Swiss citizens, Switzerland has established an effective system of shared political power. This has been achieved through a federal, collegial system of governance, with significant political responsibilities entrusted to each of the country's cantons.

Multistate nation
Nations whose members live in two or more states.

The third pattern is a **multistate nation,** in which a nation is divided between two or more states. This pattern, the least common, is rooted partly on past imperial conquests and wars, resulting in state boundaries based on the outcomes of military confrontations, not the homogeneity of peoples. For example, during the Cold War era some states were divided on the basis of superpower ideological conflicts. The separation of Taiwan from the People's Republic of China, the division of Korea (North and South), and the former division of Germany (East and West) illustrate this pattern.

In contemporary global society, the most common nation-state pattern is the multinational state. Although the multinational states vary significantly in the number of nationalities that they include, most of them are based upon a dominant nationality. According to Walker Conner, for example, of 132 states in 1971, 93 (or 70 percent) had a dominant nationality accounting for at least 50 percent of the people.[17] Although the proportion of states with a dominant nationality has declined in the late twentieth century under the growing pressures of ethnic and cultural nationalism, the bulk of the world's multinational states remain based on a dominant nationality.

The nature and strength of nation-states is important to international relations because the level of domestic cohesion and political order significantly influences the nature and character of transnational political relations of states. Because the stability of global relations depends greatly on the nature of each member state, the absence of domestic order is likely to influence greatly the character of world politics. Indeed, most major conflicts in the post–Cold War era have been rooted in ethnic, cultural, and religious conflicts that have challenged the authority of governments and threatened the disintegration of states. In some cases the outbreak of civil war has not only resulted in tribal genocide (Rwanda) and massive famine (Somalia), but has destabilized entire regions, such as the Balkans and the Caucasus. Similarly, the ongoing Arab-Israeli conflict has threatened not only the stability of Israel and the reconciliation of Jews and Palestinians, but has also impeded peace in the Middle East.

THE NATURE AND ROLE OF NATIONALISM

Definition

Nationalism
The exclusive attachment and political commitment to one's nation, leading to demands for political self-determination and the consolidation of modern nation-states.

Michael Ignatieff defines **nationalism** as "the belief that the world's peoples are divided into nations, and that each of these nations has the right of self-determination, either as self-governing units within existing nation-states or as a nation-states of their own."[18] Although nationalism frequently involves a shared culture, language, religion, and ancestry, it is not necessarily based on the historical realities or tangible elements. Rather, it is frequently based on people's psychological predispositions and political commitments toward persons with whom they share a sense of "belonging." Such belonging is nurtured and sustained by historical myths, or as Barber has noted, "a kind of group remembering of ancient stories of founding."[19]

According to nationalists, full belonging—that is, "the warm sensation that people understand not merely what you say but what you mean"[20]—can only be realized when individuals are among their own people in their own native land. Nationalism is thus, as Hans Kohn has noted, "a state of mind, in which the supreme loyalty of the individual is felt to be due the nation-state."[21] providing an ethical justification for using force to protect the members of a nation from other foreign groups.

Nationalism is normally characterized by several key elements: (1) people prefer political affinities that coincide with their nationality; (2) people achieve their highest political fulfillment by fusing political aspirations with their nationality; (3) a major source of political power is the collective political will of a nation; (4) nationhood achieves its highest fulfillment when it is identified with a state; and (5) the highest political loyalty is to the nation.

It is important to differentiate nationalism from patriotism. Whereas the latter is a people's emotional attachment to their nation, patriotism is the love of country and its political institutions. Nationalism can be viewed as the theology or ideology of a nation, whereas patriotism involves the worship of a country. Because patriotism is important to a government's promotion of foreign policy interests, nation-states encourage patriotic bonds through formal and informal educational programs, a process that social scientists commonly term "political socialization." Although patriotism, by maintaining the coherence and vigor of modern states, is a potent force in contemporary international relations, nationalism is normally a stronger political force. According to Walker Connor, when loyalty to state and loyalty to nation are in conflict, the latter has proven to be the more potent force in the international system.[22]

Among the various elements of nationalism, the most important is a people's corporate political will, which provides the basis for defining who is "we" and "they." Although religion, ethnicity, and a common historical past are important dimensions of nationalism, the indispensable element is the political determination of a people to rule themselves. One scholar has observed that "it is not the ethnic groups that disrupt national unity, but the perceived absence of national unity . . . that creates ethnic groups."[23] Thus, if a people are to successfully pursue and defend political autonomy, they must have a fixed conception of the core principles and structures necessary for national self-government. In this connection, Roman Szporluk has observed that "nationalism is a call to people to agree on constituting that unit of political organization within which they shall live and within which all their important problems will be attended to."[24]

Types of Nationalism

Nationalism came into being in the seventeenth century with the rise of the modern state. Whereas in ancient and medieval periods citizens were loyal to their local communities, the rise of nationalism resulted in shifting loyalties towards specific nations. Although the process of consolidation of nations was well underway in Europe by the eighteenth century, European nations did not become highly politicized until the last half of the nineteenth century, a period sometimes referred to as the age of nationalism. Nationalism became important during this era because of the growing role of participatory politics and mass movements.

Historically, nationalism has been expressed in a number of different forms, including political, ethnic, religious, social revolutionary, and anticolonial. *Political (or civic) nationalism,* which first emerged in Europe in the eighteenth century as people challenged existing political structures and sought to replace them with institutions rooted in consent, is based on the demand for political self-rule and the establishment of legitimate political structures. Fundamentally, civic nationalism is rooted in a political creed. Ethnicity, color, gender, religion, and culture are all subservient to political doctrine. Examples of this type of nationalism include the French Revolution, which was inspired by the claim of popular sovereignty and the early nineteenth century independence of Latin American countries, which was based on the demand for political self-rule. This type of nationalism was also expressed in the 1980s in Eastern European states when popular movements pressed for increasing liberation from Soviet communist domination. For example, in Poland, the Solidarity Movement, led by Lech Walesa, was successful in bringing about major political and economic reforms,[25] and in Czechoslovakia, Charter 77 and Civic Forum, led by Vaclav Havel, effectively challenged and ended the communist-dominated government in December 1989.[26]

A second type of nationalism, and the one receiving the most media headlines in the post–Cold War era, is *ethnic nationalism*. Such nationalism, also known as *ethnonationalism,* assumes that people's deepest communal affinities and attachments are rooted in culture and ethnicity, not in economic circumstances or political choices. As a result ethnic nationalism assumes that nationalism is based on inherited attachments, not on choices made by individuals. "It is the national community that defines the individual," writes Ignatieff, "not the individuals who define the national community."[27] The quest for increased political autonomy by ethnic groups is illustrated by the Jewish Zionist movement, which sought a separate homeland and fulfilled its quest with a creation of Israel in 1947. In the post–Cold War era this nationalism has been especially pronounced in some former Soviet republics (especially Armenia, Azerbaijan, and Georgia), the former Yugoslavia, and selected African countries.

A third type of nationalism is based on religion. *Religious nationalism* claims that the basis of a nation should be the religious faith of persons. Although religion is frequently an element in the consolidation of nations, on some occasions religion has served as the primary inspiration for nationalism. When the Islamic fundamentalists toppled the Shah of Iran in 1979, for example, they did so because they believed that he was an infidel and was propagating values and practices that were inconsistent with Islam. Similarly, the continuing strife in Northern Ireland between Catholics and Protestants, in Israel between the Jews and Muslims, and in Sudan between Christians and Muslims attests to the continuing impact of religious nationalism.

A fourth type of nationalism is *social revolution,* epitomized by the revolutionary demands to transform a country's economic, social, and political structures. Frequently inspired by Marxist ideological claims, such nationalism is often based on perceptions of exploitation and injustice and the demand for radical restructuring of society. Whereas political nationalism is concerned chiefly with the popular transformation of the political order, social revolutionary nationalism is concerned with radical socioeconomic reform. Examples of such nationalism include the communist social revolutions of China, Cuba, and the Soviet Union, as well as the social revolutions of Mexico in the 1910s and in Nicaragua during the early 1980s. Because communism provided the major impetus for twentieth-century social revolutions, the demise of the Soviet Union in 1991 has significantly reduced the influence of social revolutionary nationalism.

The fifth type of nationalism, *anticolonialism,* is rooted in the desire for self-determination by people formerly ruled by a foreign colonial power. This type of nationalism, which developed in the aftermath of World War II, became an especially potent political force during the 1950s and 1960s when some seventy countries in Africa and Asia became politically independent. Because the political structures of nineteenth-century imperialism no longer remain, this type of nationalism is no longer important.

Since the end of the Cold War, ethnonationalism has become the dominant expression of nationalism in the world. Indeed, because of the growing demands for political autonomy by religious, ethnic, and tribal minorities, one observer has suggested that ethnic nationalism has become "the key language of our age."[28]

The Impact of Nationalism on World Politics

Nationalism is one of the major forces influencing world politics. By protecting and encouraging cultural and ethnic diversity, nationalism helps to maintain and promote a heterogeneous global community. It also contributes to domestic political cohesion among homogeneous states by strengthening ethnic, social, cultural, and political bonds. Domestically, nationalism promotes political cohesion in homogeneous and pluralistic countries, but tends to weaken political authority in multinational states in which minorities compete for power. Internationally, nationalism exacerbates conflicts among states as differences are emphasized among states and as the authority of existing regimes is challenged by minorities seeking increasing self-government. It is difficult enough for states to reconcile their competing and conflicting interests in global society, but when nationalistic aspirations influence international affairs, the quest for international order becomes a daunting task, especially when key values, beliefs, and ideological aspirations are at stake.

Many domestic and international conflicts in the twentieth century have been rooted in conflicting nationalisms. The origins of World War I, for example, have been attributed partly to ethnic divisions and rivalries within the Balkans.[29] In the contemporary era, the ongoing Arab-Israeli conflict (see case 3.1), the Bosnian war in the former Yugoslavia (see case 1.2), the demand by Chechnya for increasing political autonomy from Russia, and the early post–Cold Ward conflict between Armenia and Azerbaijan over Nagorno-Karabakh (a region with an overwhelmingly Armenian population that was formerly controlled by Azerbaijan but is now controlled by Armenia) are all rooted in conflicting nationalistic claims. In view of the significant number of ethnopolitical conflicts in the post–Cold War era, it is clear that a major threat to the international community's stability derives from ethnic, religious, and cultural conflict.

To a significant degree, the growth of global multicultural conflict in the post–Cold War era has been rooted in the quest for increasing political autonomy—a principle enshrined in the norm of **self-determination** of peoples. This norm was first popularized in the early twentieth century by President Woodrow Wilson and was incorporated into the United Nations system in 1945 by making the pursuit of peace dependent partly on the "self-determination of peoples." (art. 1.2) During the Cold War era colonial peoples in Asia and Africa used this norm to justify their demands for national independence. As a result of their claims for self-determination, more than seventy new countries became politically independent. This norm also helped justify the quest for political power by groups seeking to transform domestic society through social revolution. Such claims have been the basis of numerous postwar revolutionary conflicts in the developing nations, including the Indochina war of the 1950s and 1960s and the Central American conflicts of the 1980s.

Since the 1970s, the self-determination principle has been used increasingly by ethnic minorities seeking greater political autonomy or even statehood. For example, Biafrans in Nigeria, Kurds in Iraq and Iran, and Tamils in Sri Lanka have demanded greater self-rule. Some of these efforts have resulted in new states, such as Bangladesh, Croatia, and Eritrea. Other efforts, such as the Biafran and Kurdish insurgencies, not only failed to expand self-rule but led to increased political oppression by the ruling authorities.

The "self-determination of peoples" norm is a problematic principle in global society. It is problematic because the quest for political autonomy cannot be

Self-determination
The claim, first popularized in the twentieth century by President Woodrow Wilson and subsequently enshrined in the United Nations system, that peoples have a right to political self-rule.

automatically reconciled with the norm of state sovereignty. Because the international order is based on the stability of its member-states, domestic conflicts among minorities can weaken states and thereby destabilize the international system. A League of Nations report describes the counterproductive impact of self-determination as follows:

> To concede to minorities, either of language or religion, or to any fractions of a population the right of withdrawing from the community to which they belong, because it is their wish or their good pleasure, would be to destroy order and stability within States and to inaugurate anarchy in international life; it would be to uphold a theory incompatible with the very idea of the State as a territorial and political unity.[30]

One reason for the problematic nature of the self-determination norm is that the UN Charter does not say what a people is. It affirms the right of political self-rule but does not specify who has the right. Moreover, because the UN Charter prohibits the UN or any state from interfering in the internal affairs of states, assistance to minorities seeking political autonomy is expressly forbidden.[31] Thus, the quest for self-determination by ethnic and religious minorities depends ultimately on their own capabilities to challenge the ruling authorities. Minorities that succeed are presumably legally entitled to self-determination; but those that fail may or may not be.

INDIVIDUALS AND NATION-STATES

One of the unhappy features of the existing international system is the large number of people suffering from poverty, malnutrition, political instability, and war. A large part of human suffering is due to political oppression and economic mismanagement of ruling authorities. In spite of human suffering caused by governments, most citizens seek to live within their country of origin. Occasionally, however, domestic political and economic conditions become so threatening to basic rights that citizens attempt to leave their home state by whatever means possible. After the communists took control of South Vietnam in 1975, for example, several hundred thousand people fled Vietnam, many of them escaping in small, overcrowded boats. Similarly, throughout the 1980s and early 1990s tens of thousands of Haitians fled their land in an effort to find a more hospitable political and economic environment.

Political and economic oppression within contemporary societies has given rise to two types of displaced citizens: *emigrants*—those who leave their home state and are successfully incorporated into another state, and *international refugees*—those who flee their country of origin because of civil war, persecution, or discrimination, but who remain displaced and unincorporated. The lack of a homeland for refugees presents a major social and ethical problem in the international community.

Regulating Immigration

Emigration
The right of persons to leave their country of habitation.

Immigration
The process by which citizens leave their homeland and enter another country.

One of the most widely recognized human rights is the freedom of movement. This right entails the freedom to leave the country of origin **(emigration),** but it does not entail the obligation to be accepted by another state **(immigration)**. Indeed, most states carefully monitor their borders to control the entry of foreigners.[32] Ordinarily, permission to visit a country requires a tourist visa from the host state, whereas permission to immigrate permanently normally involves long, complex procedures.

Most governments carefully regulate entry of new immigrants. Some states, such as Denmark, Norway, and Switzerland, maintain highly restrictive immigra-

In recent decades a large number of people have tried to flee their homeland by sea.

tion policies, allowing few foreigners to settle in their land. The United States, by contrast, maintains a comparatively liberal immigration policy, allowing more than 600,000 new immigrants each year, of which nearly four-fifths are given visas on the basis of family reunification. The remaining 120,000–140,000 are allowed entry as political refugees, that is, immigrants fleeing politically repressive conditions.

One of the difficult immigration issues facing governments is how to differenti-ate between foreigners seeking improved living conditions (**economic refugees**) and those fleeing political oppression (**political refugees**). This issue is important because some countries, including the United States, are more hospitable to politi-cal refugees than to persons seeking an improved standard of living. The moral dilemma of immigration was dramatically illustrated in the fall of 1991, when thou-sands of Haitians tried to flee to the United States after a military coup deposed elected president Jean-Bertrand Aristide. Because most of these "boat people" were classified as "economic refugees," they were immediately repatriated to Haiti. When a federal district judge temporarily halted the repatriation, the U.S. govern-ment built a detention camp at the U.S. Naval Base in Guantanamo, Cuba, to tem-porarily hold refugees picked up in Caribbean waters. Although the Haitian refugee problem eased in early 1992 after U.S. courts allowed refugee repatriation to resume, the moral dilemma of how to treat "boat people" continued in 1994.

Economic refugees
Displaced persons seeking improved living conditions in a foreign country.

Political refugees
Persons who have fled their homeland because of a well-founded fear of persecution.

Refugees: Citizens without a Country

According to the 1951 UN Convention on the Status of Refugees, a refugee is "a person who owing to well-founded fear of being persecuted for reasons of race, religion, nationality, membership of a particular social group or political opinion, is outside the country of his nationality and is unable or, owing to such fear, is un-willing to avail himself of the protection of that country. . . ." Fundamentally, **refugees** are displaced people without a political home. They are persons who have fled their country of origin because of fear of persecution, discrimination, and political oppression.

During the 1970s and 1980s the world's refugee population grew significantly—from about 4.6 million in the early 1970s to more than 14.4 million in 1995 (see table 2.3)—in great part due to growing religious, ethnic, and political disputes within and among states. For example, throughout the 1980s Afghanistan was caught in a bitter civil war that had been precipitated by the Soviet Union's in-tervention in 1979. As a result civil war raged between the governing, pro-Moscow regime, supported by more than 100,000 Soviet troops, and the antigovernment guerrillas (mujahedin). As of 1992, some six million persons had been displaced by the Afghan war.

Refugee
A person who flees his or her country of origin because of fear of persecution, discrimination, or political oppression. A refugee is a displaced person without a political home.

TABLE 2.3   Major International Refugee Groups, 1995

Country of Origin	Number (thousands)	Country of Asylum (principal country of origin in parentheses)	Number (thousands)
Afghanistan	2,743	Iran (Afghanistan, Iraq)	2,236
Rwanda	2,257	Zaire (Rwanda)	1,724
Liberia	794	Pakistan (Afghanistan)	1,055
Iraq	702	Germany (Bosnia)	1,005
Somalia	536	Tanzania (Rwanda)	883
Eritrea	442	Sudan (Eritrea)	727
Sudan	399	USA	591
Burundi	389	Guinea (Liberia)	360
Bosnia and Herzegovina	321	Ethiopia (Somalia)	348
Other	5,906	Armenia	304
Total Refugees	*14,489*		

Source: United Nations High Commissioner for Refugees, *The State of the World's Refugees, 1995)* (New York: Oxford University Press, 1995), p. 251.

More recently, the plight of refugees was dramatically illustrated by the flight of some two million Iraqi Kurds to Turkey and Iran in March 1991. The mass exodus was precipitated by a brutal attack on the Kurds by Iraqi military forces after they had gained temporary control of the oil-rich area of Kirkuk in northern Iraq. Similarly, the 1992–94 war among different ethnonationalistic groups in Bosnia-Herzegovina resulted in more than one million refugees, with more than half of these fleeing to western European countries. Finally, the tribal wars in Rwanda and Burundi in 1994–96 between the Hutus and Tutsis resulted in the death of some 800,000 persons and the migration of more than two million refugees to neighboring states.

The problem of refugees is significant for ethical and political reasons. Ethically, industrial democracies and other middle-income states bear a moral responsibility to assist displaced people. Although the UN High Commissioner for Refugees (UNHCR) is chiefly responsible for administering refugee camps worldwide, developed countries can provide invaluable material and political assistance. Specifically, states and international organizations can support refugees in three ways: (1) assisting in their voluntary repatriation to their homeland after domestic conditions have improved; (2) helping in their temporary resettlement in a nearby region or neighboring state; and (3) assisting in their permanent resettlement in a foreign country. From a long-term perspective, the most desirable solution is the first; the most problematic is the last.

The refugee problem is also significant politically.[33] Because the unrealized dreams of refugees can result in domestic and international instability, world politics has been, and continues to be, influenced by the plight of major refugee groups, especially those committed to establishing an autonomous political homeland. The political instability in the Middle East, for example, derives largely from the absence of a political homeland for the Palestinian people. Although the Arab-Israeli tensions derive from religious, cultural, historical, and political sources, the root cause of contemporary regional tensions is the quest for a Palestinian state.

In sum, although states are responsible for the welfare of persons within their territorial jurisdictions, many individuals suffer, nonetheless, from domestic instability, economic deprivation, oppression, and war. And when regimes institute discriminatory policies against ethnic and religious minorities and persecute those who demand increased political autonomy, human suffering can increase greatly, leading large groups of people to flee to neighboring countries. The plight of migrants, especially refugees, is thus an important issue in contemporary IR.

NONSTATE ACTORS

Although the nation-state has been and will continue to be the major actor in world politics, it is not the only unit that participates in world events. Other actors involved in international relations include intergovernmental organizations (IGOs), international nongovernmental organizations (INGOs, usually shortened to NGOs), multinational corporations (MNCs), international political movements, religious movements and organizations, and individuals.

Intergovernmental Organizations

Intergovernmental organizations (IGOs) are public international organizations in which membership is limited to states. These institutions, which include regional and universal organizations, have increased enormously in number and influence in the twentieth century. In 1909 there were approximately thirty-seven IGOs but by the late 1980s the number had increased to slightly more than 300.[34]

IGOs can be classified in terms of membership and purpose. From a geographical perspective, IGOs can be classified as general-membership organizations or limited-membership organizations. The former refers to IGOs with a global membership, such as the International Labor Organization (ILO), the World Bank, and the United Nations Educational, Scientific and Cultural Organization (UNESCO). Limited-membership organizations include IGOs, such as the Arab League, the Latin American Free Trade Association (LAFTA), and the Organization of African Unity (OAU).

A more comprehensive membership classification system has been developed by the Union of International Associations. According to the Union, IGOs can be divided into the following four categories: (1) *federations,* which include three or more autonomous international bodies; (2) *universal membership organizations,* which involve a near global representation of states; (3) *intercontinental membership organizations,* in which membership exceeds a particular region, but does not justify its inclusion in the universal category; and (4) *regional organizations,* which limit membership to the states in a particular continental or sub-continental region.

IGOs can also be classified in terms of their basic goals and purposes. Some organizations are general, multipurpose organizations. Their purposes are broad and diffuse and involve a variety of different tasks, such as national security, peacemaking, economic development, and human welfare. Examples of general-purpose organizations include the Organization of American States (OAS), the European Union (EU), and the United Nations. Other organizations have limited purposes, focusing on a specific task, such as regional security, promotion of health, and the regulation of international finance. Examples of such organizations include the International Monetary Fund (IMF), the North Atlantic Treaty Organization (NATO), and World Health Organization (WHO). Figure 2.2, which combines the classifications presented above, illustrates each different category of IGOs.

IGOs play an important role in world affairs. Not only do they provide a means for expressing the individual and collective wills of states, they also assert

IGOs
An international organization whose members are states.

FIGURE 2.2
Classification of
IGOs in Terms of
Membership
and Purpose

		Purpose	
		General	**Specific**
Membership	**Universal**	• United Nations	• Food and Agriculture Organization • International Monetary Fund • World Health Organization • World Trade Organization
	Regional	• European Union • League of Arab States • Organization of African Unity • Organization of American States	• Council for Mutual Economic Assistance • European Free Trade Association • Inter-American Development Bank • North Atlantic Treaty Organization

independent influence on interstate relations by promoting socioeconomic interdependence and contributing to the management and resolution of international conflict. For example, transnational governmental organizations such as the International Monetary Fund (IMF), the Organization of American States (OAS), and the European Union (EU) have had significant impact on Cold War international relations and continue to influence contemporary global politics.

The most important IGOs are the general-purpose organizations at both the global and regional levels. They are more directly involved in transnational political issues than the more narrowly oriented organizations. In effect, general-purpose organizations tend to provide greater opportunity to facilitate transnational cooperation and coordination among states than more limited-purpose IGOs. Because of their importance, the role of IGOs in world politics, focusing on the United Nations and the European Community, the foremost regional institution, will be examined in chapter 14.

International Nongovernmental Organizations

NGOs
Multinational
nongovernmental
groups and associations
that influence
international affairs.

International nongovernmental organizations (NGOs) are private international groups and associations pursuing common interests transnationally. Unlike IGOs, NGOs are not initiated, supported, or directed by governments. Rather, they are organized, funded, and managed by citizen groups from many different nations. Examples of NGOs include the International Red Cross, the International Olympic Committee, Amnesty International, the Committee for Nuclear Disarmament, the International Council of Scientific Unions, the International Refugee Organization, and the International Federation of Airline Pilots' Association.

The number of NGOs has risen dramatically this century, especially since the end of World War II. Whereas fewer than 100 NGOs existed at the turn of the century, by 1990 the number had increased to more than 4,600. To a significant degree, their dramatic growth has been due to the rise in global interactions, stimulated and facilitated by increased efficiency and decreased cost of transnational communication and transportation. As the world has become more interdependent, the need for organizations that facilitate and coordinate functional interactions transnationally has grown greatly.

As with IGOs, NGOs can be differentiated in terms of their geographic scope and focus. Of the 4,646 known NGOs in 1990, the Union of International Associations classified 3,406 or 73 percent of the total, as regional organizations. The remainder were classified as either global NGOs (425) or intercontinental NGOs (770).[35] Moreover, NGOs also vary greatly in terms of size and purpose. As a general rule, however, NGOs are much smaller organizations, have more limited budgets, and pursue more narrowly defined purposes than IGOs.

NGOs have considerably less direct influence on international politics than IGOs. This is partly due to the lack of governmental involvement in supporting and administering NGOs, as well as to the almost wholly technical focus of most NGOs. To a significant degree, the major purposes of NGOs are the promotion of greater transnational cooperation in specific functional issue-areas. The level of impact of NGOs on the individual and collective state behavior varies. Some NGOs, such as the European Broadcasting Union, a transnational association promoting the private interests of professional broadcasters, have little influence on the international behavior of states. By contrast, other NGOs play a key role in world politics by influencing not only state behavior but the environment of world politics itself. For example, Amnesty International, an organization that issues reports on human rights violations, has had significant impact on world affairs, influencing not only the views of government officials but also the opinions of the general public.

Sometimes NGOs serve political purposes even though their aims and composition are entirely nongovernmental and nonpolitical. In 1980, for example, President Jimmy Carter called on the United States, along with other Western nations, to boycott the Moscow Olympic games in response to the Soviet invasion of Afghanistan in 1979. The U.S. Olympic Committee subsequently agreed to support Carter's initiative, but the introduction of East-West tensions in the Olympic community had the regrettable effect of further politicizing international athletic competition.

Multinational Corporations

The **multinational corporation (MNC),** a third nonstate actor, is a business firm that owns and manages economic assets in two or more countries. Ordinarily, MNCs are owned in one country and achieve their transnational character from foreign production and sales of goods and services. Although MNCs are a relatively recent development, foreign direct investment has been practiced for many centuries. During the eighteenth and nineteenth centuries, for example, European imperial powers carried out extensive investments in their colonies, often under joint public-private ownership (e.g., the British East India Company). In the twentieth century, private corporations, such as Singer Sewing Machines, Nestlé, and IBM have greatly expanded the scope of foreign enterprise. The development and expansion of MNCs in the second half of the twentieth century is thus a by-product of international commercial and financial practices established much earlier.

MNC
A business enterprise that has production or marketing activities in two or more states.

The growing significance of MNCs derives from a number of factors. First, many MNCs are as large economically as many states (see table 2.4). In 1991, for example, the gross annual sales of Exxon Corporation, Royal Dutch/Shell Petroleum, and General Motors were each over 100 billion dollars, exceeding the gross national product of most states. Second, whereas traditional MNCs generally concentrated production in the home state and used their foreign offices to acquire primary products and sell finished goods, the modern MNC has relied heavily on the establishment of foreign subsidiaries to carry out production itself. Finally, the significant impact of MNCs on world politics is a result of the growing transnational economic activity.

In the early 1970s an increasing number of social scientists believed that the expansion of MNCs had begun to threaten state sovereignty and was reducing state autonomy. The title of Raymond Vernon's influential 1971 study of multinationals—*Sovereignty at Bay*—aptly captured a widely shared sentiment.[36] For many social scientists, the increasing economic interdependence, facilitated and encouraged by the growth of MNCs, was leading to fundamental changes in the international economic and political order. Since the mid-1970s, however, the

TABLE 2.4 World's Largest Corporations Compared with GDP of Selected States, 1995 (in billions of dollars)

GDP/Revenues	States	Corporations
$100–199	Denmark (172)	General Motors (168)
	Thailand (167)	Ford Motor Co. (146)
	Norway (145)	Mitsubishi (140)
	Hong Kong (143)	Royal Dutch Shell Group (128)
	South Africa (136)	Exxon (119)
	Saudi Arabia (125)	Wal-Mart (106)
$60–99	Israel (91)	General Electric (79)
	Greece (90)	IBM (75)
	Malaysia (85)	AT&T (74)
	Singapore (83)	Mobil (72)
	Ukraine (80)	Daimler-Benz (71)
	Columbia (76)	British Petroleum (69)
	Philippines (74)	Volkswagen (66)
$30–59	New Zealand (57)	U.S. Postal Service (56)
	Peru (57)	Unilever (52)
	Egypt (47)	Sony (50)
	Hungary (43)	Nestlé (49)
	Algeria (41)	IRI (49)
	Romania (35)	Toshiba (48)
	Morocco (32)	Honda Motor Co. (47)

Sources: GDP data from *The State in a Changing World: World Development Report, 1997* (New York: Oxford University Press, 1997), p. 236–7; data on economic size of corporations, based on 1996 total corporation revenues, is from *Fortune* (4 August 1997), p. F-2.

projections of increasing MNC power and the decline of state sovereignty have not materialized. State autonomy has not been qualified by MNCs. Three reasons have been given for the failure of investment firms to qualify state sovereignty.

First, the increasing multilateralism of foreign direct investment has reinforced political and economic competition among corporations and states. During the first three postwar decades, American corporations dominated foreign direct investment. But since the 1970s, European and Japanese corporations and banks have increased significantly in global influence. Whereas French journalist Jean-Jacques Servan-Schreiber had warned in *The American Challenge* that Europe faced the possibility of American economic domination because of the spread of MNCs in Western Europe, by the mid-1980s American MNCs had not only lost significant overseas markets to other foreign corporations, but had begun to lose a large portion of the American domestic market as well. Indeed, the expansion of Japanese MNCs was so significant that many Americans had begun to express concern about their role in American economic life.

Secondly, the nature of MNC expansion has changed significantly. Whereas MNC development in the 1960s and 1970s had led people to fear American economic domination, by the mid-1980s Americans had begun to question their own vulnerability to foreign investment. The major reason for this radical shift in focus is best explained by the change in the nature of foreign investment. Whereas earlier investment was used to establish foreign subsidiaries producing industrial goods similar to those manufactured in the home state, the MNC strategy of the 1980s had shifted toward the manufacture of components. This development has resulted in the *internationalization of production,* involving multinational production of specialized components. For example, it has been estimated that nearly three-fourths of the manufacturing cost of an IBM PC is incurred overseas.

Thirdly, the power of the state has been increasingly manifest in the multitude of bilateral and multilateral agreements worked out between MNCs and host governments. Stephen Krasner has argued that the dramatic changes in the international economic order have been brought about by the growing power of the Third World nations. They have used the international forums, especially the UN and its agencies, to structure a new set of rules for trade, development, and foreign investment. In Krasner's view, governments and MNCs have "come to accept, tacitly if not always explicitly, the legitimacy of greater national control of multinational corporate activity. Sovereignty is not at bay."[37]

International Political Movements

The fourth group of nonstate actors are international political organizations and movements. There are two basic types. The first involves international political movements seeking to alter economic and political institutions of the global system. The second involves groups concerned with domestic political liberation, either the creation of a new state or the radical reform of existing governmental institutions. Examples of the first type of international political actors include the **Nonaligned Movement (NAM)** and the **Group of 77 (G-77).** NAM originated in the 1950s as a Third World effort to combat colonialism and to avoid entanglement in East-West conflicts. The movement sought to promote national economic and political well-being of developing nations by avoiding alignment with either the Western democracies or the Soviet-bloc states. Although the movement formally came into being in 1961, its roots were established in 1955 when some twenty-nine African and Asian countries gathered in Bandung, Indonesia, to stimulate economic and political cooperation. As table 2.5 suggests, since 1961 the movement has sponsored conferences triennially, increasing its membership more than fourfold.

The Group of 77, like the nonaligned movement, comprises most Third World nations. G-77, which now numbers more than 120 states, came into being in the mid-1970s when Third World nations joined together in proposing major international economic reforms, known as the New International Economic Order. Whereas the nonaligned movement has been concerned with social, political, and economic cooperation among the poor nations, the major goal of the G-77 has been the expansion of economic power of the developing nations.

The second type of international political organizations includes separatist groups and secessionist movements of ethnic minorities seeking increased political self-determination. Examples of such movements include the Kurds in Turkey and Iran, the Basques in Spain, and the Tamils in Sri Lanka. This type of group also includes organizations seeking statehood, such as the Palestinian Liberation Organization (PLO), and those seeking to topple an existing government and to establish a new regime. Examples of the latter group include the African National Congress (ANC), the organization that successfully brought an end to white rule in South Africa and which currently governs the country, and the Faribundo Martí Liberation Front (FMLN), the Marxist guerrilla movement that unsuccessfully sought to topple the government of El Salvador during the 1980s.

NAM
A movement, formally begun in 1961, to encourage Third World states to remain independent from the East-West ideological conflict.

Group of 77 (G-77)
An informal alliance of developing nations that emerged in the 1960s to promote Third World economic development.

TABLE 2.5   Nonaligned Movement Conferences

Year	Place	Attendance	Issues/Concerns
1961	Belgrade, Yugoslavia	25	Calls for further combating of colonialism Encourages disarmament Highlights Third World economic development
1964	Cairo, Egypt	40	Calls for increased international economic cooperation Condemns South African apartheid Calls on U.S. to lift Cuban sanctions
1970	Lusaka, Zambia	53	Adopts Lusaka Declaration, encouraging political independence and Third World cooperation Grants observer status to Vietcong No criticism of 1968 Soviet-bloc intervention in Czechoslovakia No comment on Indo-Pakistan war
1973	Algiers, Algeria	75	PLO gains observer status, while condemning Israel Calls for greater economic cooperation among developing nations
1976	Colombo, Sri Lanka	94	N. Korea participates, while S. Korea is excluded from conference New International Economic Order is launched, calling on increased transfers from the rich countries to the poor lands Hails victory of Vietnam over the U.S.
1979	Havana, Cuba	94	Cuban leader Fidel Castro attributes major world ills to the U.S. and China Egypt is censored for signing the Camp David Accord No mention of Vietnamese invasion of Cambodia (Kampuchea)
1983	New Delhi, India	100	Pro-Soviet groups suffer several setbacks Calls for a peaceful resolution of the Afghanistan war Focus on international economic reforms
1986	Harare, Zimbabwe	101	Calls for increased international pressure against South Africa to eliminate apartheid Calls for international monetary reform, especially in view of Third World debt crisis
1989	Belgrade, Yugoslavia	100	Encourages continuation of detente Calls for global promotion of human rights Calls for closing the economic gap between the First and Third World
1992	Jakarta, Indonesia	108	Despite the end of the Cold War, NAM pledges continued work for Third World needs Calls for ending "ethnic cleansing" in Bosnia-Herzegovina
1995	Cartagena, Colombia	110	Calls for greater credit from the developed economies, as well as greater access to their markets Condemns continued French nuclear testing

Although each of these organizations and movements is primarily concerned with achieving domestic political objectives, each organization also participates as an international actor in the world community. For example, the ANC, which until it was unbanned in 1990 was headquartered in Lusaka, Zambia, carried out a global public opinion campaign seeking to gain support for its liberation of South Africa from a white, minority government. Similarly, the PLO, which was headquartered in Tripoli until 1993, has maintained a large international presence, with officers in many major industrial countries.

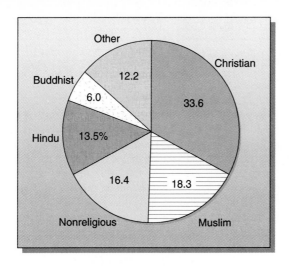

FIGURE 2.3
Estimated Membership of Major World Religions, 1994 (in percentages)
Source: Data from Otto Johnson, ed., *The 1996 Information Please Almanac* (Boston, MA.: Houghton Mifflin Co., 1996), p. 411.

Religious Movements and Organizations

A fifth type of nonstate actor is religion—and in particular the religious organizations and movements associated with it. As suggested in figure 2.3, the largest religion in the contemporary international order is Christianity, followed by Islam, Hinduism, and Buddhism. Although the major religions differ in their degree of politicization and concern with temporal issues, to the extent that religious values and practices influence political beliefs and customs, they contribute importantly to domestic and international politics.

The primary method by which religions influence world politics is through the values they espouse. For example, the emphasis of Christianity on the individual worth of every human being has encouraged Christian believers to support human rights and constitutional governments. Moreover, Christianity, especially its Protestant element, has regarded work as a means of fulfilling a divine mandate to use gifts and abilities in productive, creative service to God and humankind. As a result, some scholars argue that Christianity has helped to establish values and habits that are conducive to democratic capitalism.[41] Regardless of how religious norms are assessed, it is clear that religions influence domestic and international social and political life by the norms that are articulated and practiced by its believers.

Although religious influence on political affairs is generally diffuse and indirect, occasionally religions attempt to affect public affairs directly. This has been the case with Islam in the Middle East in recent decades. As the second largest religion in the world, with more than 800 million followers, Islam has had extraordinary influence in recent decades as it has challenged the spread of Western values and sought to establish Muslim regimes that insulate societies from the relativism, materialism, and secularism common to Western, pluralistic cultures. Although not as well institutionalized as other religions, Islam has profoundly influenced Middle Eastern affairs because of the religious zeal of some of its fundamentalist sects. Although Muslim fundamentalists are concerned with the propagation of their faith, they are primarily committed to the purification of their own societies by establishing monistic Islamic societies. In 1979, fundamentalists gained control of the Iranian government and began immediately transforming Iranian society in conformity with Islam. In addition, the Iranian regime became a major source of political, military, and financial support to fundamentalist movements throughout the Middle East.

Although religion is much less influential politically than nationalism, religious values and movements function in a similar manner, encouraging consensus through shared beliefs and moral values, and stimulating dissent when religions

Issue 2.1 Is Religion Conducive to Peace?

Religion is a vital element of national identity, contributing significantly to the cohesion of nations as well fomenting conflict within and between states. Because of the growth of ethnic and religious conflict in the contemporary world, it is commonplace to regard religion as impediment to international order and to peaceful conflict resolution. Modern history clearly suggests that religion, because of its absolutist claims, can be a source of domestic civil strife and global disorder.

But religion can also contribute to global order and peaceful conflict resolution. Douglas Johnston, reflecting the perspectives of a growing number of scholars who regard religious communities as conducive to the peace process, has written: "the use of a religious rationale to justify a conflict creates opportunities for spiritually motivated peacemakers. They can appeal to the parties on the basis of universal religious principles or on the basis of the specific warrants for conflict resolution that exist in each religion's theology.[38] Moreover, religious institutions, such as the Roman Catholic Church and Quaker agencies like the American Friends Service Committee, can play an important role in community-build-

ing and dispute settlement. Indeed, organized Protestant and Catholic organizations have played a vital role in Third World development, as well as in pacific settlement of regional disputes—a role clearly illustrated in the case study at the end of this chapter.

American public officials and scholars have been slow to recognize the important role of religion in modern social and political life. The failure to appreciate religion's positive public role is due in great part to what Edward Luttwak terms the "Enlightenment prejudice"—the belief that "progress of knowledge and the influence of religion were mutually exclusive, making the latter a waning force."[39] But the spread of modernization has not resulted in a decline in religion. Rather, the opposite has occurred. As a result, if scholars are to develop an adequate understanding of the major forces influencing contemporary international relations, and if Western diplomats are to contribute fully to global peacekeeping, they will have to develop a greater appreciation of the role of religion in the modern world. As Barry Rubin notes, "to neglect religious institutions and thinking would be to render incomprehensible some of the key issues and crises in the world today."[40]

President Fidel Castro greets Pope John Paul II on his historic 1998 visit to Cuba, one of the last remaining communist states in the world.

are in conflict. (See fig. 2.4 on regional distribution of religions.) From a political perspective, religion can contribute to the development of community consensus as well as community conflict. From a global perspective, religion can serve both as a positive force in building international harmony and as a negative force in sustaining and expanding transnational discord and conflict. For example, in the seventeenth and eighteenth centuries, a number of wars were rooted in theological disputes. The Iran-Iraq War of the 1970s was based, in significant measure, on a conflict between Sunni and Shia Muslims. Similarly, the Arab-Israeli dispute, the

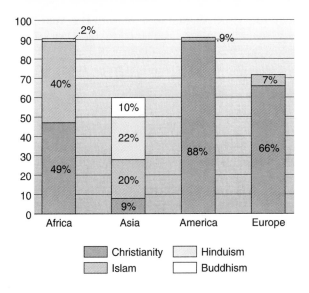

FIGURE 2.4
Distribution of Major Religions, by Region, 1994
Source: Data from Otto Johnson, ed., *The 1996 Information Please Almanac* (Boston, MA.: Houghton Mifflin Co., 1996), p. 411.

strife within Lebanon in the 1980s, and the early-1990s civil war in Sudan are all conflicts rooted in part in religion.

Religious organizations serve as important actors in global society. Examples of such institutions include the Roman Catholic Church, with headquarters in the Vatican, and the World Council of Churches, the association of Protestant churches in Geneva. Besides providing institutional leadership to their respective religions, such organizations serve as actors in global politics itself, indirectly contributing to global solidarity through the values and interests they espouse and directly by advocating public policies. The Roman Catholic Church, a highly institutionalized religious organization, is one of the most sophisticated and influential religious actors in the global community.[42]

The influence of religious organizations has been considerable in recent decades. For example, throughout the 1980s religious organizations played a key role in condemning South African apartheid by supporting governmental economic sanctions. Moreover, religious organizations have promoted such causes as human rights, hunger relief, and opposition to infant formula use in poor, developing nations. The latter campaign forced the Nestlé Corporation, the leading international manufacturer of infant formula, to alter significantly its advertising and sales practices in the Third World. Religious organizations also played a key role in the antinuclear movement in the United States but especially in western Europe in the early 1980s.

Individuals

Internationally influential persons can also be viewed as key actors in the global community.[43] Political leaders who carry out domestic or foreign policies that alter the behavior of other states, or that result in new or modified global structures, are key actors of the international community. Similarly, religious leaders, human rights activists, and other nongovernmental officials can also influence global politics profoundly. Interestingly, of the sixteen political leaders chosen as "Man of the Year" by *Time* during the 1971–1993 period, most were selected because of their global political influence. (See table 2.6.) The following examples illustrate the impact of individuals on international affairs.

Mikhail Gorbachev, who served as president of the Soviet Union from 1985 to 1991, initiated domestic reforms, including economic decentralization (*perestroika*) and greater political openness (*glasnost*), that eventually led to the collapse of the

TABLE 2.6   Selected Time Magazine's "Man of the Year," 1971–1993

Year	Individual	Country
1971	Richard Nixon	United States
1972	Richard Nixon and Henry Kissinger	United States
1974	King Faisal	Saudi Arabia
1976	Jimmy Carter	United States
1977	Anwar Sadat	Egypt
1978	Deng Xiaoping	China
1979	Ayatollah Khomeini	Iran
1980	Ronald Reagan	United States
1981	Lech Walesa	Poland
1983	Ronald Reagan and Yuri Andropov	US and Soviet Union
1985	Deng Xiaoping	China
1986	Corazon Aquino	Philippines
1987	Mikhail Gorbachev	Soviet Union
1989	Mikhail Gorbachev	Soviet Union
1990	George Bush	United States
1992	Bill Clinton	United States
1993	Yitzhak Rabin and Yasser Arafat	Israel, PLO
	Nelson Mandela and F. W. de Klerk	South Africa

communist government and the disintegration of the Soviet Union. Internationally, the decay of Soviet communism led to the end of the Cold War, which had dominated the international system for more than four decades following the end of World War II. Lech Walesa, the leader of the Polish Solidarity Movement and subsequent president of noncommunist Poland, has similarly influenced modern international relations by his championing of workers' rights and political freedom during the 1980s. Through his leadership, he not only mobilized Polish workers and helped reform the Polish regime, but contributed to the collapse of communism in Poland as well as other Eastern European states.

During the Gulf Crisis of 1990–1991 two political leaders—Saddam Hussein, the dictator of Iraq, and President George Bush—played key roles in the international community. Iraq's August 2, 1990 intervention of Kuwait was designed to increase Suddam's political and economic power in the Middle East. Iraq, a major oil-exporting state, already had the largest armed forces in the Middle East, and by conquering and annexing Kuwait, was increasing national influence even further. President Bush responded to Iraq's invasion and occupation by declaring publicly that those actions were wholly unacceptable and would not stand. Saddam had to withdraw from Kuwait or face military force. To some extent, the politics of the Persian Gulf in the fall of 1990 were dominated by the political wills of two leaders—Hussein, who was committed to keeping the conquered land, and Bush, who was determined to liberate Kuwait. Thus, both Hussein and Bush were key actors in determining not only the fate of Kuwait but also the long-term international relations of the Middle East.

Archbishop Desmond Tutu, head of South Africa's Anglican Church, has also played an important role in global politics. He helped direct opposition against the former South African government and encouraged foreign states to impose and expand economic sanctions against the white regime. Moreover, as leader of the human rights movement in South Africa, Tutu has not only contributed to the elimination of racial discrimination (apartheid) in his own country, but has helped to mobilize public opinion against all racial oppression.

In Conclusion

States are the primary, although not sole, actors in global politics. Other key actors include IGOs, NGOs, MNCs, transnational movements, religious organizations, and even individuals. Indeed, because the world is becoming more interdependent socially, economically, and technologically, nonstate actors are playing an increasingly important role in global society as governments struggle to regulate cross-border flows and movements. The growing foreign scientific, informational, economic, and cultural penetration has decreased a government's capacity to regulate domestic society as well as to influence foreign developments. But because states possess sovereign power (a topic examined in the next chapter), the state continues as the dominant actor in global society.

SUMMARY

1. The dominant actor of the global society is the nation-state. Although states are nearly as old as civilization, the nation-state dates from the mid-seventeenth century. The current international system comprises more than 180 states, most of them dating from the 1950s.

2. The key feature of the state is its authority to make binding rules within a particular territory. This authority is symbolized by sovereignty—a concept used to define the supreme power of government within a state. A nation is people sharing a common language, culture, and political identity. Nationalism is the loyalty that people have toward their own nation.

3. In the modern world there are many more nations than states. As a result, most countries are multinational states. In some cases, nations are divided between two states.

4. Because of poverty, political oppression, and persecution of minority groups, many people emigrate to other countries. Emigrants are those individuals who leave their own country and are successfully incorporated into another state. Refugees are those individuals who flee their own country because of civil war and persecution, but remain displaced without a state. The number of refugees greatly increased in the 1970s and 1980s.

5. Nonstate actors also play a key role in world politics. The most important of these are IGOs, especially the general-purpose universal and regional organizations like the United Nations and the European Community. Other important nonstate actors include NGOs, MNCs, international political movements, and religious organizations.

KEY TERMS

state	multinational state	political refugees	multinational corporation (MNC)
sovereignty	multistate nation	refugee	Nonaligned Movement (NAM)
nation	nationalism	intergovernmental organizations (IGOs)	Group of 77 (G-77)
strong state	self-determination		
weak state	emigration	international nongovernmental organizations (NGOs)	
failed state	immigration		
coherent state	economic refugees		

RECOMMENDED READINGS

Barber, Benjamin R. *Jihad vs. McWorld: How Globalism and Tribalism are Reshaping the World.* New York: Times Books, 1995. An illuminating analysis of the impact of consumer capitalism and tribal and religious fundamentalism on post–Cold War international relations.

Barnet, Richard J., and Ronald E. Muller. *Global Reach: The Power of the Multinational Corporations.* New York: Simon & Schuster, 1974. An influential study calling attention to the rising influence of MNCs in global society. The study presents a critical view of global corporations because of their enormous economic and political power.

Brown, Peter G., and Henry Shue, eds. *Boundaries: National Autonomy and Its Limits.* Totowa, N.J.: Rowman and Littlefield, 1981. This volume of six essays on moral dimensions of statehood analyzes two questions: (1)who can be a member of a nation? and (2)what are the moral obligations of nations toward nonmembers?

Hanson, Eric O. *The Catholic Church in World Politics.* Princeton: Princeton University Press, 1987. An examination of the nature and evolution of Catholic social and political thought and its impact in national, regional, and international politics. Despite its title, only two of the nine chapters focus on the role of the Catholic church in global politics.

Gilpin, Robert. *U.S. Power and the Multinational Corporation: The Political Economy of Foreign Direct Investment.* New York: Basic Books, 1975. A study of the political economy of direct foreign investment, focusing on U.S. corporations in the postwar era. In this prescient study, Gilpin argues that the costs of foreign investment are beginning to outweigh the benefits, and suggests that the U.S. foreign economic policy should be reformed to ensure vigorous national economic expansion.

Gottlieb, Gidon. *Nation Against State: A New Approach to Ethnic Conflicts and the Decline of Sovereignty.* New York: Council on Foreign Relations, 1993. This short study illuminates how growing ethnic conflicts within states have diminished state sovereignty and the potential for global stability.

Holsti, Kalevi, J. *The State, War, and the State of War.* Cambridge: Cambridge University Press, 1996. In this important study, Holsti argues that international peace requires "strong" states that enjoy significant domestic and international legitimacy. The growth of "weak" states in the contemporary world has led to the displacement of traditional institutionalized wars with domestic wars of a "third kind." Chapters 5 and 6 provide a superior analysis of the foundation of strong and weak states.

Ignatieff, Michael. *Blood and Belonging: Journeys into the New Nationalism.* New York: Farrar, Straus and Giroux, 1993. This prize-winning study by an internationally acclaimed journalist explores the growth of ethnic nationalism in the post–Cold War era. The nationalism of six regions is examined: Croatia and Serbia, Germany, Ukraine, Quebec, Kurdistan, and Northern Ireland.

Modelski, George, ed. *Transnational Corporations and World Order: Readings in International Political Economy.* San Francisco: W. H. Freeman, 1979. This collection of readings examines the nature and role of MNCs in the global system.

Moynihan, Daniel Patrick. *Pandaemonium: Ethnicity in International Politics.* New York: Oxford University Press, 1993. Examines the growing impact of ethnicity in the post–Cold War international order. Chapter 2 analyzes the tensions and uncertainties created by the "self-determination of peoples" doctrine.

Porter, Bruce D. *War and the Rise of the State: The Military Foundations of Modern Politics.* New York: The Free Press, 1994. A wide-ranging exploration of the domestic and international effects of war. Porter illuminates how wars have influenced the historical evolution of modern states, fostering national integration and governmental expansion as well as revolution, economic hardship, and destruction. An important book.

Rosecrance, Richard. *The Rise of the Trading State: Commerce and Conquest in the Modern World.* New York: Basic Books, 1986. This provocative and path-breaking study suggests that the territorial state is being replaced by the trading state because trade is replacing territorial expansion and military power as the key determinants of national influence and wealth.

RELEVANT WEB SITES

Chiefs of State and Cabinet Members of Foreign Governments	www.odci.gov/cia/publications/chief
International Relations and Security Network (ISN) See the following subjects: International Relations Government Minorities/Migration Population/Migration	www.isn.ethz.ch/
Inter-University Consortium for Political and Social Research (ICPSR)	www.icpsr.umich.edu
UN High Commissioner for Refugees	www.unhcr.ch

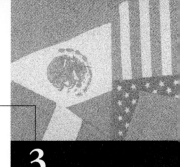

The International Community 3

In August 1990, Iraq invaded Kuwait, quickly taking control of the small state. Although Saddam Hussein, Iraq's president, was well aware that the international legal order did not allow states to resolve disputes through force, Hussein ordered the invasion anyway, believing that his bellicosity would be rewarded with additional revenues from Kuwait's abundant oil fields.

Beginning in 1991, a bitter civil war raged between Croats, Bosnians, and Serbs, threatening the rights, human dignity, and personal security of tens of thousands of citizens in the former Yugoslavia. In one of the most ominous developments of this bitter conflict, journalists reported in mid-1992 that thousands of Muslim Bosnians were being detained in Serbian "ethnic-cleansing" camps in which extensive human rights violations were taking place.

In late 1992, the total collapse of civil authority in Somalia brought a halt to humanitarian relief to that land, thereby threatening mass starvation. UN officials estimated that more than 300,000 Somalis had already died from hunger, and in the absence of restoring civil order to permit continued humanitarian relief, more than a million additional persons would likely die.

Who is responsible for protecting states from foreign aggression? Who is responsible for protecting people from the civil war or from war-induced starvation? This chapter implicitly addresses these questions by examining the nature of the international community. It begins by contrasting alternative visions of the world community and then identifies major characteristics of the international political system, calling attention to recent developments in the contemporary system. This chapter then examines the nature of global politics, focusing on the dilemma states face in promoting their national security without threatening other states. Finally, it explores the quest for national security with a case study—the Arab-Israeli dispute. This conflict illustrates the quest for self-determination of a people (the Palestinians) as well as the quest for national security of a Jewish state surrounded by Arab states.

States, like people, are insecure in proportion to the extent of their freedom. If freedom is wanted, insecurity must be accepted. Organizations that establish relations of authority and control may increase security as they decrease freedom.[1]

Kenneth Waltz, *international relations theorist*

A nation is a people tough enough to grab the land it wants and hang onto it. Period.[2]

John le Carré, *contemporary novelist*

Given the asymmetries of power, diversity of interests, and the weakness of institutionalizing mechanisms in the international system, it would be more productive to stop thinking of the Westphalian model as some ideal or historical reality and to treat it as a reference point or convention that is useful in some circumstances but not others. Some states have the power to preserve their territory and autonomy; others do not.[3]

Stephen D. Krasner, *political scientist*

An implicit argument made in this chapter is that, although the international community does not have any central authority to direct the actions of states, there is nonetheless order and stability. This order is achieved through the voluntary, independent actions of states as they balance their own self-interests with the shared interests of other nations.

THE IDEA OF INTERNATIONAL SOCIETY

Throughout the history of Western political thought, philosophers and political writers have defined the nature of global society in a variety of ways. Three of the most important perspectives are those of the realist, the idealist, and the internationalist.[4] The first two conceptions of international society derive from the realist and idealist approaches to politics examined in chapter 1. The internationalist version is a hybrid perspective, derived from the empirical orientation of realism and the normative orientation of idealism.

Realism
A political approach that emphasizes the conflictual nature of global politics, the priority of national security, a pessimistic assessment of human nature, and a consequentialist moral perspective.

Idealism
This approach to politics assumes that law, institutions, and morality can contribute to the development of peaceful, just international relations. An optimistic perspective toward world politics.

Internationalism
A view of the international community that incorporates both the realities of power and sovereignty and the idealistic claims of transnational moral and legal obligations.

Realism denies the existence of global society. Rather, it views the international community as a disparate collection of independent political societies, each seeking its own security and economic and social well-being. Because few values and cultural norms are shared in the international system, the world is not a coherent, cohesive community, but an anarchic system in which every state competes for limited resources and in which security is achieved through self-help. States promote their individual well-being through power. The common good, to the extent that it can be promoted, is realized by the combined effect of individual self-interests.

In contrast to realism, **idealism** affirms the existence of global society. Although it recognizes that the cultural, social, political, and economic bonds of international society are comparatively weak and undeveloped, especially when compared to those of a typical domestic society, the idealist perspective, nonetheless, regards global society as a developing political community. To a significant degree, the cohesion of global society is rooted in the universal values and humanitarian norms that affirm human dignity, regardless of peoples' nationality, ethnicity, state of residence, or level of economic prosperity. But the coherence and development of the international community is comparatively low because the community's legal and governmental institutions are undeveloped. As a result, idealism seeks to strengthen the international community by strengthening international structures.

Historically, two different major structural reforms have been recommended—a radical plan, calling for the establishment of a single unitary government, and a reformist plan, calling for the creation of a global federal state. In his essay "Of Monarchy" (*De Monarchia*), Dante, the noted medieval Italian poet, sets forth the radical conception by arguing for the establishment of a central government. According to him, an ideal world community can best be realized when sovereignty is transferred from states to a single monarch. Establishing a single political authority is desirable, because a unitary authority can settle disputes decisively.

Some five centuries later, Immanuel Kant set forth his reformist conception of global society in *On Perpetual Peace*. According to Kant, the world system must be transformed from a decentralized political order to a federal structure if peace and justice are to be realized in the world. Although less radical than Dante's vision, Kant's conception assumes that the ideal world comprises quasi-independent, constitutional states that peacefully collaborate in promoting common interests. Peace is maintained, in his view, not only by an established international federal authority but also by the peace-loving behavior of constitutional regimes.

Internationalism, located between the extremes of idealism and realism, provides an intermediary conception of global society. Following the ideas of

TABLE 3.1 Three Perspectives of International Community

Type	Nature of System	Moderation of Conflict	View of Future
Realism	Conflictual	Power and self-help	Maintain system
Internationalism	Harmonious and conflictual	Law and common morality	Maintain system, strengthen moral/legal obligations
Idealism	Transnational unity, uncertain	Centralize authority through international organizations	Transform system

Hugo Grotius, the seventeenth-century Dutch jurist and diplomat, internationalism assumes that peace and justice are possible in global society when states fulfill their respective legal and moral obligations. Whereas the Kantian vision requires the transformation of the international system, the Grotian perspective assumes that peace and justice can be achieved within the existing structures, provided states behave in accordance with global society's legal, rational, and moral norms. Although recognizing the problems posed by the existing decentralized political organization, this perspective assumes that states can overcome the barriers of self-interest and cultural pluralism and pursue harmonious, productive international relations by developing and cultivating shared norms and aspirations. Thus, whereas realism assumes that states will be guided solely by increasing their power, the internationalist vision assumes that statesmen are guided by common moral and legal norms that make peace and justice possible.

The contemporary world community reflects, in varying degrees, empirical and normative elements of each of the three versions. (See table 3.1.) Each contributes distinctive orientations that are invaluable for understanding international relations. In particular, these orientations include realism's emphasis on international anarchy, internationalism's emphasis on governmental legal and moral obligations, and idealism's emphasis on the centralization of global political authority and the strengthening of interdependence. Thus, no view alone can provide an adequate framework for assessing contemporary international society.

THE STRUCTURE OF THE INTERNATIONAL SYSTEM

The roots of the contemporary world system were established in the mid-seventeenth century with the development of nation-states. As noted in chapter 2, the centralization and consolidation of governmental authority began in the medieval age, culminating in the development of nation-states with the **Treaty of Westphalia** (1648). The treaty is important because it marks the development of the classical international legal and political order—commonly referred to as the **Westphalian system.** The treaty, which ended thirty years of religious wars among European states, codified the principle of state sovereignty by recognizing the undisputed authority of secular rulers within designated territories. Among other things, it affirmed the ruler's right to determine the religion of a state. According to Joseph Nye, Jr., international order was "based on the sovereignty of states, not the sovereignty of peoples."[5]

Although the global nation-state system has undergone a number of changes since its beginnings more than 300 years ago, the international community's basic structure has remained largely intact. However, since the end of World War II, and especially since the 1970s and 1980s, the global community has witnessed a number of major structural changes that have resulted in a reformed or **post-Westphalian system.** Next we will examine key features of the traditional

Treaty of Westphalia
This mid-seventeenth century treaty, ending thirty years of religious wars among European states, is significant because it affirmed the notion of state sovereignty, thereby establishing the foundation of the modern state-based global order.

Westphalian system
The anarchic nation-state system established with the 1648 Treaty of Westphalia.

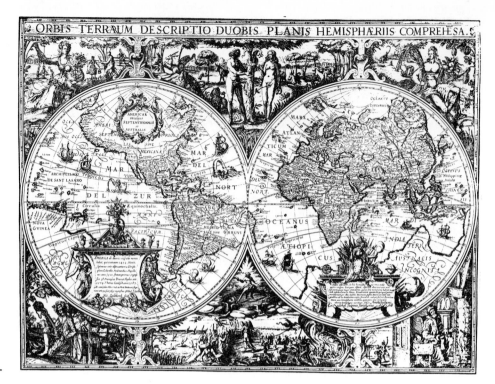

MAP 3.1
A seventeenth-century depiction of the world
This beautiful early seventeenth-century map depicts the emerging Westphalian international system.

Westphalian order and then specify some of the system's principal rules and norms that regulate interstate relations. In addition, we describe some of the major emerging features of the post-Westphalian order.

The Westphalian System

Fundamentally, the Westphalian system is a weak and underdeveloped political community—a loose multinational *society of societies*. Four features have characterized this traditional international order: the primacy of states, sovereignty, the inegalitarian distribution of national power, and the absence of a common authority to resolve disputes.

State Dominance

A key element of the modern global order is the preeminence of states. Although the global society involves many nonstate actors (e.g., NGOs, private associations, groups, individuals), the major actors in this system are states and more specifically the governments of states. International relations are basically the result of the decisions and actions of states as they seek to maximize their national interests within the international community. Because international relations are ultimately developed and regulated by states, the international system is essentially a state-centric system.

The growth of functional interdependence among states has somewhat reduced the role of state actors in global society. Post–World War II developments, such as the increase of international production and consumption, the growth of global telecommunications, and the expansion of international transportation networks, have increased the scope and depth of global interdependence, thereby making state borders more permeable. Although the power of nation-states has eroded in recent decades, it remains the key actor in global society. As historian Paul Kennedy has noted, "no adequate substitute has emerged to replace it as the key unit in responding to global change."[6]

Post-Westphalian system
The emerging system of global society that is characterized by a decline in state sovereignty, growing influence of nonstate actors and the declining role of military force.

Sovereignty

Another major feature of the Westphalian order is **sovereignty**—that is, supreme, legitimate authority within the territorial boundaries of a state. As Daniel Philpott has shown, before the Peace of Westphalia, there was no sovereignty because there was no central, legitimate authority within states.[7] The development of sovereignty had two important implications: domestically, it gave national governments final authority within the territorial boundaries of states; and internationally, it recognized states as self-determining political communities, subject to no other political authority.

From an international legal perspective, sovereignty has two key dimensions: political independence and equality. If a state is to have ultimate control over political affairs within its territorial boundaries, it must possess governmental institutions that are not subject to foreign control. To a significant degree, independence is a precondition of state sovereignty. Of course, no state—unless it is a major power—has the capabilities to pursue unlimited interests in disregard for, or at the expense of, the interests of other states. Indeed, a state's ability to pursue its national interests in the world will depend on its relative power. Moreover, a state's freedom of foreign policy action is circumscribed by external factors, such as the power of other states, the role of international governmental organizations, and the influence of international law and world public opinion.

Equality is the second legal pillar of sovereignty. Although states differ in their size and capabilities, they are fundamentally equal in their legal position in the world community.[8] The doctrine of equality is enshrined in the United Nations system and is expressed in the shared rights and obligations of member-states. For example, every nation-state has a right to exist, to use force to defend its territorial boundaries, and to determine its domestic affairs as it wishes. On the other hand, states bear common obligations, such as to settle disputes peacefully and to avoid threatening other states or interfering in their internal affairs. Although the notion of juridical equality serves as a cornerstone of the contemporary international order, it remains more fiction than reality. Because each state's security and welfare is dependent on its own resources, states have developed vastly different economic, political, and military capabilities.

Sovereignty
Supreme authority to make binding decisions within states; from an international perspective, sovereignty implies states' legal equality and political independence.

The Oligarchic Distribution of Power

A third feature of the classical international system is the inegalitarian or oligarchic distribution of power among states. Historically, the political influence of states has always been highly unequal. International relations scholar Robert W. Tucker notes that states are born unequal, and uneven rates of development only exacerbate those inequalities. Thus, "the history of the international system," writes Tucker, "is a history of inequality par excellence."[9] Since the sixteenth century, only eleven states have been considered major powers, and from the nineteenth century until 1935 only five states held this status. From the end of World War II to 1990, two states—the United States and the former Soviet Union—monopolized international relations. But since the Soviet Union disintegrated and ceased to exist in December 1991, the United States has been the sole superpower. Table 3.2 provides a rough classification of states as of 1997.

The inegalitarian or oligarchic nature of world politics is illustrated by the distribution of nuclear weapons. In 1993, of more than 180 countries in the international system only about a dozen had nuclear weapons or the capacity to build them.[10] In effect, the "nuclear club" comprised at most 7 percent of the world's member-states. Moreover, of these, only two—United States and Russia—possessed the bulk (more than 80 percent) of the world's destructive capability. Indeed, throughout the first twenty years of the Cold War the United States and the Soviet Union were the sole nuclear states, and in the remaining twenty-five years they never controlled less than 90 percent of the world's nuclear weapons.

TABLE 3.2   A Classification of States, 1997*

Type of State	Name of States		
Super Power	United States		
Major Powers	Britain	China	Germany
	France	Japan	Russia
Medium Powers	Argentina	Iran	South Africa
	Australia	Iraq	South Korea
	Austria	Israel	Spain
	Belgium	Italy	Sweden
	Brazil	Mexico	Switzerland
	Canada	Netherlands	Syria
	Cuba	Nigeria	Thailand
	Egypt	North Korea	Turkey
	Greece	Pakistan	Ukraine
	India	Poland	Venezuela
	Indonesia	Saudi Arabia	Vietnam

*This subjective ranking is based on population, GNP, and the size and quality of military forces.

Another indicator of the inegalitarian nature of global society is the wide inequalities in national income (see fig. 3.1). The United States, the leading power in the contemporary community, has a gross national product about five times that of France, Italy, and Britain, and about eighteen times that of Russia and China. Moreover, if per capita income is compared among the Western industrial states and the developing nations, the economic disparities become even more pronounced. The 1994 per capita income of Germany, Japan, and the United States was above $25,000, while the per capita income of Bolivia, Peru, and Tunisia was less than $3,000. Low-income states, like Haiti, Malawi, and Zaire, had a per capita income of less than $1,000.[11]

No Common Authority

A fourth key feature of the international system is the absence of a competent authority to mediate and resolve disputes among member-states. Scholars define this condition as **anarchy.** Anarchy in IR does not mean disorder but a lack of authoritative governmental structures.

Anarchy
The absence of governmental authority.

As noted in the Introduction, politics is the means by which societies establish and maintain community life. Politics normally involves the making and implementation of authoritative decisions for human communities. In domestic society sovereign governments have the responsibility for maintaining order by making and implementing public decisions. In international society, however, there is no international authority with the power to settle disputes and establish and implement common policies. According to Roger Masters, the international system is similar to a primitive, stateless society. In his view, the international society shares three features with stateless societies: no formal governmental institutions to judge and punish violators of the law, no structures to enforce community obligations and protect legitimate individual interests (except through

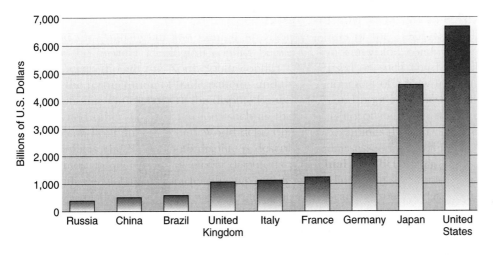

FIGURE 3.1
GNP of Leading States, 1994 (in billions of U.S. dollars)
Source: World Bank, *From Plan to Market: World Development Report 1996* (New York: Oxford University Press, 1996), p. 211.

individual initiative or "self-help"), and no recognized institutions to make rules (except through bargaining relationships or through accepted community customs and practices).[12]

The global community is an anarchic or primitive system because it lacks authoritative decision-making institutions. Its key symbol, according to the late Frenchman Raymond Aron, is war, because war is the ultimate instrument for settling interstate disputes.[13] Because there is no transnational government to regulate the international behavior of states, the well-being and security of states is ultimately dependent on each state's resources and capabilities. The international order is thus fundamentally a **self-help system,** which Kenneth Waltz defines as "one in which those who do not help themselves, or who do so less effectively than others, will fail to prosper, will lay themselves open to dangers, will suffer."[14]

Because of the absence of a global institution, military security is a top priority of all governments. Indeed, more money is devoted to the armed forces than to any other area of government. In 1994, total world military expenditures—estimated at $840 billion or roughly 3 percent of total world gross national product—were about $149 per person. Whereas developed and developing nations devoted roughly the same percentage of the GNP to military resources (3.1 percent for developed nations and 2.6 percent for developing countries), per capita expenditures in the developed countries ($587) were nearly sixteen times those of the developing nations ($37).[15] It is important to stress, however, that the high level of governmental expenditures on military forces is not solely for national security. Armed forces also serve as a means of domestic social control. As a result, some scholars argue that for most Third World countries the top priority is internal cohesion and that the chief duty of the armed forces in such states is domestic control, not the defense of territorial boundaries.[16]

The absence of developed institutions and the prevalence of force and conflict in the global community has led some to erroneously conclude that the world is devoid of order and cooperation. Although international society is an underdeveloped political system, it nonetheless achieves a significant level of stability and order. This *ordered anarchy*[17] is realized not by supranational institutions but by voluntary behaviors of state and nonstate actors. More specifically, the order and stability of global society is rooted in the distribution of power among member-states and in their voluntary cooperation and coordination in areas of common concern. Even if more developed political institutions existed in the international community, the absence of widely shared political interests and values would be a major stumbling block to world order.

Self-help system
A system where each actor is ultimately responsible for its own welfare and security.

Rules of the Westphalian System

Political philosopher John Rawls has argued that social systems require two types of rules. The first kind, called "constitutive rules," defines the major players of a system and specifies the criteria for determining which actors can join the system. The second type, "regulative" rules, specifies norms governing the actors' behavior.[18] Applying Rawls' classification of rules to international political society, we define international constitutive norms as those that specify (a) which actors are members of global society and (b) what criteria must be fulfilled before prospective members can become members of the international community. The international community's regulative norms, by contrast, provide the fundamental rules governing international relations. Because the international community's constitutive and regulative norms provide the foundational rules of global society, they can be regarded as the world's "constitution."

Constitutive Norms

The major constitutive norm of the international system is that states are the chief actors in global society. States that exhibit sovereignty—that is, whose governments maintain effective control within defined territories—are entitled to membership in the international community. But how are state boundaries to be determined? And because national groups can claim political self-rule based on the widely accepted norm of self-determination, which nationalities are entitled to statehood? When the international community began affirming the norm of self-determination, it did so not to undermine existing states, but to provide justification for political self-determination to former colonies. Thus, article 6 of the General Assembly's 1960 "Declaration on the Granting of Independence to Colonial Countries and Territories" states: "Any attempt aimed at the partial or total disruption of the national unity and the territorial integrity of a country is incompatible with the purposes and principles of the Charter of the United Nations."[19] Thus, as originally developed, the norm of self-determination applied chiefly to non self-governing territories. Former colonies were entitled to statehood; nations and tribes, either within colonies or other sates, were not necessarily entitled to claims of political self-rule. Not surprisingly, the bulk of states joining the international community in the aftermath of World War II were former colonies of European imperial systems.

Traditional constitutive norms favor existing states. Indeed, the presumption in favor of the international community's member states has contributed to the stability of the Westphalian system. In recent years, however, as the norm of self-determination has been increasingly used by ethnic and religious minorities to challenge the authority of existing states, the norms of self-determination and state sovereignty have come into increasing conflict. This has been the case especially in countries formerly dominated by the Soviet Union (e.g., the Tartars in Ukraine and the Chechens in Russia), and in selected other states, such as Canada (where the Quebecois have demanded greater political autonomy) and Iraq (where the Kurds have pressed for greater self-rule). The growing demands for self-determination by ethnic minorities have not only undermined many states and threatened the viability of others, but they have weakened the foundations of the Westphalian order itself. Moreover, although states are the basis of the international system, there is no provision for determining which groups are entitled to political autonomy. How states and subnational groups resolve their conflicting claims is solely a domestic issue, not subject to external determination. As Daniel Moynihan has observed, a group's demands for political autonomy may result in a quest for secession from the state, but secession and civil war are "none of the world's business."[20] Thus, whether minorities succeed in establishing self-rule is entirely up to each group's resources and capabilities.

Michael Mandelbaum has argued that the modern international system must be based on some norm, and that support for the status quo—that is, acceptance of the existing states and their respective territorial boundaries—is the simplest available principle. If this norm is discarded, he argues, all borders become suspect and the potential for international chaos is considerable. From a moral perspective, the defense of the status quo is problematic because it presumes that the world's cartography is morally legitimate. Existing territorial boundaries, however, were not established following any normative principle, but were the result of military and political contests. As Mandelbaum observed, "[h]istorically, the prize of independence has gone to those powerful or clever or fortunate or merely numerous enough to achieve it."[21]

Regulative Norms

Although no single document provides a comprehensive listing of the international community's core behavioral norms, the United Nations Charter defines some of the major shared goals of global society and some of the major rights and duties of states. The Charter thus provides a fundamental legal framework for contemporary global politics. The international community's member-states have adopted numerous other treaties and conventions that specify basic rules and principles regulating international relations. After examining these multilateral declarations, conventions, and treaties, Dorothy Jones concludes that the international community is governed by a set of rules that she terms a "code of peace." Because the **code of peace** specifies the acceptable behavioral norms of the international community, it provides not only a regulatory structure but an ethical system as well. The key elements of the code of peace are:

Code of peace
The fundamental rules governing the international behavior of states. The rules are derived from widely accepted treaties and conventions.

1. Sovereign equality of states
2. Territorial integrity and political independence of states
3. Equal rights and self-determination of peoples
4. Nonintervention in the internal affairs of states
5. Peaceful settlement of disputes between states
6. Abstention from the threat or use of force
7. Fulfillment in good faith of international obligations
8. Cooperation with other states
9. Respect for human rights and fundamental freedoms.[22]

In addition to these nine basic norms, Jones argues that since World War II two additional principles have become increasingly accepted by states, but because they are not universally accepted at this time they must be classified as auxiliary norms. These two emerging principles are the protection of the environment and the creation of an equitable international economic order.

Michael Walzer has developed a similar peacekeeping framework based on sovereignty and other widely accepted states' rights. Walzer, a political theorist, bases his regulatory system on the "domestic analogy"—an argument about states' rights based on a comparison of domestic political communities with the international system. According to him, states have rights in the international community just as individuals have rights in domestic society. States' rights, he argues, comprise a framework, or **legalist paradigm,** that defines the fundamental rules of interstate behavior and the role of force in protecting legitimate state interests. Walzer's regulatory framework involves the following six principles:

Legalist paradigm
The international legal framework that specifies basic rights and duties of states.

1. An international society of independent states exists;
2. The states comprising the international society have rights, including the rights of territorial integrity and political sovereignty;

3. The use of force or threat of force by one state against another constitutes aggression and is a criminal act;

4. In response to aggression, states are justified in carrying out two types of action—a war of self-defense by the victim and a war of law enforcement by the victim and other members of international society;

5. Nothing but aggression justifies war;

6. After the aggressor has been militarily repulsed, it can also be punished.[23]

Although Walzer's theory is based on a hypothetical argument, it provides, nonetheless, an illuminating structure based on the basic rights and duties of states. Jones' argument, by contrast, provides a useful listing of regulatory norms that states have already accepted as binding in their global relations. Despite the differences in Jones' code of peace and Walzer's legalist paradigm, both sets of regulatory norms provide a normative structure that, if followed, would contribute to global order and international peace. Indeed, both Jones and Walzer view their regulatory rules as ethical because their observance is designed to inhibit aggression, facilitate international conflict resolution, and foster global order.

The Post-Westphalian System

Although the contemporary international system continues to be based on the four pillars of the Westphalian order, the modern system has changed in recent decades in response to significant cultural, religious, social, economic, political, and technological developments in global society. In significant measure, the development of the post-Westphalian order is a response to the rise of post-industrial economic life and post-modern political life in the late twentieth century. Some of the most important features of this reformed global system, highlighted in table 3.3, are briefly examined below.

One feature of the modern international order is the *growing influence of non-state actors*. Of special importance are the growing number of technical, scientific, economic, social, and religious nongovernmental organizations that foster and sustain global interdependence. Although growth in the number and role of nonstate actors has not displaced the nation-state as the major international actor, it has reduced its relative influence and resulted in more complex transnational relations.[24]

A second important feature of the post-Westphalian system is the *decline of state sovereignty* and the loss of governmental control over events within the state. This development is due to a number of factors, but in particular to the increasingly permeable boundaries of states and the growing disintegrative cultural, ethnic, and religious forces within societies. The loss of state autonomy is not a wholly new development, however, because sovereignty has been compromised in a variety of ways in previous eras. Indeed, one scholar has argued that the prevalent idea that the loss of sovereignty is a new development is "historically myopic," because the qualification of state sovereignty has been "an enduring characteristic of the international environment."[25] What is new, however, is the manner in which sovereignty has been compromised. Whereas the traditional order qualified sovereignty through voluntary agreements and involuntary imposition, the modern reductions in sovereignty are largely the result of increasing functional interdependence within global society, as well as the rising ethnonationalistic claims of subnational groups.

A related feature of the modern global order is the *rise of weak states*. As noted in chapter 2, states can be differentiated along a continuum of strong and weak states. Strong states are those characterized by a comparatively high level of social, political, and economic unity, governmental institutions perceived as legitimate, effective governmental authority to make, enforce, and interpret rules, and military and police forces capable of defending territorial boundaries. Weak states

TABLE 3.3 Comparison of the Westphalian and Post-Westphalian Systems

	Westphalian	Post-Westphalian
Actors	States	States, quasi-states, IGOs, NGOs
Nature of states	Sovereign	Decline in sovereignty
Condition of states	Strong States are coherent	Strong and weak Many states are fragmented, some are nonviable
Nature of power	Based chiefly on military and economic resources	Military resources become less important Social, cultural, religious resources more significant
Distribution of power	Oligarchic Inequalities are important	Oligarchic Inequalities lose some significance
Global institutions	Limited role	Moderate role

are those with few of these attributes. During the nineteenth century, the so-called classical Westphalian era, states were strong and coherent and their governments enjoyed significant authority. But the post-World War II explosion in new states, involving the addition of 120 new states to the international community, has resulted in a growing number of weak, fragmented, and ineffective states. As Kalevi Holsti has noted, the rise of weak states has led to increased domestic instability and increasing civil wars—or what he terms "wars of a third kind."[26]

Fourth, the post-Westphalian system is characterized by a *decline in the influence of military power*. Even though major powers with significant military resources can still use force to compel a weaker state, significant military capabilities do not automatically translate into political influence. To be sure, military power continues to provide the ultimate resource for national security, but the ability of states to influence events in global society is increasingly dependent on resources other than force. In chapter 6 on power we examine some of the major developments that have resulted in significant modifications in the nature of power in the modern international system.

A fifth, related feature of the post-Westphalian order is the *loss in political significance of power inequalities*. In the classical era, especially during the nineteenth century, well-armed states had major influence in the international system. In that system, strong states made and enforced the rules of global society. In the modern system, by contrast, the inequalities in power have become less important because small, well-armed groups can exert significant influence on global affairs. For example, when Chechnya, a small republic within the Russian Federation, tried to secede from Russia in the early 1990s, President Boris Yeltsin sent a large armed force to put down the rebellion. Even though Russia possessed large and well-equipped military forces, Chechen rebels were able to inflict such heavy losses on Russian forces that Yeltsin was ultimately forced to settle the dispute by giving the Chechens significant political autonomy.

Finally, *international institutions play a more important role* in the contemporary system. This growing influence is due partly to the rising impact of two global forces—globalism and tribalism. The first fosters international integration and community, whereas the second contributes to conflict and fragmentation. In connection with the growth of globalism, international governmental and nongovernmental institutions play a significant role in facilitating transnational cooperation and coordination. And in connection with rising disintegration, IGOs and NGOs also contribute to the management and resolution of global conflict.

CONTEMPORARY DEVELOPMENTS
IN THE INTERNATIONAL SYSTEM

As noted before, two features characterize the modern post–Cold War international system—*globalism* and *tribalism,* which Benjamin Barber defines as the "forces of McWorld" and the "forces of Jihad."[27] To be sure, the forces of integration and fragmentation are not new developments in global society. But because these forces have dramatically influenced the nature and structure of world politics on the international community, we examine the nature of each of them below.

Globalism

Globalism
The growing role of transnational interactions among people, groups, states, and other actors.

Globalism involves the expansion of social, economic, cultural, and scientific transactions across national boundaries and is a direct consequence of the rise of the postindustrial order in the late-twentieth century. Whereas the industrial era was characterized by efficient mass production of goods, postindustrial societies are characterized by a service economy, efficient information processing, and rapid communications. As a result of major technological, scientific, and economic innovations, transnational interdependence has expanded dramatically in the postwar era, thereby reducing the importance of national boundaries.

Several developments have contributed to the expansion of globalism. First, *modern transport technologies* have increased the efficiency of global transportation. A modern jumbo jet (such as the Boeing 747), for example, can carry 400 or more passengers at speeds in excess of 500 miles an hour on a nonstop flight of 8,000–10,000 miles. Whereas transatlantic travel used to take more than one week at the turn of the century, now the supersonic Concord jet can carry passengers from New York to Paris in less than three and a half hours. Moreover, jet cargo allows countries to export perishable goods throughout the world.

Second, *modern telecommunications systems* have also contributed to the growth of transnational information flows. According to UNESCO, the number of television transmitters increased from 8,550 in 1965 to 60,570 in 1985, and the number of television receivers increased from 186 million to 661 million during the same period.[28] Even in remote areas of Third World nations, citizens often have access to satellite receivers that permit immediate access to foreign news. As a result of the expansion of television stations and receivers and the development of global communications networks, modern telecommunications systems have greatly expanded global coverage of news, sports, and entertainment. For example, major athletic events, such as the World Soccer Cup, are now televised instantaneously throughout the world. Because major sporting events are covered globally, outstanding athletes—such as Chicago Bulls basketball star Michael Jordan—are recognized throughout the world, even in remote Third World areas. The CNN television network, with cable access in more than sixty countries, has greatly expanded global news coverage. For example, during the January 1991 Persian Gulf War and the August 1991 abortive coup against Soviet President Mikhail Gorbachev, CNN provided nearly continuous on-site television coverage to hundreds of millions of homes throughout the world. When the United States intervened in Somalia in December 1992, media officials were on hand to provide live coverage of the arrival of U.S. Marines on the Somali coast. Finally, and most significantly, the rise of computer-based communications, including electronic mail and the Internet, is revolutionizing not only communications but also commercial and financial transactions. Because of the instantaneous, efficient low cost of cross-border computer communications, the volume of global transactions has expanded dramatically since the early 1980s.

A third related development is the *globalization of popular culture* as seen by the growth in brand names such as Levis, McDonald's, Coca-Cola, IBM, Apple, Microsoft, Pierre Cardin, and Sony. Because brand labels convey an image of modernity, the names tend to be as important as the products themselves. Another expression of global culture is the growing export of entertainment. *The Bill Cosby Show,* for example, was for many years one of the most popular television programs in South Africa, and U.S. soap operas have been a major export commodity to Latin America. In November 1991 *Terminator 2* was briefly the number 1 movie in Switzerland, a land that has generally prided itself on its political neutrality and cultural insularity. During the author's brief visit to Gaza in 1988, he was told that *Rambo* was the most widely rented movie among several small video rental shops. In light of the growing influence of American popular culture, Barber observes: "What is the power of the Pentagon compared with Disneyland? Can the Sixth Fleet keep up with CNN? McDonald's in Moscow and Coke in China will do more to create a global culture than military colonization ever could."[29]

A fourth factor contributing to global interdependence is the *growth of the international market.* As modernization has spread throughout the world, the demand for modern, specialized goods and services has increased. As a result, the level of global trade has expanded dramatically in the last half of the twentieth century, with annual exports increasing to more than 6 trillion dollars in 1996. And to facilitate cross-border transactions, the volume of global foreign exchange markets has increased even more dramatically, rising to an estimated daily average of more that $1.3 trillion. Moreover, financial markets have become more globally interdependent. Although cross-border trade of stocks and bonds accounted for less than 10 percent of the U.S. GDP in 1980, by the early 1990s, international equities transactions accounted for more than 100 percent of the U.S. GDP.[30] In view of the dramatic rise in the size and impact of global capital and financial markets, the value of securities and foreign currencies is increasingly influenced by international investors and currency traders. For example, the dollar remained overvalued in the early 1980s in great measure because of high foreign (primarily European investors) demand for dollars, whereas the rise in the New York Stock Exchange in the mid 1980s was greatly influenced by Japanese demand for U.S. securities. More significantly, modern economic expansion has become increasingly globalized with the rise of multinational production. No longer are computers, machinery, automobiles, and other industrial products made solely in one country. Rather, modern goods are constructed from components made in many different countries.

The growing web of international interdependence of people, products, and information has had the ironic effect of reducing government control over transnational flows, especially information and other intangible resources. For example, while the former Soviet government tried to limit contact with Western political and economic ideas, the spread of modern technology, especially copying machines, televisions, and VCRs, provided a means of disseminating Western ideas that contributed to the growing demand by Soviet elites for greater political and economic freedom. When the Chinese government carried out its crackdown against student dissidents at Beijing's Tiananmen Square in 1989 and halted foreign television coverage, dissidents were able to bypass government controls by sending messages overseas through FAX machines. Moreover, although governments have tried to limit the growth of the deadly AIDS virus, they have been largely unsuccessful to date in controlling its global proliferation.

Because many modern networks of global interdependence operate without government knowledge or participation, transactions across national boundaries are often beyond government control. As a result of the growth in global transactions, the classical international order, characterized by the dominance of

international relations, has given way to a modern global system in which non-governmental **transnational relations** play a more important role in global society (see fig. 3.2). Although scholars are divided on the extent to which interdependence has transformed the classical Westphalian order, it is clear that the international order has been modified, not displaced. Although nonstate actors play a more important role in the contemporary global system, the modern global system has not displaced the traditional, decentralized order. States are still sovereign. They still remain the primary actors in global politics.

One of the most important consequences of the growth of functional interdependence has been the rise of global consciousness—that is, the development of global affinities and concerns. As citizens increase contact with foreigners and as they become more aware of global issues, their concerns, allegiances, and psychological affinities tend to shift toward the international system. The rise of social and cultural interdependence thus tends to encourage a cosmopolitan culture, decreasing nationalistic parochialism and encouraging global perspectives. In effect, the growth of global interactions makes people more aware of the world as a "global village," thereby strengthening international solidarity.

Of course, the growth in cosmopolitan consciousness is not inevitable. Interdependence can promote conflict as well as cohesion. As one scholar has noted, high levels of economic interdependence have not prevented domestic strife and civil wars. Moreover, when states distrust or fear each other, interdependence tends to exacerbate conflict, rather than promote peace and tranquility.[31] Thus, global interactions can contribute to peaceful and productive living conditions only when people are positively predisposed to work harmoniously, cooperate in promoting shared concerns, and resolve issues peacefully. In the absence of such positive psychological predispositions, interdependence is unlikely to promote global solidarity and reduce conflict, competition, and insecurity among nations.

Tribalism

Tribalism, the second feature of the contemporary global system, involves the disintegration of existing states. Because most countries are multinational states, civil wars have been a periodic feature of the global international order. Some of these wars have been tribal in nature, such as the domestic conflicts in Zaire in the 1960s, in Rwanda and Burundi in the 1970s and mid-1990s, and in Somalia and South Africa in the early 1990s. Other conflicts have been religious in nature, such

FIGURE 3.2
Comparison of Classical and Modern International Systems

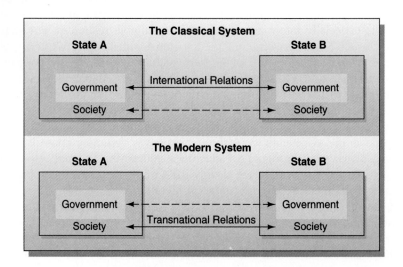

as the bitter struggle between Muslims and Hindus in India and the Muslim-animist/Christian feud in Sudan. Still others, such as the intense Lebanese civil war of the early 1980s, combined ethnic, religious, economic, and political dimensions. What is unprecedented about the factionalism and tribalism of the post–Cold War era is the high degree of ethnic, religious, and political division within countries, making cultures, sects, and dissenting minorities more influential in global society.

Throughout the world—but especially in Africa, Asia, and eastern Europe—ethnic, religious, and political minorities are seeking to counter the universalist pressures of modernity and the market by cultivating stronger tribal, ethnic, and religious bonds through increased claims of self-determination. In a major study of ethnopolitical groups, Tedd Gurr found that the number of minority groups involved in significant conflict increased from 1945 to mid-1990s. (See fig. 3.3.) In Canada, for example, French-speaking citizens from Quebec are pressing for increased political independence, thereby threatening the Canadian federation. In Turkey, Iraq, and Iran, Kurds are pressing for greater political autonomy from their respective governments.

Although modern history suggests that increasing domestic and international interdependence is a precondition for economic expansion, sects, factions, clans, and minority groups continue pressing for political self-determination and the disintegration of existing nation-states. Indeed, the disintegration and destruction of Beirut—the "pearl" of the Mediterranean—dramatically illustrates what can happen when religious and ethnic factionalism triumphs over communitarian forces.

Several factors have contributed to social fragmentation in the contemporary global system. First, the United Nations system, with its emphasis on **self-determination,** has reinforced the notion of self-rule for peoples desiring political autonomy. As designed by its founding fathers in 1945, the United Nations system provides peoples with the right to determine their own political destinies—that is, to establish political communities that are politically independent and able to make society-wide decisions without external interference. Although self-determination helped to unify countries as part of the anticolonialist movement of the 1950s and 1960s, in the modern world this principle has contributed to the weakening and growing fragmentation of countries. The demand for increased political autonomy by ethnic minorities (such as the Siks, Kurds, Tamils, and Ossetians) has resulted in increased political instability and war, and in the disintegration of a number of nation-states.

Self-determination
The claim, first popularized in the twentieth century by President Woodrow Wilson and subsequently enshrined in the United Nations system, that peoples have a right to political self-rule.

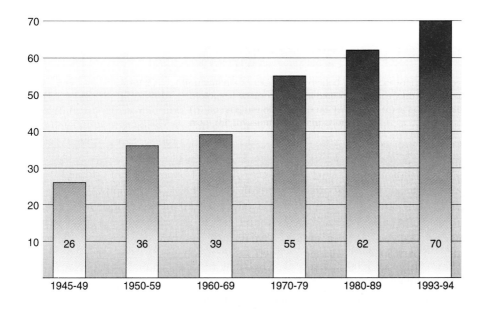

FIGURE 3.3
Number of Ethnopolitical Groups Involved in Serious Conflicts, 1945–1994
Source: Tedd Robert Gurr, "Peoples Against States: Ethnopolitical Conflict and the Changing World System," *International Studies Quarterly,* 38 (September 1994), p. 350.

Second, the failure of existing governments to effectively protect the rights of ethnic minorities has also contributed to the growth of factionalism. Because few transitional societies have achieved well-developed pluralistic cultures, developing nations generally are unable to provide effective protection to ethnic, religious, and other minorities. Although democratic culture increased in strength in the global community during the 1980s, ethnic and religious clan wars continue in countries in which pluralism and democratic institutions remain underdeveloped or absent altogether.

A third factor contributing to the growth in tribalism is the end of the Cold War. The collapse of Soviet communism has resulted in a vacuum of governmental authority in many countries, but especially in former Soviet republics and formerly Soviet-dominated Eastern European states. Even though ethnic rivalries predate the collapse of the Cold War, the end of the Soviet empire has displaced ideology as a cohesive national force, giving rise to cultural, social, and ethnic rivalries. In an essay written at the outset of the Cold War, Daniel Bell warned of the dangers of ethnic conflict: "To replace the politics of ideology with the politics of ethnicity might only be the continuation of war by other means."[32] Not surprisingly, the collapse of Soviet communism has been followed by bitter ethnic fighting in the former Soviet republics of Azerbaijan, Armenia, and Georgia, and in the former Yugoslavian republics of Bosnia-Herzegovina, Croatia, and Kosovo.

Although tribalism is unlikely to halt the move toward greater functional interdependence, the quest for stronger social and cultural identities is likely to be a major source of tensions within nations and affect global relations between state and nonstate actors. The tension between the forces of Jihad and the forces of McWorld will therefore likely continue into the next century and perhaps even grow stronger.

SECURITY IN GLOBAL SOCIETY

In describing the global political system, we observed that it was an anarchic system without authoritative conflict management institutions. As a result, we noted that each state is ultimately responsible for its security and well-being. No problem illustrates the precarious and paradoxical nature of the system's self-help character better than national security. Because each state is responsible for deterring (threatening to punish) aggression and for punishing unjust attack, each state seeks to maximize its military capabilities. But the quest for military security by one state is a double-edged sword because weapons can be used defensively or offensively. Thus, the quest for national security is ambiguous. For example, President Reagan's Strategic Defense Initiative (SDI)—designed to destroy attacking strategic nuclear weapons—could be classified either as a program of strategic defense (by the United States) or of strategic offense (by the Soviet Union).

Security dilemma
The dilemma created when states seek to enhance national security by increasing military capabilities.

As a result, when a state seeks to increase its security by increasing military capabilities, other states may perceive its actions as a threat. This leads to a **security dilemma:** *If a state seeks to increase its security, the addition of military capabilities may lead to commensurate actions by other states, and thereby reduce its overall national security.*[33]

Thus, the quest for wise, rational policies requires not only increasing military power, but also assessing how other states will respond. Failure to do so could result in a net loss of security, even though national capabilities increase. Because the security of states ultimately depends on the interaction of states' behavior, national security is always tentative and conditional.

Consider, for example, the quest for security by two hypothetical states—Beta and Gulf. In their quest for security each has fundamentally three choices: to increase, maintain, or reduce military capabilities. Suppose, for example, that Beta seeks to increase its national security by expanding its military capacity. If Beta increases its capabilities, Gulf can respond in one of two ways. First, it can disregard Beta's action and accept its relative decline, or it can respond by increasing its own capabilities. If the former condition is achieved, Beta is potentially more secure, whereas Gulf is potentially less secure. If, on the other hand, Beta chooses to promote international harmony and goodwill by decreasing its military capabilities, Gulf has two basic alternatives—to respond in kind and decrease its own capabilities, or to take advantage of the new situation by maintaining its capabilities or even increasing them. Figure 3.4 illustrates the interrelated nature of national security for these two hypothetical states.

Another illustration of the precarious nature of security is a parable, originally developed by Jean Jacques Rousseau and applied to world politics by Kenneth Waltz.[34] Five men decide to go hunting together at a time when all are suffering from extreme hunger. Because the meat of a single deer can satisfy the hunger of all five, they agree they should cooperate in trapping one. But a hare can satisfy the hunger of any one of them. As they go hunting, a hare comes within reach of one of the hunters. If he kills the hare, he will satisfy his immediate personal needs; but such action will also allow the deer to go free and cause the other hunters continued hunger and possibly death. The hunter's choice is thus: to kill the hare and satisfy personal, immediate needs or to continue hunting. His choice is all the more difficult when he recognizes that the other hunters may shortly have a similar choice and may, in fact, defect from the group and fulfill personal wants.

The parable illustrates not only the indeterminate and paradoxical character of world politics, but the ambiguity of states' external policies. The common goal of the hunters (capturing a deer) represents the general, long-term "global" interests of states, including such concerns as world peace, economic prosperity, protection of the global environment, and promotion of human dignity. The hare represents the nationalistic, short-term policies of states. Examples of such behaviors include increasing military capabilities, imposing higher tariff barriers, prohibiting immigration, and disregarding international law. In the quest for national and international goals, government officials (like hunters) must choose between general and particular interests, short-term and long-term goals. Because states must assess their interests in light of the actions of other states, economic and military self-restraint may not always be the rational policy. Nor is the pursuit of common interests in disregard for national interests the most moral policy, because self-restraint does not necessarily lead to the common good. On the one hand, a state must cooperate with other states if peace and prosperity are to be realized; on the other hand, a state must not depend wholly on joint ventures, lest it fail to adequately protect itself from aggression and to provide for the material needs of its citizens.

To illustrate some of the major concepts and themes covered in this chapter, the Arab-Israeli conflict is examined (see case 3.1). Although Israel is a small state,

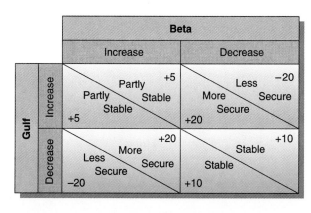

FIGURE 3.4
Pay-off Matrix
between Two
Hypothetical States

Case 3.1 The Arab-Israeli Conflict

The Dispute

The Arab-Israeli conflict involves two distinct but interrelated elements. The first is a conflict between two peoples—the Jews and the Palestinians; the second is a conflict between Israel and the neighboring Arab states. The first is an *intranational dispute,* the second an *interstate* one.

The *Jewish-Palestinian conflict* is rooted in the desire of two peoples to set up a state on the same land.[35] For religious, cultural, and historical reasons, both Arabs and Jews desire a homeland in **Palestine** (also known as the Holy Land)—the territory currently encompassing Israel, Gaza, and the West Bank. The roots of this dispute began in the early part of the twentieth century when Jews, under the inspiration of the Zionist movement, began to return to Palestine in the hope of creating a political homeland. Following the creation of the state of Israel in 1948, the Jewish-Palestinian conflict increased in intensity, resulting in numerous wars. Since 1967 the conflict has focused on the political rights of Palestinians in the West Bank and Gaza Strip—territories that were occupied by Israel following the 1967 war. To a significant degree the intifada of the late 1980s was a rebellion by Palestinians seeking increased political autonomy in Israeli-occupied lands.

The second dimension of the conflict, the *Arab-Israeli dispute,* involves international antagonisms between Israel and its Arab neighbors—Egypt, Iraq, Jordan, Lebanon, Saudi Arabia, and Syria.[36] After Israel achieved statehood, this conflict expanded from an intranational conflict between Jewish and Arab peoples to a regional interstate dispute between the governments and military forces of Israel and its Arab adversaries. From the outset, Arab states opposed the partitioning of Palestine to establish Jewish and Palestinian states. Thus when Israel declared its political independence in May 1948, Arab states refused to recognize Israel and sent military forces to attack the new state, pitting Israeli forces against Arab armies and a Palestinian militia.

Given the nature and strategic importance of the Arab-Israeli conflict, the promotion of peace and stability in the Middle East requires the reconciliation of Jews and Arabs and the moderation of transnational enmity between Israel and its Arab neighboring states. In effect, peace in the region can be promoted only by addressing both disputes simultaneously. As former U.S. diplomat Harold Saunders has noted, "states will not resolve their conflict until two peoples with claims to the same land resolve theirs. The Arab states cannot accept Israel until the Israeli-Palestinian dimension of the conflict has been justly and compassionately addressed."[37]

Historical Background

Israel came into being in 1948 when Great Britain terminated its mandate over Palestine. For several hundred years Turkey (the Ottoman Empire) had ruled the Middle East as a unified political region. After the Allied Powers defeated the Ottomans in World War I, Turkey was forced to relinquish control over a significant portion of its regional territorial acquisitions. Responsibility for Syria and Lebanon went to France, while responsibility for Jordan and Palestine went to Britain. Although Britain allowed Transjordan (modern Jordan) to become a quasi-independent principality under the leadership of Emir Abdullah in 1921, it established full control over Palestine, administering the land until May 14, 1948.

Two significant developments facilitated the creation of Israel from the Palestinian mandate. First, during the early part of the twentieth century the Jewish people, who had suffered great persecution throughout eastern Europe, began to call for a homeland in Palestine. This movement, called **Zionism,** provided an important impetus to increasing migration of Jews to Palestine. While at the beginning of the mandate in 1922 there were only about 56,000 Jews in Palestine, by 1946 this number had increased to 600,000 and by 1962 to more than 2,000,000.

Second, British policy made possible increased migration of Jews to Palestine. The first public declaration of British interest in a Jewish state was made by Lord Balfour of Britain in November 1917: "His Majesty's Government view with favour the establishment in Palestine of a national home for the Jewish people, and will use their best endeavours to facilitate the achievement of this object." Lord Balfour noted that the British commitment to this goal should not "prejudice the existing civilian and religious rights of existing non-Jewish communities in Palestine." The Arabs, of course, bitterly opposed the **Balfour Declaration,** and when Britain became the mandatory power in 1922, sought unsuccessfully to get Britain to reduce the number of Jews migrating to Palestine.

As Jewish settlements increased in Palestine, so did the frequency and intensity of Arab-Jewish conflict. As a result of rising domestic violence, Britain referred the problem of Palestine's future to the United Nations. In 1947 the UN General Assembly debated the fate of the Palestinian mandate, adopting a plan on November 30. The plan, supported by both the United States and the Soviet Union, called for the partitioning of Palestine into two states—one Arab and the other Jewish, with Jerusalem remaining as an international zone administered by the United Nations. Arab states strongly opposed this partitioning policy, and when Britain ended its mandate, followed immediately by Israel's declaration of independence, war erupted.

Arab-Israeli Wars

As noted earlier, Israel has been involved in five wars since its creation in 1948. Each has resulted in at least partial victory for Israel, leading to modifications in the territorial and geopolitical landscape of the Middle East (see map 3.2). Following is a brief description of each war.

The *1948 war* was precipitated by Israel's declaration of independence—an act that led Arab armies into battle with the armed forces of the new Israeli

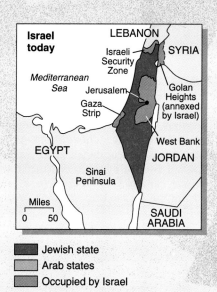

MAP 3.2
Israel and the Occupied Territories

state. After a year of fighting, Israeli forces had defeated their Arab adversaries, thereby slightly increasing the territorial borders of Israel. The more fundamental cause of the 1948 war, however, was the ongoing battle over land between Jewish and Palestinian settlers. This conflict had become especially violent in the aftermath of World War II, as large numbers of Jewish people migrated to Israel to settle in the western part of Palestine. As the violence between Jews and Palestinian Arabs intensified, thousand of Palestinian settlers were forced to flee their settlements. It has been estimated that some 800,000 Palestinians were displaced by the state-building process of Israel—400,000 before 1948 and 400,000 immediately thereafter.

The *1956 war*, a short and limited conflict between Egypt and Israel, began on October 29 when Israel attacked Egyptian forces in the Sinai Peninsula. Israel's military aims were twofold: to destroy Egyptian military bases in the Sinai that had been supporting guerrilla attacks against Israel, and to open the Gulf of Aqaba to Israeli shipping by removing Egyptian military threats at the Strait of Tiran (the opening of the Gulf). The Israeli military quickly defeated Egyptian forces and subsequently retreated following the introduction of UN peacekeeping forces. Although the Sinai remained Egyptian territory, the introduction of UN forces into the peninsula was an important gain for Israel.

The *1967 war*—also known as the **Six-Day War**—began with a surprise Israeli attack on Egypt on June 5. The Israeli preemptive strike was precipitated by two hostile actions taken by Egypt's President Gamal Abdel Nasser: first, Egypt ousted the UN Emergency Force (UNEF), which had been charged with maintaining peace in the Sinai following the 1956 war; and second, Nasser announced a blockade of the Strait of Tiran. The effect of these two actions was to deny Israel its 1956 war gains.

The Israeli strike of June 5 began with an aerial attack of Arab airfields, most of them in Egypt, and an armoured intervention into the Sinai. Within three hours Israel decimated most of Egypt's air force, damaging nearly all military runways and destroying more than 350 airplanes. In the following five days Israel's military defeated Egyptian, Jordanian, and Syrian ground forces, seizing significant Arab territories. These included the Sinai and the Gaza Strip from Egypt; the West Bank, including East

continued

Case 3.1 The Arab-Israeli Conflict—*continued*

Jerusalem, from Jordan; and the Golan Heights, the strategic high ground overlooking the Sea of Galilee, from Syria.

The fourth major Arab-Israeli war occurred in 1973. It is known as the **Yom Kippur War** because it began on the afternoon of the most important Jewish religious festival, the Day of the Atonement (Yom Kippur). Fighting began when Egyptian forces crossed the Suez Canal and broke down Israeli defenses along the canal. Within a day of the attack, Egypt had managed to cross nearly 500 tanks to the eastern side of the Suez and in the process destroy some 100 Israeli tanks. At the same time of the Egyptian surprise attack, Syrian military forces attacked well-defended Israeli positions along the Golan Heights. The Arab forces achieved some early military gains, in part because of effective Egyptian-Syrian coordination and the surprise factor.

Despite suffering early military defeats, Israeli forces were able to regain control of the entire Golan Heights region. And after an early Egyptian victory, the military situation in the Sinai turned into a stalemate as Egyptian and Israeli forces fought bitter tank battles, some as large as major World War II tank battles. The turning point for Israel occurred when its forces successfully counterattacked by crossing the Suez Canal, trapping and threatening 20,000 Egyptian soldiers and 300 tanks in the Sinai.

Although the 1973 war did not alter the map of the Middle East, the early Arab gains in the Sinai and the Golan Heights helped to restore Arab confidence shattered by the Six-Day War. The uncertain and somewhat ambiguous results of the Yom Kippur War were not insignificant, however. Indeed, the absence of victory in the 1973 war provided a necessary precondition for the *Camp David Accords* that paved the way for the **Egyptian-Israeli Peace Treaty** of March 1979. The treaty, which provided for the return of the Sinai to Egypt as part of the normalization of relations between the two states, involved, in effect, trading land for the promise of peace.[38]

The *1982 war* began with an Israeli armed intervention into Lebanon on June 6, 1982. Although numerous factors precipitated the Israeli action, the major cause of the action was the continued attack on Israel by Palestinian guerrillas living in southern Lebanon. During the 1970s Lebanon had become the principal home for thousands of fighters of the Palestinian Liberation Organization (PLO), the principal military and political organ of the Palestinian people. After King Hussein expelled PLO militia from Jordan in 1970, most PLO fighters had moved to Lebanon. Because of the weakness of the Lebanese government and the deep divisions within the country, the PLO forces grew in size and influence so that by the early 1980s they constituted a major military force within Lebanon. Israel's principal goal in the 1982 war was, thus, to destroy PLO bases that had been threatening northern Israel.

By the end of the first month of occupation, Israeli military forces had reached Beirut, trapping some 6,000 PLO fighters within the western part of the city. Because a massive attack on PLO forces would have resulted in significant civilian casualties, Israel declared a cease-fire, demanding that Palestinians lay down their weapons and leave the country. As a result of diplomatic initiatives by U.S. envoy Philip Habib, Israel reached an agreement with its adversaries, allowing for the safe exit of the encircled Syrian and Palestinian fighters. By late August 1983, some 15,000 persons had migrated to selected Arab states, including Algeria and Tunisia. After forcing the departure of PLO and Syrian soldiers from Lebanon, Israel reduced its military occupation, withdrawing its forces to the southern part of Lebanon. When Israel ended its occupation in 1985, it established a "security zone" to prevent a resumption of the guerrilla attacks on northern Israeli communities—the development that had originally precipitated Israel's intervention. By the time of Israel's withdrawal, the intervention had cost Israel some 650 Israeli deaths and about $3.5 billion.

With the exception of the Lebanon war, each of the previous Arab-Israeli conflicts resulted in gains for Israel. The war of independence, for example, expanded the state's boundaries, whereas the Sinai war opened the Gulf of Aqaba to Israeli trade, eliminated guerrilla bases in the Sinai, and established United Nations peacekeeping forces in the peninsula. In 1979 Israel agreed to return the Sinai to Egypt, but continued its military occupation of the West Bank and Gaza. However, as Palestinians began to openly oppose continued Israeli occupation in the late 1980s, the cost of holding those territories began to escalate dramatically.

The Making of Peace

The fundamental impediment to peace in the Middle East has been the desire of two peoples for separate states within Palestine. Since Jews fulfilled their political objective of statehood in 1948, their primary concern has been the security and protection of Israel's territorial boundaries. By contrast, the primary concern for Palestinian people has been the quest for political self-determination. This goal became more elusive after the 1967 war, when Israel seized the West Bank and Gaza, home to more than 1.35 million Palestinians. In the twenty years following occupation, little progress was made toward increased Palestinian self-rule within these territories. As a result, in late 1987 an indigenous uprising began in the occupied territories, involving widespread demonstrations, civil disturbances, and small-scale violence, resulting in an economic paralysis of Gaza and the West Bank. Although the *intifada* was not a war per se, it involved a large part of Israel's military forces, leading some observers to classify it as the sixth major war of the Arab-Israeli conflict. Although some Palestinians hoped that this rebellion would lead to increased political autonomy, the uprising accomplished little for them.

The first direct Arab-Israeli talks since Egypt and Israel negotiated a peace treaty in 1979, began in November 1991 in Madrid. The talks, which involved Israel, Jordan, and Syria, along with Palestinian representatives from the West Bank and Gaza, were held amid much publicity and expectation. Both U.S. President Bush and Soviet President Gorbachev participated in the launching of this historic round of diplomatic negotiations. Egypt and Saudi Arabia also supported this event and sent official delegations to assist the beginning of the dialog. Although the meeting began without a fixed agenda, the ostensible purpose of the Madrid negotiations was to help resolve the Arab-Israeli territorial conflict and to encourage resolution of the Palestinian quest for political autonomy.

Following the Madrid talks, additional rounds of diplomatic negotiations were held in Washington, D.C., but little progress was realized. Unbeknownst to the negotiators, Israeli and PLO representatives had begun meeting secretly in early 1993 in response to an intermediary initiative by the Norwegian foreign ministry. These secret sessions—known as the "Oslo connection" (see case 12.3) because most of them were held in the Oslo countryside—were first carried out between a PLO official and an Israeli professor, but subsequently between senior PLO representatives and Israeli government officials. After some seventeen negotiating sessions, the talks culminated in an unprecedented draft accord establishing a framework for increased Palestinian autonomy within Gaza and the West Bank city of Jericho. Most important, Israel and the PLO—two antagonists for more than thirty years—agreed to recognize each other. In his letter to Israeli Prime Minister Yitzhak Rabin, PLO head Yassir Arafat stated that the PLO recognized Israel's right to exist and renounced terrorism and violence. For his part, Rabin stated that Israel recognized the PLO as the "representative of the Palestinian people" and agreed to carry out negotiations with it in the quest for a Middle East peace settlement. Moreover, as a result of Arafat's recognition of Israel and his pledge to peaceful negotiations, President Bill Clinton authorized official U.S. ties with the PLO.

In September 1993, Arafat and Rabin signed the historic **Israel-PLO Accord** establishing principles governing the transition to increased Palestinian self-rule in Gaza and the West Bank. During the five-year interim period, the two parties are to establish a permanent agreement that will determine, among other things, the borders of the Palestinian-ruled territories, the status of Israeli settlements and military posts in Gaza and the West Bank, and the future status of Jerusalem. In May 1994, Israel completed the withdrawal of its military forces from Gaza and the West Bank town of Jericho and transferred governmental responsibilities to Palestinian authorities. The ending of Israel's 27-year occupation of these conquered lands paved the way for another major Israel-PLO agreement. In September 1995, Arafat and Rabin signed the **Second Israel-PLO Accord,** which expands Palestinian rule in Gaza and the West Bank. According to the agreement, Israel agreed to withdraw its troops from most of the West Bank, relinquishing control to a new 82-member elected Palestinian Council. Finally, Israel and Jordan ended their 46-year state of war by signing the 1994 **Israel-Jordan Peace Accord.** Besides terminating the state of war between the two countries, the agreement provides a basis for increased bilateral cooperation.

continued

Case 3.1 The Arab-Israeli Conflict—*continued*

Yitzhak Rabin, Prime Minister of Israel, and Yasir Arafat, Chairman of the PLO, shake hands on the White House lawn with President Bill Clinton after signing a historic peace accord in 1993 that will permit increased Palestinian self-rule in Gaza and the West Bank.

Despite these dramatic steps in reconciling historic antagonisms between Palestinians and Israelis, significant tensions remain between the two peoples. These tensions were evident when large-scale violence broke out in October 1996, after the newly elected Israeli government, headed by conservative Prime Minister Benjamin Netanyahu, opened a second entrance to an ancient viaduct beneath the Temple Mount in Jerusalem. Because the viaduct is adjacent to one of Islam's holiest sites, the government's action triggered massive demonstrations resulting in open fighting between Palestinian and Israeli security forces. But perhaps the greatest threat to the Middle East peace process has come from radical Jewish and Palestinian groups opposed to any reconciliation between the two peoples. Although some religious Jews believe that Israel should incorporate all Palestinian lands, the current conservative government, along with a majority of citizens, has remained committed to accommodation based on the principle of "land for peace." But radical Palestinian groups that are opposed to any peace accord, including such groups as *Hamas* in Gaza and the West Bank and *Hezbollah* (Part of God) in southern Lebanon, continue to threaten the peace process by acts of violence. For example, in mid-1997 major suicide bombings in Jerusalem not only brought peace negotiations to a standstill, but led to mutually de-

this fifty-year dispute has been significant not only because it has destabilized the Middle East but also because it has threatened access to the region's petroleum exports. Although progress has been achieved in reconciling historic antagonisms in the mid-1990s, the dispute still continues in 1998, with significant issues still remaining to be resolved. Some of these issues involve: (1) the status and boundaries of a Palestinian state, (2) control of Jerusalem, (3) the status of Syrian-Israeli relations and the settling of borders (along the Golan Heights), and (4) the status of Lebanon-Israel relations and the settling of borders (along the "security zone" between the two states).

The Arab-Israeli dispute has been one of the most difficult and volatile international conflicts in the last half of the twentieth century. Since achieving independence in 1948, Israel has fought five wars against Arab peoples or states (1948, 1956, 1967, 1973, 1982), and during the late 1980s faced a major domestic uprising (*intifada*) by Palestinian Arabs in the Israeli-occupied territories of the West Bank and the Gaza Strip. Because this conflict is rooted partly in the quest for a separate political homeland for the Palestinian people, the conflict illustrates the difficult and often precarious path in the transforming claims of self-determination into vi-

structive measures, including Israel's temporary halting of payments to Palestinian authorities and a Palestinian boycott of Israeli products. In sum, although significant progress has been made toward Arab–Israeli reconciliation and, more particularly, toward increased Palestinian-Israeli cooperation based on Palestinian self-rule, continuing violence has not only threatened further peace negotiations, but has threatened to destroy some of the accomplishments already achieved.

Lessons

The Arab-Israeli dispute suggests a number of important lessons relating to concepts and themes covered in this chapter. First, the ability to translate the claim of self-determination into statehood is ultimately determined by the abilities and resources of a people. As John le Carré's statement at the outset of this chapter suggests, the creation of a state ultimately depends upon the determination and capabilities of a nation. Even though the establishment of Israel was facilitated by UN initiatives, the creation and preservation of the state has depended chiefly upon the actions of the Jewish people themselves. Five major wars have threatened but have not destroyed the state.

Second, in view of the anarchic character of the international system, national security is dependent ultimately on the power of the states. Because no international organization exists that can protect states from foreign aggression, each country is ultimately responsible for its own national security. Israel's success in protecting its slender borders has been due to the fact that, despite being threatened by larger military forces, its own capabilities have been sufficient to protect its territory and to punish aggression.

Third, the Arab-Israeli dispute also illustrates the security dilemma, calling attention to the risks inherent in pursuing peace while also maintaining defensible borders. In its quest for peace with Arab neighbors, Israel's strategy has been to exchange land for political accommodation. In continuing this strategy, what additional concessions should Israel make without jeopardizing its own territorial security? More specifically, what political and territorial concessions should Israel make with the PLO? Should Israel support the creation of a Palestinian state and if so, what should be its boundaries? Should control of Jerusalem remain with Israel, or should it be shared with Palestinian authorities? Should Israel give back the Golan Heights to Syria in order to encourage accommodation with a regime that has been unwilling to recognize its legitimacy? Such issues are challenging because the quest for peace and security does not depend solely on what one state does but on what all relevant actors do. Both peace and security are conditional.

able states. At the same time, the dispute illustrates the dilemma of reconciling national security without threatening neighboring states. Finally, because the Arab-Israeli dispute involves religious, nationalistic, and territorial symbols and issues considered vital by both Jews and Palestinians as well as the governments of Israel and its Arab neighbors, it has been one of the most passionate and intractable conflicts in the contemporary international order.

In Conclusion

IR occurs within an anarchic system of states. Although scholars disagree about the nature of global system, there is wide agreement that the world, comprising many different interacting sovereign units, is an underdeveloped political community. Even though procedures and institutions exist for promoting cooperation and resolving disputes, global institutions have little authority because they depend largely on voluntary cooperation. Since the end of World War I, global interdependence has risen significantly, thereby increasing the permeability of national boundaries. At the same time, the increasing global functional interdependence has not displaced sovereign governments. Indeed, the post–Cold War has witnessed an unprecedented growth in factionalism as cultural and political minorities have sought to increase political autonomy from existing governments.

SUMMARY

1. Scholars and political writers have defined the international community in a variety of ways. Each of the major perspectives—realism, idealism, and internationalism—provides important insights into a comprehensive understanding of the contemporary global order.

2. Since the mid-seventeenth century, the structure of global society has been governed by a system of sovereign states that have resulted in a decentralized world order based on an oligarchic distribution of power. Despite significant modifications in the nature of global society, the modern post-Westphalian system remains anarchic in structure and governed chiefly by states.

3. Despite its anarchic structure, the international community is governed by a set of rules. Constitutive norms define which actors are entitled to membership in the international community; regulative norms define the standards of acceptable behavior in international relations.

4. Although unprecedented growth in international functional interactions has resulted in greater global interdependence, the contemporary global society has also experienced increasing factionalism as ethnic and religious minorities try to gain greater political autonomy.

5. Because there is no government in international society, each state is responsible for its own security. The security dilemma arises from the common quest of states to maximize their security through increases in military capabilities. But increases in military power will only yield additional security if other states do not respond by increasing their capabilities.

6. The Arab-Israeli conflict involves two distinct elements—a dispute between states (Israel and its Arab neighbors) and a dispute between two peoples (Jews and Palestinians). Since its creation, Israel has been involved in numerous wars that have resulted in the expansion of its territorial boundaries. Since 1967 Israel has occupied the Golan Heights, Gaza, and the West Bank. The Sinai, also acquired in 1967, was returned to Egypt in 1979. As a result of the Oslo peace initiative, Israel has transferred political control of Gaza and sections of the West Bank to Palestinian authorities.

KEY TERMS

realism
idealism
internationalism
Treaty of Westphalia
Westphalian system
post-Westphalian system
sovereignty

anarchy
self-help system
code of peace
legalist paradigm
globalism
international relations
transnational relations

tribalism
self-determination
security dilemma
Palestine
Zionism
Balfour Declaration
Six-Day War

Yom Kippur War
Egyptian-Israeli Peace
  Treaty
Israel-PLO Accord
Second Israel-PLO Accord
Israel-Jordan Peace Accord

RECOMMENDED READINGS

Bull, Hedley. *The Anarchical Society: A Study of Order in World Politics*. New York: Columbia University Press, 1977. A theoretical and philosophical examination of the problem of order in the international community. Bull explores three questions: (1) What is order in world politics? (2) How is order maintained in the international community? (3) What are some alternative methods of achieving world order?

Mandelbaum, Michael. *The Fate of Nations: The Search for National Security in the Nineteenth and Twentieth Centuries*. New York: Cambridge University Press, 1988. Using case studies from the nineteenth and twentieth centuries, Mandelbaum examines how states seek to maximize their national security in the anarchic international system. The six historical illustrations deal with Britain, China, France, Japan, Israel, and the United States.

Rosenau, James N. *Turbulence in World Politics: A Theory of Change and Continuity*. Princeton: Princeton University Press, 1990. Argues that the growth of interdependence is resulting in major structural changes in the international political order. Because of the rising influence of nonstate actors and the declining capabilities of governments in controlling transnational relations, Rosenau suggests that the traditional "state-centric" perspective should be replaced by a "multi-centric" approach.

Rosenau, James N., and Ernst-Otto Czempiel, eds. *Governance Without Government: Order and Change in World Politics*. Cambridge: Cambridge University Press, 1992. A collection of essays examining the nature and extent of international governance without world government. See especially: James N. Rosenau, "Governance, Order, and Change in World Politics," and Mark W. Zacher, "The Decaying Pillars of the Westphalian Temple: Implications for International Order and Governance."

Rubenstein, Alvin Z., ed. *The Arab-Israeli Conflict: Perspectives*. 2nd ed. New York: HarperCollins Publishers, 1991. A compilation of informative essays on various dimensions of the Arab-Israeli conflict, including origins of the dispute, the seven wars, and Israeli and Palestinian perspectives.

Saunders, Harold H. *The Other Walls: The Politics of the Arab-Israeli Peace Process*. Washington, D.C.: American Enterprise Institute, 1985. Although this study is chiefly concerned with the Arab-Israeli dispute, chapters 1 and 2 describe key elements of the peace process and explain central principles of conflict resolution. An insightful study by a former leading diplomat.

Shipler, David K. *Arab and Jew: Wounded Spirits in a Promised Land*. New York: Penguin Books, 1986. This study examines the roots of hostility between the Arabs and the Jews. A Pulitzer Prize-winning account by a leading journalist.

Smith, Charles D. *Palestine and the Arab-Israeli Conflict*. New York: St. Martin's Press, 1988. A useful introduction to the origins and development of the Arab-Israeli conflict. Half of the book focuses on the historical evolution of Palestine before its partition in 1947.

Tucker, Robert W. *The Inequality of Nations*. New York: Basic Books, Inc., 1977. Explains why inequality characterizes the international system, and why efforts to reduce international inequalities, especially between the developed and developing nations, is likely to be ineffective and even counterproductive.

Waltz, Kenneth N. *Theory of International Politics*. Reading, Mass.: Addison-Wesley Publishing Co., 1979. A penetrating account about how the international community achieves order without government. See especially chapters 5 and 6, which examine the nature of international community and the role of the balance of power in maintaining stability, respectively.

RELEVANT WEB SITES

Avalon Project, Yale Law School Data on U.S. diplomacy	www.yale.edu/lawweb/avalon/avalon.htm
Conflict Archive on the Internet (CAIN) Data on conflict in Northern Ireland	http://cain.ulst.ac.uk
Initiative on Conflict Resolution and Ethnicity (INCORE)	www.incore.ulst.ac.uk/
International Affairs Network (IAN) International affairs resources Peace and conflict resolution resources	www.pitt.edu/~ian/ianres.html www.pitt.edu/~ian/resource/conflict.htm
International Relations and Security Network (ISN) Under Regions (Middle East) see the following: Arab-Israeli Peace Process Israel Palestine	www.isn.ethz.ch/

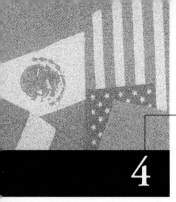

CHAPTER

4   Conflict and Cooperation in the World Community

The relations between sovereign states assume three different forms: cooperation, conflict and indifference. When they cooperate, they benefit from the creation of new values, material or nonmaterial. When they are in conflict, they attempt to gain values at each other's expense.[1]

Klaus Knorr, *international political economist*

Nations dwell in perpetual anarchy, for no central authority imposes limits on the pursuit of sovereign interest. . . . At times, the absence of centralized international authority precludes attainment of common goals. . . . Yet at other times states do realize common goals through cooperation under anarchy.[2]

Kenneth Oye, *political scientist*

. . . with many sovereign states, with no system of law enforceable among them, with each state judging its grievances and ambitions according to the dictates of its own reason or desire—conflict, sometimes leading to war, is bound to occur.[3]

Kenneth Waltz, *international relations theorist*

The international community, like all human communities, is characterized by cooperation and conflict. Because social life is possible only when actors share values, interests, and commitments, the existence of an international society presupposes some level of consensus about the nature and purposes of community life. Although the global community is a primitive political system, the quest for the world's common good is possible, though not assured, through cooperation. State and nonstate actors do pursue shared interests within global society. For example, states generally honor the territorial integrity of other states, and when this norm is compromised through overt or covert intervention, governments nonetheless continue to affirm political sovereignty. States also generally comply with treaties, international agreements, and international law, such as the law of the sea, rules of diplomatic representation, and major legal provisions of international organizations like the United Nations, World Health Organization (WHO), and the General Agreements on Tariff and Trade (GATT).

The extraordinary level of global coordination and cooperation is illustrated by the global postal system: a Chicago resident can receive a letter from a resident in Lagos, Nigeria, implying U.S.–Nigerian cooperation in the mailing, shipping, transferring, and delivery of a stamped envelope. Moreover, a St. Petersburg merchant can import corn from an Iowa firm, thereby representing U.S.–Russian commercial cooperation. To be sure, a large part of transnational cultural, social, religious, scientific, and economic transactions are undertaken apart from governments. Indeed, a significant part of global interdependence is carried out without the knowledge, consent, or support of states. But governments do contribute to the development and maintenance of global cooperation and coordination through bilateral and multilateral initiatives and through the work of political and functional IGOs. For example, because of declining fishing stocks in the North Sea, Western European governments began establishing national fishing quotas in 1976. These quotas were renewed annually until 1983, when the European Community established a common fisheries policy. Moreover, because herring had been nearly depleted, European states banned the fishing of herring altogether until its stocks were replenished.

Despite the significant coordination and cooperation within global society, disagreements, tensions, and disputes are inescapable realities of all communities. Because states pursue their national interests in disregard for, and even at the expense of, the interests of others, conflict is inevitable in global society. Wars are the most extreme expression of global conflict, but the majority of international disputes are nonviolent, involving competition for scarce tangible and intangible resources. The following recent incidents illustrate the varied and pervasive nature of global conflict:

1. In 1993 the European Union (EU) instituted trade barriers on the larger, cheaper bananas from Latin America and gave preferential treatment to banana exports from its former colonies in the Caribbean. U.S. corporations, including Dole, Chiquita, and Del Monte, which control nearly two-thirds of the world's banana trade, claimed that EU trade preferences cost them hundreds of millions of dollars annually and demanded an end to these discriminatory policies. In reply to these demands, the U.S. government challenged EU's policy in the World Trade Organization, demanding an end to its preferential policies. In 1997 the WTO ruled that EU's banana trade policies were discriminatory and had to be terminated.

2. In mid-1997 rebel forces, led by Laurent Kabila, took control of Zaire, forcing its dictator Mobutu Sese Seko to flee the country. The rebels began their campaign to topple the corrupt Mobutu regime some eight months earlier with the support of Rwandan forces. The liberation campaign not only resulted in fragile relations among Zaire's neighbors but led to much suffering, with tens of thousands of refugees fleeing areas of fighting.

3. In 1997 Hezbollah ("Party of God") guerrillas in southern Lebanon carried out numerous rocket and mortar attacks on civilian populations in northern Israel, prompting Israeli military forces to attack selected targets within Lebanon. Although Israel maintains an 8-mile security corridor along its northern border, Palestinian fighters continue to carry out periodic attacks against Israel.

4. Although Bosnian Croats, Muslims, and Serbs stopped fighting in 1995 with the signing of the U.S.–brokered Dayton Accords, the lack of accommodation among the contestants and limited support for implementing the agreement continues to threaten the Balkan peace. In mid-1997, ethnic animosity and political fragmentation continued within Bosnia and especially among the Bosnian Serb leadership, threatening the implementation of the Dayton agreement.

5. At the 1997 NATO summit in Madrid, NATO formally invited Poland, Hungary, and the Czech Republic to join the Western Alliance. The expansion of NATO came about when the United States persisted, over the strong objections of Russia, in demanding the addition of former Soviet-bloc states. In the end, Russia, which was given a voice in NATO policy, accepted the NATO enlargement.

6. Despite the historic harmonious ties between the United States and Canada, significant tensions developed in the 1990s between Canadian and U.S. salmon fishermen in the Pacific northwest. To help regulate salmon fishing, Canada and the United States adopted in 1985 the Pacific Salmon Treaty, which established a commission to monitor and regulate salmon catches along the West Coast, from Oregon to Alaska. Despite this legal framework, conflict between the two states greatly intensified in the mid-1990s as each state accused the other of overfishing. Some observers began referring to this conflict as the "salmon war" after Canadian authorities detained four American fishing vessels traveling to Alaska, and a flotilla of Canadian fishing boats carried out a three-day maritime blockade of a U.S. ferry.

This chapter explores the nature and sources of international cooperation and conflict. It first examines major areas of interstate cooperation and then explores the nature and role of international regimes—the informal networks of functional cooperation. It also examines the phenomenon of integration at both the global and regional levels. After highlighting different types and sources of international conflict, the chapter examines different ways of managing and resolving disputes. The chapter concludes with a case study on the Persian Gulf War to illustrate the conflict and cooperation themes explored earlier.

THE NATURE OF INTERNATIONAL COOPERATION

Joseph Grieco defines international cooperation "as the voluntary adjustment by states of their policies so that they manage their differences and reach some mutually beneficial outcome."[4] In global politics, international cooperation is normally characterized by three features: (1) the actions of states (and other nonstate actors) are voluntary; (2) cooperation involves the identification of, and commitment to, shared goals; and (3) cooperation results in beneficial outcomes to the participants. When cooperation is regularized and establishes patterns of behavior, it results in an *international regime,* a concept examined later in this chapter.

As noted in chapter 3, despite the absence of authoritative governmental institutions, global society is characterized by some stability and order. The ordered anarchy found in the international community is not created by a hegemonic power or international governmental institution but by the voluntary and reciprocal actions of state and nonstate actors. To better understand the nature and extent of global cooperation in the international community, this section briefly analyzes sources of transnational cooperation, the nature of functional interdependence, and the role and impact of global and regional integration.

Sources of Cooperation

Cooperation in the global community can be achieved in several ways.[5] First, it can be established *tacitly*—that is, achieved without communication or explicit agreement. As Robert Axelrod has shown, such "self-generating" cooperation is achieved when parties share common interests resulting in mutually reinforcing behaviors.[6] Tacit cooperation is difficult to establish in the short run, because actors may be tempted to cheat or gain an unfair advantage. But over the long term, they tend to realize that their own self-interests are best achieved through the implicit promise of reciprocity—"If you cooperate, I will cooperate; if you cheat, I will cheat." According to Axelrod, the foundation of voluntary cooperation lies in the norm of reciprocity.[7] This type of cooperation was no doubt responsible for the development in antiquity of diplomatic immunity, the practice of making diplomats immune from the laws of the host state. Similarly, the failure to use chemical weapons in World War II, and more recently in the Persian Gulf War of 1991, was undoubtedly due to the fear of reciprocal behavior.

Second, cooperation can be created through *negotiation.* States can initiate and institutionalize cooperation through bilateral and multilateral accords established through bargaining. Examples of cooperation based on multilateral agreements include the GATT agreements reducing tariff and nontariff trade barriers, the Mediterranean Action Plan that attempts to reduce pollution in the Mediterranean Sea, and the 1982 Third UN Law of the Sea Treaty (UNCLOS III) that codifies maritime international law. More recently, the North American Free Trade Agreement (NAFTA) was established to reduce trade barriers among Canada, Mexico, and the United States, thereby increasing international economic cooperation among the three states. Examples of bilateral accords include thousands of extradition treaties established through reciprocity, Cold War nuclear arms control agreements between the United States and the Soviet Union (e.g., SALT I, the ABM Treaty, and START I), and the 1992 Brazil-Argentina agreement halting existing military nuclear programs and pledging not to seek to develop or acquire nuclear arms.

Finally, cooperation can be strongly encouraged by a *superior power* (hegemon). The imposition of cooperation—an argument associated with the **hegemonic stability theory,**[8] which attributes global economic and political stability to the existence of a dominant power—is achieved when the dominant power establishes rules and institutions influencing the behaviors of other states. In effect, the hegemon that establishes and maintains the principal international structures is the functional equivalent of a common governmental authority in global society. The Bretton Woods international economic order, created at the end of World War II by the victorious Allies, illustrates this type of enforced cooperation. The Bretton Woods system, based on such institutions as the World Bank, the International Monetary Fund, and GATT, fostered economic cooperation through the liberal economic order established by the Western powers. Moreover, during the Cold War the Soviet Union used its status as regional hegemon to maintain order and stability within and among Eastern European states and to influence the nature and degree of economic interdependence among them.

Hegemonic stability theory
The belief that international peace and economic prosperity are a by-product of a hegemonically imposed structure.

Areas of International Cooperation

Shared interests provide the basis for international cooperation among state and nonstate actors. Some of the major areas of global cooperation include: (1) protection of national security and political independence of states; (2) reduction of the likelihood and destructiveness of war through arms control initiatives; (3) promotion of peace through the development of rules and the institutionalization of conflict resolution; (4) development and enforcement of international law; (5) development of procedures and institutions that facilitate national economic expansion; and (6) the management and effective protection of global resources. We will briefly illustrate each of these six areas of shared activity.

The most fundamental state interest is the protection of political sovereignty and territorial integrity. Because the only method of protecting political independence is through the voluntary respect for the sovereignty and independence of states, nonintervention is considered one of the most fundamental legal principles of the community of states. The rights of territorial integrity and political sovereignty can only be realized if states fulfill their legal obligation not to interfere in the internal affairs of other states. States do, of course, violate the sovereignty of other states from time to time for any number of reasons, including protection of human rights, support for an ally, or in response to a prior intervention. Even though governments bemoan the insecurity rooted in the anarchic world system, all are committed to protecting their own sovereignty, thereby sharing a common desire to preserve the existing decentralized world system.

Second, states cooperate in limiting the dangers and destructiveness of war. For example, more then 100 states have signed the 1925 Geneva Protocol banning the use of chemical and biological weapons. Similarly, most governments have signed the 1968 Nonproliferation Treaty, prohibiting states from building or acquiring nuclear arms. States also are signatories to numerous conventions regulating warfare, such as the rules of war adopted at the 1899 and 1907 Hague Peace conferences and the 1949 Geneva Convention on the Treatment of Prisoners of War.

Third, states cooperate in promoting international peace by establishing and applying rules and procedures for pacific conflict resolution. States joining the UN, for example, commit themselves to peaceful international relations, pledging to

Absolute gains
An increase in the capabilities of one actor without regard to the other actors.

Relative gains
An increase in one actor's capabilities relative to the capabilities of other actors.

ISSUE 4.1 International Cooperation: Realism vs. Neoliberal Institutionalism

Since the 1980s, international relations scholars have been involved in an intense debate over the nature and role of cooperation in global society. The principal contrasting positions have been based on different perspectives, and in particular, realism and neoliberal institutionalism.

According to the realist perspective, international cooperation is uncertain and difficult because the international community is anarchic—that is, lacking authoritative institutions that can assure the security of member-states and settle disputes peacefully and impartially. Liberal institutionalists (idealists), by contrast, are far more optimistic about the degree of cooperation that is possible in the international community because they not only view international relations as fundamentally harmonious, but they also believe that global institutions exert significant independent influence on states. As a result, international organizations, such as NATO, the European Union, and the World Trade Organization, and less formal international institutions, such as the Nonaligned Movement and the international conservation regime, not only facilitate cooperation among states, but they are themselves important actors in contemporary global relations.[9]

In the 1980s, a new liberal institutionalism, or *neoliberalism,* emerged that provided a more realistic, yet optimistic view of international collaboration. The new institutionalist paradigm is significantly different from traditional liberal institutionalism because it agrees with realism that states are the primary global units, that states are rational unitary actors, and that the international community is anarchic. At the same time, neoliberals share with traditional liberalism a belief in the efficacy of international institutions and the important role of such institutions in fostering global cooperation.[10]

According to neoliberal institutionalism, because states are "rationally egoistic," they seek to maximize national interests, even if they must deceive and break promises. Because of the possibility of deception and cheating, developing and maintaining stable international cooperation is a significant challenge in an anarchic environment. Neoliberals, however, are optimistic about cooperation because they believe that international institutions can play a decisive role in moderating fear and distrust and in reducing cheating.

Realism, by contrast, assumes that the development of international cooperation is much more difficult. Unlike the neoliberals, they do not believe that international institutions play a significant *independent* role in influencing the behavior of states. More significantly, because realists emphasize the anarchic structure of the international community, they assume that the economic welfare and territorial security of states is never assured. As a result, realists believe that states seek not only to increase their power and wealth, but to maximize their relative capabilities, which alone are considered the final determinants of a country's national security and political independence. According to Joseph Grieco, "states are positional," and are concerned not only with **absolute gains** (or losses) in economic, military, political, or other related capabilities, but also with the **relative gains** (or losses)—that is, changes in capabilities in relation to those of other states.[11] Thus, contrary to neoliberal assumptions, realists believe that international cooperation involves significant risks and dangers, because cooperation can lead to changes in states' relative capabilities.

resolve disputes without resorting to force. The sole justification for resorting to unilateral military force, according to the UN Charter, is self-defense (art. 51).

Fourth, states cooperate in maintaining and enforcing widely accepted rules of international law. For example, states cooperate in protecting the right of diplomatic immunity and the doctrine of the freedom of the high seas because it is in their mutual interests to do so. Moreover, states now recognize each country's right to an exclusive economic zone (EEZ), giving it sole economic control over the waters extending up to 200 nautical miles (NM) from its shore. As a result, mining and fishing within a state's EEZ can only be undertaken with the consent of its government.

Fifth, states' shared interest in promoting economic growth results in international cooperation in areas such as international trade and foreign aid. One of the most important means by which states cooperate economically is by maintaining stable and efficient financial institutions that facilitate foreign trade. Because there is no world government to establish and maintain rules and institutions that facilitate trade, the creation and maintenance of an international economic order is dependent wholly upon the voluntary acts of states. Thus, the need for additional financial liquidity within the International Monetary Fund (IMF) resulted in the creation of Special Drawing Rights (SDRs) in the mid-1970s in order to facilitate international financial transactions among governments.

Finally, states cooperate in protecting and preserving the global environment. Since the 1970s, governments have worked to regulate global pollution and to protect the earth's water and air, as well as its endangered species. In 1987, for example, government representatives met in Montreal to deal with the decay of the ozone layer protecting the earth from the sun's harmful ultraviolet rays. At the meeting representatives from twenty-four leading states signed the Montreal Protocol, pledging to reduce by one-half the production and use of chlorofluorocarbons (CFCs) and other ozone-depleting chemicals by the end of the century. Because of the increasing threat posed by chlorofluorocarbons, the major industrial states subsequently agreed to ban ozone-depleting chemicals altogether by the year 2000. And when the stock of African elephants became severely depleted in the 1980s, a majority of states voted at the 1989 meeting of the Convention on International Trade in Endangered Species (CITES) to ban the sale of ivory altogether.

International Regimes

The bulk of international cooperation among states is carried out in specific areas of mutual interest. To a significant degree, these common interests and shared decision-making patterns are reinforced by commonly accepted rules and norms as well as shared expectations. Scholars have increasingly used the concept of **regime** to describe these growing informal networks of interdependence.[12] As formulated by Stephen Krasner, regimes are "implicit or explicit principles, norms, rules, and decision-making procedures around which actors' expectations converge in a given area of international relations."[13] Unlike a domestic political regime, in which decision-making authority is in the hands of established organizations, international regimes represent spheres of voluntary compliance based on common interests and widely accepted rules and norms.

Regime
The rules, principles, and decision-making procedures governing international behavior in a given issue-area.

The concept of regime has been used in a wide variety of ways, from informal areas of shared activity to highly formalized and institutionalized areas of decision making. One scholar has suggested that the disparate nature in which the concept has been used has resulted in "intellectual chaos,"[14] whereas another has charged that the term has simply become a synonym for international organizations.[15] As used here, regimes are not identical with either international law or international organizations. Rather they are a half-way house between the anarchic self-government of sovereign states and the established rules of international law and existing international organizations. Whereas international law and international organizations represent well-developed institutions and rules, regimes represent emerging, less formal patterns of behavior rooted in actors' largely voluntaristic behavioral patterns. Although organizations are not necessarily a part of international regimes, as they develop and mature they often lead to formal organizations that help regulate and institutionalize behavior.

Because regimes are normally less institutionalized than international organizations and international law, their impact in global society is often underestimated. But even though regimes may not contribute decisively to international conflict resolution and functional interdependence, they influence greatly the nature and extent of global cooperation. They do so by regulating decision-making procedures based on commonly accepted rules and norms and by promoting shared interests. As one scholar has observed, regimes not only centralize enforcement procedures but "establish stable mutual expectations about others' patterns of behavior."[16] Examples of international regimes include:

1. *Whaling regime:* seeks to regulate and protect whales (administrated by the International Whaling Commission);

2. *Rhine regime:* seeks to reduce pollution in the Rhine River through the guidelines established by the International Commission for the Protection of the Rhine (established by Germany, France, Luxembourg, Netherlands, and Switzerland);

3. *Antarctic conservation regime:* protects marine life and other resources in the Antarctic based on norms of the Convention on the Conservation of Antarctic Marine Living Resources (1980);

4. *International monetary regime:* coordinates international monetary policies of states (administered by the International Monetary Fund);

5. *International trade regime:* promotes the reduction of tariff and nontariff trade barriers through the World Trade Organization (WTO);

6. *Svalbard Archipelago regime:* provides norms by which foreign states can exploit the natural and marine resources of this group of islands (located 600 miles northwest of Norway);

7. *International conservation regime:* seeks to protect endangered species through such agreements as the 1973 Convention on International Trade in Endangered Species of Wild Fauna and Flora (CITES) and the 1979 Convention on the Conservation of Migratory Species of Wild Animals;

8. *European security regime:* seeks to promote peace and harmony among European states. This regime is based on principles from IGOs like the UN, NATO, the European Union and the Final Act of the Conference on Security and Cooperation in Europe (CSCE)—commonly known as the Helsinki Act of 1975.

9. *Nuclear nonproliferation regime:* seeks to halt the spread of nuclear weapons to states that do not have them through such institutions and accords as the Nuclear Nonproliferation Treaty (NPT), the International Atomic Energy Agency (IAEA), the Treaty of Tlatelolco, and the Wassenaar Agreement.

Oran Young has identified three ways that regimes may originate.[17] First, they can develop as a result of explicit bargaining among two or more participants, as has been the case with the development of the postwar international trade regime. Second, regimes can develop as a result of the coercive or leadership role of a dominant actor. For example, the development of the nonproliferation regime (involving the regulation of nuclear weapons proliferation) originated with a bilateral U.S.–USSR agreement that was subsequently institutionalized with the 1968 Nonproliferation Treaty. Third, regimes may originate spontaneously in response to mutual self-interests. Examples of such "self-generating" regimes include the international collective conservation efforts for endangered species and for the protection of the atmosphere's ozone layer.

The level of regime institutionalization can vary greatly. Some are well developed and rely heavily on centralized organizations to collect and analyze data and to administrate decisions. For example, the international monetary regime is of this sort, with international financial affairs strongly regulated by the International Monetary Fund, the administrative offices of the regime. The deep-seabed mining regime, created to regulate the mining of the ocean floor, is also centrally administered, although by a newer and much weaker organization (the International Seabed Authority in Kingston, Jamaica). Other regimes—such as the pollution controlling regimes for the Mediterranean Sea, the Persian Gulf, and the Caribbean area—are decentralized structurally and rely largely on voluntary compliance.

Scholars have recently shown that international cooperation in functional areas, especially in technical fields, is dependent upon a diffusion of knowledge through transnational networks of technical and scientific cooperation. Scholars define these global networks of knowledge-based experts as **epistemic communities.**[18] Recent case studies in several areas, including arms control, international trade, and environmental protection, suggest that these knowledge communities play an important role as sources of policy innovation, as channels for diffusing knowledge and expertise internationally, and as catalysts of policy and institutional reform. For example, Peter Haas argues that the emerging scientific evidence that emissions of CFCs were depleting the atmosphere's ozone layer led environmental scientists and concerned government officials from many countries to push for the enactment of regulations protecting the environment.[19] Similarly, William Drake and Kalypso Nicolaidis argue that the Uruguay round of GATT negotiations succeeded in lowering trade barriers on "services" in part because of a global diffusion of knowledge about the nature and impact of the service economy.[20] Studies of these epistemic communities also illuminate how the diffusion of knowledge across national boundaries contributes to international cooperation in select issue-areas.

Epistemic community
A global network of knowledge-based professionals in such scientific and technological areas as trade, arms control, biotechnology, and environmental protection.

Global and Regional Integration

Integration refers to the increasing social, political, and economic interdependence within and among states. Unlike regimes, which result from voluntary actions of states and other international actors, regional and global integration is the deliberate process of developing increasing levels of cooperation and coordination among member-states. Normally, integration involves the consolidation of political authority, which is expressed through an increasing number of rules and procedures that are binding on the emerging association or community.

The two major types of integration relevant to the international community are economic and political. **Economic integration** refers to the process of establishing increasing economic union among a group of states. Economists have identified five levels of economic integration. Strictly speaking, the first four relate to economic life, and the last is essentially political. The five stages, listed in order of increasing integration, are:

1. Free trade area
2. Customs union
3. Common market
4. Economic union
5. Political union

Economic integration
The process of building an economic community by breaking down barriers that impede the mobility of goods, services, capital, and labor.

The economic integration process normally begins by establishing a *free trade area* in which member-states eliminate trade barriers in order to enlarge the market and foster greater economic specialization. Although member-states maintain common internal trade policies, they are free to establish their own trade policies with nonmembers. Examples of free trade areas include the Andean Pact, the North American Free Trade Agreement (NAFTA), and the European Free Trade Association (EFTA). A *customs union,* the next step in the integration process, involves the elimination of internal trade barriers among its members and the adoption of common external trade policies toward nonmembers. The third level of integration is the *common market,* which involves a customs union plus the elimination of barriers to the free movement of the factors of production—labor, capital, and technology—among its members. Establishing a customs union and common market requires increasing levels of economic coordination, which can only be achieved through the creation of transnational institutions that can help create and sustain common economic policies. *Economic union,* the fourth level, represents the complete union of the economies of two or more states. In addition to establishing the conditions for a common market, economic union requires that member-states establish common fiscal and monetary policies, coordinating national economic actions in order to establish an integrated economy. Normally, a highly developed banking system based on a common currency is necessary for economic union. Essentially an economic union signifies the creation of a single country economically, while still maintaining multiple governing authorities. Thus, the fifth and final level of integration is *political union,* which involves the political consolidation of authority so that multiple political entities become one. Because political union involves a different type of integration, we briefly examine it below. Table 4.1 summarizes the five levels of economic integration.

European Union (EU)
A regional organization of 15 Western European states that promotes increased economic, social, scientific, and political unity. The EU was formally known as the EC.

The best example of a common market is the **European Union (EU),** a fifteen-member regional association first begun with the European Coal and Steel Community in 1952 and later institutionalized with the creation of the European Economic Community in 1957. Throughout the 1970s and 1980s Western European member-states achieved significantly higher levels of economic integration so that by the early 1990s, the European Community (EC) had achieved the conditions of a common market. To continue the process of integration, member-states signed the *Treaty on European Union* (commonly known as the Maastricht Treaty), which entered into force on November 1, 1993, after twelve EC members had ratified it. The treaty calls for the creation of a European monetary union, based on a common currency by 1999, along with the establishment of common foreign and defense policies. The European Union is examined more fully in chapter 14.

Political integration
The process by which political decision making is centralized and consolidated in authoritative, supranational institutions.

Political integration refers to the institutionalization of political authority within human communities. In domestic society this process—generally defined as political development—involves increasing centralization, specialization, and accountability in decision making.[21] In the international community, political integration refers to the creation of supranational institutions whose authority is not wholly dependent on the wills of sovereign member-states. This process, whether at a global or regional level, involves a shift away from the decentralized anarchic global system. The highest level of political integration is defined as *political union.* Such a union is achieved when two or more states transfer national sovereignty to a common authority, thereby making one country. This process took place in 1789 when the thirteen states of North America, functioning under the Articles of Confederation, established one federal country, the United States of America. In the contemporary international system, the European Union represents the closest expression of political integration.

Political and economic integration can be pursued at either the global or regional levels. Although the founders of the United Nations had hoped that global-

TABLE 4.1 Levels of Economic Integration

Political Union	A central government has ultimate authority over all political, economic, and social life within a community.
Economic Union	Common Market + Members coordinate fiscal, monetary, and social policies in order to establish complete economic union.
Common Market	Customs Union + Members eliminate barriers that impede the movement of labor, capital, and technology.
Customs Union	Free Trade Policy + Members establish common trade policies towards nonmembers.
Free Trade Area	Members eliminate tariffs and other trade barriers toward each other; no common trade policies towards nonmembers.

ism would develop at a faster rate than regionalism, this has not been the case. In the postwar decades, regional integration has been more successful in some regions than global integration. Security associations like NATO and the former Warsaw Pact, and economic experiments like the EU have achieved greater interdependence than global associations like UNCTAD, WHO, and GATT. This is because regional organizations not only share greater geographical proximity but have greater cultural homogeneity and stronger functional ties.

Scholars disagree on whether regional integration is beneficial to the world community. Some argue that the strengthening of functional and regional cooperation contributes to global cohesion by weakening nationalism and developing transnational affinities. Others suggest that regional integration is counterproductive because, while increasing interdependence and cohesion among a subgroup of states, it increases cleavages among major regional groups, thereby impeding the development of global solidarity. According to this view, the development of the European Union, for example, benefits European member-states more than it benefits non-EU relations. Similarly, regional institutions like NAFTA (which involves preferential trade among the United States, Canada, and Mexico) and MERCOSUR (which involves increasing coordination of trade policies among Argentina, Brazil, Paraguay, and Uruguay), may foster close economic ties among its member-states but may be a source of cleavage with nonmembers.

THE NATURE AND MANAGEMENT
OF INTERNATIONAL CONFLICT

The Nature of Conflict

International conflict occurs when a real or perceived incompatibility exists between states and other relevant actors. Although social scientists define conflict in a variety of ways, they generally agree that social and political conflict involves the following elements: two or more actors, incompatible goals, the pursuit of actions by one actor against another in order to influence or control its behavior, and mutually opposing actions between participants. A key element of all conflict is the existence of "position or resource scarcity," for which the wants of all actors cannot be fully satisfied and for which the quest for such resources results in conflict behavior.[22]

International Participants

Because states are the final decision-making authorities in the global system, the most important international conflicts are those involving states—either with other states or with nonstate actors. The most significant disputes in global society are, of course, those between governments themselves. Such disputes arise over a variety of issues, including territorial boundaries, threats to regional peace, international economic interests, protection of nationals, and vital political interests. When states are unable to reconcile their vital interests, they resort to force, with war serving as the ultimate instrument of conflict resolution. Sometimes states resort to indirect methods to influence an opposing state, such as seeking to weaken a government through assistance to opposition groups or guerrilla movements trying to bring down a government. During the 1980s, for example, South Africa provided aid to anti-Marxist guerrillas in Angola, while the United States supported anti-Sandinista fighters in Nicaragua. Both actions were designed to weaken or topple existing revolutionary regimes.

States may also have conflicts with IGOS. Although these are normally less significant than those involving only states, conflicts with regional or global political

IGOs (e.g., the UN or the EU) can be highly significant. For example, after failing to achieve a reduction in the European Community's agricultural subsidies in December 1992, the United States threatened to impose a 200 percent tariff increase on selected European agricultural products. A disastrous trade war was fortunately averted when a compromise was worked out between the EC and the United States (see chapter 16). This type of dispute was also illustrated in the significant disagreements between Western industrial states and the developing countries over deep-sea mining at the Third UN Conference on the Law of the Sea (1973–1982).

Subnational political groups can also influence the nature and scope of global conflict. Although enthnonational conflicts typically involve domestic disputes between cultural, religious, and ethnic minorities and the state, such conflict can significantly affect international relations, either by undermining existing states or exacerbating regional tensions between states. In a major study of ethnic minorities, Ted Gurr found that from 1945 to 1994, 233 ethnic groups had suffered discrimination or had made political claims on behalf of collective rights. Gurr found that these minorities had pursued their collective claims through one of three strategies: (1) *ethnonationalism*, involving the quest for political autonomy; (2) *indigenous rights*, involving increased self-determination by conquered peoples; and (3) *communal contention for power*, involving competition for political power among tribes, clans, and other culturally distinct peoples.[23] According to Gurr, during the 1993–94 period, there were fifty major ethnopolitical conflicts in the world. The major ones are listed in table 4.2.

The least significant type of global conflict is that involving NGOs, such as religious movements, transnational political organizations, and MNCs. Only if an NGO (such as a terrorist group) resorts to violence and threatens the citizens and property of a state will the dispute be given high priority by states. For example, during the mid-1980s the U.S. government gave high priority to the release of Western hostages held by Islamic fundamentalists in Lebanon. And when investigators discovered Libyan complicity in the terrorist bombing of a West German bar where U.S. military personnel were killed, the United States responded with a large bombing raid against military installations in Libya.

Types of Conflicts

International conflicts also differ in their nature. Stephen Krasner has suggested that international politics is concerned with two distinct forms of power—*relational power*, for which states seek to increase their comparative economic and political influence within an established set of rules and institutions, and *meta-power*, for which states jointly attempt to alter the procedures and institutions themselves.[24]

Relational disputes involve concrete disputes between two or more parties over the distribution of tangible and intangible resources. Such disputes focus on issues such as land, military security, territory, and economic resources. The majority of global disputes are of a relational nature.

Institutional disputes, by contrast, focus on modifications and reforms of existing rules and institutions or the development of new ones. When a state or group of states seeks to alter existing institutional norms, it inevitably will face another group of actors opposed to the desired changes. Although relational disputes normally are settled by the immediate allocation of resources, the settlement of institutional disputes normally results in a new framework or set of rules, whose impact is not immediately evident. Because institutional disputes can involve the modification of important conflict-resolution norms, they are potentially more important than relational conflicts.

TABLE 4.2 Major Ethnopolitical Conflicts, 1993–1994

Country	Key Issues*	Nature of Conflict	Deaths (1000s)
Afghanistan	C	Civil War among Pashtun, Tajik, and Uzbek factions	575–1,000
Angola	C	Civil War rooted in Mbundu-Ovimbundu rivalry	500
Bosnia	E	Serbs and Croats seek to partition Bosnia, eliminate Muslims	200
Burma	I and E	Tribal peoples fight for political autonomy	130
Burundi	C	Hutu-Tutsi tribal war	100
Chad	C	Civil War between Anakaza and Bideyet peoples	100
China	I and E	Suppression of Tibetans	100
Guatemala	I and C	Suppression of rural peoples (Mayans) suspected of aiding insurgents	150
Indonesia	I and E	Suppression of East Timor rebels fighting for independence	200
Iraq	I and E	Repression of Kurdish rebellion	180–250
Liberia	C	Ethnic rivalries fuel a civil war	150
Sri Lanka	E	Tamils fight for political independence	78–100
Somalia	C and E	Clans fight for control of southern Somalia; Isaaq clan controls north	350
Sudan	E	Civil War between Muslim government and southern fractions	1000–1500

C=Communal Contention for Power   E=Ethnonationalism   I=Indigenous Rights

Source: Ted Robert Gurr, "Peoples Against States: Ethnopolitical Conflict and the Changing World System," *International Studies Quarterly* 38 (September 1994), pp. 369–375.

This type of conflict was illustrated by the dispute between the developed and developing nations over the reform of the international economic order. The dispute began in the mid-1970s, when the Third World began demanding a radical restructuring of the rules and procedures of the global economic system. The proposed initiative, known as the **New International Economic Order (NIEO),** sought to modify existing rules and to introduce institutions with the authority to allocate economic resources among states. In effect the NIEO sought to establish "authoritative regimes" to replace the market-oriented rules and institutions that had been established by the developed nations in the aftermath of World War II. Although the long-term aim of the proposed international economic order was to transfer wealth from the North to the South, the immediate goal of the NIEO was to increase the power and influence of the Third World. As Stephen Krasner has noted, the debate was fundamentally about how the Third World could increase its influence in global society so that it could reduce its political and economic vulnerabilities.[25]

New International Economic Order (NIEO)
The Third World's alternative economic system designed to give the developing countries more influence in the global economy and to help transfer economic resources from the rich to the poor countries.

Global conflicts can also be differentiated on the basis of their scope—that is, their international effect. Systemic conflicts are those with global impact; parochial disputes are those with limited, local impact.

Systemic conflicts are rooted in global issues, generally focusing on economic, political, or ideological sources. In the last half of this century two systemic disputes have dominated world politics—an ideological conflict between the Soviet Union (East) and the United States (West) and an economic conflict between the rich, industrial democratic states (North) and the developing nations in Africa, Asia, and Latin America (South). Both of these disputes have involved major

Systemic conflicts
Major, system-wide disputes in the international community.

ISSUE 4.2 Post–Cold War Conflict: Civilizations or States?

In a widely read 1993 article,[26] Samuel Huntington, an influential IR scholar, argued that the post–Cold War era called for a new conceptual map of international relations. During the Cold War the world was divided into three main groups of states: the West (First World), the East (Second World), and the non-aligned developing nations (Third World). Because such divisions are no longer valid, Huntington proposed an alternative paradigm that assumes that the major divisions in the world are based on alternative civilizations. Even though Cold War conflict was dominated by ideological and political conflict between superpowers, Huntington argues that post–Cold War conflict will be rooted in "the clash of civilization." Huntington writes: "It is my hypothesis that the fundamental source of conflict in this new world will not be primarily ideological or primarily economic. The great divisions among humankind and the dominating source of conflict will be cultural. Nation-states will remain the most powerful actors in world affairs, but the principal conflicts of global politics will occur between nations and groups of different civilizations"[27] Moreover, because cultural conflict is rooted in deep-seated emotional affinities, Huntington thinks that civilizational disputes are likely to be more intransigent than the superpower disputes of the Cold War and less subject to compromise.

According to Huntington, the world is comprised of seven or eight major civilizations (Western, Confucian, Japanese, Islamic, Hindu, Slavic-Orthodox, Latin American, and African), each of which has a different understanding not only of the relationship of God and humankind, but also of the nature of political authority and the rights and obligations of persons. Although Western ideas have dominated the structures and policies of global society, such notions as individualism, human rights, constitutionalism, equality, and liberty have little resonance in non-Western civilizations. As a result, Huntington argues that the "central axis" of future international relations is likely to be the conflict between "the West and the Rest."[28]

Is Huntington right? Is it true that the battle lines of future conflict will be the fault lines of civilizations, not the territorial borders of states? And is it true that future global conflict will pit the West against the non-West? Huntington's theory, which was subsequently developed into a book titled *The Clash of Civilizations and the Remaking of World Order,* has precipitated intense debate. Some scholars have argued that the growing influence of tribal, ethnic, religious, and cultural affinities in contemporary global conflict validates the civilizational model. Others, while affirming the growing influence of culture in post-modern political life, have charged that the civilizational paradigm either oversimplifies reality, underestimates the continuing role of the state and nationalism, or overestimates the role of inter-civilizational disputes. Stephen Walt, for example, argues that nationalism, not civilization, is the driving force of the post–Cold War world,[29] while Foud Ajami, argues that states, not civilizations, are the major units of global politics. Ajami writes: "civilizations do not control states, states control civilizations."[30] Moreover, since the forces of modernization and secularism are irresistible and likely to be far more dominant than Huntington acknowledges, the national quest for economic development is likely to be more influential than either religion or culture. In his view, nations would "rather scramble for their market shares, learn how to compete in a merciless world economy, provide jobs, and move out of poverty"[31] than emphasize national identity. While accepting the growing role of civilizational affinities in the post-Cold War world, Ronald Steel argues that future global conflict will focus chiefly within civilizations, rather than between them.[32] Similarly, James Kurth claims that the real cultural clash in the future will not be between the West and the non-West but within the West itself. This conflict will pit modernists supporting Western values against post-modernists supporting post-Western values.[33]

While scholars continue to debate Huntington's civilizational paradigm, the great merit of the proposed model is that it has stimulated vigorous analysis of existing IR paradigms and encouraged the development of alternative models to more effectively interpret and assess post-Cold War global politics.

confrontations between the leading world powers. At the same time, they have spawned many regional and local disputes. For example, the Vietnam War of the 1960s and the Afghanistan and Central American conflicts of the 1980s were all rooted in the broader ideological conflict between democracy and communism. Similarly, even though the North-South conflict has focused on such Third World issues as the restructuring of trade patterns and the development of a New International Economic Order (NIEO), the dispute between rich and poor countries has itself spawned other areas of tension, such as the ownership of mineral resources on the ocean floor and the Third World debt. Chapter 5 examines the first of these macro conflicts; the North-South dispute is described and assessed in chapter 15.

The most frequent type of global dispute is **parochial conflict.** Whereas systemic conflict is global in character, this type of dispute is limited in scope and duration and normally is concerned with the distribution of scarce resources. Like relational disputes, such conflicts are rooted in tangible issues such as territorial boundaries and distribution of natural resources and in intangible political issues like national honor, national security threats, and shifts in the balance of military power.

Parochial conflict
International disputes between two or more states over specific territorial political, economic, or other related issues.

International disputes can also be classified in terms of sources. K. J. Holsti has identified twenty-four issues that have contributed to armed international hostilities in the post-1945 global system.[34] Some of the most important of these include:

1. *Composition of government*—disputes over the structure of government. Because of ideological and political incompatibilities, governments have tried to topple foreign regimes and to install other governments in their place. This was the case with the Soviet military intervention into Afghanistan in December 1979; it was also illustrated by the U.S. interventions into the Dominican Republic in 1965 and into Grenada in 1983;

2. *Liberation/state creation*—armed conflict resulting from the quest for national self-determination. The demand for increased political autonomy by Palestinians and Kurds, for example, has resulted in significant global tensions in the postwar era. Similarly, the post–Cold War quest for separate statehood by Croatia, Bosnia-Herzegovina, Slovenia, and Serbia has resulted in bitter armed hostilities;

3. *Territorial claims*—international disputes over conflicting territorial claims. Such conflicts may be based on the desire for strategic resources, such as Iraq's invasion of Kuwait to gain control of its petroleum resources, or to consolidate territorial boundaries of new states, such as Bosnia-Herzegovina and Croatia;

4. *National unification*—armed conflicts over the unification of states. Such conflicts may involve disputes over the consolidation of existing nation states, such as the Vietnam War, or may involve the incorporation of territory formerly controlled by another state, such as Argentina's effort to establish sovereign control over the Falkland Islands (Islas Malvinas) in 1982.

Other important sources of postwar armed conflicts include maintaining the integrity of states, commitment to support allies, ethnic and religious unification, protection of ethnic kin in foreign lands, and protection of foreign economic interests.

Because major armed conflicts are typically based on multiple issues, it is difficult to develop a simple classification of sources of international disputes. K. J. Holsti, however, has grouped similar issues together, establishing general categories, or "mega-issues," that help to account for war. In his view, three general issues account for a significant percentage of the fifty-nine armed conflicts during the Cold War era (1946–1989): *territorial issues, state creation,* and *governmental composition.* The first, based on boundary and strategic concerns, accounts for 52 percent of the fifty-nine armed disputes; state creation, which involves disputes over national liberation, unification of nation-states and secession, also accounts for 52 percent of all postwar disputes; and governmental composition, which involves disputes over ideological liberation, support for ideological allies, and the establishment of ideologically acceptable regimes, accounts for 45 percent of the disputes.[35]

Managing International Conflict

Political conflict is commonly regarded as detrimental and counterproductive to social life, especially if conflict becomes violent and destructive. But conflict is not always destructive. Some conflicts can contribute to a better world by diffusing more serious conflict and by encouraging a more creative and dynamic international community. Moreover, international conflict can, ironically, stimulate greater cooperation.[36] Such cooperation and unity may arise, for example, in wartime when a nation is threatened by a foreign enemy. Moreover, states may overlook other incompatibilities in their shared quest to defeat a common enemy. For example, during World War II the United States and Great Britain cooperated with the Soviet Union in fighting the Axis powers even though both the democratic countries were strongly opposed to Stalin's communist regime.

In addition, conflict can itself increase international interactions and thereby strengthen transnational solidarity. As theorists of social conflict have noted, social conflict not only promotes interaction with a community, but tends to clarify positions and interests among actors. However paradoxical it may appear, an open, conflictual society encourages a more mature and stable political community than a highly regulated community without social and political conflict. Moderate, frequent conflict not only diffuses more serious conflict but promotes dialog and negotiations among opponents. Conflict, in other words, stimulates cooperation to resolve disputes. The Cold War, for example, fostered regular dialog and cooperation between the two superpowers. Indeed, one scholar has suggested that the high level of U.S.–USSR arms control negotiations during the 1970s and 1980s resulted in a high level of superpower cooperation, which may have established an arms control regime.[37]

Although numerous strategies have been devised for dealing with conflict, two major approaches exist—avoidance and management. **Conflict avoidance** disregards conflict altogether. Because of the harmful and destructive consequences associated with conflict, this approach seeks to avoid all the unpleasant and destructive consequences of conflict by avoiding it altogether. One way this approach can be applied in the global community is by minimizing international interactions. Although isolationism reduces international conflict, it also bypasses the beneficial outcomes of international cooperation and coordination. Clearly, economic self-sufficiency (autarky) and political isolationism reduce the possibility of foreign policy disputes and protect a community from unwanted external influences, but the cost of such a strategy, even if possible, is excessive. Albania, a backward and reclusive state, illustrates the destructive consequences of this approach. From the 1950s through the 1980s, Albania remained a closed, hermetically sealed nation, with the result that its society, economy, and polity stagnated for more than thirty years.

This approach can also be pursued by disregarding conflicts when they arise. According to this mindset, it is preferable to seek peace and order when the promotion of one's own interest may lead to violent or harmful conflict. Known in international politics as **appeasement,** this approach is best illustrated by the British government's response to Hitler's taking of Czechoslovakia in 1938. At the Munich Conference of 1938, British Prime Minister Neville Chamberlain accepted Hitler's annexation of the Sudentenland (the area of Czechoslovakia bordering Germany) in return for Hitler's promise not to acquire further European territories. Chamberlain returned to London announcing that "peace is at hand." But, to Chamberlain's chagrin, World War II broke out shortly thereafter.

Conflict avoidance
The effort to disregard political conflicts in the hope that neglect will help to resolve disputes.

Appeasement
A policy designed to avoid conflict by giving in to an aggressor's demands.

Neither isolation nor appeasement are adequate global strategies. The first impairs transnational relations, thereby reducing the potential for economic growth; the second simply postpones conflict, often resulting in delayed but far more destructive consequences.

In contrast to the first approach, **conflict management** assumes that conflict is, in part, constructive and beneficial. It seeks to manage social and political conflict, rather than to eliminate it altogether or to disregard its consequences. This approach seeks to resolve disputes without destroying the fabric of a free society based on the political independence of actors. Conflict management thus seeks to maintain human communities based on the free and responsible action of members, while establishing procedures and institutions that resolve conflicts and settle disputes effectively and efficiently.

The management and resolution of conflicts can be carried out directly by the participants, or indirectly through a third party. Indirect **(third-party) conflict resolution** is used by states when they are unable to resolve a dispute themselves. An outside party is used to cool passions, clarify issues, and help settle the dispute. Normally, when conflicts are resolved through a third-party strategy, the result is either a binding or nonbinding award or judgment.

The most common third-party procedures involve conciliation, mediation, arbitration, and adjudication. In *conciliation,* the outside party gathers facts, classifies issues in the disputes, and seeks to reestablish negotiation and bargaining between the parties. To a significant degree, the termination of the ten-year Iran-Iraq war in 1989 was achieved by the diplomatic efforts of UN Secretary General Javier Perez de Cuellar, who served as a conciliator between the two disputing states. The 1978 Camp David negotiations between Egypt and Israel, which resulted in the Camp David Accords, were successful largely because of the determined and indefatigable conciliation provided by President Jimmy Carter and his staff. *Mediation* is similar conciliation, except that the third party has the added task of proposing a solution. This process was successfully used by the Vatican in the early 1980s when the Pope's diplomatic emissaries helped to resolve a bitter territorial dispute between Argentina and Chile over the Beagle Channel (see case 12.2). In *arbitration,* the parties entrust the settlement of a dispute to an arbitrator (or a group of them), who issues a binding judgment. Finally, *adjudication* is similar to arbitration except that the judgment is based on international law and is rendered by an international legal body like the International Court of Justice (ICJ) in The Hague, the Netherlands. The 1979 U.S.–Iran dispute over diplomatic hostages, which resulted in the ICJ's judgment calling for the release of U.S. hostages and for the payment of reparations, illustrates this approach to conflict resolution.

The bulk of global conflict management is carried out through *direct conflict resolution.* This approach is normally implemented either through force, threat of force, or compromise. The use of **force**—often called the "politics of conquest"— occurs when one party uses its superior force to impose its will on a weaker one. The American military defeat and surrender of Japan in 1945 illustrates this approach to conflict resolution. A more recent example of this type of politics is the U.S. intervention in Panama in December 1989 to depose strongman General Manual Noriega.

When power is divided unequally between contesting parties, force can serve as a quick and efficient means of settling disputes. But when contesting parties have relatively equal power, then the use of force can result in much destruction and an uncertain settlement.

The major limitation of conquest as an instrument of conflict management, however, is that it does not assure long-term peace and stability. When conflicts are resolved through force, individuals and groups continue to prefer their original goals and interests and may continue to seek a way of rectifying the imposed

Conflict management
An approach that seeks to manage social and political conflict by seeking to reduce its harmful effects while also protecting its constructive, creative effects.

Third-party conflict resolution
An approach to dispute resolution involving an external party. Common third-party procedures include conciliation, mediation, arbitration, and adjudication.

Force
The application of military power in order to punish or compel; applied coercion.

settlement. Effective, long-term community harmony requires not only external change but also change in the inward, underlying conditions that gave rise to the dispute. Indeed, so long as participants continue to prefer their original goals and have the means to pursue them, the imposed settlement will remain vulnerable and precarious. This was the case with the Treaty of Versailles at the end of World War I. The treaty established the allied powers as victorious, but twenty years after the signing of this agreement, Germany was on the war path again, in part seeking to regain what it had lost in World War I.

A second conflict-resolution strategy relies on threats of coercive power. Such threats are of two types: **deterrence,** which seeks to *prevent* undesirable outcomes by threatening unacceptable punishment, and **coercive diplomacy,** which seeks to *bring about* desired outcomes by threatening coercive actions. As an instrument of dispute settlement, deterrence seeks to prevent unwanted actions by making credible threats; coercive diplomacy, by contrast, seeks to achieve desired behaviors by making threats. The chief difference between force and coercive threats is that the former strategy relies on the application of force, whereas the latter relies solely on threats, ranging from limited sanctions to major force. Although deterrence and coercive diplomacy have the advantage of being more efficient and economical than force, they are not always effective. The role and threat of force are examined more fully in chapter 10.

A third strategy of conflict management is **compromise.** This occurs when the contesting parties decide, either on their own accord or with encouragement of an outside party, to resolve a dispute by mutually accepting a less than ideal settlement. In effect, the parties must be willing to accept partial satisfaction, as opposed to complete realization of their goals. This means that compromise will always entail some dissatisfaction. Former Secretary of State Henry Kissinger has wisely observed that negotiated settlements will always seem somewhat unjust. "The generality of this dissatisfaction," writes Kissinger, "is a condition of stability because were any one power totally satisfied, all others would be totally dissatisfied. . . ."[38]

Compromise is normally the best way to resolve disputes because only voluntary mutual adjustments by the disputing parties can assure long-term harmony and peace. As noted above, when a settlement is achieved by force, contesting parties will continue to prefer their original positions. An imposed settlement may bring about a temporary peace, but it can also eventually erupt in a storm.

According to K. J. Holsti, the most common conflict resolution in the twentieth century has been conquest, accounting for 31 percent of the ninety-eight major international disputes from 1919 to 1990. Compromise, deterrence, and award were the next most common approaches, accounting for 20, 19, and 13 percent, respectively. Some 17 percent of the international disputes were resolved through essentially nonpolitical means: 12 percent through withdrawal and avoidance strategies and 5 percent through passive settlement—that is, by letting the dispute become obsolete. According to table 4.3, roughly the same percentage of twentieth-century international disputes were resolved through strategies of peace and through strategies of force. But whereas the role of force accounted for 63 percent of all disputes in the first part of the century, it accounted for only 43 percent of the disputes in the post-1945 era. Conversely, whereas strategies of peace accounted for 37 percent of dispute-outcomes in the first era, they accounted for 58 percent of the dispute settlements in the latter part of the century.[39]

In order to illustrate the sources and manifestations of conflict, as well as the development of cooperation, we examine the recent major territorial dispute be-

Deterrence
The use of explicit or implicit threats of coercion in order to inhibit unwanted behavior.

Coercive diplomacy
The threat or use of limited force to persuade an actor to comply with a state's foreign policy demands.

Compromise
The resolution of conflict through mutual accommodation.

TABLE 4.3 Settlement of International Disputes: Forceful and Peaceful Strategies, 1919–1990 (in percentages)

Strategy	1919–39 (% of 38 disputes)	1945–90 (% of 60 disputes)	% of Conflicts (98 disputes)
Force			
Conquest	42	26	31
Forced submission; deterrence	21	17	19
Subtotal	63	43	50
Peace			
Compromise	13	25	20
Award	21	8	13
Passive settlement	—	8	5
Withdrawal—avoidance	3	17	12
Subtotal	37	58	50
Total	100	101	100

Source: Data from K. J. Holsti, *International Politics: A Framework for Analysis,* 6th ed. (Englewood Cliffs, N.J.: Prentice-Hall, 1992), p. 363.

tween Iraq and Kuwait. The conflict, known as the Persian Gulf Crisis, is significant because it involved major geopolitical developments that threatened to destabilize a region holding the world's principal petroleum reserves. The crisis is also important because it illustrates the propensities for conflict and cooperation in global society. The failure to resolve the original dispute between Iraq and Kuwait resulted in an invasion and occupation of Kuwait—a development that increased other global tensions while also stimulating numerous new and unanticipated cooperative ventures. Because of the simultaneous proliferation of conflict and cooperation, the Iraq-Kuwait dispute illustrates the conflictual and consensual forces that are commonly found in global society.

In Conclusion

Global politics involves continuous tensions and conflicts from a variety of sources. But international relations also involve a great deal of transnational cooperation among state and nonstate actors based on a variety of shared interests. To a significant degree, global politics involves the regulation of international conflict in order to limit its harmful and destructive effects. Because no authoritative conflict-resolution institutions exist in international society, states must cooperate voluntarily in controlling international violence. Moreover, states and other actors promote shared interests across territorial boundaries in politics and many other functional areas, including economic and social life, the environment, science and technology, and religious life. International politics thus involves the ongoing promotion of transnational coordination and cooperation along with the regulation and resolution of global conflict.

Case 4.1 The Persian Gulf Crisis

On August 2, 1990, Iraq invaded its tiny neighbor Kuwait. Iraq's much larger and qualitatively superior military forces smashed through Kuwaiti defensive positions during the early morning hours of that day and within twenty-four hours controlled all key centers and installations of Kuwait, including the country's capital, Kuwait City. Within forty-eight hours Iraq had more than 120,000 soldiers and 850 tanks in Kuwait, many of them on Kuwait's southern border, thereby potentially threatening Saudi Arabia.

The Nature and Sources of the Conflict

Two major factors contributed to Iraq's invasion of Kuwait—one territorial and the other financial. The territorial dispute was rooted in Iraq's long-term quarrel over its border with Kuwait. According to Iraq, its southern Kuwait border, established by Britain in 1922 following the collapse of the Ottoman Empire at the end of World War I, unfairly limited its access to the Persian Gulf. Iraqi officials had periodically pressed for additional territory that would give them, at a minimum, sole control of the Rumaila oil field along the southern border and two swampy islands (Bubiyan and Warba) near the Iraqi port of Umm Qasr at the end of the Tigris-Euphrates delta.

The financial dispute stemmed from Iraq's $80 billion foreign debt, caused chiefly by its ten-year war with Iran.[40] During the Iraq-Iran war (see chap. 12), Kuwait had supported Iraq financially, giving it more than $10 billion, but now that the war was over, Iraq was eager to pay off part of its international debt, further modernize and replenish its military forces, and increase its relative power in the Middle East. To do this, Iraq needed additional foreign exchange from its chief export, petroleum.

According to Iraq, Kuwait was guilty of two major acts of "financial aggression." First, during 1989 and 1990 Kuwait had been pumping close to 2.0 million barrels of oil per day, or more than 30 percent higher than its assigned OPEC quota. Because Kuwait had failed to limit its production, Iraq blamed it (as well as the United Arab Emirates) for a global petroleum oversupply that had resulted in exceptionally low oil prices (about $15 per barrel, down from about $26 per barrel in 1985). Iraq estimated that for every dollar decline in the price of crude petroleum, it was losing about $1 billion of revenue annually. Second, Kuwait was charged with "stealing" nearly $2.4 billion worth of oil from the Rumaila oil field straddling the border. In the light of these two financial crimes, Saddam Hussein was demanding that Kuwait not only forgive Iraq's $10 billion debt but that it pay $13 to $15 billion in reparations.[41] Although efforts to resolve the financial dispute had been underway for two months, little progress had been achieved.

Iraq's invasion eventually led to a 46-day war spearheaded by the United States. The war, which included the largest deployment of armored forces in the history of warfare, involved more than one and a half million soldiers and more than 8,000 tanks and 1,800 aircraft. From August through mid-January, the allies prepared for war, and when Iraq failed to end its occupation, the U.S.-led coalition began the war with a massive bombing campaign. The air campaign, involving from 2,000 to 3,000 bombing sorties per day, destroyed major military, communications, and electrical power installations and inflicted heavy damage on Iraq's army and air force. After six weeks of aerial bombardment, allied forces commenced a massive 100-hour ground attack that led to the liberation of Kuwait and the destruction of a large part of Saddam Hussein's armored forces. It has been estimated that of Iraq's half a million soldiers stationed in Kuwait and southern Iraq, from 70,000 to 100,000 died in the war. Moreover, Iraqi armored forces—estimated at 4,550 tanks 2,880 personnel carriers, and 3,257 artillery pieces—were reduced to 703 tanks, 1,430 personnel carriers, and 340 artillery pieces, or roughly 15, 50 and 10 percent of the original weapons arsenal.[42] Most importantly, the war severely damaged Iraq's nuclear weapons development facilities and its chemical weapons arsenal.

The Expansion of Conflict and Cooperation

One of the ironies of conflicts such as the Iraq-Kuwait dispute is that they can lead to other tensions while simultaneously fostering cooperative ventures. Saddam Hussein had undoubtedly assumed that the occupation and annexation of Kuwait would be opposed by other states, especially other Arab states. But he also no doubt believed that, as the leading Arab military power in the Middle East, Iraq could not only prevail over Kuwait but successfully resist other Arab states that might oppose its conquest of a neighboring state. But Hussein failed to anticipate one development—a

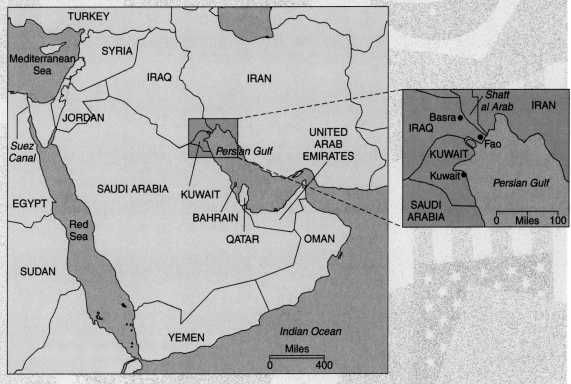

MAP 4.1
The Persian Gulf

U.S.-led coalition of states determined to protect Saudi Arabia and to liberate Kuwait. The development of this allied coalition itself resulted in unexpected international military and economic cooperation, while also breeding additional global tensions.

Immediately after Iraq invaded Kuwait, the United States froze some $30 billion of Iraq's and Kuwait's assets in the United States. More importantly, President Bush began developing a multilateral coalition of Western and Arab states that eventually resulted in the formation of a 32-state multinational military force of more than 800,000 soldiers. The major components of this force included more than half a million soldiers from the United States and major supporting forces from Britain, France, Italy, Saudi Arabia, and Egypt. Even Syria, a largely anti-Western state often charged with supporting terrorism, contributed some 15,000 soldiers. The financial cost of liberating Kuwait was also borne by a coalition of Western and Arab states—primarily by Saudi Arabia, Kuwait, Japan, and the United States. Of the estimated $61 billion cost of the war, foreign states covered about $54 billion, including $13.5 billion each from Kuwait and Saudi Arabia, $9 billion from Japan, and $5.5 billion from Germany.[43]

One of the important early developments in the Persian Gulf crisis was the action taken by the Arab League—the major international alliance of twenty-one Arab states. After meeting in Cairo on August 10 at Syria's request, the Arab League voted to condemn Iraq's invasion and to call for the liberation of Kuwait. Only Libya and the PLO joined Iraq in opposing the resolution, while Mauritania, Jordan, and Sudan expressed reservations about the League's action.[44] Most significantly, twelve of the League's member-states voted to send military forces to regain Kuwait's political independence.

continued

Case 4.1 The Persian Gulf Crisis—*continued*

This photo depicts some of the destruction from the 1991 Persian Gulf War. Just before Iraq's capitulation to UN coalition forces, thousands of military and civilian vehicles were destroyed by coalition planes as they tried to flee Kuwait.

One of the unanticipated consequences of the Iraq-Kuwait conflict was the expansion of conflict within the Pan-Arabic movement, especially between radical and moderate states. These tensions became especially pronounced between Palestinians and the Kuwaiti and Saudi Arabian governments following the war because the PLO had supported Iraq in the crisis. Both Kuwait and Saudi Arabia had historically employed tens of thousands of Palestinian workers, whose salaries helped to support families in Gaza and the West Bank. In addition, both Kuwait and Saudi Arabia had historically provided significant financial support to the Palestinian political movement seeking greater self-determination. But because Palestinian political leaders had supported Iraq's Saddam Hussein in the regional dispute, both states significantly reduced their Palestinian support following the ending of hostilities. Finally, Jordan, which also had been a major beneficiary of Saudi Arabia and Western aid, severely damaged its international stature by identifying itself with Iraq.

The most important and surprising joint diplomatic initiative during the Persian Gulf crisis was the cooperation developed between the United States and the Soviet Union. Throughout much of the Cold War, the two superpowers had competed for international influence and had used regional disputes, such as those in the Middle East, to wage their ideological conflict. But with the demise of the Cold War in 1989–1990, the two superpowers had begun to cooperate more—a development evident during the latter 1980s and especially at the September 1990 Helsinki summit meeting between presidents Mikhail Gorbachev and George Bush. At the summit, the two superpower leaders pledged to act "individually and in concert" to expel Iraq from Kuwait, stating that they were determined to end Iraq occupation, even if it required other, nonpeaceful steps. The Soviet Union's collective security actions were especially surprising since it had served as Iraq's principal weapons supplier during the 1970s and 1980s, providing Iraq with more than $23 billion in armaments during the 1982–1989 period alone.[45]

Historically, the UN Security Council had been unable to effectively carry out its responsibilities of collective security because Cold War tensions impeded the required consensus among the major powers. But with the easing of East-West tensions, the two superpowers had begun cooperating more on global concerns, and when the Persian Gulf crisis arose, the two superpowers facilitated, rather than impeded, the Security Council peacekeeping functions. Indeed, the Iraq-Kuwait crisis represents the first major international dispute in which the two major powers cooperated in promoting international peace and security in the United Nations 45-year history. Thus, one of the major cooperative achievements during the Persian Gulf crisis was the development of the U.S.-inspired coalition opposing Iraq's territorial aggression against Kuwait. This coalition was symbolized by an unprecedented thirteen Security Council Resolutions passed between August and November 1990 (see table 4.4).

TABLE 4.4 UN Security Council Peacekeeping Resolutions, Persian Gulf Crisis, 1990–1991

Resolution	Date	Major Provisions
660	Aug. 2	Condemns Iraqi invasion, calls for the immediate withdrawal of Iraqi forces
661	Aug. 6	Imposes comprehensive sanctions against Iraq for not complying with Res. 660
662	Aug. 9	Declares Iraq's annexation of Kuwait void
664	Aug. 18	Demands the safe exit of foreigners from Kuwait and Iraq and demands that Iraq rescind its orders to close foreign embassies in Kuwait
665	Aug. 25	Imposes a naval embargo to support sanctions
670	Sept. 25	Imposes an embargo on air traffic to Iraq
674	Oct. 29	Demands that Iraq stop taking foreign nations as hostages and that it stop mistreating Kuwaitis; moreover, it indicates that Iraq will be held liable for all damages and personal injuries resulting from the occupation
678	Nov. 29	Authorizes UN member-states to "use all necessary means" to implement Res. 660 if Iraq has not complied by Jan. 15, 1991
689	April 2	Implements a cease-fire, provided Iraq agrees to: (a) destroy all chemical and biological weapons and all ballistic missiles with a range of 150 km or more; (b) not acquire or develop nuclear arms; (c) accept liability for any losses resulting from the invasion and occupation

SUMMARY

1. International society is characterized by both cooperation and conflict. Realists believe that cooperation in the international community is difficult because the welfare and security of states is dependent ultimately on states' relative capabilities. Neoliberals deemphasize the challenge posed by relative gains.

2. International cooperation is chiefly rooted in the shared interests of state and nonstate actors. Some of the most important mutual interests of states include: protecting sovereignty, reducing the impact of war, maintaining international law, promoting global order, fostering national economic well-being, and protecting the global environment.

3. Global cooperation is also fostered through nonstate actors, which play a key role in promoting and facilitating socioeconomic interdependence. The development of functional cooperation in specialized areas has given rise to regimes based on shared rules and principles, resulting in patterns of interaction in well-defined issue-areas. Global cooperation can also be promoted through deliberate processes of economic and political integration.

4. Many different types of conflict occur in the international society. These can be differentiated in terms of participants (states, IGOs, and NGOs), nature (relational and institutional), scope (systemic and parochial), and sources. Some of the major sources of international conflict include territorial claims, composition of government, the creation of states, and the unification of states.

5. Two basic strategies that can be used in responding to international conflicts: avoidance and management. Conflict management, the only effective long-term strategy, can be approached in a variety of ways, including force, threat of force, and compromise. Third-party strategies, including conciliation, mediation, arbitration, and adjudication, also play an important role in resolving international disputes.

6. IR is characterized by both conflict and cooperation. Indeed, international conflicts generate global cooperation, whereas cooperative ventures frequently result in conflict. The Persian Gulf illustrates how a territorial dispute between two states generated significant international cooperation while also spawning additional tensions and conflicts.

KEY TERMS

hegemonic stability theory
absolute gains
relative gains
regime
epistemic community
economic integration

European Union
political integration
New International Economic Order (NIEO)
systemic conflict
parochial conflict

conflict avoidance
appeasement
conflict management
third-party conflict resolution

force
deterrence
coercive diplomacy
compromise

RECOMMENDED READINGS

Axelrod, Robert, *The Evolution of Cooperation.* New York: Basic Books, 1984. This path-breaking study explores conditions that facilitate cooperation among self-interested actors. Axelrod argues that reciprocity ("tit for tat") is the most fruitful way of promoting cooperation.

Diesing, Paul, and Glenn H. Snyder. *Conflict Among Nations: Bargaining, Decision Making, and System Structures in International Crises.* Princeton: Princeton University Press, 1977. An advanced theoretical and empirical investigation of how states bargain during international crises. The study provides insights into crisis decision making as well as principles and techniques of conflict resolution.

Grieco, Joseph M. *Cooperation Among Nations: Europe, America, and Non-Tariff Barriers to Trade.* Ithaca: Cornell University Press, 1990. A readable and penetrating case study of international cooperation between the EC and the United States in implementing reductions in nontariff barriers called for by the Tokyo Round regime. Based on his analysis, Grieco concludes that realism provides a more adequate explanation of international behavior of states than liberal institutionalism and more particularly its modern, revised formulation—neoliberalism.

Holsti, Kalevi J. *Peace and War: Armed Conflicts and International Order, 1648–1989*. Cambridge: Cambridge University Press, 1991. An analysis of peacekeeping in modern history, focusing on five major peace settlements—the Westphalian system, the Treaty of Utrecht, the Congress of Vienna, the League of Nations, and the United Nations. In examining these different systems, Holsti explores three issues—sources of international conflict, attitude changes toward war, and the effect of international structures on the management and prevention of international conflict.

Huntington, Samuel P. *The Clash of Civilizations and the Remaking of World Order*. New York: Simon & Schuster, 1996. In this study, Huntington, a noted international affairs scholar, amplifies the argument, first developed in an influential 1993 *Foreign Affairs* article, that political and ideological international relations among states is being displaced by cultural conflict among civilizations. Although the argument is controversial, this is essential reading for anyone concerned with the future of global politics.

James, Alan. *Peacekeeping in International Politics*. New York: St. Martin's Press, 1990. An invaluable collection of fifty-seven case studies of international conflict that illustrate the diverse nature of global disputes and the role and limits of peacekeeping initiatives.

Keohane, Robert O. *After Hegemony: Cooperation and Discord in the World Political Economy*. Princeton: Princeton University Press, 1984. This study explores the nature of, and prospects for, functional cooperation among advanced capitalist states in the light of declining American power. The author suggests that, although functional cooperation may be more difficult in the future because of the loss of American hegemony, cooperation will still be possible through international regimes.

Krasner, Stephen, ed. *International Regimes*. Ithaca: Cornell University Press, 1983. This collection of essays, which first appeared in the journal *International Organization*, provides one of the first major efforts to explore the nature, utility, and limitations of the international regime concept.

Oye, Kenneth A., ed. *Cooperation Under Anarchy*. Princeton: Princeton University Press, 1986. This collection of studies explores the conditions giving rise to cooperation in an anarchic international system. The essays examine theoretical and conceptual dimensions of the problem and illustrate the limits and possibilities of cooperation in specific areas, including national security, arms control, trade, and finance.

Young, Oran R. *International Cooperation: Building Regimes for Natural Resources and the Environment*. Ithaca: Cornell University Press, 1989. This study attempts to clarify the nature and role of international regimes by examining the evolving nature of global cooperation among states. Part I of the study is conceptual and theoretical; Part II provides case studies on international cooperation on the environment and natural resources.

RELEVANT WEB SITES

Canadian Forces College Gulf War	www.cfcsc.dnd.ca/links/milhist/gw.html
Carnegie Commission on Preventive Deadly Conflict	www.carnegie.org/deadly/sisk.html
Conflict Prevention Resource Site (Winston Foundation)	www.crosslink.net/~wfwp/
International Boundary Research Unit Data on 9,000 boundary related reports	www-ibru.dur.ac.uk/database/data.html

International Relations and Security network (ISN)
    See the following subjects:
    Conflict Management
    Conflict and Peace Studies
	www.isn.ethz.ch/

U.S. Institute of Peace
    International Relations Research Centers,
    by country
	www.usip.org/library/rcenters.html

The World Game Institute	www.worldgame.org

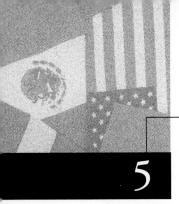

CHAPTER

5 Superpower Conflict and Cooperation

It is clear that the United States cannot expect in the foreseeable future to enjoy political intimacy with the Soviet regime. It must continue to regard the Soviet Union as a rival, not a partner, in the political arena.[1] *(1947)*

George F. Kennan, *noted U.S. diplomat*

Over $12.7 trillion in defense spending, $1.1 trillion in foreign aid, and more than one hundred thousand lives were the price the United States paid to ensure victory in the forty-five-year war against tyranny.[2] (1994)

Richard Nixon, *former U.S. president*

The cold war is over. The United States and its allies have won.[3] (1990)

William G. Hyland, *foreign affairs scholar*

Cold War
The 45-year ideological conflict between the Soviet Union and its allies and the United States and its allies.

As noted in the previous chapter, two systemic disputes have dominated the international relations of the second half of the twentieth century—an ideological conflict between the United States and its democratic allies (the West) and the Soviet Union and its communist allies (the East), and an economic conflict between the developed democratic states (the North) and the developing nations of the Third World (the South). The East-West conflict began in the immediate aftermath of World War II and ended in 1989 when the Soviet Union refused to intervene in Eastern Europe to defend embattled communist regimes. The North-South dispute, by contrast, began in the early 1960s with the dramatic growth of new nation-states and the rise in economic expectations among the poor peoples of Asia, Africa, and Latin America, and although the conflict had not officially ended by 1998, it had lost much of its strength. Despite the termination of one conflict (East-West) and the weakening of the other (North-South), contemporary international relations continue to be influenced by the lingering effects of these disputes. Knowledge of these systemic disputes is therefore important not only in developing an understanding of the important historical role that they have played in modern international relations, but also in developing an appreciation of the continuing influence of North-South and East-West structures on contemporary global politics.

The East-West conflict, known as the **Cold War,** originated in the immediate aftermath of World War II with the growing ideological and political contestation between the two leading military powers—the United States and the Soviet Union. Although the dispute was one of the most durable conflicts in world history, exceeding the length of the Peloponnesian War (431–404 B.C.), the Thirty Years' War (1618–1648), the Napoleonic Wars (1803–1815), World War I (1914–1918), and World War II (1939–1945), it ironically produced one of the longest periods of international order and global peace. John Lewis Gaddis, a distinguished historian, has described this long peace as follows: "The Cold War, with all of its rivalries, anxieties, and unquestionable dangers, has produced the longest period of stability in relations among the great powers that the world has known in this century; it now compares favorably as well with some of the longest periods of great power stability in all of modern history."[4]

This chapter examines the nature, evolution, and termination of the Cold War. It defines some of the key features of the conflict, examines factors precipitating the dispute, and compares the foreign policy perspectives of the two superpowers. The chapter then traces the historical evolution of the conflict, from its inception in 1946 to its demise in 1989. It concludes with an assessment of global politics in the post–Cold War Era. In chapter 15 we examine the North-South economic conflict.

THE NATURE OF THE CONFLICT

The Cold War was characterized by four key traits: (1) a struggle between the United States and the Soviet Union; (2) an ideological contest between two competing political and economic worldviews; (3) an avoidance of direct military conflict between the two superpowers; and (4) a distrust and antagonism rooted partly in misperception.

Superpower Conflict

Fundamentally, the Cold War was a dispute between the two dominant states of the international community—the United States and the Soviet Union. Although no major war was fought between them, these two powers were continuously engaged in a struggle for political and military dominance. The military competition between these two superpowers is best illustrated by the long and intense arms race, resulting in the development and deployment of nearly 25,000 strategic nuclear weapons. The Cold War also involved intense political competition as each superpower sought to increase its global influence. Although Europe remained the major area of contested power throughout the forty-five-year conflict, Third World regions became increasingly important areas of superpower-assisted conflict from the early 1960s to the mid-1980s.

Although the United States and the USSR were the primary actors, each superpower was supported by allies formally organized into two alliance systems. The United States and its European democratic allies established the **North Atlantic Treaty Organization (NATO)** in 1949 to combat the expansion of Soviet communism in Europe. In response, the Soviet Union established in 1955 the **Warsaw Treaty Organization (Warsaw Pact)** among its Eastern European allies to counter NATO initiatives. Table 5.1 identifies the members of each of these organizations.

Ideological Conflict

The second characteristic of the Cold War conflict was is its ideological character. Fundamentally, the Cold War was a conflict over ideas, especially principles governing the establishment and maintenance of political communities. Two political philosophies—**democracy** and **communism**—were in competition. The democratic alternative, propounded by the United States and its allies, was characterized by pluralism, contestation of political office, periodic elections, individual freedom, and capitalism; communism, by contrast, called for collectivism, authoritarian governmental rule, governmental control of political life, and state-socialism. Whereas the United States sought to advance limited, constitutional government, the Soviet Union advocated communist dictatorship. Given these sharp differences, when both nations emerged as the leading powers at the end of World War II, ideological conflict was inevitable.

North Atlantic Treaty Organization (NATO)
A military alliance of Western European and North American states established in 1949 to provide collective defense. Throughout the Cold War, NATO's chief aim was to deter Soviet aggression in Europe.

Warsaw Treaty Organization (Warsaw Pact)
A Cold War military alliance of communist states in central and eastern Europe. Created by the Soviet Union in 1955, it was disbanded in 1991.

Democracy
A system of limited government based on free, periodic, and competitive elections.

Communism
The Marxist-Leninist ideology assumes that the state should regulate the production and distribution of goods and services.

TABLE 5.1 Leading Participants in the East-West Conflict

East		West	
Warsaw Pact*	**Others**	**NATO Members**	**Others**
Soviet Union	Albania**	United States	Israel
Bulgaria	Cuba	Belgium	Australia
Czechoslovakia	China***	Canada	New Zealand
East Germany	North Korea	Denmark	Some Latin-American states
Hungary	Vietnam	France****	
Poland	Yugoslavia	Greece	
Romania		Iceland	
		Italy	
		Luxembourg	
		Netherlands	
		Norway	
		Portugal	
		Spain	
		Turkey	
		United Kingdom	
		West Germany	

*Disbanded in 1991

**Albania withdrew from the Warsaw Pact in 1966

***China was closely aligned with the USSR in the 1950s, but grew distant after a Sino-Soviet rift developed in the early 1960s.

****France participates in NATO's political affairs but not in its military operations.

The U.S. democratic ideology was fundamentally rooted in the primacy of individual human rights, especially personal freedom. According to democratic theory, because governments are the servants of people, the legitimacy to rule has to be based on consent carried out through competitive, periodic elections. Moreover, because the purpose of government is to protect and increase human rights, the authority of rulers has to be defined by law. For the West, therefore, the good life (*summum bonum*) is found in political societies characterized by constitutional government, limited governmental authority, and an open, pluralistic political culture.

The communist ideology, as espoused by the Soviet Union, was rooted chiefly in the ideas of two thinkers—Karl Marx, the nineteenth-century German political economist, and Vladimir Lenin, the leader of the Bolsheviks who became the first communist leader of the Soviet Union following the October Revolution of 1917. Marx's fundamental contribution to communist ideology was his critique of capitalism and alternative theory of production based on a labor theory of value. Lenin's most important contribution was his theory of political action and organization. The combination of Marx's political economy with Lenin's theory of political action resulted in Marxism-Leninism, or what is commonly defined as Soviet communism. Some of its key principles include:

1. The institutions, behavioral patterns, and cultural values of society are rooted in economic structures.

2. Capitalism is an unjust, evil system because it permits one class (the bourgeoisie) to exploit another (the proletariat).

3. Capitalism must be destroyed and replaced by a classless society.

4. The transition from capitalism to communism will involve forceful, revolutionary change.

5. The transition to a classless society must be directed by a group of leaders (the vanguard) of the proletariat.

The primacy of ideology contributed significantly to the intensity, intractability, and duration of the Cold War. Had the war involved only a quest for power, as had been the case in most prior great-power conflicts, the East-West dispute would have undoubtedly ended sooner. But it continued until the late 1980s in great measure because of the intense political competition between alternative political worldviews. Ideological zeal provided the fuel to keep the Cold War going for some forty-five years.

The Absence of Major War

The third key characteristic of the Cold War was the absence of a major war between the superpowers. Indeed, the Cold War produced the longest period of international stability in the modern world. This is why historian John Lewis Gaddis calls this period "the long peace."[5] Although the superpowers did not directly challenge each other through war, they were regularly involved indirectly in **proxy wars**—regional disputes in which the superpowers' influence was at stake. For example, the Soviet Union directly and indirectly helped establish and maintain revolutionary regimes in countries such as Angola, Cuba, Mozambique, and Vietnam, and supported antigovernment revolutionary movements in countries, such as El Salvador and the Philippines. The United States, by contrast, tried to halt the expansion of communism through programs of economic and military assistance to governments and anticommunist rebels. For example, during the mid-1980s the United States provided significant economic and military assistance to the government of El Salvador in order to combat indigenous revolutionary guerrillas seeking to topple the regime. It also provided economic and military aid to antigovernment forces in Afghanistan (mujahedin) and Nicaragua (Contras) as a means of checking communist expansion.

Proxy war
A war conducted through surrogate regimes. During the Cold War, the superpowers carried out a number of these conflicts in Asia, Africa, and Latin America.

Thus, by providing strategic, military, economic, and political aid to foreign actors, the superpowers fought the Cold War through surrogates. With the exception of the Cuban missile crisis of 1962—a dispute in which the superpowers implicitly threatened each other with nuclear weapons—Cold War conflicts were fought indirectly in local disputes. Superpowers became involved militarily in regional conflicts only when they were certain that the other superpower was unlikely to become directly involved militarily, as proved to be the case for the United States in Vietnam and for the Soviet Union in Afghanistan. In short, Cold Wars were fought chiefly by indigenous forces relying on foreign military and economic assistance.

Ironically, the relative stability of the Cold War was due largely to the invention of nuclear physics and its application to military weaponry. Beginning in the late 1940s, both superpowers began developing nuclear arsenals so that by the late sixties they possessed the ability to nearly destroy civilization. Notwithstanding the intense competition between United States and the Soviet Union, a direct war between them became virtually unthinkable because of the great destructive potential of their strategic weapons. Indeed, the large but balanced nuclear capabilities of the actors contributed greatly to the postwar stability of the world and especially to the peace of Europe.[6]

Misperception

A fourth characteristic of the Cold War was the high level of distrust and hostility caused by misperception. Because of the incompatibility of U.S. and Soviet ideologies, superpower elites tended to misperceive each other's behavior during the Cold War. To be sure, the Cold War involved objective conflicts; but the ideological prisms of key political leaders tended to exacerbate hostility and increase distrust. For example, Stalin's belief that capitalism and communism must continually clash tended to heighten his distrust of the United States and Britain, whereas the development and expansion of Western capitalism tended to increase Russian fears of capitalist encirclement. On the other hand, American officials' fear of communism exacerbated hostility toward communist regimes and unduly oversimplified the East-West conflict. Rather than viewing communist countries as disparate, radical regimes, Americans regarded communism as a universal, monolithic movement directed from Moscow, especially in the early years of the Cold War.

In a study of the role of perceptions in the foreign policy interactions of the United States, China, and the Soviet Union, political scientist John Stoessinger concludes that false images have commonly impaired the foreign relations of these three states—so much so that they have been "nations in darkness." According to Stoessinger, the Cuban missile crisis illustrates how misperception led the two superpowers to the nuclear abyss and how the peaceful resolution of the conflict was possible only when the superpower leaders changed their perceptions about each other. Stoessinger writes: "The story of the Cuban crisis is the story of the two most powerful men in the world who first saw what they wished to see but were able to correct their misperceptions and thus pull back from the edge of nuclear destruction."[7] Stoessinger also attributes the resumption of Cold War rhetoric in the 1980s to misperceptions of President Reagan, particularly his "devil images" of the Soviet Union. He credits the decline of East-West hostility to the displacement of image distortion. Stoessinger writes: "As official hostility began to melt away, they [Americans and Russians] also discovered that they shared more similarities than differences. And they also began to wonder why they had hated and feared one another for so long."[8] In short, government officials' misperceptions exacerbated East-West hostility, while the distortion of reality prolonged the Cold War.

ORIGINS OF THE CONFLICT

World War II Accords

Although the Cold War began immediately after World War II, the seeds of the conflict were sown much earlier. Throughout the war, Great Britain, the United States, and the Soviet Union cooperated in defeating Germany. The unity of the three allied powers was rooted not in shared political values, but in a shared desire to defeat Hitler and his forces. The cooperation was, in effect, "a marriage of convenience."

Throughout the war the United States provided significant military and economic assistance to the Soviet Union through its Lend-Lease Program. According to estimates, during the war the United States gave the Soviet Union some 9,600 cannons, 18,700 airplanes, 10,800 tanks, 427,000 trucks, 1,900 steam locomotives, along with nearly 5 million tons of food.[9] Despite wartime cooperation, significant policy differences began to emerge between the allied powers as early as 1943. Most of these concerned postwar planning over the future of Europe, especially such issues as Polish-Russian territorial boundaries, the partitioning of Germany, German-Polish borders, and the role of occupying forces in the establishment of interim European governments.

The future of Europe was first jointly addressed at the November 1943 conference in Tehran, attended by British Prime Minister Winston Churchill, U.S. President Franklin Delano Roosevelt, and Soviet leader Joseph Stalin. The "Big Three" continued negotiations throughout 1944 and 1945, seeking to resolve their differences at two other conferences—first at Yalta, on the Black Sea, in February 1945 and then at Potsdam (Berlin) in July 1945. Although these meetings established the basic principles for postwar reconstruction, they did not fully resolve the competing interests of the allied powers. Because of the great destruction wrought by German aggression, Russia's primary concern was territorial security; the American and the British, although sensitive to the need for friendly governments along Russia's western border, were chiefly interested in the establishment of freely elected governments in Western Europe.

From the outset of postwar planning, the United States opposed the partitioning of Europe in general and of Germany in particular. The notion of **spheres of influence** was considered contrary to the universal principles on which a new peaceful and stable world order should be built. But both Britain and the Soviet Union had particular interests in European regions, and the intractability of negotiations among the Big Three had led Churchill and Stalin to accept the idea of "spheres of influence" at their Moscow meeting in October 1944. Because the Red Army had already moved into Bulgaria and Romania, Churchill suggested to Stalin that Britain and Russia accept a division of responsibility and influence in the five Balkan states: Yugoslavia and Hungary were to be divided 50—50; Russia was to enjoy 90 percent influence in Romania and 75 percent in Bulgaria; and Britain, along with the United States, was to have 90 percent responsibility in Greece. In his memoirs, Churchill recounted that he put this information on a half-sheet of paper—which he called a "naughty document"—and gave it to Stalin, who signed the paper with a tick of blue pencil. "It was all settled in no more time than it takes to set down," he observed.[10]

Spheres of influence
Regions where a dominant power has major influence.

The Yalta meeting of February 1945 was the most important allied conference. At that time, the Red Army was attacking German forces from the East, while British and American military forces were pushing from the West. With an allied victory imminent, the Big Three had gathered to discuss the political future of conquered territories and to address two specific concerns—the composition of the Polish government and the future administration of Germany. Among other things, Stalin, Roosevelt, and Churchill agreed that four allied states (the Big Three plus France) would be jointly responsible for the future of Germany and would require it to pay reparations of $20 billion, half of this to Russia. More significantly, the three leaders signed a "Declaration of Liberated Europe," pledging to assist former enemy (Axis) satellite states in establishing future governments through self-determination. The declaration called on the allied governments to (1) establish domestic order, (2) provide emergency relief where needed, (3) establish interim governments that were "broadly representative of all democratic elements in the population," and (4) help establish governments based on free elections at the earliest possible time.

At Potsdam five months later the Big Three—Stalin, Churchill, and now Harry Truman, who had become president upon Roosevelt's death—met to establish principles guiding the future governance of Germany. The United States had wanted a unified German state, but because of the increased polarization between the East and the West, had decided to accept a partitioned Germany. A divided Germany had the advantage of ensuring self-determination for at least part of Germany and of limiting the area from which Russia could seek wartime reparations.

The Division of Europe

A major outcome of World War II was the division of Europe into two *spheres of influence*—one dominated by the Soviet Union and the other by the United States

Issue 5.1 Three Perspectives on the Origins of the Cold War

What caused the Cold War? Why did the two leading powers become involved in a long, intractable conflict after cooperating during World War II in defeating the Axis powers?

There are three major schools of thought on the roots of the Cold War. The first group of scholars, the *traditionalists,*[11] argue that in the aftermath of World War II, the Soviet Union posed an increasing threat to European and other states seeking to recover politically and economically from the war. According to this perspective, the Cold War was due to a growing Soviet threat, fueled in part by a revolutionary communist ideology. Traditionalists argue that the Soviet Union's unwillingness to radically reduce its military forces in Central Europe and to honor its commitment to allow self-determination and free elections in countries along its western border forced the United States and its democratic allies to forcibly "contain" Soviet expansionism.

The second group, the *revisionists,*[12] believes that both the United States and the Soviet Union bear culpability for the Cold War, but places primary responsibility on the United States because of its misperception of Soviet foreign policy and its overreaction to its postwar foreign policy. According to the revisionist perspective, the U.S. perception of a "Soviet threat" was a myth fabricated in order to justify American imperial hegemony. Because the Soviet Union was a major victim of German aggression, suffering more than 20 million casualties, it legitimately sought economic reparations and the establishment of secure borders by ensuring that regimes along its Western border were "friendly." But the United States misinterpreted Soviet behavior and overreacted by establishing an overly confrontational and paranoid foreign policy.

The third group of scholars, the *moderates,*[13] view the roots of the Cold War from an intermediary perspective between those emphasizing communist expansionism, on the one hand, and American misperception and overreaction, on the other. According to this perspective, Soviet foreign policy was not fueled by ideological considerations but by great power imperialism, fueled in part by insecurity and by political and economic acquisitiveness. John Lewis Gaddis, a leading American historian of the Cold War, argues, for example, that Soviet foreign policy was "motivated by insecurity and characterized by caution," but was "also incapable of defining limits of security requirements," thereby leading the Soviet Union "to fill power vacuums where this could be done without encountering resistance."[14] While admitting to U.S. misperceptions and overreactions, the moderates argue that the Soviet Union's early postwar behavior was expansionistic, alarming not only the United States but other countries as well.

and Britain. At the beginning of World War II, communism had a negligible impact on Europe. Weak communist parties existed in Romania and Hungary and not at all in Albania, Germany, and Poland. Only in Bulgaria, Czechoslovakia, and Yugoslavia did communist parties have any significant role. But after the defeat of Germany, Stalin wasted no time in consolidating Soviet control over neighboring states. He established control over the Soviet sector of Germany (later called East Germany), helped establish a pro-Moscow government in Warsaw, forced a communist government on Romania, and helped establish communist elements in elected governments in Bulgaria, Hungary, and Czechoslovakia. In Albania and Yugoslavia, communist governments were established by indigenous guerrilla forces receiving Soviet help.

To a significant degree, Soviet influence expanded throughout Eastern Europe because of the presence of the liberating Red Army. Having destroyed Hitler's military forces, the Soviet Union consolidated its power by filling the political vacuum left by a defeated Germany. Although Russia had pledged to support self-determination, the presence of its military forces proved to be a more important determinant of the evolution of European politics than the promises made at Yalta. Thus, by 1946 the Soviet Union had extended its sphere of influence westward, establishing de facto control over parts of Finland, Germany, Poland, and Romania, and all of Estonia, Latvia, and

Germans celebrate the opening of East Germany's borders atop the Berlin Wall in 1989.

Lithuania. Moreover, communism had spread in different degrees to Albania, Bulgaria, Czechoslovakia, Hungary, and Yugoslavia (see map 5.1).

Although Russia had pledged at Yalta to establish interim governmental institutions that were broadly representative of all elements of society, the manipulation of the electoral system in Poland made it clear to Britain and the United States that the Soviet Union's desire for establishing "friendly" border regimes superseded its commitment to self-determination.

EVOLUTION OF THE EAST-WEST CONFLICT

During its forty-five years, the East-West conflict evolved through four distinct historical phases: (1) emergence, (2) hostility and confrontation, (3) detente, and (4) renewal and demise of confrontation. The disintegration of the Eastern European Soviet bloc in 1989 brought on the post–Cold War era. Table 5.2 highlights some of the key superpower agreements and confrontations from 1946 to 1991.

The Emergence of the Cold War (1946-1948)

During this first phase of the conflict, the Soviet Union became increasingly intransigent and expansionistic. Rather than withdrawing its military forces from the occupied Eastern European territories (Poland, Hungary, East Germany, Bulgaria, and Romania), as Britain and the United States expected, the Soviet Union not only continued its military occupation but sought to extend its influence in other surrounding territories. By providing overt and covert support to communist movements, the Soviet government sought to solidify or install communist regimes in Albania, Azerbaijan (a northern province of Iran), Czechoslovakia, Greece, Turkey, and Yugoslavia.

Following British and American opposition, coupled with Iran's public condemnation in the United Nations of continued Soviet occupation of Azerbaijan, the USSR withdrew its forces from northern Iran in May 1946. This was the only time

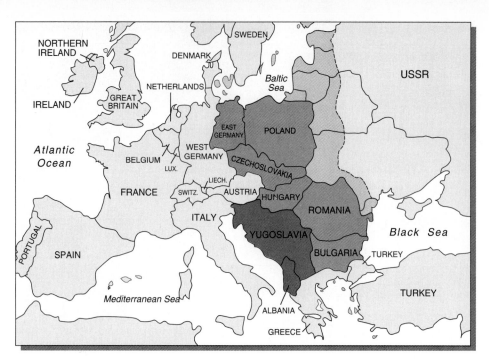

MAP 5.1
The Soviet Union's Sphere of Influence During the Cold War

Territory added to USSR, 1939–45
Soviet-dominated states, 1947–89
Independent communist state

in the early postwar period that the Soviet government voluntarily backed down in the face of Western opposition. In October and November of 1946, communists manipulated elections in Bulgaria and Romania, leading to communist parliamentary control in both nations.

In 1947 the primary area of East-West conflict shifted to Turkey and Greece. The disputes in Turkey concerned territorial boundaries with the Soviet Union, while in Greece communist insurgent forces were threatening the ruling monarchy. Perhaps the most blatant acts of postwar Soviet expansionism occurred in 1948, when the Soviet-backed communists seized power in Czechoslovakia and Soviet military forces undertook a ten-month blockade of West Berlin—an act that led the allies to airlift essential supplies to that city.

In response to the obdurate and expansionistic Soviet foreign policy, U.S. policy attempted to maintain the 1945 status quo and to assist European countries in rebuilding their economies. Three important doctrines defined this policy: containment, the Truman Doctrine, and the Marshall Plan.

Containment
The U.S. Cold War strategy designed to limit Soviet expansionism.

According to the strategy of **containment,** the major aim of U.S. foreign policy was to limit Soviet expansionism. The doctrine received its most explicit enunciation in one of the most famous articles ever published in the leading U.S. journal *Foreign Affairs* in 1947. Authored by diplomat George F. Kennan, Jr., but published under the pseudonym of "X," the article, "The Sources of Soviet Conduct," analyzed postwar Soviet foreign policy and then outlined the rationale for the strategy of containment. Kennan's central thesis was that Soviet expansionism could be contained by the "adroit and vigilant application of counterforce." In effect, the United States should use its military, economic, and political resources to stop the expansion of Soviet influence.

Truman Doctrine
A policy, set forth by President Harry Truman in 1947, committing the United States to support peoples threatened by communist aggression.

The **Truman Doctrine,** the second key element of postwar policy, was a response to communist threats in Greece and Turkey. In early 1947, after the British

TABLE 5.2   Major U.S.-USSR Agreements and Confrontations, 1946–1991

Cooperation	Year	Confrontation
Soviet withdrawal from Azerbaijan	1946	
	1948	Berlin blockade
	1950	Korean War
Austria State Treaty between U.S., USSR, France, and Britain	1955	
	1956	Soviet invasion of Hungary
	1960	U-2 Incident
	1961	Berlin Wall constructed
	1962	Cuban missile crisis
Limited Test Ban Treaty	1963	
	1965	U.S. escalation in Vietnam War
	1968	Soviet invasion of Czechoslovakia
SALT I Accord, ABM Treaty	1972	
	1974	Soviet-Cuban involvement in Angola
SALT II Treaty signed	1979	Soviet intervention in Afghanistan
	1981	Martial law declared in Poland
	1983	U.S. deploys INF in Europe
INF Treaty	1987	
USSR begins troop withdrawals from Afghanistan	1988	
Berlin Wall opens	1989	
East-West Conventional Arms Reduction Treaty	1990	
Unification of Germany	1990	
START I Accord signed	1991	
Dissolution of the USSR	1991	

government announced its termination of military and economic assistance to these two countries, the Truman administration decided to support those regimes. In an address to Congress on March 12, 1947, President Truman argued that the U.S. government should "support free peoples who are resisting attempted subjugations by armed minorities or by outside pressures." Accordingly, he called on Congress to approve $400 million in economic and military aid to the Greek and Turkish governments. Although Truman's address was primarily concerned with the immediate needs of Greece and Turkey, the doctrine was subsequently used to justify support for other regimes threatened by communism.

Finally, the **Marshall Plan,** first articulated by Secretary of State George C. Marshall in a 1947 commencement address at Harvard University, called for massive economic assistance to European nations to encourage postwar economic recovery. In response to this initiative, the U.S. government provided massive aid to Western European states (about $12 billion in the first four years of the program), and contributed greatly to the rapid recovery of Europe.

Marshall Plan
A 1947 plan, set forth by U.S. Secretary of State George Marshall, committing the United States to assist Western Europe's post-World War II economic recovery.

The Era of Confrontation (1949–1969)

During this second phase of the Cold War two important developments took place: first, both superpowers helped create military and political alliances; and second, direct and indirect conflict between the two superpowers increased.

In 1949 Western states, led by the United States, established NATO. Created by twelve states and subsequently increased to sixteen, the chief purpose for the alliance was to provide collective defense against possible Soviet aggression. NATO sought to deter Soviet aggression by threatening unacceptable retaliation. To achieve a credible threat, NATO relied on a strategy of flexible response, based on conventional and nuclear capabilities, coupled with the direct linking of U.S. security with the defense of Western Europe. Throughout most of the postwar era, the United States maintained more than 300,000 troops in Europe, thereby ensuring that any major attack on Western Europe would involve a direct attack on the United States.

The Soviet Union's counterpart alliance was the Warsaw Pact, a military organization created in 1955 to provide collective defense to the Soviet Union and its Eastern European satellites. But as a result of the ending of the Cold War, the Soviet alliance was disestablished in early 1991, and as of 1998 virtually all Russian troops had been withdrawn from Eastern Europe.

A second alliance system created by the Soviet Union was the Council for Mutual Economic Assistance (*COMECON*), established in 1949 to facilitate trade among the Soviet-bloc socialist states. Its original members included Albania (which withdrew in 1961), Bulgaria, Czechoslovakia, East Germany, Hungary, Poland, Romania, and the Soviet Union. Mongolia and Cuba joined subsequently. This organization ceased functioning in 1991 with the disintegration of the Soviet empire.

During this Cold War phase, the superpowers engaged in numerous direct and indirect conflicts. Of these, three stand out: the Korean War (1950–1951), the Cuban Missile Crisis (1962), and the Vietnam War (1965–1973). Because the Cuban crisis will be analyzed in chapter 8, here we briefly sketch only the Korean and Vietnam conflicts.

The Korean Conflict

The Korean War broke out in 1950 when Chinese- and Soviet-supported North Korean forces attacked South Korea, quickly defeating its ill-equipped soldiers and forcing them to retreat to the southern area of the Korean peninsula. Although the war may have been prompted by a desire for national unification, the United States interpreted it as a test case of the East-West resolve, and dispatched military forces to save South Korea from communist aggression. On September 15, 1950, General Douglas MacArthur carried out a successful surprise amphibious landing at Inchon, subsequently recapturing the capital of Seoul. He then proceeded into North Korea, prompting Chinese communist forces to enter the war. After brief but intense fighting, Chinese and North Korean forces regained control of the territory north of the 38th parallel, while the United States maintained control in the southern territory. (See map 5.2.) The conflict ended with a cease-fire in July 1953.

From an IR perspective, the Korean conflict is significant because it greatly intensified the geopolitical conflict between communism and democracy. And from a U.S. foreign policy perspective, the war convinced many Americans of the increasing threat of global communism. According to Robert Art, the Korean conflict reinforced Americans' growing convictions that (1) communism was an increasingly global and monolithic threat, (2) the Soviet Union was the international leader and manager of communism, and (3) communists would not hesitate to use direct military force to expand their international power and influence.[15]

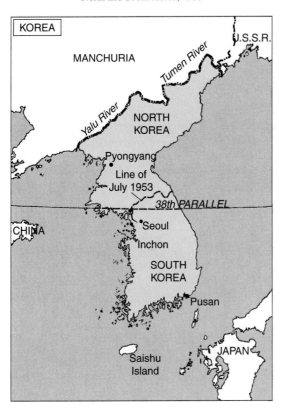

MAP 5.2
Two Cold War Conflicts: Korea and Vietnam

The Vietnam War

The United States became involved militarily in Vietnam ostensibly to contain the expansion of communism in Southeast Asia. After Vietnamese revolutionary forces defeated the French colonial forces at Dien Bien Phu in 1954, a provisional agreement was reached in Geneva calling for a cease-fire. The cease-fire was based on three elements: (1) a temporary division at the 17th parallel between the communists in North Vietnam and noncommunists in South Vietnam (see map 5.2); (2) national elections to be held in July 1956; and (3) the eventual reunification of the country.

Because of the failure to hold free, competitive elections in 1956, communists began using force to try to establish a unified, communist state. To counter the growing insurgency of communist guerrillas, the United States began assisting the South Vietnamese government in the early 1960s. The guerrillas—known as the **Vietcong**—were supported by North Vietnam, which in turn was receiving substantial military and economic assistance from China and the Soviet Union. As the guerrilla war intensified, the United States increased its military assistance from a small group of advisers in 1960 to more than 15,000 by 1963.

A critical turning point of U.S. involvement in Vietnam came in August 1964, when North Vietnamese gunboats allegedly attacked two American destroyers. This event led to a much disputed congressional resolution—known as the **Gulf of Tonkin Resolution**—that authorized President Johnson to take whatever military actions he deemed necessary to defend U.S. forces as well as to prevent further aggression. Accordingly, the United States began an intensive bombing campaign of North Vietnam and increased the number of American military forces. By late

Vietcong
South Vietnamese communist guerrillas who sought to topple the government of South Vietnam.

Gulf of Tonkin Resolution
A Congressional resolution authorizing the president to take whatever military actions were considered necessary in order to protect U.S. military forces in Vietnam.

Tet offensive
A major 1968 military offensive by communist guerrillas against the South Vietnam regime.

1965 the total number of American soldiers had reached 200,000; by early 1968, they numbered more than half a million.

In January 1968, communist forces staged a massive, countrywide, and wholly unexpected assault known as the **Tet offensive.** Although the communist forces were defeated decisively after several weeks of fighting, the offensive marked another important turning point in the war, as American public opinion turned increasingly against the war. Before the Tet offensive, U.S. political leaders and military planners had assumed that continued fighting would eventually lead to communist defeat. But the offensive's broad scope, unanticipated character, and level of penetration in Saigon, coupled with an increasingly critical media, undermined the optimistic military assessments that had governed the war. Thus, instead of focusing on how to win the war, political leaders began to focus on how to disengage from it. One of the major foreign policy concerns of President Richard Nixon, who assumed office in 1969, was the withdrawal of American military forces while simultaneously assuring "peace with honor." This process, which involved continuous diplomatic negotiations coupled with some of the most extensive bombing campaigns of the entire war, culminated with the **Paris Peace Treaty** of January 27, 1973.

Paris Peace Treaty (1973)
This peace accord, signed by the United States, South Vietnam, North Vietnam, and the National Liberation Front, ended the Vietnam War, thereby bringing to an end the long and costly U.S. involvement in Southeast Asia.

During this second Cold War phase, the Soviet Union intervened militarily in two Eastern European states—in Hungary in 1956 and in Czechoslovakia in 1968. In both cases Soviet military forces intervened in order to halt indigenous reform movements. According to the so-called **Brezhnev Doctrine,** coined at the time of the Prague spring uprising, Soviet-bloc states have the right to determine their domestic affairs, but only so long as the policies do not conflict with the Soviet-directed movement of international communism.

Brezhnev Doctrine
The doctrine, articulated in 1968 by President Leonid Brezhnev, that the Soviet Union had the right to intervene in Eastern-bloc states in order to preserve communist government.

These two Eastern European crises did not result in East-West confrontations because Hungary and Czechoslovakia were regarded as within the Soviet sphere of influence. Moreover, because the Soviet Union had vastly superior conventional military forces within the immediate region, it would have been unwise for the West to provide military aid to the reform movement. The two crises are significant, however, because they reinforced the Western perception of Soviet expansionism.

Detente (1969–1979)

This third phase of the Cold War was characterized by a growing relaxation of tensions between the United states and its two arch-rivals—China and the Soviet Union. The shift toward greater flexibility and accommodation derived largely from the growing isolationism of the American electorate, coupled with increased Soviet military and political influence in the world. By the late 1960s the Soviet Union had achieved strategic nuclear parity with the United States. In 1968 the Soviet Union had flexed its military muscles by invading Czechoslovakia, while in the mid-1970s it supported the placing of Cuban troops in Angola and Ethiopia to support and consolidate communist regimes in those states. Rather than directly challenging and competing with the Soviet Union, the United States chose the path of accommodation and compromise, referred to as **detente.**

Detente
The policy of relaxing tensions through accommodation.

A number of major developments expressed the growing accommodation during this eleven-year Cold War phase: (1) withdrawal of the United States from Vietnam, (2) American-Chinese accommodation after twenty-two years of hostility, and (3) arms control negotiations.

Nixon Doctrine
A 1969 promise that the U.S. would support countries threatened by aggression, provided indigenous forces assumed primary responsibility for defense.

In 1969, President Nixon announced the so-called **Nixon Doctrine,** which promised U.S. support to countries threatened by external aggression, but placed the primary responsibility for defense on indigenous forces. Applied to the Vietnam War, the doctrine resulted in a new strategy known as *Vietnamization,* calling for increased training and support for the South Vietnamese armed forces, coupled with diplomatic negotiations with North Vietnam. After four years of negotiations, the United States and North Vietnam signed the Paris Peace Treaty in 1973. The treaty provided for a cease-fire, withdrawal of U.S. military forces, the release of American prisoners of war, the self-determination of South Vietnam, and the maintenance of a divided Vietnam at the demilitarized zone (DMZ).

But after American forces disengaged from Vietnam, the South Vietnamese government was unable to defend itself from communist forces. When the North Vietnamese crossed the DMZ on March 12, 1975, they began a series of battles that eventually resulted in the conquest of South Vietnam. On April 30, 1975, South Vietnam surrendered unconditionally, thus ending a protracted conflict begun some thirty years earlier by Ho Chi Minh. Vietnam was now a single state governed by communists.

The second important manifestation of detente was the increased accommodation between China and the United States. After communism had been established in China in 1949, Sino-American relations became strained and almost nonexistent. But after taking office, President Nixon ordered a reexamination of U.S. foreign policy toward China, leading to secret exploratory meetings with Chinese leaders. These diplomatic initiatives resulted in the termination of the twenty-one-year U.S. ban on direct trade with China, Nixon's decision to visit China in 1972, and the establishment of liaison offices in Washington and Peking. The process of Sino-American accommodation culminated in 1979 with the establishment of full diplomatic relations between the two countries.

The growing relaxation (sometimes called *rapprochement*) in U.S.-Chinese relations was not a result of increased ideological compatibility between the two countries, but rather a by-product of mutual hostility to the Soviet Union. Operating under the dictum that "the enemy of my enemy is my friend," President Nixon and his National Security Advisor Henry Kissinger sought to strengthen Sino-American relations to offset Soviet expansionism.

A third highlight of detente was arms control. Believing that the management of strategic nuclear weapons was mutually beneficial, both U.S. and USSR officials began major arms control negotiations. These negotiations, known as *Strategic Arms Limitations Talks (SALT)*, resulted in two sets of agreements. The first, signed in 1972, involved an interim five-year *SALT I Accord*, establishing limits on offensive strategic nuclear weapons, and an *Anti-Ballistic Missile (ABM) Treaty*, placing limitations on strategic defensive systems. In 1979, another agreement—the *SALT II Treaty*—was signed by President Jimmy Carter and Soviet leader Leonid Brezhnev. The treaty, which established further limits on strategic warheads and launchers, was never ratified, however, because President Carter withdrew the treaty from the Senate ratification process after Soviet troops invaded Afghanistan in December 1979.

Resurgence and Demise (1980-1988)

Soviet intervention in Afghanistan marked the end of detente and the beginning of an eight-year period of intense superpower conflict, sometimes called the "new Cold War." Although the East-West conflict had decreased during detente, the Soviet regime had continued expanding and modernizing its military forces despite several arms control agreements. As Harold Brown, U.S. secretary of defense in the Carter administration, observed in the late 1970s: "When we build, they build; when we don't build, they still build." As a result of the Soviet intervention in Afghanistan coupled with the continuing growth of Soviet military forces, some American military and political leaders became disillusioned with detente and began to call for a more confrontational foreign policy, backed by a stronger military.

After assuming office in 1981, President Ronald Reagan developed a two-pronged challenge to Soviet adventurism. First, the government embarked on an unprecedented buildup of U.S. military forces, seeking to alter the perceived U.S.-USSR imbalance of military power. Second, the administration established a more confrontational foreign policy toward the East, seeking to hold the Soviet Union accountable for its foreign policy behavior. U.S. Department of Defense expenditures increased dramatically during the first Reagan administration, climbing at the fastest rate since the Korean War. The rapid increase in the defense budget produced new and more modern conventional and nuclear weapons systems and larger and better trained military forces. For example, the number of Navy ships grew by almost one third, to nearly 600, while a massive research program, the Strategic Defense Initiative (SDI), was launched to explore the feasibility of developing a comprehensive system to defend against a strategic attack. Even though the SDI never became operational, the program had an important psychological effect on the Soviet perception of U.S. military power, thereby stimulating arms control.

Reagan Doctrine
The U.S. policy of supporting weak democratic states from communist revolutionaries and of assisting anticommunist insurgencies seeking to overthrow communist regimes.

A key element of U.S. foreign policy during this fourth phase of the Cold War was the so-called **Reagan Doctrine,** which called for the support of anticommunist movements seeking greater self-determination and assistance to democratic regimes threatened by communist insurgency. It translated into covert and overt military support for anticommunist movements in such countries as Afghanistan and Nicaragua, causing increased civil strife. In both states the antigovernment assistance resulted in a loss of Soviet influence. In Afghanistan, U.S. aid to the guerrillas (*mujahedin*) helped bring about the 1988 withdrawal of Soviet troops, while U.S. aid to the anti-Sandinista rebels (contras) contributed to a regional peace plan that led to competitive presidential elections in 1990—won by anti-Sandinista candidate Violeta Chamorro. Under the Reagan Doctrine, the United States also gave military and economic assistance to governments threatened by communist insurgencies, such as El Salvador and the Philippines. As of 1991, total assistance to El Salvador exceeded $3 billion.

Beginning in the mid-1980s, U.S.-Soviet hostility again declined. Two factors contributed to the relaxation of superpower tensions. First, after coming to power in 1985, Soviet leader Mikhail Gorbachev instituted domestic reforms in order to halt his country's growing economic paralysis. The reforms would unleash forces that brought unanticipated and unprecedented developments in the Soviet Union as well as in Eastern European states. Gorbachev's two major reform policies, **glasnost** and **perestroika,** involved greater cultural, social, religious, and political freedom in Soviet society, along with increased economic decentralization.

Glasnost
The USSR policy of increased openness, developed and pursued by Soviet leader Mikhail Gorbachev in the late 1980s.

A second major development, rooted in the decline in Soviet power, was the growing willingness of the Soviet Union to curtail its military expansionism and reduce its overseas support of revolutionary regimes. This was perhaps best expressed by the willingness of the Soviet Union to agree to a complete elimination of medium-range strategic missiles. The Intermediate Nuclear Forces (INF) Treaty, signed at the Reagan-Gorbachev Summit in Washington, D.C. in 1987 and subsequently ratified by both governments, is significant because it did away with an entire class of strategic nuclear weapons.

Perestroika
Economic reform policies established by Soviet President Mikhail Gorbachev in the late 1980s, resulting in some economic decentralization.

The Soviet diplomatic retrenchment was perhaps most dramatically illustrated by Gorbachev's 1988 announcement that the Soviet Union would withdraw its military forces from Afghanistan. Foreign Minister Edward Shevardnadze, in an unprecedented admission, apologized for the Soviet Union's intervention in Afghanistan, indicating that its behavior had been contrary to the legal and moral norms of the international community. A year later, President Gorbachev admitted that the Soviet Union's intervention in Czechoslovakia in 1968 had been wrong.

At the same time, the Soviet Union reduced its support of foreign revolutionary movements in countries such as Angola, Cuba, Ethiopia, and Mozambique. As a result, the international influence of communism declined noticeably, and forced the Marxist regime to establish more moderate foreign policies. Cuba, for example, began reducing its overseas military commitments and by mid-1991 had withdrawn all of its troops formerly stationed in Ethiopia and Angola. Moreover, the Soviet Union and the United States signed a peace accord with Angola, each pledging not to assist warring factions within the country. Finally, the seventeen-year-old Marxist regime in Ethiopia, headed by Lieutenant Colonel Mengistu Haile Mariam, was overthrown by antigovernment rebels in May 1991.

THE POST–COLD WAR ERA

The Decline and Death of Soviet Communism

The collapse of communism in Eastern Europe in 1989 marks the beginning of a new era in global politics. Originating with modest political reforms in Poland and Hungary, the anticommunist movement spread throughout Eastern Europe, culminating in the "fall" of the Berlin Wall on November 9. Throughout the Cold War political leaders in Eastern Europe had attempted periodically to reform Leninist-styled communist regimes, but the Soviet Union had always brutally crushed these efforts. The last major challenge to Eastern European communism had been in Poland in 1980–1981 by **Solidarity,** a union-based political movement led by Lech Walesa, an electrician. But his efforts to increase political freedom had resulted in the imposition of martial law in 1981 and the banning of the movement.

Solidarity
A union-based political movement, led by Lech Walesa, that challenged the communist government in Poland throughout the 1980s. After winning the country's first democratic elections, Solidarity assumed power in 1989.

By the late 1980s anticommunist movements were again stirring in Eastern European countries, especially in Poland and Hungary. In Poland the continuing demands by Solidarity led to the first free parliamentary elections in any Eastern European state in forty-five years. The June 1989 elections, which Solidarity won decisively, established the first noncommunist government in Eastern Europe in the postwar era and paved the way for the eventual collapse of communist governments in other Soviet-bloc states. The pressure for increased government accountability and political freedom shifted first to Hungary, then to East Germany, Czechoslovakia, Bulgaria, and Romania. Because of the increasing rapidity with which the anticommunist reforms spread in Eastern Europe, some have suggested, albeit simplistically, that the fall of communism took ten years in Poland, ten months in Hungary, ten weeks in East Germany, and ten days in Czechoslovakia.

Following the cataclysmic events of 1989, Central European states held elections in 1990 that brought to power anticommunist governments in East Germany, Czechoslovakia, and Hungary, and severely weakened socialist regimes in Bulgaria and Romania. The East German parliamentary election in March, won decisively by antigovernment parties, was especially significant because it increased the pace of unification of East and West Germany.

Besides dramatic political reforms within Eastern European countries, the demise of Cold War rivalries resulted in a relaxation of East-West military relations, the reunification of Germany in 1990, and the collapse of communism in the Soviet Union itself—a development resulting in the political independence of the three Baltic republics (Estonia, Latvia, and Lithuania) and the establishment of a new confederal union among the remaining Soviet republics.

For nearly forty-five years democratic states had sought to thwart Soviet aggression in Europe through a defensive alliance (NATO). But as the perception of the Soviet threat decreased, Western political and military leaders began to reassess the nature and role of NATO. One of the early important by-products of reduced East-West hostility was the November 19, 1990 signing of the *Conventional Armed Forces in Europe (CFE) Treaty,* the first major conventional arms reduction agreement between NATO and Warsaw Pact member-states. Since the 1960s the two superpowers had carried out ongoing *Mutual Balanced Force Reductions (MBFR)* talks in Vienna, but had been unable to achieve any agreements. But the emergence of less hostile East-West relations created an environment conducive to reductions in conventional weapons.

Another important by-product of increased East-West cooperation was the Soviet government's decision to dissolve the Warsaw Pact. The Pact's military alliance was disestablished on March 31, 1991, while its political elements were dissolved shortly thereafter.[16] Once Eastern European countries began establishing noncommunist regimes, the demise of the Warsaw Pact was, of course, inevitable. Hungary became the first country to announce its withdrawal from the military alliance in June 1990, and by the end of the year several other Eastern European states had followed suit. Thus, by the time that the Warsaw Pact's dissolution was made official, the process was well under way. With the end of the Warsaw Pact, the Soviet Union began withdrawing its large military force (more than 600,000 soldiers) stationed in the Baltics and Eastern European states. By 1994, more than half a million troops and dependents had been withdrawn from Germany alone—a development representing the largest peacetime withdrawal of military forces not defeated in battle.[17] And by 1996, virtually all Russian (formerly Soviet) military forces had been withdrawn not only from European states but from bases around the world.

Because of a relaxation of East-West relations in the emerging post–Cold War, the United States announced in May 1991 that it would reduce its NATO forces by 50 percent (roughly 160,000 soldiers) by mid-1994. Throughout the 1970s and 1980s, the United States had maintained more than 300,000 soldiers in Europe, most of them in Germany, as a means of assuring European nations that American and European security interests were inextricably connected. But with the growing democratization of the Soviet Union and the reduction in superpower ideological rivalries, significant military reductions had become possible. And with the subsequent disintegration of the Soviet Union, further NATO force reductions were not only possible but politically prudent. Thus, the United States continued its NATO force reduction so that fewer than 80,000 U.S. troops remained stationed in Europe in 1997.

The second major post–Cold War development was the reunification of the German state. Following the establishment of a Christian Democratic government in Eastern Germany in March 1990, formal negotiations on the reunification of Germany began. Bilateral discussions were subsequently broadened to include the four allied powers (the United States, the Soviet Union, France, and Britain) that had been responsible for governing Berlin throughout the Cold War. A major breakthrough in these multilateral discussions—known as the "two plus four"—occurred in July 1990, when Soviet leader Mikhail Gorbachev announced that the Soviet government would withdraw its 350,000 troops from East Germany by 1994 and permit the unified Germany to be aligned with NATO.

The third and most significant post–Cold War development was the demise of communism in the Soviet Union itself. In August 1991, hardline communist leaders carried out an unsuccessful coup against the government of Mikhail Gorbachev. During the three days that Soviet President Gorbachev was under house arrest in Crimea, Boris Yeltsin, the head of the Russian republic, rallied public opinion against the illegal government takeover, eventually persuading military forces to return to their barracks and forcing coup leaders to flee from Moscow. In the aftermath of the coup, Gorbachev—proded by Yeltsin and supported by prodemocratic elected legislators—resigned his position as leader of the communist party and further shifted whatever political authority remained in the party to elected institutions. Yeltsin, for his part, confiscated all communist party property in the Russian Republic, placing party and government offices under continuous police control.

MAP 5.3
The Former Soviet Union

The disintegration of the Soviet Union rapidly accelerated in 1991 with the growing transfer of political authority from the central government to its fifteen republics. (See map 5.3.) On September 6, the Soviet government formally recognized the political independence of Estonia, Latvia, and Lithuania, ending Soviet control begun in 1939. And on December 8, the three leading Soviet republics—Russia, Belarus, and Ukraine—implicitly announced their independence from the Soviet state by establishing a **Commonwealth of Independent States (CIS),** an informal confederal alliance designed to facilitate economic, political, and military cooperation. On December 21, eight of the remaining nine Soviet republics (Armenia, Azerbaijan, Kazakstan, Kyrgystan, Moldova, Tajikistan, Turkmenistan, and Uzbekistan) joined the CIS. Only the small republic of Georgia declined to join the new alliance.

Although Gorbachev continued to defend the Soviet state and oppose the CIS, the transfer of political authority to the republics made the demise of the Soviet Union inevitable. Not surprisingly, on December 25 Gorbachev resigned as president of the Soviet Union, thereby confirming the death of the Soviet state. Following his resignation and the transfer of nuclear weapons control to Boris Yeltsin, the Soviet flag was lowered at the Kremlin and replaced with the Russian flag—an event signaling the end of the Soviet communist state.

Commonwealth of Independent States (CIS)
An organization that seeks to promote economic, political, and military cooperation among eleven of the fifteen former Soviet republics.

The End of the Cold War

The disintegration of the Soviet Union and the end of the Cold War came as a surprise to most Western policy makers and scholars. Because of the authoritarian character of the Soviet regime and its significant military capabilities, most policy makers in the late 1980s continued to believe that the Soviet Union, although facing significant domestic political and economic challenges, would continue indefinitely as a superpower. Moreover, most Western political leaders believed that bipolar configuration of power would continue to characterize global society.

International relations scholars were similarly surprised when the Soviet-led coalition began to dissolve in 1989, eventually resulting in the collapse of Soviet communism itself. Some of the explanations that have been given for scholars' failure to anticipate the collapse of the Soviet regime include: (a) theories of international relations had become insensitive to important and unexpected developments, in great part because of reliance on inappropriate scientific methodologies;[18] (b) the study of the Soviet Union (Sovietology) had succumbed to "group think" and was influenced by "revisionist" scholars who were overly sympathetic to the USSR;[19] and (c) because the Cold War had brought about global stability, scholars were unconsciously sympathetic to a continuation of a bipolar global system dominated by the superpowers.

Why did the Cold War end? As noted below (see issue 5.2), policy analysts and scholars attribute the fall of the Soviet Union and the end of the Cold War to many different sources. Even though historians and international relations scholars will continue to debate the causes of the Soviet empire's collapse, two competing perspectives have been especially influential, representing the major alternative orientations of many Western scholars and political leaders. The first perspective, based on an international or systemic level of analysis, attributes the fall of communism to external factors and in particular to the military containment of Soviet expansionism. During the 1980s this perspective was articulated by the Reagan administration through the strategy of "peace-through-strength."[20] The second perspective, based on a domestic or state level of anlaysis, attributes the end of the ideological conflict and collapse of the Soviet Union to internal economic and political weaknesses. Whereas the first approach credits the United States for the victory of the West, the second attributes the collapse of the Soviet Union to the flawed principles and institutions of communism.

As noted at the outset of this chapter, although the Cold War was one of the most durable disputes in world history, it also, ironically, resulted in one of the longest periods of global peace. John Lewis Gaddis, who calls this era **the long peace,** has identified several theories and arguments that help to explain the longevity of Cold War peace: first, nuclear arms, by making war unthinkable, helped to promote global peace; second, the bipolar distribution of power contributed to the stability of the international system; third, the development of a liberal international economic order was made possible by the hegemonic role of the United States; fourth, the increasing obsolescence of great power war, the increasing permeability of state borders, and the failure of command economies—tenets that Gaddis associates with an approach termed "triumphant liberalism"—have contributed to the strengthening of global society; finally, the long peace can be partly explained by the cyclic nature of history, which has, according to some scholars, demonstrated recurring patterns of hegemonic dominance.[31]

The long peace
The 45-year Cold War era that resulted in one of the longest periods of international peace.

Effects of the End of the Cold War

The precipitous decline of communism and the disintegration of the Soviet Union are the most important political events in post–World War II international relations. Even though the economic power of the United States declined relative to Europe and Japan during the 1970s and 1980s, the demise of the USSR left the United States as the undisputed power in the international system. That fact was underscored during the Persian Gulf crisis, during which time the United States led a UN-sanctioned military coalition in defeating Iraq in February 1991.

The decline of communism and the dissolution of the Soviet empire has had a number of important effects on the structures of the international community. First, *the expensive U.S.-USSR arms race ended,* resulting in a peace dividend not only for the two contestants but also for their allies. Although both Russia and the United States continue to maintain comparatively large and well-equipped armed forces in the late 1990s, the financial resources allocated to defense by Russia and the United States in 1997 were at least 35 to 40 percent less than would have been the case had the Cold War not ended. In addition, the United States has greatly reduced its overseas military forces, cutting, for example, its NATO forces in Europe

Issue 5.2 Explanations of the End of the Cold War

What caused the Cold War to come to a surprising, abrupt, and peaceful end? Although no consensus exists among scholars as to why the Soviet Union collapsed and the Cold War ended, two theories—one based on geopolitics and the other based on domestic political economy—have dominated. The first emphasizes the role of international developments and especially the role of the United States in challenging Soviet power; the second emphasizes the structural shortcomings of socialist economics and authoritarian and totalitarian politics. Following are some selected views on the meaning and causes of the Cold War's end:

> Democracy won the World Series. In some large part this happened due to modern communications. The victory was cultural and ideological; the weapons were informational.[21]
>
> Ben J. Wattenberg, social scientist

> Nobody—no country, no party, no person—"won" the Cold War. It was a long and costly political rivalry, fueled on both sides by unreal and exaggerated estimates of the intentions and strength of the other party. It greatly overstrained the economic resources of both countries, leaving both, by the end of the 1980s, confronted with heavy financial, social and, in the case of the Russians, political problems that neither had anticipated and for which neither was fully prepared.[22]
>
> George F. Kennan, former U.S. diplomat and noted scholar

> The real victor in the Cold War is not the policy of any particular administration or the activities of any particular movement, but the Western system itself . . . .The real genius of the Western system has not been its coherent and far-sighted policy, but the vitality and attractiveness of its policy.[23]
>
> Daniel Deudney and G. John Ikenberry, political scientists

> The United States and its allies won the Cold War for two reasons. First, the United States formed a new coalition after the war with its allies, Britain and France, and eventually the defeated powers—Germany, Japan, and Italy. The new coalition proved far too strong for the Soviet Union, especially after the defection of communist China . . . .The United States did not win the Cold War only because the Soviet Union was contained . . . .The Soviet system failed because it was inherently and fatally flawed.[24]
>
> William G. Hyland, former senior U.S. government official

> What happened in the revolutionary year 1989 was that liberty suddenly found itself pushing against an open door. The balance swung away from power with breath-

taking speed; the authoritarian alternatives that have dominated so much of twentieth-century history were revealed to be, for the most part, hollow shells. We have good reason to hope that liberty will flourish in the next few years as it has not in our lifetime, and it is in that context that the real nature of the West's "victory" in the Cold War becomes clear. For it was authoritarianism that suffered the real defeat, and in that sense all of us—including our old Cold War adversaries—have won.[25]

> John Lewis Gaddis, diplomatic historian

> No, the end of the old [Soviet] system was due to its complete inherent rottenness and non-viability and when the facts left no alternative, its new rulers tried by new policies to save rather than to abandon the system.[26]
>
> Robert Conquest, historian of the Soviet Union

> The West did not, as is widely believed, win the Cold War through geopolitical containment and military deterrence. Nor was the Cold War won by the Reagan military buildup and the Reagan Doctrine, as some have suggested. Instead, "victory" for the West came when a new generation of Soviet leaders realized how badly their system at home and their policies abroad had failed. What containment did was to successfully stalemate Moscow's attempt to advance Soviet hegemony. Over four decades it performed the historic function of holding Soviet power in check until the internal seeds of destruction within the Soviet Union and its empire could mature. At that point, however, it was Gorbachev who brought the Cold War to an end.[27]
>
> Raymond L. Garthoff, Cold War scholar and former diplomat

> The Cold War ended on the terms set by the United States . . . .I believe the Cold War ended because, in the mid-1980s, we had the coincidence of (1) a policy that combined strength and firmness, with a willingness to negotiate fairly and (2) a Soviet leadership that finally realized that the country could not go on as it had, that it had to change internally, but that it could do this only in cooperation with the outside world. Gorbachev, Reagan, and America's allies all deserve full credit for the essential roles they played in this process.[28]
>
> Jack F. Matlock, Jr., last U.S. ambassador to the Soviet Union

> In hindsight, it is apparent that Gorbachev's initiatives began the process that brought the Cold War to an end.[29]
>
> Richard Ned Lebow and Janice Gross Stein, international relations scholars

> The proponents of liberal society were proven right. After seventy years of trial, communism turned out—by the confession of its own leaders—to be an economic, political, and moral disaster. Democracy won the political argument between the East and the West. The market won the economic argument.[30]
>
> Arthur Schlesinger, Jr., noted U.S. historian

A statue of Lenin is removed from Bucharest, Romania, symbolizing the end of forty years of Communist rule.

from about 300,000 troops to less than 80,000. Finally, Russia and the United States have carried out significant reductions in the number of nuclear weapons and placed its strategic arsenals on a low alert status.

A second consequence of the end of the Cold War is that *communism has become a discredited theory of political economy*. After the Soviet Union collapsed, political leaders in Russia and other former communist republics embarked on the implemention of economic reforms based on privatization and free enterprise. Russia's repudiation of state socialism and adoption of market-based economic reforms had an especially profound impact in the discrediting of Marxist-Leninist principles of political economy. Robert Heilbroner has described the loss of socialism's influence as follows:

> Less than seventy-five years after it officially began, the contest between capitalism and socialism is over: capitalism has won. The Soviet Union, China, and Eastern Europe have given us the clearest possible proof that capitalism organizes the material affairs of humankind more satisfactorily than socialism: that however inequitably or irresponsibly the marketplace may distribute goods, it does so better than the queues of a planned economy; however mindless the culture of commercialism, it is more attractive than state moralism; and however deceptive the ideology of a business civilization, it is more believable than that of a socialist one.[32]

The discrediting of central economic planning in the former Soviet empire, coupled with the relative economic success of free enterprise in East Asia and se-

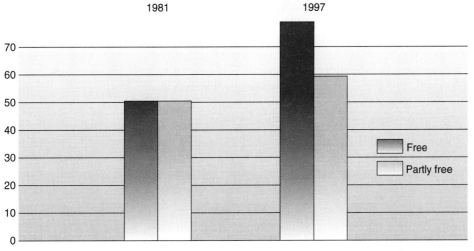

FIGURE 5.1
Comparison of
Political Freedom,
1981 and 1997
Sources: Raymond Gastil,
Freedom in the World: Political Rights & Civil Liberties, 1981 (Westport:
Greenwood Press, 1981),
p. 102; and Adrian Karatnycky et. al., *Freedom in the
World: The Annual Survey
of Political Rights & Civil
Liberties,* 1996–1997 (New
York: Freedom House,
1997), p. 5.

lected states in Latin America and elsewhere, has resulted in a growing popularity of capitalism. In Latin America, for example, a number of countries, including Argentina, Brazil, and Mexico, are following Chile's example of market economics. In Asia and Africa, too, a growing number of states, including India, Ghana, Zambia, and Zimbabwe, have abandoned state planning in favor of privatization of state enterprises and market-oriented domestic and international economic policies.

A third important consequence of the end of the Cold War and the death of Soviet communism has been *the expansion of political freedom and democratic governments.* As noted in figure 5.1, the number of states classified as "free" increased by 55 percent (from 51 to 79) during the 1981–1997 period, while the number of "partly free" countries increased by 16 percent (from 51 to 59). Even though the total number of persons governed by free and partly free regimes increased from 2.58 billion to 3.51 billion during this seventeen-year period, the percentage of the world's population ruled by democratic or partly democratic governments increased only marginally (from 57 percent of the world's population in 1981 to 61 percent in 1997) because of dramatic increases in the world's total population.[33] To be sure, although the post–Cold War expansion of democracy has been due to many factors, the end of the Cold War and the dissolution of the Soviet Union have surely contributed significantly. As of 1997, communist governments remained in power in only a few countries including Belarus, China, Cuba, and North Korea.

The death of Soviet communism has greatly weakened radical regimes and communist political parties worldwide. Because the Soviet Union served as the chief source of economic, political, and military aid in propagating the communist faith during the Cold War, the demise of the Soviet state has greatly handicapped foreign communist movements and political organizations. For example, Marxist revolutionary governments, such as the Sandinistas in Nicaragua and the Mengistu revolutionary regime in Ethiopia, were replaced in 1990 and 1991, respectively. Moreover, communist guerrilla movements, such as those in El Salvador (FMLN) and in the Philippines (NPA), have ceased to pose credible military threats to ruling authorities.

Finally, the end of the Cold War has resulted in *greater harmony and cooperation between Russia and the West.* The increased accommodation and cooperation between the United States and Russia has been encouraged and facilitated by Russia's adoption and implementation of democratic structures and free enterprise reforms. Although Russia continues in 1997 to institutionalize democratic capitalism, relations between Russia and the West have become increasingly cooperative. For example, despite Russia's strenuous opposition to NATO membership for former

Soviet-bloc states, Russia accepted, in the end, NATO's inclusion of Hungary, Poland, and the Czech Republic in mid-1997 after it was promised a voice in NATO affairs. Similarly, in 1997 Russia became a member of the so-called Group of Seven (G-7), the Western economic summit, thereby further consolidating Russia's increasing participation in the global economy. Although Russia is now part of the Group of Eight (G-8), it still awaits membership in the World Trade organization (WTO). Membership is likely in the near future after it has implemented more comprehensive economic liberalization policies.

THE FUTURE WORLD ORDER

Even though post–Cold War regional security arrangements are still emerging, it is clear that, with the collapse of the Soviet Union and the contraction of Russian influence, power is becoming more diffuse in the international system, especially within Europe and Asia. As noted above, the United States has emerged as the preeminent power in the world, and although its military and economic power will continue to dominate into the next century, it is unlikely that U.S. power will translate into a unipolar structure. Rather, given the absence of the U.S. imperial ambitions, the growing economic power of China, Japan, and the European Union, and the increasing interdependence of global society, the structure of world order will continue to evolve. Even though it is impossible to predict the future, the international system of the twenty-first century is likely to be characterized by four features: (1) increasing international instability, (2) conflicts based on nonideological sources, (3) growing fragmentation of nation-states, and (4) a uni-multipolar global structure.

International Instability

Although the bitter ideological conflicts of the Cold War no longer persist in the international community, future global relations will continue to be conflictual. In the early 1990s one scholar bemoaned the ending of the Cold War because he foresaw increasing political instability due to the rising multipolarity and growing inequality of military power among states.[34] Others, however, have rejected this pessimistic assessment, arguing that an increasingly multipolar world, supported by an increasingly integrated Europe, could provide a stable foundation for not only economic expansion but also for stable political relationships.[35] Regardless of how one interprets the end of the Cold War, it is evident that the collapse of communism has not ushered in a new world order.

Although some analysts may have hoped for a more peaceful world, international conflict not only persists, but has become more diffuse. Throughout the Cold War, the bipolar military balance of power not only enhanced global order but also inhibited "hot" wars primarily because the East-West polar structure provided a framework for managing international conflict. Because of the pervasive influence of the two superpowers, the domestic politics and international relations of many developing nations were greatly influenced by the U.S.-USSR ideological conflict. However, the collapse of the bipolar order has not ushered in a peaceful new world order in Asia, Africa, and Latin America; rather, it has resulted in increased state fragmentation and growing international conflict. As one scholar has observed, the end of the Cold War has not been a historical watershed, as some have alleged, but rather a continuation of the anarchic, decentralized political order that has characterized IR since the eighteenth century.[36]

Nonideological Conflict

Although ideology was the principal source of international disputes during the Cold War era, the major sources of future domestic and international political conflict in the post–Cold War era are religious, ethnic, and economic, rather than ideological. Samuel Huntington has argued that culture has replaced ideology as the major source of communal cohesion and conflict. In his view, because communal affinities are increasingly rooted in religion, culture, and ethnicity, the most significant international conflicts in the future will be based on civilizational ties. Huntington thus argues that future global politics will involve a fundamental "clash of civilizations."[37] Whether one agrees with Huntington's thesis, it is clear that cultural, tribal, ethnic, and religious factors have contributed to the growth of domestic and interstate conflict in the post–Cold War years.

Economic issues have also become more important sources of post–Cold War conflict. Although international trade has periodically contributed to global competition in previous eras, commercial, environmental, and developmental issues have become increasingly important in global politics. Two factors have contributed to the rising importance of economic conflict. First, the economic development of the Third World has resulted in a significant growth in economic production and a dramatic rise in consumer exports from some developing economies to the developed nations. As a result, a number of industrial states have developed significant trade imbalances, thereby heightening protectionist demands from labor groups. The U.S.-China trade conflict of the 1990s, for example, has been rooted in large U.S. trade deficits with China (more than $40 billion annually) and in the belief that China's economy is not sufficiently open to Western goods and services. A second source of post-Cold War economic conflict is the high levels of unemployment in Western Europe and the increasing difficulty in maintaining generous state-sponsored social and welfare services. In 1997 the unemployment rate in most European states was above 10 percent, with a total Western European unemployment estimated at 18 million persons. Because government revenues had declined in response to modest economic growth, most developed governments have been forced to reduce welfare programs. In response to continuing high unemployment and public sector cutbacks, workers have demanded greater protection from perceived unjust foreign competition, thereby heightening international economic tensions.

Fragmentation of States

The post–Cold War era is also characterized by growing fragmentation of states, as ethnic, religious, and political groups demand increasing political self-determination. During the Cold War, ethnonationalistic claims were held in check by ideologies, but with the ending of the East-West dispute, tribal, ethnic, religious, and political groups have demanded more political autonomy. Ethnonationalistic claims have been especially powerful in multinational territories of the former Soviet Union and in eastern and central Europe. For example, Czechoslovakia divided in two states—the Slovak Republic and the Czech Republic—while Yugoslavia disintegrated into Slovenia, Croatia, Bosnia and Herzegovina, and Macedonia, leaving the Federal Republic of Yugoslavia with less than one-third of its original territory. Moreover, ethnonationalism was especially strong in such former Soviet republics as Armenia, Azerbaijan, Georgia, Turkmenistan, and Tajikistan, as well as in such African states as Burundi, Congo (formerly Zaire), Liberia, Rwanda, Somalia, and Sierra Leone. Whether state fragmentation continues to increase is impossible to predict, but based on the post–Cold War rise in ethnonationalistic claims in international affairs, continued state fragmentation is likely to continue in the foreseeable future.

Uni-Multipolar World

A final feature of the post–Cold War world is its uni-mulitpolar structure. In the late twentieth century it is clear that the United States is the only superpower. Although other states exert significant influence in global society, the economic and military power of the United States is unrivaled. Although the United States remains the dominant power, and may account for a "unipolar moment" in the immediate aftermath of the collapse of the Soviet Union,[38] the structure of global society in the late 1990s is also increasingly multipolar, with states such as Germany, Japan, and China exerting growing influence in global society and regional blocs, especially the European Union and the Pacific Basic states, commanding greater influence in global decision making. As a result, although the United States remains the preeminent power, the structure of the international community is increasingly multipolar. Thus, the international system is uni-multipolar and likely to remain so in the foreseeable future.

In Conclusion

Even though the long and bitter Cold War is over, the quest for peace and justice still remains. Because the global system continues to be anarchic, international conflicts will continue, although their shape and form will no longer be influenced by the superpower contest between Western democracy and Soviet communism. Whether or not another ideological conflict will replace the East-West dispute is unclear. What is certain is that international political disputes will continue but in a new form.

Currently Eastern European nations and the former Soviet republics are carrying out unprecedented economic and political reforms—shifting their economies from command to market systems, and transforming political cultures and institutions from centralized, autocratic regimes to pluralistic, competitive political systems. To the extent that these reforms succeed, they are likely to result in more powerful global actors that will significantly impact international relations in the future.

SUMMARY

1. The dominant systemic conflict in the postwar international system was the Cold War. The conflict, which began in 1945 and lasted until 1989, is characterized by the dominance of superpowers, emphasis on ideological conflict, an avoidance of direct military conflict between the superpowers, and a high level of misperception.

2. Although the Cold War began shortly after the end of World War II, the seeds of the conflict were sown earlier. Scholars interpret the origins of the East-West conflict from radically different points of view.

3. During its forty-five-year history, the Cold War evolved through four distinct phases:

emergence, hostility and confrontation, detente, and renewal and demise of conflict. In the first phase, the United States established the policy of containment, which was to serve as the dominant aim of its foreign policy during the Cold War. Two major conflicts epitomize the era of hostility—the Korean conflict and the Vietnam War. In the era of detente, the superpowers increased their cooperation, concluding, among other things, SALT I and the ABM Treaty. The fourth phase involved increased conflict, as the United States sought to directly challenge Soviet expansionism with the Reagan doctrine. The rise to power of Mikhail Gorbachev resulted in significant domestic reforms and a moderation of Soviet foreign policy.

4. The Cold War ceased with the fall of the Berlin Wall on November 9, 1989. The fall of the wall resulted from the growing democratization in Eastern Europe, coupled with a declining ability and willingness of the Soviet government to maintain communist regimes beyond its borders.

5. As a result of the demise of the Cold War, East and West Germany were reunified in 1990, while the Soviet Union dissolved the Warsaw Pact and announced the withdrawal of its military forces with Eastern European states. The United States, for its part, has greatly reduced its NATO forces.

6. The most extraordinary post–Cold War development occurred in the Soviet Union itself in 1991 with the collapse of the USSR.

Since then, former Soviet republics have, in differing degrees, implemented democratic institutions and practices and sought to decentralize domestic economic structures, privatizing a growing number of state enterprises. The end of the Cold War has had a number of effects, including: the ending of an expensive superpower arms race, the discrediting of socialism, the expansion of democracy, and the growth of cooperation between Russia and the West.

7. Although it is impossible to predict the future, in the light of post–Cold War developments, the international system is likely to be characterized by : (1) increasing global instability, (2) conflicts based on nonideological sources, (3) increasing fragmentation of states, and (4) a uni-multipolar global structure.

KEY TERMS

Cold War

North Atlantic Treaty Organization (NATO)

Warsaw Treaty Organization (Warsaw Pact)

democracy

communism

proxy war

spheres of influence

containment

Truman Doctrine

Marshall Plan

Vietcong

Gulf of Tonkin Resolution

Tet offensive

Paris Peace Treaty

Brezhnev Doctrine

detente

Nixon Doctrine

Reagan Doctrine

glasnost

perestroika

Solidarity

Commonwealth of Independent States (CIS)

the long peace

RECOMMENDED READINGS

Colton, Timothy J., and Robert Legvold, eds. *After the Soviet Union: From Empire to Nations*. New York: W.W. Norton, 1992. A penetrating collection of essays by leading scholars on post-communist regimes in the former Soviet Union. Topics addressed include politics, economics, national security, nationalism, and foreign policy.

Gaddis, John L. *The Long Peace: Inquiries into the History of the Cold War*. New York: Oxford University Press, 1987. A collection of readable and insightful essays on the origins and evolution of the Cold War.

———. *The U.S. and the End of the Cold War*. New York: Oxford University Press, 1992. This leading historian sets forth his views on the ending of the Cold War.

———. *We Now Know: Rethinking Cold War History*. New York: Oxford University Press, 1997. Drawing on recently declassified materials, Gaddis uses Soviet, East European, and Chinese sources to explain what is currently known about the nature and evolution of the Cold War, from its inception to the Cuban missile crisis.

Garthoff, Raymond L. *Detente and Confrontation: American-Soviet Relations From Nixon to Reagan*. Washington, D.C.: The Brookings Institution, 1985. An exhaustive study of the historical development of American-Soviet relations from 1969 to 1984 based in part on the author's role as a former U.S. diplomat.

———. *The Great Transition: American-Soviet Relations and the End of the Cold War*. Washington, D.C.: The Brookings Institution, 1994. An authoritative and comprehensive account of U.S.-Soviet relations in the 1980s. Garthoff provides an illuminating account of the forces and developments that brought about a collapse of the Soviet communist system and the end of the Cold War.

Hyland, William G. *The Cold War: Fifty Years of Conflict*. New York: Random House, 1990. A succinct, well-organized, and readable overview of the Cold War by a leading foreign affairs scholar and former senior White House official.

Kegley, Charles W., Jr. *The Long Postwar Peace: Contending Explanations and Projections*. New York: HarperCollins, 1991. This collection of essays, based on papers given at a 1989 conference, examines alternative perspectives on the nature, origins, and impact of the postwar peace.

Lebow, Richard Ned and Janice Gross Stein. *We All Lost the Cold War*. Princeton: Princeton University Press, 1994. A study of the role of nuclear deterrence and compellence during the Cold War based on two case studies—the Cuban missile crisis and the 1973 Middle East crisis. The authors argue that, contrary to the conventional wisdom, superpower strategies tended to provoke and exacerbate conflict, rather than to restrain it.

Mearsheimer, John. "Back to the Future: Instability in Europe After the Cold War," *International Security,* 15 (Summer 1990), pp. 5–56. A provocative and influential article suggesting that the end of the Cold War is likely to be destabilizing to Europe.

Spanier, John. *American Foreign Policy Since World War II.* 12th ed. New York: Holt Rinehart and Winston, 1991. This widely used text provides a lucid historical overview of the evolution of the Cold War.

RELEVANT WEB SITES

Avalon Project, Yale Law School
    Data on U.S. diplomacy

www.yale.edu/lawweb/avalon/avalon.htm

Cold War International History Project
    (Woodrow Wilson Center)

www.cwihp.si.edu/default.htm

Library of Congress
    The Soviet Union and the United States

http://lcweb.loc.gov/exhibits/archives/intro.html

NATO

www.nato.int

U.S. Department of State
    U.S. Foreign Relations Series

www.state.gov/www/about_state/history

Power in World Politics   6

International politics, like all politics, is a struggle for power.[1]

Hans J. Morgenthau, *political scientist*

There is nothing more difficult to take in hand, more perilous to conduct, or more uncertain in its success, than to take the lead in the introduction of a new order of things.[2]

Niccolò Machiavelli, *sixteenth-century political thinker and diplomat*

. . . defense is more important than economic growth, political ideology, or the legal principle pacta sunt servanda. More important, that is, to the state, to national government and those who shape these policies.[3]

Susan Strange, *British political economist*

Power is one of the most important concepts in international politics. Because the world's tangible and intangible resources are limited and the wants of states are unlimited, conflict among nations is inevitable. States that have greater power will tend to be more successful in protecting and promoting their national interests than other states. Moreover, each state needs power because it is responsible for its own security and the promotion of vital interests in the world. Kenneth Waltz, a leading international relations theorist, observes that power provides states with four important resources: (1) maintenance of autonomy, (2) increased freedom of action, (3) greater margin of safety, and (4) greater influence in the international community.[4]

Despite its significance, power remains one of the most elusive concepts in international relations. Although the term is widely used by lay and professional people alike, few understand it. But if government officials are to effectively advance national interests, they must be able to anticipate world political conditions and to accurately assess the barometer of power. That is, they must understand existing distributions of power as well as the ongoing shifts of power among the world's leading states. Just as a meteorologist seeks to predict the weather and anticipate storms, so a statesman seeks to anticipate potential conflicts and cataclysmic wars.

One of the most widely debated themes in world politics is the extent to which power determines the international relations of states. On the one hand, scholars of the tradition of realism characterize world politics as "power politics," in which the map of the world is made and sustained by the coercive, competitive actions of states. On the other hand, idealists assume that building a stable harmonious international community is possible by developing international legal and governmental institutions. This text, rooted in idealist and realist perspectives, assumes that politics involves an interplay of power and ethics, political organization and moral purpose. It is an error to regard politics as purely a struggle for power, but it is equally dangerous to view it as purely a quest for justice through cooperative human ventures. The distinguished historian E. H. Carr has wisely observed that "political action must be based on a co-ordination of morality and power. . . . It is as fatal in politics to ignore power as it is to ignore morality."[5]

This chapter examines the nature and role of power in world affairs. First, power is defined by comparing it to other related concepts and by identifying some of its key characteristics. Second, some of the important tangible and intangible elements of power are examined. Third, some of the challenges posed by the measurement of power are discussed. It concludes with an examination of some major patterns of power, giving special emphasis to the role of balance and hegemonic distribution.

THE NATURE OF POWER

To better clarify its nature, power must be differentiated from the related concepts of influence, authority, and force. After defining the concept, this section examines some important features of power in world politics.

Definition

Influence
The ability of an actor to alter the preferences and behavior of another actor.

Influence involves the ability to alter another person or group's behavior. Thus one state (A) is considered to have influence over another state (B) when A can get B to do something it would not do otherwise. Influence can be achieved through noncoercive or coercive methods. Noncoercive influence involves the altering of behavior through peaceful, nonthreatening means such as persuasion, manipulation, deceit, propaganda, and the promise of rewards. Coercive influence involves the use of threats or force to alter behavior.

Authority
The capacity to command obedience through voluntary, noncoercive means.

Authority, the most important form of noncoercive influence, is the capacity to command obedience without compulsion or threat of coercion. Authority does not rest on the superior force of those issuing commands but derives from voluntary acceptance of the right of persons or institutions to make society-wide decisions. In other words, authority is based on the inherent or consensual right of rulers and governing institutions to make binding decisions for a political community. Because authority is the most efficient way of building and maintaining consensus, it is an essential element of decision making within domestic political communities. But authority is almost totally absent in world politics because there is no commonly accepted governmental institution that can make binding decisions on member-states. As a result, whereas authority is the basis of domestic politics, power is the foundation of world politics.

Power
The capacity to determine outcomes.

Power, the most common form of coercive influence, is the ability to determine outcomes. Power can be realized through a variety of methods ranging from positive inducements ("carrots") to negative threats ("sticks"); from "soft," co-optive strategies to "hard," coercive commands. Regardless of how it is realized, power involves being able to control other individuals, groups, or states, as well as to establish partial control over the environment. Political scientist Karl Deutsch has defined power as "the ability to prevail in conflict and to overcome obstacles."[6] Deutsch's definition calls attention to the capability of prevailing—of getting one's way in spite of the wills and interests of other governments. If a state is to prevail against the interests of other states, it must be able to overcome the goals of opposing states. This will require tangible and intangible resources with which to induce, if not compel, another state to alter its behavior.

Force
The application of military power in order to punish or compel; applied coercion.

Force involves the implicit or explicit use, or threat of use, of coercion to punish or to compel. In effect, it is coercive power. Force is the most violent and costly method of bringing about political influence because it depends on military and police power to achieve goals. Force may be applied in different ways. The

128

most extreme application is war, which involves the use of military power to compel or punish an enemy. At the opposite extreme is deterrence, which involves solely the threat, but not use, of coercion. Deterrence is the most efficient use of coercive power because it seeks to inhibit undesirable outcomes only by threatening punishment. It is a more efficient use of force because it does not use the coercive resources of a state.

Characteristics of Power

Power has several important features. First, *power is relational.* Like influence, power is not a tangible resource but a dimension of interpersonal, intergroup, or interstate relations. To say that the United States is a powerful nation means that it has significant capabilities relative to other states. Because power is defined relative to other countries, a state's power can increase either by a rise in its own capabilities or by a decline in the power of other states. For example, although the power of the United States had undoubtedly declined from the 1950s to the 1980s relative to Europe and Japan, American power increased substantially in the late 1980s relative to the Soviet Union.

Second, *power is primarily a means, not an end.* Karl Deutsch has written that power is the currency of politics, just as money is the currency of economies. Money provides the means for acquiring goods and services; by contrast, power provides the means for getting one's way.[7] In domestic affairs, power provides the means for developing and sustaining community life; in international politics, power is the means by which states protect and maximize their interests in the world system. Given the anarchic structure of the international community, power is a major determinant of a state's ability to protect and expand its national interests. In effect, national power will determine the state's freedom of action in the world community.

Not all students of world politics accept the instrumental view of power. A central tenet of political realism is that politics is itself a quest for power. Political realists, like Niccolò Machiavelli, Thomas Hobbes, and Hans Morgenthau, argue that political power, while providing a state with the means to achieve its interests, is fundamentally an end in itself. Power is an end because without it nothing else is possible. In his classic study *Politics Among Nations,* Morgenthau writes that "statesmen think and act in terms of interest defined as power."[8] He goes on to suggest that "if the desire for power cannot be abolished everywhere in the world, those who might be cured would simply fall victim to the power of others." It is imperative, therefore, for the statesman to acquire and manage power.[9]

Third, *power is based on perception.* Power is not a tangible good but a belief that an individual or community can prevail. A reputation of power confers power. Although tangible resources are important in providing a credible basis for people's perceptions, ultimately power is based on what people think. A state may have significant economic and military resources, but if people do not believe in the final analysis that those resources will be used to coerce and compel another state, they will contribute little to power. For example, Israel's success on the battlefield (e.g., the Six-Day War in 1967) and in covert operations (e.g., the successful 1976 Entebbe raid to rescue Jewish hostages in Uganda) significantly enhanced its reputation, whereas the U.S. failure in the Vietnam War and its unsuccessful hostage rescue operation in Iran in 1980 contributed to a decline in perceived American power.

Fourth, *power is multidimensional.* That is, there are many ways by which power can be exerted over others. If, as the distinguished political realist Hans Morgenthau has noted, power comprises "anything that establishes and maintains the control of man over man,"[10] then it may be exerted through a variety of means, including military, economic, psychological, cultural, and technological instruments. Because the international environment in which power is used is continually shifting with the changing wants, interests, and vulnerabilities of states, the ability to control other states and aspects of the international environment will depend on the relative usefulness of the instruments of power. For example, the dependence of some industrial states on oil imports, coupled with the cohesion of oil-exporting nations (achieved largely through the Organization of Petroleum Exporting Countries) has resulted in a relative increase in economic power to the major oil-exporting states and a relative decline in the most vulnerable oil-importing states.

Fifth, *power is dynamic*. It is continually changing as the relative capabilities of states rise and decline. Because power is the political currency of international relations, states can increase or decrease their levels of power, depending on the rate at which power is created and used. If states use power carelessly, or if they overspend their currency of power, they may end up politically bankrupt. As in economic life, states must save and invest resources in order to expand their political stock of power.

The relative changes of power among states are rooted in the shifting political, economic, and military resources of states. During the eighteenth century, for example, countries like the Netherlands, Spain, Sweden, and the Ottoman Empire were major international powers, but by the beginning of the nineteenth century, they had lost their dominant status. During the nineteenth century Great Britain ruled the seas virtually unchallenged, but by the mid-twentieth century its power and prestige had declined dramatically. Table 6.1 illustrates the changing configuration of great powers since the eighteenth century.

Meta-power
The ability to make, sustain, and reform the fundamental rules and institutions of the international system.

Finally, *power can be institutionalized* by establishing rules, regimes, and institutions that reflect the distribution of power among groups and communities. Political scientist Stephen Krasner defines the capacity to create and modify procedures, rules, and institutions as **meta-power**.[11] Unlike relational power, which

TABLE 6.1 Great Powers in the World, 1700–2020

	1700	1800	1875	1910	1935	1945	1990	2020 (projection)
*Turkey**	x							
Sweden	x							
Netherlands	x							
Spain	x							
*Austria***	x	x	x	x				
France	x	x	x	x	x			x
*England****	x	x	x	x	x			x
*Prussia*****		x	x	x	x			x
*Russia******		x	x	x	x	x		x
Italy			x	x	x			
Japan				x	x			x
United States				x	x	x	x	x
China								x

*Ottoman Empire **Austria-Hungary ***Great Britain ****Germany *****Soviet Union

Source: Kenneth Waltz, *Theory of International Politics* (Reading, MA: Addison-Wesley, 1979), p. 169 and the author's own estimates and projections.

involves, the maximization of influence within established boundaries, meta-power is the capacity to create, modify, or transform institutions and systems. In creating the United Nations at the end of World War II, for example, the five major states (United States, USSR, Britain, France, and China) institutionalized their power in the new organization by giving themselves permanent membership in the Security Council and requiring that all of its substantive decisions be made with their consent. More recently, the developing nations used meta-power in attempting to alter the existing rules and institutions of the international economic system and establish norms that were more favorable to them. As noted in chapter 15, although the developing nations were able to make some modest changes in the rules of the global economy, they were unsuccessful in implementing their proposed New International Economic Order (NIEO).

Power can also be differentiated in terms of the methods used to exert control. Two fundamentally different approaches are available. The direct strategy—sometimes defined as command or **"hard" power**—seeks to influence behavior through coercive threats or positive inducements. Examples of "hard" power include war, the threat of military intervention, and economic sanctions. Additionally, the U.S. nuclear strategy of deterrence and NATO's Cold War policy of "flexible response," designed to counter any Soviet military threat against Western European states, are based on "hard" power resources.

The indirect strategy—called co-optive or **"soft" power**—seeks to achieve behavioral outcomes by establishing environmental preconditions that facilitate and encourage desired results.[12] The aim of "soft" power is to get foreign actors to pursue the goals and behaviors of the home state—to get others to want what you want. Some resources that are important in co-optive behavioral power include political ideals and ideologies, cultural patterns, and global and regional economic and political structures. During the Cold War the United States used its influence to

Hard power
The ability to influence the behavior of international actors through coercive threats or positive inducements.

Soft power
The ability to influence international affairs through co-optive strategies involving political ideals, cultural values, and economic and social norms.

Aircraft carriers, capable of carrying about 100 planes and 5,000 sailors, are one of the most important instruments for projecting military power in distant lands.

foster democratic systems and to encourage capitalist economies, whereas the Soviet Union sought to encourage Communist regimes committed to state-regulated and state-owned enterprises. But with the collapse of the Soviet Union, democratic capitalism has become the dominant norm in the post–Cold War world. In former Soviet republics and central European countries governments have increased privatization and encouraged private enterprise. Similarly, throughout the Third World leading Asian, African, and Latin American countries, including such influential states as Argentina, Brazil, India, and Mexico, have adopted market-based economic strategies and have embarked on the privatization of state-owned enterprises.

ELEMENTS OF POWER

Political scientists commonly define power as the ability to control or alter behavior. Although such a definition is useful to scholars analyzing the historical evolution of international relations, it is of little help to government officials responsible for the affairs of state. What statesmen need is a framework to guide decision making, not an elusive or ephemeral standard for measuring power. In effect, government officials need to define power in terms of widely accepted elements rather than in behavioral abstractions. Although power is ultimately a subjective assessment about the ability to determine events, the judgments about a state's power are rooted in its capabilities, which are dependent in great measure on tangible and intangible resources. Tangible elements, such as wealth, population, and territory, and intangible elements, such as national morale and quality of government, provide a state with **potential power.** The effective use of resources to control other states and the international environment results in **actual power.**[13]

Potential power
The anticipated capacity of a state to determine outcomes based on its tangible and intangible resources.

For example, in 1990 Japan had the second largest gross national product in the world, yet its power was considered less than that of nations like Britain, France, and Germany. Japan's potential power was thus higher than its actual power. By contrast, Israel, though a small state with limited natural resources and a middle-income economy, was widely regarded as a major Middle East power. Its enhanced power reputation was due to its military successes, especially the Six-Day War of 1967. In a sense, Israel's actual power was greater than its potential power.

Actual power
An actor's ability to determine other actors' behavior in view of its effective utilization of tangible and intangible resources.

Tangible Elements

Numerous physical attributes contribute to a nation's power. Some of the most important are: territory, population, natural resources, level of economic development, and military capacity.

Territory

The physical size, location, and terrain of a country can contribute significantly to its power. A large territory is generally considered advantageous to a state, although there is no necessary connection between size and power. The size of a country is generally considered important insofar as it serves as a source of plentiful raw materials and provides strategic military advantages for defending the territory. Large countries like Canada, Russia, and the United States benefit not only from an abundance of material resources, but also from extensive land in which to mobilize military forces.

A nation's terrain also contributes to the power of a state. Mountainous terrains as found in the Andean countries of Ecuador, Peru, and Bolivia, or in the Alps in Switzerland and northern Italy, can serve as a deterrent to foreign aggression. At the same time, terrain can impede national economic and political integration and thereby inhibit the economic potential of a state.

Finally, the location of a state is of crucial significance. Morgenthau suggests that a nation's location is "the most stable factor upon which power of a nation depends."[14] He argues that the power of the United States is influenced significantly by the fact that its territory is separated from other continents by large bodies of water. Similarly, Britain's location as an island has historically contributed to its national power by providing greater ease in protecting national boundaries from foreign aggression.

Population

National populations, and especially population densities, vary greatly from state to state. Although the size of a nation's population is not a key determinant of power, it nevertheless contributes to the power potential of a country in part because it determines the size of the pool from which soldiers are selected for military service. In general, the most influential states in the world are those with large military forces, and these, with few exceptions, tend to be nations with large populations. (See fig. 6.1.) Of course, states allocate different levels of manpower to national defense. States confronting regional hostilities, such as Cambodia, El Salvador, and South Korea, devote a relatively large portion of their manpower to the armed forces.

A most important quality of a national population is its esprit de corps and professional competence. Because an educated and highly motivated population is indispensable to national economic and political development, nations with high levels of illiteracy, limited social mobility, and high levels of apathy are much less likely to generate national power than those with highly skilled and determined populations.

A large population also contributes to a nation's economic potential by providing a large supply of laborers as well as a large market for goods and services. What is important, of course, is not the size of the population per se but its overall potential. Although both India and China are the most populous states, the national power of both states is limited by their low level of economic development. By contrast, Israel, with a population of less than 5 million, enjoys a reputation of a medium-size power, in great measure because of its citizenry's strong morale and cohesion. In short, population contributes importantly to power, but only in combination with other intangible qualities, such as health, education, national cohesion, morale, and efficient organization.

FIGURE 6.1
Manpower of Largest Military Forces, 1995 (in thousands)
Source: U.S. Arms Control and Disarmament Agency, *World Military Expenditures and Arms Transfers,* 1996 (Washington, D.C.: GPO, 1997), p. 5.

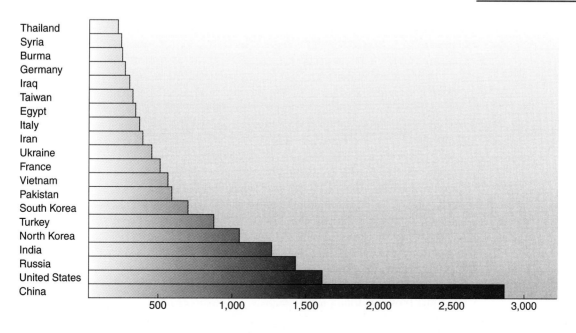

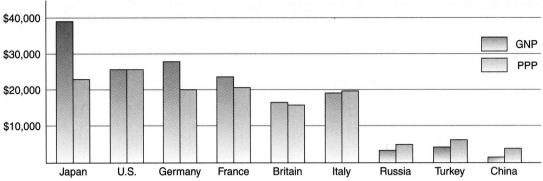

FIGURE 6.2

GNP Per Capita and Purchasing Power Parity (PPP)* Estimates of Selected Countries, 1996 (In U.S. dollars)

*GNP per capita comparisons provide an inadequate measure of economic well-being because people's purchasing power varies greatly among states. To provide a more effective international comparison of economic welfare, the U.N. International Comparison Programme has developed a purchasing power index based on the purchasing power of local currencies. The PPP conversion rate is defined as the number of units of a country's currency that are required to buy the same amounts of goods and services in the domestic economy as one dollar would buy in the United States.
Source: World Bank, *World Development Report,* 1997 (New York: Oxford University Press, 1997), pp. 214–15.

Natural Resources

Raw materials are important because they provide resources essential to national economic expansion. Countries that are richly endowed in mineral resources (like Canada, Russia, Saudi Arabia, South Africa, and the United States) are more secure economically than countries that have few natural resources (such as Great Britain, Japan, and the Netherlands). Not only do vital raw materials contribute to increased economic self-sufficiency, they provide needed foreign exchange from exports. The extraordinary oil reserves of Iraq, Iran, and Saudi Arabia, for example, have been a major contributing factor to their regional and international influence in the 1970s and 1980s.

Natural resources do not guarantee economic development per se. Although some resources, such as oil, gold, and diamonds, are the major basis for the wealth of some states, increased productivity has caused the economic expansion of most states. Modern wealth is not based on raw materials but on intangible elements, such as entrepreneurship, efficient technology, and effective marketing skills. This explains why the Netherlands, Switzerland, and Japan—all countries with limited resources—have achieved such high levels of economic modernization.

Level of Economic Development

Two useful measures of the relative economic capacity of states are the total gross national product (GNP) of countries and their per capita GNP. The latter is an especially useful measure of the economic capacity of a country because it provides a relative index of the average personal productive capacity of different states. (See fig. 6.2.) Other useful but less significant indicators of economic capacity include national production capabilities in such key sectors as industry, agriculture, and energy.

National economic capacity is an especially important element of power because it provides a state with the means to acquire and maintain effective, well-equipped military forces. According to Paul Kennedy, the rise and fall of great powers has been related historically to the rise and fall of their economies. Empires, writes Kennedy, are based on wealth, and when a nation's economy declines, it inevitably results in a loss of international influence.[15] Even though some critics have suggested that Kennedy overemphasizes the role of economics in determining the power of states,[16] it is clear that wealth is essential for national power. States with a high gross national product are able to devote more economic resources to military defense. Table 6.2 shows the high correspondence between the gross national product and the level of military expenditures. A high level of economic development does not itself assure national power. But although wealth may not be a sufficient condition for power, it is clearly a necessary element.

One reason why a state's economic capacity does not necessarily translate into national power is that a state's economic resources can be used for purposes other

TABLE 6.2 GNP and Total Military Expenditures of Major Powers, 1995

Gross National Product (billions of U.S. $)		Rank	Military Expenditures (billions of U.S. $)	
United States	7,247	1	United States	277.8
Japan	5,153	2	Russia	76.0
China	2,759	3	China	63.5
Germany	2,172	3	Japan	50.2
France	1,521	4	France	47.7
United Kingdom	1,110	5	Germany	41.1
Italy	1,082	6	United Kingdom	33.4
Russia	664	7	Italy	19.4
Brazil	656	8	Saudi Arabia	17.2
Spain	553	9	South Korea	14.4
Canada	541	10	Taiwan	13.1
South Korea	424	11	Brazil	10.9
Netherlands	390	12	Canada	9.1
Australia	342	13	Israel	8.7
India	326	14	Spain	8.6

Source: U.S. Arms Control and Disarmament Agency, *World Military Expenditures and Arms Transfers, 1996* (Washington, D.C.: GPO, 1997), pp. 36 and 38.

than national security, such as improving living conditions and promoting national health and education. States vary greatly in the percentage of national income and general government budget that they devote to the armed forces. As table 6.3 suggests, no relationship whatever exists between the level of economic development and the proportion that governments spend on military defense: the level of governmental spending on the military is completely unrelated to GNP per capita. For example, Japan, which has the second largest gross national product, devotes 1 percent of its GNP to national security, whereas Laos, one of the poorest countries in the world, devotes more than 7 percent of its GNP to military defense.

Because national power is relative, a nation's absolute economic capacity is less important than its relative level of economic development. Absolute improvements in the economic capabilities of a nation will result in better living standards, but not necessarily in increased power. For economic capacity to contribute to national power, the economic capacity of a nation must improve relatively as well. for example, the Netherlands in the mid-eighteenth century was richer in absolute terms than in the seventeenth century, although its relative wealth had declined. Similarly, although Britain's share of world industrial production declined from 25 percent in the mid-nineteenth century to 3 percent in the 1980s, its absolute level of economic development increased substantially during this period. In absolute terms, Britain became a richer country in the twentieth century while losing much of its imperial influence and prestige.[17]

Military Capacity

Military resources are undoubtedly the most important element of power. National security is ultimately based on each state's ability to protect its territorial boundaries

TABLE 6.3 Relative Burden of Military Expenditures, 1995

ME/GNP* (%)	GNP Per Capita (1995 dollars)					
	Under $200	$200–499	$500–999	$1,000–2,999	$3,000–9,999	$10,000 and over
10% and over			Bosnia & Herzegov.+ North Korea Iraq+	Serbia & Montenegro+	Oman Saudi Arabia Russia Croatia	Kuwait
5–9.99%	Sierre Leone Mozambique	Pakistan Sudan+ Rwanda	Egypt	Jordan Botswana	Syria Libya Greece Bahrain	Israel Brunei Cyprus
2–4.99%	Burundi Chad Ethiopia	Gambia Laos Mauritania Cambodia Burkina Faso Haiti Guinea-Bissau Zambia Vietnam Central African Rep. India Mongolia Uganda Kenya Togo Nicaragua	Sri Lanka Zimbabwe Tajikistan Afghanistan+ Macedonia Angola Liberia Congo Bolivia	Djibouti Morocco Turkey Burma Uzbekistan Ecuador Algeria Ukraine Azerbaijan Iran Swaziland Colombia Thailand Georgia China Moldova Namibia	Chile Lebanon South Korea Malaysia Slovakia Suriname Bulgaria Gabon Romania Uruguay Czech Republic Poland South Africa	Taiwan United Arab Emir. Singapore Qatar United States France United Kingdom Sweden Norway Portugal Australia Netherlands
1–1.99%	Tanzania Malawi	Mali Bangladesh Equatorial Guinea Guinea Ghana Benin Niger	Cameroon+ Lesotho Indonesia Senegal Honduras Guyana Ivory Coast Cape Verde	Tunisia Fiji Peru Turkmenistan Belize Cuba Philippines Papua New Guinea Paraguay Panama Dominican Republic Guatemala Albania El Salvador	Argentina Trinidad & Tobago Brazil Hungary Venezuela Malta Estonia	Finland Germany Denmark Italy Canada Belgium Switzerland Spain Slovenia New Zealand Ireland
Under 1%	Bhutan+ Zaire Somalia	Nepal Madagascar Sao Tome & Princ.+	Nigeria+ Yemen+	Kyrgystan+ Mexico Kazakstan Armenia Jamaica Costa Rica	Latvia Barbados Belarus Lithuania Mauritius	Japan Austria Luxembourg Iceland

*Countries are listed within blocks in descending order of the military expenditures/gross national product ratio.

+Ranking is based on a rough approximation of one or more variables, for which 1995 data or a reliable estimate is not available.

Source: U.S. Arms Control and Disarmament Agency, *World Military Expenditures and Arms Transfers, 1996* (Washington, D.C.: GPO, 1997), p. 31.

from foreign aggression and to promote its vital interests abroad. Even though states resort to military force infrequently, military capacity is the foundation of a country's national power. The ability to deter aggression or to influence other actors is ultimately rooted in the capacity to achieve its objectives through force.

To a great degree, a country's reputation for power is based on the quality and quantity of its armed forces. Obviously, the quality and size of military forces depend on a variety of elements, including the level of a country's economic development, the size of the population, the quality of education, the quality of military training, the degree of national cohesion, and the size of budgetary resources devoted to national defense. Because rich, developed countries can allocate more resources to military defense than poor ones (see fig. 6.3), modern, industrial states generally have more capable military forces than developing nations.

The proportion of resources that states devote to national defense is of course determined largely by political and security considerations, including the nature and scope of global conflicts as well as the overall level of political order within the international community. During the Cold War, for example, the East-West conflict fueled an arms race between the United States and the Soviet Union, but with the relaxation and eventual ending of this dispute, military expenditures by the major contestants and their allies declined significantly—from a total of $1,025 billion in 1985 to $567 billion in 1995.[18] The ending of the Cold War also had a significant impact on total world expenditures—falling 34 percent from an all-time peak of $1.36 trillion in 1987 to $864 billion in 1995.[19] This decline is also evident in the dramatic fall in the world arms trade, which decreased from a peak of $82 billion in 1987 to $31.9 billion in 1995 (see fig. 6.4).

Regional instability can also contribute to high levels of military expenditures. This has been the case for the Middle East, a region that has devoted the highest proportion of its GNP to military defense since 1980. And although its expenditures have declined significantly since the mid-1980s, when they accounted for nearly 18 percent of the region's GNP, the Middle East continued to devote more public funds to defense in 1995 (7.9 percent of GNP) than any other region.[20] Not surprisingly, the Middle East has been, and continues to be, the major arms importing region of the world, accounting for about 43 percent of the world's total weapons imports.[21]

Domestic political conditions can also escalate militarism. For example, the division of states—such as Korea (between North and South Korea) or China (between the People's Republic of China and Taiwan)—can contribute to a perception

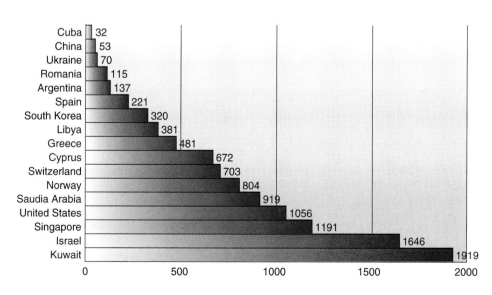

FIGURE 6.3
Annual Per Capita Military Expenditures of Selected States, 1995 (in U.S. dollars)
Source: U.S. Arms Control and Disarmament Agency, *World Military Expenditures and Arms Transfers,* 1996 (Washington, D.C.: GPO, 1997), p. 40.

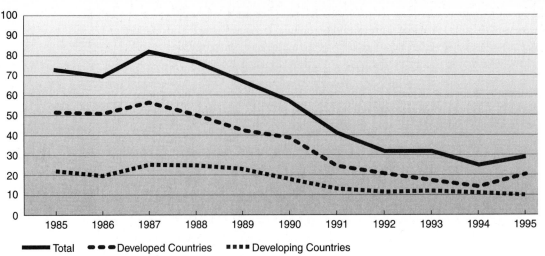

Total ●●● **Developed Countries** ■■■■ **Developing Countries**

FIGURE 6.4
World Arms
Imports,
1985–1995 (in
billions of dollars)
Source: U.S. Arms Control
and Disarmament Agency,
World Military Expenditures and Arms Transfers,
1996 (Washington, D.C.:
GPO, 1997), p. 100.

of national insecurity. Indeed, the fear of aggression explains why North Korea, South Korea, and Taiwan have maintained disproportionately large military forces. Similarly, a regime's political ideology can also influence the size and character of a country's military force. For example, during the early 1980s, when the leftist Sandinista regime was consolidating its power in Nicaragua, it spent annually between 11 and 17 percent of its GNP on military defense.[22] And even after the collapse of the Cold War, some radical regimes, such as Cuba and North Korea, continue to maintain comparatively large military forces.

Morale, training, and level of experience of armed forces are also important in assessing military capacity, because highly motivated, well-trained, and experienced soldiers will fight better than inexperienced and poorly trained ones. The German defeat of France in 1940 was accomplished not by larger military forces, but rather by forces of roughly the same size that were better organized. The importance of training, organization, and leadership is also evident in contemporary Israel, which enjoys the reputation of a medium power despite its small population and territory. Israeli pilots are considered among the best in the world. When the Israeli air force engaged Syrian fighters during Israel's 1982 invasion of Lebanon, its jets overwhelmed the Syrian air force. Israel claims to have destroyed more than eighty modern Soviet-built Syrian jets (MIGs) and to have lost less than five of its own fighters.

The quality and modernity of armaments contribute to a perception of power. Normally, a weapon's military value is determined by its lethality or destructive potential. Lethality, in turn, is based on two factors—the destructive power of the weapon, and the accuracy and distance with which it can be delivered, even when faced with electronic countermeasures. As a general rule, the more modern a weapon is, the more efficient its power and the more effective its delivery capacity. The two most destructive types of armaments are chemical weapons, such as nerve or mustard gas, and nuclear weapons.

Intangible Elements of Power

Just as physical attributes do not ensure victory in sports, physical endowments do not translate directly into power. Periodically, a physically and athletically weak team may defeat a stronger one because of better teamwork, superior coaching, and fewer mistakes. In effect, the intangible elements are agents of converting physical elements into actual power. The three most important intangible elements of power are (1) national morale, (2) the nature of government, and (3) leadership.

CHAPTER 6: POWER IN WORLD POLITICS

138   CHAPTER 6: POWER IN WORLD POLITICS

National Morale

An important, though elusive, attribute of power is the nature and character of a nation's morale or corporate will. The national will of people is expressed by the degree of support that the citizens give to the policies of their government, whether in peace or war. Morale, in other words, represents the depth of community. It reflects the strength of relationship between the government and the people and among the people themselves. A nation deeply divided about its foreign policies will obviously be unable to effectively mobilize its tangible resources in pursuit of those decisions. Moreover a society deeply divided along ethnic, religious, or political lines will be unable to effectively project power internationally.

One of the major reasons why the United States failed to meet its objectives in Vietnam was the lack of domestic support for the Vietnam War. In the end, only a minority of the American people believed it was in the national interest to be directly involved militarily in defending South Vietnam from communist aggression. This lack of commitment contrasts sharply with the high morale of the Vietcong (the guerrillas from South Vietnam) and North Vietnamese soldiers, who demonstrated remarkable determination and persistence in the pursuit of their military objectives despite great obstacles.

The Nature of Government

The structure and character of government also has an important impact on the power potential of a state, especially because a state's ability to project power in the world is dependent on the quality, coherence, and efficiency of its decision making. Authoritarian regimes—military governments, such as those in Africa and Latin America, and traditional autocratic regimes, such as those in Jordan and Saudi Arabia—are generally able to make decisions rapidly and to achieve a high degree of predictability and continuity. Because power is highly centralized in such systems, only a handful of people need to be involved in the decision-making process. These characteristics are even more evident in totalitarian communist systems in which the authority and power of the ruling elites is even greater than in authoritarian systems.

Because competitive regimes are more open and less centralized, their decision-making process generally involves broader participation, slow execution, and limited continuity. But competitive regimes have two important advantages over autocratic regimes: first, they are much better able to gain the support of the citizenry, and second, they are more likely to develop wise policies because of greater openness in the decision-making process.

Leadership

The quality of political and military leadership also contributes to a nation's reputation of power. Political leadership involves effective steering of a country. This entails identifying national goals and developing a strategy to achieve such goals. At the same time, leadership must mobilize resources and citizenry to implement national strategies.

Lenin, Stalin, Hitler, F. D. Roosevelt, Churchill, and deGaulle are generally considered great leaders because they influenced not only domestic affairs, but international developments as well. Many believe that Britain's heroic stand against Hitler's expansionist foreign policy must ultimately be credited to Sir Winston Churchill, Britain's wartime prime minister, who rallied the British people to oppose Germany's aggression. In the late twentieth century, such leaders as Lech Walesa from Poland, Nelson Mandela and F. W. de Klerk from South Africa, and Mikhail Gorbachev and Boris Yeltsin from the former Soviet Union, have all demonstrated courageous and farsighted leadership skills. Walesa almost single-handedly helped create and sustain the Solidarity Movement, whereas Mandela and de Klerk provided the leadership to dismantle apartheid and establish a new constitutional order. Similarly, Gorbachev initiated major economic and political reforms (e.g., *glasnost* and *perestroika*), which were subsequently expanded and institutionalized by President Yeltsin.

An especially important element of political leadership is the quality of diplomacy—that is, the capacity to effectively use resources to maximize national interests in the international system. Indeed, Hans Morgenthau argues that the quality of diplomacy is the most important attribute of power.[23] During the 1990–1991 Persian Gulf crisis, for example, Saddam Hussein enhanced his relative power greatly by his brazen and recalcitrant attitude toward ending the military occupation of Kuwait. Had he accepted the demands set forth by the UN Security Council, he no doubt would have saved from destruction a large part of his military forces. But his excessive brinkmanship led to war, military defeat, the decimation of his armed forces, and ultimately to Iraq's loss of regional influence. On the other hand, President Bush's skillful diplomatic initiatives resulted not only in numerous Security Council resolutions condemning Iraq and the eventual liberation of Kuwait, but in the significant enhancement of American power in the international system.

Finally, the quality of military leadership also influences a nation's power. Military leadership not only contributes to the cohesion and morale of the armed forces, but to the development of strategies and tactics for applying force. Leadership is especially important in wartime when military commanders must make important strategic decisions that can mean the difference between victory and defeat.

THE CHANGING NATURE OF POWER

As noted above, national power depends not only on the mix of tangible and intangible resources, but on the context in which such resources are used. In recent decades both the relative significance of different power resources and the global political context have changed. Although these changes have not diminished the significance of power in international politics, the character of power has shifted.

One important development affecting global power has been the expanding functional interdependence of the international system. The growing economic, technological, and scientific integration of global society has resulted in the increasing porosity of state boundaries and the decline of government control over international events. According to Joseph S. Nye, Jr., even though the major powers continue to have substantial power over other states, the growing complexity of the international system has resulted in a declining capacity to determine international behavioral outcomes.[24] In effect, the complexity of the modern world has decreased the capacity of powerful states to determine international events.

Although rising interdependence has decreased governmental control abroad, it has ironically resulted in increased domestic vulnerability. The increased need for foreign natural resources has increased the dependence of states on imported resources, whereas the expansion of modern telecommunications has increased the influence of global public opinion on domestic decision making. There can be little doubt that the global televising of the coup against Mikhail Gorbachev in August 1991 contributed significantly to the coup's ultimate failure. Similarly, the U.S. humanitarian intervention in Somalia in December 1992 was undertaken in great measure because of the media's publicizing of the famine.

A second shift in power has been the growing significance of nonmilitary resources. Although the perception of power has been based historically on the ability to protect and enhance vital interests, power has typically been associated with the capacity to deter aggression and to prevail in military conflict. Although military force continues to serve as the ultimate instrument of national security, non-military resources have become more prominent in response to the rising significance of nonmilitary threats.[25] Because of growing global interdependence, national security is increasingly threatened in nonmilitary ways, including ecological degradation, scarcity of nonrenewable resources (e.g., petroleum, minerals, coal), illicit drugs, health epidemics (e.g., AIDS), and decreased control over the dissemination of information. For example, although the United States remains the sole superpower, it has been unable to effectively stem the influx of illegal drugs. Moreover, private international media networks continue to exert great influence over the opinions and concerns of citizens in developing nations, even though such organizations lack the power resources of governments of the major states.

Third, power has become less transferable from one sphere to another. Whereas traditional military and economic resources have provided states with the means to determine outcomes in a variety of societal areas, power has become increasingly less transferable from one arena to another. In Nye's view, power has become "less fungible."[26] For example, nuclear weapons may enhance a nation's power, but they do not assure economic power. Similarly, a strong national economy may provide a comfortable standard of living for citizens, but it will not guarantee regional political influence. In short, governments seeking to influence behavior need to use appropriate resources to achieve the desired outcomes.

Power continues to play an important role in international relations. But because of the changing context and significance of power resources, the realist paradigm—the traditional conception of international relations—has become less valid in the late twentieth century.

PATTERNS OF POWER

As noted in chapter 3, power can be potentially concentrated in one state (unipolar), two states (bipolar), or three or more states (multipolar). Historically, the latter two patterns have been far more common than the first. Indeed, with the possible exception of the Roman Empire era, no other historical period can be classified as unipolar. To be sure, the collapse of the Soviet empire has left the United States as the undisputed power in contemporary global society, but its power is challenged and qualified by the growing role of other actors, especially the European Community and Japan.

Another method of classifying international systems is in terms of the level of centralization of power. Fundamentally, the power patterns of the global system can be differentiated along a power continuum defined by two extreme conditions—balance and preponderance. Even though most power patterns represent different points along this continuum, we classify systems in terms of two "ideal" or extreme patterns because most power distributions tend toward one extreme or the other. The *balance of power pattern,* the most prevalent distribution in modern times, is characterized by a fundamental parity among the major actors or groups of actors. The *hegemonic power pattern,* by contrast, is characterized by a concentration of power in one or more states.

Historically, the global system has vacillated between these two patterns, although scholars differ greatly not only on when those patterns have existed but also on their probable effect on the peace and stability of the international system. Indeed, one of the most widely debated subjects among international relations scholars is the impact of power patterns on the stability of the world. In the following sections we describe the theory and practice of two major approaches to power—balance of power and hegemony.

Balance of Power

Theory

Balance of power theory
The belief that peace and global stability are best achieved and maintained through a fundamental equilibrium of power among major actors.

The **balance of power theory,** perhaps the oldest and most widely accepted theory of world politics, assumes that states behave in the international system in such a way that no single state can dominate the others. States oppose the preponderance of power of other states not only because such imbalance might threaten their own security, but also because such dominance poses a threat to the stability of the international community itself. A fundamental premise of the theory is that national security is best assured when the power of leading states is in fundamental equilibrium. Balance, not superiority, is the key to a stable international community of states. Moreover, because weakness is assumed to encourage aggression, the most effective way of preventing war is to ensure that no state, or group of states, gains a preponderance of power. Thus, the balance of power theory postulates that states, as a method of increasing national security, will always align themselves with the weaker states in order to achieve international equilibrium.

James E. Dougherty and Robert L. Pfaltzgraff, Jr., have identified eleven techniques by which states maintain a balance of power: (1) the policy of divide and conquer, (2) territorial adjustments following war, (3) creation of buffer states, (4) establishment of alliances, (5) maintenance of regional spheres of influence, (6) military intervention, (7) diplomatic bargaining, (8) peaceful settlement of disputes through negotiation, mediation, or arbitration, (9) reduction of armaments, (10) arms races, and (11) war itself.[27] During the past two centuries, the most important method of maintaining a balanced pattern of power has been the formation of alliances.

The theory assumes that maintaining a balance of power is a dynamic process. Because power among states is continuously shifting, stability can only be achieved if increases in power are checked by countervailing power. Some scholars and statesmen have argued that this equilibrium is achieved by the deliberate policies of states. For example, the English statesmen Sir Eyre Crowe wrote in 1907 that it had "become almost a historical truism to identify England's secular policy with the maintenance of this balance by throwing her weight now in this scale and now in that, but ever on the side opposed to the political dictatorship of the strongest single state or group at a given time."[28] Others argue, however, that states will automatically align themselves in such a way as to prevent a centralization of power. Kenneth Waltz, for example, writes that "states will ally with the devil to avoid the hell of military defeat."[29] Thus, for Waltz and other neorealists, the global equilibrium of power that is achieved does not derive from "balance of power" foreign policies, but is a by-product of the collective self-interested pursuits of states.[30]

Some scholars argue that balance of power does not promote international stability and order. A. F. K. Organski, for example, argues that stability and peace are associated with preponderance of power, not balance. In his view, "The relationship between peace and balance of power appears to be exactly the opposite of what has been claimed. The periods of balance, real or imagined, are periods of warfare, while the periods of known preponderance are periods of peace."[31] Inis Claude, Jr., also notes that there is no necessary correlation between peace and balance, and that the superiority of power could possibly help keep harmony if the "right" state has superior power. Even Hans Morgenthau, an advocate of political realism, calls attention to the shortcomings of the theory, including its uncertainty, unreality, and inadequacy.[32]

Practice

It is commonly assumed that since the development of the Westphalian nation-state system (1648), international relations have been based on the balance of power system. Some scholars have suggested that this system was common even in medieval and ancient times. Philosopher David Hume, for example, noted in the eighteenth century that the "maxim of preserving the balance of power is founded so much on common sense and obvious reasoning that it is impossible it could altogether have escaped antiquity."[33] Although balance of power patterns may have been practiced in ancient times, scholars agree that the modern era offers the clearest evidence of this pattern, with the nineteenth century providing the classic expression of the balance of power theory.

Following Napoleon's defeat, representatives from the major European powers gathered at the Congress of Vienna (1815) to establish an informal framework for maintaining peace. At the conference, an informal, flexible balance of power system was established that brought peace and stability to Europe for nearly a century. Although conflicts occurred from time to time, these were comparatively minor, resulting in modest transnational adjustments. There were no religious, ideological, or national liberation wars involving the masses. If force was used, the armies were small and the wars were limited.

The major features of this European system were (1) a multiplicity of states; (2) a broad dispersion of power; (3) widely shared political beliefs about the nature and role of government; (4) a common commitment to the balance of power system and a belief that national interests were served by it; and (5) a commitment to flexibility in making and dissolving alliances.

This system worked especially well in nineteenth-century Europe for a number of reasons. First, the leaders of European states (England, France, Prussia, Austria-Hungary, and Russia) shared common political beliefs and were committed to the preservation of the existing system. Second, European leaders were deeply opposed to concentrated power. Indeed, the system of collegiality and moderation established at the Congress of Vienna was chiefly designed not as a peacekeeping system, but as a method of avoiding the concentration of power that had resulted from Napoleon's military conquests. And third, rulers were committed to the peaceful resolution of disputes through negotiation. Not only was diplomacy emphasized, but the values and practices of negotiation, including secrecy and flexibility, promoted diplomatic compromise.

Although the balance of power system has functioned in a modified form throughout the twentieth century, the structure of world power has changed greatly, especially since the end of World War II. Unlike the classical era, which was characterized by a broad distribution of power, moderation in disputes, shifting alliances, and secret diplomacy, the Cold War era was characterized by concentrated, bipolar power, intense and deeply ideological conflicts, and rigid alliances. Since the disintegration of the Soviet Union in 1991, the United States has become the sole dominant actor, resulting in a shift from bipolarity to unipolarity. Charles Krauthammer describes the post–Cold War system as follows:

> The most striking feature of the post–Cold War world is its unipolarity. No doubt, multipolarity will come in time. In perhaps another generation or so there will be great powers coequal with the United States, and the world will, in structure, resemble the pre–World War I era. Now is the unipolar moment.[34]

The balance of power system is an important conceptual development. By serving as a halfway house between total anarchy and world government, the balance of power approach provides a framework for establishing community order without the creation of authoritative governmental structures backed by a monopoly of power. The balance of power system is therefore significant because it demonstrates how imperfect order can be achieved as a by-product of the collective wills of independent actors, each pursuing its individual interests. In effect, stability in a decentralized system is possible without government.

Hegemonic Power

Theory

Hegemonic stability theory
The belief that international peace and economic prosperity are a by-product of a hegemonically imposed structure.

In view of the assumed preponderance of power in the global system, some scholars have advanced an alternative theory to balance of power. This thesis—commonly defined as the **hegemonic stability theory**[35]—asserts that international order is a consequence of a monopoly of power. Organski argues that a preponderance of power creates and sustains international stability. According to him, "In the nineteenth century . . . there was almost continuous peace. The balance of power is usually given a good share of the credit for this peaceful century, but . . . there was no balance at all, but rather a vast preponderance of power in the hands of England and France."[36]

George Modelski similarly observes that peace derives from a preponderance of power, and suggests that the most prevalent power pattern in the modern world has not been a balance of power distribution but rather a hegemonic pattern. In *Long Cycles in World Politics,* Modelski argues that, since 1500, four major powers have played a dominant role in world politics: Portugal, the Netherlands, Great Britain, and the United States. Each of these states has served as a world leader in a particular historical era. Because each of these historical eras or cycles is roughly one hundred years long, Modelski defines his analysis as "the long cycles of world leadership." Modelski's five major cycles are depicted in table 6.4.

The stability of the modern world, according to Modelski, is rooted in the long periods of global dominance by a leading power. Each of these cycles begins in the aftermath of a major war that establishes the supremacy of the leading state and then is followed by a period of decline until another major global conflict erupts that either confirms the status of the leading power, as was the case with Britain in 1792, or results in a transfer of power to the successful challenger, as was the case in each of the other cycles. Although changes from one cycle to the other are highly conflictual, the cycle itself is highly stable.

Collective security
A theory of world order, first applied by the League of Nations, that seeks to deter aggression by promising collective retaliation against any community member committing aggression.

Another theory of preponderant power is **collective security,** which, like the hegemonic stability theory, assumes that peace can best be realized through a centralization of power. But unlike the hegemonic stability theory, collective security assumes that dominance will be achieved collectively rather than individually. In effect, peace is realized by the creation of peacekeeping arrangements in which member-states commit themselves to collectively punish aggression. Collective security is not based on the permanent superiority of power of some members; rather, the predominance of power is achieved only temporarily in order to punish unacceptable behavior.

TABLE 6.4 Modelski's Leading States, Sixteenth to Twentieth Centuries

Historical Cycle	Time	Leading Power
First cycle	1516 to 1580	Portugal
Second cycle	1580 to 1688	Netherlands
Third cycle	1688 to 1792	Great Britain
Fourth cycle	1792 to 1914	Great Britain
Fifth cycle	1914 to present	United States

Source: George Modelski, *Long Cycles in World Politics.* (Seattle: University of Washington Press, 1987), passim.

TABLE 6.5 Leading States and Power Resources, Sixteenth to Twentieth Centuries

Period	Leading State	Key Resources
16th century	Spain	gold bullion, colonial trade, mercenary armies, dynastic ties
17th century	Netherlands	trade, capital markets, navy
18th century	France	population, rural industry, army, public administration
19th century	Britain	industry, political cohesion, finance and credit, navy, liberal norms, island location (easy to defend)
20th century	United States	economic scale, scientific and technical leadership, universalistic culture, military forces and alliances, liberal international regimes, hub of transnational communications

Source: Data from Joseph S. Nye, Jr., *Bound to Lead: The Changing Nature of American Power* (New York, N.Y.: Basic Books, 1990), p. 34.

If collective security is to effectively promote international peace, three conditions must exist: first, member-states must be strongly committed to the regional or global peacekeeping associations; second, states must be opposed to aggression and assume that the collective punishment of aggression will keep peace; and third, states must be committed to use their power to implement the collective security regime. In short, collective security is a political arrangement that seeks to keep peace by deterring aggression through the promise of collective punishment. Like the balance of power system, collective security operates within the existing state system. But unlike it, collective security uses the superior force of all peace-loving states to punish the aggressor nation.

The theory of collective security has been implemented by the League of Nations and the United Nations, and by Latin American states that are signatories to the Rio Pact, formally known as the Inter-American Treaty of Reciprocal Assistance of 1947. Regional security alliances, such as NATO or the Warsaw Pact are not forms of collective security because they are not concerned with punishment of aggression among its own members. The theory and practice of collective security is examined more fully in chapter 14.

Practice

Some states have periodically amassed a preponderance of power, thereby giving them the ability to dominate other states and to dictate the rules and arrangements by which international relations are carried out. In ancient times, for example, the Greek and Roman empires had virtual control of the major centers of world power. Modern hegemonies, however, have had proportionately less influence in the world system. Even at the height of the *Pax Britannica,* for example, Britain's empire encompassed only 20 to 25 percent of the world's population. And during the 1950s and 1960s, the heyday of the *Pax Americana,* the United States had the most potent military forces and served as the leader of the world economy, yet it had no colonies and its influence in foreign lands was limited.

States have historically achieved a preponderance of power through a variety of means. According to table 6.5, some of the most important sources of hegemonic power have been increased economic efficiency, a large maritime capability in order to regulate world trade, the export of raw materials, and significant military capabilities.

In Conclusion

Power is a key component of global politics. Although power exists in all types of politics, it is especially important in the international community. Because of the absence of authoritative governmental institutions in global society, the pursuit of national interests in the world rests in great measure on a state's power. As a result, governments devote significant resources to the enhancement of national power, especially to its military and economic dimensions.

Historically, the quest for power among states has resulted in a variety of different patterns that have vacillated between the extremes of balance and preponderance, equilibrium and dominance. These patterns of power have not been created by a leading state or an international organization, but are the by-product of the competitive ambitions and interests of states themselves. Historically, the most common distributional pattern has been the balance of power, although a hegemonic pattern has appeared from time to time. Although scholars have analyzed the relative merits of each of these different patterns of powers, there is little agreement as to which pattern is more conducive to peace and justice.

SUMMARY

1. Power, one of the most important concepts in world politics, is the ability to determine outcomes.

2. Power has numerous characteristics. It is relational; it is a means; it is rooted on perception; it is multidimensional; its totality is fixed; it is dynamic; and it can be institutionalized.

3. Numerous tangible and intangible elements contribute to power. Tangible elements involve territory, population, level of economic development, and military capacity. Intangible elements include national morale, the nature of government, and leadership.

4. Although power continues to be a key determinant in international relations, its nature has shifted in recent decades—in part because of the growing interdependence of global society, the diminishing impact of military resources, and the declining transferability of power from one sphere to another.

5. There are two basic patterns of power—balance and hegemony. The balance of power pattern is characterized by a diffusion of power among several states so that no single country or group of countries can monopolize power in the international system. The hegemonic power pattern exists when one state, or a group of states, is able to dominate others and thereby dictate the rules of international relations.

6. These two power patterns have given rise to competing theories of international order. According to the balance of power theory, equilibrium promotes peace and stability in the international system. The hegemonic stability theory, by contrast, assumes that a preponderance of power is more conducive to peace and global stability.

KEY TERMS

influence	force	soft power	balance of power theory
authority	meta-power	potential power	hegemonic stability theory
power	hard power	actual power	collective security

RECOMMENDED READINGS

Art, Robert J. "To What Ends Military Power?" *International Security, 4* (Spring 1980). 3–35. A useful analysis of the different types of military power and the role that each plays in global politics.

Baldwin, David A. "Power Analysis and World Politics: New Trends versus Old Tendencies," *World Politics, 31* (January 1979): pp. 161–194. A penetrating assessment of the nature and role of power in international relations.

Claude, Inis L., Jr. *Power and International Relations.* New York: Random House, 1962. Although dated, this readable study remains a useful conceptual introduction to the three major systems of managing international relations—balance of power, collective security, and world government.

Kennedy, Paul. *The Rise and Fall of the Great Powers.* New York: Random House, 1987. A historical investigation of the relationship of national wealth to military power and foreign political influence. Kennedy argues that the rise and fall of the "Great Powers" is associated with the rise and fall of their national economic capacities.

Knorr, Klaus. *The Power of Nations: the Political Economy of International Relations.* Princeton: Princeton University Press, 1975. A conceptual analysis of how states convert political, economic, and administrative resources into national power and influence.

Nye, Joseph S., Jr. *Bound to Lead: The Changing Nature of American Power.* New York: Basic Books, 1990. While recognizing that the relative international economic position of the United States has declined in recent decades, Nye refuses to accept the widely accepted view that the United States no longer has the resources necessary for influencing the course of global politics. Instead, he argues that the United States still has the basic capacity to lead.

Odell, Peter R. *Oil and World Power,* 8th ed. New York: Penguin Books, 1986. An informative introductory study of the international political economy of oil—the world's leading industry.

RELEVANT WEB SITES

Central Intelligence Agency Factbook — www.odci.gov/cia/publications/nsolo/wfb-all.htm

International Relations and Security Network (ISN) — www.isn.ethz.ch/
    See the following subjects:
    Arms Control/Disarmament
    Military/Defense

NATO — www.nato.int

World Military Expenditures and Arms Transfers (ACDA) — www.acda.gov/wmeat95/

7 Ethics in World Politics

History shows no exact and necessary correlation between the quality of motives and the quality of foreign policy.[1]

Hans J. Morgenthau, *influential political scientist*

What passes for ethical standards for governmental policies in foreign affairs is a collection of moralisms, maxims, and slogans, which neither help nor guide, but only confuse, decision. . . .[2]

Dean Acheson, *former U.S. Secretary of State*

The "necessities" in international politics . . . do not push decision and action beyond the realm of moral judgment; they rest on moral choice themselves.[3]

Arnold Wolfers, *noted mid-twentieth-century IR scholar*

Saints can be pure, but statesmen, alas, must be responsible.[4]

Arthur Schlesinger, Jr., *distinguished historian*

Empirical
Objective, observable phenomena.

Normative
Prescriptive, value-based norms.

In his description and analysis of the Peloponnesian Wars of the fifth century B.C., Thucydides suggested that international relations are primarily determined by considerations of power and security. Although Thucydides recognized that moral values influence the thinking and behavior of statesmen, he observed that when political leaders must choose between security and considerations of justice, the former supercedes the latter. "The strong do what they have to do," he wrote, "and the weak have to accept."[5] Ever since Thucydides penned his powerful account of the wars between Athens and Sparta, realism has served as the dominant paradigm of international politics. Despite the continuing appeal of human rights and the growing functional interdependence within the contemporary international system, realism continues as the dominant tradition among statesmen and soldiers because the anarchic international community does not assure the territorial security and economic prosperity of member-states. Ultimately, each state is responsible for its own security and well-being.

Although morality is an inescapable dimension of most aspects of human life, scholars and public officials are often reticent to acknowledge the moral dimension of international relations. The neglect of morality in global politics is clearly evident in the international relations literature. For example, few international relations texts emphasize the role of morality in global politics. There is a widespread conviction that power, not morality, determines the international actions of states. Because of the profound influence of realism in postwar United States, American international relations scholars have focused on the quest for national security and the promotion of economic prosperity in the anarchic international system. They have neglected the ethical dimensions of global relations.

Another reason for the neglect of ethics is the scientific orientation of contemporary social science scholarship. Most contemporary political scientists are concerned primarily with describing how the world functions. The emphasis is on **empirical** (factual) generalizations, rather than on **normative** (value) judgments. Although the modern emphasis on distinguishing facts from values is important, the development of a "value-free" social science is not only impossible but undesirable. Human beings are moral agents. Their behavior is guided not only by the realities of the existing world (what "is"), but also by hopes and moral aspirations for a better world (what "ought to be"). The choices they make, either for themselves or for the communities to which they belong, are thus partly rooted in moral values. In effect, politics is also concerned with what ought to be—with what is right, fair, and just. Thus, because the aim of studying world politics is not only to describe and understand the world but also to make it more just, analysis and assessment of the moral dimension of political life are not only desirable but essential.

As noted earlier, because political behavior is guided by both morality and power, ideals and security, an analysis of global politics that fails to take into account ethics will provide an inadequate account of international relations. The Greek philosopher Aristotle long ago observed that politics is fundamentally a moral enterprise—an activity rooted in ethics—and any sound theory of domestic or international politics must take into account moral purposes and arguments. This is why historian E.H. Carr has written that a "sound political thought" must be based on both utopia and reality, realism and idealism.[6]

This chapter, comprised of four major parts, examines the nature and role of ethics in world politics. The first part defines the nature of political morality and ethical analysis and then compares two ethical approaches—consequentialism and moral absolutism. The second part defines and contrasts three ethical traditions of international relations—skepticism, communitarianism, and cosmopolitanism. The third section explores the nature of justice in global society, contrasting the quest for justice among states with the quest for justice among people. Two cases studies—one on caning in Singapore and the other on the female genital mutilation—illustrate the difficulty of defining human rights in light of the world's diverse cultural traditions. Finally, the chapter examines the contribution and limitation of moral norms in the development and implementation of foreign policy. A case study on famine relief is presented to illustrate the important role of moral values in inspiring and guiding foreign policy.

MORALITY AND ETHICS IN GLOBAL SOCIETY

The word morality comes from the Latin *mores,* meaning custom and common usage based on shared values. The term ethics is rooted in the Greek *ethos,* also meaning common practices based on shared moral values. Because the terms have a common root meaning, they are often used interchangeably. Strictly speaking, however, the terms represent different elements of the normative process— **morality,** referring to the widely shared values and beliefs about what is good and bad, right and wrong, and **ethics,** referring to the examination, justification, and critical analysis of morality. It is therefore important to distinguish between moral principles—that is, norms that define what is just and unjust, good and bad—from the process of ethical reasoning that seeks to integrate morality into the fabric of moral decision making in foreign affairs.

Morality
Values of right and wrong, good and bad.

Ethics
The critical analysis of moral values and their application.

Political Morality

Moral norms are characterized by three features: (1) they command universal allegiance; (2) they demand impartiality; and (3) they are largely self-enforcing. Morality's claim of universality means that moral norms are binding on all peoples of all nations. Immanuel Kant articulated this requirement with his famous "categorical imperative," which demands that persons treat others as having intrinsic worth.

The second feature of morality—impartiality—helps to ensure that moral principles are used to advance the common good. Because of the human propensity for selfishness, moral language is frequently used to clothe and advance self-interest. Impartiality requires that morality be defined and applied irrespective of who is affected. John Rawls, in his classic *A Theory of Justice,* makes this claim by arguing that social and political justice must be based on moral principles derived impartially through a "veil of ignorance"—that is, without knowing who will benefit from them.[7] Finally, moral norms are self-enforcing. The English jurist John Fletcher Moulton argued early in this century that the moral domain involved "obedience to the unenforceable." According to Moulton, human affairs consisted of action in three distinct realms—legal, moral, and voluntary. Morality, which involved the intermediary domain between governmentally enforced rules and the realm of free choice, was concerned with human action based on "consciousness of duty."[8]

Although personal morality is frequently identified with political morality, the two are different. Individual morality entails principles, rules, and norms that are applicable to the conduct of persons in their personal or private relations. The Ten Commandments is an example of such morality. Political morality, by contrast, involves norms that are applicable to the life of political communities. Examples of such norms include the fundamental equality of persons, the freedom of conscience, the collective right of self-determination, and the national right of self-defense. Because individual and political morality are not identical, Lea Brilmayer has noted that "the prohibitions found in interpersonal morality cannot be mechanically transplanted into a code of conduct for public officials."[9]

Ethical Analysis

Ethics involves choosing or doing that which is right and good and avoiding that which is bad or evil. Ethical decision making is often difficult in personal life, but this is especially the case in political life in which governmental actions are rarely subject to simple moral verdicts. As a result, the development of just public policies will necessitate *ethical reasoning* in order to identify the most desirable action from morally legitimate alternatives. Such a process will involve, at a minimum, the identification of relevant moral values, the application of moral norms to the problem, the critical assessment of potential alternatives, and the implementation of the chosen policy.

In international relations, ethical reasoning is important for at least three reasons. First, global issues and problems rarely involve only one moral value. Rather, most foreign policy issues and international concerns involve numerous moral norms, some of them competing and some of them complementary. The process of ethical reasoning must therefore identify, prioritize, and apply the relevant values and beliefs, often resulting in trade-offs among competing moral norms. For example, President Truman's decision to drop the atomic bomb on Japan in 1945 involved a difficult moral calculus: on the one hand, using the bomb could help to end the war and avoid a costly and highly destructive land invasion of Japan; on the other hand, the use of the bomb would cause great human suffering, destroy two urban centers (Hiroshima and Nagasaki), and involve the use of a new type of weapon that was incompatible with traditional strategic thought.

Second, ethical reasoning requires the application of morality to the goals, means, and ends of public policies. Intending to do the right thing is not enough; the means and consequences must also be moral if a policy is to be completely just. There are two important challenges in developing a moral foreign policy. First, relevant moral values must be identified and applied to the specific foreign policy behaviors of states and to the general problems of global society, including international conflict resolution, economic development, protection of human rights, and environmental protection. Second, ethical foreign policies must be devised that are likely to advance the greatest good and occasion the least evil. In carrying out this task, relevant moral norms must be applied not only to foreign policy goals, but also to the means and likely outcomes of states' actions. This is an especially challenging task because the morality of foreign policy goals, means, and anticipated consequences are rarely, if ever, complementary. Some policies, for example, may involve partially evil methods while achieving good results, whereas other policies may have morally desirable objectives and just means but result in bad outcomes. Thus, foreign policies inevitably involve trade-offs among competing and conflicting moral claims.

Third, moral reasoning is important because ethics is made up of different competing ethical approaches. Two of the major ones, as noted in the section that follows, are moral absolutism, which seeks to assure moral purity ("clean hands"), and consequentialism, which seeks to weigh the merits of decision making by assessing the "utility" of expected outcomes. In addition, the field of international ethics comprises traditions that provide different perspectives in the quest for global justice. Thus, when officials and scholars morally assess the problems and policies of the international community, they must choose among alternative ethical approaches and traditions. The selection of these ethical traditions will influence significantly the process of moral argumentation and the conclusions that are likely to be drawn.

Consequentialism versus Moral Absolutism

According to Max Weber, political ethics are of two types—one concerned with results and the other emphasizing moral rules and intentions. Weber defined these traditions as the "ethic of responsibility" and the "ethic of ultimate ends."[10] These two perspectives are not original to political ethics, but are rooted in two dominant traditions of philosophical ethics: consequentialism and moral absolutism.[11]

Consequentialism assumes that ethical behavior must be judged primarily by outcomes. It assumes that the promotion of human rights, for example, may involve some unjust political act. One of the most important schools of thought of the consequentialist tradition is utilitarianism, developed in Britain in the nineteenth century by James Mill and Jeremy Bentham. According to them, the ethical norms by which personal action as well as public policies should be judged is the utilitarian norm of "the greatest good for the greatest number."

The second approach to ethics is **moral absolutism,** or what philosophers commonly define as "deontological ethics." This approach insists on the strict adherence to moral principles and rule, regardless of consequences. It opposes the notion that the end justifies the means. According to the purist perspective, because both goals and methods must be morally legitimate, promoting justice and the common good by using evil means is morally unacceptable. Immanuel Kant, an apostle of absolutist ethics, illustrated this perspective by arguing that lying to protect a child from a madman was wrong because it compromised the norm of truth-telling.

Consequentialism
An ethical tradition that assumes that actions should be judged by their consequences.

Moral absolutism
An ethical tradition that insists on strict adherence to moral rules, regardless of consequences.

ETHICAL TRADITIONS

There are three distinct conceptions of how ethical values relate to world affairs. These three traditions are: moral skepticism, communitarianism, and cosmopolitanism.[13] The first is based on consequentialist ethics, whereas the cosmopolitan tradition is rooted in moral absolutism. The communitarian tradition relies on both perspectives.

Issue 7.1 Consequentialism Versus Moral Absolutism[12]

You have arrived in a small village in Haiti. Upon entering the village square you realize that military personnel have blindfolded five men and are getting ready to shoot them. When you ask why the men are being killed, you are told that a soldier was killed the previous evening by one member of the group, but that all of them are being executed because military officers have been unable to uncover the person responsible for the crime. You inform the officer in charge that it is wrong to kill innocent people. To prove that he is ethically sensitive to the value of human life, the officer hands you a rifle and says that if you will kill one member of the group, the other four will be freed. If not, all five will be shot.

What would you do? Would you follow the moral absolutist tradition and keep your hands clean and not participate in this immoral game, or would you apply a utilitarian ethic that seeks to maximize the greatest good and minimize harm? Would you, in other words, try to minimize evil by getting your hands dirty by participating in the killing of one person who may or may not be culpable of the alleged crime?

Moral Skepticism

Moral skepticism
The belief that moral principles do not apply directly to international relations.

Moral skepticism, based on the approach of political realism, is advocated by international relations scholars such as Hans Morgenthau and George F. Kennan. Unlike cynics, who deny the validity of morality, skeptics affirm the reality of moral norms, but challenge their applicability to international affairs. Skeptics argue that because there is an absence of widely shared standards of international morality, it is impossible to develop a body of widely accepted ethical values by which to guide and judge the behavior of states. Moreover, skeptics assume that morality applies primarily to individuals, not to institutions, organizations, and states.

One of the central tenets of moral skepticism is the belief that global politics poses extraordinary conditions because of the anarchic structure of international affairs. Because the security of states cannot be guaranteed in global society, the chief moral responsibility of the statesmen is to assure public safety. Former British Prime Minister Winston Churchill once observed, "National security is so fundamental to the state that it requires no mandate." Because of the primacy of national security, skepticism assumes that a radical discontinuity exists between ordinary life, which is shaped by morality and law, and the extraordinary conditions of global politics, in which a survival ethic is essential in view of the possibility of war and conquest.

Prudence
The virtue of selecting and implementing policies in the light of alternative moral actions.

Finally, moral skeptics argue that states should be guided by **prudence,** or practical wisdom. Fundamentally, prudence involves the weighing of alternative actions in light of anticipated consequences. Although advocates of the prudence tradition have historically recognized a significant tension, if not discontinuity, between ethics and politics, prudence does not necessarily involve the negation of ethics. Indeed, Aristotle argues that prudence is the means by which morality can be effectively applied to political action. Thus, although some secular realists, such as sixteenth-century Italian author and diplomat Niccolò Machiavelli and the seventeenth-century English philosopher Thomas Hobbes, view prudence as unrelated to morality, other skeptics, including the eighteenth-century British parliamentarian Edmund Burke and contemporary Christian realists like Reinhold Neibuhr and Kenneth Thompson, view prudential decision making as the only way of reconciling morality and political action.[14]

As a consequentialist ethic, skepticism assumes that the common good can best be promoted by the application of prudent decision making—that is, by giving practical judgment priority over moral verdicts. This is why Hans Morgenthau writes that "there can be no political morality without prudence."[15] Indeed, Morgenthau, following Aristotle, regards this norm as the supreme virtue in politics.

Communitarianism

Communitarianism is based on the tradition of "common morality," which views ethical norms as rational and universal. Although global society is comprised of many different nations and cultures, morality is not rooted in the values and traditions of specific cultures but in the shared sentiments and values of all persons. In effect, common morality is a transcultural morality rooted in universal rational reflection. Examples of global ethical norms include basic human rights (such as freedom from torture and the freedom to emigrate), the conditional authority of government, the obligation to avoid unnecessary suffering in wartime, the sanctity of treaties, and the obligation not to intervene in the domestic affairs of other states. The idea of common morality is often denoted as "natural law" or "moral law," and its precepts apply both to states (communitarianism) and to individuals (cosmopolitanism).

> **Communitarianism**
> A tradition that assumes that states are morally legitimate and subject to widely accepted legal and moral norms.

The communitarian perspective is represented by such thinkers as seventeenth-century German international lawyer Samuel Pufendorf, eighteenth-century Swiss jurist Emmerich de Vattel, nineteenth-century British political thinker John Stuart Mill, and contemporary political philosopher Michael Walzer. Unlike moral skeptics, who deny the relevance of morality to world affairs, these thinkers share the conviction that precepts of international morality exist and must guide the statesmen if the world is to be peaceful and just. At the same time they reject the view that politics is solely motivated and guided by national interests and power politics. Charles Beitz says that this perspective assumes that "states have obligations to conform to relevant moral rules that are capable, in principle, of requiring sacrifices of self-interest."[16]

The communitarian perspective assumes that the political behavior of states must be guided and judged by the norms of international morality. Such norms consist either of broad general norms—such as freedom, economic prosperity, human dignity, political equality, and justice—or more specific moral rules, such as those found in the *just war theory,* a doctrine providing norms for judging when war is morally legitimate and how it should be prosecuted. (See chap. 11.) Although specific rules can provide in some instances simple categorical verdicts about actions of states, most foreign policy decisions do not lend themselves to simple moral judgments. Indeed, the major value of general moral principles is not to offer moral verdicts about foreign policy but to encourage *ethical reasoning* about international affairs, especially in molding and reforming conceptions of the national interest. Most problems in foreign affairs are complex and often intractable, and devising an ethical perspective is not easy. Thus, whether applying moral rules or general principles, the prudent statesmen should pay heed to journalist H.L. Mencken who once observed, "For every complex problem there is a simple solution—and it is always wrong."

Cosmopolitanism

Cosmopolitanism, like the communitarian perspective, is rooted in the tradition of common morality and more specifically in the Western tradition of individual rights. It assumes that international morality is global in scope, applying to all peoples and all nations; rational in nature, because people apprehend its content through thoughtful reflection; and personalistic, because it is concerned chiefly with human rights and the social and economic well-being of persons.

> **Cosmopolitanism**
> An ethical tradition that assumes that persons, not states, are morally significant in global society. Humanitarian intervention is thus morally permissible.

Moreover, cosmopolitanism is rooted in the tradition of moral absolutism and therefore emphasizes the imperative of behavior in accord with recognized moral rules, regardless of outcomes.

This perspective is represented by thinkers such as sixteenth-century Spanish theologian Francisco Suarez, nineteenth-century German philosopher Immanuel Kant, and contemporary political philosophers Charles Beitz and Henry Shue. Two prominent American political leaders who have articulated this ethical approach are Presidents Woodrow Wilson and Jimmy Carter, both of whom carried out activist foreign policies in defense of basic human rights.

Ethical cosmopolitanism is similar to the communitarian perspective in that it affirms the relevance of ethics to international relations. But whereas cosmopolitanism adheres stringently to the tradition of moral absolutism, the communitarian approach attempts to judge the public policies in light of goals and possible consequences. Moreover, whereas the communitarian perspective is concerned with the moral rights and duties of states, and especially with the protection of state sovereignty from foreign intervention, this perspective gives moral precedence to the rights of individuals. Thus, although the communitarian approach attempts to promote an ethical global society by working through existing state systems, the cosmopolitan perspective attempts to build global society by focusing on the well-being of people themselves. As a result, cosmopolitanism does not view state boundaries as morally significant.

According to cosmopolitanism, states are obligated to defend and protect human rights. When significant injustices occur within countries, such as massive human rights violations perpetrated by the ruling authorities, governments lose their moral standing within international society. Foreign intervention is not only ethically permissible but, in exceptional circumstances, obligatory. Similarly, when a nation's health is seriously threatened by disease and massive hunger, foreign regimes have an ethical responsibility to assist its suffering peoples. For example, when the Khmer Rouge, the radical revolutionary communists ruling Cambodia in the late 1970s, carried out a massive genocide campaign against their own people, killing as many as two million persons, foreign governments had a moral obligation to halt the wanton killing of innocent civilians. Similarly, when hundreds of thousands of Ethiopians were faced with starvation in the mid-1980s because of drought and civil war, developed countries were morally obligated to provide humanitarian assistance.

Both communitarianism and cosmopolitanism provide alternative ethical paradigms for assessing world politics as well as devising foreign policies. More specifically, they provide alternative conceptions for defining justice and applying its norms to the contemporary world system. Because moral skepticism denies the relevance and significance of morality to international relations, it contributes little to the moral conduct and assessment of world politics. Table 7.1 presents key features of the three ethical traditions examined here.

JUSTICE AND THE INTERNATIONAL SYSTEM

The Idea of International Justice

In order to ethically assess the structures and policies of the international community, it is necessary to have a normative standard—a conception of justice—by which to judge foreign policy behaviors and international institutions. Although the idea of international justice is generally associated with the rightness and fairness of the institutions, procedures, and decisions within global society, defining the norms of justice is an especially difficult and elusive task for at least two reasons.

TABLE 7.1 Comparison of Three Ethical Traditions

	Ethical Approach	Type of Morality	Ethical Precedence
Moral Skepticism	consequentialism	prudence	state
Communitarianism	consequentialism/ moral absolutism	moral rules/ general principles	state
Cosmopolitanism	moral absolutism	moral rules	individual

First, defining international justice is difficult because there is little consensus on what political justice is. Even though justice is one of the most frequently analyzed concepts in Western political philosophy, political thinkers have held widely different perspectives about what the concept of justice entails.[17] Historically, most political thinkers have associated political justice with the rightness and fairness of rules, procedures, and institutions and their consistent and impartial application. This approach is generally called **procedural justice** because it seeks to regulate the process for achieving justice, rather than to realize particular outcomes considered just. This approach is illustrated by the American judicial system, which is based on the pursuit of justice through the impartial application of rules. In recent decades, however, a growing number of thinkers have approached justice from an alternative perspective that emphasizes the rightness or fairness of results. This approach, called **distributive (or substantive) justice,** associates justice with the achievement of particular outcomes. International justice from this perspective is thus concerned with the promotion of an equitable distribution of resources among states and other international actors.

Second, the idea of international justice is elusive because the international community is comprised of many distinct societies, each with its own social structures, historical traditions, and cultural and religious norms. As a result, cultural pluralism is a fact of global society. Although domestic societies frequently are based on a plurality of cultural and moral norms, domestic societies normally have much more moral consensus than global society. Stanley Hoffmann has observed that because the international community is based on a "cacophany of standards," justice becomes either "a matter of sheer force—carried at the point of a sword—or, when force does not prevail, a matter of fleeting bargains and tests of fear or strength."[18] Because of the widespread relativity of values found in the world, some thinkers have concluded that there is no universal morality. The only morality that exists, according to them, is subjective, relativistic values associated with each country. This notion—known as the **doctrine of cultural relativism**—holds that the international community's norms about right and wrong, justice and injustice, are based on the different moral norms and cultural traditions of each society. And because the world is comprised of many cultures and moralities, the doctrine holds that there is no universal, binding morality. Because cultural relativism challenges the claims of international ethics, the doctrine is examined and critiqued later in this chapter.

Communitarian Justice Versus Cosmopolitan Justice

The pursuit of justice in international society may involve two different approaches—**communitarian justice** and **cosmopolitan justice.** The first, based on the perspective of communitarianism, is concerned with international justice—that is, the equity and fairness of relations among states. The second is based on cosmopolitanism and focuses on the rights and well-being of persons, regardless of where they live.

Procedural justice
According to this instrumental approach, justice requires strict, consistent, and impartial adherence to rules and procedures.

Distributive justice
According to this substantive approach, justice requires a fair or equitable distribution of goods and resources.

Doctrine of cultural relativism
The belief that, since the world is comprised of many different cultures, each with its own moral norms, there is no universal, binding international morality.

Communitarian justice
Justice focusing on equitable and fair relations among states.

Cosmopolitan justice
Justice focusing on equitable and fair relations among persons.

Communitarian justice—sometimes defined as international justice—focuses on the morality of international behavior, giving special attention to the rights and duties of states. Just as individuals bear rights and responsibilities to one another within domestic society, states must fulfill mutual obligations to other states if peace and justice are to be realized in the world. Examples of widely accepted obligations, examined earlier in chapter 4 (see the "code of peace"), include such norms as: the right of self-defense, the peaceful settlement of disputes, nonintervention in domestic affairs, and the sanctity of treaty obligations. Because sovereignty and territorial integrity are basic states' rights, peace and justice are possible in global society only when the political independence of states is respected. Foreign intervention, military aggression, or other similar violations of state autonomy thus represent basic threats to global order and international justice. In his seventeenth-century classic study *The Law of War and Peace,* Hugo Grotius argues that international society is based on fundamental legal and moral precepts. Even though states are sovereign, they are obligated to fulfill the international community's legal and moral norms. According to Grotius, these norms are rooted in historical precedents, natural law, the Bible, and the joint decisions of states. Even in wartime, states are not free to pursue victory at all costs, but must behave in accordance with widely recognized norms governing warfare. According to Grotius, international justice is possible when states fulfill their legal and moral obligations.

Cosmopolitan justice is concerned with justice among people within global society. Whereas communitarian justice considers states morally significant, the cosmopolitan perspective regards individuals and groups as the primary moral actors. In effect, this approach views the world as a society in which principles of distributive justice apply to persons. Thus, when states commit gross human rights violations or commit genocide against their own citizens, they forfeit their moral standing as legitimate members of global society. Because state boundaries are not morally important, bringing a halt to such evil through foreign intervention is not only permissible but necessary.

If international order and justice are to be strengthened in global society, both communitarian justice and cosmopolitan justice must be encouraged. The former is important because it provides the framework in which an orderly international community can function. Because the world community is a weak society, respect for different cultures and values is indispensable to a stable transnational political system. But because the world is threatened by egregious inequalities among states, the cosmopolitan perspective is important because it gives priority to human beings, regardless of where they live.

These contrasting approaches to justice offer radically different foreign policy implications. A foreign policy rooted in the communitarian paradigm, for example, will foster international order and justice by honoring its international treaty obligations and fulfilling widely accepted rules and legal obligations. In particular, states will attempt to promote world order by respecting the autonomy of states, ensuring collective punishment of aggression, and establishing international structures that promote global economic, political, and social cooperation. In addition, a communitarian foreign policy will provide economic assistance to poor, developing nations and seek to establish an international economic order that is conducive to global economic expansion. Although this paradigm regards states as the primary actors, it assumes that international organizations can contribute to the development of mutual cooperation and peaceful settlement of disputes. A cosmopolitan perspective, by contrast, will tend to de-emphasize political sovereignty and the quest for national security, encourage a strong global commitment to human rights and transnational economic prosperity, and seek to develop strong nonstate actors, especially regional and global IGOs, to facilitate the development of global political solidarity and economic well-being.

The problem of foreign intervention illustrates the different foreign policy implications that are likely to result from these two alternative ethical paradigms. A commitment to cosmopolitan justice, for example, is likely to result in foreign policies deeply committed to the protection of human rights, even if military intervention is required. The communitarian approach, on the other hand, will likely resist foreign intervention, even when humanitarian needs are involved, because it assumes that international justice must protect sovereignty and respect territorial boundaries.

As noted in chapter 10, foreign intervention is normally considered illegal and immoral—illegal, because it violates the sovereignty of another state and immoral, because it violates the moral norms underlying the anarchic international political order. But intervention may also be considered morally legitimate in exceptional circumstances—such as when a regime commits gross human rights violations or when another foreign power intervenes to influence the course of a civil war.[19] Although scholars disagree on the legal and moral circumstances legitimizing **humanitarian intervention,** two conditions commonly accepted as preconditions are: (1) the existence of gross human rights violations, such as genocide or mass starvation, and (2) the intervention must be a last resort, with other peaceful alternatives having been fully exhausted.

Humanitarian intervention
Foreign intervention justified on humanitarian grounds.

Case study 7.1, on U.S. intervention in Somalia, illustrates the important role of a cosmopolititan foreign policy perspective.

Human Rights and the Problem of Cultural Relativism

Human rights are those rights to which persons are entitled by virtue of their humanity. Individual rights may be defined and justified from a positive (empirical) or normative perspective. *Positive rights* are those personal entitlements specified by existing domestic and international statutes and conventions. *Normative rights,* by contrast, are those human rights claims based on morality—on the belief that such claims ought to be upheld. Although the positive rights enumerated by international legal conventions have helped to make human rights claims more prominent in contemporary global politics, the foundation of international human rights is morality, not political agreements and legal conventions. Because of the normative basis of rights claims, human rights are an essential element of the ethics of global politics. Indeed, one scholar has observed that human rights have become "a kind of *lingua franca* of ethics talk so that much of the discussion about ethics in international relations takes place making use of the vocabulary of rights. . . ."[22]

Human rights
The fundamental political, civil, socio-economic, and cultural rights of human beings.

Although human rights are defined from a number of different perspectives (see case 7.2), there is widespread international political consensus about human rights.[23] This political agreement is evident in the significant body of international law of human rights that has developed under the leadership of the United Nations. The first and most important international legal document on human rights is the UN Charter, which affirms faith in "fundamental human rights" and calls on states to promote "respect for human rights and for fundamental freedoms" (art.1). In 1948, the UN General Assembly adopted the **Universal Declaration of Human Rights,** which, because of its comprehensive, global character, is generally regarded as the charter of international human rights. Other important international human rights agreements are the International Covenant on Civil and Political Rights and the International Covenant on Economic, Social and Cultural Rights (see table 7.2).

Universal Declaration of Human Rights
This statement, adopted by the UN General Assembly in 1948, is regarded as the international charter of human rights.

Despite widespread public support for conventions such as these, states hold widely different perspectives on the nature and priority of human rights. This plurality of human rights conceptions has been reflected in the ever-expanding list of international rights—a growth that has tended to undermine political liberalism's

Case 7.1 U.S. Intervention in Somalia

The Problem

Somalia, a poor, developing nation along the Horn of Africa with a population of about 6–8 million people, is an inhospitable country with few natural resources. The country became politically independent in 1960 when British Somaliland (the northern half) and Italian Somaliland (the southern half) were united. Unlike most other African states, Somalia has largely one people—the Somalis, who make up about 85 percent of the total population—but they are deeply divided among rival clans and subclans. In 1969 General Mohammed Siad Barre seized power in a military coup and ruled the country tyrannically and corruptly until his government was overthrown in January 1991. In the aftermath of Siad Barre's ouster, bitter fighting broke out among the major clans. Ironically, the most intense fighting developed between two warlords of the same (Hawiye) clan—General Mohammed Farrah

Periodically military forces are used for humanitarian purposes. Here U.S. troops help distribute food in Somalia in 1992.

Aidid, whose guerrillas had forced Siad Barre from the country, and Ali Mahdi Mohammed.

In 1992 a major famine developed in Somalia, causing the death of 300,000 persons and threatening the lives of another 2 million. Although drought was a contributing factor, the major reason for the hunger and starvation was the bitter civil war that had destroyed agricultural production and was impeding the distribution of humanitarian relief. Because of the complete breakdown of civil authority, a small UN peacekeeping force—known as *UN Operation in Somalia (UNOSOM I)*—had been introduced to keep humanitarian supplies arriving from foreign states. But as lawlessness intensified in 1992, the distribution of humanitarian relief became virtually impossible. In the wake of growing anarchy, UN Secretary-General Boutros Boutros-Ghali pleaded with the major powers that a much larger peacekeeping force was needed if massive starvation was to be prevented.

U.S. Intervention

Because of the possible starvation of some 1–2 million Somalis, President Bush, after consulting with other major powers, authorized a limited military intervention into Somalia. coined "Operation Restore Hope," the military action was a temporary emergency measure designed to achieve limited objectives—namely, to restore civil order, halt looting and crime, and allow humanitarian relief programs to continue functioning. Unlike other U.S. foreign interventions, the Somali action had no strategic or political purpose; its sole aim was humanitarian.[20] In the words of President Bush, the action involved doing "God's work."[21] To ensure broad multilateral support, the UN Security Council unanimously endorsed a resolution authorizing a U.S.-led interventionary task force—known as *United Task Force (UNITAF)*. Although the operation was to be directed by the United States, the 35,000-member operation would involve some 7,000 sol-

emphasis on such foundational claims as freedom from torture, freedom of conscience, freedom of speech, and freedom of assembly. Thus, the political, social, and economic rights listed in table 7.2 are increasingly regarded as fundamentally equal.

The growing confusion over human rights was evident at the 1993 World Conference on Human Rights, the largest international gathering on human rights in twenty-five years. The goal of this UN-sponsored conference was to develop a post-Cold War declaration on international human rights.[27] After a week of meet-

diers from other countries. Moreover, once U.S. forces had achieved their peacemaking mission, they would turn over authority to a UN peacekeeping force.

The decision to intervene in Somalia contrasts sharply with the government's reticence to become involved in former Yugoslavia. Beginning in 1991, a bitter civil war raged among Bosnians, Croats, and Serbs as they fought over the partitioning of the former communist state. The war had resulted in tens of thousands of deaths and more than a million refugees, and despite the introduction of a 22,000-member UN peacekeeping force, fighting continued sporadically, with many isolated communities threatened with starvation. Athough the genocide and suffering in Croatia and Bosnia-Herzegovina provided compelling moral justification for foreign military action, the Bush administration opposed military involvement because (1) it would be excessively costly in human and economic terms, and (2) there was little likelihood that such an operation would succeed in ending the war. By contrast, the Somali civil war provided a clear moral justification for foreign military intervention at an estimated low cost and with a high probability of success.

The U.S. military intervention in Somalia began in mid-December with the landing of a 3,000-member marine force. By the time the U.S. forces had arrived, many Somali guerrillas had fled to the interior or outside of the country. As a result, the military intervention was swift and unopposed. After consolidating control over Mogadishu, the major port city, and its surrounding area, U.S. forces moved to other cities and villages in central Somalia, where famine was most severe, establishing secure transportation and distribution networks for humanitarian supplies of food and medicine. Within a month of the intervention, U.S. forces had successfully established control over key transportation channels, thereby allowing the resumption of humanitarian relief. After achieving its original mission, the United States began withdrawing its troops, so that by May 1993 only about 5,000 soldiers of the original 28,000-member task force remained in Somalia. The United States then transferred the responsibility for the relief operation back to a UN peacekeeping force—*UNOSOM II*.

UN Peacekeeping

Once the United Nations assumed control of the Somali operation, it began shifting the peacekeeping mission toward nation-building. In particular, UN officials believed that if clan warfare was not to resume in Somalia, it was important to demilitarize the country. The need to reduce the military power of the clans became evident in early June when General Aidid's forces ambushed a group of Pakistani peacekeepers, killing twenty-four and wounding fifty-four. Subsequently, U.S. forces got involved in a bitter fight with Aidid guerrillas, resulting in many casualties, including seventeen Americans killed and seventy-seven wounded. This development prompted President Bill Clinton to more than double the number of U.S. troops in Somalia by adding 1,900 soldiers and placing a 3,600-member marine force on ships offshore. In deploying these new forces, Clinton pledged to withdraw all troops from Somalia by March 31, 1994.

From an ethical perspective, the original U.S. decision to intervene in Somalia was wholly just: the aims, means, and expected outcomes of "Operation Restore Hope" were moral. But once the mission was expanded to include nation-building, the Somalia operation became increasingly morally ambiguous, in part because of the operation's rising military cost of the operation and the decreasing likelihood that the broader goals could be realized in the near future.

ings, the delegates from 171 countries approved, by consensus,[28] a final declaration, known as the **Vienna Declaration of Human Rights,** which lists basic principles and an action program to advance human rights in the international community. The Vienna Declaration reflects the growing emphasis of multicultural interpretations by its emphasis on social, cultural, and economic rights, while de-emphasizing rights associated with limited, constitutional government. This is why the declaration omits such core rights as the freedom of religion, freedom of assembly, and freedom of speech. One Western conference critic calls the Vienna

Vienna Declaration of Human Rights
A comprehensive statement on international human rights, adopted in Vienna in 1993, emphasize social, economic, and cultural rights.

TABLE 7.2 International Human Rights

International Covenant on Civil and Political Rights (1966)
States are obligated to respect and promote such rights as:
life and physical security of persons;
freedom of thought, religion, and expression;
freedom of association and peaceful assembly;
due process of law and a humane penal system;
freedom from torture; and
legal equality and nondiscrimination.
International Covenant on Economic, Social and Cultural Rights (1966)
States are obligated to respect and promote such rights as:
to work and to enjoy an adequate standard of living;
to "just" working conditions, including fair compensation, a safe and healthy working environment and periodic holidays;
to form trade unions and to strike;
to social security; and
to participate in the cultural life of a nation.

Declaration a "hodge-podge collection of high principles, stolen wording and bad compromises" that would likely be used by authoritarian rulers "to justify old and new human rights violations."[29]

The belief in international human rights is, of course, inconsistent with the doctrine of cultural pluralism. As noted earlier, the doctrine alleges that morality is completely relative to the norms and practices of each society, and that there is, therefore, no universal morality and no international human rights. All that can be affirmed are the particular rights claims of each society. Because the doctrine of cultural pluralism poses an important challenge to the idea of human rights, the doctrine is critiqued empirically and normatively.

Empirically, the claim of total moral diversity is simply untenable. As one scholar has noted, moral diversity cannot be total because "certain moral principles are necessary for social life." Indeed, he argues that people share a common morality that is expressed in such norms as respect for human life, fellowship, and freedom from arbitrary interference.[30] Michael Walzer has similarly argued that there is a universal commitment to such notions as "truth" and "justice," as well as agreement about such norms as the dignity of persons, the impartial application of the law, and freedom of conscience. Walzer calls this shared morality "minimal" or "thin" in order to differentiate it from the more substantive "maximal" or "thick" morality of each culture. Moral minimalism, he observes is a "thin" morality not because it is unimportant or makes few claims on persons, but because its claims are general and universal.[31]

Normatively, the doctrine of cultural relativism is also untenable because cultural relativity is not an ethical argument. To affirm that the world is comprised of different cultures is a descriptive statement. Its validity depends upon its truth. But the doctrine of cultural relativism seeks to make not only descriptive claims but prescriptive claims as well. It asserts that, based on the fact of pluralism, there can be no moral hierarchy among different cultures. Thus, a moral doctrine is derived from the fact of cultural pluralism. But, as R.J. Vincent has noted, the doctrine can-

Case 7.2 | Human Rights and Caning in Singapore

The Conflict

In 1994, Michael Fay, an 18-year-old American youth living with his mother in Singapore, was found guilty of vandalism (spray-painting automobiles). Singapore's court sentenced him to six lashes with a cane, four months in prison, and a $2,200 fine—a punishment that was grossly inconsistent with Western legal norms, but consistent with the Singapore's own draconian political and social rules. Because the punishment involved flogging—a practice long considered inhumane in the West—the court's judgment precipitated an intense debate in the United States over the justice of the punishment as well as over the morality of the East Asian approach to human rights.

Singapore, a modern, prosperous city-state on the southern tip of Malaysia, is an authoritarian regime with limited personal freedoms and strict social and cultural controls. Although Singapore's economic system is relatively free, the social and political life is highly regulated by the state. For example, Singapore permits the detention of suspects for up to two years, whereas meetings with five or more persons require a police permit. Socially, its rules seem even more severe: chewing gum, spitting, or feeding birds are not permissible in public areas, and violations are subject to severe fines.

International law forbids punishment involving torture. Article 7 of the International Covenant on Civil and Political Rights states that "No one shall be subjected to torture or to cruel, inhuman or degrading treatment or punishment." Still, a number of states, including Singapore, continue the practice of caning. As practiced in Singapore, a prisoner is tied to a wooden trestle and struck on the buttocks with a damp rattan cane. Although the effects of caning depend on the number and intensity of the strokes, flogging frequently results in permanent scars.

After Fay was sentenced, an intense public debate emerged in the United States over the appropriateness of caning. The debate became officially important when President Bill Clinton condemned the punishment as "excessive" and called on Singapore's president to commute the sentence. In response to Clinton's appeal, Singapore decreased the punishment from six lashes to four, and after serving his punishment, Fay was released from prison and returned to the United States.

The Moral Debate

The debate precipitated by the caning of Fay was fundamentally a controversy over alternative theories of political society and human rights—a debate between the "Asian School," which stresses order and communal obligations, and Western political liberalism, which emphasizes economic and political freedom and individual rights. Did Singapore violate international law when it flogged Fay? More fundamentally, did it carry out an act of torture that was contrary to basic ethical norms of global society? Or did Singapore simply apply its own cultural and political perspective of social justice? If the latter, is the East Asian human rights perspective morally valid?

If Singapore were a poor, corrupt developing nation, it is unlikely that its action would have gained much attention in the West. But Singapore is a modern, sophisticated, and productive society, providing ample economic, educational, and social benefits to its people. It has minimal poverty, a low crime rate, and its students' achievement scores in science and mathematics are among the highest in the world. By contrast, the United States, the leading liberal society in the world, has experienced significant social and cultural decay in recent decades with the breakdown of the family unit, the disintegration of inner-city neighborhoods, and the explosion of crime. This decay is especially evident when social life of Singapore and Los Angeles, cities of roughly the same size, are compared: in 1993 Singapore had 58 murders and 80 rapes, whereas Los Angeles had 1,058 murders and 1,781 rapes.[24]

According to Lee Kuan Yew, Singapore's former long-term prime minister and the architect of the nation's political and social system, his country's economic and social development has been due, in great measure, to the priority given to communal obligations and the refusal to follow Western liberalism's emphasis on individual rights. The East Asian approach to political society has the advantage, he believes, in more effectively balancing communal goods with individual claims.[25] Some East Asian officials suggest that the social and cultural decline of the United States is due to its excessive emphasis on individualism and freedom. For example, Kishore Mahbubani argues that American social and cultural decay is due to its ideology of individualism and personal freedom. In his view, the excessive celebration

continued

of individual freedom has had an ironic outcome, contributing to social decay and cultural decline, which itself now threatens the personal security and economic and social well-being of individuals. Mahbubani writes: "It is obvious that this enormous reduction of freedom in America is the result of a mindless ideology that maintains that freedom of a small number of individuals (criminals, terrorists, street gang members, drug dealers), who are known to pose a threat to society, should not be constrained . . . even if to do so would enhance the freedom of the majority."[26] For Mahbubani and other East Asian officials, Western liberalism has encouraged excessive emphasis on individual freedoms, thereby undermining the family and weakening social institutions, and impairing the criminal justice system.

In sum, Westerners believe that the East Asian approach to political society provides insufficient individual freedom and does not adequately respect human rights. Flogging is but one instance of Singapore's flawed, authoritarian political order. East Asians, by contrast, believe that it is Western liberalism, with its celebration of individual rights, that is threatening community order and the social well-being of persons. What do you think?

not logically rank cultures. All that it can do is assert that values are rooted in the particularities of each culture.[32]

In short, despite cultural pluralism, statesmen and citizens alike continuously judge the political behavior of foreigners, while seeking to justify their own actions. The fact that people argue about the rules and institutions of the global economy, the legitimacy of war in response to aggression, the legality of foreign intervention, and the obligation to assist nations suffering from poverty and political oppression suggests that some shared morality exists. Walzer, for example, has observed that people's debates and arguments about war imply the existence of moral norms about war. Walzer writes: "The moral world of war is shared not because we arrive at the same conclusions . . . but because we acknowledge the same difficulties on the way to our conclusion, face the same problems, talk the same language."[33] Walzer suggests that the hypocrisy and dishonesty expressed by citizens, soldiers, and statesmen in and about war signify the existence of an ethical code of war. "The clearest evidence for the stability of our values over time," writes Walzer, "is the unchanging character of the lies soldiers and statesmen tell. They lie in order to justify themselves, and so they describe for us the lineaments of justice. Wherever we find hypocrisy, we also find moral knowledge."[34.]

Because the world is comprised of many societies, each with its own customs, cultural norms, and moral traditions, the quest for justice in the world is an especially difficult challenge. Not only does cultural pluralism impede the development of binding international norms, but thinkers and public officials must reconcile widely divergent ethical theories and approaches. The daunting task of developing an authoritative political morality for the world is illustrated by the debate over female genital mutilation (see case 7.3).

MORALITY AND FOREIGN POLICY

The Role of Morality

One of the reasons why students of world politics have doubted the role of ethics in foreign affairs is that moral values have sometimes been used to promote na-

Case 7.3 Female Genital Mutilation: Tradition or Torture?

Every year some 2 million adolescent girls undergo a tribal ritual involving genital cutting. The practice, rooted in traditional customs dating to ancient Egypt, is generally called "female genital mutilation" by Western opponents and "female circumcision" by African multiculturalists.[35] The ritual involves the removal of part or all of a girl's genitalia in order to eliminate sexual sensation, to ensure virginity, and to thereby make a woman marriageable. The practice, which is found in some rural areas of Asia and the Middle East, is especially prevalent in Africa, in which more than 100 million women are estimated to have undergone the ritual. Despite efforts by some African governments to restrict the practice, genital mutilation remains popular in approximately twenty-eight African countries because it is regarded as a rite of passage from adolescence into adulthood. Indeed, the rite is generally viewed in some cultures as an occasion for celebration.

As Western citizens have become more aware of this traditional custom, they have voiced increasing condemnation of the practice, calling for international sanctions against countries that permit it. Although international organizations have devoted resources to publicize the health hazards of the ritual, limited collective actions have been undertaken—in great part because the dispute about female genital mutilation involves a fundamental conflict between indigenous traditional cultural norms and modern Western values. For a Western citizen, the African ritual is a form of torture, and a violation of international law and fundamental human rights. For an African traditionalist, however, the practice is legitimate because it is rooted in customs and mores that give meaning to peoples living in traditional tribal societies.

Several Western states, including the United States, have enacted laws to prohibit female genital cutting within their own territorial boundaries.[36] Laws have been passed so that immigrants coming from traditional societies in which the ritual is practiced will not perform it on their own children. Moreover, the recognition that genital cutting is inconsistent with basic human rights has resulted in some requests for political asylum in Western countries. In an important test case in the United States, a 17-year-old woman from Togo, who fled her homeland to avoid genital cutting, requested asylum in the United States. Although her appeal was at first denied, the U.S. Board of Immigration Appeals overturned the original decision and granted asylum based on the woman's legitimate fear of a ritual involving torture.[37]

tional self-interest, rather than universal rights. Throughout its history, but especially in the late nineteenth and early twentieth centuries, U.S. political leaders have based foreign policy behavior on moral values such as peace, human rights, and freedom. For example, President McKinley supposedly relied on divine guidance in order to decide whether or not to use military force against Spain in the Philippines. And when Woodrow Wilson ordered U.S. military forces to intervene in Veracruz, Mexico, in 1914, he did so because he thought it would promote human dignity in that land. More recently, President Jimmy Carter gave expression to the universalistic and moralistic motif in his human rights policy—a diplomacy based on the belief that the United States had a moral obligation to defend basic rights wherever possible.

The propensity to misuse values for national gain (moralism) has of course resulted in increased skepticism, if not cynicism, about ethics. Arthur Schlesinger, Jr., for example, writes that in foreign affairs moral values should be applied only in questions of last resort.[38] Similarly, former U.S. Secretary of State Dean Acheson observes that the "vocabulary of morals and ethics is inadequate to discuss or test foreign policies of states." He suggests that there are no moral standards of universal applicability that can be used by the diplomat. "When we look for standards [of political morality]," writes Acheson, "we find that none exist."[39]

George Kennan has expressed in numerous writings his skepticism about the value of ethics in making and implementing foreign policy. According to Kennan, morality can contribute little to foreign policy decision making because (1) there are no widely accepted international standards of morality and (2) the decisions of governments must be based on values other than personal morality. Kennan writes:

> Moral principles have their place in the heart of the individual and in the shaping of his own conduct. . . . But when the individual's behavior passes through the machinery of political organization and merges with that of millions of other individuals to find its expression in the actions of a government, then it undergoes a general transmutation, and the same moral concepts are no longer relevant to it. A government is an agent, not a principal; and no more than any other agent may it attempt to be the conscience of its principal. In particular, it may not subject itself to those supreme laws of renunciation and self-sacrifice that represent the culmination of individual moral growth.[40]

Kennan, like other realists, argues that the only legitimate basis of foreign policy is the national interest—which he defines chiefly in terms of national security, the integrity of political life, and the well-being of citizens. These interests, he observes, have no moral quality but arise from the decentralized character of international order.

One limitation of Kennan's argument is that it is based on a purely instrumental view of politics—a perspective that assumes that the process of governing is a "practical exercise," not a moral task. Even though governing does of course concern the maintenance of order, the provision of economic well-being, and the resolution of conflict, politics also has a nobler cause—the promotion of justice, peace, and human dignity.

Second, Kennan assumes that morality is primarily a list of fixed rules of right and wrong for guiding human behavior. But morality does not consist of simple categorical norms but of broad principles that guide and inform human choices. In foreign affairs, as in much of life, there are no simple moral judgments on most issues. Therefore, ethics is valuable in IR not because it provides moral solutions, but rather because it can help mold and reform the general conception of a state's fundamental interests and illuminate morally acceptable methods of promoting them.

Foreign policy is inescapably a moral enterprise. Although the priority of national security decreases the realm of moral choice for statesmen, it does not eliminate ethics. As with other areas of life, human choices are ultimately based on values, many of them moral in nature. The ethical challenge in foreign affairs is not whether moral values influence foreign policy, but which ones and to what degree. Foreign policy is not and cannot be value-free. International politics does not push decision and action beyond the realm of moral judgment. It is based on moral choice itself.

The priority of moral values is illustrated in Robert Kennedy's account of the Cuban missile crisis. According to him, morality was the most important factor in defining U.S. response to the Soviet introduction of missiles into Cuba. Kennedy says that top U.S. officials spent more time weighing and assessing the moral consequences of military action than on any other matter during the early stages of the crisis. According to Kennedy, the major reason why the United States did not launch a military attack against Cuba was that such an act would have eroded the "moral position" of the United States.[41] To be sure, moral discourse does not itself assure ethical behavior. But as political theorist Michael Walzer has noted, moral discourse is "coercive" in that it shapes our thinking, arguments, and justifications for behavior.[42]

The Aims of Morality

Moral values contribute in three ways to the development and implementation of foreign policy. First, they provide direction; second, they provide a basis for judgment; and third, they provide inspiration.

Direction

Moral values provide general guidance to states by clarifying and molding state interests. John C. Bennett suggests that values can offer "ultimate perspectives, broad criteria, motives, inspirations, sensitivities, warnings, moral limits" to statesmen.[43] They do not, however, provide directives for policies. Moral values are like a beacon that provides direction to a ship in a storm. If there is no vision, no reference point, diplomacy will lack consistency and continuity and will be tossed about in the stormy waters of world politics. As Henry Kissinger has noted, "It is not possible to conduct a foreign policy without a vision of the world that one wants to bring about. . . . If one does not have that vision, one runs the risk of a series of unrelated decisions."[44] The importance of moral values was clearly demonstrated during the presidencies of Jimmy Carter and Ronald Reagan. During Carter's administration, one of the major values inspiring foreign policy was the promotion of human rights. During his two-term presidency, Ronald Reagan championed the cause of freedom, making the liberation from communist oppression a moral crusade. Moreover, the decision to intervene militarily in Somalia in 1992, a case examined earlier in this chapter, was inspired chiefly by the moral concern for human dignity, not the strategic interests of the United States.

Judgment

Moral values also serve as a basis for assessing foreign policy decisions and behavior. Moral norms are like a plumb line, providing standards for judging human actions. Without morality, foreign policy succumbs to the game of power politics, for which military might becomes the primary standard.

An even more important contribution of morality is that it provides a basis for self-judgment. Because of the human propensity for pride and selfish behavior, one of the most difficult challenges is to apply moral values to ourselves. It is easier to judge others than ourselves, and easier to judge foreign states than our own nation. This is why Herbert Butterfield used to observe that the cause of morality is furthered insofar as self-judgment is applied to human choices.[45] For the same reason Reinhold Niebuhr wrote that there could be no moral action without self-criticism.[46]

Inspiration

Finally, morality can contribute to foreign policy by providing emotional appeal for the actions that are undertaken by government. Political leaders have a responsibility for initiating policy, but if its implementation is to be effective, it will have to capture the imagination of the public. For example, after the Soviet Union requested humanitarian aid in 1921, U.S. public officials galvanized public and Congressional support for the famine-relief efforts by appealing to morality. And during the 1960s President Kennedy captured the moral imagination and aspirations of a large segment of people throughout the developing world through programs such as the Alliance for Progress and the Peace Corps. Indeed, one of the reasons why his memory lingers in Third World cities, towns, and villages is that he articulated a vision of a better, more just world. Nelson Mandela, the former head of South Africa's liberation movement and the first president of South Africa's nonracial, democratic regime, has similarly provided moral inspiration for ending racial discrimination in South Africa. Though imprisoned from 1964 until 1990, Mandela served as the moral leader of the anti-apartheid movement in South Africa.

To illustrate the important role that moral values play in providing direction and inspiration to foreign policy decision making, we examine U.S. humanitarian relief to Russia in the early 1920s (see case 7.4). From a strictly strategic perspective, U.S. food aid was contrary to the principal U.S. foreign policy objective,

Case 7.4 U.S. Famine Relief to Russia

The Famine

In 1921 a massive famine developed in the Soviet Union, threatening the lives of millions of Russians. War had greatly reduced agricultural production during the 1915–1920 period, and when the famine hit in 1921 some 20 million Russians were threatened with starvation and famine-related epidemics, especially typhus and smallpox. Hundreds of thousands of refugees had begun fleeing farms and rural villages in search of food and medical care, flooding Russia's major cities with refugees. In view of the great suffering caused by the famine, the Soviet government issued an appeal for foreign humanitarian assistance. The appeal was first made by Russian author Maxim Gorky, who, among other things, called on "cultured European and American people" to provide assistance, especially food and medicines.

At the time the Soviet Union made its appeal, international humanitarian assistance was being increasingly accepted as a moral obligation by the major powers.[47] Throughout the nineteenth century, governments had intermittently provided international disaster relief. But following the First World War, **famine relief** became not only more widely accepted but also morally expected among the major powers. One expression of this was the Allied cooperation in postwar humanitarian relief. Because agricultural production in the central European countries had virtually stopped during the war, at the time of the Armistice (1918) some 200 million persons were suffering from disease, hunger, and malnutrition, especially in Austria, Germany, Hungary, and Poland. In response to the growing starvation, the United States, supported by Britain, France, and Italy, responded with a major multilateral famine-relief effort.

The growing acceptance of humanitarianism was demonstrated by the increased institutionalization of famine relief. To better coordinate international assistance, for example, a centralized International Red Cross was established in 1921. Moreover, the newly established League of Nations articulated the international humanitarian-relief norm by explicitly calling on its member-states (in art. 25) to support international humanitarian aid. Thus, by the time famine struck Soviet Russia, international humanitarian relief was a widely accepted norm in global society.

At the time of the famine, the U.S. government (along with Britain and France) was seeking to isolate the Soviet communist regime, with the hope that it would be overthrown. Following the Bolshevik Revolution, the United States had opposed the recognition of the government and had refused to accept Russian gold to pay for U.S. imports because it regarded the gold as "stolen" property. To isolate Soviet Russia, Britain and France had instituted a trade blockade, while the U.S. had implemented a slightly less punitive measure—outlawing foreign trade—because it viewed blockades as contrary to international law.

In the early 1920s Western opposition to the Soviet regime intensified after the Bolshevik government instituted a number of revolutionary policies contrary to Western interests. The initiatives most strongly opposed by the West were the Soviet Union's efforts to destabilize Western governments through propaganda; the regime's repudiation of Russia's prerevolutionary debts to foreign countries; and the expropriation, without compensation, of foreign investments.[48] Although its loans and investments in Russia were comparatively small, the U.S. government viewed debt repudiation and property confiscation with alarm, setting a dangerous international precedent. Thus, when Warren Harding became president in 1921, he reaffirmed the U.S. policy of commercial and diplomatic isolation established by his predecessor, Woodrow Wilson. The United States would not intervene militarily to topple the Soviet communist regime, but it would continue isolating the Soviet economy, hoping that domestic economic needs would destabilize the Soviet political system.

which was to undermine and topple the revolutionary communist regime. But U.S. officials, following a cosmopolitan ethic, determined that humanitarian values should take precedence over strategic goals. Interestingly, when a major famine developed in North Korea in 1997, the U.S. government, notwithstanding its official opposition to this revolutionary communist regime, authorized significant humanitarian relief.

The Soviet appeal for famine relief presented U.S. policy makers with a dilemma. On the one hand, the famine promised to destabilize and possibly weaken the Soviet regime. Lenin, the Bolshevik head of the new government, had warned his comrades at the Tenth Party Congress in March 1921 that a major crop failure would undermine his government and could possibly result in the fall of the regime and the end of Soviet communism. Thus, when crop failure became even more severe than had been anticipated, the famine appeared to advance the very goals that the United States and its allies were pursuing through diplomatic and commercial channels. On the other hand, the suffering in Soviet Russia presented the American people with an opportunity to help alleviate human suffering in a far away land. By providing food and medical supplies, the U.S. government could alleviate human suffering and thereby fulfill an international moral obligation.

American Humanitarian Relief

When faced with the choice of responding to or disregarding human needs, U.S. government officials chose to provide humanitarian assistance and to sacrifice politics. They did so, according to Robert McElroy, because they recognized that international morality "obliges nations with food surpluses to aid famine-stricken countries regardless of their political regime."[49]

Herbert Hoover, Harding's secretary of commerce, played a key role in developing the government's response to the Soviet famine. Because he had played a key role in coordinating humanitarian relief to Europe both during and after World War I, he was qualified to devise a competent relief program. Moreover, Hoover had continued his involvement in humanitarian affairs, serving as chair of the American Relief Association (ARA), the agency that had coordinated European famine relief. After receiving Soviet Russia's appeal, Hoover recommended to Secretary of State Charles Evans Hughes that the United States as-sist the Russian people, provided the famine relief was based on principles that had guided the European reconstruction efforts. Implicit in Hoover's recommendation were four preconditions: first, the government needed to declare a need for aid; second, the government needed to approve the American assistance plan; third, relief workers needed to have full freedom of movement in Russia; and fourth, aid needed to be distributed impartially.[50] After brief consultations, the Soviet government announced its approval of the American relief initiative.

Although initial relief was funded from existing ARA resources, the bulk of the aid was funded by the U.S. government. In 1921, the U.S. Congress approved President Harding's Russian relief request of $24 million ($20 million for food purchases and $4 million for medical supplies), a sum roughly equivalent to 1 percent of the 1921 federal budget.[51] By early 1922, some 35,000 ARA distribution centers had been set up in the Soviet Union and were feeding some 10.5 million persons daily. In addition, more than 7 million persons were inoculated for typhus and smallpox, greatly reducing the spread of these diseases. By mid-1923, most regions in Soviet Russia had regained food self-sufficiency, leading to the phase-out of U.S. relief programs by the end of the year.

From an ethical perspective, the U.S. famine-relief policy was moral in its goals and means but morally problematic in its consequences. The famine-relief program was morally problematic because it unwittingly helped to keep in power a revolutionary communist regime. By meeting human needs, the U.S. government contributed to the stabilization of Soviet society, thereby contradicting its stated policy of undermining the government. Although numerous factors contributed to the U.S. response, the fundamental norm guiding U.S. policy was the desire to relieve famine. Thus, in reconciling the geopolitical goal of weakening the Soviet regime and the humanitarian goal of famine relief, U.S. officials gave precedence to the alleviation of human suffering.

The Dangers of Morality

The effort to explicitly apply moral values to foreign policy will not necessarily result in ethical behavior. Indeed, history suggests that moral norms can be misused and lead to moralistic policies that bring not only harm to states but discredit morality itself. In applying ethical values to the conduct of foreign affairs, it is therefore important to be aware of potential dangers. The following sections briefly examine three harmful effects—moralism, self-righteousness, and cynicism.

Moralism

This danger derives from the application of simplistic moral stereotypes to complex foreign policy issues. **Moralism** results when problems are oversimplified and when moral values are applied as if issues were either good or bad, true or false. For example, during the 1950s and 1960s, many U.S. government officials viewed the Cold War as a conflict between good and evil. Thus, in 1983 President Reagan referred to the Soviet Union as an "evil empire." Although judgment was no doubt historically correct in view of the Soviet Union's long record of human rights violations, this simple verdict was viewed by many scholars and news commentators as overly simplistic. Similarly, during the 1990 Persian Gulf crisis, President Bush compared Saddam Hussein to Hitler because of his dictatorial methods of governing Iraq and the brutality with which his military forces had occupied Kuwait. Even though news commentators agreed that many of Hussein's policies involved significant evil, they also opposed the simple moral verdict offered by the president.

Most issues in foreign affairs do not lend themselves to simple moral verdicts, in great measure because issues involve overlapping and even competing moral values. As a result, decision makers must choose among potential alternatives, selecting policy alternatives that promote the most good and bring about the least harm. But moralism impedes the process of moral reasoning because it assumes that political morality is monolithic. One of the most destructive effects of moralism in world politics is that it intensifies conflicts among states. When statesmen become crusaders rather than diplomats, they decrease the flexibility with which they can pursue global interests. Hans Morgenthau has noted that,

> The morality of the particular group, far from limiting the struggle for power on the international scene, gives the struggle a ferocity and intensity not known to other ages. For the claim to universality which inspires the moral code of one particular group is incompatible with the identical claim of another group; the world had room for only one, and the other must yield or be destroyed.[52]

Self-Righteousness

This second danger arises from overconfidence in one's own moral rectitude—often a direct outcome of applying morality to others but not to oneself. According to Reinhold Niebuhr, self-righteousness is especially pronounced in nations because they are less capable than individuals of being self-critical. Moreover, nations often seek to clothe their interests in moral language in order to gain universal public approbation.

One of the regrettable consequences of self-righteousness is hypocrisy—the pretentious use of moral slogans for national gain. This problem arises from the confusion between principles, which may be just and correct, and behavior, which often is not. Because all political activity is partly an exercise in self-interest, there can never be a completely just nation or wholly moral foreign policy. No matter how inspired they are by transcendent moral values, foreign policies always are partly unjust. One of the essential requirements of a humane, ethical foreign policy is humility—the recognition that no person or state possesses all truth. Stanley Hoffmann wisely notes that an essential norm of the international community of states is moderation, or what he terms "the morality of self-restraint."[53]

Cynicism

A third danger resulting from the misuse of morality is cynicism—that is, the denial of transcendent standards. When states use moral values pretentiously and self-righteously in justifying their foreign policy behavior, they encourage hypocrisy and ultimately cynicism itself. According to E.H. Carr, one of the major contributions of political realists to the analysis of international relations is their exposure of the weaknesses of idealists who profess to have identified universal moral values. Carr writes that the most damaging criticism of idealists is not that they fail to live up to their moral standards, but that the supposedly absolute and universal principles have not always been moral principles but norms rooted in the national interest.[54]

Despite these dangers, moral norms can and must play a role in developing and executing foreign policy, particularly if the world is to become more peaceful and just. But how can power and morality be integrated? How can moral values be applied to foreign policy without compromising values or distorting the foreign policy process?

The Need for a Comprehensive Strategy

Political ethics are commonly associated with intentions and purposes. Because moral purity is far easier to achieve in thought than in deed, scholars and philosophers have tended to avoid "the problem of dirty hands" by emphasizing the religious, theoretical, and conceptual dimensions of ethics and to avoid the problems associated with political implementation and results. But although the purity of motives is important in religion, it is not the deciding factor in politics. As Peter Berger notes, "When it comes to politics, we get no moral Brownie points for good intentions; we will be judged by the results."[55] The aim of morality is not to purify goals, but to uplift the quality of life—to bring peace and justice to the world. A morality that provides vision and purpose is important, but vision alone is not enough. Morality must guide the process of policy selection and policy implementation as well.

Joseph Nye, Jr., has suggested that a moral foreign policy must be concerned with goals, means, and consequences.[56] The challenge in applying moral principles to foreign policy is to reconcile the demands of morality at each of these three levels. Because foreign policies are rarely able to achieve moral goals, moral means, and moral outcomes, foreign policy decision making inevitably involves trade-offs among competing moral obligations at these three levels. For example, some policies—like the U.S. effort to topple Manuel Noriega's government in Panama—may involve moral goals and outcomes but involve dubious means. Other policy decisions may have noble intentions but lead to morally questionable outcomes. During the 1990–1991 Gulf War, for example, the United States encouraged Kurds, a minority group in northern Iraq, to rebel against Saddam Hussein's regime. After allied forces had defeated Iraq decisively, the Kurds tried to establish political autonomy, but Hussein, using his remaining military forces, was able not only to defeat the Kurdish resistance, but to force more than one million Kurds to flee to sanctuaries along the northern borders.

President Reagan's proposed Strategic Defense Initiative (SDI) illustrates the difficulty of reconciling moral values with goals, means, and outcomes. The aim of SDI—providing strategic protection—was morally unassailable. The means and likely consequences of SDI, however, posed many ethical problems. For example, because a comprehensive strategic defense system was estimated to cost from $250 billion to $500 billion, allocating such large amounts of money to this program raised moral issues about alternative uses of public funds. More importantly, by politically undermining the system of nuclear deterrence, SDI was potentially contributing to increased international instability. Even though an internationally shared comprehensive strategic defense system would have undoubtedly been more moral than existing conditions, the transition from nuclear offense to strategic defense would have been highly destabilizing and fraught with great dangers. Finally, SDI posed moral concerns at the level of consequences. What would be the outcome of a successful SDI program? Would the world be safer with strategic defense than strategic offense? Because of uncertainties about the means and likely outcomes of SDI, the shift toward strategic defense raised numerous ethical concerns, making the initiative morally problematic.

U.S. imposition of economic sanctions against South Africa also illustrates the moral ambiguity of foreign policy. (see case 9.1) Because of **apartheid,** South Africa's policy of racial segregation, the United States instituted economic sanctions in the mid-1980s as a means of promoting democratic reforms and social justice in that land. But sanctions are morally problematic because they fail to discriminate between the intended target (usually government officials, the business elite, and political and military leaders) and the citizenry. For example, trade sanctions reduced demand for labor-intensive minerals and agricultural products, resulting in massive unemployment and underemployment in the black townships in the late 1980s. Additionally, economic sanctions are morally problematic because of their uncertain impact on policy reform. Although the aim of sanctions is to inflict pain in order to alter undesirable policies, the relationship between economic hardship and policy reform is unclear—a truth demonstrated during the Persian Gulf War, when Saddam Hussein, facing some of the most comprehensive and effective sanctions ever imposed on a foreign state, refused to withdraw his forces from Kuwait. Although the dismantling of apartheid might suggest that sanctions have "worked," it is not clear that the government's democratic initiatives were precipitated, or even encouraged, by Western economic pressures.

As these examples illustrate, developing a moral foreign policy is an especially challenging task because foreign policies are seldom fully in accord with morality at the levels of goals, means, and results. More likely, policies are likely to involve moral trade-offs among competing and sometimes conflicting moral norms, resulting in morally ambiguous foreign policies. In the last analysis, the challenge in forging an ethical policy is to choose the action that promotes the greatest good and occasions the least evil.

Apartheid
The policy of racial segregation that was implemented in South Africa from 1948 to 1990.

In Conclusion

Because politics is inescapably an ethical enterprise, a satisfactory account of global politics must take into account power and morality. The quest for justice in global society is much more difficult than in domestic society because in the international community there is less consensus about moral values and because international institutions are less developed. But although moral and cultural pluralism may make the quest for international justice more difficult, the diversity of values does not signify that the global society is devoid of moral order. Indeed, the arguments and justifications about the promotion of a more humane, equitable, and just global society provide evidence that citizens, soldiers, and statesmen are concerned with normative politics, even though they may disagree on goals and means.

If a foreign policy is to be effective over the long term, it must be consistent not only with the basic moral values of its citizens but also with the shared moral aspirations of other nations. To the extent that states carry out ethical foreign policies, they increase the possibility of peace and justice in global society.

SUMMARY

1. Morality is inextricably a part of global politics. Some thinkers argue that morality should be applied in light of expected results (consequentialism), whereas others believe that ethical rules should be strictly observed, regardless of anticipated outcomes (moral absolutism).

2. Three major traditions have dominated international ethics: skepticism, communitarianism, and cosmopolitanism. The first assumes that ethics, although illuminating important decision-making principles, does not apply directly to foreign policy or to the issues and problems of global politics; the second assumes that ethical norms apply directly to the foreign policy behavior of states; and the third assumes that morality applies chiefly to persons and derivatively to states.

3. It is important to differentiate between communitarian justice and cosmopolitan justice. The pursuit of justice in world affairs is morally ambiguous because the quest for equity among states will not necessarily assure justice among people. The defense of states' rights may require at times the toleration of injustice within countries, whereas the defense of human rights may occasionally necessitate foreign intervention.

4. Human rights are moral rights that people possess by virtue of their humanity. Although different cultures hold different perspectives about the nature and role of human rights, there is international political consensus about the concept of human rights. This consensus is expressed in numerous international declarations and conventions.

5. Moral values contribute to foreign policy behavior by providing direction, inspiration, and judgment. The explicit application of morality to foreign policy needs to be carried out with caution, lest its misuse results in moralism, self-righteousness, and cynicism.

6. Moral norms are commonly applied to policy aims and purposes. But an ethical policy must also ensure that the means and likely outcomes are also in accord with moral principles. Thus, the development of an ethical foreign policy must be based on a comprehensive integration of morality and the policy's goals, methods, and results.

KEY TERMS

empirical
normative
morality
ethics
consequentialism
moral absolutism
moral skepticism

prudence
communitarianism
cosmopolitanism
procedural justice
distributive (substantive) justice

doctrine of cultural relativism
communitarian justice
cosmopolitan justice
humanitarian intervention
human rights

Universal Declaration of Human Rights
Vienna Declaration of Human Rights
famine relief
moralism
apartheid

RECOMMENDED READINGS

Beitz, Charles R. *Political Theory and International Relations*. Princeton: Princeton University Press, 1977. Beitz argues that international ethics—traditionally identified with political realism and the state duties of nonintervention and promotion of self-determination—are inadequate. Global ethics must incorporate concerns of distributive justice.

Coll, Alberto R. *The Wisdom of Statecraft: Sir Herbert Butterfield and the Philosophy of International Politics*. Durham: Duke University Press, 1985. A penetrating analysis of Butterfield's Christian perspectives on world politics.

Hare, J.E., and Carey B. Joynt. *Ethics and International Affairs*. New York: St. Martin's Press, 1982. Hare, a philosopher, and Joynt, a political scientist, provide a penetrating philosophical assessment of the problem of ethics and foreign affairs. The study focuses on war, deterrence, arms control, and the legitimacy of the contemporary international order.

Hoffmann, Stanley. *Duties Beyond Borders: On the Limits and Possibilities of Ethical International Politics*. Syracuse: Syracuse University Press, 1981. A conceptual examination of the role of ethics in foreign affairs, focusing on the role of morality in foreign policy, the use of force, the promotion of human rights, and the problem of distributive justice.

Kennan, George F. "Morality and Foreign Policy," *Foreign Affairs,* 64 (Winter, 1985–1986): 205–18. Kennan, a distinguished scholar and diplomat, restates his argument that the conduct of foreign policy should be guided by instrumental values, not ethical norms.

McElroy, Robert W. *Morality and American Foreign Policy: The Role of Ethics in International Affairs.* Princeton: Princeton University Press, 1992. The thesis of this study is that moral norms influence foreign policy through three mechanisms—the conscience of decision makers, the role of public opinion, and international reputational pressures. Four case studies are used: famine relief to Russia in 1921, America's renunciation of chemical and biological warfare, the termination of control over the Panama Canal, and the bombing of Dresden.

Nardin, Terry. *Law, Morality, and the Relations of States.* Princeton: Princeton University Press, 1983. Although the bulk of this study concerns the nature and role of law in the world, the last four chapters focus on the interrelationship of morality, law, and world order.

Nardin, Terry, and David R. Mapel, eds. *Traditions of International Ethics.* Cambridge: Cambridge University Press, 1992. A superior collection of essays describing and analyzing major ethical traditions and influence moral judgment in global politics. Some of the traditions examined include: international law, realism, natural law, Kantian rationalism, utilitarianism, liberalism, Marxism, and the Bible.

Nye, Joseph S., Jr. *Nuclear Ethics.* New York: Free Press, 1986. A readable, authoritative account of the moral challenge posed by nuclear weapons. After examining essential elements of moral analysis, Nye outlines a moral defense of nuclear strategy.

Thompson, Kenneth W. *Morality and Foreign Policy.* Baton Rouge: Louisiana State University Press, 1980. An analysis of the relationship of moral norms to the conduct of foreign policy from an Anglo-American perspective.

RELEVANT WEB SITES

Human Rights	www.un.org/rights
International Affairs Network (IAN)	www.pitt.edu/~ian/resource/human.htm
U.S. Department of State Annual Human Rights Reports	www.state.gov/www/global/human_rights/index.html
U.S. Institute of Peace Religion, Ethics, and Human Rights Program	www.usip.org/research/rehr.html

CHAPTER

Foreign Policy: Defining and Pursing National Interests

8

In December 1989 President George Bush ordered U.S. military forces to topple the Panamanian dictatorship of General Manuel Noriega and to help reestablish democracy in that country. U.S. federal courts had indicted Noriega for drug trafficking, while his Panamanian Defense Forces (PDF) had periodically harassed North Americans living in Panama. As a result, President Ronald Reagan declared in the mid-1980s that a major U.S. foreign policy goal was the ouster of General Noriega from power. To achieve this end, the U.S. government pursued a variety of means, including bilateral and multilateral diplomatic initiatives and severe economic sanctions. These initiatives, however, failed to achieve the desired objective. As a result, when General Noriega declared late in 1989 that "a state of war" existed with the United States and his military forces killed an American serviceman and harassed another U.S. military officer and his wife, President Bush ordered the invasion, immediately toppling the government.

At the same time that Panamanian events were unfolding, the communist dictatorship of Romanian President Nicolae Ceausescu was also coming to an end, but in very different circumstances. As noted earlier, in the fall of 1989, anticommunist movements gained significant influence in Bulgaria, East Germany, Czechoslovakia, and Hungary. But in Romania the government not only resisted change but became even more repressive and intransigent. As a result, popular revolution broke out, encouraged in great part by a brutal assault by security forces on demonstrators in the western city of Timisoara. This event caused the Romanian army to halt its support of the government and to shift its allegiance to the anti-Ceausescu forces and to protect the masses demonstrating against the regime. Although a brief bloody conflict ensued between the army and the pro-Ceausescu security forces, the dictator, sensing imminent defeat, fled Bucharest. He was captured shortly thereafter, secretly tried and then executed, signaling the victory of the antigovernment forces.

Even though the fall of the dictatorship was carried out solely by the Romanian people, the rapidly unfolding events in the country resulted in a variety of different responses from foreign governments. Even before

---

If we could first know where we are and wither we are tending, we could better judge what to do, and how to do it.

Abraham Lincoln, 1863

We have no perpetual enemies. Our interests are eternal, and those interests it is our duty to follow.[1]

Lord Palmerston, *nineteenth-century member of British Parliament*

The one indispensable factor in forming reliable partnerships is not democracy or the lack of it, but self-interest, and there is not the slightest reason to think that will change.[2]

John L. Harper, *foreign policy scholar*

International politics is not a game with its own rules, actors, and stratagems. Ultimately, most foreign policy initiatives are taken to meet domestic requirements or needs. To understand foreign policy, then, we have to look not only at the external environment but at the domestic politics of the major actors.[3]

Kalevi J. Holsti, *international relations scholar*

Ceausescu had fled his presidential palace in Bucharest, Warsaw Pact leaders met to consider whether military aid should be given to the popular uprising. Soviet leader Mikhail Gorbachev, for his part, announced his country's support for the antigovernment forces and implied that Soviet armed forces could potentially be used to defend the uprising![4] Shortly after the dictator had fled Bucharest, France (the Western European country with deepest ties to Romania) announced that it would provide economic assistance to a new Romanian government. The United States, following France's lead, also pledged financial support and recognized the new Romanian government immediately after Ceausescu's execution.

These two political events illustrate the important role of foreign relations in the contemporary political world. Although states are regarded as sovereign political communities, none of them is immune from foreign governmental and nongovernmental developments. States can and do influence other states. In both the Panamanian and Romanian crises, foreign governments were involved directly or indirectly in helping to foment, sustain, and resolve political conflicts.

This chapter and the next examine the nature, goals, decision-making methods, and implementation strategies of foreign policy. What are the vital interests of states? What major factors determine foreign policy? Which models (conceptual frameworks) are most helpful in illuminating foreign policy decision making? What strategies are most important in pursuing foreign policy objectives? In addressing some of these questions, this chapter (1) examines the nature and purposes of foreign policy, (2) explores the role of national interest in defining foreign policy objectives, and (3) describes some of the major determinants of foreign policy. In the next chapter we examine the foreign policy decision-making process and some of the principal tools of policy implementation.

THE NATURE OF FOREIGN POLICY

International relations involve relationships among governmental and nongovernmental actors resulting in three types of interaction: (1) intergovernmental, (2) governmental-societal, and (3) nongovernmental. (See fig. 8.1.) The first type of interaction involves actions among governments and other regional or global intergovernmental organizations (IGOs). Fundamentally, foreign policy refers to this type of interaction. Although international interactions are most frequent among nongovernmental actors, the most significant relations are among states.

The second type of international interaction occurs between the government of one state and societal elements in another. It includes activities such as Third World relief efforts by foreign governments, propaganda designed to influence foreign society. CIA and KGB efforts to penetrate a foreign society in order to influence its government illustrate this level of interaction. Similarly, when Greenpeace, an international environmental group, sought to halt French nuclear testing in the South Pacific in the late 1970s and early 1980s, they exhibited this type of interaction.

The third type involves international interactions among different elements of society, including the religious, social, cultural, technological, and economic aspects. For example, events such as the quadrennial world soccer tournament or the Olympic Games involve global participation and presuppose a high of level transnational cooperation and coordination. Such functional cooperation is significant because it encourages greater global integration and fosters transnational understanding. Indeed, functionalism—a theory of integration examined in chapter 14—assumes that an effective way to build and sustain political community is through transnational nongovernmental interaction.

Normally, states are unable to fulfill all their social, political, and economic wants within their national borders. As a result, governments generally seek to in-

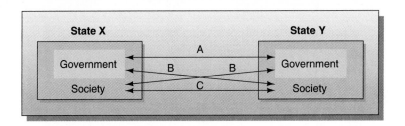

FIGURE 8.1
Tri-Dimensional
International
Relations

crease economic welfare, social well-being, and political influence by pursuing national interests beyond territorial boundaries. The process by which states pursue such national goals within global society is commonly defined as foreign policy. In this text, we define **foreign policy** as the *explicit and implicit actions of governmental officials designed to promote national interests beyond a country's territorial boundaries.*[5]

Foreign policy
The actions of governmental officials designed to promote national interests beyond a country's territorial boundaries.

Elements of Foreign Policy

Figure 8.2 identifies the principal elements of the foreign policy process. National interests, the fundamental wants of states, are the foundation of foreign policy. The **national interest,** a concept examined more fully later in this chapter, is rooted in a country's dominant values and orientations and, in particular, in the nature and character of nationalism and ideology of the state. Because national interests define the fundamental wants of states, they provide not only a broad vision and direction to society but a foundation for identifying the more specific and concrete **national goals.** Whereas national interests include security, political independence, and economic well-being, national goals include the pursuit of short- and long-term objectives, such as the regulation of immigration, the reduction of illegal drug trafficking, the development of regional trade agreements, and the promotion of basic human rights.

National interest
A concept denoting the basic corporate interests of a nation-state.

National goals
The specific objectives pursued by states.

   National strategy is the means by which a state seeks to implement its foreign policy. To be effective, foreign policy must be based on realistic goals and defined in terms of a state's existing capabilities. National strategy is the process by which states assess their relative power capabilities and devise creative, yet credible, methods for using their political, economic, and military resources to achieve desired goals.

   Because states compete for scarce resources in the international community, conflict is inevitable in foreign affairs. In the game of foreign policy, states with larger relative capabilities will ordinarily achieve greater success in pursing their foreign objectives than states with more limited resources. However, superior military and economic resources alone will not assure a successful foreign policy. A state needs a strategic plan to effectively advance its national interests. This requires a clear vision of what is desired, a deep commitment to national goals, and a coherent plan for implementing them.

National strategy
The design and implementation of foreign policy based on a state's interests and capabilities and in terms of the interests and capabilities of other states. See statecraft.

   Although foreign policy is frequently associated chiefly with political objectives, foreign policy actually seeks to advance a vast array of state interests, including the security of the state and the political independence of the government, the promotion of economic development, the protection of a nation's culture, and the protection of the global environment, especially its natural resources and endangered species. The most fundamental interests of governments, however, concern territorial security, economic well-being, and international peace. As a result, the most important domains of foreign policy are *national security policy, international economic policy,* and *diplomatic policy.*

   National security policy (also called defense policy) centers around the territorial integrity and political independence of a state. Because each state is

National security policy
The dimension of foreign policy concerned with a state's territorial security and political independence.

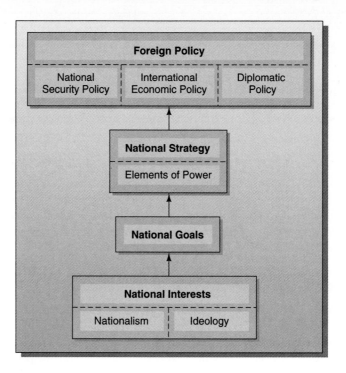

FIGURE 8.2
Elements of
Foreign Policy

ultimately responsible for its own existence and safety, governments give highest priority to the protection of their territory from foreign aggression. National security policy is therefore concerned with the development of strategies and military capabilities that can effectively deter aggression and, if necessary, defend vital interests with force. Elements of such policy include weapons development and procurement, defensive alliances, military doctrine, intelligence, and arms control. This type of policy is illustrated by President Clinton's 1997 national security strategy report in Issue 8.1.

International economic policy
The international economic dimension of foreign policy.

The second sphere of foreign policy, **international economic policy,** involves the pursuit of foreign economic objectives. Because countries seek to improve economic well-being through international economic initiatives, a country's international economic policy is a central component of foreign policy. Examples of this type of policy include trade negotiations, foreign economic assistance, support for international economic institutions, and coordination of international monetary policies. During the Cold War, the Soviet Union's international economic policy involved significant foreign economic support in helping to sustain and to expand the number of socialist economies in the world.

Diplomatic policy
The political dimension of foreign policy.

Diplomatic policy, the third domain of foreign policy, is concerned with the advancement of states' political and ideological interests. For example, a primary aim of U.S. diplomatic policy in the post–Cold War has been the promotion and strengthening of democracy in the developing nations and the former Soviet-bloc states. As a result, the United States has implemented numerous pro-democratic initiatives, including the assistance of former Soviet-bloc in consolidating democratic structures, the expansion of NATO to include three central European states, and the restoration to power of Haiti's democratically elected president, Bertrand Aristide. Diplomatic policy is also concerned with the development of norms, institutions, and relationships that are conducive to global order. As a result, this type of foreign policy seeks to foster global accommodation through bilateral and multilateral diplomatic initiatives, such as arms control and disarmament measures,

Issues in International Relations

Issue 8.1 The National Security Strategy of the United States

The president of the United States annually issues a report that defines the fundamental foreign policy aims of the country. The 1997 document defines U.S. national security as follows:

> [T]he goal of the national security strategy is to ensure the protection of our nation's fundamental and enduring needs: protect the lives and safety of Americans; maintain the sovereignty of the United States, with its values, institutions and territory intact; and provide for the prosperity of the nation and its people.
>
> We seek to create conditions in the world where our interests are rarely threatened, and when they are, we have effective means of addressing those threats. In general, we seek a world in which no critical region is dominated by a power hostile to the United States and regions of greatest importance to the U.S. are stable and at peace. We seek a climate where the global economy and open trade are growing, where democratic norms and respect for human rights are increasingly accepted and where terrorism, drug trafficking and international crime do not undermine stability and peaceful relations. And we seek a world where the spread of nuclear, chemical, biological and other potentially destabilizing technologies is minimized, and the international community is willing and able to prevent or respond to calamitous events.[6]

environmental protection accords, the development of institutions to more effectively manage scarce global resources, and the development of international legal norms, such as those relating to the space law and law of the sea.

Increasingly scholars and statesmen have begun to regard all vital foreign policy concerns as security interests.[7] During the Cold War, the concept of national security was used chiefly to define the freedom from potential military threats, especially war. With the end of the Cold War and the decline of the threat of major global war, the concept of national security has broadened to cover other core interests as well. Some of these include: protection of shared global resources, protection of the earth's environment, establishment of strategies of sustainable economic growth, managing the earth's natural resources, maintenance of an open and equitable international trading system, maintenance of available energy resources, and protection from drug trafficking.

As a result, analysts now argue that states need to devise *environmental security* policies that protect the environment from further degradation and from increasing scarcity of natural resources. Similarly, fear of inadequate energy resources has led to increased emphasis by public officials to enhance *energy security*. Moreover, in view of the continuing rapid population growth in the poor nations, some analysts have emphasized the need for *demographic security*. For example, some scholars have suggested that, in view of the rising population densities in many low-income states and the growing social and economic inequalities between the rich and poor nations, mass human migrations from the poor/high-density states to the rich/low-density states could be highly destabilizing and threaten the political stability and social and economic well-being of developed societies.[8] For example, from 1995 to 2025 the population of Mexico and Central America is expected to increase at more than double the rate of the United States, whereas the population of northern African countries is expected to increase by more than ten times the rate of southern European countries.

Dimensions of Foreign Policy

In assessing countries' foreign policies it is also important to differentiate goals, announced policies, and actions. *Intentional policy* refers to the real interests and objectives of government, whether they are publicly announced or not. *Declaratory policy* is concerned with the goals and interests articulated by government officials. And *operational policy* describes the foreign policy decisions and actions taken by government.

For example, nearly a decade before the United States established diplomatic relations with the People's Republic of China (PRC) in 1979, it sought closer political and economic ties with China. Beginning in the early 1970s, the United States adopted an intentional policy of exploring the feasibility of closer ties with the PRC. To give effect to this policy, President Nixon sent his national security advisor Henry Kissinger on several secret trips to the PRC. These exploratory trips were part of the United States' operational policy towards China. Finally, after publicly disclosing the exploratory secret trips, President Nixon announced, in 1973, the establishment of a U.S. Liaison Office in Peking. This phase of American declaratory policy culminated in 1979 with the establishment of full diplomatic relations between the U.S. and China.

In assessing foreign policy, it is important to distinguish between its intentional, declaratory, and operational dimensions. Sometimes all three aspects of foreign policy are explicitly defined. Generally, however, only one or two dimensions are clearly articulated or self-evident. Sometimes governments refuse to publicly express their foreign policy goals. In other cases they seek to keep their interests and intentions obscure and to pursue goals indirectly or to carry out actions through covert means.

One of the major challenges in foreign affairs is to accurately ascertain the intentions of foreign governments. This can be especially difficult, because a state may pursue goals that are at times inconsistent with its official declarations and overt actions. A classic example of a duplicitous foreign policy is Adolph Hitler's promise, at Munich in 1938, to be a peaceful country if Germany was allowed to incorporate part of German-speaking Czechoslovakia (Sudetenland). At Munich Hitler promised the leaders of Britain and France that Germany would make no further territorial demands. After accepting Hitler at his word, Neville Chamberlain, the British prime minister, returned to London declaring that he had achieved "peace in our time." Because Hitler had no intention of fulfilling his territorial promise, the Munich Accord is best remembered as a foreign policy betrayal that illustrates the dangers of equating foreign policy declarations with real goals and intentions.

A second problem confronting the statesman is the lack of consistency among the three dimensions of foreign policy. Ideally, intentions, declarations, and actions should be complementary and consistent. Unfortunately, this is not always the case. Indeed, governments may announce a particular decision but carry out actions inconsistent with the articulated policies. For example, France's declared policy toward terrorists is never to negotiate with them. Yet, on several occasions in the 1980s the French government negotiated with terrorist groups, repatriating incarcerated terrorists in order to gain the release of hostages. Similarly, in 1989 the United States publicly condemned the Chinese government for its massacre of untold numbers of Chinese demonstrators in Tiananmen Square and established sanctions. Shortly after announcing the new policy, however, President Bush secretly sent national security advisor Brent Scowcroft on a secret mission to China to improve relations between the two states. Many criticized the operational policy of sending a high-level government official because it was not only against U.S. democratic sensibilities, but it was also inconsistent with the announced policy of cool and distant relations. To be credible, declaratory policy must be consistent with the behaviors of government.

THE NATIONAL INTEREST AND FOREIGN POLICY

Definition

One of the widely used concepts in the discipline of IR is the idea of national interest.[9] This concept is generally used by scholars and practitioners to denote the *fundamental needs and wants of states in terms of the basic needs and wants of other states*. Subjective in character, the national interest is based on the perceived long-term collective interests of a country's citizenry. Thus, even though states pursue a variety of foreign policy goals in the global system, the concept of national interest is a singular, unitary notion.

The citizens of countries generally share a variety of common interests. Some of these are more significant than others. One way of clarifying the nature of national interest is to distinguish among different types of states' interests. One scholar has identified three major standards for classifying such interests—level of priority, degree of specificity, and level of permanence. These three categories yield six ideal-type interests.

1. *Vital interests*—(also known as *core or strategic interests*) these include the fundamental, long-term state goals, such as national security;
2. *Nonvital interests*—secondary concerns on which states may be willing to compromise;
3. *General interests*—the diffuse, global concerns of states, such as the maintenance of regional peace and the promotion of economic well-being;
4. *Specific interests*—the limited, clearly defined objectives of states;
5. *Permanent interests*—the unchanging goals of states, such as the protection of territorial boundaries; and
6. *Variable interests*—the changing interests of states that arise in response to particular geographic or political developments.[10]

Because states' interests generally share two or more of these dimensions, it is possible to integrate them into a typology (see table 8.1). Although not limited exclusively to them, the national interest is rooted in the fundamental, long-term interests found in the upper left part of the table.

Limitations

Despite the widespread use of the idea of national interest, the concept is conceptually deficient in several respects. One difficulty is the subjective character of the concept. Significant disagreement exists about how and by whom the national interest should be defined. What is the national interest? Is the national interest rooted in the nation or in the state? Who should decide what it is—the people or the government?

Second, the national interest is based on the assumption that states are rational and coherent actors. But as noted in the next chapter, the assumption that states are unitary, rational actors is not realistic. States and nations comprise numerous elements, each of which has its own particular interests. Similarly, government is not a coherent organization but includes different bureaucratic offices and political elements, each with its own goals and distinct perceptions of the national interest. To the extent that a national interest exists, then, it must be based on the perceived interests of relevant governmental and nongovernmental actors.

A third problem is the difficulty of distinguishing national interests from global interests. Are national interests and global interests complementary or conflictual?

TABLE 8.1   Classification of U.S. Interests, 1997

		Vital	Nonvital
Permanent	**General**	Maintain peace Promote world order	Promote international goodwill Increase foreign appreciation of U.S. culture
	Specific	Maintain secure territorial borders Promote national economic growth	Encourage international free trade Regulate level of immigration
Variable	**General**	Maintain integrity of NATO Promote nuclear nonproliferation	Strengthen the UN and other international institutions Support the economic unification of Western Europe
	Specific	Encourage democratic transition of Russia Encourage human rights in China	Restrict Third World imports made with child labor Encourage protection of tropical rainforest

Are national interests based on short-term or long-term perspectives? A cursory review of modern history suggests that foreign policies are often guided by a parochial and short-term perspective. But as global interdependence increases and the world's resources become more limited, the quest for short-term gains is clearly inadequate.

Despite these definitional and conceptual problems, the notion of national interest can be a useful tool in describing and assessing foreign policy. Just before the outbreak of World War II, Winston Churchill called attention to the importance of the national interest by observing: "I cannot forecast to you the action of Russia. It is a riddle wrapped in a mystery inside an enigma, but perhaps there is a key. The key is Russian national interest." Thus, exploring the underlying long-term state interests can help define and explain the competing and often conflicting foreign policy behaviors of states.

Hierarchy of Interests

According to psychologist Abraham Maslow, human needs can be ranked according to their level of significance. They are: (1) physical needs, such as air and food; (2) personal security and safety; (3) the need for love and belonging; (4) self-esteem; and (5) self-actualization—that is, the development and fulfillment of a person's capabilities.[11] Like human needs, the interests of states can also be prioritized. Although states pursue a variety of goals, widespread agreement exists that interests considered to be fundamental interests are more important than those considered transitory and nonpermanent. And although statesmen may define these interests differently, there is general agreement that national security, economic prosperity, and the protection and promotion of a nation's national identity rank among the most important universal state interests. The first two interests are tangible, but the third is intangible. We shall briefly examine each interest.

Security

Former U.S. Secretary of State Henry Kissinger has said that "foreign policy must start with security." Security is the most basic concern of states because the international political system is a decentralized, anarchic political order in which the responsibility for preservation and security is wholly up to each member-state. According to Kenneth Waltz, self-preservation is the most important tangible interest because the fulfillment of all other interests depends on the territorial integrity and political independence of the state. Waltz observes that the survival motive is taken as the ground of action, not because states always explicitly seek security, but because the anarchic world structure requires that states take care of their own survival.[12]

National security involves two distinct but essential elements. First, it requires the preservation of the nation-state and in particular the protection of the state's territorial boundaries. Second, it presupposes the protection of national sovereignty—that is, national self-determination. Security means that a state can defend its land and people. It also means that a people must have the freedom to act independently from other states. Michael Walzer writes that the legal foundation of the international community—what he titles the "legalist paradigm"—is based on two fundamental states' rights—territorial integrity and political sovereignty. He argues that when a foreign state violates these rights, it commits aggression, thereby justifying the use of force by the victim states. According to Walzer, the victim of aggression not only has the moral and legal right to use force to repulse an attack, but also the right to punish the aggressor.[13]

In his classic study, *Politics Among Nations,* Hans Morgenthau argues that the fundamental concern of countries is national security. National security "is the irreducible minimum that diplomacy must defend with adequate power without compromise."[14] He suggests that the only way of assuring a nation's security is through national power. As a result, Morgenthau argues that the immediate motive of all states is national power. "We assume," writes Morgenthau, "that statesmen think and act in terms of interests defined as power."[15] Morgenthau does not deny that states pursue a variety of goals, but he suggests that the fundamental drive is always the same—increasing national power.

Throughout most of the Cold War, many international relations scholars defined national security largely in military dimensions. But since the 1980s, a growing number of scholars has called attention to other dimensions of national security, including drug trafficking, economic development, environmental threats, international migration, and population growth.[16] Although such traditional issues as military force, strategy, and arms control continue to be significant in national security research, these themes are now less prominent than they were during the Cold War era.

Economic Well-Being

The second basic state interest is economic prosperity. There are two fundamental reasons why the economy is important. First, governments pursue national wealth in order to increase their political and military influence in the international system. Historian Paul Kennedy has investigated the relationship of wealth to military power and found that the two attributes are closely linked historically.[17] This should surprise no one, because an economically prosperous state is better able to build and maintain a strong army and navy than an economically weak state. Of course, states need not use their wealth to secure increased military power. Some developed countries—notably Austria, Japan, Luxembourg, and Iceland—devote less than 1 percent of their GNP to national defense (see table 6.3).

Countries have pursued national wealth in numerous ways. In the seventeenth century, some European powers, following the doctrine of *mercantilism,* attempted to acquire revenues by strictly regulating economic life, especially international trade. Britain sought to increase its economic power through free trade, a pattern that has been greatly expanded since 1945. The United States led in establishing international economic institutions and practices that greatly reduced tariff and nontariff barriers to world trade.

The second reason economic prosperity is a national priority is that the citizenry demands it. Modernization in the twentieth century has increased the transnational flow of information, leading to greater awareness of living conditions in foreign states. The expansion of a global economic market has spread modern goods throughout the world. Telecommunications, then, coupled with the global distribution of advanced consumer goods, has fueled rising consumer expectations. Whether rich or poor, people are demanding improved living conditions and greater access to consumer goods.

Economic prosperity is important to all nations. Whether countries are developed or developing, there is a widespread expectation that governments are responsible for a growing economy. Much of the political unrest in the Third World has been due to the inability of governments to establish policies and institutions that foster job creation. For example, Soviet President Mikhail Gorbachev tried to reform the country's economy in the late 1980s in order to advance his country's national output. Recognizing that the Soviet Union's power could not be maintained with a stagnating economy, Gorbachev sought to restructure the economy (*perestroika*) through increasing decentralization. The priority of economic welfare was demonstrated even more vividly in Eastern European states—especially in Bulgaria, East Germany, Czechoslovakia, Hungary, and Romania—in which popular uprisings in the last half of 1989 led to the installation of noncommunist governments committed to free enterprise initiatives to stimulate economic growth.

National Identity

The third basic interest of states is the protection and preservation of a nation's way of life, including its cultural, social, religious, and political distinctives. Although the national character of a state comprises a number of dimensions, two elements are especially important—nationalism and ideology.

Nationalism, as noted in chapter 2, refers to the loyalty of a people toward their nation. It functions as a collective will binding together a people sharing a common historical past, a shared culture, a common language, and, most importantly, shared political aspirations. Occasionally, nations share a common religion and ethnic origin. Regardless of its nature, basis, or origins, nationalism has been a major influence in contemporary global relations, providing the inspiration and direction for a large share of global interactions. Nationalism has been both an integrative and disintegrative force. As the former, nationalism has contributed to group cohesion and the consolidation and protection of nation-states. Jewish Zionism, which has encouraged the development and consolidation of the state of Israel, illustrates such nationalism. However, the increasing demand for self-rule among Muslims, Croats, and Serbs in Bosnia-Herzegovina illustrates the disintegrative consequences of narrowly defined self-determination.

Throughout the last half of the twentieth century, the quest for national identity has been an especially potent force in international relations. Because of its emphasis on self-determination, nationalism has contributed to the fragmentation of the international system by encouraging the political independence of former colonies and other dependent territories. Indeed, during the 1950s and 1960s, nationalism served as the major engine of decolonization. And in the aftermath of the end of the Cold War, nationalism contributed to the further breakup of former communist states, including Czechoslovakia, the Soviet Union, and Yugoslavia. Indeed, in the

Nationalism
The exclusive attachment and political commitment to one's nation, leading to demands for political self-determination and the consolidation of modern nation-states.

early 1990s, the most intense ethnic conflicts in global society were in former communist-ruled territories, such as Armenia, Bosnia-Herzegovina, Georgia, and Tajikistan. Although nationalism has contributed to the expansion of new states, it has also fostered national integration, especially in coherent states in which a large part of the citizenry belong to one nationality. In such nation-states, nationalism has helped to consolidate national power and to energize foreign policy.

An **ideology,** commonly defined as a simplified and coherent *belief system,* is rooted in the fundamental norms, values, and orientations of a political system (*political culture*). Because an ideology provides a simplified view of political reality, it inspires and guides domestic and international political activity of a state. Whereas nationalism provides the noncognitive, emotional forces that bind people together, an ideology provides political and moral values that direct and inspire national goals. Nationalism and ideology thus serve as powerful complementary political forces within contemporary states.

Ideologies influence foreign policy decision making in a number of specific ways, including: influencing people's perceptions about international affairs; providing a framework for foreign policy decision making, thereby constraining choices and enhancing continuity; providing a means for justifying foreign policy actions; and enhancing national unity.[18]

The importance of ideologies and belief systems in foreign policy is illustrated by the dramatic changes in Iranian foreign policy following the fall of the Shah's government in 1979 and the establishment of a radical Islamic regime. Until the Shah was deposed, Iran pursued a largely pro-Western foreign policy. Its domestic and foreign policy interests were pragmatic and secular, involving modernization, economic expansion, and increased educational opportunities for citizens. But with the accession of the Ayatollah Khomeini, Iran embarked on a reconstruction of its society based on Islamic values and the pursuit of a radical, anti-Western foreign policy. Similarly, the intractability and intensity of the Cold War was due, in great measure, to the strong ideological commitments of each superpower and its allies. Indeed, conflicting worldviews—one proclaiming liberty, self-determination, and democracy and the other proclaiming equality, socialism, and communist party political domination—provided the fuel for the East-West geopolitical conflict.

Ideology
A simplified political belief-system that inspires and guides governmental decision making.

DETERMINANTS OF FOREIGN POLICY

What factors influence the making of foreign policy? Although many elements affect the foreign policy actions of states, scholars' research on the foreign policy decision-making process has stressed three major factors: the role of political and governmental leaders; the impact of domestic society, especially the role of economic and political structures; and the role of international influences (see fig. 8.3). In the following sections we examine how each of these elements affects the making of foreign policy.

The Role of Individuals

Foreign policy is made by individuals. Although foreign policy is frequently viewed as developed by the impersonal structures of government, human beings, as individuals, play a key role in the formulation and implementation of foreign policy, whether as political leaders, government officials, media representatives, interest group leaders, or even citizens. Because government leaders play a crucial role in foreign affairs, we first sketch the important role of leaders in global society and then examine two factors—leadership style and belief systems—that frequently affect leaders' decision making.

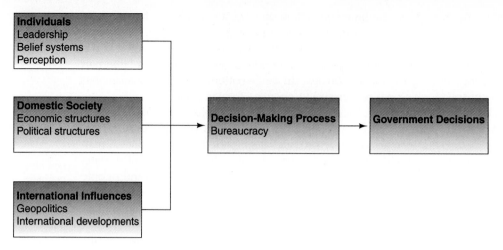

FIGURE 8.3
Major
Determinants of
Foreign Policy

Political Leadership

Leadership involves the ability to shape the actions and beliefs of others. In exercising leadership two elements are required: power (i.e., the ability to shape events) and purpose (i.e., the ability to project ideas and principles about the effective ordering of politics).[19] In examining the evolution of the world's map, it is clear that the creation and maintenance of states, along with their respective territorial boundaries, has been profoundly influenced by leaders like Napoleon, Bismarck, Adolf Hitler, and Joseph Stalin. Following are some example of leaders who have decisively influenced IR during the second half of the twentieth century:

Ho Chi Minh—The leader of North Vietnamese Communists from the mid-1940s until his death in 1969. Ho first defeated the French armed forces in 1954 and then, by challenging U.S. military intervention in the 1960s, helped to create the conditions that led to U.S. withdrawal from Vietnam in 1972.

Richard Nixon—He secretly initiated in 1970–1971 the improvement of U.S.-Chinese relations—a development that led to the reestablishment of formal diplomatic relations in 1979.

Anwar Sadat—In 1979 this Egyptian president courageously traveled to Jerusalem, to the consternation of other Arab political leaders, to improve Israeli-Egyptian relations. His leadership made possible the Egyptian-Israeli Peace Treaty.

Margaret Thatcher—When Argentinian military forces captured the Falkland Islands in 1982, the British prime minister—also referred to as "The Iron Lady"—dispatched a naval task force to recover the islands.

Lech Walesa—This Polish union worker and champion of human freedom led the Solidarity Movement during the 1980s until political pluralism was introduced into Poland, leading to the establishment of the first noncommunist government in Eastern Europe.

Mikhail Gorbachev—Beginning in 1985, he set in motion political and economic reforms that eventually led to the collapse of Soviet communism and the end of the Cold War.

The so-called "great-leader" theory of history seeks to explain foreign affairs from the perspective of governmental leadership. According to this theory, the history of international relations is primarily the result of the actions of major political leaders. Although leadership clearly plays an important, if unpredictable, role in world politics, it is simplistic to attribute foreign policy solely to the idiosyncratic elements of human personality. Leaders function within institutional and systemic

Annual economic summits among the Western leaders of the major industrial powers (G-7) provide an opportunity for formative international economic cooperation and encourage policy coordination on the related issues. Here G-7 leaders meet at the 1993 Tokyo summit.

constraints. Domestic political dynamics and bureaucratic structures, for example, establish parameters for foreign policy decisions. Similarly, the legal, moral, political, and economic dimensions of the international system provide additional constraints on foreign policy behaviors. Thus, although it is important to recognize the distinctive role of leadership in foreign policy, scholars have sought to understand what factors help to explain the foreign policy behavior of leaders, as well as to assess the role of other foreign policy influences.

Leadership Style

Leaders' decision-making approaches are influenced by many factors, including their personality traits, their personal histories, and their core values. They are also rooted in the environmental context in which leaders emerge. Henry Kissinger, following Max Weber, has observed that leadership style is rooted in the political, social, and cultural conditions of nations. According to him, three leadership styles have characterized contemporary international relations: bureaucratic-pragmatic, ideological, and revolutionary-charismatic.[20]

The bureaucratic-pragmatic style, represented by developed democratic states, emphasizes constitutional processes and bureaucratic procedures and deemphasizes goals and judgment. Because procedures and techniques are paramount, this style is appropriate for dealing with technical and constitutional issues, but much less effective in dealing with historical purpose.

The ideological leadership style, expressed by communist or Islamic fundamentalist regimes, is characterized by a rigid adherence to a political or religious worldview. Because the ideological style is guided by zealous dedication to principles and beliefs, its approach is inflexible, single-minded, and determined. During the Cold War, Soviet government leaders manifested this leadership style. And after Islamic radicals gained control of Iran's government in 1979, the new regime, headed by the Ayatollah Khomeini, pursued a rigid, fundamentalist foreign policy rooted in Islamic values.

The revolutionary-charismatic leadership style, represented by radical Third World leaders like Fidel Castro of Cuba, Mohammar Qaddafi of Libya, and Saddam Hussein of Iraq, expresses a revolutionary commitment to change. A charismatic leader is essentially a prophet with a vision of the future. The revolutionary-charismatic leader is not so much concerned with the economic improvement of society as with the transformation of society. Because charismatic leaders are totally absorbed and committed to stated political and moral goals, little room exists for compromise, flexibility, and negotiation. As a result, foreign relations involving revolutionary-charismatic leaders are likely to be unstable and unpredictable.

Leadership style also depends upon its context. One scholar, for example, has suggested that international leadership can be rooted in structural, institutional, and situational factors.[21] Structural leadership seeks to influence international affairs by shaping the geopolitical distribution of power within the international community; institutional leadership seeks to influence events by defining the rules and norms of global society; and situational leadership seeks to shape international events through initiatives and actions that are neither structural nor institutional. Leadership thus tends to vary in accordance with the nature of goals and purposes being pursued, as well as power resources with which to implement policies.

Belief Systems

Because religious and political values profoundly shape how individuals view the world and how they interpret events, foreign policy scholars have carried out extensive research on the nature and role of belief systems in decision making.[22] A **belief system** is the collection of core values, beliefs, and images that make up an individual's worldview. Belief systems are composed of two types of preconceived "images"—those relating to facts (what has been, is, and will be) and those relating to values (what ought to be). These images serve as the lenses through which individuals see the world, filtering information in light of the system's norms.

Belief systems are important not only because they structure people's core values but also because they provide an image-filtering system by which new information is processed and interpreted. Although such filtering systems make information processing more efficient, they also can distort images. Such distortion typically results from the desire to maintain *cognitive consistency* by interpreting new information in a manner compatible with existing beliefs and images. Thus, when new images are not in accord with a person's belief system, it leads to a process that psychologists call **cognitive dissonance.**

Because individuals dislike mental dissonance, they seek to reduce such conflict in a variety of ways. Some of the information-screening processes that individuals use to maintain cognitive harmony include: (1) *image denial,* by which individuals simply neglect to perceive an inconsistent image; (2) *information compartmentalization,* by which individuals process conflict images by subdividing information in distinct categories, such as moral, scientific, political; (3) *selective perception,* by which individuals emphasize developments that are consistent with their worldview and neglect those events that appear inconsistent with their beliefs; and (4) *wishful thinking,* by which individuals underestimate negative consequences and overestimate desired outcomes.

Even though these screening devices can help maintain cognitive consistency, they can result in **misperception** and thereby impair rational decision making.[23] Examples of common misperception in foreign affairs include: underestimating enemy capabilities, overestimating one's own relative power, misperceiving enemy intentions, underestimating an opponent's resolve, and overestimating one's own goodness and morality, while attributing evil and immorality to the enemy.

In an important case study of belief systems and foreign policy, Ole Holsti examined the impact of John Foster Dulles' worldview on his role as U.S. secretary of state from 1953 to 1959. According to Holsti, Dulles held a negative, moralistic view of the Soviet Union based in great measure on "the trinity of atheism, totalitarianism, and communism." Dulles' anti-Soviet worldview comprised three dichotomies: (1) the Russian people were "good," but the Soviet leaders were "bad"; (2) the Russian national interest was "good," but international communism was "bad"; and (3) the Russian state was "good," but the Soviet communist party was "bad." In order to ascertain whether Dulles' belief system influenced his perceptions, Holsti carried out a *content analysis* of the declarations and speeches made by Dulles during his tenure as secretary of state. Holsti found that Dulles did in-

Belief system
A collection of core values, beliefs, and images that make up an individual's world view.

Cognitive dissonance
Psychological conflict between existing beliefs and newly-acquired information.

Misperception
Distortions of reality caused by such factors as human biases, personal values, and ideological presuppositions.

deed perceive and interpret information about the Soviet Union in a manner consistent with his belief system. In fact, Holsti found that even though Soviet capabilities and success and the general evaluation of the USSR tended to change during the 1950s, Dulles' overall negative perception of the Soviet Union remained unchanged—thereby confirming the powerful influence of belief systems on perception. In light of his findings, Holsti concluded that Dulles had a closed image of the Soviet Union and interpreted data to maintain a belief system rather than to adjust it according to a changing environment.[24]

Almost thirty years later President Ronald Reagan held a similar belief system, one that assumed that the Soviet Union was an "evil empire" whose aggressiveness could only be checked through a strong, forceful military posture. As a result, Reagan championed the cause of anticommunist insurgencies ("freedom fighters," as he called them) in Afghanistan, Angola, and Nicaragua, and built a strong military defense to challenge Soviet expansionism.

The Impact of Domestic Society

Domestic society is a second major source of foreign policy influences. Two elements of national society that are especially influential in foreign policy decision making are the nature of a country's economy and the character of a country's political system.

Economic Structures

Among national economic factors that influence foreign policy, two are of special significance: the level of economic development and the nature of the economic system itself. Because wealth is an important element of power, countries with large national incomes will tend to have greater influence than those with smaller incomes. Historian Paul Kennedy has noted that national economic capacity has played a major part in the rise and fall of states.[25] Wealth alone, of course, will not guarantee global influence, but it is an important element in a credible foreign policy. Wealth increases the range and flexibility of foreign action. High-income countries like France, Germany, and Japan have a greater range of choices than do poor countries like Bangladesh, Bolivia, and Zaire.

The nature of economic systems also influences foreign policy, especially foreign economic policy. For example, *socialist* states, such as Albania and Cuba, have tended to favor strict international economic controls and to encourage reforms in the world economy that would reduce international economic inequalities. *Democratic socialist* states, like the Netherlands and Denmark, have also supported major bilateral and multilateral economic transfers from the rich to the poor nations. Indeed, the highest rates of foreign aid to the Third World have come from the Western European socialist countries. *Capitalist* countries, by contrast, have tended to oppose governmental intervention in domestic or international economic life. Capitalist regimes, like the United States and Britain, have been staunch defenders of free enterprise and of open trade within the global economy. To a significant degree, the liberal (free) international economic system created at the end of the Second World War was based largely on capitalist principles, in great measure because the states that established that system were themselves capitalist regimes. Since the mid-1970s, Third World countries have sought to redress international economic inequalities by favoring significant reforms in the international economic order.

Political Structures

A country's governmental structures can significantly affect the nature of foreign policy. Indeed, one scholar has suggested that the level of openness of a regime's structures is one of the major bases for comparing foreign policies.[26] Because a major difference between democratic and nondemocratic regimes is in the level of participation in electing government officials and in formulating public policies, this section briefly explores the role of public opinion and then contrasts the nature of decision making in democratic and authoritarian systems. Finally, the impact of domestic governmental structures on the peacefulness of international relations is examined, focusing in particular on the belief that democratic systems are more conducive to peace than autocratic regimes.

The Role of Public Opinion According to democratic theory, the legitimacy of governmental decision making is based on consent. This consent is expressed through periodic elections as well as through participation in policy debates. Typically, only a small percentage (3–5 percent) of the electorate in democratic regimes is well informed and politically active, and an even smaller percentage (1–2 percent)—those classified as *political elites*—is directly involved in organizing and mobilizing participation and in influencing public opinion.

Although public opinion plays a vital role in decision making in democratic regimes, its impact in foreign affairs is more modest than in domestic affairs.[27] One reason for this is that, with the exception of national security and economic prosperity issues, citizens generally perceive international affairs as less important than domestic issues. As a result, citizens tend to be less interested in, and less informed about, international relations than about domestic political issues.[28] Another factor that may account for the limited impact of public opinion on foreign policy is the complexity of many international issues—a fact that might account for some of the differences in foreign policy beliefs and orientation between leaders and the public. U.S. public opinion surveys have consistently shown, for example, that leaders have a more global perspective than the mass public and are more eager for U.S. involvement in world affairs.[29] Moreover, leaders have generally given precedence to strategic interests and obligations to allies. The general public, by contrast, has generally given priority to social and economic issues, such as domestic employment, illegal immigration, and drug trafficking (see table 8.2).

Notwithstanding the modest role of public opinion in foreign policy making, the general opinions and sentiments of the masses do affect the development and implementation of foreign policy in democratic systems. One important function of public opinion is that it provides a framework of acceptable government action. By establishing general parameters for decision making, public opinion provides the foundation for defining and assessing the legitimacy of policies. Another important function is that it constrains foreign policy formulation by limiting the range of potential actions. Thus, the American public's general opposition to using military force for nonvital missions has helped to circumscribe an expansionistic U.S. foreign policy in the post–Cold War era.

Of course, foreign policy issues can periodically become highly salient in society, greatly expanding the impact of public opinion on foreign policy making. For example, the growing public opposition to the Vietnam War led to significant domestic and international policy changes that eventually led to the U.S. withdrawal from Vietnam. Similarly, public opinion played an important role in influencing U.S. policy debates over strategic policy in the early 1980s, over Central American policy in the mid-1980s, and over approval of the **North American Free Trade Agreement (NAFTA).** In Western European democracies, public opinion has similarly played a decisive role in selected regional issues, such as NATO's deployment of intermediate-range nuclear ballistic missiles in the early 1980s and the further consolidation of European unity under the Maastricht Treaty in the early 1990s.

As with domestic affairs, interest groups play an important role in organizing and mobilizing public opinion when foreign affairs issues are involved. When in-

North American Free Trade Association (NAFTA)
A 1993 accord that reduces trade barriers among Canada, Mexico, and the United States.

TABLE 8.2   Perceived U.S. Foreign Policy Goals of Leaders and the Public

Issue	The Public	Leaders
	(percentage who consider goals "very important")	
Halting the flow of illegal drugs into the U.S.	85	57
Protecting the jobs of American workers	83	50
Controlling and reducing illegal immigration	72	28
Combating world hunger	56	41
Strengthening the United Nations	51	33
Defending the security of U.S. allies	41	60

Source: John E. Rielly, ed., *American Public Opinion and U.S. Foreign Policy 1995* (Chicago: Chicago Council on Foreign Relations, 1995), p. 15.

ternational developments threaten the vital interests of groups, their representatives will attempt to lobby legislators and other relevant government officials. For example, even though farmers are less than 4 percent of France's labor force, they exert significant influence on French foreign policy. Thus, when European governments sought to reduce agricultural subsidies in 1992 as part of the Uruguay Round of trade negotiations, French farmers organized massive demonstrations, blocked roads, and threatened to halt agricultural production and sales. In the United States, labor unions and business groups similarly have sought to influence foreign policy making by carrying out media campaigns to influence public opinions and by lobbying decision makers. This was especially the case in the fall 1993 debates preceding the congressional vote on NAFTA (see case 8.1) and during the summer 1997 congressional vote over continuation of most-favored-nation trading status for China.

Authoritarian Versus Democratic Decision Making   Some scholars have argued that nondemocratic regimes are better equipped to develop and execute foreign policy than representative governments. For example, Alexis de Tocqueville in his classic study *Democracy in America* suggested that autocratic regimes are better able to manage foreign affairs than democratic systems because the requirements of successful foreign policy—competence, persistence, secrecy, and judgment—are more likely to be found in the former regimes.[36] In the early twentieth century the American journalist Walter Lippmann suggested that the foreign policy of democracies was likely to be inadequate because public opinion was largely uninformed and unlikely to undertake bold initiatives in times of crises.[37]

From a structural perspective, authoritarian governments are likely to be superior to democratic regimes in several areas of foreign policy making. First, decision making is likely to be more efficient in authoritarian governments. In democracies policy development and implementation is often slow and cumbersome because of the bargaining involved among different governmental organizations and prolonged discussions and debates carried out in the public at large. In an autocracy, by contrast, decision making is normally carried out swiftly and with limited intergovernmental negotiation.

Second, decision making is likely to be more consistent in an authoritarian regime. In a democracy, foreign policy is likely to be more inconsistent because of the transitory nature of public opinion. At the same time, presidential democracies can become paralyzed when different political parties are involved in the decision-making process. During the 1980s, for example, the inconsistency in U.S. foreign

Case 8.1 Making Foreign Policy: The Case of NAFTA

Background

NAFTA is a comprehensive trade accord calling for the elimination of trade barriers among Canada, Mexico, and the United States. The accord, which went into effect on January 1, 1994, establishes rules and principles by which cross-border trade barriers will be reduced or eliminated over a 15-year period. The accord covers goods and services, including banking, securities investing, and trucking. For example, NAFTA immediately eliminated more than half of all trade barriers on agricultural products and established a schedule for eliminating all remaining barriers on agricultural products within 15 years. Similarly, NAFTA allows increasing cross-border financial transactions, including U.S. banking operations within Mexico. To assure a gradual transition toward a more open, transnational banking system, NAFTA establishes a timetable for phasing in U.S. bank operations in Mexico.[30]

The foundation for NAFTA was set in 1988, when the United States and Canada signed a free trade agreement calling for the elimination of most trade barriers between the two countries within ten years. In 1990, Canada and the United States invited Mexico to join the free trade area, believing that a larger free trade zone would encourage job creation in each country and would help to consolidate Mexican democratic and market-based reforms begun in the mid-1980s. Because Mexico's standard of living was considerably lower than that of Canada or of the United States, the trilateral negotiations were much more complex and time-consuming than those originally carried out between the United States and Canada, requiring more than two years of painstaking talks. After NAFTA negotiations were completed, government leaders signed the accord in December 1992, opening the way for congressional approval in each of the three states. Because President George Bush had carried out NAFTA negotiations under "fast track" authority, Congress could approve or reject the accord but could not amend the legislation once it had been submitted for a vote.

The Politics of NAFTA

Even before NAFTA had been approved in the United States, numerous domestic political groups began to oppose the agreement. They believed that NAFTA would result in a loss of U.S. jobs because of Mexico's lower wage scale and in harmful environment effects because of Mexico's weaker environmental standards and less effective implementation of existing laws. As a result, some influential environmental groups claimed that pollution within Mexico and along the U.S.-Mexican border would increase significantly if NAFTA was implemented. Similarly, U.S. labor groups claimed that NAFTA would lead to the transfer of manufacturing jobs and selected agricultural production from the United States to Mexico.

Because of the growing concern about potential harmful economic and ecological effects, NAFTA became a major issue of contention in the 1992 U.S. presidential elections. President George Bush, who initiated NAFTA and was responsible for negotiating the accord, vigorously supported the agreement, arguing that it would foster job creation in each of the three member-states. Democratic candidate Bill Clinton, by contrast, provided qualified support for the accord, arguing that he supported freer trade with Mexico only if U.S. jobs and the environment were adequately protected. The most vociferous critic was independent candidate Ross Perot, who claimed that NAFTA would result in "a giant sucking sound" as U.S. jobs moved from the United States to Mexico. Although many economists argued that NAFTA would help create jobs in the United States, Perot asserted that the U.S. economy would lose some 5 million jobs and destroy the middle class.

policy towards Central America occurred because the Reagan administration favored interests in Central America that were not shared by a congress controlled by the Democratic party.

Third, authoritarian regimes are likely to present a more coherent front than democratic governments. Because authoritarian regimes are much more centralized, they normally present a higher degree of external unity than representative, participatory systems. Moreover, because public debate and open discussion are uncommon in authoritarian systems, public opinion is unlikely to affect the devel-

After assuming office in January 1993, President Clinton sought to appease NAFTA critics by making a number of supplemental agreements to protect the United States from potential harmful effects from increased U.S.-Mexico trade. In particular, the Clinton administration signed two side agreements to protect the environment from increased Mexican pollution and U.S. jobs from unfair competition. In addition, in order to get the support from uncommitted legislators, President Clinton made a number of deals affecting such products as beef, peanut butter, wheat, orange juice, and vegetables.[31]

The campaign to approve NAFTA was highly contentious. From the outset, numerous groups opposed the accord for economic, environmental, cultural, political, and ideological reasons. These groups included organized labor (principally the AFL-CIO), fruit and vegetable growers (such as South Florida farmers), and environmental groups (such as the Sierra Club and Greenpeace). The major support for the accord came from officials and leaders who were ideologically committed to freer international trade, from business groups that expected to gain from the trade accord, and from economic and political groups that believed that closer U.S.-Mexican cooperation would be mutually beneficial. Such groups included most large business groups and professional associations, including such organizations as the National Association of Manufacturers (NAM), the U.S. Chamber of Commerce, and the Council of the Americas, which represents U.S. business interests in Latin America. Similarly, the vast majority of social scientists concerned with U.S.-Latin American political and economic concerns also supported the agreement. Given the staunch opposition to NAFTA among some Democratic Party officials, populist figures like Ross Perot and labor and environmental leaders, public opinion was deeply divided over the issue.[32] One poll taken in November 1993, shortly before the congressional vote on NAFTA, found that 37 percent of the respondents supported the agreement, while 41 percent opposed it.[33]

Because a majority of Democratic Party members in the House of Representatives were either undecided or opposed to NAFTA, President Clinton made a determined effort in the weeks preceding the congressional vote to gain support for this trade pact. This task was made even more difficult because two Democratic leaders in the House—the Majority Leader, Richard Gephardt, and the Majority Whip, David Bonior—vigorously opposed the accord. It has been estimated that in the month before the vote, Clinton devoted eighteen public events to the NAFTA debate, personally met with more than 150 wavering members of the House of Representatives, and used his entire cabinet to lobby wavering members. The president even called on Vice-President Gore to debate Ross Perot, the arch-NAFTA critic, on television. In the end, presidential leadership paid off, with the House approving NAFTA 234 to 200, with 75 percent of Republicans supporting the accord and only 40 percent of Democrats doing so. As expected a majority of House members from the South (63 percent) and the West (65 percent) voted for NAFTA, although a majority of House members from Northeast (65 percent) and Midwest (52 percent) voted against NAFTA.[34] Shortly thereafter, the U.S. Senate, as expected, easily approved the accord (61 to 38).

Despite President Clinton's victory, some leaders have continued to oppose NAFTA and its possible extension to other Latin American countries. As a result, when Clinton sought "fast track" negotiating authority in November 1997 in order to extend NAFTA to Chile and possibly other Latin American countries, organized labor led the public opposition to this congressional measure. As a result of their opposition, the House of Representatives was unable to get the necessary support to approve this initiative.[35]

opment or modification of governmental policies. In democracies, by contrast, policies can vary significantly in response to shifts in public opinion. Additionally, the existence of decentralized decision making in democracies frequently leads to open conflict among different agencies and government institutions, sometimes leading to policy confusion and uncertainty. When legislatures and executives espouse different foreign policy views and interpretations, policy articulation and implementation will often be compromised. This is especially the case when different political parties control the presidential and legislative branches of government, as was the case in the United States in the mid-1980s. As a result, U.S. foreign policy, particularly towards Central America, lacked consistency.

Fourth, authoritarian regimes are less likely to be influenced by sudden shifts in public opinion and popular mood swings than democratic systems. Because it is widely agreed that the media can profoundly influence the political agenda in democratic societies, the exposure of violence and inhumane suffering—as was the case in the Somalia in 1991 and in Rwanda and Zaire in 1994—can evoke a public outcry to "do something."[38] Because authoritarian regimes are characterized by a tightly regulated media, television and radio are unlikely to have much impact on governmental decision making in such systems. As a result, the so-called **CNN effect**[39]—the creation of public pressures to halt human suffering, violence, and gross human rights violations in response to media exposure—is unlikely to have much impact in such societies. Thus, authoritarian regimes are protected from pressures arising from televised imagery that may encourage unwise and unrealistic policies.

Finally, authoritarian systems may be superior in negotiation. This superiority derives not only from factors such as those previously mentioned but also from their ability to control and protect information. Stated bluntly, authoritarian regimes are better able to keep secrets. Because of their openness and decentralization, democracies are more vulnerable to the disclosure of sensitive information, including information that might compromise the negotiating process itself. In 1970, for example, the *Los Angeles Times* published the SALT negotiating fallback strategy, an act that incensed National Security Advisor Henry Kissinger so much that it led to the wiretapping of telephones to determine which White House officials were compromising classified information.[40]

Democracies of course enjoy a number of major advantages in foreign affairs. One strength of democratic decision making is that government policies are likely to enjoy greater public support. This is because the principal officials in executive and legislative institutions have been elected by the public. To be sure, a president or prime minister appoints key foreign affairs officials, such as the ministers of defense and foreign affairs or key foreign policy advisors, but these serve at the pleasure of the elected chief executive.

A second advantage of an open, participatory decision-making approach is that it is likely to yield superior, long-term choices. This advantage derives in part from the increased opportunity to discuss and assess policy alternatives and their likely outcome, thereby ensuring maximum opportunity for anticipating problems and estimating intended and unintended outcomes of policy alternatives.

A third advantage of democratic regimes is that decisions that enjoy popular support are likely to be more credible and effective in global society. Moreover, national morale, manifested in the sacrificial and dedicated service of public officials and citizens, is likely to be stronger in participatory regimes than in authoritarian systems.

Fourth, democratic decision making is likely to be more flexible and adaptable. Given the changing political and economic conditions in the global system, policy innovation is essential in foreign affairs. Authoritarian regimes are not well equipped to adjust to the ongoing changes because decision making is highly centralized and because governments often impede the free flow of information in society. Democratic regimes, by contrast, are better able to carry out policy reform because political pluralism and institutional decentralization increase flexibility.

In sum, despite significant tactical advantages enjoyed by authoritarian regimes, democratic, representative decision making is, on balance, superior to centralized, undemocratic decision making. Although the development of policies may be slower and more cumbersome in democratic systems, participatory decision making is likely to result in superior policies that enjoy greater and more intense popular support.

CNN effect
The impact of immediate television exposure of major political developments on public opinion.

The Peacefulness of Political Regimes   Are some types of regimes more conducive to peace than others? Does the quest for international security among states lead to similar foreign policies, as realists assert, or is the nature of a regime important, as liberal institutionalists contend? More particularly, are democratic states more prone to peace, as some scholars have claimed?

One of the most cherished liberal propositions about international politics is that constitutional democracy breeds peace. The idea of democratic peace is not new but dates from the early nineteenth century. One of the first thinkers to articulate this belief was the nineteenth-century German philosopher Immanuel Kant, who argued in his essay *Perpetual Peace* that the proliferation of representative regimes would encourage the pacification of interstate relations. Democratic regimes were less likely to go to war than autocratic governments, Kant suggested, because the political participation by citizens would inhibit war. Kant wrote: "if the consent of the citizens is required in order to decide that war should be declared . . ., nothing is more natural than that they would be very cautious in commending such a poor game, decreeing for themselves all the calamities of war."[41] During the first half of this century, a number of political leaders, from Woodrow Wilson to Dwight Eisenhower, popularized the notion of democratic peace, while some scholars called attention to pacific effects of representative political systems. For example, Quincy Wright, observed in his monumental *A Study of War* that democracies are less prone to go to war, but that once they begin fighting they do so even more intensely than authoritarian regimes.[42]

Beginning in the early 1980s scholars began to examine systematically the propensity toward war of democratic systems and came to the astounding conclusion that *democracies don't fight each other*. R.J. Rummel, for example, found that "in all the wars from 1814 to the present [1989], there has been no war between stable democracies, even though the number of democracies has grown to fifty-one today, or 31 percent of all nations, governing 38 percent of the world's population."[43] One scholar argues that the absence of war between democracies "comes as close as anything we have to an empirical law in international relations."[44] In view of the analysis of democracy and war, scholars have developed the so-called **democratic peace thesis (DPT),** one of the most important postulates to emerge from the social sciences during the second half of this century. This argument is explained in Issue 8.2.

Democratic peace thesis (DPT)
This theory attributes the absence of war among democratic states to the ideals and values of constitutional regimes and procedures of democratic institutions.

International Influences

The international environment also influences foreign policy by providing not only the operational context for action but also the challenges and opportunities as well as the threats and rewards, to which states must respond. Among the external factors that influence foreign policy, geography, international legal and moral norms, the nature of official international interactions, and the scope of transnational relations are especially noteworthy.

Geography

Because the size, location, and terrain of a country influence national power, some scholars have argued that geography is an important determinant of foreign policy. This conviction has generally been supported by research in the area of **geopolitics,** a field exploring the relationship of geography, national power, and foreign policy. A central premise of geopolitics is that geographical dimensions of states affect the projection of national power and thereby influence global relations. During the nineteenth and early twentieth centuries, geopolitics was a fashionable approach to international relations. In the United States, for example, Alfred Thayer

Geopolitics
The field that examines the interrelationship of geography, national power, and foreign policy.

Issue 8.2 The Democratic Peace Thesis

The DPT claims that (1) democracies do not go to war against other democracies and that (2) when conflict arises among democracies, they rarely use force because it is "illegitimate" to do so.[45] What explains the pacific nature of democracy? Scholars have developed two general explanations to support the democratic peace argument (see fig. 8.4). First, it is suggested that democracies foster peace because of *structural and institutional constraints*. Because constitutional regimes maintain limited government through institutional mechanisms (e.g., checks and balances and separation of powers), and because the legitimacy of decision making is rooted in consent, democracies maintain structures and procedures that impair centralized, autocratic decision making. The second explanation is *normative and cultural*. It assumes that liberal ideas encourage freedom, public debate, tolerance, and compromise and that the diffusion of such ideas encourages peaceful conflict resolution. Although both institutional and normative elements help to constrain foreign policy decision making, Russett argues that the normative/cultural explanation is the more "powerful."[46]

It is important to stress that the DPT does not hold that democratic states are less war-prone. Studies

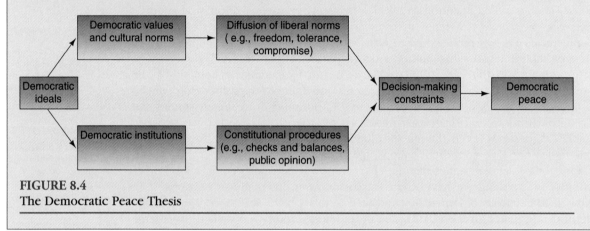

FIGURE 8.4
The Democratic Peace Thesis

Mahan, a nineteenth-century American naval officer, argued that because control of the seas was essential in projecting power, international influence was ultimately dependent on naval power.[53] In Great Britain, by contrast, Sir Halford Mackinder argued in the early twentieth century that control of the Eurasian "heartland" (basically central Europe and western Asia) was the key to controlling the world.[54] But in the early 1940s Nicholas Spykman modified Mackinder's thesis by suggesting that controlling the "rimland" or perimeter of World Island (Europe, Asia, Africa) was the key to global influence. In Spykman's words: "Who controls the rimland rules Eurasia; who rules Eurasia controls the destinies of the world."[55] Even though geopolitics has lost some of its influence in this century, some scholars have continued to emphasize geopolitics in the contemporary analysis of IR.[56]

Geography clearly has implications on a country's security. Of various geographical elements that affect territorial vulnerability, location, the character of neighboring states, and topography have been especially important. The geographical location of a state is important because it can affect the nature and scope of international relations. For example, location can affect international access. Countries that are islands, like the United Kingdom and Japan, are more likely to develop maritime military power than standing armies. Indeed, S.E. Finer suggests that the rise of democracy in Britain was facilitated by Britain's concentration on naval power and the absence of a large army.[57] Island nations are also likely to encour-

have shown that the type of political regimes does not affect a country's general propensity for international conflict. Bruce Russett, for example, argues that "the consensus of systematic studies is that the type of political system is not related in general to the probability that a country will be involved in war or international conflict in general."[47] Jack Levy similarly concludes that "the evidence is conclusive that democratic states have been involved, proportionately, in as many wars as nondemocratic states."[48] How, then, do we reconcile the DPT with the conclusion that the type of political regimes is statistically unrelated to peace?

To begin with, because most countries of the world have been nondemocratic, a large portion of international relations have involved nondemocracies. Moreover, the propensity to conflict is inherent in the anarchic international structure. Whether regimes are democratic or not, they face similar external challenges in pursuing their global interests. Additionally, major powers, regardless of their political character, are likely to be more involved in global conflicts than small powers. The fact that the United States has been more conflict-prone than many other countries is due to factors that derive from its "great power" status. Russett notes that great powers are more conflict-prone because they have wider interests, have greater military capabilities that they can use in distant places, and are involved with many more states than small powers.[49] In sum, although democracies have been proportionately involved in as many conflicts as nondemocracies, they are inherently more prone to peace with other democracies.

The DPT has generated a significant scholarly debate.[50] Nevertheless, there is a growing recognition among government officials that promoting democracy may be one of the more fruitful post–Cold War strategies to foster global order. For example, during a visit to Czechoslovakia in 1990, British Prime Minister Margaret Thatcher said: "if we can create a great area of democracy stretching from the west coast of the United States . . . to the Far East, that would give us the best guarantee of all for security—because democracies don't go to war with one another."[51] And in his 1994 "state of the union" address U.S. President Bill Clinton reiterated the democratic peace thesis, claiming that "the best strategy to ensure our security and to build a durable peace is to support the advance of democracy elsewhere. Democracies don't attack each other."[52] Thus, although scholars may continue debating the theoretical validity of the thesis, public officials have increasingly accepted its claims.

age greater international trade because of their need to import essential goods and services and also because of the relative ease in carrying out trade through shipping. The condition of being landlocked can also influence foreign policy. Lack of direct access to the sea for countries like Bolivia, Chad, and Switzerland means that a significant part of a state's commerce must traverse through other states. Zambia, for example, is highly dependent on South Africa for its international trade, while Bolivia must rely on Chile or Peru for an outlet to the sea.

The number and nature of neighboring states also affects the foreign policy of a state. Some countries, such as China, Brazil, Russia, and Germany, each have borders with nine or more states. Other states, like Canada, Ecuador, Spain, and the United States have borders with two or fewer states. Although the number of bordering states is not itself a cause of foreign policy, states with many contiguous states are potentially more vulnerable and more likely to face border disputes and territorial threats than states with few bordering states. Even more important than the number of contiguous states is the nature of relations between neighbors. Canada and the United States, for example, share a largely unprotected territorial border of more than 5,000 miles, whereas China and Russia share a slightly shorter border that remains one of the most heavily protected territorial boundaries in the world. The location of other states is also important. One of the reasons for the perceived vulnerability of European states is the large number of countries within close proximity. For example, most continental European countries are within 1,000 kilometers of at least twenty other states. Moreover, at least twenty-eight countries exist within 1,000 kilometers of Russia. In contrast to European powers, the United States is not only protected by two oceans, but is located far from other continents. Moreover, even though the United States has fought in several wars in its 200-year history, these have been, with few exceptions, international wars fought abroad rather than on domestic soil.

The impact of geography on perceived territorial vulnerability is most graphically illustrated by Israel, a slender state bordered by four Arab countries. Since Israel was created in 1948, it has been involved in five major wars with its Arab neighbors, in great part because of their unwillingness to accept the Jewish state. The antagonism between the Jewish and Arab peoples has been exacerbated by the territorial vulnerability of the Israeli state. In the 1967 Six-Day War, Israel decreased its territorial vulnerability by gaining control of the strategic Golan Heights, bordering Syria, and of the West Bank, thereby increasing Israel's width from approximately fifteen kilometers to sixty-eight kilometers. (Israel also gained control of the Sinai Peninsula but returned it to Egypt with the signing of the Egypt-Israeli Peace Treaty of 1979.)

Finally, a nation's topography also affects foreign policy by the protection it affords the state. Deserts and mountains, for example, can provide a barrier to foreign conquest. The Alps and the Pyrenees have historically provided a northern buffer to Italy and Spain, respectively, while the Andes Mountains have served as a territorial barrier between Argentina and Chile. Similarly, even though Switzerland is surrounded by four states and is in the center of continental Europe, its rugged terrain has served a major obstacle against aggression.

International Legal and Moral Norms

A second determinant of foreign policy is international law and international morality. Although international law is relatively weak compared to domestic law (see chap. 13), it still provides a rich body of international rules that regulate the behavior of state and nonstate actors. Some of the major areas of international law include maritime law, space law, environmental protection, diplomatic practices, jurisdiction, pacific settlement of disputes, war, and human rights. Although no superior force exists to enforce widely accepted rules, states generally follow international law both because norms are viewed as authoritative and because states believe that compliance is in their self-interest to do so. Some states might consider disposing toxic wastes in the open sea in order to avoid the more costly process of domestic disposal through environmentally safe practices, but such action would be clearly contrary to widely accepted international legal norms.

A more elusive constraint on the state behavior is international morality. According to Hans Morgenthau, international morality is a major restraint on the foreign policy behavior of states.[58] However, because little agreement exists about what constitutes good and bad behavior in the international community, international morality is perceived as weak, with even less authority than international law. It is clear, nonetheless, that governments desire to act in accord with ethical norms in order to be perceived as acting rightly. Robert Kennedy observes, for example, that the major reason why the United States did not carry out a preemptive attack against Cuba during the 1962 missile crisis was the belief that such an action would have been detrimental to the country's international reputation as a moral leader.[59] Another more recent illustration of the important role of morality is the widespread condemnation of "ethnic cleansing" within Bosnia-Herzegovina.

The Nature of Official Interactions

A third type of international determinant of foreign policy is the nature of intergovernmental transactions. Such interactions include bilateral and multilateral relations between states. When states share a high degree of cultural, political, and economic consensus, their interactions are likely to be far more harmonious and productive than if their values are highly divergent. The close bond between the United States and Britain, for example, derives from a shared history, common democratic institutions and practices, and a profound commitment to political, social, and economic freedom—that is, to a liberal conception of society. Moreover, the high commitment to common political ideals, such as individual liberty and political competition, has provided the foundation for the North Atlantic Treaty Organization (NATO). The powerful role of religion and culture is also illustrated by the strong ties among Arab states. Despite significant economic and political differences among states, the Arab nations have been major supporters of the Palestinian Liberation Organization.

Formal multilateral agreements, conventions, and treaties also help to determine foreign policy by structuring, constraining, and guiding policy making. Examples of formal structures that influence the development of foreign policy include regional organizations (e.g., the organization of African Unity, the European Union), security alliances (e.g., NATO), and multilateral organizations (e.g., the International Monetary Fund and the World Trade Organization). Other less formal initiatives can involve international initiatives and cooperative ventures, such as periodic global conferences (e.g., the 1997 Summit on Global Warming in Kyoto, Japan, and the 1996 UN Conference on Trade and Development in Midrand, South Africa), along with specific international initiatives (e.g., the international campaign to ban land mines). The pressures created by a high level of international consensus were especially evident with the signing of the antipersonnel mine treaty in late 1997. Even though more than 150 states signed the treaty, the United States did not sign the accord because it believed that continued use of mines was essential in defending South Korea from potential aggression from North Korea.

The Scope of Transnational Ties

The level and quality of socioeconomic transactions can also influence foreign policy. As noted earlier in chapter 3, the world has become increasingly interdependent culturally, socially, and economically, with countries becoming more vulnerable to transnational forces. For example, the expansion of trade and the integration of global financial markets, economies are increasingly influenced by global market forces. Thus, when foreign investors begin to lose confidence in the economic structures and policies, as was the case in Mexico in 1994 and in several South Asian states in 1997, the impact of international markets can be overwhelming. In late 1997, several South and East Asian countries were facing severe economic pressures due to a substantial decline in the value of their national currencies and loss of credit-worthiness. The pressures on South Korea, the eleventh largest economy in the world, were so large that the IMF, supported by the United States and other industrial states, provided a $55 billion line of credit. In short, interdependence has significant repercussions on states carrying out their domestic and international affairs.

IN CONCLUSION

Because national self-sufficiency is not a viable, long-term option for states, each country must develop a strategy for pursuing its basic interests in global society. The challenge for each state is to fashion a credible foreign policy that advances its national interests in light of its needs and capabilities. Numerous factors, including leadership, economic development, the nature and quality of the government, and geography, influence the priorities and goals pursued by states in the international community. But despite the cultural, political, economic, and social diversity among states, there is a high degree of consensus in the security, political, and economic goals of countries. Clearly, states want peace and economic prosperity, but especially national security.

SUMMARY

1. International relations involve interactions among state and nonstate actors. Fundamentally, IR entails intergovernmental relations, international governmental-societal relations, and transnational relations among nations. Foreign policy refers chiefly to interactions among governments.

2. The basis of foreign policy is the national interest of states. Foreign policy involves the pursuit of national interests in global society in terms of other states' interests. Vital state interests comprise several major concerns, but the most fundamental involve national security, economic well-being, and political and diplomatic affairs. National strategy is the means by which a state promotes its interests in the international community.

3. Foreign policy can be differentiated in terms of the intentions, declarations, and actions of states. In assessing foreign policy it is important to distinguish between each of these three dimensions.

4. Three major determinants of foreign policy are individuals, domestic society, and the international system. Factors that influence the impact of individuals on foreign policy include leadership style and belief systems. Domestic economic and political structures also affect the formulation and implementation of foreign policy. Finally, foreign policy making is influenced by several international influences, including geography, international legal and moral norms, the nature of official interactions, and the scope of transnational ties.

5. Although scholars differ on whether democracies are more peaceful than nondemocracies, there is substantial empirical evidence that democracies do not fight each other. Of course, democracies, as with all states, get involved in international conflicts, but they do not go to war against other democratic states.

KEY TERMS

foreign policy
national interests
national goals
national strategy
national security policy

international economic
  policy
diplomatic policy
nationalism
ideology

belief system
cognitive dissonance
misperception
NAFTA

CNN effect
democratic peace thesis
  (DPT)
geopolitics

RECOMMENDED READINGS

Brown, Michael E., Sean M. Lynn-Jones, and Steven E. Miller, eds., *Debating the Democratic Peace* (Cambridge: MIT Press, 1996). A superior anthology of readings on the democratic peace thesis.

Brzezinski, Zbigniew. *Power and Principle: Memoirs of the National Security Advisor, 1977–1981*. New York: Farrar, Straus and Giroux, 1983. An informative and penetrating account of the major foreign policy issues of the late 1970s by President Carter's national security advisor.

___. *The Grand Chessboard: American Primacy and Its Geostrategic Imperatives*. New York: Basic Books, 1997.

Using a geopolitical perspective, Brzezinski argues that, because Eurasia remains the geographical center of world power, the United States, as the sole superpower of the post–Cold War era, must be globally engaged in the Eurasian continent. In his view, American foreign policy must "employ its influence in Eurasia in a manner that creates a stable continental equilibrium, with the United States as the political arbiter."

Goldstein, Judith, and Robert O. Keohane, eds. *Ideas and Foreign Policy: Beliefs, Institutions, and Political Change*. Ithaca: Cornell University Press, 1993. Ideas— whether worldviews, principled beliefs, or assumptions about the cause and effect of relationships—have consequences. This collection of essays explores how ideas influence foreign policy and help to bring about outcomes in global society.

Hermann, Charles F., Charles W. Kegley, Jr., and James N. Rosenau, eds. *New Directions in the Study of Foreign Policy*. Boston: Allen & Unwin, 1987. A compilation of advanced essays on a variety of methods and approaches used in the comparative study of foreign policy.

Jervis, Robert. *Perception and Misperception in International Politics*. Princeton: Princeton University Press, 1976. A seminal study of the role of perception in foreign policy making, calling attention to the impact of misperception as a source of global conflict.

Kissinger, Henry. *The White House Years*. Boston: Little, Brown, 1979; and *Years of Upheaval*. Boston: Little, Brown, 1982. These two volumes provide a comprehensive account of the major foreign policy issues faced during the Nixon presidency. The first volume focuses on the years when Kissinger served as national security advisor, the second when he served as secretary of state. Both provide vivid accounts of some of the personalities and institutions shaping U.S. foreign policy.

Nincic, Miroslav. *Democracy and Foreign Policy: The Fallacy of Political Realism*. New York: Columbia University Press, 1992. This study challenges the prevailing realistic assumptions that popular pressures from below or democratic, competitive structures from above are counterproductive to sound foreign policy. On the contrary, the search for the national interest can be realized only from "authentically democratic aggregation of domestic preferences."

Rizopoulos, Nicholas X., ed. *Sea-Changes: American Foreign Policy in a World Transformed*. New York: Council on Foreign Relations Press, 1990. A stimulating collection of essays, written in light of the end of the Cold War, on different areas of U.S. foreign policy.

Russett, Bruce. *Grasping the Democratic Peace: Principles for a Post–Cold War World*. Princeton: Princeton University Press, 1993. International relations among democracies are inherently more peaceful than among nondemocracies. According to Russett, this is due not to their wealth, alliances, or distance from each other, but to values and cultural norms that restrain violence and to institutional structures that inhibit war.

Wiarda, Howard J. *Foreign Policy Without Illusion*. Glenview: Scott, Foresman, 1987. A short, readable introductory study on the elements that contribute to the making of U.S. foreign policy. The book focuses on factors such as public opinion, the mass media, interest groups, political parties, and think tanks.

RELEVANT WEB SITES

Foreign Policy Association   www.fpa.org/links.html
   See the following:
   Domestic and foreign newspapers
   "Great Decisions" Program

International Affairs Resources   http://data.fas.harvard.edu/cfia/links/

National Endowment for Democracy   www.ned.org

Think Tanks:
   Heritage Foundation   www.nationalsecurity.org
   The Brookings Institution   www.brook.edu

U.S. Department of State   www.state.gov/index.html
   See Current Issues

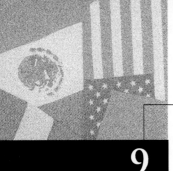

CHAPTER

9 Foreign Policy Decision Making

On September 29, 1991, President Jean-Bertrand Aristide was overthrown in a military coup, bringing an end to democratic rule in Haiti. Aristide, a radical Roman Catholic priest, had been elected the previous December in the country's first democratic elections. Led by the United States, Western leaders strongly condemned the military coup and tried to pressure the new government to return power to civilian authority.

To pressure the Haitian military to reinstate Aristide, the Organization of American States (OAS), a regional organization of thirty-seven Western Hemisphere countries, imposed a trade ban in October 1991 and other more stringent trade restrictions in May 1992. Although these measures decreased access to foreign goods, Haiti was still able to secure vital resources, including food and petroleum. In order to further increase economic pressure on Haiti's military, the UN Security Council imposed a worldwide oil embargo in June 1993. This ban resulted in immediate oil shortages and led Haiti's rulers to the bargaining table.

In July 1993, at UN-sponsored negotiations at Governors Island, N.Y., General Raoul Cedras, the head of Haiti's army, agreed to a transition plan based on the establishment of an interim government, amnesty to military officers who had been involved in the coup, and the return of Father Aristide as president. After the interim government was installed in August, the Security Council lifted the oil embargo. Two months after the transition plan was put into operation, however, it began to unravel. The military refused to cooperate with the creation of a new, more professional police force, and it refused to relinquish power to civilian, elected authorities. As a result, the Security Council reimposed the oil embargo and threatened even more severe trade restrictions.

Although promoting democracy has been a major U.S. foreign policy objective throughout the postwar era, implementing this goal has never been easy, as the Haitian case illustrates. How should the United States foster democratic rule in poor, developing nations? Should it rely on positive (carrots) or negative (sticks) sanctions? How much military pressure should be put on a small country like Haiti to promote human rights and political democracy? Should the U.S. government promote its democratization goals through regional or global organizations, like the OAS and the UN, or should it pursue such goals unilaterally?

This chapter analyzes the process of foreign policy implementation. It begins by examining alternative models of foreign decision making, contrasting idealistic and realistic explanations of foreign policy and reviewing some major impediments to rational policy formulation. The chapter then compares routine and crisis decision making, illustrating the latter with a case study on the Cuban missile crisis. Thirdly, major instruments of foreign policy implementation are examined, focusing on the role of economic and military statecraft. Finally, the chapter assesses the role of intelligence in foreign policy decision making.

Models of Decision Making

Foreign policy decision making is an aspect of a state's governing system. Because the concept of governing is rooted in the Greek verb "to steer," foreign policy decision making can be viewed as the process of steering the state within the seas of global society. Fundamentally, such steering involves choices (*decisions*) by political leaders and government officials (*decision makers*) to advance states' transnational interests (*goals*). As with all human decision-making processes, individual and collective self-interest are assumed to be the major motives for determining foreign policy goals.

In an effort to explain the foreign policy process, scholars have developed a number of simplified models of decision making. The most basic of these is the rational actor model, which conceives of decision making as a deliberate process by which decision makers calculate the cost and benefits of alternative actions. Even though such a model is useful in providing a simple and intelligible foreign policy model, such an approach is insufficient because it is based on ideal conditions that rarely characterize contemporary foreign affairs. Moreover, decision making is rarely influenced by rational utilitarian estimates alone. Typically, other nonrational factors, including ideological and religious biases, organizational dynamics, bureaucratic procedures, and group dynamics, can affect foreign policy decision making. As a result, scholars have developed alternative decision-making models to take into account the institutional, organizational, and psychological impediments to rational decision making. The two major alternative models are the organization process model and the bureaucratic bargaining model.[5] In the following sections we examine major features and limitations of the rational actor model and then sketch some key features of alternative paradigms.

The Rational Actor Model

From an ideal and rational perspective, making and implementing foreign policy involves identifying interests and goals, developing a strategy for achieving goals, and successfully implementing policy. According to the ideal perspective, states behave in purposeful ways, seeking to maximize short- and long-term goals. International relations are not random, unintelligible interactions among states, but are rooted in the goal-oriented choices and actions of political communities. If the foreign relations of states were totally random and irrational, the study of foreign affairs would be impossible. Indeed, because states are assumed to behave in intelligent and purposeful ways, the analysis of foreign policy is possible.

The **rational actor model** assumes that states are coherent actors that seek to maximize their interests by rationally weighing the costs and benefits of alternatives. Some of the major elements of the rational actor model are:

Rational actor model
A model that assumes that individuals make decisions by, among other things, gathering the necessary evidence, weighing the alternatives, and then selecting the action that is most likely to advance the desired goals.

1. Problems are defined thoroughly and accurately.
2. National goals and interests are identified, especially in light of defined problems.
3. National goals and interests are prioritized.
4. Alternative strategies for pursuing goals are identified.
5. Policy alternatives are assessed in light of potential consequences.
6. The optimum strategy is selected in light of anticipated policy outcomes.[6]

Although the rational actor model is helpful in illuminating the rational character of international relations, it suffers from several shortcomings. First, the model assumes that states behave as *coherent actors*. Countries are viewed as communities ruled by a cohesive, well-organized government in which the decision-making process is regarded as a by-product of deliberate and rational assessment. But governmental decision making is not carried out by a single individual or a unified, coherent organization. Rather, it is undertaken by numerous officials, each representing a variety of political and governmental agencies, and each representing interests and perspectives that are not necessarily complementary. Indeed, decision making is frequently a slow and cumbersome process because of conflicts among officials, groups, agencies, and governmental institutions involved in the formation of policies.

For example, the making of U.S. foreign policy not only involves the president and his White House staff, but also appointed officials and civil servants in the Department of State, the Department of Defense, and other related government agencies, as well as the Congress. The multiplicity of foreign policy actors is typically represented in medium to large embassies, in which ten to twenty distinct government agencies are represented. Thus, at U.S. embassies in countries such as Argentina, India, Nigeria, and Spain, one is likely to find officials not only from the Department of State, but also from the Drug Enforcement Agency, the Department of Commerce, the Department of Agriculture, the Treasury Department, the Agency for International Development, and the Department of Defense. Because of the multiplicity of actors involved in developing and implementing foreign policy, decision making often results from intense competition among relevant government institutions and personnel. This is especially the case in modern, pluralistic regimes in which political power is dispersed among a variety of governmental agencies and political institutions.

Second, the model assumes that decision making is based on *a rational dispassionate assessment of long-term, strategic interests*. In effect, it assumes that governments pursue the national interest. But decision makers are seldom motivated solely by the general, future interests of the state. Because governmental decision making is the result of a multitude of agencies and organizations, each with its own particular interests, foreign policy is often the product of limited and short-sighted interests of people and organizations. In effect, government officials do not always pursue public policy with dispassion. Sometimes they place their personal or institutional loyalties above the general interests of the nation. For example, some have suggested that Israel's foreign policy in the 1980s was focused excessively on its short-term interests in expanding control over the occupied territories (West Bank and Gaza) and did not give sufficient priority to the growing demands for Palestinian political autonomy in those areas.

Third, the model assumes that decision makers have *adequate time and information* on which to make rational choices. Accurate, dispassionate goal setting and goal implementation requires reliable information. It also presupposes time to analyze and prioritize alternative strategies. But governmental decision making is often undertaken with limited information and under severe time constraints. Despite efforts to gain as much information about the interests and capabilities of other states, information about foreign governments is always incomplete. Moreover, decision making is often undertaken under time constraints, especially during international crises. As a result, foreign policy decision making is generally based on incomplete information.

Finally, the model does not take into account the *role of misperception*.[7] As noted earlier, foreign policy decision makers act in light of their perceptions, not in light of reality itself. Because people's psychological preconceptions serve as a lens for filtering data, ideological worldviews can easily distort reality and this, in turn, can impair governmental decision making. Misperception decreases the availability of accurate information and impairs the analysis of goals and strategies. Thus, when external stimuli are distorted, sound, dispassionate decision making becomes difficult, if not impossible.

Table 9.1. highlights the discrepancy generally found between the ideal-rational model and the realities of world politics.

Alternative Models

The **organization process model** emphasizes governmental decision making as the outcome of choices from diverse government agencies, each with its own *standard operating procedures (SOPs)* and interests. Because most foreign policy decisions involve several government agencies, decision making is the result of the interaction of these quasi-independent organizations. According to Allison, the behavior of these organizations is not determined by dispassionate assessment of issues, but primarily by the routines established in these organizations beforehand. Government leaders can, of course, influence the outputs of their organizations, but they cannot substantially control their behavior. As a result, decision making in this model is less a result of deliberate choices of leaders and more a result of outputs of large, complex organizations functioning according to standard patterns of behavior.[8] For example, although Bill Clinton was critical of President Bush's foreign economic policy toward China during the fall 1992 presidential campaign, after becoming president he continued most-favored-nation (MFN) treatment toward China—in great part because of the overwhelming support for such a policy from relevant governmental agencies.

The **bureaucratic bargaining model** views governmental decision making as a result of bargaining among the different relevant government actors. Unlike the

Organization process model
A decision-making approach that emphasizes the role of standard operating procedures and established behavior patterns within complex bureaucratic and governmental agencies.

Bureaucratic bargaining model
The analysis of policy making that stresses bargaining among different relevant governmental actors.

TABLE 9.1 Comparison of Ideal and Actual Governmental Policy Making

Task	Ideal Process	Actual Practice
Information	Accurate, timely data available to define issues, problems	Information about the world is only partially accurate and fragmentary
Goal Selection	National goals defined clearly and dispassionately	Nonrational factors influence goal setting
Ranking of Goals	Interests and goals are ranked in light of immediate gains	Goals are ranked in light of short-term, ideological interests and long-term interests
Policy Selection	Policy based on rational assessment of likely outcomes	Policy selection is based on collective negotiating among relevant government agencies
Articulation of Policy	Policy is defined clearly and coherently	Multiple agencies describe policy in different and, at times, conflicting ways

rational actor model, which assumes that the development and implementation of public policies is carried out by a simple, coherent structure, this model emphasizes the multiplicity of different agencies that seek to influence the decision-making process. Because decision makers represent specific institutions, they tend to interpret decision making from their agencies' perspective. Thus, this model emphasizes competition, bargaining, and negotiation among relevant decision makers, each fighting for their respective agencies' interests.

Thus the bureaucratic bargaining politics model views decision making as a consequence of interagency power politics, in which the influence and skill of government heads will significantly influence public policy. During the Cuban missile crisis, bureaucratic bargaining was continuously evident in the secret meetings of the National Security Council. For example, during the missile crisis, heads of military agencies ("hawks") tended to favor greater use of force, whereas those from nondefense agencies ("doves") tended to support a more moderate course of action. After intense bargaining, the government decided to pursue the option of a naval blockade, an intermediate position between the extremes of a military intervention and doing nothing.

Although conflict and competition among governmental agencies can contribute to improved decision making, some scholars have questioned the effectiveness of bureaucratic organizations in developing innovative policies. For example, Roger Fisher, in his insightful study *Conflict for Beginners,* suggests three reasons why bureaucracies produce inadequate decisions: first, subordinate officers tend to act as policy judges rather than as advocates for a particular decision; second, governments place a premium on success, thereby discouraging new initiatives and proposals among civil servants; and third, prior governmental decisions are enormously influential, because it is easier to make choices based on precedent than to define problems in new, creative ways.[9]

Theory of bounded rationality
A theory suggesting that decision makers frequently fulfill minimal conditions, rather than optimize utility, because they rely on simplified world views based on limited or "bounded" perspectives.

In addition to governmental and bureaucratic influences, rational decision making can also be compromised by nonstructural constraints, including psychological influences and group dynamics. For example, Herbert Simon, a Nobel laureate economist, has argued that decision makers may not wish to maximize their goals and to optimize their choices, as rational utilitarian theory might predict. Instead, they may simply wish to satisfy limited gains. According to Simon's **theory of bounded rationality,** some decision makers may be guided by a simplified worldview based on limited or "bounded" rationality. Thus, to avoid the cumbersome and time-consuming process of weighing alternatives, they may simply seek to fulfill minimal conditions (*statisfice*), rather than to *optimize* utility.[10]

Prospect theory
This theory suggests that, since humans are more concerned with minimizing losses than with maximizing gains, policy makers are more risk-prone in seeking gains and less risk-prone with respect to potential losses.

Another theory that offers an alternative explanation to a rational-utilitarian approach to decision making is **prospect theory.**[11] According to this theory, decision makers make choices by evaluating alternative options in light of a known "reference point." How a problem is framed and what reference point is used in estimating gains and losses is thus likely to significantly influence leaders' decision making. Moreover, because people are assumed to be far more concerned with minimizing losses than with maximizing gains, the theory claims that people are likely to assume greater risks when potential gains are involved and less risk-prone when potential losses are likely. Prospect theory thus suggests rational decision making is likely to be impaired by the human propensity to be more hopeful and risk-prone about future policies than to risk criticism for halting failed policies.

Groupthink
The tendency of groups to encourage conformity of thought and thereby impair open, creative deliberation.

Finally, decision making can be influenced excessively by group dynamics. Even though interactions among persons and groups can contribute to a more informed and logical process of decision making, groups can also impair open, rational deliberation by creating a climate that impedes creative analysis and encourages excessive conformity of thought. This phenomenon—called **groupthink**[12]—impedes innovative, creative analysis and breeds a bureaucratic mind-set within organizations. Groupthink can be especially damaging in foreign policy when it encourages a belief in one's invulnerability or moral superiority. During the Cold War the latter belief was periodically expressed by U.S. officials who tended to categorize Soviet communists simplistically and pejoratively. More recently, Western officials have similarly tended to brand radical Third World leaders, such as Omar Qaddaffi and Saddam Hussein, as irrational and fanatical.

ROUTINE VERSUS CRISIS DECISION MAKING

Routine Decision Making

Most foreign policy is formed and implemented through multiple governmental actors following well-established decision-making patterns and routines. **Routine foreign policy making,** which is based on the organizational process and bureaucratic bargaining models, is normally highly conflictual, slow, and frequently cumbersome. Moreover, in a democratic system the number of governmental and nongovernmental actors involved is must greater than in authoritarian systems, thus making routine decision making much more dynamic and complex, involving significant discussion and debate among legislative and executive actors, bureaucratic agencies, interest groups, the media, and the public at large.

Routine foreign policy making
Slow, incremental, bureaucratic decision making using standard operating procedures (SOPs).

In democratic systems, routine foreign policy making is generally characterized by four features. First, such decision making involves *multiple organizations and institutions,* each with their own interests and perspectives. In the United States, for example, the initiation and implementation of foreign policy making is carried out by: (1) the president and his White House advisors (especially the national security advisor), supported by the National Security Council; (2) major departments and agencies concerned with national security and foreign affairs (the Departments of Defense and State and the Central Intelligence Agency); (3) miscellaneous supporting agencies (e.g., Office of the U.S. Trade Representative, the Agency for International Development, the Arms Control and Disarmament Agency, the U.S. Information Agency, and the National Security Agency); and (4) domestic departments and agencies whose work frequently involves international concerns (e.g., the Department of Agriculture, the Treasury Department, the Commerce Department, the Drug Enforcement Agency). Congress, along with its respective committees and subcommittees, plays a key role in debating international trade proposals and foreign policy and national security issues, approving major foreign affairs initiatives, ratifying international treaties, and authorizing funding for the work of departments and agencies in carrying out international relations policies and programs. Finally, nongovernmental actors, including think tanks, specialized interest groups, business associations and labor groups, and the media play an important role in influencing foreign policy decision making. Because the executive is given primary responsibility for foreign policy, public opinion, as noted in chapter 8, serves to support and to constrain the initiatives of the executive, rather than to provide the basis for decision making.

A second feature of democratic decision making is the *inevitability of conflict.* Because numerous actors are involved in foreign policy making, each with specific interests and perspectives, conflict is a natural by-product of decision making in democratic structures based on the doctrine of pluralism—that is, the belief that good policies emerge from the contestation of ideas and competing interests. Conflicts occur between leading public officials, relevant departments, different branches of government, and governmental and nongovernmental actors. Such conflicts can become especially pronounced when the executive and legislative branches are represented by different political parties or when the executive initiates policies that are strongly opposed by particular groups. From time to time, foreign policy consensus cannot be achieved, and foreign policy becomes unpredictable and variable. This was the case for President Reagan's Central America foreign policy in the mid-1980s, which sought to weaken the Sandinista regime in Nicaragua by supporting anti-Sandinista counterrevolutionary forces (known as the Contras). But the difficulty and then failure to secure legislative approval for these initiatives resulted in a vacillating and frustrating policy. Moreover, if the mass public opposes a major foreign policy initiative, the government may simply refuse to make a decision. In 1984 and 1985, after NATO began deploying nuclear-tipped cruise missiles, the government of the Netherlands refused to make a decision on whether or not to deploy such missiles because it was widely assumed that any decision by the parliament would have led to the collapse of the government. Because of the highly contentious nature of the nuclear debate, the Dutch government simply refused to make a decision on the deployment of missiles on its land.

A third feature of routine decision making is the *necessity of compromise.* According to the bureaucratic bargaining model, decision making is a by-product of negotiation and bargaining among relevant governmental actors. As noted in case 8.1, gaining congressional support for NAFTA required a major White House initiative to build and sustain support, especially among members of the House of Representatives. In the end, in order to get necessary congressional support, President Clinton was forced to make a number of concessions ("side agreements") to special interests, including labor, environmental, and agricultural groups. In short, the successful development, adoption, and implementation of foreign policy initiatives, as with all democratic decision making, requires the building of coalitions through the give-and-take of negotiation.

Finally, foreign policy decision making is characterized by *incrementalism*—slow, piecemeal change. Because decision making is often a time-consuming and complex process, David Braybrooke and Charles Lindblom have suggested that policy makers frequently lack a clear idea of what they are trying to achieve. As a result, governmental decision making tends to be a process of "muddling through," rather than a process of establishing clear goals and of selecting the most effective and efficient strategies for achieving such goals.[13]

Incremental decision making
Routine, piecemeal decision making by relevant bureaucratic and governmental agencies.

The **incremental decision making** style is illustrated by the evolution of U.S. foreign policy towards the former Soviet-bloc countries in the wake of the precipitous decline of Soviet communist influence in Eastern Europe, followed by the collapse of the Soviet Union itself. Beginning with the establishment of a noncommunist government in Poland in August 1989, the winds of democratic reform swept through Eastern Europe with unprecedented speed and force, resulting in the fall of communist governments in East Germany, Czechoslovakia, Hungary, Romania, and Bulgaria. The demise of the Soviet state, coupled with the dramatic reforms in Eastern Europe, resulted in vigorous public policy debates within and outside the U.S. government. After patiently and incrementally examining policy alternatives, the Bush administration devised a policy of qualified support for the reforms and developments in the Soviet Union and Eastern Europe. Even though the U.S. government sought to provide food credits to the Soviet Union and limited financial assistance to several other former communist states, it did not encourage self-determination for Soviet republics. For example, although the Baltic republics had sought political independence from the Soviet Union as early as the spring of 1990, the United States did not move to recognize these states until after the Soviet government had formally allowed them to secede in September 1991. In short, the United States responded to the decline of the Soviet Union and the end of the Cold War with limited, incremental adjustments in its policies.

Crisis Decision Making

Periodically, significant international conflicts arise that cannot be handled through the normal routines of government.[14] Such conflicts, generally defined as **international crises,** are characterized by the perception of significant threat, limited time in which to respond, the heightened expectation of possible use of force, and the involvement of the top leaders of government. A classic illustration of a crisis is the Cuban missile crisis (see case 9.1). Although crises are normally of short duration, sometimes they last many months. Perhaps the longest crisis in recent history was the U.S.-Iranian hostage crisis of 1979, which began with the Iranian revolutionary students' takeover of the U.S. Embassy in Tehran and ended more than a year later when the Iranian government freed fifty-three diplomatic hostages.

One major difference between routine and **crisis decision making** is seen in the level of control by the government's top leadership. In the United States, for example, crisis decision making has generally involved the president, the vice-president, the secretary of defense, the secretary of state, the director of central intelligence, and the president's national security advisor. In the former Soviet Union, crisis decision making generally involved the head (general secretary) of the Soviet Communist Party along with the party's top leadership. During the Cuban missile crisis, for example, decision making was carried out almost exclusively by Nikita Khrushchev and the party's Politburo (the Political Bureau of the Party's Central Committee).

Another important difference between these two types of decision making is the number of relevant actors involved. Whereas routine decision making involves numerous governmental agencies, crises, by contrast, are controlled almost exclusively by the government's top leadership. This is so for several reasons. First, crises normally involve issues of vital national concern, often involving either a direct or indirect military threat. Because the prime responsibility of government is to protect the sovereignty, territorial integrity, or vital political and economic interests of the state, when a foreign state threatens these, the head of government and his or her top advisors will automatically assume prime and immediate responsibility. Second, the standard operating procedures of bureaucratic agencies are too slow, cumbersome, and disjointed to allow a government to act with the needed swiftness. The time constraints in crises preclude executive-legislative debates or a comprehensive analysis of issues by appropriate bureaucratic offices. Third, crises generally involve highly sensitive issues requiring secrecy. Because the probability of unwanted disclosure of information is generally proportional to the number of agencies and officials involved in the decision making, governments generally limit the number of officials involved in crisis decision making in order to decrease the risk of unwanted disclosure of information to the public.

International crises
Unexpected short-term international conflicts involving vital interests of states.

Crisis decision making
Decision making during an international crisis.

STATECRAFT: INSTRUMENTS OF POLICY IMPLEMENTATION

Historically, statecraft has been defined as the art of conducting the affairs of state. Although such a conception includes both domestic and foreign domains, comtemporary use of the term is usually limited to international relations. **Statecraft** is here defined as the deliberate and organized actions governments take to influence foreign state and nonstate actors in order to maximize national interests.[28] By influence, we mean that states seek to persuade other actors to do something they would not otherwise do (positive influence) or to stop doing something considered unacceptable (negative influence).

As noted in chapter 6, states can influence other state and nonstate actors through a variety of policy instruments.[29] Some of the most important include:

Statecraft
The actions undertaken by government officials towards foreign state and nonstate actors in order to maximize national interests. Similar to national strategy.

(continued on p. 210)

CASE STUDY

Case 9.1 The Cuban Missile Crisis

The Cuban missile crisis of October 1962 was a brief but extraordinarily dangerous confrontation between the United States and the Soviet Union. The crisis, which brought the superpowers to the brink of nuclear war, began on October 16, when President Kennedy was informed that, based on photographic intelligence, the Soviet Union was installing intermediate nuclear missiles in Cuba.

The thirteen-day crisis had a private and public phase. During the secret phase high-level government officials (known as the Executive Committee, or simply ExCom) analyzed the Soviet challenge and deliberated about the strategy that should be pursued. This secret phase ended a week later when President Kennedy gave a nationally broadcast speech in which he announced the Soviet introduction of missiles into Cuba and outlined a number of initial military and diplomatic initiatives the U.S. government was taking in response to this development. The public phase lasted six days, until Sunday morning, October 28, when Soviet leader Nikita Khrushchev announced that the offensive weapons would be dismantled and withdrawn.

The Nature of the Dispute

Fundamentally, the Cuban missile crisis was a Cold War quarrel over the power status of the United States and the Soviet Union in the Western Hemisphere. When President Kennedy became aware of Soviet missile installations in Cuba, he determined that the missiles could not remain. Not only did they immediately threaten U.S. national security, they directly challenged the existing balance of power. The Soviet government's official explanation for introducing missiles in the Western Hemisphere was to protect Cuba from a U.S. invasion.[15] The Soviets pointed to the 1961 Bay of Pigs invasion as evidence of U.S. aggressive intentions. But however much the Soviet Union may have wished to support its new revolutionary ally, the defense of Cuba did not fully explain Soviet action. Raymond Garthoff, a former U.S. diplomat who was directly involved in the crisis, has noted that only one explanation is satisfactory— the desire to redress the perception that the Soviet Union was inferior in strategic nuclear weapons.

Fundamentally, three options were available to the United States—*persuasion, invasion,* and *compellance.* In the words of General Maxwell Taylor, the United States could "talk 'em out, shoot 'em out, or squeeze 'em out."[16] The first option assumed that rational dialogue and flexibility could resolve the conflict. With the exception of UN Ambassador Adlai Stevenson, no senior American official favored negotiating Western military assets for the withdrawal

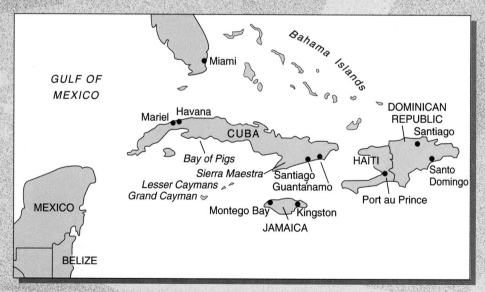

MAP 9.1
Cuba and Surrounding Countries

of Soviet weapons from Cuba. The second option, championed by such "hawks" as General Maxwell Taylor, Paul Nitze, Douglas Dillon, and John McCone, along with former Secretary of State Dean Acheson, relied on military force to solve the problem—either through an air strike, an invasion, or a combination of the two. A third alternative, representing an intermediate position between diplomacy and force, involved a **naval quarantine** (blockade) of Cuba. President Kennedy chose this latter option because it provided additional time for the withdrawal of the missiles without resorting to an air-strike or an invasion. Although the blockade would not guarantee the removal of the missiles, it would place immediate pressure on the Soviet Union without resorting to force.

The Confrontation

In his nationally televised speech, President Kennedy declared that the stationing of strategic weapons in Cuba was a "reckless and provocative threat to world peace and to stable relations between our two nations" and that the United States would not accept this unilateral change in the status quo. To reinforce the aim of securing a withdrawal of the missiles, Kennedy instituted a number of initial diplomatic and military measures, including a "quarantine" on all offensive military weapons, whereby all Soviet ships bound for Cuba would be inspected and those with offensive weapons cargoes would be turned back. In addition, Kennedy warned that any missile launched from Cuba would be regarded as an attack by the Soviet Union on the United States, resulting in a "full retaliatory response upon the Soviet Union."

To convey its resolve, the U.S. government initiated military actions, including the dispersion of its strategic forces in order to decrease their vulnerability to attack, the deployment of some 180 ships in the waters surrounding Cuba, the call-up of reserve

The construction of these missile sites in Cuba in 1962 resulted in the most dangerous Cold War crisis between the United States and the Soviet Union.

continued

Case 9.1 The Cuban Missile Crisis—*continued*

forces, and the transfer of a large number of troops to Florida. Most significantly, the United States placed its nuclear forces at a high state of readiness. To provide additional time to Soviet ships proceeding toward Cuba, the United States reduced the original quarantine line from 800 miles to 500 miles.

On Friday evening Kennedy received a long letter from Khrushchev stating, among other things, that if the United States would agree not to invade Cuba and halt its blockade, the Soviet Union would withdraw its missiles from Cuba. Khrushchev concluded his letter with an appeal for reason: ". . . you and I should not now pull on the ends of the rope in which you have tied a knot of war, because the harder you and I pull, the tighter this knot will become. And a time may come when this knot is tied so tight that the person who tied it is no longer capable of untying it, and then the knot will have to be cut."[17] The next day Kennedy responded by demanding that the Soviet Union halt constructing missile bases and that all its offensive weapons in Cuba "be rendered inoperable, under effective United Nations arrangements."[18]

On Saturday evening Attorney General Robert Kennedy, the president's bother and closest advisor during the crisis, met with Soviet Ambassador Anatoly Dobrynin to discuss the crisis. Although there is some dispute about exactly what the attorney general told Dobrynin, evidence shows that Kennedy conveyed three important points: (1) time had run out and either the Soviet Union would withdraw its missiles or the United States would take them out; (2) the promise of no invasion and elimination of the quarantine was contingent on the removal of missiles; and (3) the United States would eventually withdraw its Jupiter missiles from Turkey. McGeorge

Bundy, one of the key participants in the crisis, subsequently noted that the promise to withdraw the "Jupiter" missiles was conditioned on secrecy. Had the Soviet Union made the withdrawal public, the agreement would have been "null and void."[19]

The Settlement

The crisis ended on Sunday, October 28, when Khrushchev announced that the Soviet Union would remove the weapons it had recently introduced into Cuba. In his announcement, Khrushchev emphasized again that the weapons were entirely defensive in nature and then, after acknowledging President Kennedy's promise not to attack or invade Cuba, indicated that the missiles would be removed.[20] Although the decision to withdraw the missiles immediately reduced the gravity of the conflict, the crisis itself did not come to an end until other key issues, including the status of forty-two Ilyushin L-28 bombers, were resolved.[21] Although Fidel Castro wanted to keep the bombers, Khrushchev announced, after intense Soviet-Cuban negotiations, that the bombers would be withdrawn. In response, Kennedy announced the lifting of the quarantine.

Lessons

Some theorists have suggested that the missile crisis was beneficial because it forced policy makers to confront the reality of the nuclear age. Other, more specific lessons, include the following: First, because of the danger of escalation involved in crises, major powers, especially nuclear states, should pursue strategies of crisis prevention, rather than of crisis management. Recent revelations about the missile crisis suggest that the risk of losing control was far greater than had been considered at the time of the

1. *Rational persuasion:* using logic and data to persuade (e.g., peaceful negotiation)
2. *Manipulative persuasion:* using deception to persuade (e.g., some types of propaganda)
3. *Inducement:* using positive and negative sanctions to persuade (e.g., foreign aid)
4. *Deterrence:* using military threats to prevent behaviors deemed unacceptable (e.g., nuclear retaliation)
5. *Coercive diplomacy:* using military threats to persuade actors to alter their behavior (e.g., threat of military intervention)
6. *Force:* using coercive power to compel an actor to change its behavior (e.g., war)

conflict—but for reasons different than are usually assumed. According to one scholar, the greatest risks did not originate from the leaders themselves but from actions, events, and errors beyond their control.[22] For example, a senior Soviet military-intelligence officer who was spying for the United States was arrested on October 22, the night Kennedy gave his televised speech about the crisis. Shortly before his arrest he sent a prearranged coded signal to his U.S. intelligence handlers indicating that the Soviet Union was about to launch a nuclear attack. Secondly, because Khrushchev had prohibited the firing of SAM missiles at American planes, the downing of the U-2 plane on October 27 was in direct violation of Soviet military orders. Thirdly, General Thomas Power—the head of the Strategic Air Command (SAC)—ordered an increased level of military preparedness without authorization from the president or the secretary of defense. The alert, which increased readiness to Defense Condition (DefCon) 2, the next highest level, was sent in unencrypted form rather than in code so that the Soviets would be sure to learn about it. Fourth, on October 27, the same day that an American reconnaissance plane was downed in Cuba, another U-2 plane inadvertently flew into Soviet airspace.[23]

A second important lesson is the priority of intelligence—that is, the need for accurate information about the capabilities and intentions of an opponent. Despite regular reconnaissance flights, U.S. intelligence was woefully incomplete during the crisis. For example, prior to the conflict the U.S. government had estimated the number of Soviet military personnel in Cuba at about 4,000; during the crisis this estimate was increased to between 8,000 and 10,000; and in the immediate aftermath it was further increased to between 12,000 and 16,000. During the late 1970s Fidel Castro confirmed that there were about 40,000 Soviet military personnel in Cuba at the time of the crisis, and more recently Soviet officials have confirmed the number at 42,000.[24]

A third important lesson is the necessity of discussion and debate in defining and responding to a foreign policy problem or crisis. According to Robert Kennedy, the missile crisis demonstrated the value of basing decisions on competing and conflicting opinions and recommendations.[25] In the ExCom, opinions were divided among three groups—"hawks," "doves," and "owls."[26] The "hawks" believed that the United States should destroy the missile sites, either through an air strike, or an invasion, or both; the "doves" believed that the crisis should be resolved peacefully through negotiation, avoiding military action at all costs; and the "owls" believed that a middle road option of coercive diplomacy, based on diplomacy and military threats, should be pursued. The existence of a plurality of perspectives inhibited spontaneous actions and contributed to the development of prudent policies during the crisis.

Finally, the crisis demonstrated the need for empathy. According to Robert Kennedy, the crisis demonstrated the need to place ourselves in the other country's shoes. In his view, the president spent more time trying to assess the likely effect of particular policies on the Russians and Khrushchev than on any other phase of decision making. "What guided all his [the president's] deliberations," wrote Kennedy, "was an effort not to disgrace Khrushchev, not to humiliate the Soviet Union, not to have them feel they would have to escalate their response because their national security or national interests so committed them."[27]

From a moral perspective, the most desirable of these instruments is rational persuasion, and the least acceptable is generally military force. Diplomatic negotiation is normally considered the most ethical approach because it seeks to achieve behavioral change peacefully while using truthful communication. Force, by contrast, frequently is considered unethical because of the death and destruction involved in military combat. But as suggested in chapter 11, force can be morally justified when it is an instrument of last resort and applied in defense of legitimate state interests against foreign aggression. Deterrence and coercive diplomacy, like force, rely on military power, but whereas force uses coercion to compel an opponent, deterrence and coercive diplomacy rely on coercive threats. Even though military threats do not bear the same evil as overt force, military threats are nonetheless morally problematic because they involve some of the evil effects of force. Finally, manipulative propaganda is also morally problematic because the actor seeks to influence the behavior of other actors through dishonest forms of communication.

Although peaceful persuasion is regarded as the most desirable method of carrying out foreign policy, actors are frequently unable to resolve disputes through diplomatic negotiation. As a result, they resort to other policy instruments. For example, during the 1990–1991 Persian Gulf crisis, precipitated by Iraq's aggression against Kuwait, the United States used propaganda, UN mediation, and international sanctions to induce Iraq to withdraw from Kuwait. However, after these initiatives failed to persuade Iraq to abandon its occupation, a U.S.-led international coalition resorted to military force to expel Iraq from Kuwait.

Statecraft is normally carried out either through positive or negative sanctions. Positive sanctions use rewards (carrots) like economic or military aid, the granting of most-favored-nation trading status, the transfer of technology, or the conditional granting of concessions. Negative sanctions involve threats or use economic or military punishment (sticks) to promote desired behavioral outcomes. Examples of negative statecraft, listed in order of increasing coerciveness, include: public condemnation, propaganda, modest economic sanctions, economic embargoes, military threats, limited military operations, military intervention, and major war.[30]

If statecraft is to be effective, a government must have clear foreign policy goals and develop appropriate strategies for implementing national objectives. Roger Fisher has observed that one of the major shortcomings of international negotiations is the lack of clear goals. According to him, governments often have greater knowledge of what they do not want than of desired outcomes. As a result, states often pursue ambiguous foreign policies, relying on threats and punishment, rather than on explicit articulation of desired outcomes. Despite the popularity of threats, Fisher thinks that they are used because of the erroneous belief that inflicting pain leads governments to alter their behavior. In Fisher's view, positive sanctions are far more effective in achieving desired outcomes.

Although foreign policy is carried out through a variety of policy instruments, four types of statecraft dominate contemporary international affairs: *diplomacy (peaceful negotiations), propaganda, economic statecraft,* and *military statecraft.* Next we examine the nature and role of propaganda and economic sanctions, and briefly touch on military statecraft—a topic covered more fully in chapters 10 (on force) and 11 (on war). The nature and role of diplomacy is explored in chapter 12.

Propaganda

Propaganda
The deliberate attempt to influence the attitudes and opinions of a target population through systematic dissemination of information.

Propaganda is the deliberate attempt to influence the attitudes and opinions of a target population through systematic dissemination of information. Fundamentally, the aim of propaganda is to persuade. This can be done through straightforward foreign reporting of events and actions, similar to the dissemination of information by public relations firms. But propaganda also can be undertaken through manipulative techniques, including reliance on psychological symbols, distortion of facts, disinformation, and lying—all of which have given propaganda a negative connotation. In this chapter we assume that propaganda is a legitimate instrument of foreign affairs, just as advertising is a valid method for marketing goods and services. Whether or not propaganda is a morally acceptable tool will depend partly on the truthfulness of the disseminated information.

Governments use propaganda in foreign affairs in order to influence public opinion in foreign societies. (See fig. 9.1). The U.S. Information Agency, for example, disseminates information about American economic, social, and political life through educational and cultural centers located throughout the world. It also operates the Voice of America, broadcasting programs in some forty languages. And

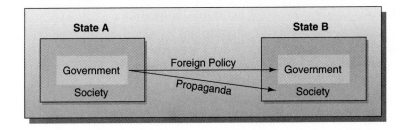

FIGURE 9.1
International
Propaganda

although the Cold War has ended, the U.S. government continues to sponsor Radio Free Europe and Radio Martí, beaming broadcasts to Central Europe and Cuba.

During the Cold War, the Soviet Union disseminated its communist perspectives to foreign countries through its state-sponsored news service, governmental publications, and radio broadcasting. One of the major instruments of Soviet propaganda was Radio Moscow, broadcasting thousands of hours of weekly programs in nearly eighty languages. Moreover, the Soviet Union subsidized the distribution of *Soviet Life,* a monthly pictorial magazine about Soviet society, to influence Western public opinion.

Sometimes governments use propaganda not only to foster greater understanding and appreciation for a country, but to manipulate public opinion. Such manipulation can be carried out through organized media campaigns based on misinformation and disinformation. Because such activities are normally carried out covertly, it is difficult to document foreign propaganda campaigns. Still, it is widely known that, from the earliest days of the Cold War, both superpowers used media campaigns in European and later in Third World states to bolster public opinion in favor of either Western democracy or Soviet communism. For example, in the early 1980s, when Western European nations were considering whether or not to deploy intermediate-range nuclear ballistic missiles, large, well-organized antinuclear campaigns took place in numerous Western European countries, highlighted by massive public demonstrations in major cities. Although the European "peace campaign" was based on indigenous sentiments, the antinuclear movement received significant external financial and organizational support.

Economic Statecraft

Economic statecraft refers to the organized economic actions used by government to influence other states. The primary difference between economic statecraft and military statecraft is not in the level of coercion, but in the instruments used: the first relies on economic tools to reward and punish foreign governments, whereas the second relies on military force.

In attempting to influence the actions of foreign states, economic statecraft can rely on economic incentives or punishment. This is achieved either through positive commerical and financial rewards or through economic coercion. Sanctions can also differ in scope, ranging from modest economic measures affecting trade or aid to major economic punishment and rewards, including massive economic transfers, embargoes, boycotts, and freezing of foreign assets. Table 9.2 identifies leading types of positive and negative **economic sanctions.**

A commonly used positive economic sanction is direct economic assistance, which can be given through grants, loans, commodity transfers (e.g., subsidized grain transfers), and other similar instruments. According to David Lumsdaine, industrial democratic states have provided more than $500 billion in foreign aid between 1950 and 1989.[31] Such aid has been given for a variety of reasons, including the advancement of ideological interests, the promotion of human dignity, the

Economic statecraft
The economic instruments used by governments in order to influence the behaviors of state and nonstate actors.

Economic sanctions
Actions that impose economic hardship on a target state in order to influence its behavior. Economic sanctions may also involve positive rewards.

TABLE 9.2 Leading Types of Economic Sanctions

Positive Sanctions
1. *Tariff Reduction:* Decrease in import taxes on goods from target state; sometimes refers to exports as well
2. *Preferential Trade Agreements:* Giving preferential treatment to imports from target state
3. *Granting "Most-Favored Nation" Status:* Treating imports from target state as favorably as those from any other state
4. *Granting Export or Import Licenses:* Giving permission to import or export particular goods or technology
5. *Increasing Foreign Aid:* Providing target state with more financial assistance

Negative Sanctions
1. *Tariff Increase:* Increase in import taxes on goods from target state; sometimes refers to exports as well
2. *Boycott:* Prohibition on imports; its scope can vary from limited (one or two goods) to comprehensive (entire category of goods and services)
3. *Embargo:* Prohibition on exports, although it can sometimes refer to a ban on all trade
4. *Quota:* Quantitative limitation on selective exports or imports from target state
5. *Blacklists:* Banning of firms involved in trade violations with target state
6. *Freezing of Assets:* Impounding overseas financial assets owned by a target state
7. *Foreign Aid Suspension:* Terminating foreign economic or military aid
8. *Expropriation:* A forceful takeover of foreign property belonging to a target state

quest for stable regional relations, and the encouragement of domestic reforms. In late 1990, for example, the U.S. government promised one billion dollars in food credits to the former Soviet Union, in great part to sustain the ongoing political and economic reform movement within that country.

Negative economic sanctions are imposed for at least three reasons. First, they can be utilized for symbolic purposes—that is, to send a message. For example, the United States' imposition of economic sanctions against South Africa in 1986 provided a means of communicating American displeasure with South African policy of racial segregation (*apartheid*). Second, sanctions can be instituted to punish a regime for unacceptable behaviors. The imposition of the U.S. grain embargo against the Soviet Union, for example, provided a method of imposing economic coercion on the Soviet Union for its intervention in Afghanistan in 1979. Third, and most importantly, sanctions are used to influence the actions of a target state. For example, comprehensive sanctions were imposed on Iraq in August 1990 in order to pressure its government to halt the military occupation of Kuwait.

The United States has relied increasingly on economic sanctions to seek to influence the behavior of other states. From 1993 to 1996, for example, it imposed sanctions or passed legislation to do so sixty times against thirty-five different countries (see map 9.2). The major reasons for imposing these unilateral sanctions included: human rights and democratization (22 times), antiterrorism (14), nuclear nonproliferation (9), antinarcotics (8), political stability (8), and worker rights/prison labor (6). The countries with the most sanctions were Iran (11), Cuba (9), Sudan (7), and China (6). These economic sanctions are significant because the thirty-five countries represent a population of some 2.3 billion persons (about 42 percent of the world's population) and a potential export market worth $790 billion (or about 19 percent of total global trade).[32] According to another

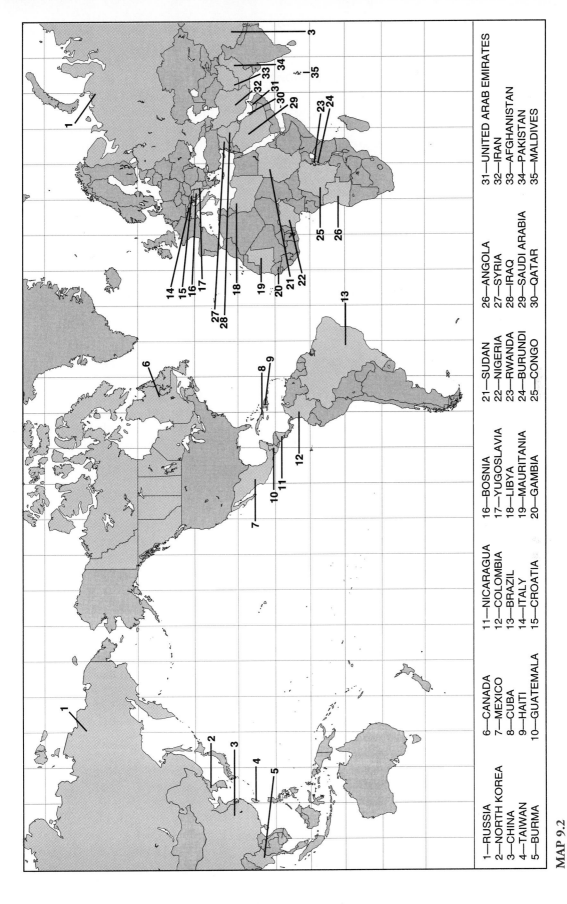

MAP 9.2

Countries Subject to U.S. Economic Sanctions, 1993–1996

1—RUSSIA	6—CANADA	11—NICARAGUA	16—BOSNIA	21—SUDAN	26—ANGOLA	31—UNITED ARAB EMIRATES
2—NORTH KOREA	7—MEXICO	12—COLOMBIA	17—YUGOSLAVIA	22—NIGERIA	27—SYRIA	32—IRAN
3—CHINA	8—CUBA	13—BRAZIL	18—LIBYA	23—RWANDA	28—IRAQ	33—AFGHANISTAN
4—TAIWAN	9—HAITI	14—ITALY	19—MAURITANIA	24—BURUNDI	29—SAUDI ARABIA	34—PAKISTAN
5—BURMA	10—GUATEMALA	15—CROATIA	20—GAMBIA	25—CONGO	30—QATAR	35—MALDIVES

study, U.S. economic sanctions were costing the United States about $15 billion annually in lost exports.[33]

The Impact of Economic Sanctions

Donald Losman has noted that economic statecraft has two dimensions—economic success and political success. The first refers to the ability of sanctions to achieve the desired economic outcomes, such as a significant decline in foreign investment, lower economic output, lower export revenues, higher unemployment, and ultimately, a net drop in living conditions. The second refers to political change brought about by the imposed economic coercion. Because a major assumption of economic statecraft is that changes in economic welfare in a target state will induce desired behavioral changes, economic success of sanctions is a precondition for political effectiveness.[34]

The economic effectiveness of economic coercion is likely to increase when the following six conditions exist:

1. *When the relationship between the sanctioning and target state is asymmetrical.* When the state imposing sanctions is economically stronger than the target state, it is better able to absorb the costs of such policies imposing sanctions and to influence other actors. One major study of 115 sanctions from World War I to 1989 found that in successful sanctions episodes the average spending economy was 187 times larger than the average target economy.[35]

2. *When the target state is economically dependent.* Because no state is completely self-sufficient, every country is vulnerable to some degree to international economic developments. Economic sanctions are likely to be most effective when a state is highly dependent on foreign resources and markets. According to one study, successful sanctions involved target states that depended on an average of 28 percent of their trade with the sender.[36] One reason for the partial success of the 1973 Arab oil embargo against Israel, the Netherlands, and the United States was their heavy dependence on petroleum.

3. *When the punished state is unable to easily substitute goods, technology and markets.* When the United States canceled Cuba's sugar quota after Fidel Castro took power in 1959, for example, Cuba arranged for the Soviet Union to buy its sugar, thereby minimizing whatever harm U.S. economic sanctions might have had on the country. Similarly, when the United States instituted a grain embargo on the Soviet Union in 1979, it turned to Argentina and other grain exporters to meet its grain requirements.

4. *When the cost of imposing sanctions is significantly higher on the target nation than on the punishing state.* The oil embargo of 1973, for example, was successful partly because the Arab states, led by Saudi Arabia, were able to reduce oil production and sustain short-term lower revenues in order to control supply. The fall in oil supply led to the quadrupling of petroleum prices.

5. *When sanctions are imposed collectively.* When the United Nations imposed comprehensive trade sanctions on Iraq following the August 1990 invasion of Kuwait, international trade with Iraq came to a virtual halt, thereby precipitating a 50 percent decline in its GNP. If the sanctions had been imposed only by some of the Western states, the economic punishment would not have been nearly so severe. The failure of U.S. sanctions against Cuba is due, in great measure, to the lack of support for such a policy by most other states of the international community, including Canada and virtually all Latin American and Western European countries.

6. *When the target state is vulnerable to foreign economic pressures.* Because open societies are more vulnerable to sanctions than closed societies, countries with democratic structures and market economies are likely to be affected much more by economic sanctions than autocratic regimes with limited political participation and a state-regulated economy. Ironically, dictatorial regimes—the systems that are most likely to violate human rights and disregard widely accepted international law norms—are less susceptible to economic sanctions than constitutional, democratic regimes. Thus, although economic sanctions against undemocratic regimes (such as Cuba, Haiti, Iran, and Iraq) have frequently imposed significant societal hardships, such economic adversity has rarely resulted in desired behavioral reforms.

The history of economic sanctions suggests that imposing economic punishment is easier to achieve than bringing about desired behavioral changes. In effect, economic success is easier to achieve than political success. Not surprisingly, a large number of scholars have held pessimistic views about the efficacy of sanctions. For example, Charles Kindleberger asserts that "most sanctions are not effective,"[37] whereas Margaret Doxey concludes a study of sanctions by noting that "in none of the cases analyzed . . . have economic sanctions succeeded in producing the desired political result."[38] David Baldwin similarly states: "It would be difficult to find any proposition in international relations literature more widely accepted than those belittling the utility of economic techniques of statecraft."[39]

Economic coercion is regarded as politically ineffective for several reasons.[40] First, some social scientists question the view that punishment encourages behavioral change, that pain and reform are causally linked. Although adversity may lead to capitulation and disintegration, it can also result in resolve. For example, the imposition of the UN arms embargo on the Republic of South Africa created short-term problems for the country; in the long run, however, the sanctions resulted in a major domestic weapons industry, making the country not only self-sufficient militarily but encouraging it to become a major weapons exporter. Moreover, the imposition of an oil embargo encouraged South Africa to develop alternative energy resources, so that by the 1980s it had become virtually self-sufficient in energy.

A second reason for the political ineffectiveness of sanctions is that the imposed economic hardship is borne by average citizens and not governmental officials. For example, although the U.S. embargo on Nicaragua in 1984 led to a significant rise in the cost of consumer goods, the resulting economic hardship was absorbed largely by urban workers and peasants, not by Sandinista political and military officials. Similarly, when the U.S. imposed comprehensive sanctions against Panama in 1988 to bring down the government of General Manuel Noriega, Panamanian economic activity came to a near halt in late 1988. But because the government continued to receive revenues from its transoceanic canal and oil-pipeline, government employees, especially members of Noriega's Panamanian Defense Force, were largely unaffected by American economic statecraft. The failure of economic sanctions was also demonstrated in the 1990–1991 Iraq-Kuwait conflict, during which time the United Nations imposed comprehensive trade sanctions against Iraq. As in other sanctions episodes, the political and military leadership remained largely unaffected by the halt in trade, whereas the common citizens had to bear the bulk of the economic hardships.

If sanctions appear to have little success in altering the foreign policy behavior of states, why are they so popular? In great part because they are cheap, powerful symbols of communication.[41] For example, the United States has repeatedly imposed economic sanctions to dramatize its opposition to behaviors of other states. For example, the U.S. imposed sanctions against the Soviet Union for its 1979 invasion of Afghanistan, against Nicaragua in the early 1980s for the regime's increasing monopoly of power and its regional support of insurgency, against Panama in 1988 to help topple the government of strongman Manuel Noriega, and against Iraq following its intervention and annexation of Kuwait in 1990 provided important international communications signals but were ineffective in achieving behavioral change. Some activists have argued that the comprehensive economic sanctions imposed in the mid-1980s against South Africa were responsible for ending institutionalized racial separation (*apartheid*) and the white monopoly of power. Although the sanctions no doubt contributed to the establishment of a nonracial democratic system in 1994, case study 9.2 suggests that such policies were nonetheless morally ambiguous and far less influential than the disinvestment by the international business community.

Although the instruments of economic coercion are unlikely to alter the behavior of governments in the short term, they can galvanize domestic and international public opinion, thereby weakening the government's authority of the target state. Ironically, sanctions are likely to be most effective against democratic, middle-income societies that protect basic human rights and least effective against authoritarian or quasi-totalitarian regimes in which human rights abuses are more common.

Military Statecraft

Military statecraft, the third general instrument for implementing foreign policy, involves the use or threat of use of force (coercive power) in order to influence the behavior of state and nonstate actors.[46] Most military statecraft is carried out through implicit or explicit threats of coercion, rather than the direct application of force. Just as police rarely utilize weapons to enforce law in domestic society, so, too, nations rarely utilize force against each other in their pursuit of global interests. Although military capabilities are rarely translated into force, this does not mean that military capabilities are not being utilized. Military power, like other types of power, is continuously being translated into bargaining capabilities through the potential use of force.

Because the lethality of modern weapons has continued to increase, major powers have tended to rely on threats rather than on overt force. As a result, the principal military strategies of the contemporary international system are deterrence and coercive diplomacy. As noted above, **deterrence** involves the use of military threats to prevent unwanted foreign behaviors. **Coercive diplomacy,** by contrast, involves threats or even limited force to persuade an opponent to desist or undo an act of encroachment. Because both deterrence and coercive diplomacy rely upon coercive threats, they offer the possibility of achieving foreign policy goals economically, with little or no bloodshed.

If deterrence and coercive diplomacy are to be effective instruments of persuasion, the threats of force must be sufficiently potent and credible to prevent unwanted behaviors and to compel behavioral change. In particular, credible threats will depend on the relative military capabilities of states and on the strategy and resolve to use them. In sum,

Military statecraft = Capabilities + Strategy + Resolve

Because power is ultimately relational and perceptual, maximizing bargaining power will require, at a minimum, the accurate measurement of relative power and national resolve. The challenge in military statecraft is to maximize bargaining power without resorting to force.

To be effective, military statecraft requires a credible declaratory policy and an effective operational doctrine. *Declaratory policy* refers to the explicit goals and strategies of a state's armed forces. An *operational doctrine* consists of the plans

Case 9.2 The Morality of Economic Sanctions: The Case of South Africa

The Development of Sanctions

International opposition to South Africa's apartheid regime began in the early 1960s as public officials became more aware of the injustices associated with the increasing institutionalization of racial segregation. In 1962 the UN General Assembly passed a nonbinding resolution condemning apartheid, calling on states to ban trade and break diplomatic relations with South Africa. Subsequently, the Security Council authorized a ban on arms shipments to South Africa and later imposed a mandatory arms embargo. Another important sanction was OPEC's oil embargo, which forced South Africa to pay much higher costs for petroleum. Although these economic sanctions resulted in a significant decline in South Africa's rate of economic growth, none of these measures had much political impact on the white Afrikaner government. Indeed, the oil embargo led South Africa to pioneer in the development of oil extraction, making the country nearly self-sustaining in energy, and the arms embargo encouraged the development of a major military arms industry whose exports subsequently became a major source of foreign exchange.

In response to growing American public opposition to apartheid, the U.S. Congress began considering economic sanctions in the mid-1980s. To forestall more severe sanctions, President Reagan instituted modest sanctions in September 1985. The following year, however, Congress, over-riding a presidential veto, passed legislation instituting comprehensive sanctions. The 1986 legislation (known as the Comprehensive Anti-Apartheid Act of 1986) imposed, among other things, a ban on selected South African imports, a ban on new investment in South Africa, a ban on exports of oil and computers, and the termination of landing rights for South Africa's Airlines (SAA). The European Community and the British Commonwealth also instituted similar, though more modest, sanctions at this time.

Although government-imposed sanctions were symbolically significant, the most influential measures were the private actions of the business community, especially the closure of MNC affiliates in South Africa. The *disinvestment* by U.S. corporations was largely in response to the widespread public *divestment* campaign, calling on municipalities and public institutions to sell stock in companies involved in South Africa. The aim of the divestment campaign was not only to force institutions to divest their stock but to force companies to withdraw from South Africa. It has been estimated that by 1991, more than twenty-eight states, twenty-four counties, and ninety-two cities had adopted divestment measures, resulting in the sale of some $20 billion of stock.[42] As a result of these initiatives, more than five hundred international companies, the bulk of these from the United States, closed their South African operations in the 1980s. In addition to disinvestment, international banks stopped lending to South Africa. As a result of disinvestment and the cutoff of loans, South Africa experienced massive capital outflows and a sharp weakening of its currency. It has been estimated that from 1985 to 1989 net capital outflows were $11 billion, leading to a significant contraction of the South African economy and a loss of at least $4 billion in export earnings.[43]

The Moral Ambiguity of Sanctions

Most Western leaders believed that apartheid was discriminatory, undemocratic, and unjust. The dilemma decision makers faced was how best to foster structural reform in South Africa while causing the least harm to the black, disenfranchised majority. Fundamentally, two strategies were available— isolation or engagement, economic sanctions or constructive diplomacy and participation in the global economy. Sanctions advocates, led by Archbishop Desmond Tutu, argued that sanctions were necessary both to express moral outrage and to compel domestic political change. In Tutu's view, sanctions were moral both because they were widely supported by the black masses and also because they were a necessary instrument of coercion on the white government. Sanctions opponents, by contrast, argued that economic sanctions were an inappropriate strategy for two reasons: first, because hardship was unlikely to lead to reform, and second, because they would lead to unnecessary harm on the poor, black working class. Alan Paton, author of *Cry, the Beloved Country* and one of the leading critics of apartheid, expressed his opposition to sanctions as follows: "I do not understand how your Christian conscience allows you [Bishop Tutu] to advocate disinvestment. I do not understand how you can put a man out of work for a high moral principle. . . . You come near to saying that the end justifies the means, which is a thing no Christian can do."[44] *continued*

Case 9.2 The Morality of Economic Sanctions: The Case of South Africa—*continued*

From a moral perspective, the major shortcoming of sanctions is the economic hardship that they inflict on the masses. Sanctions are blunt policy instruments, and the harm that they cause is not easily targeted. However, imposing direct harm on innocent civilians, even to pursue a just end, is morally problematic because it fails to discriminate between officials responsible for governmental decisions and the citizenry. According to the just war doctrine (see chap. 11), only political and military officials of a state—that is, those responsible for government policies—may be directly attacked. Arguing by analogy, some scholars have suggested that economic sanctions are moral only to the extent that they protect civilians from unnecessary harm. Thus, Chris-

tiansen and Powers support sanctions only when "adequate humanitarian provision is made for the civilian population."[45]

Even though many observers now believe that economic sanctions contributed symbolically, if not substantively, to ending apartheid and to the establishment of a democratic regime, scholars continue to disagree about the morality of sanctions. Regardless of how economic sanctions are assessed, it is clear that they frequently impose significant hardship on the masses, as was the case in South Africa.

In light of the above, were economic sanctions an appropriate policy instrument toward South Africa? Did the ends (abolishing apartheid) justify the means (comprehensive sanctions)?

---

and tactics for the application of force. A third dimension of military statecraft involves *weapons acquisitions policy,* which refers to the plans for purchasing and developing military weapons.[47] During the Cold War these three elements were illustrated by NATO's declaratory policy to deter Soviet-bloc aggression, a weapons acquisitions policy that sought to develop and acquire conventional and nuclear weapons to deter Soviet aggression, and an operational doctrine (known as *flexible response*) that sought to contain any type and level of aggression.

The effective implementation of deterrence and coercive diplomacy strategies requires diplomatic skill in communicating resolve. Although sufficient military capabilities are essential, deterrence also depends upon intentions and will. And as Craig and George have observed, signaling deterrence is not simply a matter of making threats. To be credible, a state's declarations must be perceived as involving vital interests of the deterring state.[48] Similarly, the success of coercive diplomacy will also depend upon effective communications. In particular, the coercing state must communicate a high level of urgency with its compliance demands and it must also help create an asymmetry of commitments, for which the coercing power is perceived as more committed to its demands than the opponent is in opposing them.[49] In sum, although military strategies such as deterrence and coercive diplomacy are based on force, they also involve skillful implementation. As with all foreign policy instruments, effective persuasion is dependent upon adaptation to the specific context, an asymmetry of power, and different levels of perceived commitment.

INTELLIGENCE AND FOREIGN POLICY MAKING

Throughout history leaders have attempted to learn as much as possible about foreign states. The Bible tells that Moses sent twelve men to explore Canaan and report back what type of land it was. Moses gave them the following instructions: "See what the land is like, and whether the people who live there are strong, few or many. See whether it is easy or difficult country in which to live, and whether the cities are weakly defended or well fortified; is the land fertile or barren, and does it grow trees or not." Some 400 years before Christ, the Chinese military strategist Sun Tzu wrote that the real test of statecraft was not in winning one hundred battles but rather in using intelligence to find security without fighting a war. In 1967 Israeli intelligence provided political leaders with unmistakable evidence that Arab states were ready to launch a joint attack on Israel. Israel responded with a preemptive air attack on Egypt and Syria, which ultimately resulted in Israel's victory over its Arab neighbors.

Fundamentally, **intelligence** is evaluated data or "distilled information" about foreign countries.[50] This data, which may relate to people, events, technological and scientific developments, military organization, and political dynamics of foreign countries, is useful for assessing the interests and capabilities of foreign governments, anticipating global economic and political developments, and warning of imminent danger. It also helps to identify problem areas and illuminate policy constraints. Intelligence thus helps government leaders maximize national interests within global society.

The role of intelligence in foreign policy is similar to the athletic scouting reports used by professional teams in preparing for a sports event. For example, before two professional football teams play each other, team scouts collect data on the strategies and capabilities of the opposing team. Similarly, before college athletes are recruited into professional teams, large amounts of information are gathered about the past performance and future potential of players.

The development of intelligence involves three phases: collection, analysis, and dissemination. In the first phase, intelligence may be collected openly (overt) or secretly (covert). Normally, most intelligence is gathered overtly through listening, observation, and reading. Open sources such as books, journals, newspapers, and radio and television are commonly used for gathering and developing intelligence estimates. For example, *Aviation Week & Space Technology,* a U.S. commercial aerospace magazine for professionals working in aviation and space technology, is considered one of the best data sources on U.S. commercial and military aerospace developments.

Covert intelligence involves the clandestine collection of information. A major way of carrying out covert collection is through spying (*human intelligence*), involving the placement of agents in foreign countries to secretly observe and report on developments of interest to the sending state. A second way of collecting intelligence is through high-resolution aerial photography (*photo intelligence*). During the early Cold War years, the United States collected this type of intelligence through airplanes (such as the U-2 and the SR-71), but since the 1970s it has relied almost exclusively on satellites. A third method is *signal intelligence,* which involves the interception of electronic signals through sophisticated listening posts located in foreign countries and on ships and airplanes. Because governments generally try to maintain confidentiality in their decision-making process, they rely on coded messages to protect communications from electronic monitoring. Nevertheless, governments collect coded signals and seek to break the codes in order to penetrate official communications of foreign governments. By the same token, governments try to protect their own communications from foreign interception— a task commonly defined as **counterintelligence.**

After intelligence is collected it must be analyzed and interpreted. Raw data is of little help to foreign policy decision makers. Indeed, when facts are completely clear, there is no need for intelligence assessment. All that is needed is to report the findings. Government officials need processed information that offer forecasts and estimates. In foreign policy decision making, the most useful intelligence is that which estimates probabilities and outlines the range of possible options without attempting to state definitive or sweeping conclusions.

Intelligence
Evaluated data on the goals, capabilities, and likely actions of foreign actors. Most intelligence is gathered and processed secretly.

Counterintelligence
A government's effort to protect the secrecy of its operations from foreign intelligence agents.

Providing accurate, comprehensive descriptions and interpretations of foreign developments and events is of course difficult, especially because information is always incomplete and subject to a variety of interpretations. Moreover, because it is impossible to predict the actions of leaders, the prediction of future developments will, of necessity, be incomplete and at times highly speculative. Not surprisingly, intelligence agencies failed to anticipate the rapid fall of communism, symbolized by the fall of the Berlin Wall in 1989. Similarly, U.S. intelligence agencies failed to predict Iraq's invasion of Kuwait in August 1990, although they had warned of the possibility of conflict between the two states.

One important task of policy makers and intelligence analysts is to anticipate intelligence requirements. Normally, intelligence is collected in response to specific requests. In the United States, for example, the National Security Council makes requests of the Central Intelligence Agency, whereas the Defense Intelligence Agency annually establishes prioritized collection requirements for its military attache offices in embassies throughout the world. The challenge, of course, is to identify potential future problem areas so that data can be collected and analyzed before a crisis occurs. But anticipating crises is extraordinarily difficult.

When the United States intervened in Grenada in 1983, for example, available intelligence was woefully inadequate, making the invasion a more difficult operation than had been expected. Moreover, when Argentina invaded the Falkland Islands in 1982, British forces were caught completely off guard. Indeed, the British military services did not even have a detailed map of the islands. And during the Iraq-Kuwait war, U.S. intelligence on the size and capability of the Iraqi military forces proved to be woefully inadequate, according to allied commander General H. Norman Schwarzkopf.

The dissemination of intelligence—the third phase—involves the distribution of finished reports to appropriate government officials. For example, in the United States intelligence is made available to the top government leadership in four ways. First, the president and his advisors receive a daily intelligence summary, highlighting important international developments and calling attention to potential trouble spots. Second, the intelligence community—comprising the Central Intelligence Agency, the National Security Agency, the Defense Intelligence Agency, and other smaller agencies and governmental offices—produces National Intelligence Estimates (NIEs), providing annual comprehensive assessments of vital issues, such as military and economic capabilities of major powers, major technological breakthroughs of leading industrial states, and energy supplies. Third, the intelligence community issues Special National Intelligence Estimates (SNIEs). Unlike the periodic NIEs, SNIEs are specific, one-time reports prepared in response to particular problems and issues. Finally, the intelligence community issues Interagency Intelligence Memoranda (IIM). These reports provide basic information on important technical, economic, social, and political issues. Unlike the SNIEs, which offer a prediction or forecast, the aim of the IIMs is purely informational.

The availability of good intelligence does not assure that governments will use it effectively. In a thorough study of the Japanese attack on Pearl Harbor in December 1941, Roberta Wohlstetter found that the American unpreparedness was not the result of faulty intelligence. Indeed, she demonstrates that U.S. forces had been able to provide American policy makers with ample signs of the possibility of an attack. Many of these signs were the result of decoding of top secret Japanese cables and radio messages. Thus, the reason for American unpreparedness lay not in inadequate intelligence, but in the judgments of political and military leaders in Washington who tended to believe that the Japanese were much more likely to attack bases closer to their home territory. As Wohlstetter notes, the U.S. "failed to anticipate Pearl Harbor not for want of the relevant materials, but because of a plethora of irrelevant ones. Much of the appearance of wanton neglect that emerged in various

investigations of the disaster resulted from the unconscious suppression of vast con-
geries of signs pointing in every direction except Pearl Harbor."[51]

In Conclusion

Although the formulation and implementation of foreign policy is commonly
viewed from a highly rational and coherent perspective, a realistic assessment reveals that foreign policy decision making is an extraordinarily complex and con-
flictural process. Thus, in developing prudent foreign policy goals and strategies, it
is important not to "idealize" the decision-making process. This will require, at a
minimum, a careful appraisal of national interests coupled with a realistic assessment of the role of the various instruments of statecraft. Although intelligence is always desirable in making and implementing routine foreign policy, it becomes especially crucial in crises.

SUMMARY

1. International relations are often analyzed from
   an ideal-rational perspective. Although such
   an approach is helpful in understanding
   foreign affairs, it is important to recognize that
   states are not coherent, rational actors.
   Foreign policy behavior is often influenced by
   other factors, including domestic political
   dynamics and misperception in foreign affairs.

2. When foreign policy decision making is
   carried out in routine circumstances, it is
   characterized by multiple actors and slow,
   incremental actions. During crises, by
   contrast, foreign policy decision making
   becomes much more centralized and involves
   a country's top leadership.

3. The Cuban missile crisis, arguably the most
   dangerous conflict of the Cold War era,
   brought the two superpowers to the brink of
   nuclear war. Decision-making lessons that
   have been attributed to this conflict include:
   (1) the need to avoid crises altogether, (2) the
   need for intelligence, (3) the importance of
   basing foreign policy on diverse opinion, and
   (4) the need to avoid humiliating an
   opponent.

4. Statecraft is the process by which states
   implement foreign policy goals in global
   society. It is carried out by three major
   instruments: propaganda, economic statecraft,
   and military statecraft. Propaganda is the
   means to influence public opinion in foreign
   states.

5. Economic sanctions are a commonly used
   tool of statecraft. Even though states apply
   such sanctions to foster foreign policy
   changes, economic coercion will not
   necessarily result in behavioral changes.

6. Military statecraft involves the threat or use of
   force to achieve foreign policy objectives.
   Such statecraft is based on capabilities,
   strategy, and resolve. Deterrence and coercive
   diplomacy are two major instruments of
   military statecraft.

7. A critical element in foreign policy is
   intelligence—"distilled information" about
   foreign countries. Intelligence is collected
   openly or secretly and is based on human
   sources, photography, and intercepted
   communications.

KEY TERMS

rational actor model

organization process
  model

bureaucratic bargaining
  model

theory of bounded
  rationality

prospect theory

groupthink

routine foreign policy
  making

incremental decision
  making

international crises

crisis decision making

statecraft

naval quarantine

propaganda

economic statecraft

economic sanctions

military statecraft

deterrence

coercive diplomacy

intelligence

counterintelligence

RECOMMENDED READINGS

Allison, Graham T. *Essence of Decision: Explaining the Cuban Missile Crisis.* Boston: Little, Brown, 1971. A pioneering study of crisis decision making that calls into question the widely accepted rational actor model of foreign policy. Allison suggests that alternative models emphasizing the role of bureaucracies and organizational politics can improve understanding of foreign policy making.

Baldwin, David A. *Economic Statecraft.* Princeton: Princeton University Press, 1985. A comprehensive survey of the nature and role of economic statecraft that calls into question the widely accepted notion that economic sanctions are ineffective foreign policy tools. Baldwin believes that economic statecraft is an important and effective instrument of foreign policy.

Blight, James G., Bruce J. Allyn, and David A. Welch. *Cuba on the Brink: Castro, the Missile Crises, and the Soviet Collapse.* New York: Pantheon Books, 1993. This vivid and insightful book explores the role of Cuba in the Cuban missile crisis. The study is based upon a 1992 conference in Havana that brought together leading missile crisis veterans, including Robert McNamara and Fidel Castro, and scholars from Cuba, Russia, and the United States. By providing background, proceedings, and analysis of the conference, the study illuminates important elements of this dramatic event. A tour de force.

Bundy, McGeorge. *Danger and Survival: Choices about the Bomb in the First Fifty Years.* New York: Random House, 1988. The definitive study of the role and impact of nuclear weapons on postwar global politics. Bundy provides a penetrating account of the Cuban missile crisis.

Cortright, David and George A. Lopez, eds. *Economic Sanctions: Panacea or Peacebuilding in a Post–Cold War World?* Boulder: Westview Press, 1995. A superior collection of studies on the nature, role, effectiveness, and morality of economic sanctions. Case studies cover sanctions toward Iraq, the former Yugoslavia, Haiti, and South Africa.

Garthoff, Raymond. *Reflections on the Cuban Missile Crisis.* Washington, D.C.: Brookings, 1987. Garthoff, a former diplomat and participant in the Cuban missile crisis, provides an insightful account of the crisis. He relies heavily on declassified documents as well as his own diplomatic expertise.

George, Alexander L. *Presidential Decisionmaking in Foreign Policy: The Effective Use of Information and Advice.* Boulder, Co.: Westview Press, 1980. An important study of how presidents make foreign policy, focusing on impediments to information processing as well as some of the means available for reducing such barriers. Of particular value are chapter 3 on the role belief systems play and chapter 8 on different management styles.

Hufbauer, Gary Clyde, and Jeffrey J. Schott. *Economic Sanctions Reconsidered: History and Current Policy,* 2nd ed. Washington, D.C.: Institute for International Economics, 1990. A detailed investigation of the nature and impact of economic sanctions. The book provides an excellent data source on postwar economic sanctions.

Kennedy, Robert. *Thirteen Days: A Memoir of the Cuban Missile Crisis.* New York: W.W. Norton, 1969. A short, lucid account of the most dangerous Cold War crisis by a key actor. The afterword by Richard Neustadt and Graham Allison is especially helpful in understanding this event.

Laqueur, Walter. *A World of Secrets: The Uses and Limits of Intelligence.* New York: Basic Books, 1985. This is a readable and insightful analysis of the nature, uses, and limitations of intelligence in the making of foreign policy. The case studies on the role of intelligence during the "missile gap" controversy, the Cuban missile crisis, and the Vietnam War are illuminating.

Macridis, Roy C., ed., *Foreign Policy in World Politics: States and Regions.* 8th ed. Englewood Cliffs, N.J.: Prentice-Hall, 1992. An informative introductory text to the study of comparative foreign policies. The study examines the foreign policies of Britain, France, Germany, Soviet Union, United States, China, and Japan, and analyzes regional foreign policy issues, including the European community, the Middle East, Latin America, and Scandinavia.

May, Ernest R., and Philip D. Zelikow, eds. *The Kennedy Tapes: Inside the White House During the Cuban Missile Crisis.* Cambridge: Harvard University Press, 1997. A carefully edited collection of transcripts of the most important White House meetings during the Cuban missile crisis. The editors provide invaluable introductory essays that describes the changing decision-making environment during the crisis and illuminate key issues under consideration. An indispensable source to the Cuban missile crisis.

RELEVANT WEB SITES

"Fourteen Days in October: The Cuban Missile Crisis"	http://library.advanced.org/11046
Library of Congress Cuban missile crisis	http://lcweb.loc.gov/exhibits/archives/colc.html
National Security Archive (George Washington Univ) Cuban missile crisis	www.seas.gwu.edu/nsarchive
U.S. Department of State U.S. foreign policy	www.state.gov/www/regions/internat.html
U.S. Department of Defense Information	www.defenselink.mil

Force: The Use of Military Power   **10**

On August 2, 1990, Iraq carried out a massive surprise invasion of Kuwait. Within twenty-four hours, Iraqi armed forces had taken control of all key Kuwaiti military and governmental centers and installed a puppet regime. Shortly thereafter, Iraqi president Saddam Hussein announced the formal annexation of Kuwait.

The swift conquest of Kuwait was realized through Iraq's superior military forces, which were much larger, better equipped, and more experienced than those of Kuwait. Moreover, because Iraq's attack was carried out with great surprise, Kuwaiti forces were able to provide only token resistance to the invading Iraqi forces. Saddam's aggression was no doubt based on the assumption that, even though some states would condemn his action, none would seek or be able to repel his gains through military retaliation. In effect, Hussein had calculated that his country's use of military force would greatly enhance his country's regional and global economic and military standing.

As this case suggests, military capabilities are a singularly important dimension of power because the pursuit of territorial security and other key national objectives is ultimately dependent on force. When states are unable to reconcile conflicting interests, they inevitably rely on their own resources, including military force, to get what they want.

In the previous chapter we briefly explored the different instruments of foreign policy. Although the nature and role of military statecraft was briefly sketched, here we examine more fully the role of force in world politics. In the chapter's first two sections, I describe various types of military power and then analyze the nature and role of coercive threats. The next three sections explore the role of limited force in three distinct environments—guerrilla war, terrorism, and military intervention. The chapter concludes with an analysis of the nature and impact of nuclear weapons on global politics. The phenomenon of war, the most extreme form of force, is examined in chapter 11.

THE NATURE OF MILITARY POWER

Military power performs four important functions: first, it provides prestige to a country; second, it protects through its ability to deter aggression; third, it provides military defense in the event of an attack; and finally, it provides the means to compel an adversary to alter its behavior. Each of these roles involves a distinct type of military power, which we will examine.

Prestige power
National power based on modern weaponry, symbols, and reputation.

Prestige power, or what Robert Art calls "swaggering power,"[4] involves maximizing a nation's image and reputation through the symbols of military capability. It is achieved by developing, acquiring, and demonstrating military capabilities. Unlike military force, which uses military power against another actor, prestige power only displays military potential. This type of power is demonstrated in large and pretentious military parades, the foreign port visit of a naval task force, or the acquisition of modern weapons, such as ballistic missiles or nuclear bombs. Because prestige power is dependent on large and modern military forces, historically the major powers have possessed it. During the nineteenth century, for example, British naval superiority gave the British empire significant prestige. Similarly, aircraft carriers and strategic nuclear forces are sources of prestige for contemporary world powers.

Deterrent power
The capacity to inhibit action through the credible threat of punishment.

Deterrent power is the ability to inhibit action through the implied or stated threat of punishment. It seeks to prevent undesirable actions by dissuading behavior through the threat of retaliation. Deterrence does not inhibit behavior through the use of military force, but by the promise of future military punishment. Indeed, the resort to force implies the failure of deterrence to influence behavior. For deterrence to work, goals must be supported by credible threats, and the threat of punishment must be rooted in the perceived *capacity* and *willingness* to carry out retaliation. The first relates to military capabilities and is rather easy to assess; the second is rooted in psychology and is virtually impossible to determine beforehand. For example, when Argentina invaded the Falkland Islands (Islas Malvinas) in 1982, it did so because it believed that Britain would not retaliate militarily. Although Argentine military commanders recognized that Britain possessed superior military forces, they thought that the British government would not authorize force to regain the islands. In effect, they gambled because they doubted British resolve. As a result, Argentine forces temporarily gained control of the islands until British forces recaptured the islands almost two months later. (See chap. 11 for a discussion of the Falkland War.)

Defensive power
The ability to repel an attack and limit destruction from aggression.

Defensive power is the ability to repel attack and to limit destruction from aggression. During the Cold War, this type of power was the basis of NATO, a defensive alliance whose chief aim was to protect European democracies from Soviet-bloc aggression. Although it is easy in theory to differentiate between the power to defend and the power to compel, in practice it is extraordinarily difficult to distinguish between the two, especially because the power needed to defend can also be used to compel, and vice versa. Moreover, because a good defense requires a good offense, defensive strategies are often indistinguishable from offensive postures. For example, defensive force is ordinarily used only in response to an act of aggression. But because a surprise attack provides tactical advantages, a state with evidence that an attack is imminent may carry out a preemptive attack to blunt the effect of the anticipated aggression. During the Six-Day War of 1967, Israel carried out a preemptive air strike against Egyptian and Syrian airfields because it had evidence that Arab states were about to attack it.[5]

Compellent power
The use of force or threat of force to persuade an adversary to stop unwanted action or to fulfill a desired action.

Compellent power is the capacity to get an adversary to stop some action, undo an unacceptable deed, or implement a desired behavior. To compel a foreign actor, a state must increase penalties—either in the form of physical force or economic and social costs—for not complying with the wishes of the compelling

TABLE 10.1 Comparison of Four Types of Military Power

	Purpose	Type of Military Forces	Use of Force
Prestige	Influence perceptions	Large, modern weapons	None
Deterrence	Prevention through threatened retaliation	Major conventional forces; strategic nuclear forces	Conditional
Defensive	Protect society from attack	Major conventional forces	Military force used to defeat aggression
Compellent	Get adversary to do something	Major conventional forces	Military force used to coerce adversary

state. The ultimate instrument for achieving compellence is military force. The United States used this type of power during the Christmas bombing of Hanoi in 1972 in order to get North Vietnam to return to the Paris negotiations. Compellent power was also used in early 1991 to oust Iraqi military forces from Kuwait. But compellence can also be achieved through the imposition of economic and social penalties, such as economic sanctions. For example, in 1987 the United States established comprehensive sanctions against Panama in order to pressure its military strongman General Manuel Noriega to give up power. The aim of the sanctions, like the use of bombing in Vietnam, was the same: to compel another state to change its behavior.

States use each of these forms of military power in accord with their national capabilities and foreign policy goals. (See table 10.1.) Throughout history, the most prevalent forms of military power have been compellent and defensive force. But in the twentieth century, deterrence has become the dominant form of power, in large part because of the increasing destructive potential of modern armed forces, evident in the large number of civilian and military casualties in the major wars. The increasing significance of deterrence is also due to the application of nuclear technology to the armed forces. As suggested later in this chapter, nuclear weapons have given deterrence a completely new meaning, because they provide the means not only of destroying an enemy's military forces but its society as well.

THE ROLE OF MILITARY POWER

It is not true that the primary role of military power is to carry out war. Although war is the ultimate method for resolving international disputes, the chief purpose of military power is to enhance the bargaining ability of states. Whether in peace or in war, a government's ability to pursue national interests will depend greatly on its military capabilities. Indeed, although other tangible and intangible elements contribute to an effective foreign policy, military power remains the dominant international currency for fulfilling national interests in global society. Of course, military capabilities do not automatically yield influence. If military capacity is to be translated into bargaining power, it must be combined with an effective military statecraft or strategy.

Peace Versus War

Relations among states are sometimes categorized as either in peace or in war. This view greatly oversimplifies the nature of world politics, which is best characterized as a mixture of conflict and harmony, competition and coordination.

Because military power is a part of all interstate relations, it is incorrect to divide international relations in terms of a peace/war dichotomy. Peace and war are not mutually exclusive categories. A more accurate classification of international relations includes at least four major conditions: peace, conflict without force, force without war, and war (see table 10.2). The two middle categories represent an intermediary zone between war and peace in which most international relations take place. International crises, a potential fifth zone examined in chapter 8, falls between these two intermediary categories.

In the condition of peace, states pursue their national interests without force and resolve their interstate disputes through negotiation and compromise. Reason and moderation prevail. But when states are unable to achieve their desired goals through peaceful negotiation, they resort to more coercive instruments of statecraft to achieve their objectives. Three major levels of military power used, in order of increasing coerciveness, are threats, limited violence, and unlimited force. Each of these methods corresponds to a category of international relations.

Conflict without force represents conflictual international relations without overt violence. Although states use a variety of nonviolent sanctions in seeking to influence the behavior of other states, the most commonly used instrument of statecraft is coercive threats. Such threats are used to prevent undesirable behaviors or to compel behavioral change. Because most global politics involves the reconciliation of competing and conflicting interests, the bulk of international relations are carried out in this intermediary zone of conflict without force.

Force without war, a relatively new category of international relations, refers to limited war or unconventional conflicts.[6] Historically, war has been the ultimate means of resolving interstate disputes. But because of the increasing destructive potential of military forces, governments have attempted to limit the scope of force by deliberately limiting the nature and scope of violence and by becoming involved in foreign conflicts through indirect participation and reliance on unconventional uses of force. Because disputes are settled with limited military coercion, force without war is often defined as **low-intensity conflict (LIC).**[7] Examples of LICs include border skirmishes, raids, covert operations, short-term interventions, and foreign participation in civil wars.

The two most important types of LICs are guerrilla wars and special military operations. Although **guerrilla wars** are essentially domestic revolutionary conflicts, they are included here because of direct and indirect participation by foreign governments. When civil wars involve revolutionary changes, with significant regional repercussions, major powers have periodically sought to promote or limit such changes by supporting existing regimes or aiding rebel factions to halt reforms or even to topple governments. For example, during the 1980s the U.S. government supported the elected government in El Salvador in its battle with the Marxist revolutionary forces (FMLN) by giving the regime nearly $5 billion in economic and military aid. On the other hand, during the same period the United States provided significant military aid, including sophisticated antiaircraft missiles, to the Afghan rebels (mujahedin) to force the Soviet military out of Afghanistan.

Low-intensity conflict (LIC)
Conflicts carried out by force without war—that is, with limited military coercion.

Guerrilla war
An unconventional war involving irregular forces using "hit-and-run" tactics.

TABLE 10.2   Categories of International Relations

Category	Peace	Conflict without Force	Force without War	War
Policy Instrument	Diplomatic negotiation	Coercive threats	Low-intensity conflict	Full use of armed forces

The second type of LIC, *special military operations,* involves limited short-term military activities against particular foreign governmental and nongovernmental targets. Examples of special operations include the U.S. antidrug campaign against South American cocaine producers and exporters and the U.S. bombing of military targets in Tripoli in retaliation for Libya's support of terrorism. Military intervention—such as the U.S. intervention in the Dominican Republic in 1965 and in Grenada in 1983—is also a form of special operations when undertaken for limited objectives.

The final and most extreme condition of world politics is *war,* in which military force is used to compel an adversary to alter its unacceptable behaviors. In this realm of foreign relations, states use all their military resources to overcome the opposition of an adversary.

Whether or not states resort to force will, of course, depend on the salience of the issues involved and the relative resources available to pursue foreign policy goals. States do not carry out threats or apply force simply to increase power. Rather, they make threats, use limited force, and even go to war in order to fulfill national goals. Carl von Clausewitz, the famous nineteenth-century Prussian officer and military strategist, observes that war is fundamentally "a continuation of policy by other means." Thus, force—like other instruments of statecraft—is a means to achieve national interests in global society.

Threats

Most military power is based not on actual force but on threats of force. The two major types of threats used in international relations are **deterrence** and **coercive diplomacy.** Both are instruments of persuasion. The first seeks to *prevent* undesirable behaviors by promising unacceptable punishment, whereas the second seeks to *compel* behaviors through the promise of coercive force.[8] Because both deterrence and coercive diplomacy seek to realize foreign policy objectives without resorting to violence, both are a more economical and efficient use of military power than war. Not surprisingly, coercive threats are far more common in pursuing foreign policy than the overt use of force.

The two most common methods of carrying out threats are official declarations and mobilization of military forces. Often governments use both to reinforce the threat. *Official declarations,* which can be made explicitly or implicitly, secretly or publicly, involve a government's intention to carry out military action in the event that a state does not comply with its desired objectives. Before the month-long bombing campaign of Iraq, President Bush repeatedly warned the Iraqi government that its military forces had to withdraw from Kuwait in compliance with UN resolutions. President Bush's declarations made it plain that if Iraq did not withdraw from Kuwait, allied forces would use military force to liberate the occupied country. Saddam's failure to heed the threat led to war.

The second method of threatening a foreign regime involves the *military show of force.* This method ranges from modest and peaceful military deployments to large deployments, such as the five-month mobilization of more than a half million soldiers in the Iraq-Kuwait conflict. The United States applied force this way in 1987 and 1988 when it maintained a large naval presence in the Persian Gulf in order to protect tankers flying the U.S. flag. More recently, in July 1990, the United States dispatched two aerial refueling planes to the United Arab Emirates and sent six combat ships into the Persian Gulf in order to express solidarity with both Kuwait and the United Arab Emirates after Iraq had made direct threats against them. Regrettably, this symbolic force was unsuccessful, and Iraq invaded Kuwait.

Are threats effective? Does the show of military force increase a country's ability to influence foreign policy behavior? In a significant study on the political use

Deterrence
The use of explicit or implicit threats of coercion in order to inhibit unwanted behavior.

Coercive diplomacy
The threat or use of limited force to persuade an actor to comply with a state's foreign policy goals.

of force, two foreign affairs scholars found that the United States resorted to coercive threats on 215 occasions between 1946 and 1975.[9] Of these, thirty-five incidents involved increased military readiness to cope with significant crises, such as Berlin in 1948 and 1961 or the Cuban missile crisis of 1962. In 180 less serious incidents, U.S. policy makers used armed forces to protect American interests abroad or to secure various other objectives. These incidents ranged from foreign ship visits to the deployment of major ground, air, and naval units, including increased readiness of U.S. strategic nuclear forces. The study found that although coercive threats helped realize U.S. policy objectives at first, after six months their effectiveness declined significantly. Their study implied that discrete uses of military force to attain political objectives serve mainly to delay unwanted developments abroad.[10]

When threats fail, states frequently resort to overt force by carrying out coercive operations, ranging from limited military intervention to full-scale war. In the following sections I examine the nature and role of military intervention, and in chapter 11, I describe and assess the phenomenon of international war. Before analyzing military intervention, however, I examine two types of unconventional force commonly used by nonstate actors—guerrilla war and terrorism.

Guerrilla Wars

Guerrilla wars are military conflicts using unconventional tactics. Such wars are characterized by four key features. First, they are political contests over who will rule society. Henry Kissinger notes that a guerrilla war differs from a traditional conflict in that its key prize is not control of territory, but control of people. This is done not through conventional war but through terror and intimidation, hoping to weaken a government's authority and public support.[11] Because the root cause of revolutionary wars is popular dissatisfaction with existing social and economic conditions, the strategy of the revolutionaries is to win the hearts of the people by promising radical reforms that reduce perceived injustices. Fundamentally, the aim is to promise the transformation of social and economic structures in return for popular support.

Second, guerrilla wars are chiefly rural military conflicts. A major strategy of guerrillas is to control the countryside in order to have a relatively secure base of operations and access to food. Because guerrillas seek rural support by promising land, a major element of their reform program is land redistribution. Once the guerrillas gain rural support, they can carry out a war of encirclement and eventually wear down government forces. The Chinese, Cuban, and Nicaraguan revolutions succeeded in this way.

Third, guerrilla wars are long-term conflicts of attrition that seek to wear down the enemy. Whereas conventional wars involve a direct military contest between two opposing groups, a guerrilla conflict seeks to avoid direct military confrontations altogether, preferring to weaken the enemy psychologically through hit and run tactics. Because revolutionaries do not have the military capabilities to defeat the government, their strategy is to wear down government forces. Mao Tse-tung has provided a succinct description of this strategy: "Enemy advance, we retreat; enemy halts, we harass; enemy tires, we attack; enemy retreats, we pursue."[12] Although revolutionaries may occasionally resort to terrorist tactics, their aim is not simply to create fear through random violence, but to exhaust the political will of the government and the military determination of the armed forces. They do this by carrying out surprise, small-scale attacks on military installations and by destroying key supply, communications, power, and transportation centers. Guerrillas aim to weaken the ruling authorities by imposing significant economic costs on them. During the 1980s, for example, the revolutionary forces of El Salvador (FMLN) carried out some $5 billion in economic damage.

One major aim of guerrilla war is to get government forces to overreact and attack civilian targets, thereby further alienating citizens from their government. For example, during the later phase of the Nicaragua guerrilla war of the late 1970s, the Sandinista insurgents succeeded in this strategy by causing the National Guard forces of Anastasio Somoza, Jr., to bomb urban areas, thereby further demoralizing public support for the ruling authorities. Even though such raids did little harm to the Sandinista guerrillas, they further alienated the government from the people.

Throughout the Cold War, guerrilla wars were common as antigovernment forces resorted to insurgency to topple existing regimes. Although the two superpowers occasionally confronted each other directly (e.g., the Berlin blockade and the Cuban missile crisis), the United States and the Soviet Union waged most of their conflicts indirectly in revolutionary wars in developing countries. In seeking to extend the ideology of communism and to gain political allies in its conflict with the West, the Soviet Union provided massive military and economic assistance to destabilize noncommunist regimes and to help install and sustain Marxist regimes. A key part of its global strategy was to support revolutionary insurgency. The United States, for its part, opposed the forceful expansion of communism, devoting significant economic and military resources to combat communist-influenced insurgencies. Because of the superpowers' military and economic aid, many regional Cold War conflicts, including the long-term revolutionary wars in Vietnam (1964–1973) and Afghanistan (1979–1989), were long, bloody affairs.

With the end of the Cold War, ideological insurgencies have been replaced by domestic ethnonationalist wars. Unlike the ideologically-inspired guerrilla conflicts of the past, post–Cold War insurgencies—whether in Afghanistan, Armenia, Bosnia, Chechnya, Sudan, or Turkmenistan—are inspired by ethnic, religious, and nationalistic sensibilities, rather than by ideological goals. And although the motives of guerrilla wars have evolved in the post–Cold War era, the aims and tactics of guerrilla war have remained largely unchanged—namely, to topple existing regimes by resorting to unconventional force.

TERRORISM

A second major type of unconventional force used in contemporary global society is terrorism. According to Martha Crenshaw, terrorism involves "symbolic acts of violence, intended to communicate a political message to watching audiences."[13] Terrorism seeks to promote society-wide fear through limited and unconventional force in order to bring about desired political changes.

The Nature of Terrorism

Contemporary international terrorism is characterized by a number of key attributes. They are: (1) the priority of politics, (2) the targeting of civilians, (3) the focus on psychological effects rather than physical destruction, and (4) the prominent role of nongovernmental actors.

Terrorism is a political activity, undertaken not to inflict violence and destruction per se but to communicate a political message. International terrorism, to paraphrase von Clausewitz, is the continuation of politics by other means. Like war, it is a form of violence used for political ends. But unlike war, the goal of violence is not to compel an enemy, but to weaken community solidarity and delegitimatize governmental institutions. Some of the major political goals of contem-

Terrorism
The use of indiscriminate violence for political ends. To foster fear within society, terrorists target civilians.

A massive bomb explodes in Bogotá, Colombia, in front of police headquarters. The terrorist attack, which left thirty-five persons dead, was presumed to be connected to drug trafficking.

State-sponsored terrorism
Terrorism supported or directed by a government, generally in a foreign country.

porary terrorist organizations have included: statehood for nationalist groups (e.g., the Kurds in Iran and the Basques in Spain), political liberation from existing governmental control (e.g., the Irish Republican Army's quest to free Northern Ireland from British control), and domestic political subversion (e.g., the Tupamaros' quest to subvert the Uruguayan military government in the 1970s).

In addition, governments may pursue **state-sponsored terrorism** by resorting to clandestine warfare against another regime, either directly or, more commonly, through surrogates. States that have supported "surrogate terrorism" against Western states include Iran, Libya, and Syria. For example, U.S. investigators found evidence linking Libya to the 1988 bombing of PanAm flight #103, which blew up over Scotland killing more than 250 persons. In 1991 the U.S. government indicted two Libyan officials and when Libya refused the U.S. extradition request, it imposed economic sanctions. The sanctions were still in effect in 1998. The most significant state-sponsored terrorism in the mid-1990s has been against Israel from two Islamic fundamentalist groups—*Hamas,* located in Gaza and the West Bank, and *Hezbollah* in southern Lebanon. Hamas has been responsible for training and carrying out deadly suicide bombings in Israel, while Hezbollah has carried out rocket attacks against northern Israeli settlements.

Terrorism is also characterized by the use of violence against innocent people. Every human being is a potential target—children, diplomats, businesspeople. Because terrorism makes all human beings potential victims, it is an immoral form of violence, without domestic or international legitimacy. Whereas conventional wars involve destruction aimed at soldiers and military and political installations,[14] the terrorist makes no distinction between combatants and noncombatants. Indeed, terrorists' primary targets are not military and political officials, but innocent civilians. In order to carry out their unconventional violence, terrorists rely on a limited set of tactics that include bombings, assassination, armed assaults, kidnappings, barricade and hostage situations, and hijackings.

A third characteristic of terrorism is its desire to breed widespread fear in society. Its aims are psychological rather than physical. Brian Jenkins has noted that terrorism produces "a lot of people watching, a lot of people listening, not a lot of people dead."[15] Michael Walzer has similarly written that, "If one wishes fear to spread and intensify over time, it is not desirable to kill specific people identified in some particular way with a regime, a party or a policy. Death must come by chance. . . ."[16] Because publicity is important in spreading fear within the population, terrorists carry out acts of violence that will receive prominent media coverage. One student of terrorism has noted that "you don't do terrorism to kill people. You do it to create an echo that makes you larger than life. No echo, no success."[17]

Finally, international terrorism is violence perpetrated primarily by nongovernmental agents. To be sure, governments provide support to terrorist organizations, and may occasionally resort to direct acts of terror. But if a government wishes to inflict violence on another society, it will generally do so through surrogates.

The Impact of Terrorism

The growing threat of terrorism to global society derives from several factors. First, the expansion of modern telecommunications networks provides rapid global exposure of major acts of violence. As a result, the psychological effects of modern terrorism have been greatly expanded, with the impact of terror rarely limited to the countries in which attacks are perpetrated. For example, the 1992 bombing of the Israeli embassy in Buenos Aires, the 1993 bombing of the Uffizi Gallery in Florence, the 1995 nerve gas attack on a Tokyo subway system, and the 1997 summer suicide bombing of an outdoor market in Jerusalem all received instantaneous global media coverage. Second, the availability of smaller, more lethal weapons has increased society's vulnerability to terrorist acts. The mid-air destruction of a PanAm jumbo jet over Scotland in December 1988 was achieved through the use of a small amount of plastic explosives. Third, modern societies are much more susceptible to terrorism because of their inherent complexity and fragility. Because modern societies rely on efficient communication and transportation, threats to these networks of interdependence can influence societies profoundly. Finally, terrorist networks have become more complex and sophisticated, relying increasingly for financial and material support on governments, businesses, and other multinational organizations. Because of the growing transnational character of terrorist organizations, detection of terrorists has become more difficult. Ironically, as governments have expanded domestic security efforts, they have unwittingly encouraged the internationalization of terror. One scholar has observed that terrorism is inherently international in character because, as states seek to protect themselves from such violence through improved counterterrorist measures, the incentives for terrorists to cross national frontiers tend, paradoxically, to increase.[18]

Since the 1970s, terrorism has become an increasingly prevalent problem in international relations. Before the 1970s, terrorism was chiefly a domestic political problem, carried out by dissatisfied nationals against existing regimes. But during the 1970s and 1980s terrorism became more transnational, with the planning, support, and execution of terror rarely being limited to the boundaries of a single country. Even though some terrorist attacks, such as the bombing of the U.S. federal building in Oklahoma City in 1995, originate and end within a country, the bulk of contemporary terrorism involves cross-border activities.

Beginning in the late 1960s, the frequency and impact of international terrorism increased significantly. According to the U.S. Department of State's Office of Counter-Terrorism, international terrorist incidents increased more than five times between 1968 and 1996—from 125 international incidents to 665. In 1985 alone terrorist attacks resulted in 2,223 casualties, including 900 deaths.[19] As noted in figure 10.1, during the late 1970s and 1980s, the number of international incidents averaged more than 500 incidents per year. Since the end of the Cold War, the frequency of terrorist incidents has declined precipitously, falling to 296 incidents in 1996, the lowest level in twenty-five years.

Despite the decline in the frequency of terrorist attacks, international terrorism continues to pose a major threat to the domestic tranquillity of many states, as political groups resort to such violence to dramatize demands for political self-rule, and to the order of the international system, as groups seek to dramatize opposition to the foreign policies of states. For example, in 1996 terrorist demands for increased political autonomy precipitated the suicide bombings in Tel Aviv and Jerusalem by extremist groups opposed to the Middle East peace process, killing more than sixty persons and forcing early elections and a change of government in Israel. Similarly, Peruvian Marxist guerrillas seized the Japanese ambassador's residence in Lima along with hundreds of senior political and diplomatic officials in order to dramatize their opposition to existing government policies and to demand the release of incarcerated rebels. After several months of failed discussions and negotiations, the terrorist crisis ended when government forces stormed the diplomatic compound, successfully freeing all hostages. Finally, the use of terrorism to challenge policies of foreign states was dramatically illustrated by the 1996 truck bombing of an apartment complex used by U.S. military personnel in Dhahran, Saudi Arabia. This tragic attack killed 19 U.S. airmen and wounded 240 others.

Although the frequency of terrorist acts has declined in the 1990s, the potential threat of terrorist bombings continues to escalate. With the exception of the 1995 Tokyo subway nerve gas attack that resulted in more than 5,500 casualties, including 12 deaths, international terrorists have relied almost exclusively on conventional bombs. But if terrorist groups should acquire nuclear devices or begin constructing chemical or biological weapons, the psychological impact of terrorism could dramatically escalate, giving terrorist groups even greater influence.

MILITARY INTERVENTION

Short-term military intervention is a major way to use force while avoiding a full-scale war. For our purposes, we define military intervention as the sending of military forces to a foreign land, without the consent of the host state, in order to in-

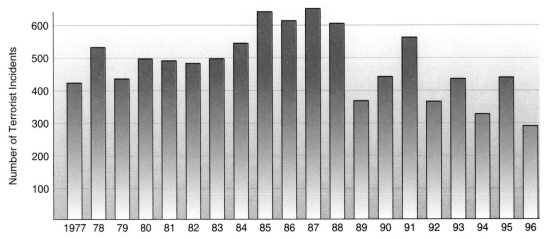

FIGURE 10.1

Frequency of International Terrorist Incidents, 1977–1996
Source: U.S. Department of State, "Patterns of Global Terrorism, 1996."

TABLE 10.3   Types of Foreign Intervention

OPEN:

Direct Military Intervention: introduction of armed forces in a foreign country without host state consent in order to influence its behavior (e.g., Israeli invasion of Lebanon in 1982, the U.S. intervention in the Dominican Republic in 1965 and Grenada in 1983).

Military Support: introduction of armed forces in a foreign country, in response to a request by host state, in order to protect a regime threatened by foreign intervention or internal insurgency (e.g., U.S. support of South Korea from 1950 to the present and British support of Belize after it became independent in 1981).

Raids: a limited incursion designed to punish or rescue (e.g., the 1976 Israeli rescue operation at Entebbe Airport, Uganda; the abortive U.S. rescue operation of fifty-three hostages in Tehran in 1980).

Open Propaganda: radio and television programs designed to influence foreign public opinions (e.g., Radio Free Europe beamed to Soviet-bloc states during the Cold War, and Radio/Television Martí beamed to Cuba).

CLANDESTINE:

Subversion: clandestine activities designed to threaten a government and its political institutions (e.g., U.S. toppling of the Arbenz regime in Guatemala in 1954; secret Cuban intervention in Venezuela and the Dominican Republic in 1960–1961).

Special Operations: secret activities designed to kill or destroy specific targets (e.g., the 1985 French sinking of a Greenpeace environmental ship in New Zealand; Israeli destruction of a nuclear reactor in Baghdad in 1981, and its destruction of PLO headquarters in Tripoli in 1985).

Secret Propaganda: dissemination of unattributable information to influence public perceptions and thereby alter the environment in which governments act (e.g., Soviet Union efforts to influence Western European public opinion on NATO's deployment of nuclear missiles in 1981–1983).

Political Action: secret assistance given to individuals and groups to influence foreign political dynamics (e.g., U.S. efforts to influence Italian elections in the aftermath of World War II; U.S. efforts to keep Salvador Allende from winning Chile's presidency in 1970).

fluence its internal affairs. As suggested by table 10.3, states can intervene in the affairs of other states in a variety of ways. These include either direct or indirect actions, overt or covert methods, and either military or nonmilitary actions. Because the primary concern of this chapter is the use of force, we will focus on direct military intervention.

Intervention and International Law

Military intervention is the most important type of intervention because it involves an extreme challenge to the sovereignty and territorial integrity of states. Raids, bombing attacks, and clandestine operations are of course important violations of state sovereignty. But direct military intervention is a much more serious action because it introduces, in a deliberate and overt manner, military forces in a foreign land.

Intervention is inconsistent with international law and, more specifically, contrary to the Charter of the United Nations. Article 2 (4) of the Charter states: "All members shall refrain in their international relations from the threat or use of force against the territorial integrity or political independence of any other state, or in any other manner inconsistent with the Purposes of the United Nations." An even more explicit defense of the **principle of nonintervention** is set forth in the Charter of the Organization of American States (OAS), article 18, which states:

Principle of nonintervention
This core principle of international law prohibits the direct or indirect interference in the domestic affairs of foreign states.

No State or group of States has the right to intervene, directly or indirectly, for any reason whatever, in the internal or external affairs of any other State. The foregoing principle prohibits not only armed force but also other forms of interference or attempted threat against the personality of the State or against its political, economic and cultural elements.

Because the principles of sovereignty and nonintervention seek to protect the status quo, international law is fundamentally a conservative system, justifying the world's existing cartography. The existing boundaries of states have not been fashioned by legal norms or principles of justice; rather, they are largely the result of power politics, with the prize of national independence going to people with the power and resolve to achieve it. According to one scholar, the norms of sovereignty and nonintervention have become the fundamental doctrines of the international system for largely utilitarian reasons: the world needs order and the status quo provides the simplest and most convenient method of protecting the existing interstate system. If the status quo is discarded, all borders become suspect.[20]

The nonintervention norm is so important in the modern international system that the United Nations is prohibited by its Charter from intervening in the domestic affairs of member-states. The Charter (art. 2.7) states: "nothing contained in the present Charter shall authorize the United Nations to intervene in matters which are essentially within the domestic jurisdiction of any states. . . ." The UN can, of course, authorize military actions (under Chapter VII of the Charter) in exceptional circumstances, when it considers international developments harmful to the world's peace and security. In general, however, international law prohibits individual or multilateral intervention.

As noted earlier (in chap. 4), Dorothy Jones argues that the international legal order provides an ethical framework that is conducive to international peace. In her view, the international community's shared political doctrines and legal principles, as expressed in existing international treaties, conventions, and declarations, provide a legal framework, or "*code of peace,*" that is binding on states. The code, which comprises nine rules, including the norms of sovereignty and nonintervention, is significant because it establishes principles that foster international order.[21]

It is important to stress that nonintervention is not the most important norm governing the international community. An even more basic principle is the right of political independence and the corollary right of self-defense, affirmed by Article 51 of the UN Charter. This right allows a state to take legitimate military actions, including the possibility of preemptive intervention, to defend its national sovereignty and territorial integrity. For example, the Israeli preemptive military attack on Egypt and Syria in the 1967 Arab-Israeli War was justified on the grounds of self-defense, because Israel had gained evidence that Arab countries were about to carry out an attack against it.[22] Similarly, in June 1981 Israel carried out a bombing raid against Iraq's nearly completed nuclear reactor in the outskirts of Baghdad on the grounds that Iraq was seeking to develop nuclear weapons. Although the aerial bombardment by jet fighters violated international legal norms, Israel justified the action on the grounds of self-defense.

Improving the political and governmental institutions of another country is not considered a legitimate basis for intervening in another country. According to John Stuart Mill, states need to be treated as self-determining communities so that they can develop the institutions and practices that best fit their history and culture.[23] "There are things that we cannot do for [other countries]," writes Michael Walzer, "even for their own ostensible good.[24] Tyranny may be harmful and democracy beneficial, but states must determine their own political practices and institutions. They must be allowed to struggle, for only during an authentic struggle can people develop the virtues and practices required to maintain a free society. Of course, political self-determination may not result in a constitutional regime that protects human rights, but this risk must be taken.

Intervention and Global Politics

Despite the legal prohibition against foreign intervention, states have periodically intervened in the affairs of other states. Indeed, intervention has been so common in modern times, according to one scholar, that the history of global politics is "in no small part the history of intervention."[25] During the nineteenth century, for example, major European powers intervened in Asia and Africa to establish colonies that could serve, among other things, as sources of raw materials and cheap labor and a market for goods. During the Cold War, the superpowers intervened to protect and promote vital interests or to advance ideological purposes.

We have suggested that intervention is legally permissible for purposes of self-defense, and it may be considered legal for other reasons as well. According to Walzer, for example, military intervention is morally legitimate when undertaken for three purposes: (1) to support a legitimate war of secession or national liberation; (2) to counter prior foreign intervention, and (3) to protect people from gross human rights violations, such as enslavement or massacre.[26] In a related manner, Lloyd Cutler has suggested that intervention is legitimate when foreign intervention has been preceded by another state's intervention and when the aim is to assist a prodemocratic movement in support of national self-determination.[27] Another commonly articulated exception to the nonintervention norm is the protection of nationals living in a foreign country. According to this principle, when a foreign government is unable to protect nationals, governments may carry out a short-term intervention, such as the rescue operation of fifty-three U.S. diplomatic hostages in Tehran in 1980. U.S. interventions in the Dominican Republic in 1965 and in Grenada in 1983 were justified, in part, to protect American lives.

Undoubtedly, the primary moral principle justifying foreign military intervention is the gross violation of human rights. In the mid-seventeenth century, Swiss jurist Emmerich de Vattel argued in his *Law of Nations* that states could intervene to protect an oppressed people. According to Vattel,

> To give help to a brave people who are defending their liberties against an oppressor by force of arms is only the part of justice and generosity. Hence, whenever such dissension reaches the state of civil war, foreign Nations may assist that one of the two parties which seems to have justice on its side. But to assist a detestable tyrant, or to come out in favor of an unjust and rebellious people, would certainly be a violation of duty.[28]

When a government threatens the basic rights of a large portion of its people through blatant massacre or enslavement or forced relocation, it violates fundamental standards of human dignity, thereby qualifying its moral standing in the community of states. Thus, when Cambodia's Khmer Rouge government carried out a massive genocide campaign against its people in the late 1970s, killing from one to two million persons, the regime forfeited its moral standing in the international community.

But columnist Charles Krauthammer has argued that humanitarian purposes are not a sufficient condition for intervention. In his view, immorality may be a necessary condition for foreign military action, but it is not a sufficient condition. "To intervene solely for reasons of democratic morality," writes Krauthammer, "is to confuse foreign policy with philanthropy."[29] In his view, a second condition must be met before force can be used: intervention must be strategically necessary—that is, it must be essential to the long-term interests of the intervening state. The strategic requirement for intervention is significant because states do not

Military intervention is a periodic occurrence in international relations. Here United States troops arrive in Port-au-Prince, Haiti, in order to restore democracy to that land. The 1994 intervention was carried out without opposition.

have unlimited resources for intervening whenever public order breaks down in foreign states or when major human rights abuses occur. When India intervened in 1971 in East Pakistan (Bangladesh), it did so not only to halt the genocide being carried out by the Pakistani (Punjabi) army against the Bengalis, but to promote its strategic interests—namely, to stabilize East Pakistan, halt the migration of Bengali refugees into India, and challenge the growing power of neighboring Pakistan. And when Tanzania intervened in Uganda in 1979 to topple the regime of Idi Amin, it did so not only because of the atrocities being committed by the regime but also because, as a neighboring state, it had a strategic interest in the stability and well-being of Uganda.

In addition, the intervention must have a high probability of success. To ensure short-term success, the intervening state must have adequate intelligence and an overwhelming preponderance of power. Because a high likelihood of success is an important requirement of intervention, human rights violations are often ignored by foreign regimes, even when they have significant power. One principal reason for the reluctance by European powers and the United States to intervene in the former Yugoslavia to halt the bitter civil war between Croats, Bosnians, and Serbs in the early 1990s was the difficulty posed by such an intervention. The intense hostility among warring factions and the region's challenging topography would have cost intervening nations too many military resources and would not have assured a long-term solution to the domestic tensions giving rise to the war. In short, although starvation and human suffering in the former Yugoslavia clearly justified foreign intervention, the high cost of such an action made foreign intervention unwise and unlikely.

In the last half of this century, three major motives have inspired foreign intervention: *national security, strategic interests,* and *humanitarian impulses.* A common justification for intervention is the perception of a threat to national security from neighboring states. When states perceive that their territorial boundaries are threatened, they frequently resort to coercive action, including military intervention. For example, when India intervened in East Pakistan (Bangladesh) in 1971 after Pakistan embarked on a war against the Bengali people, it did so because it perceived the war and the mass human rights violations as a threat to its own security. And when Tanzania intervened in Uganda in 1978, it did so not because of Idi Amin's human rights violations but because Amin's dictatorship threatened regional order.

Secondly, states have intervened for strategic reasons—that is, to advance national interests of an intervening state. Such strategic goals may include the promotion of political interests, the pursuit of economic gains, the protection of allies, and the maintenance of a regional balance of power. Examples of strategic intervention include the Soviet Union's intervention in Afghanistan in 1979, Vietnam's intervention in Cambodia in 1979, and the United States' intervention in the Dominican Republic in 1965 and in Grenada in 1983. Both U.S. interventions were undertaken to prevent radical revolutionary leaders from taking power, thereby advancing American ideological interests. To illustrate further the nature and impact of strategic intervention, we examine the U.S. intervention in Grenada in case 10.1.

Humanitarian impulses have also inspired a third type of foreign intervention. According to Jack Donnelly, humanitarian intervention is foreign intervention that seeks "to remedy mass and flagrant violations of the basic human rights of foreign nationals by their government."[35] When the United States declared war against Spain and intervened against Cuba in 1898, for example, it did so in part to overthrow an oppressive dictatorial regime that was committing gross human rights violations. Moreover, as suggested earlier in chapter 7, when the United States intervened in Somalia in 1992, it did so chiefly to reestablish political order in order to resume humanitarian relief.

Since the end of the Cold War, an increasing number of countries have experienced civil strife and political fragmentation as ethnic and religious minorities and nationalistic groups have demanded greater self-rule. In a growing number of cases, the demand for political autonomy in African and Asian countries has resulted in the collapse of existing states, leading to bitter civil strife and the displacement of millions of refugees. Faced with increasing regional instability, genocide, and refugee displacement, the international community has been faced with growing demands for UN-sponsored collective intervention to help restore domestic order and prevent further killing. Despite the significant humanitarian needs created by the decline in state legitimacy, major powers have been reluctant to undertake individual or multilateral peace-making and nation-building operations.

Nuclear Weapons and World Politics

The Nature of Nuclear Arms

The atomic age was born on July 16, 1945, when the first successful nuclear explosion took place at the Trinity test site near Alamogordo, New Mexico. Since then, nuclear power has been an important element in world politics. In his prescient volume, *The Absolute Weapon,* published in 1946, Bernard Brodie observed that "everything about the bomb is overshadowed by the twin facts that it exists and that its destructive power is fantastically great."[36]

The application of nuclear physics to the construction of weapons has provided humankind with the means of destroying a large part of civilization. Nuclear *fission* (the splitting of atoms) has enabled scientists to create atomic bombs with the equivalent energy of thousands of tons of TNT (kilotons), whereas nuclear *fusion* (the joining of two hydrogen nuclei) has resulted in hydrogen bombs with the equivalent power of millions of tons of TNT (megatons). The atomic bomb that exploded at Hiroshima on August 6, 1945, had the power of about 12.5 kilotons of TNT; the hydrogen bomb, tested by the United States at Bikini Atoll in the Pacific on March 1954, had the power of 15 megatons—or more than one thousand times the Hiroshima bomb.

The application of nuclear technology to military force has resulted in two different types of nuclear weapons—strategic and tactical. **Strategic weapons,** carried by bombers and missiles, are the powerful bombs and warheads serving as instruments of ultimate protection for a state; **tactical weapons,** by contrast, refer to short-range nuclear arms designed for battlefield use. Because strategic weapons are the armaments of last resort, this chapter focuses on them.

Strategic weapons
Long-range nuclear arms, delivered by bombers, ICBMs, and SLBMs, that are designed to protect a state's territorial integrity and political independence.

Tactical weapons
Short-range nuclear weapons designed for battlefield use.

Case 10.1 U.S. Intervention in Grenada, 1983

On October 25, 1983, U.S. military forces invaded Grenada, a Caribbean micro-state with a population of about 110,000 persons. Although U.S. forces encountered heavy resistance at first, especially from heavily armed Cubans, they quickly consolidated control over the island's southern region, capturing the island's rebel leaders and securing all key military objectives within three days. Although the United States provided numerous justifications for its military action, the fundamental reason for the U.S. intervention was strategic, aiming to halt the potential impact of radical Marxist politics and regional instability in the Caribbean basin.

Grenada had achieved political independence from Britain in 1974, and after establishing a parliamentary government, headed by Eric Gairy, an eccentric, populist leader, the new regime became increasingly repressive. The political repression, however, resulted in increased resistance, spawning a number of opposition groups, including a radical movement known as the New Jewel Movement (NJM). The NJM, headed by Maurice Bishop, stressed nationalism, Marxist ideology, and close ties with Cuba. In March 1979, while Gairy was out of the country, Bishop led a bloodless coup and established his own regime, known as the People's Revolutionary Government. Because the new government established close ties with Cuba and other communist states, relations with the United States became strained, leading to the cutoff of all aid. When Bishop's government began building a 9,000-foot runway with Cuban assistance, the Reagan administration became alarmed, regarding such a development as a threat to the region's stability and as a challenge to the U.S. goal of fostering democratic capitalism in the region. Grenadan officials claimed, however, that the new runway was being developed solely to foster increased tourism.

In 1983 the NJM was faced with growing internal political tensions between moderate and hardline Marxists. As a result of these ideological conflicts, the country's hard-core deputy prime minister, Bernard Cord, placed Bishop, the prime minister, under house arrest—an action that destabilized an already weak regime and resulted in a breakdown of public authority. When Bishop and several other officials were executed, the new regime was faced with even more civil strife and public demonstrations. As a result of Grenada's growing political turmoil, the Organization of Eastern Caribbean States

(OECS) requested U.S. assistance in restoring domestic order.

U.S. government officials gave three reasons for the military action against Grenada.[30] First, U.S. officials claimed that the United States intervened in order to protect its citizens. According to President Reagan, the "overriding" reason for authorizing military force was to protect the lives of citizens seeking to depart the island. Second, U.S. officials justified the action as a form of collective defense, responding to a legitimate request for military assistance from the OECS. According to U.S. officials, this request was deemed consistent with international legal norms of collective defense as expressed in the UN Charter (art. 52), the OAS Charter (arts. 22 and 28), and the OECS Treaty (art. 8).[31] Third, U.S. officials claimed that U.S. action was in response to a request for help from Grenada's governor-general, Sir Paul Scoon.

Despite these justifications, the underlying rationale for U.S. intervention was to halt the spread of Marxism in the Caribbean basin. The aims of the intervention were strategic, not humanitarian. During his first two years in office, President Reagan had repeatedly called attention to the threat posed by Grenada's increasing radical politics and its Marxist alignment. He believed that Grenada's alliance with Cuba and other communist regimes threatened not only the Caribbean region but, by extension, the U.S. interests as well. As he noted in a speech in March 1983, "It isn't nutmeg that's at stake in the Caribbean and Central America, it's the United States' national security."[32] Thus, when U.S. forces found a large cache of weapons, sufficient to equip a 10,000-troop army, and discovered an extensive network of secret bilateral agreements with Soviet-aligned states,[33] U.S. officials felt vindicated in their judgment that Grenada's militarization and politicization had in fact represented a threat to the spread and consolidation of democracy.

Most states of the international community, however, did not share the U.S. perspective on Grenada.[34] When the UN General Assembly discussed this action, most diplomats roundly denounced the U.S. action. At the end of the General Assembly debate on the U.S. invasion of Grenada, UN members voted overwhelmingly for a resolution calling the U.S. action "a flagrant violation of international law."

Characteristics

Nuclear weapons have five important characteristics. First, they differ qualitatively from conventional arms because of their extraordinary destructive power. For example, a one-kiloton thermonuclear bomb exploded at an altitude of 650 feet would kill virtually every unshielded living organism on the twenty-five acres immediately below it. A 25-megaton weapon would unleash greater energy than all the bombs dropped in Europe during World War II. Because of their great power, nuclear weapons can no longer be thought of as instruments of military force. This is why Thomas C. Schelling observed that military strategy could no longer be viewed as the "science of military victory" but rather, of "coercion, intimidation, and deterrence."[37]

Second, nuclear weapons have more diverse destructive effects than conventional arms. Although conventional bombs destroy with blast, nuclear arms destroy with heat and radiation, accounting for 30 and 20 percent of the damage. Following a nuclear explosion, invisible gamma rays cause problems ranging from immediate illness to death, depending upon the degree of total exposure to a bomb's radioactive fallout.

Third, because nuclear arms are relatively small, they can be delivered by land- and sea-based missiles with speed and accuracy to faraway lands. For example, a U.S. or Russian land-based missile can deliver its nuclear warheads some 8,000 miles away in approximately thirty minutes. In effect, nuclear weapons can carry out mass destruction without having to mobilize conventional armies. But the difference between nuclear weapons and bayonets, as Schelling has noted, is not in the number of persons that can be killed but "the speed with which it can be done, in the centralization of decision, in the divorce of the war from political process, and in computerized programs that threaten to take war out of human control once it begins."[38]

Fourth, unlike conventional armies, strategic nuclear weapons involve few combatants. Unlike previous conventional wars, in which the number of soldiers was important in determining the outcome, nuclear arsenals require few, highly trained personnel. A U.S. ballistic missile submarine, for example, has a crew of about 125 persons, whereas an underground land-based missile center is manned with only a few officers. The limited number of persons directly involved in operating nuclear arsenals has thus resulted in an ironic condition: unlimited power with a limited number of combatants.

Last, strategic nuclear arms are unique because there is no effective defense against them. Because nuclear weapons can be delivered with ballistic missiles, their interception is extraordinarily difficult.[39] Moreover, because a single nuclear warhead can destroy a major metropolitan area, an effective strategic defense must be virtually leak-proof. Whereas conventional defense is considered effective if it destroys only part of an attacking force, nuclear defense must be virtually 100 percent effective, because the penetration of a single missile could result in catastrophic destruction. Thus, because there is no effective defense against strategic attack, the stability of nuclear deterrence has derived, paradoxically, from mutual vulnerability.

The Triad

During the Cold War, the superpowers developed three major launching systems for delivering strategic nuclear weapons. These systems—which came to be known as the **triad**—comprised bombers, intercontinental ballistic missiles (*ICBMs*), and submarine-launched ballistic missiles (*SLBMs*). In the early phase of the Cold War bombers were the sole means of delivering nuclear arms. But in the 1960s ballistic missiles were developed capable of carrying nuclear warheads. The development

Triad
The three elements of the superpowers' strategic nuclear arsenal: intercontinental ballistic missiles (ICBMs), submarine-launched ballistic missiles (SLBMs), and bombers.

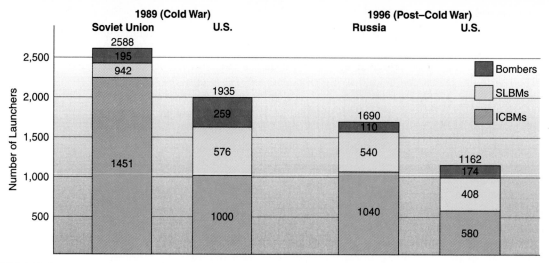

1989 (Cold War)

Soviet Union   U.S.

1996 (Post–Cold War)

Russia   U.S.

Legend: Bombers, SLBMs, ICBMs

FIGURE 10.2

United States and Russian Nuclear Launchers, 1989 and 1996

Source: International Institute for Strategic Studies, *The Military Balance,* 1996/97 (Oxford: Oxford University Press, 1996), Passim.

of ICBMs transformed military strategy because a superpower could now threaten massive destruction 5–8,000 miles away without going into combat. Subsequently submarine-launched missiles were also developed. Although SLBMs have been less powerful and less accurate than ICBMs, they have served as the most important instruments of deterrence. Whereas bombers can be shot down and ICBM silos can be destroyed by an accurate missile attack, submarines cannot be tracked and are therefore virtually invulnerable.

Before the end of the Cold War, the two superpowers had about 4,500 strategic launchers capable of carrying more than 25,000 nuclear warheads.[40] With the collapse of the Soviet Union and the defeat of communism, the nuclear arsenals of the United States and the former Soviet Union have decreased significantly. As of December 1996, the United States and Russia (which gained control of all nuclear weapons previously stationed in Belarus, Kazakhstan, and Ukraine) were estimated to jointly have less than 3,000 launchers and 15,000 warheads. (See fig. 10.2.) The START I Treaty (Strategic Arms Reductions Talks), which became effective in 1994, required that the United States and Russia reduce their stockpiles of nuclear warheads to a maximum of 6,500. The START II Treaty, which the Russian parliament (Duma) had not ratified by late 1997, will further reduce nuclear stockpiles to around 3,500 warheads for each country. In addition to the quantitative reductions in nuclear arms, the end of the superpower conflict has increased international cooperation, thereby reducing the salience of nuclear weapons. Both the United States and Russia now maintain strategic forces on a low level of alert and have shifted targeting away from major urban centers.

Strategic Defense

On March 23, 1983, President Reagan delivered his famous "star wars" speech in which he called on the U.S. scientific community to investigate the possibility of developing a defensive system against ballistic nuclear missiles. The president suggested that because it was preferable to "save lives than to avenge them," the United States should examine the feasibility of making missiles "impotent and obsolete." The aim of the **Strategic Defense Initiative (SDI)** was thus to explore the feasibility of creating a comprehensive space-based shield that would provide protection from nuclear attack. In effect, the aim was to shift national security from strategic offense to strategic defense, from a policy based on Mutual Assured Destruction (MAD) to a policy based on mutual assured security (MAS).

Strategic Defense Initiative (SDI)
A plan, initiated by President Ronald Reagan, to develop a ballistic missile defense system using space-based lasers.

As envisioned by some scientists, the idea of SDI involved a multi-layered defensive strategy. Because the trajectory of a typical ballistic missile involves four phases, strategic defense would attempt to destroy enemy missiles in each phase. If it were possible to destroy 50 percent of all enemy missiles and warheads in each phase, then only six or seven warheads out of a hundred launched would reach their targets. Even though a success rate of 93 or 94 percent would still allow for mass destruction, advocates of SDI believed that such a capability would be an effective deterrent to aggression and, most significantly, would provide some defense to citizens in the event of a deliberate or an accidental attack.

From 1984 until 1990 the U.S. government devoted more than $20 billion to SDI research. When the program was launched some defense analysts estimated that a modest strategic defense system would cost as much as $150 billion and that a comprehensive system might cost more than one trillion dollars.[41] But the most damaging criticism of SDI came from the scientific community, which argued that a comprehensive shield was technologically unfeasible in the near future. In an important article, four influential officials argued that "there was no prospect whatever that science and technology can, at any time in the next several decades, make nuclear weapons 'impotent and obsolete.'"[42]

Because the threat of strategic nuclear conflict has all but vanished in the post–Cold War era, the United States has halted its space-based defense program. At the same time, the dissolution of the former Soviet Union has increased the potential for new nuclear actors, while "rogue" states, such as Iran, Iraq, Syria, and North Korea, pose increasing regional threats as they acquire more sophisticated weapons, especially short- and medium-range ballistic missiles. In order to cope with the potential threat of limited missile attacks, both Russia and the United States continue to explore the feasibility of developing and deploying an antimissile defensive system, or **theater terminal defense.** Unlike the comprehensive space-based strategic defense, the aim of theater ballistic missile defense (BMD) is to provide limited protection from isolated missile attacks.

Although no effective defense exists against nuclear attack, both Russia and the United States continue to explore the feasibility of a limited BMD. In the mid-1990s the Clinton administration increased funding for a "thin" BMD system, and in view of the current initiatives, the United States is likely to begin deploying a limited terminal defense system early in the next century.

Theater terminal defense
An antimissile defense system that seeks to protect specific areas, especially political and military targets.

Nuclear Weapons and Force

Nuclear arms provide states with military power but not usable force. One of the first strategic thinkers to question the military usefulness of nuclear weapons was Bernard Brodie, who, in 1946, observed that the major aim of atomic bombs was to avert war.[43] Nearly forty years later former Secretary of Defense Robert McNamara reiterated this same truth in a widely read article in *Foreign Affairs*. McNamara wrote: "Nuclear weapons serve no military purpose whatsoever. They are totally useless—except only to deter one's opponent from using them."[44] McNamara did not suggest that nuclear weapons had no political usefulness, but only that they did not provide usable military power.

Historically, military force has provided the ultimate instrument for protecting and projecting state interests in the global community. The nuclear invention, however, has radically altered the relationship between force and statecraft, bringing about what Robert Jervis calls the "nuclear revolution"—a condition in which nuclear powers are mutually vulnerable to each other and in which military victory is impossible. Jervis writes:

> Throughout recorded history, all-out war has been a useful tool of statecraft; the ability of states to resort to the highest level of violence has been a major engine of

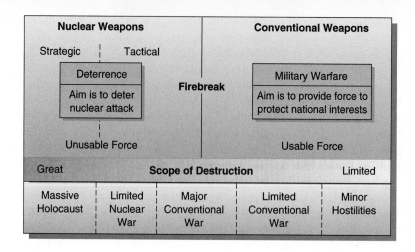

FIGURE 10.3
Comparison of Nuclear and Conventional Military Power
Source: From Mark R. Amstutz "Deterrence: An Assessment of the Bishops' Nuclear Morality" in *Evangelicals and the Bishops' Pastoral Letter,* edited by Dean C. Curry, 1984. Reprinted by permission of Christian College Coalition, Washington, D.C.

international change. Because military victory is impossible, the many patterns that rested on the utility of superior force have also been altered. Even great military success cannot limit the damage that the other superpower can inflict. As a result, force and the threat of it cannot support foreign policy in the same way that it did in the past.[45]

As figure 10.3 illustrates, conventional arms and nuclear weapons have different roles. The line dividing the two types of armaments—known as the nuclear **firebreak**[46]—represents the boundary between usable force and deterrent power. During the 1950s and 1960s, the firebreak between nuclear and conventional arsenals seemed secure and clearly defined. A major reason for this was that few weapons systems threatened the physical and psychological gap between these two weapons categories. Nuclear arms were large and much more destructive than conventional weapons. But in the 1970s and 1980s, the strategies and military capabilities of both superpowers began to blur the distinction between these two types of force, thereby weakening the perceived firebreak. Both the United States and the Soviet Union developed smaller and more accurate nuclear warheads and larger and more destructive conventional weapons. Moreover, both superpowers adopted more discriminating and flexible nuclear strategies that appeared to increase the possibility of limited nuclear war.

The fundamental function of nuclear weapons has been deterrence—prevention by threat.[47] Nuclear states accepted deterrence as the primary aim of strategic nuclear forces for two reasons—first, because there was no known effective defense against nuclear attack, and second, because winning a nuclear war was impossible. A nuclear power may win a military conflict, but it cannot win a nuclear war. Henry Kissinger described the novel problem created by nuclear arms as follows:

> In the past the military establishment was asked to prepare for war. Its test was combat; its vindication, victory. In the nuclear age, however, victory has lost its traditional significance. The outbreak of war is increasingly considered the worst catastrophe. Henceforth, the adequacy of the military establishment will be tested by its ability to preserve peace.[48]

Nuclear weapons thus produce an anomalous situation in which societies remain wholly vulnerable to attack but in which aggression is unlikely because of the great mutual destructive potential of the weapons.

Fundamentally, deterrence is a state of mind. Deterrence requires, of course, military capabilities to carry out unacceptable punishment and the political will to do so. But what is important is not the capability or strategy, but the adversary's

Firebreak
The psychological barrier between conventional and nuclear weapons.

perception of them. So long as capacity and determination are perceived as adequate, deterrence will remain credible and effective. If either element is perceived as inadequate, the credibility of deterrence will decline and eventually the bluff will be called. Because there is no effective way of protecting society from nuclear aggression, the credibility of deterrence ultimately rests on the ability to punish aggression. In the terminology of nuclear strategists, credible deterrence is achieved with the ability to carry out unacceptable damage through a **second strike** in response to a **first strike.** Indeed, the stability of deterrence rests on the certainty of being able to carry out a second strike *after absorbing a first strike.* According to nuclear theorists, the credibility of deterrence does not rest on the magnitude of the retaliation but on the *certainty* and *unacceptability* of the punishment. So long as punishment is assured and unacceptable, deterrence will remain credible.

Because nuclear victory is impossible, some have suggested that nuclear weapons are useless instruments of foreign policy. But as a *New York Times* editorial observed, "the stubborn reality is that nuclear weapons, though unusable, remain extremely useful."[49] Nuclear weapons, like other elements of national power, are instruments of national sovereignty. As such, they provide states with a means of protecting and promoting national interests. During the Cold War, for example, the United States deployed tactical and short-range nuclear arms in West Germany and South Korea, whereas NATO's principal Cold War military doctrine—*flexible response*—involved an explicit coupling of the U.S. strategic arsenal with European security. Moreover, the United States periodically used its nuclear forces, both discretely and sometimes explicitly, as instruments of coercive diplomacy in order to advance particularly foreign policy goals.[50]

The Impact of Nuclear Weapons

Scholars differ in their assessment of the impact of nuclear arms on world politics. A few IR scholars, for example, believe that nuclear weapons have been largely irrelevant to global order.[51] Others argue that the nuclear invention has been harmful to global society, wasting scarce economic resources and unnecessarily threatening civilization. For example, Jonathan Schell in *The Fate of the Earth,* an influential account of the nuclear dilemma, observes that the large nuclear stockpiles pose a major threat to the earth. In his words: "To say that we and all future generations are threatened with extinction by the nuclear peril . . . is to describe only half of our situation. The other half is that we are the authors of that extinction."[52] Many experts on nuclear strategy, however, argue that, notwithstanding the great dangers and high costs, nuclear weapons have been beneficial to global order, especially in influencing superpower relations during the Cold War.

Consequences
Nuclear weapons have had a number of important political effects on the international community. First, they have helped to keep world peace.[53] Throughout the history of the Western world, international conflict has regularly taken place. But since World War II, no major war has taken place. Paul Schroeder argues that since the second century under the Pax Romana, the world has known no long period of general peace. The modern record, according to him, was thirty-eight years, nine months, and five days, from the end of Napoleon's defeat at Waterloo to the beginning of the Crimean War. That record was broken, he notes, on May 15, 1984.[54] Of course, it is impossible to confirm that nuclear weapons are responsible for the stability and order among major states in the postwar period, because the efficacy of nuclear deterrence can only be proved by its failure. But Thomas Schelling captures a widely shared sentiment when he observes:

Second strike
The ability to carry out nuclear retaliation after sustaining nuclear aggression.

First strike
The ability to destroy the bulk of a nation's strategic nuclear weapons in a surprise attack.

Those 40 years of living with nuclear weapons without warfare are not only evidence that war can be avoided but are themselves part of the reason why it can be; namely, increasing experience in living with the weapons without precipitating a war, increasing confidence on both sides that neither wishes to risk nuclear war, diminishing necessity to react to every untoward event as though it were a mortal challenge.[55]

The conviction that nuclear arms have fostered peace has more recently been espoused by John Mearsheimer. In an influential 1990 article, he argued that the end of the Cold War was likely to be destabilizing, bringing about a shift in the "geometry of power" from bipolarity to multipolarity. He suggested that the coming decline in superpower strategic capabilities would lead to a dispersion of military power within Europe. Such a development, he suggested, would be harmful to European security because it would foster instability within the region.[56]

Second, scholars argue that nuclear arms have helped to preserve the status quo. A reason for this is rooted in the difference between deterrence and compellence. Deterrence is easier to achieve because all that is required is to refrain from forbidden behaviors. Compellence, by contrast, involves getting an adversary to change his behavior—either by stopping undesired actions or beginning desired ones. According to Mearsheimer, in international conflicts defenders have an advantage over aggressors because defenders usually value their freedom more than aggressors value new conquests.[60] Moreover, as instruments of deterrence, nuclear weapons help to stabilize world politics by making any forcible changes in the status quo extraordinarily costly to any would-be aggressor. Nuclear weapons may not provide military power to compel, but they are especially effective in maintaining existing international conditions.

Finally, nuclear weapons have encouraged egalitarian political relationships. Although nuclear states may possess different types and levels of nuclear weapons, these inequalities are not important. Once a state has achieved the military capability of assured retaliatory punishment, changes in strategic force structure are unlikely to influence political events. Moreover, because unacceptable punishment can be achieved with few nuclear weapons, strategic nuclear power is insensitive to modest shifts in strategic capabilities. As McGeorge Bundy once noted, what matters is the level of nuclear danger, not the exact state of the nuclear balance.[61]

The Future Role of Nuclear Weapons

In the aftermath of the Cold War, a growing concensus has developed among Western officials and scholars on the declining usefulness of nuclear weapons and the need for significant reductions in nuclear arsenals. Because of the end of the ideological superpower conflict, there is now no major threat involving strategic nuclear weapons. As a result, a number of groups and leading officials have called for radical cuts in nuclear stockpiles. One group of leading U.S. officials (known as the Goodpaster Committee), for example, has suggested that, because of the declining political and military utility of nuclear arms, the United States should drastically reduce its nuclear stockpile, even beyond the cuts required by existing U.S.-Russian agreements (START I and II). According to this group, "a world in which no state or group possessed nuclear weapons would be a safer place for the United States."[62] Another group (involving fifty-eight high-ranking military officials from seventeen countries, including thirty-five from Russia and the United States) has not only suggested radical cuts but has also called for the eventual abolition of nuclear weapons. In their 1996 declaration, these military officials state: "long-term international nuclear policy must be based on the declared principle of continuous, complete, and irrevocable elimination of nuclear weapons."[63]

CASE STUDY

Case 10.2 The Role of Nuclear Arms in the Cuban Missile Crisis

The Cuban missile crisis, precipitated by the Soviet Union's clandestine introduction of intermediate nuclear weapons into Cuba, was undoubtedly the most dangerous conflict of the forty-year Cold War. As noted in the previous chapter, during the thirteen-day dispute the United States placed its nuclear forces on high alert and implicitly threatened their use. Although nuclear weapons greatly increased the danger of the conflict, were such weapons harmful or beneficial to the resolution of the dispute? What role, if any, did nuclear weapons have on the crisis, and did the perceived balance of strategic weapons influence the resolution of the conflict?

One school of thought claims that the balance of strategic weapons played a crucial role in assuring American victory. Even though the United States held a superior tactical position, a higher level of resolve and superior conventional military capabilities, its victory was chiefly the result of the favorable strategic balance, according to this perspective. Khrushchev capitulated because his nuclear forces were inferior to those of the United States.

A second theory is that nuclear weapons had no effect whatsoever on the outcome of the crisis. Because both superpowers had nuclear weapons in 1962, their mutual possession meant that their only role was to deter their use by the other. General Maxwell Taylor, for example, has noted that "the strategic forces of the United States and the USSR simply canceled each other out as effectual instruments for influencing the outcome of the confrontation."[57] More recently, McGeorge Bundy has written that he has found "the attribution of [American]

success mainly to strategic superiority increasingly unpersuasive as time has passed."[58] In his view, conventional superiority on the scene was the major military determinant of the conflict's outcome.

The third thesis—a middle position between the two extremes—is that nuclear weapons played a modest role in influencing the crisis. This camp attributes two effects to nuclear arms. First, the strategic balance helped to moderate the behavior of the superpowers during the crisis due to the realization that strategic nuclear forces did not provide usable force. Both Khrushchev and Kennedy recognized that a major nuclear conflict was unwinnable. Second, because of its nuclear superiority and greater strategic readiness, the United States was better able to manipulate the risks of nuclear conflict. But as Marc Trachtenberg has noted, the slightly favorable strategic balance tended to moderate and inhibit American military action, rather than promote it. "Fear of escalation," he has written, "went a long way toward neutralizing whatever advantages might have accrued to the United States." Trachtenberg noted, however, that the strategic inferiority of the Soviet Union did affect Khrushchev's response. Indeed, he suggests that the Soviet leadership took American strategic capabilities and strategy far more seriously than did the Americans themselves.[59]

Did the threat of nuclear conflict have a moderating effect on the coercive diplomacy of the two superpowers? What effect did the perceived balance of nuclear power have on terminating the crisis? What do you think?

Although nuclear arms play a less important role in contemporary international relations than they did during the Cold War, nuclear weapons continue to have a decisive role in international security, serving as the ultimate instrument of national security for states that possess such armaments. For example, the Clinton administration issued a new set of nuclear strategy guidelines in 1997, updating the rules that were established by the Reagan administration in 1981. Although the new guidelines incorporate numerous changes, nuclear arms continue to serve as the cornerstone of the U.S. defense strategy.[64]

Some IR observers believe that the major contemporary military threat to the United States and other major powers lies in nuclear proliferation and the potential for nuclear terrorism. As a result of the weakening controls over nuclear technology and fuels following the collapse of the Soviet Union, some scholars believe that nuclear "leakage" is now, and will be in the foreseeable future, the principal military threat to the vital interests of Western countries. As a result, some scholars have suggested that the United States should increase its strategic and economic assistance to Russia and foster greater military collaboration in reducing the potential for nuclear leakage.[65] Despite the growing potential threat from small-scale nuclear devices, officials and scholars believe that the potential threat from proliferation and leakage should be contained with conventional force, not nuclear strategies.[66]

IN CONCLUSION

Whether in peace or war, states use military power to pursue national interests through implicit or explicit threats. When states are unable to reconcile conflicting interests, especially those considered vital, they may resort to limited force, such as clandestine destabilization of a foreign government, support of insurgent forces, small-scale military operations, or a limited military intervention. But if states are unable to resolve disputes over vital interests, governments may resort to full-scale war—a topic examined in the next chapter.

Nuclear weapons have had a profound impact on the postwar international system. Because of their incredible destructive power, nuclear arms are not instruments of warfare but tools of deterrence. Stability among the major powers in the postwar era has been aided by the nuclear invention, which has made nuclear conflict unthinkable. Because nuclear technology cannot be disinvented, statesmen are challenged to effectively regulate the nuclear regime. Specifically, nuclear states must vigorously pursue arms control and even more importantly, seek to halt nuclear proliferation among nonnuclear states.

SUMMARY

1. There are four major types of military power: prestige, deterrent, defensive, and compellent. Military power is important in international relations because it contributes to a state's ability to pursue foreign policy objectives.

2. Military power contributes to a state's foreign policy not only in wartime but also in peacetime. In wartime, force is used to compel an opponent; in peacetime, military capacity enhances a state's bargaining power through implicit threats.

3. Two major categories of international relations in between war and peace are conflict without force and low-intensity conflict (LIC). Two types of LICs are guerrilla wars and special military operations. Guerrilla wars differ from conventional wars in that they are chiefly political conflicts waged in rural areas using unconventional tactics and relying on a strategy of attrition.

4. During the 1970s and 1980s terrorism became more prevalent, posing an increasing threat to the order and psychological stability of the international system. Despite the fall in terrorist incidents, terrorism continues to be a major threat to global order.

5. Although international law prohibits states from intervening in the internal affairs of other states, governments periodically intervene in other countries using a variety of methods, including overt military force. Legally and ethically, military intervention can be justified only as a last resort and only when exceptional conditions exist.

6. Nuclear weapons are the most powerful armaments ever developed. Because of their incredible destructive potential, they have transformed the relationship of force to statecraft. Moreover, because nuclear weapons can be delivered with ballistic missiles, they can threaten massive destruction without going into combat.

7. Nuclear weapons are chiefly instruments of deterrence. They do not provide usable force to compel an enemy, but they do serve as the world's most effective instruments of deterrent power. Although scholars hold many different views on the role of such weapons, many officials believe that nuclear arms helped to preserve the status quo and promote global stability during the Cold War.

prestige power

deterrent power

defensive power

compellent power

low-intensity conflict (LIC)

guerrilla war

deterrence

coercive diplomacy

terrorism

state-sponsored terrorism

principle of
   nonintervention

strategic weapons

tactical weapons

triad

Strategic Defense Initiative
   (SDI)

theater terminal defense

firebreak

second strike

first strike

RECOMMENDED READINGS

Allison, Graham T., Albert Carnesale, and Joseph S. Nye, Jr., eds. *Hawks, Doves and Owls: An Agenda for Avoiding Nuclear War*. New York: W.W. Norton, 1985. Although the fear of nuclear war has greatly dissipated with the end of the Cold War, this set of essays provides an excellent overview of many of the major issues involved in superpower arms control.

Blechman, Barry M., and Stephen S. Kaplan. *Force Without War: U.S. Armed Forces as Political Instrument*. Washington, D.C.: Brookings Institution, 1978. A careful conceptual and empirical analysis of how the United States used its military forces for political purposes from 1946 to 1975. The authors identified some 215 times that American military force was used as a discrete political instrument, and found that of these, some three dozen involved diplomatic crisis. An important study.

Bull, Hedley, ed. *Intervention in World Politics*. Oxford: Clarendon Press, 1984. An illuminating study of different conceptual and practical issues of foreign intervention. Topics examined include: international legal dimensions of intervention, humanitarian intervention, intervention to secure natural resources, collective intervention, and intervention and national liberation movements.

Bundy, McGeorge. *Danger and Survival: Choices about the Bomb in the First Fifty Years*. New York: Random House, 1988. The definitive account of the role and evolution of U.S. nuclear weapons and their impact on global politics.

Craig, Gordon A., and Alexander L. George. *Force and Statecraft: Diplomatic Problems of Our Time*. 3rd ed. New York: Oxford University Press, 1995. Historical case studies are used to illuminate key issues of international politics from the seventeenth century to the present. In addition, major contemporary topics dealing with the interrelationship of force and diplomacy are examined, including the balance of power, economics and foreign policy, deterrence, negotiation, and coercive diplomacy.

Freedman, Lawrence. *The Evolution of Nuclear Strategy*. New York: St. Martin's Press, 1981. A comprehensive account of the impact of nuclear weapons on military strategy and of the evolution of American strategic thought. Freedman provides a penetrating assessment of the different strategic doctrines developed to maintain a credible deterrence policy.

George, Alexander L. *Forceful Persuasion: Coercive Diplomacy as an Alternative to War*. Washington, D.C.: U.S. Institute of Peace Press, 1991. A short, lucid study of the theory and practice of coercive diplomacy.

George, Alexander L., and Richard Smoke. *Deterrence in American Foreign Policy: Theory and Practice*. New York: Columbia University Press, 1974. A comprehensive investigation of the theory and practice of deterrence in postwar American foreign policy. The study includes eleven major case studies from the 1948 Berlin blockade until the 1962 Cuban missile crisis.

Jervis, Robert. *The Meaning of the Nuclear Revolution: Statecraft and the Prospect of Armageddon*. Ithaca: Cornell University Press, 1989. This study explores how the development of nuclear and thermonuclear armaments have transformed the meaning of war, the psychology of statesmanship, and the formulation of military policy. MAD, argues Jervis, is not a policy but the inescapable condition of shared nuclear capabilities.

Mandelbaum, Michael. *The Nuclear Question: The United States & Nuclear Weapons, 1946–1976*. Cambridge: Cambridge University Press, 1979. This exceptionally clear, nontechnical history of U.S. nuclear strategy explains how the United States learned to live with the bomb. The study gives special emphasis to strategic developments of the 1960s.

Mearsheimer, John J. *Conventional Deterrence*. Ithaca: Cornell University Press, 1983. This insightful study examines selected case studies of deterrence failures (World War II and the Arab-Israeli conflict) in order to develop a better understanding of the prospect for conventional deterrence in Central Europe and elsewhere.

Schelling, Thomas C. *Arms and Influence*. New Haven: Yale University Press, 1966. In this influential study Schelling argues that the great power of nuclear arms has radically altered the relationship of military power to diplomacy, and he seeks to show how.

RELEVANT WEB SITES

International Relations and Security Network (ISN)   www.isn.ethz.ch/
   See the following subjects:
   Extremism/Terrorism
   Military/Defense

U.S. Arms Control and Disarmament   www.acda.gov
   Agency (ACDA)

U.S. Department of State   www.state.gov/global terrorism
   Data on terrorism

CHAPTER

War and International Relations

Warfare is almost as old as civilization. From the earliest of times people have resorted to armed violence to constitute, protect, and increase the resources, territorial boundaries, and perceived needs and wants of such political communities as clans, tribes, empires, religious groups, city-states, feudal kingdoms, and nation-states. Since the establishment of nation-states in the mid-seventeenth century, the dominant form of warfare in global society has been war among sovereign states. Because of the absence of authoritative conflict-resolution institutions in the international community, states have periodically resorted to force when they have been unable to resolve conflicts through peaceful negotiation. War has thus served as an instrument of last resort for the settling of international conflicts.

Chapter 10 examined the role of force short of war; here we look at the nature and role of war in the international community. After contrasting intranational and international wars, the first part of this chapter describes the scope, evolution, and impact of modern war. The second section describes three types of wars (classical, total, and postmodern), and each is illustrated with a contemporary case study. The third section reviews some of the major theories of warfare, focusing on three types of explanations, focusing on the individual, the state, and the international system. The final section examines the relationship of ethics to war, emphasizing the role and impact of the just war doctrine.

THE NATURE, EVOLUTION, AND IMPACT OF WAR

War in the Contemporary World

In the contemporary international system, two major types of war have been prevalent: intranational wars and international wars. **Intranational wars** involve domestic armed conflict between two or more political groups, or between the state and a particular segment of society. Such wars are typically caused by political groups seeking to: (1) gain control of

Si vis pacem para bellum ("If you want peace, prepare for war.")

Vegetius, *ancient Roman general*

. . . the preservation of peace requires active effort, planning, the expenditure of resources, and sacrifice, just as was does.[1]

Donald Kagan, *distinguished historian*

Large-scale, conventional war—war as understood by today's principal military powers—may indeed be at its last gasp; however, war itself, war as such, is alive and kicking and about to enter a new epoch.[2]

Martin van Creveld, *Israeli scholar and strategist*

[T]he major sources of war in the future will derive less from the character of relations between states than what goes on within states.[3]

Kalevi J. Holsti, *IR scholar*

Perhaps war in the developed world is becoming not only rationally unthinkable, but also subrationally unthinkable. Major war, in other words, may be obsolescent.[4]

John Mueller, *IR scholar*

Intranational wars
An internal conflict between two or more domestic political groups, or between the state and a particular segment of society.

251

the government; (2) topple the existing government and thereby transform the regime; or (3) secede from an existing state by achieving military and political independence. Intranational wars are significant in contemporary global society because international order is dependent in part on the stability and political effectiveness of states, the principal actors in the international community. Because the pursuit of peace and justice in global society depends in part on the coherence and viability of its member-states, the prevalence of intranational wars can result in regional instability and impair the development of global order.

The sources of internal wars typically involve a growing demand for greater domestic political justice, for increased self-determination by ethnopolitical groups, or for greater participation in governmental decision making. As the distinguished military historian John Keegan has recently observed, war in contemporary society has not been solely a means of resolving interstate conflicts but also a "vehicle through which the embittered, the dispossessed, the naked of the earth, the hungry masses yearning to breathe free, express their anger, jealousies and pent-up urge to violence."[5] Because intranational wars are generally society-wide conflicts, they typically impact civilian populations far more than interstate conflicts. Moreover, because such wars are fought to resolve perceived injustices, such wars are passionate, all-consuming disputes, resulting in the weakening, if not the elimination, of the rules of institutionalized wars. Indeed, one of the major features of intranational wars is the loss of the fundamental distinction, developed in international wars, between combatants and noncombatants. Because intranational wars are fundamentally society-wide conflicts, it is the people, not the institutionalized military forces, that pay the major cost of fighting such wars.

International wars
Armed conflicts between two or more states.

International wars, by contrast, are armed conflicts between two or more states. Their chief characteristics include: (1) the participation of two or more states; (2) the deliberate, overt, and largely unlimited use of mass violence to settle conflict; and (3) the resort to force to compel an enemy state to alter its behavior. Unlike low-intensity conflict, which involves unconventional, covert, or indirect force, international wars involve the direct, and often unlimited, application of military power. Moreover, unlike the popular, society-wide nature of intranational wars, international wars are fought over states' interests, not people's wants. Although this chapter is primarily concerned with international wars, intranational wars are becoming increasingly more significant in global politics because they threaten the stability of existing regimes and thereby challenge the established international order.

Since the creation of the modern nation-state system in the mid-seventeenth century, international war had been viewed as a political activity in which states and other actors resort to violence in order to defend or achieve desired political objectives. The aim of warfare is not random killing and wanton destruction but rather the use of force to compel an enemy to alter his behavior. This rationalist perspective about international war has best been set forth by the nineteenth-century Prussian strategist Carl von Clausewitz, who argued in his classic study *On War* that war is not an aimless activity, but purposeful political action designed to achieve vital goals for a state. For Clausewitz, violence is the means; the end is the realization of vital national interests through the submission of the enemy. This is why he defined war as a "political instrument, a continuation of political activity by other means."[6] According to Clausewitz, a war is much like a wrestling match in which each player uses physical force to try to compel his opponent. War, therefore, is "a duel on an extensive scale"—a contest between competing states, each seeking its own interests at the expense of other states.[7] The application of collective violence will lead to a winner and a loser.

The Aims of War

Wars, which vary significantly in their intensity and destructiveness, can also be classified in terms of their purposes. To a significant degree, the character of war depends upon the ends and the means of warfare. *Limited wars* are those with defined political objectives involving proportionate and discriminating violence; *total wars* are military conflicts fought for the unconditional surrender or complete military defeat of the enemy and are carried out with unlimited use of violence.

Although the aims of warring parties vary widely, the goals of state and non-state actors can be classified along a continuum, with *unlimited ends* at one extreme and *limited ends* at the other. For example, the Falkland Islands War, discussed in case 11.1, illustrates a military conflict guided by limited objectives. After Argentine military forces established temporary control of the islands, the government of the United Kingdom announced that it would use military force to regain sovereign control of the lost territory. The aims of the British were thus limited and specific—to compel Argentinian military forces to withdraw from the islands. By contrast, such intranational wars as the Russian-Chechen "self-determination" war of the mid-1990s or the Croat-Muslim-Serb war over the partitioning of the former Yugoslavia illustrate the comprehensive and unlimited political objectives of war. Similarly, the unlimited goals of war are illustrated by the 1980s Iran-Iraq war (discussed later in this chapter in case 11.2) and the U.S.-Japan Pacific campaign of World War II. The commitment of the Japanese was so intense that it took the Japanese regime nearly a week to accept the U.S. demand of unconditional surrender following the devastating nuclear attacks on Hiroshima and Nagasaki.

The scope of wars also depends upon the means used in military campaigns. As with the goals of war, the scope of warfare can be defined along continuum, with limited, discriminating violence at one extreme and unlimited, total violence at the other. Wars of limited means are typically prosecuted by institutionalized, state-trained military forces using discriminating conventional weapons and seeking to inflict harm and destruction chiefly on military forces. A major feature of limited wars is that military forces apply violence in accord with generally accepted rules and conventions, upholding the distinction between combatants and noncombatants. It is important to emphasize that a limited war is defined not by the level of destruction inflicted but by limits placed on the use of available military resources. Thus, although the U.S. war in Vietnam was a highly costly and destructive war, the conflict involved limited means because U.S. military operations generally sought to apply proportionate and discriminating violence. Other examples of wars prosecuted with limited means include the Falkland Islands War and the Persian Gulf War.

Total wars, such as World War I and World War II, involve the full mobilization of society to prosecute war and the use of virtually all available military and economic resources in order to prosecute the military campaign. Moreover, total wars deemphasize, if not disregard, widely accepted rules and customs of war, including the distinction between combatants and noncombatants. It is important to stress that total wars are not defined so much by the level of destruction that they inflict but by the manner in which the wars are fought. The character of total wars is graphically illustrated by the terror bombing of cities during the World War II, the "ethnic cleansing" in the 1992–1994 Bosnian civil war, and the tribal genocide of the Hutus against the Tutsis in Rwanda in 1994.

The Frequency and Impact of International Wars

Throughout the history of Western civilization, interstate conflict has been a frequent phenomenon. According to Quincy Wright, 278 international wars were fought from the end of the fifteenth century to the middle of the twentieth century—roughly one war every two years.[8] American sociologist Pitirim Sorokin examined the number of years some of the major European states had been at war and found that war was more common than peace. For example, he found that Russia (his homeland) had experienced only one peaceful twenty-five-year period in the previous one thousand years, and that since the tenth century it had been at war forty-six of every hundred years. He also found that since the early eleventh century England had been at war fifty-six of every hundred years.[9]

The most exhaustive contemporary empirical research on international war has been carried out by Melvin Small and J. David Singer. For more that twenty-five years, they directed a Correlates of War Project, which sought to measure and analyze quantitative indicators that might be associated with war. According to Singer and Small, from 1816 to 1980 there were 118 wars. Of these, sixty-seven were interstate conflicts between two or more states, and the remainder were imperial or colonial wars involving entities that did not qualify as full members of the international system. The states most frequently involved in international and imperial wars during this period were: France (22), England (19), Turkey and Russia (18), Italy (12), China (11), Spain (10), and the United States (8).[10]

Throughout the Westphalian era, international wars have become less frequent but more destructive. According to Jack Levy, the historical trends of wars among the major powers over the past five centuries suggest that the frequency of war between the leading states has declined precipitously (see fig. 11.1), while violence has increased in extent, severity, and intensity, defined in terms of absolute and per capita battle deaths. Based on his analysis, Levy concludes that wars among the big powers have become less frequent but more destructive.[11] According to Francis Beer, the increasing destructiveness of war coupled with the declining frequency of war has resulted in the growing stability in the international society of states, or what he terms "peace diffusion."[12] This growth in international order is depicted by figure 11.2.

FIGURE 11.1
Great Power Wars, 1495–1975
Source: Data from Jack Levy "Historical Trends in Great Power War, 1495–1975" in *International Studies Quarterly,* 26, (June 1982) pp. 278–300.

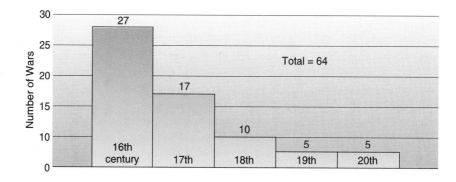

FIGURE 11.2
Relationship of Frequency and Destructiveness of War
Source: Adapted from Francis A. Beer, *Peace Against War* San Francisco: (W.H. Freeman and Company, 1981).

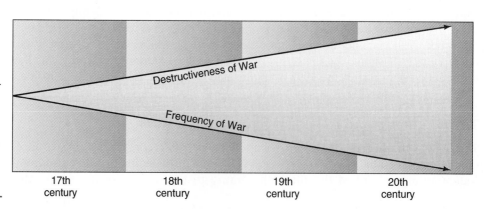

Three factors have contributed to the increasing destructiveness of war. First, the application of new scientific and technological discoveries to weaponry has resulted in more powerful military forces. Gun powder, the machine gun, and aerial bombardment, for example, are just a few of the important technological developments that have revolutionized warfare. Second, the shift from limited to total war has resulted in long, comprehensive wars of attrition that led to the weakening of the rules of warfare designed to protect civilians and to minimize human suffering among combatants. The shift in the character of war was illustrated in World War II, with the bombing of civilian targets (e.g., London, Coventry, Dresden, Rotterdam, Hiroshima) in order to weaken civilian morale. It has been estimated that the ratio of military to civilian dead in World War I was 90:10. But because of the shift to total war in World War II, the ratio of military to civilian deaths was 10:67. This dramatic shift has intensified in subsequent international and intranational wars, rising to a military/civilian ratio of 10:90—exactly the opposite of what it was at the beginning of the century.[13] Third, the increasing commitment to political and ideological objectives has led to increased political determination in wartime and greater ferocity in carrying out the battle. The brutality of modern wars is illustrated by the inhumane treatment of prisoners inflicted by both German and Japanese forces during World War II. One military historian has estimated that of about five million Soviet prisoners in Nazi captivity, more than three million died of mistreatment and privation.[14]

Data confirm the increasing destructiveness of war. Sorokin estimates that European war casualties in the fourteenth, fifteenth, and sixteenth centuries were 167,000, 285,000, and 863,000, respectively. For wars in the seventeenth, eighteenth, and nineteenth centuries, however, estimated casualties increased to 3.4, 4.6, and 3.8 million, respectively.[15] Twentieth-century wars have been the most destructive and account for more deaths than in all previous wars combined. It is estimated that civilian and military deaths were about 20 million in World War I and around 40 million in World War II.[16] And since 1945, wars—mostly civil conflicts within Third World states—have accounted for more than 40 million deaths.[17]

CLASSICAL, TOTAL, AND POSTMODERN WARS

Since the development of nation-states in the mid-seventeenth century, war has evolved both in its means and purposes. In light of the changing nature and scope of war over the past three and a half centuries, three types of war can be identified: classical, total, and postmodern. Classical wars are limited military conflicts between states designed to achieve political objectives. Total wars, by contrast, involve unlimited use of violence in seeking the unconditional defeat of the enemy. Finally, postmodern wars are small-scale wars fought within countries over the creation of new states or over the legitimacy of existing political authorities. In the following sections we discuss and illustrate the nature of each of these types of wars.

Classical Wars

The development of the Westphalian order in the mid-seventeenth century was closely linked to the capacity of the state to wage war. Because nation-states developed as rulers gained the political authority and military power to govern peoples within specified territories and to defend such territorial boundaries from potential foreign aggression, the process of state-building was directly linked to the state's domestic monopoly of coercive power and its ability to wage war internationally.[18] As nation-states became increasingly organized and institutionalized in

CASE STUDY

Case 11.1 The Falkland (Malvinas) Islands War

The Falkland Islands, located some 300 miles east of the southern tip of Argentina, consist of two large islands, East and West Falkland, and some 200 small islands and islets (see map 11.1) with a population of about 2,000. Most of the Falklanders, or "kelpers," are of British descent and nearly all are native born. Historically, the islands' most important economic activity has been the production of high-grade wool, although fishing has become an increasing source of income in recent years.

The Dispute

The Falkland Islands dispute was fundamentally about sovereignty—about the ownership of territory. Historically, both Argentina and the United Kingdom have claimed sovereignty over the islands. Although Britain has maintained continuous, uncontested control over the islands since 1833, Argentina has never recognized Britain's sovereignty over the islands. Indeed, throughout the past 150 years Argentina continued to press its sovereignty claim over the *Islas Malvinas,* as they are called in Argentina. During the 1960s and 1970s Argentina and Britain carried out intermittent but unsuccessful negotiations. Because Britain remained staunchly committed to the self-determination of the Falklanders and because they, in turn, remained committed to British rule, little progress was made diplomatically. As one

British diplomat observed, "We wanted to get rid of the place, and the wish of the islanders was only a diplomatic obstacle, not a cause worth dying for."[19]

The War

War began on April 2, 1982, when Argentinian military forces invaded Port Stanley, the islands' major city, and forced the surrender of the small contingent of British marines. After breaking diplomatic relations with Argentina, the British government resolved to regain control of the islands, even if force was necessary. Within a few days of the invasion, Britain had assembled and dispatched a large naval task force to the Falklands, some 8,000 miles away.

The Falklands War involved two distinct phases—a preparatory phase and a limited war phase. During the first phase, both Argentina and Britain carried out extensive military preparations. Argentina moved some 12,000 soldiers and a large stock of military weapons and equipment onto the islands. Meanwhile, the British assembled and deployed a large naval force, including land forces of about 9,000 soldiers. To make military reinforcement more difficult, Britain established a 200-nautical mile (NM) exclusion zone around the Falklands. At the same time, major diplomatic initiatives were developed in order to avert war. These included mediation efforts by U.S. Secretary of State Alexander

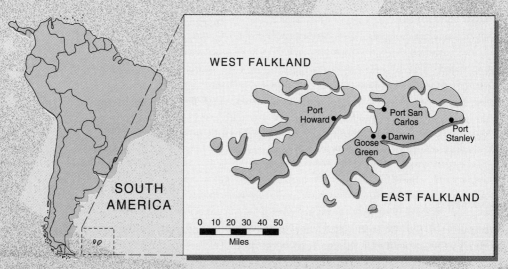

MAP 11.1
The Falkland Islands, (Islas Malvinas)

Haig and UN Secretary-General Javier Perez de Cuellar. Moreover, the UN Security Council passed Resolution 502, calling for the cessation of hostilities and the withdrawal of Argentine military forces from the islands, and the Organization of American States (OAS) urged an immediate cessation of hostilities. At the initiative of Britain, the European Community condemned Argentina's aggression and voted to ban its imports into Europe.

In the second phase, Argentine and British military forces carried an intensive six-week limited war, involving some of the largest naval battles since World War II. The first major event occurred on May 2, when a British submarine sank the cruiser *Belgrano*, Argentina's largest vessel. The loss of the ship, coupled with Britain's declaration that all waters beyond Argentina's twelve-mile territorial limit were a "war zone," forced the Argentina navy back to shore. By contrast, the British fleet played a pivotal role throughout the conflict by transporting and landing troops and armaments onto the islands and by providing air protection from attacking Argentine jets. British naval losses sustained from bomb and missile attacks were high, including the loss of five major ships.

On May 21, British forces carried out a successful amphibious landing at Port San Carlos (located some fifty miles west of Port Stanley). After consolidating its ground forces, the marine units moved quickly eastward and after fighting several ground battles, succeeded in surrounding Port Stanley. On June 14, Argentine forces, recognizing that they were completely encircled and in a militarily hopeless situation, began to raise white flags. The next day, the commander of Argentina's military forces surrendered.

The Outcome

The major result of the war was that the territory seized forcefully by Argentina on April 2 was returned to Britain after Argentina surrendered its military forces on the Falklands. The war was costly to both states. It has been estimated that troop losses were 250 for Britain and about 800 for Argentina. The major material losses for Britain included several naval and cargo vessels, whereas the major losses for Argentina included one naval warship and more than ninety jets. In addition, the war was extraordinarily expensive to both nations, especially considering the destruction of a significant portion of Argentina's air force and the loss of large amounts of war material left on the Falklands. The British government estimated the total cost of its military campaign at about $1.19 billion and the project costs for defending the islands through the 1980s at close to $2 billion[20]—or roughly $1.5 million per each inhabitant in the Falklands.

Because Argentina continues to claim sovereignty over the Falkland Islands, Britain has maintained 2,000 troops on the islands since the end of the war. In the meantime, however, the islands have prospered economically, in great measure from the lucrative sale of commercial fishing licenses. And with increased revenues, the local administration has significantly expanded infrastructure, including a modern school, a hospital, and roads. Moreover, the recent confirmation of large oil reserves—estimated at 2.5 billion barrels, or greater than those of the North Sea—could lead to a dramatic transformation of the islands after drilling begins early in the next century.[21]

During the Falklands War, both Argentina and Britain suffered significant military losses. Here the British destroyer HMS Sheffield *burns after being hit by an Exocet missile. The destroyer subsequently sank, with twenty lives lost.*

the eighteenth and nineteenth century, war-making became a more professional activity, subject to much greater training and institutionalized rules and practices. As governments expanded the training and professionalization of armed forces, rulers gained increasing power not only to protect their territorial boundaries but also to use such forces to expand state boundaries and to acquire territorial possessions in distant lands. Moreover, as institutionalized armed forces became increasingly accepted as a legitimate instrument of the state, international war was also recognized as a valid method of conflict resolution. Because the Westphalian order was based on the premise that states, like individuals, possessed the inherent right of self-defense, Clausewitz' thesis—that war is "a continuation of policy by other means"—was viewed as the accepted norm of war and politics.

Since Westphalian system wars involve military conflicts between states using government-directed armed forces, they are frequently regarded as Clausewitzian international wars. Such **classical wars** are characterized by international military conflicts involving: (1) states, (2) purposive actions carried out to attain political objectives, and (3) military force consistent with widely accepted rules and norms of the international community. Such military conflicts thus presume the existence of strong states in which government authority is clearly defined, and states possess a clear monopoly of power within their territorial boundaries. Moreover, because such wars typically are prosecuted for specific political objectives, they typically have a beginning and an end. Finally, because such wars are assumed to be rational actions in the pursuit of legitimate foreign policy objectives, they are undertaken as a last resort, only after peaceful methods of conflict resolution have been exhausted. Most eighteenth- and nineteenth-century interstate wars are classical in nature. We illustrate this type of war with a case study on the Falklands War.

Classical wars
An interstate war fought by the military forces of two or more states in order to achieve political objectives.

Total Wars

As a result of economic modernization in the nineteenth and early twentieth centuries, the military potential of industrial countries increased dramatically with the development of larger and more powerful armaments. Moreover, as a result of growing technological innovations in communications and the further expansion of transportation infrastructure, industrial countries were becoming increasingly integrated. As a result of these and other developments twentieth-century war has become increasingly lethal, giving rise to the phenomenon of total war.

A **total war** can be defined as an international dispute involving the unlimited use of force to achieve the complete defeat of the enemy. Like classical wars, total wars are rooted in interstate disputes. But they differ in that the violence and destruction inflicted in war is targeted on the entire society, with minimal effort given to the protection of the civilian population. Moreover, whereas the goals of classical wars are limited, the objectives of total wars involve the unconditional surrender of the enemy. Because both parties in such wars typically seek the complete defeat of their opponent, total wars are characterized by a high level of resolve and human destruction. Although World War I represents the first major total war, World War II, the most destructive war in the history of humankind, is the most dramatic illustration of this type of conflict. Since 1945, numerous intranational and regional total wars have been fought over geopolitical disputes. These include Cold War conflicts such as the Korean and Vietnam Wars as well as regional disputes such as the Iran-Iraq War of the 1980s. Each of these wars have involved prolonged military conflict involving society-wide participation and a high level of resolve by the contestants. Moreover, these wars have involved a high level of destruction to the society's economic and social infrastructure while also resulting in a significant level of civilian and military casualties. To illustrate the contemporary role of total war, we briefly describe the key elements of the Iran-Iraq war of the 1980s in case 11.2.

Total war
An international dispute involving unlimited use of force to achieve the complete defeat of the enemy.

CASE STUDY

Case 11.2 The Iran-Iraq War

On September 22, 1980, Iraq carried out a major air and land attack on Iran, commencing one of the longest and most brutal wars of modern times. The war, which lasted eight years, is estimated to have resulted in one million deaths and cost more than $400 billion.[22] Unlike the Falklands War, which resulted in a decisive settlement of a territorial dispute, the Iran-Iraq war did not achieve any tangible gains for either combatant.

The Conflict

Three factors contributed to the outbreak of the Iran-Iraq war: (1) a territorial dispute, (2) religious tensions between Islamic moderates (Sunnis) and fundamentalists (Shiites), and (3) a personality conflict between Saddam Hussein, Iraq's president, and the Ayatollah Khomeini, the leader of Iran.

The first and most immediate factor precipitating the war was a territorial conflict over the Shatt al-Arab River, an estuary serving as a border between Iran and Iraq and as a major waterway for Iraqi trade. Because the Shatt al-Arab is Iraq's only direct access to the sea (see map 11.1), the waterway is of critical economic importance. Given the strategic significance of the estuary, Iraq had made exclusive claims over the estuary until 1975, when it agreed to share the waterway in return for Iran's ceasing to support antigovernment Kurdish rebels in northern Iraq.[23]

The second source of the Iran-Iraq conflict was religious tensions between Islamic moderates and radicals. Throughout the 1970s religion seemed to play a relatively unimportant role in both countries, in great measure because both states were governed by secular regimes. But religious and political moderation came to an abrupt halt in the region in early 1979 when the Iranian revolution forced the Shah from office and established a fundamentalist Islamic regime, headed by the Ayatollah Khomeini. As the religious and political leader of Iran, Khomeini was not satisfied to set up an Islamic theocracy in his own land but was deeply committed to supporting Islamic revolution elsewhere, especially in nearby Iraq. After the 1979 Iranian revolution the rivalry between the Iraqi moderates and Iranian radicals intensified, leading Iraq to deport an estimated 100,000 fundamentalists.

The third source of the war was personal animosity between Hussein and Khomeini. Both men were powerful, determined political leaders, committed to radically different ideologies. Hussein considered Khomeini a threat to his Baathist government. Khomeini, in turn, regarded Hussein as an infidel—a leader who had betrayed the true faith of Islam. And once war began, Khomeini spurned the rules of limited war, demanding Iraq's total and unequivocal surrender. Indeed, Khomeini declared that the price of peace was the fall of the Baathist regime and the death of Hussein.

The War

The war began with a surprise Iraqi air and land attack on Iran, and within two months, Iraq had seized some 4,000 square miles of Iranian territory. By mid-1982, however, the military advantage had begun to shift toward Iran. Although Iraq maintained superiority in military armaments, especially in tanks and airplanes, Iran had begun to capitalize on its three to one manpower advantage. By July 1982, Iran had not only recovered most of its lost territory but was beginning to threaten Iraq. Once it became clear to Iraqi military commanders that they could not win a war of attrition against Iran, they settled into a defensive posture. This strategy worked well until 1986, when Iranian forces crossed the Shatt al-Arab and captured the port city of Fao, holding it for more than two years.[24]

In 1983 and early 1984, the numerically superior Iranian ground forces increased military pressure on Iraq by launching periodic offensive raids. In response to growing Iranian successes, Iraq expanded the scope of the war by resorting to chemical weapons, carrying out terror bombing of cities, and expanding attacks on oil shipping. These shipping attacks—known as the "tanker war"—drastically curtailed oil exports for both states but especially Iran.

The Outcome

Military hostilities ceased on July 20, 1988, when a UN-sponsored cease-fire took effect. At that time Iraq held about 1,000 square miles of territory formerly controlled by Iran. The Ayatollah's acceptance of the cease-fire was due in great measure to the vigorous diplomatic efforts of UN Secretary-General Javier Perez de Cuellar, coupled with the growing economic and military hardship experienced by Iran.

Three developments contributed to Iran's acceptance of the cease-fire. First, Iraq's missile attacks on

continued

Case 11.2 The Iran-Iraq War—*continued*

Iranian cities had a demoralizing impact on citizens. The "war of the cities" kept millions of people in terror. Second, Iraq's bombing appeared to have severely damaged the Iranian economy. And although Iraq was receiving significant aid from Arab oil exporting states, Iran was receiving virtually no external support. Third, and most important, U.S. entry into the Persian Gulf conflict increased the cost of Iran's continued belligerence. In July 1987 the United States had begun to provide protection to Kuwaiti tankers flying the American flag. Although the United States attempted to stay clear of the fighting, its escort service to tankers resulted in sporadic military conflicts with Iranian speedboats. When a U.S. navy ship hit an Iranian mine in April 1988, the United States retaliated by sinking or crippling six Iranian ships and destroying two Iranian oil platforms.

Finally, on July 3 a U.S. cruiser (USS *Vincennes*) accidentally downed an Iranian plane, killing 290 passengers. Ali Akbar Rafsanjani, the speaker of the Iranian parliament, indicated that Iran decided to accept the cease-fire after the Iranian plane was shot down. According to Rafsanjani, this was the "turning point" in Iranian thinking because it indicated that the United States was ready to commit "immense crimes" if Iran continued the war.

Following the cease-fire, both states continued to hold some 100,000 prisoners of war, and Iraq continued to control some Iranian territory along the Shatt al-Arab gained early in the war. In the next two years, little progress was made in resolving the conflicting territorial claims to the Shatt. However, in September 1990 the dispute was abruptly settled when Iraq voluntarily relinquished its claim over the disputed territory and returned its war prisoners to Iran. Iraq's actions were not motivated by generosity or increased sensitivity to Iran but were rooted in self-interest: Iraq was facing the possibility of another military conflict after it had invaded and annexed Kuwait in August 1990. The settlement of the Shatt al-Arab dispute was thus a by-product of another dispute.

In sum, the Iran-Iraq war began with dubious purposes and appears to have settled nothing. The war broke out in part because of the personal animosity between the two countries' leaders. Moreover, although this total war lasted nearly ten years and cost nearly one million lives, the conflict itself was based on ephemeral, symbolic issues. In the end, it accomplished nothing except death and destruction.

Postmodern Wars

Historically, classical wars and total wars have been the most important types of military conflicts in global society. But since the end of the Second World War, and especially since the end of the Cold War, such conflicts have become less important as intranational political, religious, and ethnic wars have become more frequent and more significant in global society.

Postmodern wars

Intranational conflicts fought over the legitimacy of existing political regimes.

Postmodern wars—or what Holsti terms "wars of a third kind"[25]—are characterized as intranational conflicts fought within states over the legitimacy of existing state structures. As noted earlier, the contemporary international system is increasingly characterized by the expanding influence of nonstate actors and greater global interdependence. Even though states were comparatively few in number and strong in structure throughout the first three centuries of the Westphalian order, the dramatic rise in the number of new states in the last half of the twentieth century, coupled with the increasing weakness of many new regimes, has resulted in a significant rise in intranational wars.

According to one study, of the 164 wars during the 1945–1995 period, only 38 (23 percent) were classical, interstate conflicts, while 126 (77 percent) were intranational, internal conflicts.[26] Of these 126 internal wars, about half were based on internal ideological disputes and the other half were state-nation conflicts involving the quest for increased political autonomy by national and separatist political groups. Moreover, the bulk of these wars were in two Third World regions, with

Africa accounting for 44 wars and the Middle East accounting for 33. As a result of the prevalence of intranational war in the contemporary world, Holsti argues that the problem of war in future global politics will be concerned chiefly with domestic politics rather than with international politics. In his view, "security *between* states in the Third World, among some of the former republics of the Soviet Union, and elsewhere has become increasingly dependent upon security *within* those states."[27]

As noted earlier, the post–Westphalian order is a world characterized by global politics in which quasi-states and nonstate actors have increasing influence. In the classical, Westphalian order, states are strong and are able to effectively regulate political affairs within their territorial boundaries. The problem is to achieve peaceful and humane international relations in global society. In the post–Westphalian system, the authority of a growing number of states, especially within the Third World, is either limited or altogether absent, and the lack of domestic authority threatens not only political order within "weak" and "failed" states but also regional stability as well as the international community itself. The post–Cold War collapse of domestic authority in such countries as Haiti, Liberia, Rwanda, Somalia, Sudan, Yugoslavia, and Zaire has resulted in the death of hundreds of thousands of persons, massive starvation, millions of refugees, and the destabilization of regional order. Case 11.3 on the 1994 Rwanda civil war and its subsequent international effects illustrates the profound impact of domestic instability on global order.

In sum, war poses a major problem to the international community. At the domestic level, internal wars threaten the viability and legitimacy of existing states and foster regional insecurity and instability. At the international level, interstate wars threaten global order, impairing international cooperation, fostering international insecurity, and distorting national priorities. Even though international war remains the major immediate threat to the stability of the international community, intranational war is increasingly important in global society. The Charter of the United Nations—the constitution of the international community—lists the rights and obligations of member-states, but it fails to specify the norms by which regimes should govern the people or to define which peoples are entitled to the right of self-determination. Because the international community is largely silent on the issue of state creation and domestic governance, political groups will continue to challenge domestic regimes and demand for increased self-rule.

THEORIES OF WAR

One of the most difficult and elusive questions in international relations is "why war?" Ever since Thucydides analyzed the Peloponnesian War, scholars have offered a wide range of explanations for the phenomenon of war. Some of these explanations focus on the imperfections of human beings; others emphasize the role of states; and still others focus on the nature of the international political order. Despite these different emphases, it is important to recognize that war, like other social problems, is rooted in a multiplicity of sources. No single-factor explanation is adequate.

In *Man, the State and War,* Kenneth Waltz sets forth a useful framework for understanding the causes of war. According to him, there are three factors or "images" that help account for war: people, states, and the world system.[32] War is rooted in the imperfections and moral inadequacies of people, the unjust behavior of national governments, and the anarchic character of the international community. Wars occur in the global system not only because people and states behave unjustly but also because there is nothing to stop them. According to Waltz, aggressive behavior of individuals and the unjust policies of states are the immediate causes of war, and because

Case 11.3 The Rwanda Genocide and Its Aftermath

Background

Rwanda, a small nation of some 7.5 million inhabitants in central Africa, is populated by two different tribal peoples—the Hutus and the Tutsis. Although both peoples speak the same language, enjoy the same type of food, share similar religious beliefs, and have lived side by side for centuries, they differ slightly in appearance and in the vocations they have typically pursued. The Hutus, a Bantu people, have historically lived as peasants cultivating the land; by contrast, the Tutsis, a taller people from northern Africa, have generally worked in cattle grazing. More significantly, Rwanda's Hutu majority (85 percent of the population) has been historically ruled by the Tutsi minority (15 percent of the population). Even during the colonial rule that began in the late nineteenth century, German and Belgian colonial rulers governed through the Tutsi authorities.

In 1959 Rwanda gained its independence from Belgium, in large part in response to growing demands by the Hutu majority for self-determination. After gaining control of the new government, Hutu rulers sought to redress historic political, social, and economic inequalities. These initiatives precipitated increased civil strife, resulting in a growing number of Tutsi refugees. By 1964 more than 300,000 Tutsis had fled Rwanda, and by 1973 the total number of refugees exceeded 600,000. By the end of the 1980s the Tutsi diaspora was estimated to include nearly one million Tutsis living in neighboring countries, especially Uganda and Burundi. Because of the continuing Hutu domination of government and systematic exclusion of Tutsis from Rwandan society, Tutsis established a guerrilla force (known as the *Rwandan Patriotic Front—RPF*) in the late 1980s. In 1990, the RPF attacked Rwanda, demanding an end to tyranny and exclusion. The Hutus, in turn, retaliated against the Tutsis, killing several hundred leading officials and further reinforcing racial extremism.

In order to halt the cycle of violence, Hutu President Juvenal Habyarimana and RFP leaders signed a power-sharing peace accord in Arusha, Tanzania in 1993. The aim of the *Arusha Accords* was to bring the ongoing conflict between the ruling Hutus and the RPF guerrillas to a halt by establishing a cease-fire, power-sharing among competing groups, supervised democratic elections, repatriation of refugees, and the integration of RFP with the government's armed forces.[28] To ensure the accord's implementation, the UN Security Council created an

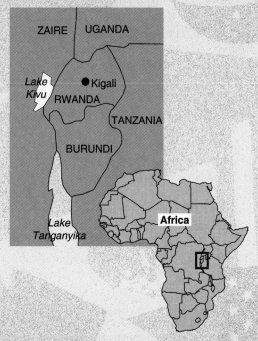

MAP 11.2
Rwanda and Surrounding States

observer force of 2,500 troops, known as the *UN Assistance Mission to Rwanda (UNAMIR)*.

The Genocide

On April 6, 1994, as President Habyarimana was returning to Kigali, Rwanda's capital, his jet was hit by two antiaircraft missiles as it approached the airport, resulting in a crash that killed all passengers. Within hours of Habyarimana's death, Hutu militia, led by the Presidential Guard, began a systematic massacre of Tutsis and Hutu moderates. Some of the first assassinations involved moderate leaders, including the government's Hutu prime minister and ten Belgian members of UNAMIR assigned to protect her. This action led Belgium to withdraw its 400 other troops, virtually paralyzing the UN force.[29] Encouraged by political and civic extremists, Hutu killing spread quickly throughout the land, leading to the systematic killing of tens of thousands of Tutsis and moderate Hutus. One of the largest massacres occurred in mid-April in the western city of Kibuye, when more than 5,000 Tutsis were rounded up in a stadium and then slaughtered. Although the government forces were well equipped with modern weapons, the genocide was carried out by tens of thousands of Hutus at close quarters with primitive weapons. "If people murdered with machetes." writes David Rieff, "it was because the Hutu leadership had conceived of a genocide that would involve the entire Hutu people."[30]

The genocide did not end until the RPF forces took control of most of Rwanda by mid-June. By that time, the Hutus had killed at least 800,000 Tutsis, making this genocide campaign one of the deadliest and most destructive in modern times.[31] Moreover, the RPF's rapid conquest of Rwanda, which was achieved not through military battles but by the rapid flight of Hutus terrified by their mass murder, resulted in one of the largest and fastest movements of refugees in the history of civilization. In one 25-hour period, a quarter of a million Hutus fled into Tanzania. By the time that the Tutsis had gained control of all Rwanda in August, it was estimated that some 2.2 million refugees had fled Rwanda, principally to Burundi, Tanzania, and Zaire. In the first two weeks of the refugee exodus, an estimated 2.2 million Hutus fled to neighboring states, with more than one million fleeing to Goma, Zaire, alone.

Regional Implications

Although the new government immediately encouraged the return of refugees, few had done so by the end of 1996. This was because the Hutu militia, who controlled most refugee camps, refused to allow refugees to return, hoping to consolidate their power within the camps and to create an armed force that could eventually topple the new Rwandan government. Fearing the growing power of the Hutu militia, the Rwandan government demanded the closure of Zairian refugee camps. After Hutu guerrillas began carrying out border raids, the Tutsi-led Rwandan defense forces (renamed the *Rwandan Patriotic Army—RPA*) intervened in the Zairian camps to destroy the remaining Hutu guerrilla forces and to free all refugees who desired to return home. In November 1996 the RPA attacked the Zairian refugee camps, routing the militia and thereby precipitating the return of some 700,000 Hutu refugees.

The defeat of the Hutu militia also reinforced the campaign of Zairian rebels who were seeking to topple the dictatorship of the country's long-term dictator, Mobuto Sese Seko. The Zairian rebel forces, which were supported by Rwandan Tutsi militia, began controlling Zaire's western border area in early 1997. Within two months, however, the rebels had gained control of the western half of Zaire, including the mineral-rich area in the southwest area of the country, and threatened to topple the governing regime. The success of the rebel forces was due, in significant measure, to the support from Rwandan Tutsis, who were seeking to capture and kill Hutu militia still hiding in the jungles of Zaire. When rebel forces began threatening Kinshasa, the country's capital, Mobutu resigned the presidency and was replaced by Laurent Kabila, the leader of the victorious rebel forces. Thus, the 1994 Rwandan genocide not only influenced domestic political affairs, but also transformed the regional political landscape of central Africa. As this case study suggests, although wars of a "third kind" may involve limited interstate military conflict, they can profoundly influence regional international relations.

Although most destruction in wars is carried out with modern weapons, killing is sometimes carried out with traditional weapons. The machetes pictured above were used in the 1994 Rwanda massacres, which resulted in the death of more than one-half million Tutsis.

TABLE 11.1 A Typology of Theories of War

Actor	Sources of War	Causes of War
The Individual	Human nature Leadership Misperception Loss of control Expected utility of war	Human condition
The Nation-State	Economic structures Military-industrial complex Undemocratic regimes Nationalism	Behavior of states
The International System	Power symmetry Power transition Arms races	International system

international institutions are unable to prevent them, the international system serves as a permissive cause of war. Using Waltz's triparitite framework, we will examine some major theories and hypotheses about the source of wars. (See table 11.1.)

The Individual

Many prominent theorists believe that individuals—not states or the world system—are chiefly responsible for war. Those that emphasize the role of individuals in causing war have developed numerous hypotheses and theories. Some of these emphasize the fundamental nature of persons; other emphasize the nature, role, and constraints on decision makers. We will examine five different theories related to the individual: human nature, political leadership, misperception, loss of control, and the expected utility of war.

Human Nature

This perspective assumes that the basic cause of war is rooted in the essential nature of persons. Wars occur because of people's unjust and aggressive behavior, attributed to factors such as psychological drives, biological instincts, and moral depravity. In the following paragraphs we briefly examine three prominent theories representing the human nature perspective: psychological impulses, biological instincts, and moral deprivation.

The *psychological drives* thesis has been most forcefully set forth in the early twentieth century by psychiatrist Sigmund Freud, who argued that the root cause of human conflict is the aggressive impulse within people. "I take up the standpoint," he wrote, "that the tendency to aggression is an innate, independent, instinctual disposition in man."[33] Because these impulses are grounded in human nature, it is impossible to eliminate them. Despite his pessimistic view of human nature, Freud was not wholly pessimistic about the possibility of eliminating war. He identified two ways to promote harmony. First, civilization can continue to domesticate and tame human instincts, making war culturally less acceptable. Second, people who subordinate instincts to reason can encourage domestic tranquility and international peace.

The thesis that human aggression is a *biological instinct* has best been articulated by the eminent biological scientist Konrad Lorenz. Based on his animal research, Lorenz concluded in his book *On Aggression* that people, like all other animals, are instinctively aggressive. But whereas animals use threats rather than violence to establish a hierarchy within the species, human aggression leads to injury and even death. Indeed, Lorenz believes that human aggressive instincts have become "grotesquely exaggerated" and have "gone wild" in people.[34] Despite his pessimistic belief that human aggression is innate, Lorenz holds hope for the future, believing that people can become more peaceful and harmonious by developing greater self-knowledge and by directing their aggressive instincts toward nonhuman objects.

The view that human conflict is rooted in the *moral depravity* of persons is central to the Christian religion. According to Christian doctrine, conflict and aggression are rooted within persons. Christian theologians, such as St. Augustine, St. Thomas Aquinas, and John Calvin, have taught that people commit aggression because of a sinful, corrupt nature. According to the Bible, the corruption of people is universal—affecting all persons regardless of race, intelligence, or social position—and total—encompassing all of a person's life, including human reason. Belief in human sinfulness does not imply, however, that human beings are completely devoid of good. The Bible teaches that the essence of people is good, for God created human beings in his image. As Reinhold Neibuhr has noted, human sinfulness did not destroy the true essence of a person, only corrupted it.[35] Although Christians can agree with Freud and Lorenz that the individual is a source of conflict, they disagree with them by asserting that aggression is based on people's imperfect moral condition, not an inherited biological or psychological precondition.

Although humanists and traditional political philosophers emphasize the role of human nature in fostering conflict, contemporary international relations scholars pay limited attention to this factor—in great part because they believe that few new insights and findings can be uncovered on human nature that will help promote a more peaceful world. Because human nature is regarded as largely unchanging, little incentive exists to analyze the roots of human behavior.

Leadership

Some theorists assert that wars can result from the whims and impulses of government leaders. This theory, rooted in the great-leader theory of history, applies chiefly to autocratic regimes and other governments in which executive authority faces limited checks on its power. It is less relevant to democracies in which contesting factions can check the power of each other and in which a decision to go to war will generally involve popular participation. The role of leadership is clearly illustrated in the Iran-Iraq War case 11.2 examined earlier. As the case suggests, that war began because of Khomeini's personal animosity with Hussein. Ten years later, Iraq's invasion of Kuwait was undertaken largely because of Hussein's belief that such action would increase his country's regional influence and increase oil revenues substantially. Because it is doubtful that either conflict could be explained by strategic imperatives or the innate aggressiveness of the Iraqi people, the most convincing explanation lies in the ambitions of leaders.

Regardless of what scholars may conclude about this theory, it remains a favorite explanation of those who must fight and die when nations wage war. In Erich Remarque's *All Quiet on the Western Front,* a soldier offers this explanation for war: ". . . Every full-grown emperor requires at least one war, otherwise he would not become famous. You look in your school books."[36]

Misperception

Another explanation for war is the failure of accurate communication because of misperception. Although numerous factors contribute to the distortion of reality, including fear, overconfidence, and absence of accurate information on people and events, a major source of misperception (see chap. 9) is an individual's belief system or political worldview. Every individual holds preconceived "images" about the international system (e.g., the nature of the global system, the role of power in world affairs, the intentions of friendly and enemy states), and these images serve as filtering devices to process and interpret information.

According to Levy, decision makers can be influenced by three types of misperception: (1) the exaggeration or underestimation of an adversary's capabilities; (2) the exaggeration or underestimation of an adversary's intentions; and (3) the misperception of third states.[37] John Stoessinger similarly argues that the distortion of an adversary's power can be highly damaging to foreign relations. In particular, he argues that "a leader's misperception of his adversary's power is perhaps the quintessential cause of war. . . . It is not the actual distribution that precipitates war; it is the way in which a leader thinks that power is distributed."[38] In an important case study of World War I, Ole Holsti, Richard Brody, and Robert North argue that the outbreak of World War I could be traced to the distortion of communication among statesmen of the major European powers.[39] And in a similar study of the Cuban missile crisis, these three scholars conclude that the peaceful resolution of the conflict was facilitated by the low level of misperception of each other's statements and actions.[40]

Loss of Control

A related theory attributes war to decision makers' loss of control during international crises. The loss of control may be due, among other things, to the organizational interests of the military, the preference of military leaders for offensive strategies, and the rigidity of military doctrines and war plans. Because of the difficulty of controlling the momentum of military operations once they have begun, some scholars argue that the loss of political control over military operations can contribute to war. For example, several scholars have suggested that a major cause of World War I was the military's reliance on offensive strategies, coupled with the loss of political control once military mobilization had commenced.[41] More recently, scholars have emphasized the dangers posed by miscalculation and by incentives to preemptive use of force during nuclear crises. Because of the destructive potential of nuclear forces and the limited time to respond to perceived threats, secure and effective command and control of military forces is essential if decision makers are to manage crises effectively. According to Richard Ned Lebow, the most effective way to reduce miscalculation and the possibility of losing control in times of crises is to develop sound military strategies and command and control systems that ensure full political control of nuclear forces.[42]

Expected Utility of War

Expected utility of war theory
A theory that attributes the outbreak of war to decision makers' estimated gains. According to the theory, the higher the expected gains (utility) from war, the greater the likelihood that leaders will resort to war.

Another closely related explanation for war is the **expected utility of war theory,** advanced by Bruce Bueno de Mesquita. According to him, war can best be explained as a rational decision-making process in which political leaders risk war only when their expected gains outweigh expected losses. Bueno de Mesquita takes issue with theories that seek to explain war in terms of different distributional patterns of power. Using data from the Correlates of War Project, he concludes that "no particular distribution of power has exclusive claim as a predictor of peace or war either in theory or in the empirical record of the period 1816–1965."[43] Instead, he argues that a better explanation can be achieved by taking into account the risk-taking behaviors of national leaders. Although most people would ordinarily regard the initiation of war as an irrational act, Bueno de Mesquita assumes that leaders' decision to go to war is a rational act based on their calculated assessment of probable gains and losses.

According to the expected utility of war theory, the probability of war increases as expected gains exceed anticipated losses. The theory assumes that the decision to go war typically involves three types of calculations: first, leaders estimate the expected gain from a bilateral war; second, they estimate the expected gain from a multilateral war in which third parties support the initiator of war; and third, they estimate the expected utility from a multilateral war in which third parties align themselves with the victim state. According to Bueno de Mesquita, the higher the overall expected utility of war, the greater the likelihood of war. In effect, the theory posits that wars are more likely when leaders believe that their anticipated gains are greater than their costs. Bueno de Mesquita tested his theory and found that the modern history of war corroborates the expected utility hypothesis. According to him, of the seventy-six wars from 1816 to 1974, sixty-five of them (86 percent) were initiated by states having a positive expected utility score.[44]

The Nation-State

The second source of war is the nation-state. According to this perspective, if peace is to be promoted in the world, the nature and behavior of states needs to be reformed. In the following sections we examine four theories attributing war to different aspects of states—economic structures, the military-industrial complex, autocratic government, and nationalism.

Economic Structures

In the nineteenth century, political economist Karl Marx argued that the expansion of capitalism would inevitably lead to economic conflict within societies. Although Marx called attention to the economic sources of international conflict, the development of the Marxist explanation of war was left to his disciple Vladimir Lenin, the founder of the Soviet Union. Whereas Marx had predicted that capitalism would begin to suffocate from its inherent contradictions, capitalism in fact was becoming stronger, not weaker, in the early twentieth century. Lenin argued that the reason for this was that capitalist states were extending the life of capitalism by exporting surplus capital overseas and finding new sources of cheap labor and raw materials, as well as new markets for excessive industrial production.

In *Imperialism: The Highest Stage of Capitalism,* Lenin argued that the expansion of capitalism led to intense international competition among leading capitalist states and inevitably to war. The root cause of conflict was **monopoly capitalism,** characterized by an increasing concentration of wealth. As financial monopolies gained political influence, governments inevitably became instruments for industrial and financial elites, who sought to dominate and exploit workers domestically and to extend their influence internationally. The establishment of colonies in Asia and Africa by European empires was thus an inexorable byproduct of monopoly capitalism. Because of the increasing competition for foreign sources of raw materials, markets, and cheap labor, wars among capitalist states were thought to be an inevitable result of the expansion of global capitalism. For Lenin, the outbreak of World War I vividly illustrated this truth.

Monopoly capitalism
The Marxist-Leninist belief that capital would become increasingly concentrated in the hands of a small number of industrial and financial elites.

In short, war is primarily the result of imperialistic policies of advanced capitalist states. The root cause of war is not human nature or even economic greed. Rather, the source is the economic system of capitalism, which perpetuates class conflict domestically and internationally. The way to peace is to promote a classless society in which economic classes and territorial borders cease to be significant.

The Military-Industrial Complex

Military-industrial complex

A concept that calls attention to the convergence of interests between the armed forces, major weapons industries, and government agencies responsible for national security.

A variant of the Leninist explanation is the view that war is the product of specific elite groups who profit from military spending and international conflicts. Such elite groups, generally referred to as the **military-industrial complex,** comprise the armed forces, the major weapons industries, and government officials responsible for foreign and national security policy. Although C. Wright Mills argued in *The Causes of World War III* that a military-industrial complex can exist in both capitalist and socialist societies, the more common view in the United States has been that the source of international conflict is the domestic economic structures of industrial democracies.

For example, in *Roots of War* Richard Barnet argues that "war is primarily a product of domestic social and economic institutions."[45] Wars will cease, according to him, only when the military, political, and economic structures of society are organized to make peace, not war. As long as the preparation for war is economically profitable, wars will continue. Barnet identifies three important factors contributing to war: (1) the national security establishment is too powerful and too insensitive to long-term national interests; (2) national economic expansion is overly dependent on military weapons procurement; and (3) military and industrial elites manipulate public opinion excessively. If the United States is to become a force for peace in the world, its social and economic structures must be reformed so that military-industrial institutions no longer control the foreign policy process.

Undemocratic Regimes

This theory assumes that warfare is more likely when regimes are undemocratic than when they are based on consent. As noted in chapter 8, Immanuel Kant argued in *Perpetual Peace* that limited, constitutional governments are much less likely to go to war than autocratic regimes. The modern historical record has confirmed Kant's thesis. According to R. J. Rummel, no war occurred between stable democracies from 1814 to 1989. Some democracies, such as Britain and France, were involved in colonial or imperialist wars in the nineteenth century, but no war took place between two mature democratic states. In Rummel's words: "Democratic states do not make war on each other."[46] Because of the absence of war among democracies, scholars have developed the so-called *"democratic peace thesis,"* which claims that democracies are conducive to peaceful international relations. As described earlier (see issue 8.2), the democratic peace thesis claims that democracies foster peace by propagating liberal ideas (e.g., freedom, tolerance, compromise, and decision making based on consent) that inhibit the use of force and by developing institutional structures (e.g., checks and balances, periodic elections) that inhibit a resort to force.

Not only are democratic states more peaceful toward foreign countries, they are also less violent domestically. Authoritarian and totalitarian regimes, by contrast, are not only more prone to war but are more violent toward their own people. According to Rummel, more than 119 million people have been killed by government genocide, massacres, and other mass killings in the twentieth century, whereas less than 36 million have died in battle in all foreign and domestic wars. Of those killed by civil wars, as many as 95 million were killed by communist regimes alone.[47]

Nationalism

Another source of war is nationalism—the passionate desire for collective group identity. As noted in chapter 2, because there are many more nations than states, few countries are based on a close correspondence of one people with one state. Moreover, because the drawing of territorial boundaries was rarely based on nationality but was the consequence of war and imperial conquest, the map of the

Issue 11.1 Selected Empirical Findings on War

ALLIANCES RARELY RESULT IN INCREASED SECURITY. States generally enter into alliances in order to increase their national security. Empirical research suggests, however, that alliance formation may result in arms races, thereby reducing national security in the long term. Based on numerous studies, John Vasquez concludes: "alliances do not prevent war or promote peace; instead they are associated with war, although they are probably not a cause of war."[49]

ALLIANCES EXPAND THE SCOPE OF WAR. Once wars begin, alliances tend to increase the magnitude and severity of wars. Randolph Siverson and Joel King, for example, found that alliances tended to serve as a contagion mechanism for spreading and expanding war.[50] As a result, an increase in the number of alliances in the international community potentially increases the number of states that could be drawn into war.

ARMS RACES INCREASE THE POSSIBILITY OF WAR. Although war is not inevitable in an arms race, the existence of an arms race increases the probability of international crises that could escalate into war. Michael Wallace, for example, examined ninety-nine serious disputes between 1816 and 1965 and found that serious disputes involving an arms race were more likely to result in war than serious disputes in which no arms race occurred.[51]

PREPARATIONS FOR WAR RARELY ENSURE PEACE. Although realists have generally assumed that military defense is the best deterrent against aggression, empirical research has cast doubt on the validity of this proposition. According to Vasquez, the findings of the Correlates of War project suggest that preparation for war against equals "produces neither peace nor victory . . . , but increased insecurity, coercion, and entanglement in a process that may lead to war."[52]

BIPOLARITY MAY, OR MAY NOT, PROMOTE PEACE. Scholars have long tried to determine whether a bipolar system (two major centers of power) or a multipolar system (three or more centers of powers) is conducive to peace and stability.[53] Because of conceptual and empirical difficulties, scholars have been unable to resolve this issue. J. David Singer, Stuard Bremer, and John Stuckey, for example, examined nineteenth- and twentieth-century wars and found that the degree of dispersion of military power had virtually no impact on the likelihood of war. However, when war-proneness during the ninteenth and twentieth centuries was analyzed separately, power concentration was associated with war in the nineteenth century but with peace in the twentieth century.[54] One possible explanation for the increasing peace associated with great powers in the twentieth century is due to the rule of the superpowers in the post–World War II era.

---

world is rooted in boundaries established by force. For example, the map of Africa is rooted in boundaries established by European imperial powers, not by the wishes and desires of ethnic and tribal groups. As a result, most states in the contemporary world are multinational, and many nations are distributed among two or more states.

Nationalistic wars, which are rooted in the aspirations of a people for increased self-rule, are generally of two types—separatist and irredentist. A **separatist war** occurs when a nationalist group seeks increased politial autonomy or even secession from an existing nation-state. Examples of this type of conflict include Moslems in northern Chad seeking greater independence from the Christian-controlled government in the south; Sikhs in India, especially in Punjab, seeking greater political autonomy; Tamils in Sri Lanka fighting for greater independence from the Sinhalese-dominated government; and in 1991, Kurdish rebel forces in Iraq rebelling against the government of Saddam Hussein in the wake of his military defeat in the Persian Gulf War to gain temporary control of the oil-rich area of Kirkuk in northern Iraq.

Irredentist wars, by contrast, result from a foreign state's claim on a people and territory of another state. Examples of irredentist claims include Argentina's claim on the Falkland Islands, China's claim on Taiwan, the Palestinian claim to

Separatist war
A conflict precipitated by a group's demand for political secession from a state.

Irredentist war
A war that results from a foreign state's claim on a people and territory of another state.

the Holy Land, and India's and Pakistan's claim on Kashmir. The danger of nationalist and irredentist wars is dramatically illustrated by the August 1990 Iraq military invasion of Kuwait, leading to the annexation of that formerly independent state and precipitating the most severe crisis in the Middle East since the Yom Kippur War of 1973.

The International System

A third source of war is the decentralized world system itself. At a fundamental level, wars happen because no institutions or structures exist to stop them; the anarchic system thus permits wars but does not directly cause them. But the probability of wars is also influenced by the distribution of power within the international system. Indeed, most scholarship on the causes of war in the past two decades—much of it based on empirical data from the Correlates of War Project identified earlier—has sought to uncover the systemic conditions and patterns of power that are associated with war. Because of the complexity invovled in this research, many of the conclusions are highly tenuous and even contradictory.[48] Some of the most significant findings are outlined in issue box 11.1.

As noted in chapter 6, the balance of power theory is one of the most widely accepted ideas in international relations. According to the theory, peace and stability are a consequence of a fundamental power equilibrium. When the power of one or more states increases and thereby threatens the balance of power, states will align themselves against the great power that seeks to alter the fundamental power equilibrium. We will briefly examine three theories rooted in balance of power: power asymmetry theory, power transition theory, and arms races.

Power Asymmetry

This theory assumes that the probability of war increases when power is distributed unequally among states and when aggressive moves are not countered by individual and collective military action. Failure to confront an increase in national power, and especially military aggression, may encourage short-term peace but will inevitably lead to increased future instability. The classic illustration of this theory is the Allied appeasement of Adolf Hitler before World War II. At the 1938 Munich conference, at which British, French, Italian, and German leaders had gathered to discuss the German demand that Czechoslovakia give up the Sudetenland, French and British foreign ministers gave in to Hitler's territorial demand in the hope that this action would appease him and bring peace to Europe. Although Neville Chamberlain, Britain's prime minister, announced on his return from Berlin that "peace is at hand," his hopes were dashed less than a year later when Germany, after taking the Sudetenland, invaded Poland in 1939, thereby precipitating World War II. According to the power asymmetry theory, had Britain and France been more resolute in opposing Hitler's early aggressive moves, the possibility of war might have been reduced.

Hegemonic stability theory
The belief that international peace and economic prosperity are a by-product of a hegemonically imposed structure.

Interestingly, some leading theorists argue just the opposite of the above. Their theory, called the **hegemonic stability theory,** maintains that peace is best assured when one state has superior power.[55] In such a system, in which the leader, or hegemon, has the capability to impose its will on others, stability and order are maintained when the hegemon uses its power to establish and maintain formal and informal international structures. According to these theorists, the most dangerous development occurs when two or more states achieve comparable power. In such a case, each state, fearing for its own position, is likely to initiate a war of rivalry with the other. Only when one power emerges victorious can world order be restored.

Power Transition

The **power transition theory,** which assumes that power distributions among states are always in flux, asserts that sudden or radical changes in the pattern of power are destabilizing and can contribute to war. A key insight of this theory is its emphasis on a dynamic assessment of power patterns, rather than a static analysis. Because national power depends partly on economic capabilities, differential economic growth rates will result in shifting military capabilities among the major powers. Because states are unable to maintain their relative power position indefinitely, danger lurks when significant power transitions begin to occur.

According to A.F.K. Organski, a leading advocate of this theory, the probability of war increases as the "power gap" between two rival states decreases.[56] Changes in the relative power of major states can threaten peace and stability, especially when a rival state increases its power and begins to challenge the role of the dominant country. When a challenger-state is convinced that military victory is possible, it may resort to war to gain economic benefits and political influence commensurate with its newly acquired capabilities. War does not result from the equality of capabilities per se nor from changes in those capabilities. Rather, it is rooted in the interaction between the original conditions and the newly acquired changes. Moreover, wars do not commence solely with challenges but may also start with the dominant power. When a leading power perceives its declining status, it may resort to a **preventive war** in order to avoid a future military confrontation when its power is even further eroded.[57]

Another theory related to power transition is Modelski's **long-cycle theory,** explored in chapter 6. According to Modelski, wars result when the power of the dominant state declines and a succession struggle ensues. As with wars rooted in power transitions, wars erupt at the end of long historical cycles when challengers seek to displace the leading power in the international system.[58]

Arms Races

Because each state is ultimately responsible for its own national security, countries seek to increase their national power, especially their military capabilities. In trying to maximize military potential, adversarial states inevitably enter arms races as each competes for military supremacy. One of the first efforts to systematically examine the dynamics and impact of arms acquisitions between two rival states was carried out by English mathematician Lewis Richardson. In *Arms and Insecurity,* he sets forth a formula for predicting military expenditures for two adversarial states. Two types of action-reaction processes are possible: stable and unstable. If two competing states seek to respond in kind to actions undertaken by an opponent, the interaction is likely to be stable, for an increase in military capabilities and expenditures will lead to similar responses by an enemy state. On the other hand, if the relationship between the two states involves a high level of hostility and distrust, the interaction of the two adversaries is likely to be unstable, involving escalating reactions. For example, if a state believes that it needs military capabilities larger than its adversary's to ensure national security, any increase in the enemy's military capabilities will require a greater increase in its own capabilities, resulting in an escalating arms race that could result in war.

Although Richardson's mathematical insights call attention to the dangers of arms races, his theory does not satisfactorily explain either arms races or war. For one thing, military competition may be due to factors other than an adversary's increasing military capabilities. Three other explanations may account for military competition. First, continued militarization may be due to political and ideological competition among leading states. The large expenditures on and continuous modernization of military capabilities of NATO and Warsaw Pact forces throughout the Cold War era illustrate this view. Second, arms races may derive from conflict over spheres of influence, such as the effort by the Soviet Union to introduce missiles into Cuba in 1962, thereby challenging the historic dominance of the United States in the Western Hemisphere. Third, arms races may be due to domestic political dynamics. Graham Allison, for example, found that the development and procurement of sophisticated weapons, such as a MIRVed ICBMs, required such a long time for planning and development that an arms race could not be attributed to an action-reaction dynamic. Rather, the development and deployment of modern weapons was rooted in domestic bureaucratic politics, not international politics.[59]

Although the "arms race" thesis wisely calls attention to the potentially destabilizing effects of escalating military competition, militarism does not adequately explain war. Just as the existence of oxygen fails to explain fire, or the existence of political freedom fails to explain political unrest, so, too, escalating military expenditures fail to account for war. As James Dougherty and Robert Pfaltzgraff, Jr., have pointed out, it is virtually impossible to show that arms races are a primary cause of war. Weapons permit and facilitate wars, but they are not the sole or even primary source of transnational conflicts.[60] To be sure, arms races contribute to insecurity and instability in international society, but they are not themselves the root cause of global insecurity.

This brief review of war theories suggests that no single factor can fully account for war. As with all major social and political problems, war is rooted in a multiplicity of sources. An adequate explanation for war must therefore take into account the role of individuals, nations, and the international system.

ETHICS AND WAR

War is one of the most challenging moral problems of international politics. Because of the growing destructive potential of military forces, a key ethical issue is whether modern war is legitimate and if so, under what conditions. If war is morally sanctioned, under what constraints may it be waged? To explore the relationship of morality and warfare, we first examine three dominant ethical perspectives on war and then describe the major elements of the just war doctrine, the most important ethical theory of warfare.

Ethical Perspectives on War

Three ethical traditions have dominated the analysis of war: *moral skepticism, pacifism,* and *principled realism.* These three traditions differ in their assumptions of the applicability of moral norms to international politics and in the ethical acceptability of force.

Moral skepticism
The belief that moral principles do not apply directly to international relations.

Moral skepticism, which assumes that survival is the highest norm of global society, asserts that ethical considerations are of little importance to the statesman or the soldier, especially when vital interests are at stake. The statesman's chief responsibility is to maximize the interests and security of the nation, not to promote the well-being of the world or to do that which is considered "right" or "good." If war breaks out, the armed forces must use their power to achieve the desired objectives. According to the skeptical view, morality is silent in wartime.

The ancient historian Thycydides depicts this viewpoint in his classic account of the Athenian aggression against the Spartan colony of Melos. Athens, which had been at war with Sparta, decided that to maintain its regional influence it needed to take control of Melos, as it had done with many of the other surrounding Peloponnesian islands. The Melian citizens, however, refused to surrender, preferring freedom to safety and war to political subjugation. In the end, Melos was conquered by the superior Athenian military forces. Thucydides recorded the Melian defeat as follows: "The Melians surrendered unconditionally to the Athenians, who put to death all the men of military age whom they took, and sold the women and children as slaves. Melos itself they took over for themselves, sending out later a colony of 500 men."[61]

Pacifism, advocated by religious groups like the Mennonites and Quakers and by secular movements espousing the strategy of nonviolence, assumes not only that ethical norms apply to international relations but that violence is immoral. Because life is sacred, states are morally obliged to protect life and to avoid any action that might endanger it. Indeed, the sanctity of life is so significant that violence can never be ethically sanctioned even to protect and promote justice. The prohibition against violence is absolute. The only morally legitimate defense of human life and justice is nonviolent resistance. Thus, war is morally unacceptable not because it fails to bring about justice, but because it is a morally illegitimate instrument.

Pacifism
A tradition that prohibits the use of violence to settle conflicts.

The third tradition, **principled realism** assumes that ethical norms are relevant to interstate relations and that war, although evil, is not the sole or even most important wrong. According to this tradition, sometimes war is justified as a last resort to defend the legitimate rights of individuals and states. States may resort to force to defend themselves from unjust aggression or to participate collectively in punishing aggression committed against another state. The moral problem of war is therefore to define the conditions under which state violence is ethically permissible.

Principled realism
A realist perspective that incorporates and applies moral norms.

Just War Doctrine

One of the most coherent and historically influential approaches to the morality of war is the **just war doctrine,** which has its roots in Greek and Roman philosophy and in the teachings of the early and medieval Christian church. The doctrine, which provides ethical principles for determining when a war can be waged and how it may be carried out, does not seek to justify war but to specify the moral conditions for undertaking a just war, and the means by which the violence of war can be circumscribed. The aim of the just war theory is to bring war under the control of ethical norms so that, if the norms were consistently followed by disputing parties, it would eliminate war altogether. According to the doctrine, war is morally legitimate when it promotes justice between states (international justice) or within nation-states (world justice). When a state carries out unjust aggression against another state, it commits an illegal act, giving the injured state the right to repulse and even punish the attacking state. But in exceptional cases states may also use force to protect people from governmental oppression and from gross human rights violations.

Just war doctrine
A body of moral principles, developed from ancient secular and religious sources, that establishes a framework for judging the justice of going to war and the justice in war.

The just war doctrine is conventionally divided into two parts: the ***jus ad bellum,*** covering the justice of resorting to war, and the ***jus in bello,*** covering justice in war. If a war is to be considered just, it must be ethically acceptable in terms of both elements. A war could be waged for a just cause using immoral means (e.g., killing civilians and torturing war prisoners), whereas a war begun unjustly could be carried out in a just, moral manner. Neither case would be acceptable according to the just war doctrine. The just war doctrine provides a number of principles for ascertaining the justice of resorting to war and the justice of prosecuting a war. (See issue box 11.2.) The role of just war norms in assessing the morality of war is illustrated in case 11.4 on the ethics of the Gulf War.

Jus ad bellum
Just war principles utilized in deciding whether or not to go to war.

Jus in bello
Just war principles relevant to the use of violence in war.

Of all the norms of the just war doctrine, the most fundamental is the first. The justice of resorting to war is the most important norm because the contemporary world system rests on the territorial and political rights of its member-states—rights

Issue 11.2 Principles of the Just War Doctrine

JUS AD BELLUM (war-decision moral law): The following principles must be fulfilled if a war is to be considered morally legitimate:

1. _Just Cause._ The cause of a war must be just. Specifically, the chief moral reason for going to war is to halt injustice, especially unjust aggression.
2. _Last Resort._ All peaceful means must be exhausted before resorting to war. War can be legitimate only when it is the final action taken by states.
3. _Competent Authority._ The use of force is just only if it is carried out by competent governmental authority. Because war must serve a public good, military force can be used only when a government has officially declared and prosecuted war. Violence by private groups or individuals is immoral.
4. _Limited Objectives._ The aims of war must be limited and proportional to the goal of a just peace. The total destruction of society is unacceptable. Unlimited wars are immoral.
5. _Reasonable Hope of Success._ The use of force against an aggressor must have a reasonable chance of success. Good intentions are not enough. There must be a high probability of achieving a just peace by carrying out war. It is immoral to prosecute a war in vain.

JUS IN BELLO (war-conduct moral law): States are morally bound to fight wars in a just manner, following two key principles:

1. _Discrimination._ According to this principle, war should discriminate between combatants and noncombatants, soldiers and civilians. Every effort needs to be made to spare the lives of those who are not bearing arms for the state. Direct attack against civilian targets, such as hospitals, cities, etc., is morally impermissible.
2. _Proportionality._ The means used to achieve victory must be proportionate to the goals being achieved. Destruction and violence carried out by military forces must be justified by the military gain expected from such action. Unlimited destruction is morally unacceptable.

that can be enjoyed only if states respect each other's sovereignty. This is why the principle of nonintervention is one of the pillars of the present international system and a cornerstone of the United Nations. The UN Charter affirms this principle in Article 2.4: "All members shall refrain in their international relations from the threat or use of force against the territorial integrity or political independence of any other state." Thus, because states' territorial rights are basic, the threat or use of force against another state justifies a war of self-defense.

In _Just and Unjust Wars,_ contemporary political theorist Michael Walzer develops a theory of war based on the "domestic analogy"—a comparison of domestic political communities with the international system. According to him, states have rights in the international community just as individuals have rights in domestic society. Among these rights are territorial independence and political sovereignty, and their violation by another state is a criminal act. Any use or imminent threat of military force by one state against another constitutes aggression and justifies the use of force to repulse aggression and to punish an aggressor.[62]

IN CONCLUSION

If states are unable to reconcile their vital interests through peaceful negotiation, they may resort to coercive diplomacy or even force. Although scholars have identified numerous causes of international violence, a fundamental source of war is the inability of states to resolve their incompatible interests through peaceful compromise. While most international wars are undertaken to punish perceived ag-

CASE STUDY

Case 11.4 The Gulf War: Was It Just?

As noted in chapter 4, a U.S.-led coalition of military forces began a massive month-long bombing campaign against Iraq on January 16, 1991. The air campaign was followed by a four-day land assault resulting in the liberation of Kuwait. Was the resort to military force morally justified, and was the war prosecuted in a moral manner? Was the Gulf War, in other words, consistent with the major principles of the just war doctrine?[63]

After Iraq invaded Kuwait, a broad international consensus emerged that Iraq's action was illegal and unjust, providing allies with a *just cause* to liberate Kuwait. As moral theorist James Turner Johnson has noted, Iraq's intervention "was as clear and unambiguous a case as one could hope to find in the real world, and the brazeness of Iraq's action remained on public display even as the international community tried to expel the Iraqis through a variety of non-military means."[64]

The U.S.-led military liberation was also consistent with the norm of *competent authority*. The resort to force was not only carried out by legitimate governmental authorities but was sanctioned by the United Nations Security Council. In fact, in the forty-five-year history of the UN, never had the major powers achieved so much unanimity over the use of collective force as in this conflict.

The resort to force was also in accord with the *last resort* principle. The problem in applying this norm is that, as political theorist Michael Walzer has observed, there is no moral theory providing guidance for its application.[65] As a result, the decision to use force will ultimately depend on military and political judgment, and here theologians and moral philosophers have no special competence. Because the major powers had attempted individually and collectively to resolve the dispute peacefully during the six-month interregnum between Iraq's invasion and the allied military operation, it is doubtful that additional time would have led to a peaceful resolution of the conflict.

Note that the most significant moral opposition to the Gulf War came from political and religious leaders who believed that nonmilitary options had not been exhausted by early January. According to them, more time was needed to allow the UN-imposed sanctions to work. But those that defended sanctions were themselves unaware that a siege—one of the oldest and most destructive forms of warfare—is fundamentally at odds with the just war doctrine because it fails to discriminate between combatants and civilians.

During the war, allied forces made every effort to discriminate between military and civilian targets. Two factors contributed to the successful application of the **discrimination norm**: first, the United States used highly sophisticated weapons, including cruise missiles and laser-guided "smart bombs," to limit civilian destruction; and second, bombs were dropped only when targets could be seen. As a result, of the 50,000 to 100,000 Iraqis killed in the war, only a small percentage were civilians.

For a number of theorists and critics, the most troubling aspect of the Gulf War, from the just war perspective, was the issue of proportionality. According to the **proportionality norm**, the evil resulting from war must be commensurate to the good (justice) achieved by it. But how can one ascertain the value of political independence or, more particularly, of the liberation of Kuwait? Is it worth 1,000, 2,000, 5,000, or even 100,000 lives? Like the norm of last resort, proportionality ultimately involves a prudential judgment between means and ends, between the good expected by the war and the evil inflicted by force. Some, like international relations scholar Robert Tucker,[66] argue that the Gulf War was disproportionate because of the large number of Iraqis killed relative to allied deaths. But proportionality does not pertain to the relationship between combatants but to the relation between the end and means of war.

gression or to compel an adversary to alter its foreign policy behavior, wars can also result from transnational, systemic developments that result in a perceived loss of national power or an increase in territorial insecurity. Indeed, some wars are the byproduct of leaders' misperceptions, unrealistic expectations and passions, and can lead to senseless military conflicts, such as World War I and the Iran-Iraq war. Finally, some wars result from domestic political disputes. Such intranational conflicts may result from demands for increased self-determination by ethnic, religious, and political groups, as well as from demands by political groups seeking to transform a political regime.

Although every effort needs to be made to resolve disputes peacefully, not all wars are morally equivalent. Purposive wars involving the defense of sovereignty, the reclaiming of lost territory, the protection of human rights, or the punishment of wrongdoing have much more legitimacy than senseless, nonpurposive wars such as the Iran-Iraq war. Even though war always involves some evil, the pursuit of peace and justice may justify, in the final analysis, the use of force in order to promote a stable, more humane regime, or to defend nations from unjust foreign policies. The challenge, however, is to promote peace and justice in the international community through peaceful accommodation, utilizing force or the threat of force only in exceptional circumstances.

SUMMARY

1. Although warfare is as old as human civilization, modern war dates from the beginning of the nation-state system in the mid-seventeenth century. Two major types of war have been common in global society: international wars among states and intranational wars.

2. In light of the different means and ends of war, three major types of war have been prevalent in the international system over the past three and a half centuries. These wars are defined as classical, total, and postmodern. Classical wars involve military conflicts using limited force to settle disputes between states. Total wars are international conflicts involving unlimited violence in the pursuit of unconditional defeat of the enemy. Postmodern wars involve intranational conflicts based on the creation, consolidation, or transformation of states.

3. As nation-states became more powerful in the eighteenth and nineteenth centuries, war became increasingly institutionalized and accepted as the ultimate means of settling interstate disputes. Even though international wars have become less frequent during the past five centuries, they have become much more destructive.

4. War in the post–Cold War era has become increasingly prevalent in weak and failed states. Such wars are carried out not to resolve interstate disputes but to topple, reform, or divide existing regimes. Because of the growing frequency of intranational wars, domestic conflicts are an increasingly important dimension of global politics.

5. Three major factors help to explain war—the individual, the nation-state, and international society. From the perspective of the individual, wars occur because of human nature, misperception of rulers, the nature of leadership, and leaders' perceived gains from war. From the perspective of the nation-state, wars occur because of militarism, economic exploitation, undemocratic governments, and nationalistic passions. From the perspective of global society, wars occur because of arms races, power disparities, and shifts in international power.

6. There are three major ethical traditions on war: skepticism, pacifism, and principled realism. The first assumes that war is an activity divorced from ethics; the second assumes that ethics is fundamentally opposed to war; and the third assumes that war is subject to moral rules.

7. The major expression of principled realism is the just war doctrine, which consists of principles for judging both the resort to war (*jus ad bellum*) and the conduct of war (*jus in bello*).

KEY TERMS

intranational war
international war
classical wars
total war
postmodern wars
expected utility of war
theory

monopoly capitalism
military-industrial complex
separatist war
irredentist war
hegemonic stability theory
power transition theory

preventive war
long-cycle theory
moral skepticism
pacifism
principled realism

just war doctrine
jus ad bellum
jus in bello
discrimination norm
proportionality norm

RECOMMENDED READINGS

Clausewitz, Carl von. *On War.* Trans. by Michael Howard and Peter Paret. Princeton: Princeton University Press, 1976. A classic study of the nature and logic of war by a nineteenth-century Prussian author and military officer.

Creveld, Martin van. *The Transformation of War.* New York: The Free Press, 1991. A historical and theoretical analysis of the goals, rules, and strategies of war. Creveld argues that low-intensity conflict has displaced conventional war as the major manifestation of force in contemporary global politics. As a result, Clausewitzian strategic analysis—based on the "trinity" of the people, the army, and the government—is no longer applicable to modern war.

Gilpin, Robert. *War and Change in World Politics.* Cambridge: Cambridge University Press, 1981. A penetrating and provocative study of how major war is both a cause and consequence of economic growth and decay.

Johnson, James Turner. *Can Modern War Be Just?* New Haven: Yale University Press, 1984. Relying on the historic and widely accepted just war doctrine, Johnson shows how moral principles can guide reasoning about nuclear weapons and strategic policy. Despite the difficulty of the subject matter, this is a clear, readable study.

Kagan, Donald. *On the Origins of War and the Preservation of Peace.* New York: Doubleday, 1995. Kagan, a distinguished classical historian, argues that peace is best achieved through the management of power. After examining four wars (the Peloponnesian War, the Second Punic War, the First World War, and the Second World War) and one crisis (the Cuban missile crisis), Kagan concludes that "the preservation of peace requires active effort, planning, the expenditure of resources, and sacrifice, just as war does."

Keegan, John. *A History of Warfare.* New York: Alfred A. Knopf, 1993. Keegan, a noted British military historian, argues that war is not the continuation of policy by other means, as Clausewitz had contended. Rather, war making is a learned activity with its own inner logic—a habit developed from 4,000 years of experimentation and repetition. A significant anthropological interpretation of the development and evolution of war.

Porter, Bruce D. *War and the Rise of the State: The Military Foundations of Modern Politics.* New York: The Free Press, 1994. A study of the impact of domestic and international wars of societies, states, and the international system itself. According to Porter, some of the important integrative effects of war include the expansion of nationalism, increased state unity, social reform, and governmental expansion; some of the major disintegrative developments include wartime destruction, revolution, and economic hardship.

Russett, Bruce. *Controlling the Sword: The Democratic Governance of National Security.* Cambridge: Harvard University Press, 1990. A study of the domestic politics of national security policy in representative regimes. Chapter 5 provides a lucid analysis of the relationship of democratic structures and war.

Small, Melvin, and J. David Singer, eds. *International War: An Anthology and Study Guide.* Homewood, Ill.: Dorsey Press, 1985. An informative collection of readings on the history, sociology, causes, and prevention of war by two leading scholars of the subject.

Stoessinger, John G. *Why Nations Go to War.* 4th ed. New York: St. Martin's Press, 1985. Using twentieth-century case studies, the author argues that wars are ultimately caused by leaders' misperception. Some of the wars examined include World War I, World War II, Korea, Vietnam, India-Pakistan, and Israel-Arab states.

Vasquez, John A. *The War Puzzle.* Cambridge: Cambridge University Press, 1993. Using empirical findings of the past twenty-five years, this study describes factors that give rise to territorial wars among states of relative equality. The study suggests that a foreign policy based on power politics is likely to encourage, rather than limit war. Vasquez also argues that wars are typically enlarged through alliances, territorial contiguity, and rivalry.

Waltz, Kenneth N. *Man, the State, and War: A Theoretical Analysis.* New York: Columbia University Press, 1959. Using the ideas of classical political philosophy, Waltz argues that wars occur because of the nature of people, the behavior and organization of states, and the decentralized nature of international society. A classic.

Walzer, Michael. *Just and Unjust Wars: A Moral Argument with Historical Illustrations.* New York: Basic Book, 1977. A powerful and penetrating study of how morality applies to force in world politics. By using numerous case studies, Walzer shows the limits and possibilities of moral reasoning on some of the most intractable problems in world affairs.

Welch, David A. *Justice and the Genesis of War.* Cambridge: Cambridge University Press, 1993. Examines the role of the justice motive in the outbreak of five great power wars—the Crimean War, the Franco-Prussian War, World War I, World War II, and the Falklands War—and finds that the demands of justice played an important role in the genesis of conflict. An important study that challenges the prevailing realist notion that wars are solely a by-product of conflicting national interests.

Wright, Quincy. *A Study of War.* Abridged ed. Chicago: University of Chicago Press, 1969. This edited version of the classic study on war includes all materials of the unabridged version except for the extensive statistical appendices.

RELEVANT WEB SITES

Fletcher School of Law and Diplomacy Database: Rules of War

www.TUFTS.EDU/fletcher/multilaterals.html

Stockholm International Peace Research Institute (SIPRI)

www.sipri.se/

U.S. Arms Control and Disarmament Agency (ACDA)

www.acda.gov

CHAPTER

Diplomacy: Promoting Cooperation and Conflict Management

An Ambassador is an honest man sent to lie abroad for the good of his country.[1]

Sir Henry Wooten, *seventeenth-century British diplomat*

Intellectuals analyze the operations of international systems; statesmen build them. . . . The analyst has available to him all the facts; he will be judged on his intellectual power. The statesman must act on assessments that cannot be proved at the time that he is making them; he will be judged by history on the basis of how wisely he managed the inevitable change and, above all, by how well he preserves the peace.[2]

Henry Kissinger, *U.S. Secretary of State and scholar*

Diplomacy must be judged by what it prevents, not only by what it achieves.[3]

Abba Eban, *former Israeli prime minister*

On February 5, 1995 the U.S. government announced the imposition of one billion dollars in economic tariffs on selected Chinese goods. The sanctions, the largest economic penalties ever imposed by the United States on another country, were instituted because of China's deliberate piracy of U.S. software, music recordings, and film. At the time that sanctions were announced, officials estimated that some twenty-nine Chinese factories, some of them state-owned, were illegally making more than 70 million copies of compact disks and video-disks per year.[4] Because these firms were duplicating patented and copyrighted materials without licenses, China was, in effect, stealing billions of dollars of intellectual property from U.S. firms and artists. Thus, after failing to heed threats from U.S. negotiators, Mickey Kantor, the U.S. trade representative at the time, announced the imposition of economic sanctions on a carefully selected list of goods that included plastic products, footwear, apparel, cellular telephones, and bicycles. Although China is a major exporter of toys and electronic equipment, these goods were exempted because U.S. officials believed that their inclusion would unnecessarily harm retailers and anger consumers.

As is frequently the case, the imposition of sanctions was delayed for three weeks in order to exempt goods shipped before the announcement was made. More importantly, however, the delay provided a final opportunity for negotiators to resolve the dispute. Partly in response to the threatened sanctions, Chinese and U.S. officials continued negotiations and reached a settlement on February 27, ten hours past the sanctions deadline. Based on the accord, China agreed to embark on an intensive crackdown of the illegal production of software, music recordings, and film.[5] Because the imposition of economic sanctions could have resulted in a bitter trade war involving more than $45 billion in goods and services, the negotiated accord was an important development for both countries.

Frequently international disputes involve issues much more important than the piracy of intellectual property. When conflicts involve vital national security issues, the stakes in negotiations are much higher, and the failure to resolve harmoniously such disputes through negotiation can lead to costly and destructive outcomes, including war. The high cost of the failure of diplomatic negotiation is illustrated by the tragic failure of Iraq and Kuwait to resolve their territorial dispute peacefully. As a result, Iraq invaded the little country in 1990, toppling its hereditary government and setting up a puppet regime. Subsequently, the United Nations demanded that Iraq withdraw from Kuwait. After failing to comply with UN demands and, more particularly, to U.S. diplomatic initiatives, allied military forces, led by the United States, carried out a massive month-long bombing campaign, followed by a four-day ground battle that resulted in Iraq's defeat. Although Saddam gained temporary control of Kuwait and increased his reputation for power, in the end his country was fragmented territorially and weakened economically and militarily and has been vulnerable to various forms of international intervention.

The U.S.-China trade dispute and the Iraq-Kuwait conflict point to the importance of reconciling conflicting interstate interests peacefully through diplomatic negotiation. Because international conflict is an inevitable by-product of global politics, a central task of public officials concerned with foreign affairs is to manage and resolve such clashes of interest in the most efficient and peaceful manner possible. Whether the international disputes involve territorial, economic, political, or symbolic issues, the pacific resolution of international tensions and conflicts is a central task of public officials.

This chapter will examine the nature and role of diplomatic negotiation in the contemporary global political community. More specifically, the chapter (1) examines important elements of diplomacy and diplomatic practices, highlighting key features of modern diplomacy; (2) discusses the role and function of contemporary diplomats; (3) analyzes the role of peaceful negotiation in the contemporary world; (4) sets forth principles for successful negotiation; and (5) explores the role of third-party conflict resolution.

THE NATURE OF DIPLOMACY

Definition

Diplomacy is defined in a variety of ways. Some, like Elmer Plischke, define diplomacy as the political process by which states carry out official relations with one another.[6] Others, like British diplomat Harold Nicolson, define diplomacy more restrictively as the management of international relations through peaceful negotiation.[7] Building on Nicolson's and Plischke's conceptions, we define **diplomacy** as *the process by which states and other international actors pursue official international relations, reconciling competing and conflicting interests through peaceful means.*

Diplomacy
The process by which states and other international actors pursue peaceful international relations, reconciling competing and conflicting interest through negotiations.

Diplomacy is not synonymous with statecraft. Earlier we defined the latter as the process by which states make and implement foreign policies. Statecraft is essentially concerned with foreign policy making. Diplomacy, by contrast, involves the peaceful pursuit of foreign policy through negotiation. Moreover, whereas statecraft is the responsibility of elected government officials, diplomacy is the responsibility of a trained cadre of professionals.

The process of diplomacy involves a number of elements. First, diplomacy concerns the *official international relations* of states. It focuses on government-to-government communication and interaction. As noted earlier, in addition to interstate relations, international relations are carried out at two other levels—between or among state and nonstate actors and between or among nonstate actors themselves. Although transnational communication and interaction at these two other levels can foster global cooperation, we are primarily concerned here with the first level of interactions. Thus our focus here is on the role of diplomats, the government officials charged with defending and promoting states' interests within the global system, hopefully promoting cooperation rather than increasing conflict.

Second, diplomacy involves *communication* among states. One of the important tasks of diplomacy is to encourage transnational understanding, ensuring that government officials accurately perceive the behaviors of other states and clearly articulate their own intentions and goals. Harold Nicolson has observed that although diplomacy entails international communication, it is not simply the "art of conversation," but rather "the art of negotiating agreements in precise and ratifiable forms" based on effective communication.[8]

Third, diplomacy involves *peaceful* bargaining. Because conflict is inevitable among states, a major goal of diplomacy is the nonviolent resolution of disputes. Because of the importance of resolving conflict peacefully, diplomacy and peaceful negotiation are often regarded as synonymous. But although diplomatic negotiation is most evident in peacetime, bargaining is an ongoing process, whether in periods of peace, heightened tensions, or even war. Even though most bargaining is carried out peacefully, it frequently relies on a variety of sanctions, including the threat of force and war itself. For this reason, international relations cannot be divided simply between conditions of peace and war; as noted in chapter 10 most international relations are found along a continuum between these two extremes.

Fourth, diplomacy involves *mutual decision making*. As a form of transaction, diplomacy cannot be undertaken in isolation. It requires the mutual cooperation of two or more states. As a former U.S. diplomat has observed, negotiation involves "shared decision making on a shared problem."[9]

Fifth, because diplomacy is essentially international communication, it is a *continuous process,* whether it involves explicit interaction between diplomats or implicit signaling by governments. Cardinal Richelieu, who served as key emissary for King Louis XIII of France, was one of the first diplomats to call attention to the need for ongoing negotiations between states. In his *Political Testament,* Richelieu wrote:

> States receive so much benefit from uninterrupted foreign negotiations. . . . I am now so convinced of its validity that I dare say emphatically that it is absolutely necessary to the well-being of the state to negotiate ceaselessly, either openly or secretly, and in all places, even in those from which no present fruits are reaped and still more in those for which no future prospects as yet seem likely.[10]

The Evolution of Diplomacy

Origins

Diplomacy, being a human activity, is probably as old as civilization itself. Its origins are found in antiquity in the ordered communication and interaction between political communities. In ancient times, for example, tribes and other primitive political communities selected emissaries to conduct negotiations on their behalf and in some instances to serve as hostages to good faith. And during the era of the Greek city-states (fifth to second centuries, B.C.), the role of diplomacy increased in scope and sophistication as political leaders began to send representatives, grant diplomatic immunities, manage and resolve conflict, and form alliances. In his account of the Peloponnesian War (431–404 B.C.), Thucydides describes in detail diplomatic practices and procedures used by Greek city-states. He details, for example, how the Spartans called a diplomatic conference in 432 B.C. to decide whether Athens had violated its treaties and whether it should be punished by war. After hearing long speeches from Athenian representatives, the Spartan Assembly voted to declare war.

The origin of formal diplomacy dates from the fifteenth century, when Italian city-states began sending permanent representatives to other cities. Because of intense rivalry between the city-states, major cities began establishing permanent diplomatic missions to facilitate communication and negotiation. It is believed that the city of Milan originated the practice of sending permanent diplomatic representatives in 1450. Another important development in the evolution of diplomacy was the appointment of distinguished individuals, such as Dante, Petrarch, and Machiavelli, to serve as temporary or permanent emissaries of city-states.

During the seventeenth century, diplomacy gained further significance as the newly formed European states began to maintain continuous communication and interaction with each other through a cadre of appointed diplomatic emissaries. But the diplomats of the seventeenth and early eighteenth centuries were not part of a cadre of professionals, but a group of distinguished persons who offered their personal services to rulers. The rise of diplomacy as a professional vocation began to take shape in the early nineteenth century, partly in response to the rise of democratic sentiments in Europe and America and the growing involvement of the general public in governmental affairs. The diplomatic corps, however, was unequivocally elitist, as befits a profession. At the Congress of Vienna (1815), European representatives agreed to conventions that formalized the structure of diplomatic ranks and accepted longevity in the host state as the basis of **diplomatic precedence.** The convention on diplomatic precedence meant that the seniority of diplomats in a particular state was to be determined on the basis of length of continuous service in the host country, not on its wealth or power. Although both conventions have been refined, the principles established in the early nineteenth century on diplomatic ranks and precedence are still effective today.

Diplomatic precedence
A tradition that the seniority of diplomats in a particular state is determined on the basis of continuous service in the host state.

Traditional Diplomacy

The nineteenth century is generally considered the era of classical diplomacy. During this time there were relatively few states, power was centered in Europe, and a small group of European states (France, Britain, Russia, Prussia, and Austria) dominated diplomatic affairs. Moreover, despite the emergence of popular, democratic sentiments in America and Europe, business, political, and religious elites continued to dominate government. Not surprisingly, officials in the diplomatic corps tended to reflect the elitist character of the governments they served.

Three features characterized nineteenth-century diplomacy—formality, flexibility, and secrecy. Diplomatic formality, which was expressed stylistically in protocol and substantively in negotiating procedures, was due to the aristocratic character of governments and to the important political role played by diplomats. Because ambassadors served as personal representatives of sovereigns, they were granted significant privileges and immunities along with special honors.

The second characteristic of traditional diplomacy, flexibility, resulted from the significant authority diplomatic emissaries enjoyed. Because international travel and communication was slow and at times difficult, diplomats were given significant responsibility and latitude to negotiate on behalf of their governments.

The third feature of traditional diplomacy, secrecy, was facilitated by the small, aristocratic, and elitist character of nineteenth-century international relations. Because governmental responsibilities were entrusted to a relatively small group of persons, the maintenance of confidentiality within and between governments was comparatively easy to maintain.

The Rise of "New" Diplomacy

Toward the end of the nineteenth century, as nationalism and democracy began to spread throughout the international system, a new form of diplomacy began to emerge. This "new" diplomacy sought to respond to the rise in the number of states, the increased impact of public opinion in foreign affairs, and the growing dispersion of power, and in particular, the rising influence of parliaments within democratic governments.

In contrast to the "old" diplomacy of the nineteenth century, the "new" diplomacy was characterized by greater openness, increased emphasis on international law as a tool for regulating conflict, and increased international participation on the basis of legal equality. The call for public diplomacy received its greatest impetus in the early twentieth century from President Woodrow Wilson, who pleaded for an end to secret diplomacy and for the institution of "open covenants openly arrived at." According to Wilson, because war was largely a by-product of irresponsible, dictatorial governments, the promotion of democratic practices was essential to world peace. Reliance on public opinion was the road to global harmony. In order to avoid the misuse of power, Wilson argued that international negotiations should be public and open. Unfortunately for him, in his attempt to achieve a viable peace, he did not practice what he preached at the Paris Peace Conference ending World War I.

The second distinctive feature of the "new" diplomacy was an emphasis on international law. Given the ferocity of World War I, proponents of the "new" diplomacy assumed that peace could not be achieved by balancing power but by developing an institutional framework in which aggression would be punished collectively by peace-loving states. Instead of relying on bilateral negotiations, they advocated the creation of binding international legal commitments. The ineffectual Kellogg-Briand Pact of 1928, which "outlawed" war, best illustrates this faith in legalism.

Finally, the "new" diplomacy was characterized by an emphasis on universality. The Hague Peace Conventions of 1899 and 1907, which brought together diplomatic representatives from more than thirty states, represented the first major effort at universal political cooperation. The conferences were concerned with developing conflict-resolution measures and codifying rules of war. Although they were successful in this regard, the real achievement of the conferences was the development of international cooperation and coordination, which would greatly assist in the creation of the League of Nations in 1919.

Harold Nicolson has suggested that the diplomatic innovations of the twentieth century have been detrimental to the process of negotiation. According to him, the ideal diplomacy is one in which international relations are carried out by professionals who exhibit such virtues as truthfulness, calmness, patience, modesty, and loyalty.[11] Because effective negotiation requires flexibility, Nicolson argues that confidentiality is indispensable to diplomacy. The shift towards open, parliamentary diplomacy is therefore counterproductive and harmful to the settlement of international disputes. Nicolson pleads for a return to secret, flexible diplomacy practiced by a highly trained corps of intelligent, tactful, and skilled professionals.

Contemporary Diplomacy

Modern diplomacy, which dates from the end of World War II, represents the continuation and further development of "new" diplomacy. Three key features of modern diplomacy are (1) the centralization of foreign policy decision making, (2) the rise of summit diplomacy, and (3) the expansion of multilateralism.

Centralized Decision Making A major characteristic of modern diplomacy is the increasing centralization of foreign policy decision making in the home state. This development is due in great part to major technological revolutions that have transformed global communications and transportation. Because of the development of satellites, computers, fax machines, and the like, embassies are now able to maintain instantaneous, secure communication with the home foreign ministry. Moreover, because of the development and proliferation of modern jet aircraft, diplomatic personnel can now travel easily and rapidly between the home country and foreign states. As a result of the increasing efficiency of global communications and international travel, major decision making has shifted from the embassy toward the home office. Rather than serving as a major foreign policy decision maker, the ambassador increasingly serves as an administrator of a complex bureaucracy and multifaceted overseas mission. Diplomats are increasingly limited to representation and reporting, with negotiation becoming an infrequent ambassadorial responsibility.

Summits
Face-to-face negotiations among leaders of major states.

Summit Diplomacy Modern diplomacy is also characterized by **summits**—periodic face-to-face negotiation between government leaders. The rationale for summits is to provide, first, an environment in which political leaders can meet directly to better understand each other and their respective political and economic national interests, and second, a forum for cultivating shared goals and reconciling conflicting aims.

Although monarchs practiced summitry in the eighteenth and nineteenth centuries, the modern era has dramatically increased the frequency and significance of this type of diplomacy. The first contemporary efforts at summitry were made by the allied powers during World War II at Tehran (November 1943) and Yalta (February 1945). At these meetings British Prime Minister Winston Churchill, Soviet leader Joseph Stalin, and U.S. President Franklin D. Roosevelt met to discuss common military and strategic interests as well as the division of Germany after the conclusion of the war. And at Potsdam (July 1945) Joseph Stalin met with Clement Attlee and Harry Truman, the new leaders of Britain and the United States, to discuss territorial boundaries of the defeated states. But the development and widespread acceptance of summit diplomacy did not come until the mid-1950s during the heightened tensions of the Cold War between the United States and the Soviet Union.

Two major types of summit diplomacy have been practiced in the contemporary era: superpower summits and economic summits. As the name implies, **superpower summits** involve direct discussions and negotiations between the heads of state of the two major powers—the United States and the Soviet Union. These summits originated in the mid-1950s in order to foster greater understanding and cooperation between the dominant military and ideological rivals of the world. The first summit was held in Geneva in 1955 and focused on German reunification and the general easing of East-West tensions; during the remaining years of the Cold War, nineteen other summits were held. Some of the most significant of these are listed in table 12.1. Although Cold War superpower summits covered a variety of political, economic, and military issues, the most frequent topic was nuclear arms control.[12] Indeed, the summits provided a forum for concluding arms control negotiations that resulted in such accords as the Strategic Arms Limitations Talks (SALT) I, the Anti-Ballistic Missile (ABM) Treaty, SALT II, and the Intermediate Nuclear Forces (INF) Treaty. Since the collapse of the Soviet Union in 1991, the United States and Russia have continued to hold periodic summits. Although these summits have been held frequently (nine were held during the 1992–1996 period), they are less important than those of the Cold War era, not only because Russia does not have the power and influence of the former Soviet Union but also because the two states are not involved in a bitter ideological and military rivalry.

Superpower summits
Face-to-face Cold War negotiations between the heads of the two superpowers, the United States and the Soviet Union.

Economic summits
Annual face-to-face negotiations among the heads of state of the major industrial powers.

Economic summits seek to promote economic cooperation and to coordinate international economic policies among the leading industrialized states. Economic summits—also known as the *Group of 7 (G-7)*—involve the heads of government of Canada, France, Germany, Britain, Italy, Japan, and United States. In 1997 Russia was admitted into the economic summit, thereby transforming the G-7 into ***Group of Eight (G-8).*** Russia will remain a qualified member of the summit, however, until it consolidates its economic transformation to a free enterprise economy and until it is admitted into the World Trade Organization (WTO).

Group of Eight (G-8)
An alliance of the world's seven leading industrial democratic countries (Britain, Canada, France, Germany, Italy, Japan, and the United States), plus Russia.

TABLE 12.1 Selective Cold War Superpower Summits, 1955–1991

Date and Place	Leaders	Key Issues
July 1955 *Geneva*	Eisenhower, Khrushchev, Bulganin	East-West relations, German reunification
September 1959 *Camp David*	Eisenhower, Khrushchev	Disarmament, scientific exchanges
May 1960 *Paris*	Eisenhower, Khrushchev	East-West tensions, Berlin (cut short because of U-2 spy plane incident)
June 1961 *Vienna*	Kennedy, Khrushchev	Berlin and Laos
May 1972 *Moscow*	Nixon, Brezhnev	Arms control (SALT I and ABM Treaty)
August 1975 *Helsinki*	Ford, Brezhnev	SALT II, European security
June 1979 *Vienna*	Carter, Brezhnev	Signing of SALT II accord
November 1985 *Geneva*	Reagan, Gorbachev	Nuclear arms reductions, strategic defense
October 1986 *Reykjavik, Iceland*	Reagan, Gorbachev	Nuclear arms reductions, strategic defense
December 1987 *Washington, D.C.*	Reagan, Gorbachev	Signing INF Treaty, Central America, human rights
June 1990 *Washington, D.C.*	Bush, Gorbachev	Proclaim end of Cold War, German reunification, European security
July 1991 *Moscow*	Bush, Gorbachev	Signing of START I Treaty, U.S.-Soviet economic relations

The G-8, which meets annually in late spring or early summer, is supported by periodic meetings of finance ministers and central bank governors in order to coordinate and implement established policies. Although the economic summits have covered a wide-range of issues, the dominant concern of the G-8 has been economic prosperity, coupled with monetary stability and low unemployment (see table 12.2). Since the end of the Cold War, the G-8 has emphasized the integration of Russia and other former Soviet-dominated countries into the global economy and the encouragement of privatization and market-based reforms.

The popularity of summitry is a direct result of the growing belief that face-to-face dialogue is conducive to better international relations. According to this view, direct communication not only provides a means for increasing awareness about the interests of other states, but also facilitates better understanding about the possibilities and constraints of other countries' foreign policies. More than any other contemporary head of state, President George Bush relied heavily on personal diplomacy, using the telephone to keep in touch regularly with leading political figures. For example, during the Iraq-Kuwait conflict, he used direct telephone communications with other heads of state to gain their support in opposing Iraq's conquest of Kuwait.

There are both advantages and disadvantages to summit diplomacy. On the positive side, summits: (1) provide a forum for broadening understanding about issues, especially those on which states have opposing positions; (2) provide an opportunity for leaders to become personally acquainted and to develop a greater appreciation for the constraints under which they work within their respective

TABLE 12.2 Western Economic Summits, 1986–1998

Date and Place	Major Issues	Declarations
May 1986 Tokyo	Trade liberalization, global environment	Reform agricultural trade policies, promote open trade, cooperate in combating terrorism
June 1987 Venice	Third world debt, U.S. deficit, East-West economic relations	Maintain stable dollar, promote agricultural trade liberalization
June 1988 Toronto	Third World debt, trade, global environment	Third World debt relief, support further trade liberalization
July 1989 Paris	Eastern Europe, Third World debt, global environment	Condemn Tiananmen Square massacre, economic aid for Poland and Hungary
July 1990 Houston	East-West ties, economic aid to Eastern Europe	Endorse Brady debt relief plan, support market reform in Eastern Europe
July 1991 London	East-West economic ties, Soviet economy	USSR given special ties with IMF and IBRD, Soviet market reforms encouraged
July 1992 Munich	U.S.-EC trade, financial aid to Russia, civil war in Bosnia	Warn Serbia of possible UN armed action, increase aid to Russia
July 1993 Tokyo	Trade and job creation, the management of trade	Trade liberalization, increase aid to Russia, U.S.-Japan trade accord
July 1994 Naples	Trade and job creation	Ratify new GATT accord, aid to Ukraine, support Bosnian peace initiatives
June 1995 Halifax	Bosnia and global trade	Call for further trade liberalization and stabilization of financial markets
June 1996 Lyons	Terrorism, Bosnia, UN budget	Adopted multilateral antiterrorist plan, states promise to meet UN obligations
June 1997 Denver	Global warming, peace process, aid to Africa	Call for democratic elections in Hong Kong and continuing peace initiatives in the Middle East
May 1998 Birmingham	Nuclear testing, East Asian economic problems	Criticized India for carrying out nuclear tests and expressed concern for breakdown of law and order in Indonesia

states; (3) help to highlight areas of common concern and to increase coordination in political and nonpolitical areas; and (4) occasionally help to bring about crucial diplomatic concessions that result in agreements. The positive aspects of summits were especially evident in the superpower summits during the late 1980s, when Presidents Reagan and Bush were able to develop close and productive working relationships with Soviet leader Mikhail Gorbachev.

Summits also pose dangers. Some of these include: (1) the temptation to make unwarranted concessions because of the general public's high expectations of summit diplomacy; (2) the making of unwise declarations and choices because of inadequate opportunity to assess decision-making implications; and (3) the failure to negotiate effectively because of leaders' ineffective face-to-face negotiating skills or because of lack of foreign affairs expertise.

The dangers of summitry are illustrated by the negotiations at Reykjavik Summit in 1986. At that summit President Reagan put forward a proposal to ban all ballistic missiles within ten years and to reduce strategic warheads from existing levels (about 11,000) to a ceiling of 6,000. Although reduction in strategic weapons had been a major aim of the Reagan government, the "breathtaking" proposal caught most American officials by surprise. When the Soviet Union countered that it would accept the proposal only on the condition that the United States halt its strategic defense program, Reagan balked. In retrospect, many defense experts think that Reagan's offer to ban ballistic missiles was unwise, because the initiative had not been examined thoroughly beforehand. One former secretary of defense noted that the president offered to alter the strategy of nuclear deterrence, the foundation of the Western alliance's thirty-year-old strategy, without even consulting the Congress, European allies, or defense (including U.S. Joint Chiefs of Staff) and foreign policy experts within the U.S. government.[13] Not surprisingly, most European leaders and U.S. strategic planners were greatly relieved when the Soviet Union refused to accept the radical reductions in strategic weapons without the halt in the strategic defense program.

Increased Multilateralism Finally, modern diplomacy is characterized by its multilateral character. **Multilateral diplomacy,** which involves joint negotiation between three or more states, is normally carried out within formal organizations, such as UN agencies, the Arab League, the Organization of American States, and informal contexts, such as the mid-1980s peace negotiations among Central American states and the peace negotiations over the fate of Bosnia-Herzegovina in 1992–1993. Such multilateralism also includes large plenary conferences and summits that involve widespread participation by governments and relevant NGOs. Examples of such *parliamentary diplomacy* include recent global summits such as the 1992 Earth Summit in Rio de Janeiro, the 1994 Population Conference in Cairo, the 1995 Social Summit in Copenhagen (see case 12.1), and the 1995 Conference on Women in Beijing. Because such conferences involve thousands of official delegates and carry out their work in open, plenary session, such meetings do not permit significant diplomatic negotiation. Rather, they serve as public relations events, highlighting important international concerns and ratifying by consensus documents that have been prepared beforehand.

Three factors have contributed to the expansion of multilateralism. First, the proliferation of international government organizations (IGOs) has stimulated the growth of multilateral diplomacy. As the number of universal, regional, and specialized IGOs has increased in the postwar years, so has the volume of multilateral negotiation. Examples of multilateral negotiation include the UN Economic Commission for Latin

Multilateral diplomacy
Diplomatic discussions and negotiations among three or more nations, such as the G–8 or specialized UN-sponsored conferences.

Serbian President Slobodan Milosevic (left), Bosnian President Alija Izetbegovic (center), and Croatian President Franjo Tudjman (right) sign the Dayton Peace Accords at Wright-Patterson Air Force Base in Dayton, Ohio. The November 1995 peace agreement brought an end to the Bosnian war.

Case 12.1 The 1995 Social Summit

The World Summit for Social Development, held in Copenhagen in March 1995, was one of the largest UN-sponsored conferences ever held. A total of 187 states participated, including 110 heads of state, along with thousands of delegates from some 2,000 nongovernmental organizations. The event was covered by some 2,500 media representatives from around the world.

After five days of deliberation, conference delegates adopted the Copenhagen Declaration and Programme of Action. The declaration declared in part: "We share the conviction that social development and social justice are indispensable for the achievement and maintenance of peace and security within and among our nations. In turn, social development and social justice cannot be attained in the absence of peace and security or in the absence of respect for all human rights and fundamental freedoms. We are deeply convinced that economic development, social development and environmental protection are interdependent and mutually reinforcing components of sustainable development, which is the framework for our efforts to achieve a higher quality of life for all people."[14]

The declaration specifies ten goals that governments, international organizations, and nongovernmental organizations (NGOs) should pursue. These include the eradication of poverty, the promotion of human dignity, the fostering of full employment, the promotion of social integration, and the expansion of health care and educational opportunities. The Programme of Action recommends actions that will foster social development and help promote the specific goals of poverty eradication, increased employment opportunities, and enhanced social integration.

The Social Summit is also noteworthy for the priority assigned to NGOs. Never before had a major international conference stressed the importance of NGOs in promoting common goals. Indeed, the declaration describes the role of NGOs as "essential," while many of the plenary speeches stressed the vital role of such institutions in bringing about economic prosperity, social development, and a more humane world. UN Secretary-General Boutros-Ghali called NGOs a catalyst between the UN and the nations of the world.[15]

Because the conference documents are not binding on states, the results of the Social Summit are chiefly symbolic rather than substantive. Unlike the 1992 Earth Summit, which resulted in two conventions (one on climate and another on biodiversity), the major outcome of this large and costly conference was the raising of global awareness about the interdependence of economic and social development.

America (ECLA), the World Trade Organization (WTO), and the UN Conference on Trade and Development (UNCTAD) and at periodic international conferences dealing with population, urban development, and environmental protection.

Second, as states have become more sensitive to the global dimensions of social, political, and economic problems, they have increasingly sought to establish cooperative strategies through international conferences. Such multilateral forums have addressed issues like trade, the environment, disarmament, and disease control. The Third UN Conference on the Law of the Sea (UNCLOS III), for example, which involved more than ten major negotiating sessions from 1972 through 1983 and representatives from some 130 states, successfully updated many important maritime rules, including laws about the width of territorial waters, the use of international straights, and rights over exclusive economic zones and the continental shelf.

A third reason for the growth in multilateral diplomacy is the increased importance of regional problems and concerns, leading to greater social, political, and economic cooperation within particular geographic regions, such as Western Europe, the Middle East, and Latin America. In addition, regional perspectives and approaches have become more important in dealing with international conflicts. In Central America, for example, five Central American states devised a peace framework that ultimately led to democratic elections in Nicaragua in early 1990 and helped reduce regional civil strife.

THE STRUCTURE OF DIPLOMACY

Official communication and negotiation between governments is carried out at two distinct levels. At the formal level, governments rely on their diplomatic institutions to communicate and bargain with other states. Governments also carry out official relations through specialized, nondiplomatic channels. Along with diplomats, large embassies of major powers have specialists in such areas as economic development, drug enforcement, the armed services, intelligence, agriculture, science, and the arts. Given the increasing level of social, economic, and cultural interaction among states, nonpolitical specialists, known as attachés, are playing a growing role in foreign relations. But the key agent of foreign policy continues to be the diplomat, and the key governmental agency is the foreign ministry (or State Department).

Agents of Diplomacy

The responsibility for conducting foreign policy falls on the state's foreign ministry. Ordinarily, the head of the government appoints the foreign minister along with the department chiefs and the ambassadors in its overseas diplomatic posts. These officials are supported by a cadre of professional diplomats, whose expertise and training vary from state to state. Obviously, as states become more modern and complex, the specialization and professionalism of its diplomats are likely to increase as well. Ordinarily, the diplomatic corps is made up of government employees who are knowledgeable about international politics, sensitive to foreign cultures, fluent in foreign languages, and skillful in diplomatic negotiation.

The U.S. diplomatic corps, for example, includes some 3,200 foreign service officers (FSOs), specializing in one of four areas: politics, economics, consular affairs, and administration. Although other types of professionals serve in the Department of State, such as specialists from the civil service and political appointees, the major task of diplomacy is entrusted to FSOs serving in Washington and overseas in more than 140 embassies, 100 consulates, and 10 missions. Even though most states select ambassadors from the trained diplomatic corps, a number of states, including the United States, appoint leading political officials to ambassadorial posts. For example, President Bill Clinton appointed Pamela Harriman, a leading Washington, D.C., socialite and long-time Democratic Party supporter, as ambassador to Paris. By all accounts, Ambassador Harriman, who was fluent in French and had direct access to President Clinton, carried out her responsibilities with skill and tact, earning the respect of both U.S. and French public officials. Of course, not all political appointments are successful. Occasionally, such appointees have limited experience in foreign affairs and little knowledge of the country to which they are assigned.

The Accreditation of Diplomats

The head of an embassy is normally an ambassador. The next most senior official is frequently the deputy chief of mission (DCM), who coordinates and oversees the work of the various offices within an embassy. Typically, the DCM is known in diplomatic jargon as the ***chargé d'affaires,*** because he or she is authorized to act on behalf of the ambassador in his or her absence. Embassies vary greatly in size, which is determined largely by the wealth and influence of the home state and by the importance assigned to relations with the host state. Thus, the U.S. embassy in London, with more than 600 employees, is nearly ten times the size of the U.S. embassy in Santiago, Chile. Issue 12.1 describes the major components of a typical U.S. diplomatic mission.

Chargé d'affaires
The senior diplomat authorized to act on behalf of the ambassador during his/her absence.

Issue 12.1 Organization of a Typical U.S. Embassy

The heart of a typical U.S. diplomatic mission is, of course, the ambassador's office, supported by a small staff. As the president's personal representative to the host country, the ambassador is charged with representing the concerns and interests of the United States in the host nation. In addition, the ambassador is responsible for protecting the lives and property of its citizens, for fostering friendly bilateral relations, and for reporting to the Secretary of State all significant developments in the host country. Although the ambassador is ultimately responsible for the functioning of an embassy, the effective management and operation of an embassy is ordinarily carried out by the DCM, thereby allowing the ambassador to emphasize ceremonial and representational duties.

In carrying out the many duties assigned to a typical diplomatic mission, a medium-sized embassy is generally organized around eight to ten major sections. These include the following:

- A *political section,* comprised of three to five foreign service officers (FSOs), monitors host-country political developments, prepares regular reports, highlights significant political developments, and maintains contact with important governmental and political officials.

- An *economics section,* comprised of three to five FSOs, prepares reports on host-country economic conditions and fosters stable, productive, and expanding bilateral economic relations.

- A *consular section,* headed by an FSO and supported by host nationals, oversees the well-being of nationals in the host country and issues tourist visas for persons wishing to visit the United States. If the host country is large and a high demand exists for visas, an embassy may establish additional consular offices in other major cities.

- An *administrative section,* managed by one or two FSOs, oversees embassy support functions, including travel, housing, compensation, security, and local support staff.

- A *defense attaché office (DAO),* comprised of military attachés from the army, navy, and air force, maintains contact with host-state military leaders, reports on important civil-military developments in the host country, and facilitates bilateral military programs, including U.S. military assistance programs.

- A *commercial section,* staffed by commercial attachés, facilitates bilateral trade relations and encourages U.S. investment in the host country.

- An *information and press office,* headed by a cultural attaché from the U.S. Information Agency (USIA), oversees the embassy's public relations and disseminates information about the United States and its policies.

- A *communications section* oversees the sending and receiving of all classified messages.

Other U.S. government agencies that are represented in a typical embassy include: the Central Intelligence Agency (CIA), which gathers intelligence considered important to the home government; the Agency for International Development (AID), which manages economic assistance to the host country; and the Drug Enforcement Agency (DEA), which monitors the production, movement, and distribution of narcotics and assists the host government in combating drug trafficking.

In the wake of the 1979 Iranian revolutionaries' takeover of the U.S. embassy in Tehran and the discovery in the early 1980s of listening devices in the U.S. embassy being constructed in Moscow, the U.S. government has made embassy security a top priority. Special attention is given to ensure adequate control over new construction, while all new structures must meet stringent security standards to assure adequate physical protection from potential terrorist or mob attacks. Additionally, greater care is being given to the security of all classified information.

According to widely shared diplomatic customs, the appointment of the ambassador and other high-ranking diplomatic officials is subject to the consent of the host state. Normally, before making its diplomatic appointments, a government will determine whether the host state considers the candidate acceptable. Consent is generally automatic from friendly states, although unfriendly ones may occasionally oppose nominations. For example, when Nicaragua's Sandinista government nominated as its ambassador to the United States a woman allegedly involved in a political assassination, the Department of State refused to give consent and Nicaragua was forced to propose another candidate.

Before an ambassador and other diplomats can officially begin their duties in the host state, they must be officially *accredited*—that is, accepted—by the host state. When the designated ambassador arrives in the host state, he or she immediately presents a letter of accreditation to the chief of state in a short ceremony. Only after the host state has formally accepted the senior diplomat is he or she considered *persona grata* and thus free to engage in formal diplomatic activities. It is important to stress that the freedom of diplomats to carry out their duties is subject to the continuing consent of the host state. If a diplomat should undertake activities deemed undesirable, the receiving state may revoke its approval and declare the diplomat *persona non grata.* States can also ask diplomats to leave for other reasons.

Diplomats are accorded many privileges and immunities. The most basic immunity is the **inviolability of diplomats.** This means that a diplomat, as the emissary of a foreign state, is not subject to the laws of the host government. This does not mean that diplomats are free to violate the laws of the host state, but only that the diplomat is not subject to its legal jurisdiction. Another important diplomatic right is **inviolability of embassies.** Beginning in the seventeenth century, some international lawyers, including Hugo Grotius, argued that embassies were like islands in foreign capitals enjoying the sovereignty of the sending state. This principle, known as *extraterritoriality,* is no longer an accepted diplomatic norm. The accepted view is that the premises and property of an embassy are simply immune from the host government's jurisdiction. This means that the land and buildings of an official diplomatic mission may not be entered without the consent of the head of mission.

A corollary of the inviolability of embassies is the right of **diplomatic asylum,** allowing embassies to protect political refugees from the host government. For example, the Peruvian political leader Victor Haya de la Torre escaped into the Colombian Embassy in Lima, Peru, in 1951 and remained there for more than three years until the Peruvian government guaranteed safe exit to him. More recently, General Manuel Noriega, the head of Panama's Defense Forces, found asylum in the Papal nuncio's diplomatic quarters in Panama City. Noriega fled to the nuncio's quarters to escape capture by U.S. forces that had intervened in Panama in December 1989, toppling his military government. Although the U.S. military forces were eager to capture Noriega, they respected the inviolability of the nuncio's legation. Only after he turned himself over to U.S. authorities was Noriega taken into custody and flown to the United States.

Finally, diplomats have the right of confidential communication. Embassies communicate with their home state through the mail and through electronic signals. Diplomatic mail, normally carried in a diplomatic pouch, is inviolable and may not be inspected or confiscated. In some instances, governments employ diplomatic couriers in order to send secret documents overseas. And to assure that telecommunications are kept confidential, governments employ codes and ciphers.

Persona grata
A diplomat who is considered acceptable by the host state.

Persona non grata
A diplomat who is declared unacceptable by the host state.

Inviolability of diplomats
Diplomatic personnel are immune from the governmental jurisdiction of the host state.

Inviolability of embassies
Diplomatic premises are immune from the governmental jurisdiction of the host state.

Diplomatic asylum
The granting of temporary asylum within a foreign embassy to a political refugee wanted by the host government.

Functions of Diplomats

The Vienna Convention on Diplomatic Relations of 1961—the fundamental charter of diplomatic duties, rights, privileges, and practices—defines the key functions of a diplomatic mission as follows:

1. Representing the sending state in the receiving state
2. Protecting in the receiving state the interests of the sending state and of its nationals, within the limits permitted by international law

3. Negotiating with the government of the receiving state

4. Ascertaining by all lawful means conditions and developments in the receiving state, and reporting thereon to the government of the sending state

5. Promoting friendly relations between the sending state and the receiving state, and developing their economic, cultural, and scientific relations

As noted above, however, as foreign policy decision making has shifted toward the home state, diplomats' responsibilities have shifted toward the first and fourth tasks—*representation* and *reporting*. We briefly explore these two responsibilities.

Diplomats carry out two major types of representation—symbolic and substantive. *Symbolic representation* involves participation in formal functions, such as diplomatic receptions and ceremonies, as well as informal visits and public relations types of gatherings. To a degree, an ambassador personifies the state that he or she represents, acting as the personal representative of the chief of state of the sending country. Indeed, symbolic representation is based on the ambassador's status as the chief of state's personal representative in the host country.

Substantive representation involves communicating a government's interests and concerns to the host government, as well as defending and explaining abroad the state's actions and policies. In addition to communicating concerns directly to the host government through its foreign ministry, an ambassador or senior diplomat may also communicate indirectly through informal channels, such as meetings with associations, labor unions, dissident groups, etc. The latter approach was illustrated in the mid-1980s by the U.S. ambassadors to Chile and Paraguay, both of whom sought to promote human rights, political freedom, and democratization by meeting with groups opposed to the military government of General Augusto Pinochet, the president of Chile, and the dictatorial rule of General Alfredo Stroessner in Paraguay.

Reporting, the second major diplomatic task, involves observing, analyzing, and describing significant developments in the host country. Typically, diplomatic missions emphasize reports in three areas—politics, economics and commerce, and military and security issues. In embassies of the United States, the first two tasks are typically carried out by diplomats (foreign service officers) assigned to either the embassy's political or economic sections, whereas military reporting is carried out by military attachés. Attachés are basically military diplomats called to represent their respective military services (i.e., the navy, army, or air force). They collect and report on military developments in the host state and coordinate any military assistance programs. Given the prominent role of the military in the Third World, military attachés play a significant diplomatic role there.

The aim of embassy reports is to keep the home government appraised of foreign conditions and to call attention to developments that could influence, directly or indirectly, bilateral or multilateral relations. Much of the diplomatic reporting involves the description of conditions, events, and activities reported openly by the government or by the local press or media. Some reporting involves highly sensitive developments known by only a few people who have a significant bearing on the conduct of a nation's foreign relations. For example, should embassy personnel become aware of an imminent *coup d'etat* against an existing friendly government, a diplomatic warning might inhibit such a development. The vast majority of diplomatic cables, however, report developments such as trade data, political party reorganization, the rise of new governmental leaders, vital statistics, acquisition of new military weapons, etc. The task of the diplomat, of course, is not simply to report events and developments but to assess their significance. The aim is therefore to provide *intelligence*—that is, data and analysis on political, economic, and military developments in the host state—so that the home government might develop and implement a prudent foreign policy.

THE NATURE AND ROLE OF NEGOTIATION

The Negotiating Process

According to Harold Saunders, the "peace process" involves five distinct phases: defining a problem, committing to a negotiated solution, developing a framework, negotiating, and implementing the negotiated settlement.[16] The first four phases comprise the process of **negotiation.**

Negotiation
The bargaining process designed to achieve a mutually acceptable settlement.

The first phase involves identifying the key elements of a dispute and reaching a definition of the nature and scope of the problem. In academic life, the nature of a question will determine the answer given. Similarly, in political life, how an international political dispute is defined will predetermine how it will be addressed and possibly resolved. The challenge in this phase is for the negotiating parties to develop an understanding about the level of differences within each of the contesting communities as well as between them. Because contesting parties are seldom coherent actors, bargaining strength will be influenced in part by the degree of domestic coherence of each of the actors. As a result, developing a common negotiating strategy from the multiplicity of competing and often conflicting viewpoints is a vital precondition to effective negotiation. One reason for the intractability of the Arab-Israeli conflict is that the Israelis and Arabs/Palestinians have been deeply divided over how to define the problem and how to proceed in a negotiated settlement. Indeed, the issues that have divided them are so great that when officials met in November 1991 in Madrid for the first major Arab-Israeli talks since the Camp David negotiations of 1979, there was little opportunity for dialogue and discussion. Indeed, this highly publicized diplomatic gathering was essentially a series of speeches from Israeli, Jordanian, Syrian, and Palestinian officials.

The second phase—sometimes defined as the "precommitment phase"—involves the development of a commitment to negotiate. So long as existing conditions are tolerable and preferable to possible alternatives, states are unlikely to bargain in good faith. In this phase informal initiatives must convince the contestants that their vital interests can be satisfied only through a negotiated settlement. According to Saunders, developing the commitment to negotiate is the heart of the negotiation process, for without such commitment, negotiation cannot begin. Saunders suggests that before negotiation can begin leaders need to make four key judgments: (1) that the present condition no longer serves a party's interests, (2) that a fair settlement is possible, (3) that leaders on the other side are willing and able to negotiate such a settlement, and (4) that a balance of forces will permit a fair settlement.[17] Thus, although negotiation is normally associated with bargaining, the indispensable element of the negotiation process is the commitment to a shared solution.

The third phase involves establishing a negotiating framework. Here the focus is on the nature of representation, the mechanics of bargaining, and the development of mutually acceptable principles and strategies to be employed in the negotiating sessions. When conflicts involve specific, well-defined issues, statesmen can generally establish a suitable framework without external assistance. But when conflicts are highly contentious, a third party is often indispensable in establishing a favorable bargaining milieu and in providing political "cover" for efficient, creative negotiations. The Camp David talks were successful in part because of meticulous planning by negotiation experts and Middle East specialists preceding those talks. Moreover, President Jimmy Carter placed his own credibility on the line by directly guiding and influencing the bargaining process and ultimately persuading President Anwar Sadat and Prime Minister Menachem Begin to reach accommodation. (See description of Camp David negotiations in case 12.2.)

Often one of the most difficult problems in this phase is the determination of which participants should be at the bargaining table. For example, in preparing for the November 1991 Middle East peace talks (Madrid), one of the most contentious issues involved the question of Palestinian representation. Because the future self-determination of Palestinians has been one of the key issues in the Middle East peace process, Palestinian participation was considered essential. But at that time Arabs and Israelis were deeply divided over who could legitimately represent the Palestinian nation. The Arabs argued that the only legitimate political voice of the Palestinian nation was the Palestinian Liberation Organization (PLO), whereas Israelis, who regarded that organization as illegal and criminal, strongly opposed its participation. Indeed, Israel made its own involvement in the Madrid talks conditional on the nonparticipation of the PLO. After many weeks of difficult negotiations, facilitated largely by U.S. Secretary of State James Baker, Arabs agreed that Palestinian interests would be represented by officials from the West Bank and Gaza.[18]

In the fourth phase of the negotiating process, states try to achieve a mutually acceptable solution through negotiation. Here the parties may negotiate directly or they may rely on a third party to clarify communication and facilitate the search for common ground among conflicting interests. The anticipated degree of success of negotiation will of course depend on how the international problem is perceived. If the dispute is assumed to be based on misperception and miscommunication, then the task of negotiation will be much simpler, involving clarification of misperceptions and the improvement in communication.[19] But if a dispute is assumed to be based on objective incompatibilities, then negotiation will be much more difficult, because conflict resolution will require not only clarification of misperceptions, but the development of mutually acceptable alternatives.

The extent to which states are committed to peaceful negotiation will depend partly on the perceived degree of goal compatibility and the extent of commitment to those goals. Figure 12.1 illustrates four possible bargaining scenarios based on the level of foreign policy goal compatibility and the degree of commitment to such goals. Of the four hypothetical environments, the one most conducive to successful negotiation is the one for which shared interests are high and the level of commitment to goals is low (quadrant D). This type of negotiation was illustrated in the drafting in the late 1980s of the North American Free Trade Agreement (NAFTA)—an accord designed to reduce trade barriers among Canada, Mexico, and the United States. Although the three signatories were concerned with NAFTA's potential economic dislocations, the three states were strongly committed to the goal of increased trade liberalization because of the potential economic gains from greater trade. Moreover, because trade liberalization did not fundamentally

FIGURE 12.1
Negotiating Environments Based on Level of Mutuality and Intensity of Interests

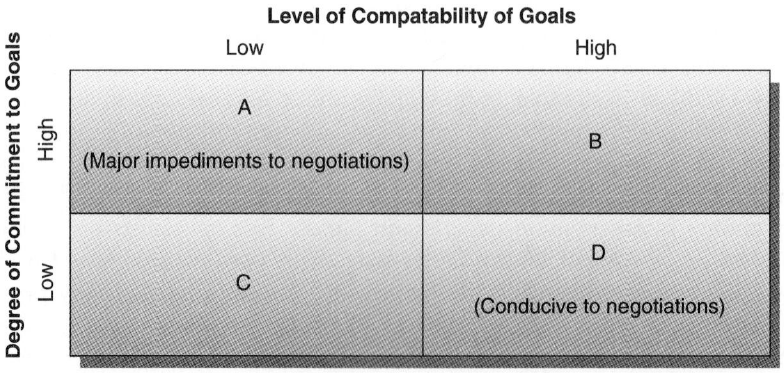

Level of Compatability of Goals

	Low	High
High (Degree of Commitment to Goals)	A (Major impediments to negotiations)	B
Low	C	D (Conducive to negotiations)

threaten vital national interests, the NAFTA negotiating environment was conducive to diplomatic bargaining.

The most difficult negotiating scenario is one in which there is little compatibility of goals and the level of commitment to the conflicting interests is high (quadrant A). The Arab-Israeli conflict, characterized by a deep commitment of two peoples (Jews and Palestinians) to statehood on the same land, illustrates this environment. The intractability of the Arab-Israeli conflict derives not from the failure of statesmanship per se, but from the vital but mutually incompatible interests of two peoples.

Negotiating environment C, characterized by low goal compatibility and relatively insignificant interests, is illustrated by the UN Third Law of the Sea Conference from 1972 to 1982. One of the most contentious issues throughout the bargaining sessions was the legal status of the deep seabed and the right to mine its resources. The Third World's position was that the deep seabed was part of the "common heritage of mankind" and that mining of the ocean floor should therefore be regulated by a transnational government organization. The industrialized states, including the United States, France, Italy, Japan, and West Germany strongly opposed this position, arguing that the historic doctrine of "freedom of the seas" allowed any state to mine the deep seabed. In the end, the two groups of states were unable to resolve this dispute during the law-making negotiations. Subsequently, however, compromise was achieved between the two groups, resulting in the Law of the Sea Convention coming into force in 1994.

Negotiating scenario B is characterized by a high commitment to goals and a high level of goal compatibility. This negotiating environment is illustrated by the U.S.-USSR Intermediate Nuclear Forces (INF) negotiations held in Geneva from 1980 to 1987. In these negotiations both superpowers wanted to reduce the number of INF forces, without reducing the adequacy of their respective military capabilities in Europe. In the final analysis, the signing of the 1987 INF Treaty banning intermediate nuclear forces in Europe was realized because of the strong common interest in reducing the military threat of NATO and Warsaw Pact forces.

Principles of Effective Diplomacy

The nature and role of diplomacy in world politics have changed dramatically in the past three centuries as a result of developments in the character of world politics and in the instruments by which official international relations are conducted. The increased interdependence of the world, the improvements in communication and travel, the development of nuclear technology, and the propensity for summit and parliamentary diplomacy have all decreased the role of diplomacy in the contemporary world order. A number of students of world affairs have expressed concern that twentieth-century developments have impeded diplomacy. Hans Morgenthau, for example, suggests that the contemporary world has denigrated diplomacy because of three vices: publicity, the application of parliamentary procedures (especially majority voting) to negotiation, and fragmentation of international issues. In his view, for negotiation to be revived, secrecy must increase, parliamentary procedures must be discarded, and diplomats must view and address the fundamental issues of international relations not in a piecemeal fashion but as part of a complex integrated web.[20]

The strengthening of diplomacy in world politics can only be undertaken if the diplomats themselves carry out their work in a responsible and professional manner. Some principles of effective diplomacy that have been emphasized by international relations scholars include:

1. *Don't Be a Crusader or Moralist.* When political leaders define their nations' interests in terms of moralistic, ideological, or legalistic causes, they tend to sacrifice diplomacy for the sake of morality. To be sure, applying moral, legal,

and fundamental political norms to foreign policy interests of states is important, but diplomacy should not be defined solely in terms of higher normative causes, because diplomacy can succeed only with compromise. The moralistic approach to the Carter administration's human rights foreign policy no doubt contributed some positive developments, but it also increased friction among some states and led to a number of counterproductive developments. Moreover, the crusading spirit of Iran's Muslim fundamentalism contributed to the senseless 1980s Iran-Iraq war. Of course, religion need not foster rigid moralism. Indeed, as suggested in chapter 2, a growing number of scholars have suggested that religion can contribute to conflict resolution and the development of a more humane world (see issue 2.1).

2. *Define Foreign Policy Interests Realistically.* To be effective, diplomacy must be based on an accurate assessment of foreign policy conditions. For Hans Morgenthau, this means that "the objectives of foreign policy must be defined in terms of national interests and must be supported with adequate power."[21] Specifically, this means that the political leadership must define vital national interests accurately, and they must do so in light of their capabilities. Failure to relate foreign policy goals to a state's available resources can lead to either defeat or ridicule. Moreover, as noted in chapter 8, the problem of misperception exists in foreign affairs. When political leaders are unable to perceive accurately the events within the global system, they are likely to overreact to the behaviors of foreign states, especially those viewed as enemies. A goal in diplomacy, then, is to reduce the effect of personal preconceptions and values to a minimum.

3. *Be Empathetic.* Effective diplomacy requires good communication, and good communication requires knowledge of one's own interests as well as those of other states. Articulating goals and objectives is not enough; an understanding of the views and perspectives of an opponent is also required. Without clear knowledge of the interests and values of the different negotiating states, there can be no sound diplomacy. But diplomats then must also be empathetic and be able to put themselves in the shoes of their opponents. In his account of the Cuban missile crisis of 1962, Robert Kennedy suggested that one of the important lessons of that crisis was the effort by some American statesmen to define the available options from the Soviet point of view. Kennedy indicated that this effort accounted for greater flexibility and tolerance on the part of the United States and contributed significantly to the successful termination of the conflict.[22]

4. *Compromise on Nonessentials.* Politics is often defined in terms of accommodation and compromise. Because conflict is inevitable in states and the international society, the development of political order in human communities always entails some reconciliation of actors' competing and conflicting interests. **Compromise,** the most fundamental method of building community order, involves settling disputes by voluntarily accepting partial, or "second best," gains. In other words, conflict resolution through compromise is based on the partial, rather than complete, fulfillment of actors' interests. If statesmen are to effectively promote national interests while also fostering global order, they must be prepared to compromise on issues not considered vital to the security and well-being of their nation. Effective diplomacy, thus, requires the clear conceptualization of national interests and the skill to protect vital interests and to promote nonvital interests in light of other states' interests. According to Morgenthau, effective compromise can be enhanced by applying the following guidelines: (1) goals should focus on substantive interests and not symbolic issues; (2) do not place yourself in a position from

Compromise
The resolution of conflict through mutual accommodation.

which you cannot retreat without losing face and credibility; (3) never allow a weak ally to make decisions for you; (4) the armed forces are the instrument of foreign policy, not its master; and (5) the government is the leader of public opinion, not its slave.[23]

5. *Focus on Desirable Actions and Decisions, Not on Values or Positions.* One of the most common errors in diplomatic negotiation is the focus on ideologies, values, and positions rather than on interests. Another common error is the concern with change in an opponent's behavior rather than on clarifying one's own interests. According to Roger Fisher, diplomats should devote more attention to identifying what they want from others and less time repeating what will happen if they do not get it. "The formulation and reformulation of the decision we seek," writes Fisher, "is . . . the single most important element in the successful conduct of foreign affairs."[24]

6. *Make Offers That Are Specific, Concrete, and Positive.* The goal of diplomacy is to bring about change. Negative sanctions (threats) are seldom the most effective way of changing an opponent's actions or policies. According to Fisher, a more effective way of increasing the likelihood of successful diplomacy is to make "yesable propositions"—to define specifically and concretely several positive alternatives, each one better than the existing conditions. To do this, Fisher suggests subdividing or "fractionalizing" problems.[25]

THE ROLE OF THIRD PARTIES

As noted in chapter 4, third parties (intermediaries) can greatly assist conflict resolution by diffusing passions, gathering relevant information, generating possible alternative solutions, and facilitating communication between antagonists. The most frequent type of intermediary in international conflict resolution is an individual state that assists two warring countries or political groups in resolving a dispute. This approach is illustrated by the decisive role of the United States in facilitating the Dayton Peace Accords, which brought an end to the war in Bosnia among Croats, Muslims, and Serbs. It is also illustrated by the role of Britain in bringing about the Lancaster House Accord, which ended the Rhodesian civil war and resulted in a new democratic state in 1980. International governmental organizations such as the UN or the European Union, or informal groups of states, such as the Contadora Group,[26] can also play an important role in facilitating the peaceful resolution of disputes. In addition, individuals can also play an important role. For example, Oscar Arias, Costa Rica's president in the mid-1980s, played an important role in bringing an end to Central America's revolutionary wars by providing a framework (known as the Arias Plan) for facilitating negotiations among Honduras, Nicaragua, El Salvador, and the United States.

The three case studies that follow illustrate the role of three types of intermediaries—governments, nongovernmental institutions, and unofficial parties. Case 12.2 on the Camp David Accords illustrates the role of a foreign government (the United States) in sponsoring and facilitating the peace negotiations between Israel and Egypt at Camp David in 1978. These negotiations are significant because they resulted in the Egypt-Israel Peace Treaty. Case 12.3 on the Beagle Channel dispute illustrates the role of a nongovernmental intermediary (the Vatican) in successfully resolving a bitter territorial dispute between Chile and Argentina. Finally, case 12.4 on the Israel-PLO peace process illustrates the potential role of unofficial intermediaries in creating preconditions for negotiation. The so-called "Oslo Connection," which began with unofficial Israeli and Palestinian contacts, secretly facilitated by

Case 12.2 | The Camp David Accords

At the invitation of President Jimmy Carter, Prime Minister Menachem Begin of Israel and President Anwar Sadat of Egypt met for nearly two weeks in early September 1978 at Camp David, Maryland, in order to promote Middle East peace. Using his influence as leader of the free world, President Carter offered to facilitate negotiations between Egypt and Israel and thereby achieve some resolution of the volatile Arab-Israeli conflict (see chap. 3). To avoid distractions and possible press leaks, Carter suggested that the two heads of state, supported by a number of aides, meet in the secluded presidential retreat center at Camp David.

The decision of the U.S. government to initiate and promote direct discussion between Israel and Egypt was a consequence of its long-term Middle East interests. Since the creation of Israel in 1948, and especially since the 1967 war, the United States had been deeply committed to the peace, stability, and political evolution of the Middle East. Three major interests had guided U.S. policy makers: (1) promoting the security of Israel, the only democratic state in the region; (2) limiting the Soviet Union's influence in the Middle East; and (3) ensuring continued Western access to Arab petroleum. Recognizing the importance of these objectives, President Jimmy Carter made the Middle East a top priority of his administration, and his initiatives and persistence were richly rewarded with an agreement establishing peace between Egypt and Israel.

At Camp David, President Carter functioned as conciliator and mediator, promoting dialogue and trust between Begin and Sadat and facilitating and directing negotiations. Because of Camp David's seclusion, the leaders were able to concentrate solely on the relevant issues, with few distractions and interruptions from their governments, the press, or other external concerns. After thirteen days of intense negotiations, Begin and Sadat concluded two agreements, known as the **Camp David Accords.** The first document, "Framework for the Conclusion of a Peace Treaty Between Egypt and Israel," is especially important because it provided the foundation for the **Egypt-Israel Peace Treaty** signed in March 1979. As a result of the treaty, Egypt regained control of the Sinai Peninsula, which had been lost to Israel in the 1967 war, and the condition of peace was reestablished between these two states. The second agreement, titled "Framework for Peace in the Middle East," established a basis for subsequent negotiations of a "transitional arrangement" for the West Bank. Although Sadat and Begin were unable to agree on increased political autonomy for Gaza and the West Bank, or to resolve the major issue of a Palestinian homeland, they were successful in paving the way for a territorial settlement, thereby partially promoting regional peace.

The success of the Camp David talks is a personal credit to President Carter. He initiated the meeting, convinced Egyptian President Anwar Sadat and Israeli Prime Minister Menachem Begin that a U.S.-supported gathering would be mutually beneficial, provided a neutral and secluded setting in which uninterrupted talks could be carried out, and directly contributed to the structuring of the talks and negotiations. As William Quandt, a Carter advisor on Middle Eastern affairs, has observed, the president was the "architect" of the Camp David Accords, playing "the role of draftsman, strategist, therapist, friend, adversary, and mediator."[27]

the Norwegian foreign ministry, was significant because it helped pave the way for formal governmental negotiations that resulted in the mutual recognition of the two political groups and to the 1993 Israel-PLO Accord.

These three case studies suggest that third parties can play an important role in international conflict resolution. Intermediaries, whether governmental, nongovernmental, or unofficial, can help to foster the preconditions for negotiation, serve as a channel of communication, help to clarify shared and opposing goals, facilitate the structuring of negotiations, and, where appropriate, help to mediate contentious issues. To be effective, a third party must be perceived as impartial and have the confidence of the contestants.

Case 12.3 The Beagle Channel Dispute

The Beagle Channel dispute between Argentina and Chile centered on three small, uninhabited islands—Picton, Lennox, and Nueva (**PLN islands**)—in the Beagle Channel. The channel, located in Patagonia on the southern tip of South America, is a 125-mile waterway joining the Atlantic and Pacific oceans and separating the Tierra del Fuego from numerous islands toward Cape Horn to the South (see map 12.1). Like many other territorial quarrels in Latin America, the Beagle Channel dispute grew out of unclear territorial boundaries at the time of independence from Spain in the early nineteenth century.[28] When Chile and Argentina became independent, each received title to the territory formerly claimed by Spain. But because not all boundaries between the two countries were completely settled, the transfer of sovereignty led to continuing territorial disputes, such as the Beagle Channel.

The first major effort to clarify the indeterminate status of the Beagle Channel occurred in 1881, when both Chile and Argentina signed a treaty granting Argentina all territory north of the channel and Chile all territory to the south. Although the treaty's terms were unambiguous, the two states did not agree on the exact location of the channel. The dispute in the region was thus whether the Beagle Channel proceeded east and west or toward the south around the Navarino Island. Numerous efforts were made in the late nineteenth and early twentieth centuries to resolve the dispute, but little progress was achieved. After several decades of relative neglect, the dispute surfaced again in the late 1950s and 1960s. In 1971 both countries agreed to have Great Britain arbitrate the dispute. Under the terms of the agreement, the British government could either accept or reject the decision given by a court of five international jurists. If Britain accepted it, the court's decision was to be legally binding on both Argentina and Chile. In May 1977, the court issued its decision, giving the three islands to Chile. Subsequently, Argentina announced that it considered the decision "fundamentally null," saying that the court had distorted its arguments and claims.

The failure to resolve the dispute through arbitration led to increased tensions between the two states. As demands for an honorable resolution to the dispute increased, both the Chilean and Argentinean governments intensified their efforts to

continued

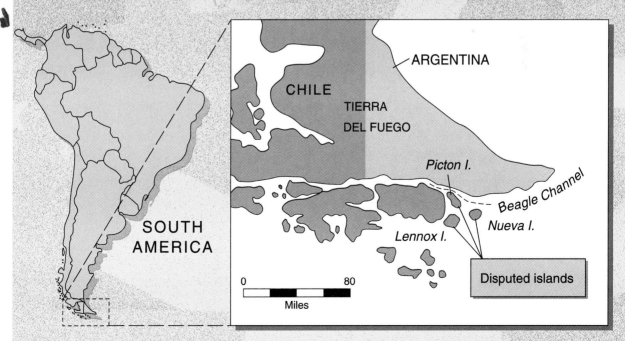

MAP 12.1

Case 12.3 The Beagle Channel Dispute—*continued*

secure legal title to the disputed boundary zone. In 1978, both countries increased their military readiness in the southern Patagonia region, sending naval vessels to the disputed territory as a show of force. Argentina evacuated civilians from Patagonia, reduced the number of flights allowed from Chile, closed parts of its Chilean border, and called up its military reserves. In addition, it expelled some 3,000 Chileans living in Argentina. Because of these and other ominous developments, some thought that military conflict was imminent.

In December 1978, Pope John Paul II offered to mediate the controversy—a development that was greeted with optimism because of the historic influence of the Catholic church in both countries. On January 8, the foreign ministers of Argentina and Chile met in Montevideo, Uruguay, and signed the Act of Montevideo, committing both countries to papal mediation of the dispute and a return to the *status quo ante*—that is, to military conditions as they existed in early 1977 before the parties deployed naval forces in the southern region. After hundreds of meetings and to speed up lagging negotiations, the Pope broke with tradition and pro-

posed a solution of his own in December 1980. The proposal, which would become the basis of the final agreement, granted the PLN islands to Chile but limited its maritime rights. Chile immediately accepted the papal proposal, but Argentina refused, bringing negotiations to a virtual halt.

During the next three years the Vatican-led negotiations continued and greatly intensified in 1984.[29] In October of that year, after more than 500 meetings, an acceptable agreement was finally reached. The final accord provided, among other things, that Chile would have sovereignty over the islands, but that its maritime rights would be restricted.[30] This would thereby limit Chile's claim to the Atlantic Ocean and preserve Argentina's maritime claims to the east of the disputed islands. On November 29, 1984, the foreign ministers of Argentina and Chile and the Vatican's Secretary of State signed the **Beagle Channel Treaty** in the Vatican, thereby concluding the long but successful papal mediation. The treaty became effective on May 2, 1985, when foreign ministers from both Argentina and Chile formally expressed ratification.

In Conclusion

Diplomats play a key role in defending and promoting national interests in the international community. As the agents of the state responsible for foreign relations, they encourage international interaction, facilitate transnational economic, social, and political cooperation, help to resolve interstate disputes, and protect the interests of nationals in foreign countries. Diplomatic negotiation is of course essential in building and maintaining a stable and just international community. Although the structure and patterns of diplomacy have changed greatly in recent centuries and especially in the last half of the twentieth century, the processes of negotiation and nonviolent conflict resolution have remained largely unchanged. Fundamentally, the successful promotion of international cooperation and the peaceful settlement of international disputes depend on the skills, knowledge, and moral commitments of public officials. Peace may be a divine gift, but generally it is the result of diligent and competent labor of professional diplomats. Occasionally, it involves unofficial representatives who help to establish conditions on which subsequent negotiations can build.

Case 12.4 The Oslo Connection

In the aftermath of the 1991 Middle East Peace Conference in Madrid, the U.S. sponsored bilateral peace talks in order to facilitate negotiations between Israel and Palestinian representatives. But after six rounds of Washington-based meetings, little progress had been realized. As a result, a number of Israelis, Palestinians, and selected foreign officials began to explore alternative avenues of peaceful accommodation. One of these exploratory journeys ultimately succeeded, leading to the mutual recognition of Israel and the PLO and to a framework for facilitating reconciliation between two political enemies. The path used to bring about reconciliation was most unusual, involving two Israeli university professors as unofficial intermediaries together with PLO representatives. In addition, the Norwegian government provided invaluable support services to facilitate discussions and negotiations, to provide a climate conducive to mutual understanding, and to ensure the secrecy of the initiative. Because of Norway's vital role in bringing together political enemies and in facilitating reconciliation, this Israeli-Palestinian peace initiative is known as the **"Oslo Connection."**

The development of the Oslo initiative began in early 1992 when Yossi Beilin, then an opposition Labor member of the Knesset, Israel's parliament, got to know Terje Rod Larsen, head of the Oslo-based Institute for Applied Social Sciences (known by its Norwegian acronym, FAFO). Because Larsen was carrying out a study of living conditions in Israel's occupied territories of Gaza and the West Bank, he had developed numerous contacts with Palestinians. As a result of his work, Larsen offered to assist Beilin in making contact with leading Palestinians. After the Labor Party won the June 1992 parliamentary elections, Yitzhak Rabin became Israel's prime minister and appointed Shimon Peres as foreign minister and Beilin as deputy foreign minister. Soon thereafter Larsen traveled again to Jerusalem and reiterated his offer to Beilin, who now was a key official in the Israeli government. Beilin urged that Larsen meet with Yair Hirschfeld, a history professor at Haifa University who was deeply committed to Israeli-Palestinian reconciliation, to explore potential avenues of unofficial Israeli-Palestinian discussions. In September, Larsen returned to Israel with Jan Egeland, Norway's deputy foreign minister, and in a meeting with Beilin and Hirschfeld, Egeland offered his country's assistance in facilitating contact with the PLO. Beilin

indicated that although he appreciated their offer, it would be impossible for him to be a part of any exploratory initiatives with the PLO, because it was an outlawed organization and all contact with its officials was prohibited by Israeli law. He suggested that they work with Hirschfeld in making contact with Palestinians.

In December, Hirschfeld traveled to London to participate in an academic meeting. While there, he met with Larsen, who introduced him to Abu Alaa, a senior PLO official. At their first breakfast meeting Abu Alaa indicated that he was interested in broad Israeli-Palestinian talks. Hirschfeld indicated that, although he was not a government official, he would be willing to serve as a channel of communication with Israeli officials. He suggested that they hold an exploratory meeting in Norway, a country that had offered its "good offices." Later that day the two men met again for further discussions and agreed to meet the following month in Norway in order to "brainstorm" about the potential value of informal, unofficial discussions.

On January 20, 1993, Hirschfeld, along with Ron Pundik, an academic colleague from Tel Aviv University, met in utmost secrecy with Abu Alaa and two aids in an elegant country home in Sarpsborg, a village sixty miles east of Oslo.[31] To assure secrecy and to ensure that the meeting did not violate Israeli law banning contract with the PLO, the first meeting was structured as an academic conference, with a keynote lecture on living conditions in the West Bank by a FAFO researcher. Hirschfeld noted that this was "the funniest" conference he had ever attended, because the three Palestinians and two Israelis, having come to hold bilateral discussions, had to listen to academic papers![32] After this perfunctory beginning, the parties shifted to the real purpose of the meeting, and for two days they carried out intensive exploratory discussions. At the outset they agreed on three ground rules: (1) they would not dwell on historical grievances; (2) their work would be secret; and (3) all positions put forward would be retractable.[33] FAFO personnel and senior officials from the Norwegian foreign ministry provided support, but were not directly involved in the discussions. Their role was that of facilitators, not mediators. Larsen and his wife Mona Juul, a senior Norwegian diplomat, provided an informal, relaxed environment that included meals shared together.

continued

Case 12.4 The Oslo Connection—*continued*

As a result of their successful first round of talks, the two academics and Abu Alaa decided to continue meeting in the future. Thus, during the subsequent three months four additional weekend meetings were held that resulted in a framework to facilitate Israeli-Palestinian dialog. In early May, Abu Alaa informed the Israelis that he would not continue the talks if the talks did not become official. Because these backchannel talks had yielded far more progress than the official U.S.-sponsored Middle East peace talks, Prime Minister Rabin and Foreign Minister Peres decided to upgrade the Oslo talks, placing a senior government official—Uri Savir, the director general of Israel's Foreign Ministry—in charge of the negotiations.

With the decision to upgrade the talks, the audacious and unusual "pre-negotiation" phase of the Oslo Connection came to an end. Although much of the substantive negotiation work still needed to be carried out, the role of the two Israeli academics should not be underestimated. As one Israeli government official observed, "Bureaucracies are too clumsy. They rarely lend themselves to starting something big. For this you need a couple of nuts."[34] Another observer noted that the professors "prepared the practice and the psychological ground that enable the professionals to join them."[35]

During the subsequent four months, the pace of secret negotiations quickened, with numerous weekend meetings held in several locations near Oslo. After significant progress in the talks, the negotiations deadlocked in July, leading to the virtual collapse of the negotiations. Abu Alaa threatened to quit the negotiations. Only the direct personal intervention of Prime Minister Rabin and PLO Chairman Arafat prevented the collapse of the Oslo talks. The Oslo Connection was saved by the brinkmanship of Rabin and Arafat when they, creating a "backchannel within a backchannel," exchanged secret letters known only to a few individuals but not to the negotiating parties themselves.[36] Their direct involvement led to compromises that settled core disputes and established the conditions for bringing the talks to a swift and successful conclusion. As a result of the Oslo initiative, the PLO recognized Israel's right to exist, accepted UN Security Council resolutions 242 and 338, committed itself to the Middle East peace process, and to the renunciation of terrorism. For its part, Israel recognized the PLO as the representative of the Palestinian people. In addition, the two parties agreed to a framework for establishing a permanent peace settlement and for an interim Palestinian authority and elected Council for governing the Palestinian people in Gaza and the West Bank. This framework—known as the **Israel-PLO Declaration of Principles**—was signed with much fanfare on the White House lawn on September 13, 1993.

SUMMARY

1. Diplomacy is the process by which states carry out international relations through peaceful negotiation. The roots of diplomacy lie in antiquity, although modern diplomacy has increased greatly in scope and sophistication.

2. Traditional diplomacy is characterized by formality, flexibility, and secrecy. Toward the end of the nineteenth century a new type of diplomacy began to emerge involving greater openness, increased emphasis on international law, and greater universality.

3. Three distinctive features of modern diplomacy are the centralization of decision making, the practice of summitry, and multilateral diplomacy. The two major types of summitry are superpower summits and economic summits.

4. The practice of diplomacy is normally carried out by officials of a diplomatic corps. An embassy is normally headed by an ambassador, who delegates the mission's ongoing operations to a DCM or *chargé d'affaires*. Both the embassy premises and the diplomats are immune from the laws of the host state.

5. The primary responsibilities of a diplomatic mission are to represent the sending state and to report on important developments in the host country.

6. Diplomatic negotiation, which has increasingly been taken over by officials in the central government, involves several phases, including definition, precommitment, establishing a framework, and bargaining. The most conducive environment for negotiation is one in which there is limited goal incompatibility with low level of commitment to goals.

7. When antagonists are unable to resolve a dispute themselves, third parties can greatly assist the negotiation process by diffusing passions and facilitating and clarifying communications. Third parties can only be effective if they enjoy the confidence of all the leading antagonists. The success in resolving the Egyptian-Israeli territorial dispute and the Beagle Channel conflict was due in great part to the credibility and influence of the United States and the Vatican. But as the Oslo Connection suggested, nongovernmental personnel can also occasionally contribute to conflict resolution by creating preconditions necessary for negotiations.

KEY TERMS

diplomacy	multilateral diplomacy	diplomatic asylum	PLN islands
diplomatic precedence	*chargé d'affaires*	negotiation	Beagle Channel Treaty
summits	*persona grata*	compromise	Oslo Connection
superpower summits	*persona non grata*	Camp David Accords	Israel-PLO Declaration of Principles
economic summits	inviolability of diplomats	Egypt-Israel Peace Treaty	
Group of Eight (G-8)	inviolability of embassies		

RECOMMENDED READINGS

Barston, R. P. *Modern Diplomacy*. London: Longman, 1988. An informative, introductory study of the nature and role of contemporary diplomacy.

Cohen, Raymond. *Negotiating Across Cultures: Communication Obstacles in International Diplomacy*. Washington, D.C.: U.S. Institute of Peace Press, 1991. Using numerous U.S. examples, this illuminating study shows how cross-cultural differences influence international negotiation.

Fisher, Roger. *Conflict for Beginners*. New York: Harper & Row, 1969. This simple, but not simplistic, study of negotiation provides many insights and principles for facilitating conflict resolution. An invaluable guide for students.

Kennan, George F. *Memoirs, 1925–1950*. Boston: Little, Brown, 1967. Kennan, one of the most influential postwar diplomats and scholars, provides a graceful and illuminating account of his diplomatic service during the pre– and early Cold War eras.

Kissinger, Henry. *Diplomacy*. New York: Simon & Schuster, 1994. Despite its title, this book covers much more than an overview of diplomacy. Rather, this study is fundamentally a historical assessment of the grand strategies of the great powers from the mid-seventeenth-century statesmanship of Cardinal Richelieu through the development of the post–Cold War "New World Order." Based on major nineteenth- and twentieth-century geopolitical developments, as well as his own intimate knowledge of foreign affairs acquired as U.S. statesman, Kissinger illuminates the principles leading to a sound foreign policy. A realistic tour de force, this study is considered Kissinger's most important work.

Makovsky, David. *Making Peace with the PLO: The Rabin Government's Road to the Oslo Accord*. Boulder, Colo.: Westview Press, 1996. A concise, informative account of the genesis, development, and conclusion of the Oslo Israel-PLO negotiations that resulted in the 1993 peace accord. The appendix includes important bilateral documents involved in the Oslo agreement.

Nicolson, Harold. *Diplomacy*. 3rd ed. New York: Oxford University Press, 1973. A concise survey of the evolution, nature, role, and procedures of diplomacy by a noted British statesman.

Plischke, Elmer, ed. *Modern Diplomacy: The Art and Artisans*. Washington D.C.: American Enterprise Institute, 1981. A useful reader on the nature, evolution, and changing functions and practices of contemporary diplomacy.

Princen, Thomas. *Intermediaries in International Conflict*. Princeton: Princeton University Press, 1992. A study of the nature and practice of international mediation. After exploring concepts and theories, the study provides four case studies: Egypt and Israel (1978), Russia and Japan (1904), Chile and Argentina (1978–1984), and the Biafran Civil War (1967).

Quandt, William. *Camp David: Peacemaking and Politics*. Washington, D.C.: Brookings Institution, 1986. A meticulous description and analysis of the mediating role of the United States at the Camp David peace talks that resulted in the Egypt-Israel Peace Treaty of 1979.

Raiffa, Howard. *The Art and Science of Negotiation.* Cambridge: Harvard University Press, 1982. A theoretical examination of factors that facilitate conflict resolution. Some of the case studies deal with international disputes, including the Panama Canal Treaty negotiations, the Arab-Israeli talks at Camp David, and the negotiations at the Third Law of the Sea Conference.

Shultz, George P. *Turmoil and Triumph: My Years as Secretary of State.* New York: Charles Scribner's Sons, 1993. An engaging, comprehensive memoir of Shultz' tenure as President Reagan's Secretary of State (1982–1989). This brilliant and illuminating book provides a detailed firsthand account of the making and implementation of U.S. foreign policy during the last decade of the Cold War. Essential reading for those concerned with superpower relations of the 1980s.

RELEVANT WEB SITES

International Affairs Network (IAN)
    Peace and conflict resolution resources
www.pitt.edu/~ian/resource/conflict.htm

International Relations and Security Network (ISN)
www.isn.ethz.ch/

U.S. Department of State
www.state.gov/www/regions/internat.html

U.S. Institute of Peace: Virtual Diplomacy Program
www.usip.org/oc/virtual_dipl

CHAPTER

International Law and Conflict Resolution

13

On November 4, 1979, Iranian revolutionaries stormed the U.S. Embassy in Tehran, taking fifty-three diplomats hostage. After failing to gain their release, the United States asked the **International Court of Justice (ICJ)**—commonly known as the World Court—to intervene in the dispute. Specifically, the U.S. government requested that the Court declare Iran's actions a violation of international law and to order the immediate release of all hostages.

The World Court gave a preliminary judgment on December 15. After rejecting Iran's claim that it had no jurisdiction in the case, the Court indicated that there was no more fundamental prerequisite for peaceful interstate relations than the inviolability of diplomatic envoys and embassies, and that Iran was obligated to immediately return the embassy to the U.S. government and release the hostages.

Throughout the legal dispute, Iran held that the Court had no jurisdiction in the dispute and refused to participate in any of the legal proceedings. In its final judgment, delivered on May 24, 1980, the Court decided that (1) Iran had violated and was still violating international law, (2) the Iranian government must restore the embassy premises to the U.S. government, and (3) reparations must be made to the U.S. government. Because Iran did not recognize the World Court's jurisdiction, it disregarded the judgment, allowing the student militants to hold the hostages until January 1981, when they were released immediately after Ronald Reagan became president.

In contrast to the limited impact of the ICJ in the hostage dispute, some four years later the Court successfully settled a territorial dispute between the United States and Canada. The dispute involved some 30,000 nautical square miles of sea off the northeastern coast of North America, including the Georges Bank, considered one of the richest fishing grounds in the world. Although claims to the territory had long been contested, the conflict became significant in the 1970s with the rising acceptance of exclusive economic zones (EEZ), which allow states to claim territorial waters up to 200 nautical miles (NM) off their coastline for exclusive economic use. In view of the economic potential for fishing and off-shore oil

> The major difficulty with international law is that it converts what are essentially problems of international morality, as defined by a particular political community, into arguments about law that are largely drained of morality.[1]
>
> Judge Robert H. Bork, *U.S. Supreme Court nominee, 1988*

> War and trade are the most obvious constants in the relationships between states in the international system. The constant that is much less obvious—in fact, almost hidden—is the search by those same states for international standards of behavior.[2]
>
> Dorothy V. Jones, *historian of international affairs*

> International law is the law which the wicked do not obey and which the righteous do not enforce.[3]
>
> Abba Eban, *former Israeli Prime Minister*

International Court of Justice (ICJ)
This 15-member world court, a formal UN organ, is the highest institution charged with adjudicating international law. It is located in The Hague, Netherlands.

drilling in the contested waters, both Canada and the United States began to press their respective interests more vigorously. And after failing to resolve the dispute through negotiations, the parties asked the World Court to arbitrate the conflict. Specifically, Canada and the United States requested that the Court appoint a panel of five Western World Court judges (United States, Canada, Italy, France, and West Germany) and issue a binding settlement. After nearly three years of study, the Court's panel settled the dispute in October 1984 by awarding the United States about two-thirds of the contested waters in the Gulf of Maine and Canada the rest.

These two cases illustrate some of the possibilities and limits of international law in resolving interstate disputes. U.S. Senator Daniel Moynihan has written: "International law exists. It is not an option. It is a fact."[4] This is especially true of the principle of inviolability of diplomatic premises and personnel, perhaps the most basic and widely accepted norm of the law of nations. Still, after violating this basic principle, Iran refused not only to accept the World Court's jurisdiction, but also refused to follow its subsequent verdict. But in the *United States v. Canada* case, both states willingly accepted the judgment of an international legal tribunal, in part because both states shared common Western political and legal perspectives and also because the dispute involved specific territorial questions that were subject to legal settlement.

This chapter examines the nature, role, and impact of international law in global society. After describing the nature and sources of international law, it analyzes how the World Court applies and interprets the law, and then discusses some of the major legal and extralegal ways of enforcing it. Finally, the chapter examines the role of international law in conflict resolution.

THE NATURE OF INTERNATIONAL LAW

Definition

International law
The customs, rules, and principles that states accept as binding in their mutual relations.

International law is commonly defined as a body of rules that states and other agents accept as binding obligations in the world community. This definition calls attention to three important features of international law.

First, international law is a body of rules comprising an integrated and logically related set of imperative norms. These norms cluster around key topics of international concern, such as the rights and duties of states, jurisdiction over nationals and aliens, the law of the sea, and the law of international organizations. Table 13.1, which lists some key norms of international law, illustrates some of those topics.

Second, international law applies chiefly to states. Historically, the major aim of international law has been to provide norms for guiding and judging the behavior of states. Because states have been the primary subjects of international law, corporations, transnational associations, and individuals have been viewed as secondary subjects that could receive legal protection only through their respective states. In the latter part of the twentieth century, however, individuals and other nonstate actors have increasingly been recognized as subjects of international law themselves. The Nuremburg and Tokyo Military Tribunals, for example, brought legal charges against Nazi and Imperial Japanese military officers for violating fundamental norms of international law. Specifically, the Axis leaders were charged with committing three types of crimes—war crimes, crimes against humanity, and crimes against peace. Most cases adjudicated by the European Court of Justice, the regional court of the European Union, deal with nonstate agents. In short, although states remain the primary subjects of international law, other actors are being increasingly accepted as well.

TABLE 13.1 Examples of Generally Accepted Rules of International Law

Category	Rules of International Law
State Rights	1. Right of independence
	2. Right of legal equality
	3. Right of self-defense
State Duties	4. Refrain from armed and unarmed intervention in other countries
	5. Refrain from fomenting civil strife in other states
	6. Honor treaty obligations
	7. Settle disputes peacefully
Jurisdiction	8. States have exclusive jurisdiction over people and property within national boundaries.
	9. Diplomats and diplomatic premises are exempt from host state jurisdiction.
	10. States may prosecute their nationals for crimes committed abroad.
	11. States may prosecute aliens for crimes committed in their territory according to their own legal procedures and standards, not those of the alien's state.
	12. States may expropriate foreign property provided it is done for public purpose and compensation is adequate and prompt.
Law of the Sea	13. States have exclusive jurisdiction over territorial waters, extending up to 12 NM.
	14. States may claim an exclusive economic zone of up to 200 NM.
	15. States can enforce their laws against foreign merchant ships in their internal waters.
	16. Ships have a right of "innocent passage" through international straits.
	17. States have the right to use the high seas.
	18. Every ship in international waters must be under the jurisdiction of a state (the flag state).
Airspace/ Outer Space	19. States have exclusive jurisdiction over their airspace.
	20. Airplanes do not possess the right of innocent passage. Use of airspace requires consent.
	21. In international airspace, aircraft must be under the jurisdiction of the flag state.
	22. States may not use celestial bodies for military purposes; spacecraft, however, may be so used.
War	23. The intentional killing of unarmed civilians is not permitted.
	24. Soldiers may not kill or wound military personnel who have surrendered.
	25. Hospitals may not be seized or attacked in wartime.
	26. Prisoners of war may not be treated inhumanely or tortured.
	27. The taking or killing of hostages is not permitted.
Human Rights	28. States are responsible for protecting human rights.
	29. Slavery, servitude, and forced labor are prohibited.
	30. States are responsible for caring for refugees.
	31. Genocide is prohibited and must be prevented and punished.
Environmental Law	32. States must refrain from polluting oceans and international airspace.
	33. States must reduce the use of ozone-depleting chemicals (CFCs).
	34. States must reduce the use of greenhouse gases.
	35. States must protect flora and fauna, especially endangered species.

Third, international law depends on a higher degree of voluntary compliance than domestic law. Because there is no central political authority in the international community to make, interpret, and enforce international law, compliance with international law is dependent ultimately on the voluntary actions of states. Indeed, international law is paradoxical in that states are both subject to its norms but also, as sovereign, independent political communities, above the law. For example, when Iran refused to participate in the *United States v. Iran* case, there was no international organization that could compel Iran to participate in the ICJ proceedings and no global executive authority that could enforce the court's judgment.

The Nature of Law

One of the continuing debates in international relations is whether international law is law or simply a moral aspiration or common expectation. Whether international law is regarded as law or merely a preference depends chiefly on how the law itself is defined.

Fundamentally, there are two approaches to law—the realist and the behavioralist. The realist school, based on the **command theory of law,** holds that only law that can be upheld by force is law. This is the view of the famous seventeenth-century British political theorist Thomas Hobbes, who wrote in *Leviathan* that "covenants without swords are but words" and that "where there is no common power, there is no law." The chief requirement for an effective legal system, according to this conception, is the ability of government to ensure compliance through the threat or use of the state's monopoly of force. During the nineteenth century the English writer John Austin provided the most celebrated articulation of this legal perspective when he defined law as "the command of the sovereign." According to Austin, because law requires not only clear rules but an institution to enforce them, international law is not properly "law" but "positive international morality." The noted newspaper columnist George Will also reflects the realistic perspective when he writes that "the very idea of international law is problematic, partly because there is no international consensus about norms." "Besides," asks Will, "can there be law among sovereign nations—law where there is no sovereign to adjudicate and enforce judgments?"[5]

In contrast to the realist approach, behavioralists emphasize the **voluntary habits of compliance.** For them law embodies the rules and norms that community participants are in the habit of fulfilling and find it in their interest to do so. The key to an effective legal system, according to the behavioralists, is *legitimacy*—that is, the public's voluntary acceptance of the laws and the public institutions that make them. If the institutions for making, interpreting, and enforcing rules are considered acceptable by subjects and if the rules themselves have widespread support, then there will be a high degree of voluntary compliance. In effect, a credible legal system needs to be based on implicit or explicit consent.

Those who suggest that international law is largely a myth rather than a reality do so because they assume that sovereign authority is essential for compliance; they recognize that the world community is a primitive political community without authoritative institutions that can make, interpret, and enforce law. As noted earlier, the world is underdeveloped politically not because of the high level of conflict among states but, rather, because of the absence of authoritative structures for settling disputes. Thus differences between domestic and international politics and law are not in kind but in degree. International society, however, is not a totally anarchic community but an "ordered anarchy" in which rudimentary political and governmental institutions facilitate transnational interactions. The problem in the international system is not the absence of law and government, but the absence of developed political institutions.

Command theory of law
The view that law exists only when backed by force.

Voluntary habits of compliance
Voluntary compliance based on habit and self-interest.

Obviously, no domestic or international legal regime can rest solely on force. If most people oppose the law, there will never be sufficient force to ensure compliance. If the law is to be effective, a large portion of the population must accept the laws and the law-making institutions as legitimate. Only significant voluntary support can ensure widespread compliance. In the United States, for example, most citizens obey traffic lights and complete annual federal and state income tax reports not because they fear prosecution, but because they are in the habit of complying with the law. They recognize that compliance with government is not only in their interest but is essential for maintaining community life. If most citizens decided to disregard traffic laws and federal and state income tax statutes, government would be unable to hire sufficient law enforcement personnel to ensure compliance.

Of course, a regime cannot rest solely on voluntary compliance. Some force is necessary, for without it those who willfully disregard the law cannot be punished. Thus an adequate theory of law must be based on both enforcement and legitimacy. An effective legal system must have institutions that can ensure compliance, even when individuals choose to disregard the law, as well as widespread public support in order to maintain a high degree of voluntary compliance.

The Making of International Law

In domestic society governments make and change law. But in global society there are no widely accepted institutions with the authority to make law. As a result, the development of international law depends on informal processes, such as conferences, international agreements, and conventions, as well as the imposition of rules by the great powers.

Article 38 of the Statute of the ICJ lists four major sources of international law: international treaties and agreements, custom, general principles of law, and judicial decisions and teachings of influential writers on international law. (See table 13.2.) Because the first two sources are the most important, we confine our analysis to them.

Treaties

An **international treaty** (or convention) is a formal written agreement between states, creating binding legal obligations for the signatories. Treaties include specific agreements between two or more states as well as general conventions and charters for universal, regional, and specialized organizations. Most scholars now regard treaties as the major source of international law and the foundation on which international legal compliance is based. Michael Akehurst, for example, writes that "treaties are the maids of all work in international law."[6] Treaties in international law are important because they create explicit norms based on the consent of states. They codify common goals and expectations and create, on the basis of voluntary consent, binding obligations.

Not all treaties are considered sources of international law. Bilateral agreements between states covering specific issues or problems normally will not lead to the creation of international law. A commercial or extradition treaty between the United States and Mexico, for example, creates binding obligations for the two signatory states but not for other countries. As a result, such bilateral conventions are not likely to contribute to an international code of law. The only treaties that are sources of international law are what Gerhard von Glahn terms "law-making treaties"—multilateral agreements based on mutual state interests and aimed at creating new international rules through explicit formal state consent or implicit

International treaty
A formal written agreement between states, creating binding legal obligations for the signatories.

TABLE 13.2   Major Sources of International Law

Source	Definition	Example
Treaties	agreements, conventions, declarations accepted as legally binding	Charter of the United Nations 1958 Law of the Sea Convention 1961 Vienna Convention on Diplomatic Privileges and Immunities
Custom	customary rules accepted as legally binding	inviolability of embassies delimitation of territorial waters rules of war
Principles	general principles of law accepted as legally binding	freedom of the seas equity *(ex aequo et bono)* treaties must be followed *(pacta sunt servanda)*
Judicial Decisions and Writings	decisions of national and international courts (especially the International Court of Justice), arbitration tribunals, and the writings of leading jurists when they influence the definition and interpretation of the law	the ICJ declared that some international organizations have legal personality the influence of the writings of such scholars as Hugo Grotius, Emmerich de Vattel, and Hans Kelsen

observance of the new rules.[7] Examples of multilateral treaties include the UN Charter, the Third Law of the Sea Convention (1982), and the 1987 Montreal Protocol, an agreement that seeks to eliminate the production and use of ozone depleting chlorofluorocarbons (CFCs).

The extent to which law is created through treaties depends of course on the nature of the treaty and the level of compliance with its provisions. Some treaties simply codify existing customs. This was the case of the Vienna Convention on Diplomatic Relations of 1961, which codified numerous customs on the rights and responsibilities of diplomatic agents. Other treaties establish new norms through deliberate joint action of government leaders. For example, the Nuclear Nonproliferation Treaty of 1968 established new standards for regulating the use and transfer of nuclear technology and fissionable materials.

Most treaties involve a combination of codification of existing practices and creation of new norms. For example, the Third Law of the Sea Convention of 1982 established a new legal category of international sea known as the **exclusive economic zone (EEZ),** giving each state sole control over the economic resources of the sea adjacent to each state. The creation of this legal norm began in 1952, when Chile, Ecuador, and Peru began claiming exclusive fishing rights over waters up to 200 NM. At the time that these three South American states made this claim, most states considered it contrary to the historic doctrine of the "freedom of the seas" and therefore illegal. But during the 1970s, when more states began claiming economic zones, the 200-NM EEZ became increasingly accepted. And by the time the Third U.N. Law of the Sea Convention concluded in December 1982, the economic zone had become part of international law, explicitly recognized in the new Law of the Sea Treaty.

Traditionally, state consent has been expressed through *signature, ratification,* and *accession.* The first two methods are generally used during the original creation of a treaty, whereas accession allows nonsignatory states to formally adhere to an existing, valid convention. Ordinarily, the creation of treaties involves both the signing and ratification of a treaty. In the first phase, authorized representatives

Exclusive economic zone (EEZ)
According to the 1982 Third Law of the Sea Treaty, territorial states have exclusive economic control over ocean waters extending up to 200 NM from the coastline.

of states sign a treaty, thus indicating the government's willingness to be bound by the terms of the agreement. This was done, for example, by former President Ronald Reagan and Soviet General Secretary Mikhail Gorbachev in December 1987 in Washington, D.C., when they signed the Intermediate Nuclear Forces Treaty. But a treaty does not become binding until ratification—that is, approved by the government itself. Although the requirements for ratification of treaties vary among states, ordinarily it is viewed as an executive act, undertaken either by the chief of state (such as a constitutional monarch) or the head of government (such as a president or prime minister). In the United States the responsibility for ratification is in the Senate, which must approve a treaty by a two-thirds vote before it becomes binding.

One of the foundational principles of international law is **pacta sunt servanda**—treaties must be observed. Although this norm is generally regarded as the bedrock of international law, jurists argue that exceptional conditions can make treaties invalid. Perhaps the most important of these is the principle of **rebus sic stantibus,** which provides that parties are not bound to fulfill the terms of a treaty when there has been a fundamental change in original treaty conditions or circumstances. In addition to this legal exception, scholars have also argued that states may unilaterally suspend treaty obligations for moral reasons. Some specific justifications given for repudiating treaties include: (1) the signing of a treaty under duress; (2) the signing of a treaty involving exploitation by a major power over a small state; (3) the use of treaties as instruments of power; and (4) the creation of a treaty through fraud.

Pacta sunt servanda
A basic principle of international law stipulating that states must fulfill treaty obligations.

Rebus sic stantibus
A principle of international law providing that treaties lose their validity when the original conditions change.

Custom

The second most important source of international law is custom. Custom does not include any regular pattern of state behavior but only those widely accepted rules and principles that are recognized as binding on the international behavior of states. What makes customary rules important sources of international law is their universality and repeated usage. Examples of customary international law include the practice of diplomatic immunity, the exemption of noncombatants from direct attack during wartime, the acceptance of a three-mile territorial sea limit for nearly two-and-a-half centuries (the territorial jurisdiction has now been extended to 12 NM for most states), and the custom of exempting unarmed fishing vessels from capture during wartime.

The *Paquette Havana* case, heard by the U.S. Supreme Court in 1900, illustrates the important role of customary norms in international relations. The case involved two Spanish fishing vessels that U.S. naval forces had captured off the coast of Florida at the start of the Spanish-American War. The owners of the Spanish vessels sued the U.S. government to recover the loss of the ships and cargo. The Supreme Court ruled in favor of the Spanish claimant because the U.S. naval vessels had violated the customary legal norm of exempting unarmed coastal fishing vessels from capture in wartime when they are solely engaged in peaceful commercial activities.

The Problem of Peaceful Change

One of the key issues of international law is the problem of how to change law peacefully. Fundamentally, there are two ways of altering laws in domestic society—through peaceful means using the institutional machinery of government and through violence. When the institutional structures of society fail to bring about needed reforms through peaceful means, political groups may resort to violence to bring them about or, in the extreme, topple a regime. Because the use of violence is an "illegal" form of political change, it is normally used only as a last resort. The responsibility of government, of course, is to maintain law and order and to thwart and punish "illegal" behavior.

Violence is relatively infrequent in domestic political society, especially in free, democratic countries. This is particularly so when compared to international society. The reason for higher levels of naked power and violence in the world community is that there are no developed institutional mechanisms for articulating popular interests and for making laws when sufficient support warrants it. Whereas interest groups, political parties, and legislatures facilitate peaceful change in domestic society, international society lacks these institutions. This does not mean that there are no accepted procedures for changing international law, but only that the procedures and institutions available for carrying out global reforms are underdeveloped.

An important vehicle for making and changing international law is the periodic *specialized conference*. Examples of such law-creating conferences include the Hague Conferences of 1899 and 1907, which codified, among other things, rules of war and procedures for international arbitration and conflict resolution, and the **Third UN Conference on the Law of the Sea,** which resulted in the 1982 UN Convention on the Law of the Sea (UNCLOS III). The UNCLOS III convention codified existing international maritime customs and established new norms in a number of major areas, including territorial waters, the high seas, and economic zones. Although international conferences can contribute to the making of conventions and treaties, they are not equivalent to domestic legislatures. States are not bound by the proposed norms until they ratify the conventions or treaties.

Another vehicle for bringing about international legal change is an **international regime.**[8] As noted in chapter 4, regimes are widely accepted rules, norms, and behavior patterns within a particular issue-area of the international community. As countries establish closer cooperation in specialized areas of shared concern (e.g., foreign investment, refugees, deep-sea fishing, environmental protection, and waste disposal), they develop informal principles and procedures codifying the shared, voluntary patterns of behavior. Regimes are important because they encourage the development of procedures and norms that facilitate coordination and cooperation among states. Although such rules and procedures are not themselves international law, they provide the shared practices on which international law can be developed. In effect, regimes serve as a "half-way house" between the anarchic system and a community based on law, contributing quasilegal norms that can be subsequently transformed into law as the procedures and rules gain acceptance.

A third approach to changing international law is through informal and incremental actions of individual states. When a large number of states begin to challenge existing norms, their "illegal" behaviors can in time precipitate a change in the law. As noted earlier, when Chile, Ecuador, and Peru began claiming a 200-NM exclusive fishing zone in the early 1950s, customary international law allowed states a maximum of 12 NM of exclusive control over adjacent waters. As a result, the United States refused to recognize the extended fishing claims, and when U.S. vessels were confiscated off the Ecuadorian coast, the U.S. government provided financial aid to fishing vessels to cover fines for "illegal" fishing and for the release of the captured ship. By the late 1970s, however, a growing number of states, including the United States, had begun accepting the larger zone, thereby precipitating a change in international law. This change was codified in the UNCLOS III (see case 13.1).

In altering international law through incremental adjustments, it is important that the proposed norms be widely accepted. If the new norm is effectively challenged by other states, especially more powerful states, it is unlikely that it will become part of the body of international law. Thus, when Muhammar Qaddafi began

Third UN Conference on the Law of the Sea
A series of negotiating sessions from 1973 to 1982 leading to the Third UN Law of the Sea Treaty—the most comprehensive legal convention on maritime law.

International regime
The rules, principles, and decision-making procedures governing international behavior in a given issue-area.

Case 13.1 Iceland versus Britain: The Codfish Dispute

In September 1972, Iceland unilaterally extended its economic (fishing) zone from 12 miles to 50 miles, thereby prohibiting foreign fishing vessels from these waters without Icelandic permits. This action, taken in great part because of the economic importance of fishing to Iceland's economy, precipitated strong opposition from Britain, whose fishermen had for centuries fished the cod-rich waters off the Iceland coast. In April 1972, the United Kingdom took the dispute to the International Court of Justice, claiming that Iceland's unilateral extension of its economic zone was contrary to international law.

In September 1972, the ICJ temporarily prohibited Iceland from enforcing the 50-mile conservation zone. But Iceland, which denied the court's jurisdiction in the conflict, declared the order invalid and directed its coast guard vessels to halt foreign fishing in the 50-mile zone. From the fall of 1972 to the spring of 1973 numerous clashes took place between Icelandic and British vessels, eventually prompting the British government to order warships to protect British fishermen. The British-Icelandic dispute greatly eased after both countries concluded a temporary agreement in October 1973 that effectively limited British fishing in the 50-mile conservation zone in accord with specific Icelandic stipulations.

In July 1974, the World Court issued its judgment in the dispute. It ruled against Iceland and in favor of Britain, and indicated that Iceland could not unilaterally exclude British fishing vessels in the new 50-mile economic zone. Because Iceland had earlier refused to admit the court's jurisdiction, it disregarded the judgment altogether, thereby precipitating a renewal of the so-called "codfish war." Because of repeated clashes and ramming incidents between British frigates and the Icelandic coast guard, Iceland broke diplomatic relations with Britain in early 1976 and threatened to withdraw from NATO. Later that year the British government withdrew its warships and British-Icelandic negotiations were resumed, eventually resulting in an agreement that, in effect, ratified Iceland's original claim. British vessels would be allowed to fish in the 50-mile conservation zone but only to the extent provided by the government of Iceland.

In June 1979, Iceland extended its economic zone to 200 NM. By this time numerous other states, including Belgium, West Germany, and the United States, had begun claiming a 200-mile conservation zone. In effect, Iceland's unilateral and "illegal" action in extending its economic zone from 12 to 50 miles helped to modify a key rule of the law of the sea.

claiming in 1981 that the Gulf of Sidra, located off the coast of Libya and historically regarded as international waters, was part of Libya's territorial waters, the United States decided to challenge a claim it regarded as arbitrary. To affirm the Western claim that the Gulf of Sidra was a part of international waters, President Reagan ordered a naval task force into those waters in August 1981. When Libya sought to challenge the action by sending up fighters, U.S. F-14 jets protecting the task force shot down two incoming Libyan planes. In short, modifying or extending existing norms can only be realized if there is broad support for such changes.

THE INTERPRETATION AND APPLICATION OF INTERNATIONAL LAW

In a municipal legal system, adjudication plays a vital role in conflict resolution. Its significant role is due to the authority of courts to settle disputes by interpreting and applying law. In the international system, however, the resolution of disputes through courts is far more difficult for two reasons: (1) supranational courts lack competence to settle conflicts, and (2) in world politics the distinction between politics and law is ambiguous and uncertain. As a result international courts play a much less significant role in the international community than do courts in domestic society.

TABLE 13.3   Selected ICJ Contentious Cases, 1974–1997

Year	Countries	Issue
1974	U.K. v. Iceland	Fisheries jurisdiction
	W. Germany v. Iceland	Fisheries jurisdiction
1974	Australia v. France	Nuclear testing
	New Zealand v. France	Nuclear testing
1976	Greece v. Turkey	Aegean Sea continental shelf
1981	U.S. v. Iran	Diplomatic hostage crisis
1982	Tunisia v. Libya	Mediterranean Sea continental shelf
1984	Canada/U.S.	Gulf of Maine maritime boundary
1985	Libya/Malta	Mediterranean Sea continental shelf
1986	Nicaragua v. U.S.	U.S. military and paramilitary acts against Nicaragua
1986	Burkina Faso/Mali	Frontier dispute
1994	Qatar v. Bahrain	Maritime and territorial boundaries
1995	Guinea Bissau v. Senegal	Maritime boundaries*
1995	Portugal v. Australia	East Timor
1996	Bosnia/Herzegovina v. Yugoslavia	Genocide
1997	Hungary/Slovakia	Construction and operation of river locks
Pending	Iran v. U.S.	Oil platforms
Pending	Cameroon v. Nigeria	Maritime and territorial boundaries
Pending	Spain v. Canada	Fisheries jurisdiction

*discontinued by parties

The International Court of Justice

The most important court in the international system is the International Court of Justice, a fifteen-member judicial body located in The Hague, the Netherlands. Because the ICJ is a formal organ of the United Nations, all UN members are automatically members of the Court, although other states can also bring cases to it provided they sign its statute. Although the Court discharges its duties as a full Court, it may also establish a special chamber to arbitrate particular disputes, as was done with the Gulf of Maine dispute between the United States and Canada noted at the outset of this chapter. Since the first World Court chamber was constituted in 1982, several other chambers have been established.

Contentious cases
Cases that deal with legal disputes betwen two or more states.

Advisory cases
Cases that deal with issues of legal interpretation raised by agencies of the UN.

The full Court hears two types of cases: **contentious cases,** which deal with issues of legal disputes between two or more states, and **advisory cases,** which deal with issues of legal interpretation raised by agencies of the UN. In contentious cases, the Court issues judgments; in advisory cases, it issues advisory opinions. From 1946 to 1997, the Court heard ninety-six cases, offering sixty judgments and twenty-three advisory opinions. Although the Court generally issues only one or two judgments per year, its ongoing caseload ranges from five to ten cases. In 1995, for example, the ICJ presided over nine contentious cases and rendered two judgments.[9] Table 13.3 lists selected contentious cases from 1980 to 1997.

Although the ICJ is the world's highest judicial body, it plays a limited role in world affairs. Whereas domestic courts are generally backlogged with cases, the World Court is underutilized. To a significant degree, this is due to states' unwill-

The international Court of Justice, located in the Peace Palace in The Hague, the Netherlands, hears Bosnia's case against Serbia in 1996. In the case, Bosnia charged Serbia with violating the international convention against genocide.

ingness to grant the ICJ jurisdiction over its international disputes, especially those considered of vital national interest. Unlike domestic courts, the World Court does not have automatic jurisdiction over international legal disputes. Its jurisdiction is established only when states voluntarily consent to its authority.

One way by which states have attempted to strengthen international adjudication is by giving the World Court compulsory jurisdiction before conflicts develop. This can be done through unilateral written declarations submitted to the Court in accordance with the **optional clause** (art. 36) of the ICJ's Statute. This clause provides that states "may at any time declare that they recognize as compulsory *ipso facto* and without special agreement, in relation to any other state accepting the same obligation, the jurisdiction of the Court in all legal disputes."

Although more than sixty states have adopted the optional clause, few have done so without reservations. The United States, for example, accepted the court's compulsory jurisdiction in 1946, but passed laws qualifying that acceptance. One of them, known as the Connally Amendment, established that the World Court did not have competence over domestic issues, and whether or not an issue was domestic or international was itself an issue of domestic affairs. In October 1985, the United States announced that it was ending its policy of automatic ICJ jurisdiction. This action was taken in great measure because the Court had established jurisdiction in the *Nicaragua v. United States* case (see case 13.2) against the wishes of the U.S. government.

One major difficulty in international adjudication is the determination of which disputes can be settled through international adjudication. To begin with, not all international disputes involve a violation of international law, just as many domestic quarrels are not the result of violations of federal and state statutes. According to British international law professor Michael Akehurst, one of the reasons for popular skepticism about international law stems from the common misconception that all international disputes must involve a violation of law. But this is clearly false. Some conflicts have their root in different interpretations of facts; others may involve uncertainties about the law; some are the result of efforts to change the law; and still others are the consequence of an unfriendly but legal act.[10]

An important task in international adjudication is to determine which disputes are essentially **justiciable** (that is, legal in character and subject to settlement in court) and which are not. In domestic society all major disputes can potentially be

Optional clause
In accordance with Article 36 of the ICJ Statue, states may give the world court compulsory jurisdiction beforehand in certain types of disputes.

Justiciable
Disputes that are legal in character and subject to settlement by a court.

Case 13.2 Nicaragua Versus United States

Facts

During the early 1980s the U.S. government assisted Nicaraguan antigovernment forces (known as *Contras*) in their insurgency against the Sandinista regime. The justification for U.S. aid to the anti-Sandinista guerrillas was that the Sandinista government had (1) provided military and logistical support to the leftist guerrillas in El Salvador and (2) had betrayed the democratic goals of the Nicaraguan revolution by establishing a Marxist state.

The scope of U.S. aid to the contras greatly intensified in March 1984 when the CIA supported the mining of three Nicaraguan ports (Corinto, Puerto Sandino, and El Bluff). The mining, carried out without warning, resulted in damage to seven Nicaraguan vessels and six from other states. In response to this increased use of force, Nicaragua filed suit against the United States on April 9, 1984.

Jurisdiction

Because the ICJ has no enforcement power of its own, it must establish jurisdiction in each case. The U.S. government argued that the ICJ had no jurisdiction because the dispute was fundamentally a political conflict, not a legal one. Furthermore, the United States challenged Nicaragua's right to plead in the World Court because Nicaragua had not explicitly given it compulsory jurisdiction. Finally, the United States insisted that in order for the proceedings to be legitimate, all parties in the dispute needed to be present. This meant, at a minimum, that El Salvador, the victim of Nicaraguan supported insurgency and on whose behalf the United States had been acting, had to be present for the Court to rule on the dispute.

In its ruling on jurisdiction, issued on November 26, 1984, the Court declared that it was competent to hear the case for three reasons: (1) the dispute was fundamentally a legal conflict, not an international armed dispute; (2) although Nicaragua had not filed a document giving the ICJ compulsory jurisdiction, a 1929 Nicaragua declaration was sufficient; and (3) the U.S. decision of April 6, 1984, to withdraw compulsory jurisdiction was unacceptable because a six-month notice must be given before suspension can take place.

Interim Measures

After rejecting preliminary U.S. objections, the Court issued on May 10, 1985, provisional measures to be carried out while the case was being heard. The interim measures called on the United States to respect the sovereignty, territorial integrity, and political independence of Nicaragua and to cease all military and paramilitary activity there. Specifically, the Court said that "the United States should immediately cease and refrain from any action restricting, blocking or endangering access to or from Nicaraguan ports, and in particular the laying of mines."

The Verdict

Even though the United States withdrew from the case in January 1985, the Court heard Nicaragua's arguments and on June 27, 1986, ruled against the United States on several counts. It rejected the U.S. plea of collective self-defense and cited breaches of obligation to Nicaragua, including intervention in internal affairs, interruption of peaceful maritime activity, and threats to state sovereignty. It also condemned illegal threats and uses of force, and found that the U.S. trade embargo and the mining of ports violated the 1956 Treaty of Friendship, Commerce, and Navigation. Finally, the Court declared that the United States had ignored general humanitarian principles and customary law on numerous occasions. As a result, the U.S. government owed reparations in an amount to be decided by the parties involved.

In judging the case, the Court indicated that the United States had violated customary international law by mining harbors, attacking naval bases and oil installations, infringing on air space, supporting antigovernment forces, and instituting a trade embargo. The justices set aside arguments of ideological intervention and dismissed the U.S. plea of collective self-defense because they thought that there was insufficient evidence to support the U.S. claim that Nicaragua was supporting insurgency in El Salvador. Additionally, the Court found that the United States had neglected principles of nonintervention, sovereignty, and basic humanitarian law.

The U.S. judge, Stephen Schwebel, disagreed with his peers' verdict, and in his dissenting remarks argued that Nicaragua was the first nation in the region to commit aggression. He cited instances of armed attacks by the plaintiff into other states and applauded the U.S. acts in defense of El Salvador, Costa Rica, Honduras, and Guatemala. The American justice concluded by disclaiming the right of Nicaragua to press charges against the United States and by reiterating that the problem was political and therefore nonjusticiable.

settled in court. This is because most societies have adopted a wide range of rules governing significant elements of economic, political, and social life. In the international system, by contrast, the most significant disputes are political and therefore not subject to legal settlement. The proportion of politics to law is much higher in the international community than in domestic society because of the former's limited political consensus and underdeveloped regulatory mechanisms and governmental institutions.

Some have argued that international adjudication can be strengthened by expanding treaty law. But this, by itself, is not enough. During the early part of this century, for example, several treaties were passed declaring war unlawful, but these acts had little impact on the behavior of states because they were not related to any significant transnational political developments. The reason for the limited role of adjudication in international society is that law can only be effective if, as noted historian E.H. Carr has pointed out, it is a by-product of political settlements in society and is dependent on, and consistent with, the underlying values and political assumptions within society.[11] Moreover, whether or not an international dispute is legal or political is itself a political issue. Carr has written:

> . . . the strengthening of international law, and the extension of the number and character of international disputes recognized as suitable for judicial settlement, is a political, not a legal, problem. There is no principle of law which enables one to decide that a given issue is suitable for treatment by legal methods. The decision is political; and its character is likely to be determined by the political development of the international community or of the political relations between the countries concerned. . . . In modern international relations, the machinery of judicial settlement has been developed far in advance of the political order in which alone it can effectively operate. Further progress towards the extension of judicial settlement of international disputes can be made, not by perfecting an already too perfect machinery, but by developing political co-operation.[12]

In short, adjudication can play a role in the settlement of international disputes, but its role is limited by the high level of political, social, and cultural pluralism. Moreover, the absence of authoritative institutions for making, changing, enforcing, and interpreting rules makes the application of law to international disputes highly tenuous. These shortcomings are well illustrated by *Nicaragua v. United States,* a widely publicized ICJ case discussed in Case 13.2.

Other International Courts

The UN Charter (art. 33) provides that "parties to any dispute...shall, first of all, seek a solution by negotiation, enquiry, mediation, conciliation, arbitration, judicial settlement, resort to regional agencies or arrangements, or other peaceful means of their own choice." In addition to the ICJ, three other types of international courts play an important role in international adjudication and the peaceful settlement of international disputes: regional courts, international criminal courts, and arbitration tribunals.

Regional courts are typically established to interpret the laws and rules governing regional organizations and to adjudicate disputes among its members. Examples of regional courts include:

> *EUROPE: European Court of Justice and European Court of Human Rights*
> *AFRICA: Commission of Mediation, Conciliation and Arbitration*
> *LATIN AMERICA: Inter-American Court of Human Rights and the Andean Court of Justice*

The most important of these is the **European Court of Justice (ECJ),** the fifteen-member court of the European Union (EU). The ECJ is the supreme court

Regional courts
International courts of regional organizations that adjudicate disputes among member-states.

European Court of Justice (ECJ)
The regional court of the European Union.

of the EU, issuing binding decisions on the meaning and application of EU statutes, rules, and decision. Because of the high level of EU's institutionalization, community law is regarded as authoritative and binding on governments, public and private institutions, commercial organizations, and citizens of member-states. Indeed, it is commonly accepted by European judicial authorities that EU law has precedence over national law. Thus, unlike the ICJ, the ECJ has automatic jurisdiction on all issues relating to the interpretation and application of EU treaties as well as the acts and omissions of institutions established to fulfill the aims of the EU. Additionally, the ECJ differs from the ICJ and most other regional courts and tribunals in that individuals and corporations may directly bring claims to the court. Since its establishment in 1952, the ECJ has heard more than 8,500 cases, with an average of more than 400 cases per year since the late 1970s. To cope with the increasing burdens placed on the Court, the EU established a supplementary judicial body known as the *Court of First Instance*. This fifteen-member body hears cases from individuals, corporations, and other agencies, thereby allowing the ECJ to concentrate on its basic responsibility of interpreting EU law.

International criminal court

A court established to deal with specific wartime crimes (e.g., the Nuremburg Tribunal, The Hague War Crimes Tribunal).

Another type of court is the **international criminal court.** Although states have been discussing the creation of a permanent international criminal court for much of this century, to date the only criminal courts that have been established are those to deal with specific wartime crimes. In the aftermath of World War II, the victorious powers established two International Military Tribunals to prosecute soldiers and political leaders for crimes against peace, war crimes, and crimes against humanity. The *Nuremburg Tribunal* and the *Tokyo Tribunal* together convicted more then 3,600 German and Japanese officials, imposing the death sentence on 1,019 of them.[13] In 1993, the United Nations established an international wartime tribunal in The Hague in order to prosecute officials, soldiers, and paramilitary personnel for gross human rights violations committed in the Bosnian civil war. Unlike the World War II tribunals, however, *The Hague War Crimes Tribunal,* as case 13.3 suggests, faced the daunting task of gathering war crimes data and of apprehending indicted officials in territories that had not been defeated militarily. Moreover, because the UN stipulated that indicted criminals could not be tried in absentia, the apprehension of alleged wartime criminals was critical to the Tribunal's success. But the NATO Stabilization Force in Bosnia (SFOR) had been reluctant to use force to apprehend indicted war criminals, lest such initiatives impair implementation of other, more significant aspects of the Bosnia peace plan, known as the Dayton Accords. But in 1997, SFOR made the first attempt to arrest two of the more than seventy indicted criminals that are not in custody in The Hague, successfully capturing one and killing the other when he resisted capture. Moreover, the prosecution of war criminals has been a difficult and time-consuming process, with the first court judgment issued in mid-1997, more than three years after the tribunal was established.

Arbitration tribunal

An international court that settles disputes by issuing binding judgments.

The third type of international courts is the **arbitration tribunal.** Although the work of such panels, commissions, or tribunals is frequently based upon international legal principles, arbitration, unlike adjudication, resolves disputes by issuing judgments based upon rules and principles accepted by the parties beforehand. Arbitration, in other words, is not based upon the interpretation of the law but on a tribunal's interpretation of the facts in light of accepted guidelines. But like adjudication, arbitration is binding on the parties. It is therefore a more authoritative method of conflict resolution than either conciliation or mediation (see chap. 12 for a comparison of these procedures).

Arbitration tribunals are either temporary or permanent. Historically, most tribunals have been ad hoc, created to resolve particular conflicts at specific times.

Case 13.3 The Hague War Crimes Tribunal

The United Nations established The International Criminal Tribunal for the former Yugoslavia in 1993 after it became clear that Croats, Muslims, and Serbs were committing gross human rights abuses in the Bosnian civil war. The most dramatic claims involved alleged crimes of "ethnic cleansing" by Serbs against Muslims, in which tens of thousands of Muslims were either killed, tortured, or abused. As a result, the Security Council authorized the creation of the Tribunal to investigate these allegations and to establish the institutional machinery in order to impartially prosecute indicted criminals.

The International Tribunal, supported by a staff of 375 persons, is comprised of a court of justices, a prosecutor's office, a twenty-four-cell detention center, and a secretariat. The court, which is comprised of two chambers and a court of appeal, is comprised of eleven justices, elected by the General Assembly for four-year terms. The Tribunal's chief prosecutor during the 1993–1995 period was Richard Goldstone, the distinguished South African jurist. As of mid-1996, the Tribunal had indicted fifty-seven persons—forty-six Serbs, eight Croats, and three Muslims—but only three of the fifty-seven were in custody.[14] The most important indictments were against the Bosnian Serb political leader, Radovan Karadzic, and the Bosnian Serb military commander, General Ratko Mladic. Although the Tribunal had issued warrants for their arrest, Karadzic and Mladic remained free

in 1998. And because Serbian authorities remained skeptical of the Tribunal's work, it appeared unlikely that high-level officials would be turned over to the court for prosecution. Moreover, neither the UN's Bosnia peacekeeping mission (UNPROFOR), which functioned from 1992 until 1995, nor the NATO Implementation Force for Bosnia (IFOR), which superseded UNPROFOR's role in December 1995, viewed the capture of indicted war criminals as a key part of their mission. Indeed, because pursuing indicted criminals might destabilize the region and impair the quest for peace, the quest for justice remained secondary to the establishment of a stable order among the three waring factions.

Notwithstanding its limited success in bringing to trial indicted wartime criminals, the Tribunal has helped to raise the awareness of human rights abuses. As chief prosecutor Richard Goldstone has observed, the work of the Tribunal is significant not only because pursuing justice is essential to the long-term political stability of Bosnia-Herzegovina, but also because the prosecution of human rights violations is essential for the further internationalization of human rights norms.[15] The task of internationalizing norms was illustrated when the UN Tribunal indicted eight Bosnian Serb military and police officers for repeated wartime rape, marking the first time that sexual assault was used as the sole basis for a war crime.[16]

Permanent arbitral panels are, however, playing an increasingly important role in the international community. Examples of permanent arbitration tribunals are included in table 13.4.

THE ENFORCEMENT OF INTERNATIONAL LAW

How is international law applied? When one state commits an illegal act against another state and refuses to resolve the dispute peacefully, how is law enforced? In effect, what methods are available to ensure compliance with the law?

In domestic society, authoritative institutions exist to adjudicate disputes and enforce the binding judgments of courts. But in international society no such authoritative institutions exist. To a significant degree, states need not accept a new rule unless they agree to it, and need not appear before an international tribunal unless they consent to do so. Because there is no centralized executive body capable of enforcing the law, some observers have concluded that international law is not law. But as noted earlier, law is not based solely, or even primarily, on force but on the widespread acceptance of rules. Because the global system does not

TABLE 13.4   Selected International Courts of Arbitration

Tribunal	Location	Role
Chambers of the International Court of Justice	The Hague	States may request a special three-judge panel to arbitrate disputes
UN Administrative Claims Tribunal	New York City	Resolves claims between the UN and its employees
International Centre for Investment Disputes	Washington, D. C.	Resolves investment disputes between states and individuals from other states
Court of Arbitration of International Chamber of Commerce (ICC)	Paris	Commercial disputes of ICC members are resolved through binding arbitration
World Trade Organization	Geneva	Member-states must resolve trade disputes using a mandatory system of dispute settlement
UN Compensation Commission	Geneva	Resolves claims against Iraq resulting from its invasion of Kuwait

have courts to make binding judicial settlements and executive institutions to implement such judgments, enforcement procedures, or sanctions, are different—not absent—from those in domestic society.

The Limited Role of Force

One of the most widely held beliefs about law is that superior force is required to ensure compliance. But as Roger Fisher, a scholar of international law and negotiation, notes, the idea that law requires force is based on several misconceptions.[17] First, law does not work only because it is a command backed by force. There are times, he argues, when governments obey the decisions of courts, even though they possess superior force to disregard such legal action. For example, when steel workers went on strike in 1950 and forced the steel mills to close, President Truman used executive power to open the mills and keep them running. The Supreme Court, however, ruled that Truman's action was illegal and ordered him to cease running the companies. He complied with the action, even though he could have used the military forces at his disposal to defy the Court. Similarly, when the Supreme Court declared in 1972 that President Richard Nixon had to turn over secret tapes, the president complied with the Court verdict because of the widely accepted binding authority of the court.

A second misconception regarding international law is that the only way to influence foreign governments is through force. According to this myth, international legal norms are incapable of influencing the actions of states because only individual or collective military power can effectively bring about behavioral change in another state. But as noted earlier, military power is only one instrument of statecraft. Other significant elements of power that do not involve military compellence include widely shared norms and procedures, international public opinion, rational argumentation and negotiation, and moral suasion. Although force may serve as the ultimate arbiter of international decision-making, force is not the only means to influence another state.

A third misconception is that law only restrains. According to Fisher, law is not only a set of rules prohibiting action but also a set of guidelines and principles affecting choices and interests of individuals and political communities. Law, in other words, is both a positive force in guiding the aims and goals of states and a restraining force in restricting selfish behavior.

The emphasis on the absence of international governmental machinery and the weakness of negative sanctions tends to focus attention on the failure and weakness of international law and to obscure the extent to which it is obeyed. Louis Henkin has correctly emphasized the role of compliance with the law:

> What matters is not whether the international system has legislative, judicial, or executive branches, corresponding to those we have become accustomed to seek in a domestic society; what matters is whether international law is reflected in the policies of nations and in relations between nations. The question is not whether there is an effective legislature; it is whether there is law that responds and corresponds to the changing needs of a changing society. The question is not whether there is an effective judiciary, but whether disputes are resolved in an orderly fashion in accordance with international law. Most important, the question is not whether law is enforceable or even effectively enforced; rather, whether law is observed, whether it governs or influences behavior, whether international behavior reflects stability and order. The fact is, lawyers insist, that nations have accepted important limitations on their sovereignty, that they have observed these norms and undertakings, that the result has been substantial order in international relations.[18]

Hedley Bull has noted that compliance with international law is generally higher than is commonly supposed. Bull writes: ". . . when states live at peace with one another and are involved in diplomatic relations and exchange money, goods and visitors with them they are, in effect, in compliance with important norms of the law of nations."[19]

There can be little doubt that states violate and disregard commonly accepted norms of international law. But even when states violate basic legal rules, they often seek to justify their illegal acts with legal justifications, thereby further reinforcing the legitimacy of international law. For example, when the United States intervened in Grenada in 1983, it justified its action in terms of international legal principles. Similarly, when Argentina invaded the Falkland Islands (Islas Malvinas) a year earlier, it defended its military action by claiming that its use of force was a last resort act and that it was undertaken to regain territories that were legally Argentina's.

Enforcement

Because there is no executive authority in global society, the enforcement of law is much more difficult in the international community than in domestic society. There are two major types of **sanctions** or enforcement procedures—legal and extralegal.

Sanctions
Measures designed to enforce compliance with international legal norms.

Legal Sanctions

Such enforcement procedures involve legally approved measures for ensuring compliance with international law. Although such instruments may be based on customary legal norms, most treaties provide for specific enforcement procedures. Such enforcement may be carried out either collectively through organizations like the United Nations, NATO, or the 1947 Inter-American Treaty of Reciprocal Assistance (known as the Rio Pact), or they may be carried out individually. Although the UN Charter provides some measures for collective enforcement of international law, the chief **legal sanctions** in the international community are based on individual action, commonly defined as *self-help*.

Legal sanctions
Enforcement procedures based on international law and implemented by states and international governmental organizations.

According to the self-help principle, an injured state may use its resources, including force, to redress a wrong it has suffered. Examples of self-help actions include public condemnation, rupture of diplomatic relations, withdrawal from organizations, retorsion, and reprisal. The last two are the most significant actions and are normally undertaken only if injury has been caused directly to the state implementing self-help acts.

A **retortion** is a lawful act that seeks to injure the wrong-doing state through nonmilitary means. A state, for example, may halt economic or military assistance

Retortion
A hostile, legal act carried out in retaliation for a foreign state's prior hostile action.

to a country that has carried out illegal actions against its nationals. This was illustrated in 1976 when the United States halted all military aid to Chile in response to alleged governmental complicity in the death of Orlando Letelier, Chile's ambassador to the United States during the Marxist government of Salvador Allende (1970-1973).

Reprisal
A hostile, illegal act that is rendered legal when carried out in response to a prior illegal act.

A **reprisal**—normally an illegal act—is usually a military action carried out in retaliation for a prior illegal act. An example of a reprisal was the 1986 U.S. bombing of Libyan military installations in retaliation for Libyan complicity in the bombing of a West German discotheque that resulted in the death and injury of several U.S. soldiers. A more recent illustration is the U.S. bombing in mid-1993 of Iraq's intelligence headquarters in retaliation for Iraq's terrorist plot to kill former President George Bush during his visit to Kuwait.

Legal sanctions, such as those discussed above, have not proved an effective tool of law enforcement. One reason is that they only work when the injured state is more powerful and influential than the injuring state. Generally, individual sanctions carried out by a weaker state are likely to prove more damaging to it than to the more powerful state being punished. Obviously, collective sanctions through regional or international organizations can overcome this shortcoming, but international collective action is difficult to achieve, especially when it involves the enforcement of international law. For example, the League of Nations' ineffectiveness in defining and implementing collective measures demonstrated that states are seldom willing to use their military power to defend a rule or principle in which their own national interests are not vitally at stake.

Extralegal Sanctions

Such enforcement procedures involve social, political, and economic actions designed to foster compliance with international law. Given the decentralized political character of the world system, **extralegal sanctions** play a more important role in promoting compliance with international law than do legal sanctions. Some of the most important extralegal sanctions include: habits of compliance, legal reciprocity, public opinion, and the preference for order and predictability.

Extralegal sanctions
Enforcement procedures based on norms other than law.

The habit of voluntarily obeying law, the foundation of all domestic and international law, provides the basis for national *self-restraint*. Political scientist Karl Deutsch has written that although the habits of voluntary compliance are an invisible partner of government, they do the bulk of the government's work by channeling the behavior of people. A political community is much like an iceberg, with the visible one-ninth representing the work of government and the submerged, invisible eight-ninths representing the customs, habits, and voluntary compliance with community rules.[20] Because there is no international police force to enforce international law, the practice of national self-restraint, based on the habits of voluntary compliance, is the bedrock of effective international law.

Reciprocity is also a significant extralegal sanction. Governments often accept legal obligations because their own self-interest is achieved if other states abide by similar rules. The origins of international law developed out of the principle of reciprocity: states accepted certain rules when other states did the same. Some of the most fundamental norms of international law, such as diplomatic immunity, respect for the sovereignty and territorial independence of states, and the protection of civilians, women, and children in wartime, evolved from reciprocal practices.

The norm of reciprocity has been illustrated with the nonuse of chemical weapons. Following the abhorrent destruction caused by chemical arms in World War I, 105 states signed the *Geneva Protocol of 1925* banning the use of chemical weapons. The implementation of this legal provision has ultimately rested on the fear of reciprocity. For example, it is commonly assumed that the Nazis' refusal to use chemical weapons in World War II was based on the fear of Allied retaliation in kind. And more recently in the 1991 Gulf War, Iraq's decision not to use its chemical capabilities, even when facing a major military defeat, was no doubt grounded in the fear of unacceptable retaliation. Prior to the commencement of the war, it was widely known that Saddam Hussein had stockpiled a large quantity of chemical weapons and that these could be delivered in a number of ways, including short-range SCUD missiles. As a result, allied military planners took extreme precautions against the possible use of chemical weapons. Most importantly, President Bush and senior military leaders made clear that the resort to chemical weapons would result in grave consequences to Iraq. The president never threatened retaliation in kind or with nuclear arms, but implied that the resort to weapons of mass destruction was illegal and would be exceedingly costly to Iraq.

International public opinion is a third important extralegal sanction. Because world public opinion is rarely coherent and well defined, especially on complex problems in international relations, its major contribution to international legal compliance is to judge the behavior of states. World public opinion may not define or clarify law, but it is a potent political force in world politics. There can be little doubt that a state's credibility and influence are enhanced when its actions are perceived as legal and just. What people think is important. For example, when the United States carried out the Libyan bombing raid in response to Colonel Qaddafi's sponsorship of state-terrorism, it made every effort to use limited, discriminating force, destroying only military and political targets and avoiding civilian casualties. Besides being morally superior, the reliance on discriminating force was also rooted in the need to maximize global public opinion. Similarly, during the air campaign of the Gulf War, allied bombers were directed to attack only Iraqi military targets and to avoid population centers and religious and historic sites. And when pilots could not see their intended targets because of weather or other obstacles, they were ordered to return with their bombs. To a significant degree, the international public support for the air campaign was derived from the widespread belief that allied forces were using discriminating force against Iraq.

The fourth extralegal sanction is the preference for stability and order provided by law. In his influential *The Law of Nations,* J. L. Brierly, a leading British scholar of international law, has summarized this last extralegal sanction well:

> The ultimate explanation of the binding force of all law is that man, whether he is a single individual or whether he is associated with other men in a state, is constrained, in so far as he is a reasonable being, to believe that order and not chaos is the governing principle of the world in which he has to live.[21]

Although stability and order are no doubt essential to the long-term well-being of nations, statesmen, like individuals, do not always calculate interests in the long run. This is because of the difficulty in defining short- and long-term interests but also because leaders pursue immediate relative gains, regardless of long-term consequences. Moreover, because compliance with the law does not always benefit all parties alike, some states may be more willing to obey international legal norms than others.

In sum, despite the absence of effective enforcement, institutions, and the reliance chiefly on self-help, international law contributes in a modest but important way to the order and stability of the international system. Those who criticize international law because of its weak enforcement procedures are of course correct; but those who call attention to the widespread state conformity with rules of international law are also correct. We are thus drawn to the conclusion, articulated by political scientist Hedley Bull, that "international law is a social reality to the extent that there is a very substantial degree of conformity to its rules; but it does not follow from this that international law is a powerful agent or motive force in world politics."[22]

CONFLICT RESOLUTION THROUGH INTERNATIONAL LAW

International Law and War

One of the most important areas of international law involves the prevention of war and, in the event of an outbreak of hostilities, the minimization of human suffering. Historically, war has been recognized as an evil, but one that can be justified as a last resort for defensive purposes. As noted earlier, the doctrine of just war (see chap. 11) is the most coherent and historically influential perspective on the morality of warfare. The doctrine does not seek to justify war but rather to specify the moral conditions for undertaking a legitimate war and the means by which the violence of war can be circumscribed.

The theory of just war provides the foundation for the international law on war, commonly referred to as "the laws of war." The first major compilation of these laws of war was carried out by Hugo Grotius, regarded as the father of international law. In *The Law of War and Peace,* published in 1625, he sets forth principles, based on customary usage and on biblical and moral arguments, for when, how, and by whom a war may be justly conducted. Custom continued to be the major source of the laws of war until the mid-nineteenth century, when multilateral treaties began to replace practice with written contracts. The most important early treaties on war were the conventions signed at the 1899 and 1907 Hague Peace Conferences, which resulted in the codification of the laws of war. Following both World War I and World War II, a number of other multilateral conventions were signed dealing with issues such as the care of wounded soldiers, responsibilities for prisoners of war, and the prohibition against using weapons of mass destruction. A major aim in developing these international rules of warfare has been to decrease human suffering in wartime.

Today one of the important issues in international law is the status of war. Throughout the history of Western civilization, war has been considered an acceptable way of defending and protecting legitimate interests. From the mid-seventeenth century, when the nation-state system developed, until the early twentieth century, war continued to be regarded by jurists and statesmen as a legal means of settling international disputes. But the unprecedented suffering and destruction of the two world wars led to increasing questioning of this rule. The Charter of the League of Nations, for example, although not prohibiting war, called on states to settle disputes peacefully. According to Article 12.1, states could not resort to war until three months after submitting a dispute to arbitration or judicial settlement. Probably the most explicit condemnation of war was the General Treaty for the Renunciation of War of 1928, otherwise known as the *Kellogg-Briand Pact*. The Pact condemns war as a means of solving international conflicts, stating that the settlement of disputes "shall never be sought except by pacific means."

The UN Charter similarly calls on states to renounce war but in less stringent terms than the Kellogg-Briand Pact. Article 2.4 of the Charter calls on member-states to refrain from threatening or using force against other states, whereas Article 51 sets forth the fundamental legal right of self-defense. Article 51 reads in part: "Nothing in the present Charter shall impair the inherent right of individual or collective self-defense if an armed attack occurs against a member of the United Nations. . . ." In short, even though significant efforts have been made to modify the legality of war, states have the right to protect their basic national interests in the world community.

Nevertheless, states are prohibited from using violence to settle disputes. Indeed, any first use of armed force against another state is contrary to the UN Charter, and therefore illegal. Once military force has been used, however, states have three legal options: (1) individual self-defense from armed aggression; (2) collective action authorized by the United Nations; and (3) collective action authorized by regional agencies such as the Organization of American States.

World Peace Through World Law?

Some scholars have suggested that the only effective way to resolve the problem of war is to transform the decentralized international order into a global state. In considering the merits of world government, three issues are of paramount significance—desirability, structure, and feasibility.

First, would a world state be desirable? Would it resolve the problem of war without creating other equally serious problems? World government advocates argue that in this century more than 100 million people have perished from war and that the control of interstate violence necessitates a radical structural transformation of the world. But critics of global reform point out that a world state would increase the possibility of tyranny and political oppression. James Madison, the principal author of the U.S. Constitution, wisely observed that the creation of a central government posed two challenges—first, a government needed to govern its citizens, and second, the government needed to control itself, lest its added power result in the misuse of authority and ultimately in tyranny.[23]

The second key issue relates to structure—whether the global state should have a unitary or federal organization. Although some theorists have advocated a unitary structure, most world government advocates support the federal model, in which a government operates at a dual level. According to the global federal model, nations would continue to have significant regulatory control over social, economic, and cultural life, and would be responsible for local law enforcement. But nations would no longer have military forces. The responsibility for ensuring national security and the protection of country boundaries would be in the hands of the new federal government, which alone would have authority over the armed forces.

The final key issue concerns feasibility—perhaps the major obstacle to structural reform. Because states are unlikely to give up sovereignty, some world government advocates have suggested that the only way of reforming the international system is by transferring sovereignty through a single, quick act. This view was expressed by Robert M. Hutchins, long-time president of the University of Chicago, who once observed that "The only real step toward world government is world government itself."[24] Others argue, however, that a gradual transformation based on law is the most effective way. The most detailed and elegant proposal for the gradual transformation of world order through law has been set forth by Greenville Clark and Louis Sohn. They argue that the achievement of international peace will best be achieved by transforming world order through constitutional reform. But those who emphasize the primacy of law in creating a world community fail to grasp the central truth, articulated by E.H. Carr, that the ultimate authority of law derives from politics.[25]

Those who recommend the creation of world order through law often use the U.S. federal system as a model for the proposed world system. It will be recalled that the state delegates to the Philadelphia Convention created a constitution in which sovereignty was shifted from the thirteen states to a central government. Proponents of a transformed international legal system have suggested that a similar transfer of sovereignty needs to occur in the international system. But the American community was not established in 1789 when the U.S. Constitution became effective. Rather, the Founding Fathers completed the process of community building that had been underway for nearly 150 years.

Because law derives its authority from politics, efforts to change politics through law are unlikely to succeed without prior political settlement. If the

American experience is to serve as a model for creating international community through law, we need to recall that legal and constitutional reforms are possible only if they rest on prior political developments and common community loyalties. The dilemma in using law to create international order is this: the world needs a common power to settle interstate disputes authoritatively, but the precondition for a world government is a strong international community that does not now exist.

IN CONCLUSION

International law contributes to the peace and stability of the international system and to the prevention, management, and resolution of international conflicts. Although international law does not have the legitimacy and authority of domestic law, its principles and rules contribute nonetheless, in significant measure, to the order of global society and in particular to the development of harmonious relations among states and other transnational actors. One of the important contributions of international law is that it specifies rights and duties of states and establishes norms for acceptable international behavior. Its chief weakness is that the legislative, executive, and judicial institutions commonly found in domestic societies are underdeveloped in the global community. As a result, law is much less credible and effective in the international community than in nations.

Some scholars have argued that the most effective way to strengthen international law is by developing world government. But as noted above, the establishment of global government, while strengthening institutions involved in the making, implementation, and interpretation of the law, would raise as many problems as it solves. Because world government remains infeasible, states are increasingly using regimes to structure international relations. To be sure, international regimes are not world government. But in creating regulatory norms that govern international behaviors in particular issue areas, regimes are providing an important legislative function in the international community. Indeed, because of the increasing influence of international regimes, some scholars view them as one of the most "hopeful developments" in contemporary world politics.[26]

SUMMARY

1. International law is the body of rules that states accept as binding in their international relations. Its major sources are treaties and custom, although general principles of law and judicial decisions also have contributed to its development.

2. Because there is no global legislature to make and modify international law, the reform of international law is carried out largely through informal processes, including periodic specialized conferences and adaptation to changing customs (international regimes).

3. The principal court of the international system is the International Court of Justice, which offers judgments in contentious cases and provides the United Nations with advisory opinions. The ICJ is underutilized, in great part, because it does not have automatic jurisdiction over international legal disputes. States may give the ICJ compulsory jurisdiction by signing the "optional clause," but few states have done so without reservations.

4. Three other types of international courts contribute to international adjudication and to the settlement of interstate disputes: regional courts, international criminal courts, and arbitration tribunals.

5. The enforcement of international law is dependent on legal and extralegal sanctions. Legal sanctions include self-help actions, such as retortion and reprisal. Extralegal sanctions include habits of compliance, legal reciprocity, public opinion, and the preference for order.

6. International law prohibits the use of force to settle interstate disputes. On the other hand, states have the right of individual and collective self-defense.

7. Some scholars have suggested that a centralized world state should be established by transforming the international legal order. But because the authority of law rests on politics, any changes in international law without commensurate changes in political structures are bound to be ineffective.

KEY TERMS

International Court of Justice (ICJ)

international law

command theory of law

voluntary habits of compliance

international treaty

exclusive economic zone (EEZ)

pacta sunt servanda

rebus sic stantibus

Third UN Conference on the Law of the Sea

international regime

contentious cases

advisory cases

optional clause

justiciable

Regional courts

European Court of Justice (ECJ)

international criminal court

arbitration tribunal

sanctions

legal sanctions

retortion

reprisal

extralegal sanctions

RECOMMENDED READINGS

Brierly, J. L. *The Law of Nations.* 6th ed. New York: Oxford University Press, 1963. A succinct study of the role of international law in world politics. A classic.

Chen, Lung-Chu. *An Introduction to Contemporary International Law.* New Haven: Yale University Press, 1989. A readable introduction to the major concepts of modern international law, written in lucid, nontechnical prose.

Forsythe, David P. *The Politics of International Law: U.S. Foreign Policy Reconsidered.* Boulder: Lynne Rienner Publishers, 1990. An examination of the nature and role of international law from the U.S. decision makers' perspective. The study focuses on five cases: the ABM treaty, covert intervention in Nicaragua, overt intervention in Grenada, refugee policy, and UN financial assessments.

Glahn, Gerhard von. *Law Among Nations: An Introduction to Public International Law.* 6th ed. New York: Macmillan, 1992. A superior comprehensive international law text. A major strength of the study is its use of case studies to illustrate the nature and role of law in global relations.

Henkin, Louis. *How Nations Behave: Law and Foreign Policy.* 2nd ed. New York: Columbia University Press, 1979. A distinguished authority on international law explains through examples and cases how international law influences the foreign policy behavior of states.

Henkin, Louis et al. *Right v. Might: International Law and the Use of Force.* New York: Council on Foreign Relations Press, 1989. This collection of essays by leading authorities examines the dilemma involved in promoting democracy and human rights overseas without violating international law.

Malanczuk, Peter. *Akehurst's Modern Introduction to International Law.* 7th rev. ed. New York: Routledge, 1997. This clear, succinct, and current introduction to international law is based on the late Michael Akehurst's widely used text.

Moynihan, Daniel Patrick. *On the Law of Nations.* Cambridge: Harvard University Press, 1990. Senator Moynihan examines the impact of international law on the conduct of U.S. foreign relations. He suggests that, although U.S. leaders and thinkers have honored the ideals of international law since the late eighteenth century, the law of nations has become less important in contemporary U.S. foreign policy.

RELEVANT WEB SITES

Human Rights Library (Univ of Minnesota)	www.umn.edu/humanrts/
ICJ Opinions	www.law.cornell.edu/icj`
International Affairs Network (IAN) International law resources	www.pitt.edu/~ian/resource/law.htm
International Court of Justice (ICJ)	www.icj-cij.org/
International Criminal Tribunal	www.un.org/icty/ www.cij.org/tribunal
Law of the Sea	www.un.org/Depts/los/
Major international laws	www.un.org/law/
United Nations Treaty Database	www.un.org/Depts/Treaty/

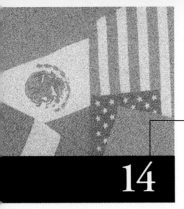

CHAPTER

14 The Role of International Organizations

IGOs
International organizations whose members are states.

International governmental organizations **(IGOs),** as noted in chapter 2, facilitate international economic, political, and social relations within global society and thereby strengthen it. Although IR scholars commonly assume that IGOs can promote a more integrated global society and a more orderly world community, they differ as to the nature and role that such organizations can and should play in global society.

This chapter focuses on three key dimensions of IGOs: first, it examines different approaches to international organizations in light of alternative theories of world order; second, it describes the nature and role of the United Nations, assessing its impact on the international system; and third, it analyzes the role of other IGOs, focusing on the European Union.

INTERNATIONAL ORGANIZATIONS AND THE MANAGEMENT OF POWER

Scholars' differing perspectives on IGOs are rooted in alternative theories of the role of power in the international community. One approach assumes that international order can be promoted most effectively through the management of power; the other assumes that power should be deemphasized, if not bypassed altogether. The first perspective is exemplified in the theories of federalism, collective security, and international peacemaking; the power avoidance approach is expressed by three major theories—international peacekeeping, third-party dispute settlement, and functionalism (see table 14.1). Each of these six theories is explored.

World Federalism

World federalism, the most radical theory of international organization, assumes that the strengthening of world community requires the creation of governmental institutions on a global level by means of a constitution. According to federalism, promoting cooperation and harmony within

TABLE 14.1 Theories of World Order

Perspectives on Power	Theories of World Order
I. Management of power	World federalism Collective security International peacemaking
II. Avoidance of power	International peacekeeping Third-party dispute settlement Functionalism

global society requires the voluntary dismantling of state sovereignty and the centralization of governmental authority in accordance with federal and democratic principles. As espoused by its proponents, world federalism would not entail global dictatorship, but it would seek to duplicate national federalism in global society.

The case for a federal world government is generally based on the assumption that establishing a central governmental authority would reduce, if not eliminate, the problem of war and would enhance human well-being. Even though a world government would no doubt reduce the incidence and intensity of conflict between states, it would not completely eradicate it. As Inis L. Claude, Jr. has observed, "government has never served as a magic wand to banish problems of disorder in any human society."[5] Just as national governments are unable to ensure tranquility and order in domestic society, so, too, a world government would be unable to assure transnational order. Religious and territorial disputes, civil wars, revolutions, and ethnic wars would no doubt continue under a world government.

One of the perennial mistakes that world government advocates make is to suppose that the centralization of power can be achieved by fiat or legal process. Those who emphasize the primacy of constitutional change in creating a world community often use the federal system of the United States as a model. They erroneously assume that the United States shifted from a confederal to a federal system of government solely through the constitutional reforms enacted at the Philadelphia Convention of 1787. They suppose that states only need to gather at an international constitutional conference and make a similar transfer in sovereignty from states to a central authority. However, the creation of the American federal system was not rooted solely in law but also in political, social, and economic factors, such as common values, shared aspirations, and growing social, cultural, and economic interdependencies. Indeed, the Founding Fathers did not create the American community with their constitution but, rather, ratified a process of national integration that had been going on for more than a century.

A stable world federation needs a centralized governmental structure and widespread shared values and aspirations. A world federal regime will require the creation of both a central authority and strong social, economic, cultural, and political affinities. The dilemma of world government is this: the international system needs world government to reduce the threat of war, but the precondition for world government is world community, which can only be solidified through the political transformation of the anarchic world system.

Collective Security

Collective security involves the creation of a peacekeeping alliance in which the combined power of member-states is used to deter, and if need be, to punish aggression. Under this arrangement, member-states pledge themselves to peaceful international relations by using their combined power against any other member-state that violates the political sovereignty and territorial integrity of another. The

World federalism
This world order approach assumes that international peace and global stability are best realized by the establishment of an international federal union of states.

Collective security
A theory of world order, first applied by the League of Nations, that seeks to deter aggression by promising collective retaliation against any community member committing aggression.

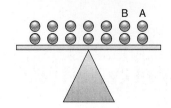 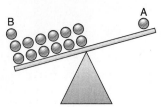

FIGURE 14.1
Operation of
Collective Security

central idea of collective security, depicted in figure 14.1, is summarized in the phrase "an attack on one is an attack on all."

Collective security is often described as a halfway house between world government and the system of balance of power. Like world government, the use of preponderant power is made available to punish aggression; but unlike world government, no central authority is formally established. An example of collective security is the 1947 Inter-American Treaty of Reciprocal Assistance (known as the Rio Pact), an agreement among most Western Hemisphere states. This treaty provides that an attack by any member against another requires the punishment of the aggressor state by all other member-states. A security alliance such as NATO is not collective security, because it seeks to protect members from external aggression or from the potential threat of civil conflicts outside the NATO area rather than from conflicts among member-states.

Several requirements are necessary for collective security to work. First, power needs to be diffused in order to ensure effective deterrence against any would-be aggressor state. Second, states need to be strongly committed to maintaining the status quo. Third, states need to be able to agree on what constitutes aggression. And fourth, states must be willing to use their resources to punish any state that violates the political and territorial rights of another. In other words, states need to be as committed to the territorial security of other states as to their own.

League of Nations
An international organization established at the end of World War I as part of the Treaty of Versailles. The League functioned until 1945, when it was replaced by the United Nations.

The **League of Nations,** established at the end of World War I, attempted to implement this theory of world organization. The league established a peacekeeping system in which all member-states were responsible for protecting victims from aggression. Article 16 of the charter states: "Should any Member of the League resort to war in disregard of its covenants under Articles 12, 13 or 15, it should *ipso facto* be deemed to have committed an act of war against all other Members of the League." The charter also placed the responsibility for determining aggression on each member-state, although the League's Council was responsible for directing the collective forces against an aggressor. Despite its commitment to collective security, the League of Nations was ineffective in preventing wars—in part because of member-states' unwillingness to commit their national forces to punish aggression. When Italy invaded Ethiopia in 1936, for example, the League's members refused to punish it, thereby confirming the perception that states are unwilling to identify their own security and welfare with that of other countries.

International Peacemaking

Peacemaking
The theory that an internationally sanctioned force can foster global order by imposing a settlement on civil wars and regional conflicts.

Peacemaking is the theory that an internationally sanctioned force can foster global order by imposing a settlement on civil wars and regional conflicts. Unlike collective security, which seeks to deter aggression among community members, peacemaking has the more ambitious goal of halting the fighting and of establishing the preconditions on which a permanent peace can be maintained. Like collective security, peacemaking uses internationally sanctioned military force to punish aggression; but unlike collective security, it seeks to develop political institutions and economic structures necessary for the creation and maintenance of a regime perceived as legitimate by the warring factions.

The United Nations, the League's successor, is authorized under the Charter's Chapter VII to carry out whatever actions it deems necessary to maintain international peace. But unlike the League, which allowed each member-state to identify aggression, the UN gives the Security Council the responsibility of determining threats to peace and for authorizing operations to keep and make peace. Because of superpower rivalries during the Cold War, the UN's ability to carry out major peacekeeping and peacemaking operations was frequently impaired. With the end of the Cold War, UN peacekeeping and peacemaking operations have greatly expanded in number and scope. The cooperation necessary for effective peacemaking was especially evident in the 1990 Persian Gulf crisis, when the Security Council passed resolutions condemning Iraq's illegal invasion and annexation and authorizing the use of force to expel Iraq. Since then the Security Council has instituted other peacemaking initiatives, including those in Cambodia, Bosnia, and Haiti.

Peacemaking is an especially challenging task because it ultimately requires the voluntary cooperation of most, if not all, antagonists. As with the League, which failed to effectively implement collective security because of the unwillingness of states to support collective punishment, major powers have similarly been reluctant to intervene in foreign wars in order to impose a peace settlement. Although the UN has authorized a number of post–Cold War operations to keep peace and foster preconditions for a long-term peace settlement, major powers have been reluctant to embark on nation-building in foreign countries because of the complexity and high cost of such an operation.

International Peacekeeping

Peacekeeping involves the introduction of multilateral military and police forces into areas of conflict in which the warring parties have achieved a preliminary cease fire. The purpose of these forces is not to impose a settlement, but simply to keep the contesting parties from fighting—to abate conflict, not to resolve it. Multinational forces hope, of course, that by inhibiting war and diffusing the passions and hatreds surrounding ethnic, religious, and political disputes, political stability will increase and a settlement will eventually be achieved.

Peacekeeping
The introduction of multilateral military and police forces into areas of conflict in which the warring parties have achieved a preliminary cease fire.

Peacekeeping and peacemaking differ in terms of context as well as mission. In terms of context, peacekeeping occurs only when a preliminary agreement has been achieved to halt fighting; by contrast, peacemaking involves the use of military force in an area of conflict when warring parties continue to use force and threats of force to demand their particular political goals. More significantly, the missions of peacekeeping and peacemaking differ significantly. Whereas the former seeks to keep the warring factions apart by maintaining buffer zones between the antagonists, peacemaking requires the introduction of military forces to compel warring parties to stop fighting. The requirements of peacekeeping and peacemaking thus differ significantly. Peacekeeping seeks neutrality; it avoids taking sides. Moreover, because such forces seek to keep warring parties apart, its forces are lightly armed. Peacemaking, by contrast, may require that its forces take sides in a dispute or to militarily oppose all major parties. And because the aim of peacemaking is to impose peace in an arena in which it does not exist, the military forces required for such an operation will, of necessity, have to be far more powerful.

Peacekeeping tends to fall between the perspectives of power management and power avoidance. Although peacekeeping does not seek to resolve conflicts through force, it does rely on UN-sponsored forces to monitor cease-fire conditions and to ensure the separation of opposing military forces. In supervising truces and cease-fires, multinational forces maintain a neutral buffer, with the ultimate aim, rarely achieved, of negotiating a final settlement. Normally, these UN forces are allowed to use military force only in self-defense. It is important to stress that peacekeeping operations can be carried out only when the contestants consent to the multinational police forces and perceive them as being impartial.

Since the United Nations instituted its first peacekeeping operation in 1948, it has authorized almost forty additional missions. These range from relatively small operations, such as the 1992 UN Observer Mission in El Salvador, established to ensure a peaceful transition to democratic rule, to large and complex operations like the 1992–1993 UN Transitional Authority in Cambodia (UNTAC), which involved a peacekeeping force of 22,000 UN soldiers and support personnel to oversee elections and to facilitate the transition to a democratic regime. The size and number of peacekeeping operations peaked in 1993, when the UN was supporting some 78,700 "blue helmet" peacekeepers.[6] Subsequently, UN forces have been dramatically reduced, so that by 1997 UN peacekeeping operations involved only about 25,000 troops. The nature and evolution of the UN's peacekeeping and peacemaking tasks are explored more fully in the following sections.

Third-Party Dispute Settlement

A fourth approach to world order is **third-party dispute settlement.** According to this theory, because international conflicts are based in part on arrogance, pride, irrationality, mistrust, and miscommunication, international organizations can promote peace by serving as an intermediary, or third party, between contesting parties. As a nonparticipant in a conflict, an international organization can help relieve tensions and even resolve disputes by clarifying issues, by improving dialogue and communication, by identifying alternative approaches, and by offering potential solutions.

A central premise of this theory is that wars are "a kind of national temper tantrum"—eruptions rooted in anger, irrationality, and passion.[7] To the extent that this is so, an external party can help reduce the incidence and intensity of international conflict. Because third parties are not emotionally involved in disputes, they can help cool passions, decrease distrust, strengthen communication, and promote rational dialogue. The aim of pacific settlement is to discourage violence by facilitating communication through the "good offices" of an international organization.

Third-party dispute settlement involves two different approaches, one legal and the other political. When a dispute involves international legal issues, states may attempt to resolve it through the International Court of Justice or a regional court, such as the European Court of Justice. But as noted in the previous chapter, adjudication remains an underutilized practice because of the unwillingness of states to entrust conflict resolution to courts.

The most important forms of third-party settlement of political disputes are good offices, mediation, and arbitration. **Good offices** refers to the use of an impartial agent or organization, trusted by both sides, that facilitates reconciliation through improved communication, clarification of issues, and the gathering of facts. During the Iran-Iraq war, UN Secretary-General Javier Perez de Cuellar provided his good offices in transmitting messages and helping to structure a cease-fire. **Mediation** is a more formal technique in which the outside party seeks not only to clarify issues and improve communication but also to offer possible solutions. The Beagle Channel dispute, examined in chapter 12, was ultimately resolved through the mediating role of Pope Paul II. The third and most comprehensive method of pacific settlement is **arbitration.** Here the disputing parties agree in advance to accept third-party decisions as binding. Like adjudication, arbitration has not been widely used because states are reluctant to give up control over issues involving vital interests.

Margin glossary

Third-party dispute settlement
An approach to conflict resolution involving an external party. Common third-party procedures include conciliation, mediation, arbitration, and adjudication.

Good offices
The use of a third party to facilitate communication between two or more disputing actors.

Mediation
The process by which a third-party facilitates conflict resolution by guiding discussions and offering nonbinding solutions.

Arbitration
The settlement of a dispute through a binding third-party judgment.

Functionalism

Functionalism assumes that world order can be developed most effectively by the strengthening of functional, nonpolitical bonds among states. Like third-party dispute settlement, this approach attempts to bypass power management altogether. Because the anarchic international system fosters conflictual and competitive international relations, functionalism attempts to build global solidarity by focusing on the shared needs and wants of people. David Mitrany, the father of functionalism, has written "[t]he problem of our time is not how to keep the nations peacefully apart but how to bring them actively together."[8]

Functionalists believe that transnational interdependence in economic, social, technical, scientific, and other related areas can promote world order in three ways.[9] First, they believe that the global efforts to alleviate poverty and improve living conditions can help reduce the tensions that foster global conflict. In effect, they believe that reducing human misery can encourage a more orderly and stable international community. Second, functionalists assume that international functional cooperation can foster transnational links that reduce state sovereignty. Because sovereignty is considered to be a major obstacle to international peace, the efforts to erode the independence of states is regarded as a step toward world order. Finally, functionalists believe that the development of global functional networks can foster international understanding and reduce misperception. Because wars are often rooted in misperception, the opportunity for direct dialogue within global organizations can help strengthen cross-cultural communication and understanding.

To a significant degree, the United Nations' specialized agencies—such as the International Development Association (IDA), Food and Agricultural Organization (FAO), UN Educational, Scientific, and Cultural Organization (UNESCO), and World Health Organization (WHO)—promote global cooperation in specific issue areas. Although they were not established to implement functionalist theory, the twenty-nine UN specialized agencies nonetheless help foster conditions that, according to functionalists, build world order.

Although improved living conditions and rising interdependence may promote domestic stability, functionalism's claims about international peace are not fully warranted. For example, even though poverty and disease no doubt contribute to human conflict, there is little evidence to support the claim that improved living conditions breed social order. Indeed, modern civil and international wars are not at all correlated with poverty and backwardness. Moreover, the claim that more global interactions results in improved understanding is also negated by modern history. World peace is not a result of a high level of interdependence but of harmonious relationships. It is the quality of human interactions, not their frequency, that determines the peacefulness of political relationships. Despite these limitations, functionalism is important because it calls attention to the fundamental role of interdependence in the development of stable human communities rooted in national self-interests.

To overcome the limitations of functionalist theory, some scholars, such as Ernest Haas,[10] have advocated **neofunctionalism,** a theory combining functional interdependence with the creation of multilateral decision-making institutions. Unlike functionalism, which assumes that global community can be created solely through increased socioeconomic interdependence, neofunctionalism assumes that international organizations must lead, direct, and coordinate the growth of transnational interactions. The most important application of the neofunctional model is the European Union, an experiment examined later in this chapter.

Functionalism
A theory emphasizing socioeconomic cooperation as the basis of community building. According to this approach, cooperation in technical, nonpolitical areas can eventually lead to cooperation in other, more difficult areas.

Neofunctionalism
A peacekeeping approach based on the promotion of functional interdependence and the creation of international organizations.

THE UNITED NATIONS

The preeminent contemporary world organization is the United Nations, established at the Conference on International Organization in San Francisco in April 1945. Its foundations were laid at two preliminary conferences (Dumbarton Oaks in Washington, D.C., and in Yalta in Crimea) at which British, Soviet, and American leaders established the key principles on which the UN is based. Following two months of deliberations at San Francisco, delegates from fifty-one countries signed the UN Charter on June 26. The new organization began operating October 24, 1945, after the required number of states had officially ratified the new accord.

Membership

According to the UN Charter (art. 4), membership in the organization is conditional on a state's commitment to international peace and to the fulfillment of the institution's aims and responsibilities. The UN began with fifty-one signatory states, and during the succeeding decade an additional nine states joined the organization. With the easing of Cold War tensions following the Korean Armistice and the death of Joseph Stalin, UN membership rose dramatically. In 1955 alone, sixteen new states were admitted, and as the drive for decolonization and political independence spread in the late 1950s and 1960s throughout the Third World, especially Africa, newly emerged nations swelled its ranks.

UN membership has increased by more than three-and-a-half times since the organization began functioning in 1945. As of 1997, nearly all nation-states (185) were UN members, with Switzerland being the most prominent nonmember (see fig. 14.2). In 1990, the UN lost two members when two divided countries—Yemen and Germany—merged into single states. But in 1991, the organization added seven states: Estonia, Latvia, Lithuania, North Korea, South Korea, the Marshall Islands, and Micronesia. And as a result of the final disintegration of the Soviet Union, eight of the remaining twelve republics joined the UN in March 1992 (Russia, Belarus, and Ukraine were already members). In addition, the principality of San Marino joined the UN at this time. A few months later Bosnia and Herzegovina, Croatia, Slovenia, and Georgia were admitted to the UN. In 1993 six other states became UN members: Andorra, the Czech Republic, Eritrea, Monaco, the Slovak Republic, and Macedonia.[11] Palau, the most recent member, joined the United Nations in December 1994.

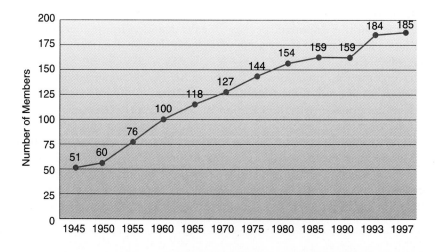

FIGURE 14.2
Growth of UN Membership, 1946–1997

The United Nations Building in New York City is the headquarters of the UN system. The building serves as home for the Security Council, the General Assembly, the Secretariat, and other organs and specialized agencies.

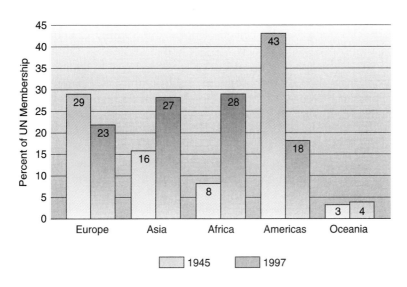

1945 ▢   1997 ▢

FIGURE 14.3
UN Membership by Region, 1945 and 1997
(in percentages)

The addition of more than eighty Third World states to the UN has radically transformed regional representation in that body. For example, from 1945 to 1990 the regional share of UN membership declined significantly for Europe and the Americas, whereas Asia's and Africa's share increased dramatically (see fig. 14.3). These shifts in regional representation have not only increased the complexity of decision making but have also altered the political dynamics of UN organs, especially the General Assembly.

Purposes

Article 1 of the UN Charter defines the organization's primary goals as:

1. maintaining peace and security
2. maintaining friendly relations among states based on the principles of equality and political self-determination

3. fostering international economic, social, humanitarian, and cultural cooperation, and promoting respect for human rights

4. facilitating peaceful and harmonious international relations among states in attaining the above goals

Because the UN is a multinational organization, its actions are ultimately determined by the collective interests of its member-states rather than the purposes and goals articulated in the Charter. This is why one scholar asserts: "The United Nations has no purposes—and can have none—of its own. It is, above all, a tool, and, like other tools, it has possibilities and limitations, but not purposes."[12]

Because members ultimately determine its activities, the UN's operations have not always been consistent with the formally specified purposes of the institution. For example, although maintaining and building world peace are generally regarded as the preeminent aims (Preamble and art. 1), throughout the Cold War the UN, limited by the superpowers' ideological conflict, emphasized nonpolitical programs, including health, literacy, and economic development. Thus, in 1988 only 5 percent of the UN regular budget of $1.7 billion was assigned to conflict-resolution activities.[13] Since the disintegration of the Soviet empire and the end of the superpowers' stalemate, however, peacekeeping has become a much more significant UN activity, rising from $230 million in 1988 to $3.6 billion in 1994.[14]

Organization

Six key agencies comprise the United Nations: the Security Council, the General Assembly, the Trusteeship Council, the Economic and Social Council, the Secretariat, and the International Court of Justice (see fig. 14.4). In addition, the UN system includes many specialized programs, such as the UN Conference on Trade and Development (UNCTAD), the UN Development Programme (UNDP), and the UN Children's Fund (UNICEF), and some eighteen autonomous agencies, including the Food and Agriculture Organization (FAO), the International Monetary Fund (IMF), and the World Health Organization (WHO). UN agencies—excluding the World Bank and International Monetary Fund and its regional offices—employ about 51,000 persons throughout the world. Of these, 10,000 work at the UN headquarters in New York City.[15]

The two primary organs of the United Nations are the Security Council and General Assembly. The first is significant because it has primary responsibility for

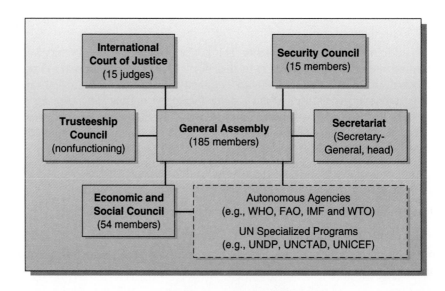

FIGURE 14.4
Major United Nations Agencies

keeping and promoting peace, the second because it serves as the plenary world parliament. In the following sections we examine the nature and role of these two institutions and briefly highlight the contribution of other agencies as well.

Security Council

This body comprises fifteen members, five permanent and ten nonpermanent. The five permanent members, which were the five leading powers when the UN was established in 1945, include China, France, Russia (formally the Soviet Union), the United Kingdom, and the United States. The nonpermanent states are elected by the General Assembly for two-year terms. In view of the significant membership increase, the rising influence of Japan and Germany, and the dramatic geopolitical developments associated with the end of the Cold War, it is clear that the structure of Security Council no longer reflects contemporary global order. In particular, the veto power of the five permanent members is no longer consistent with global power realities.[16] As a result, a number of reforms have been proposed to modify the existing structure by increasing the Security Council's membership. One proposal that was being seriously considered by the major powers in 1997 was the addition of five permanent members, including Japan and Germany and three developing countries. Although the expansion of the Security Council appears likely in the future, the decision of whether to grant additional permanent members veto power will present major challenges, especially because such a change would require amending the UN Charter.

Unlike the League's Council, the UN Security Council has substantial authority to manage and resolve international conflicts, but only if all permanent members are in agreement. Because all substantive decisions of the Security Council require nine votes, including those of the permanent members, the *veto* from any of the major powers can halt Security Council action. The veto was not designed as an obstructionist device, but as an instrument to ensure consensus among the major powers on vital issues.

According to the Charter (Chapter VII), the Security Council has the primary responsibility for maintaining peace and security in the world. It is responsible for determining the existence of any threat to peace and for taking actions it deems necessary. These can include investigation of disputes, recommendations to resolve conflict, and peacekeeping and peacemaking initiatives that include the use of force. Its decisions are binding on all states. Thus, when the Security Council imposed comprehensive sanctions against Rhodesia in 1968 and against Iraq in 1990, all UN member-states were obligated to abide by its decisions.

The most extreme form of collective action is the sanctioning of force. When diplomatic, economic, or other measures are viewed as inadequate, the Security Council may "take such action by air, sea, or land forces as may be necessary to maintain or restore international peace and security" (art. 42). During its first forty-five years, the Security Council authorized military action only once (during the Korean crisis in 1950), and this action achieved only because of the Soviet Union's temporary withdrawal from Security Council deliberations. Since then it has authorized force to liberate Kuwait in 1990, to pacify Somalia in 1991–1992, to deter Serbian aggression in Bosnia in 1993–1995, and to restore democracy in Haiti in 1994.

During the Cold War, the Security Council had limited impact on international peacekeeping in large measure because East-West antagonisms inhibited cooperation between the superpowers. During the first two decades of the Cold War, when the United States was the dominant power in the United Nations, the Soviet Union continually opposed Security Council peacekeeping actions, casting some 105 vetoes from 1946 to 1969, while the United States cast only one. From 1971 to 1986, however, the United States cast 57 vetoes (to the Soviet Union's 10),[17] in great part because the UN's political dynamics had shifted from Western democratic ideals toward Marxist socialism. But with the decline of ideological rivalries in the late 1980s, the prospects for increased UN action improved dramatically. For example, after Iraq invaded Kuwait in August 1990, the Security Council achieved its highest level of cohesion since its founding in 1945, adopting twelve resolutions that, among other things, called for an imposition of military and economic sanctions and the authorization of military force to expel Iraqi military forces from Kuwait. With the end of the Cold War and the collapse of Soviet communism, UN peacekeeping has become much more significant. During the 1988–1994 period, thirteen new peacekeeping operations were begun.

General Assembly

This institution, with representation from each of the 185 member-states, serves as the world parliament—as a forum for debate and discussion. Each member-state has one vote, and decisions on important issues (e.g., peace and security concerns, election of nonpermanent members to the Security Council, budgetary matters) require a two-thirds majority, whereas other issues are decided by a simple majority. The General Assembly meets annually in the fall with most of its work undertaken through committees. There are seven main committees, each with its own area of responsibility: First Committee—political and security issues; Second Committee—economics and finance issues; Third Committee—social, humanitarian, and cultural issues; Fourth Committee—trust territories; Fifth Committee—administrative and budgetary issues; Sixth Committee—legal issues; and the Special Political Committee—assistance to the first committee. Occasionally the General Assembly holds special sessions to consider particular issues of global concern. From 1946 to 1992 sixteen such sessions were held on topics such as Palestine (1948), the UN budget (1963), economic development and international economic cooperation (1975), Namibia (1978), disarmament (1982), and international economic cooperation (1990).

Unlike a national parliament, the General Assembly's power is limited. It does not have the authority to act on behalf of member-states. It cannot, for example, take collective action to maintain international peace or promote world order. Rather, its responsibilities (as outlined in Articles 10 through 17 of the Charter) are to discuss, study, and review international problems and then to make recommendations. These are normally given in the form of declarations, such as the famous Universal Declaration of Human Rights of 1948, and resolutions, such as the Uniting for Peace Resolution of 1950, which authorized the General Assembly to temporarily consider peacekeeping issues because of the Cold War stalemate in the Security Council.

In the early years of the United Nations, the United States had significant influence in the General Assembly. But as UN membership increased with the addition of new Third World nations, the General Assembly, like the Security Council, became less supportive of Western interests. Although most of these countries were officially nonaligned, many were ideologically identified with Marxist socialism and were strongly supportive of the Soviet Union's foreign policy. This shift in General Assembly members' orientation is illustrated in the voting patterns. For example, during the 1946–1950 period, the General Assembly majority voted 74 percent with the United States and 34 percent with the Soviet Union; but during the 1981–1985 period, the majority voted only 14 percent with the United States and 79 percent with the Soviet Union.[18]

Like most national parliaments, the General Assembly has responsibility for UN finances. It annually approves the budget and apportions the expenses among member-states by fixing member-states' assessments for regular and peacekeeping operations (see table 14.2). The United Nations and its subsidiary organizations are financed by two types of budgets—obligatory and voluntary. Obligatory budgets

TABLE 14.2   Assessment of Selected UN Members, 1994 and 1997

Country	Percentage of Regular UN Budget* 1994	1997
United States	25.00	25.00
Japan	12.45	15.65
Germany	8.93	9.06
France	6.00	6.42
Russia	6.71	4.27
United Kingdom	5.02	5.32
Italy	4.29	5.25
Canada	3.11	3.11
Spain	1.98	2.38
Ukraine	1.87	1.09
Brazil	1.59	1.62
Australia	1.51	1.48
Netherlands	1.50	1.59
Sweden	1.11	1.23
Belgium	1.06	1.01

*Apportionment, based largely on the wealth of a country, is determined through a complex formula.

Sources: UN Secretariat, "Status of Contributions as of 30 April 1994," pp. 5-9, and "Status of Contributions as of 31 May 1997," pp. 6-10.

impose on member-states predetermined financial obligations to care for the ongoing or regular UN operations (such as common support services, humanitarian affairs, aid to developing nations, and administration) and peacekeeping operations. The bulk of the UN's specialized programs and activities are covered by voluntary contributions. Such operations involve specialized social, economic, cultural, scientific, and humanitarian programs, such as the Children's Fund (UNICEF), the Development Program (UNDP), and the World Food Program, and affiliated organizations, such as the Food and Agricultural Organization (FAO), the World Health Organization (WHO), the UN Educational, Scientific, and Cultural Organization (UNESCO), the UN High Commission for Refugees (UNHCR), and the World Trade Organization (WTO).

One of the anomalies of the General Assembly is the discrepancy between a state's population and its political influence. Countries like Dominica, Saint Kitts and Nevis, and Seychelles with populations of 78,000, 48,000, and 67,000, respectively, have the same voting power as China and India, with populations of one billion and 780 million. Indeed, China, with 20 percent of the world's population, has only 0.6 percent of the General Assembly's total vote.

A related anomaly is the discrepancy between members' financial contribution and their political influence in the General Assembly. For example, the six largest contributors provide roughly 66 percent of the regular UN budget but control only 3 percent of the vote, whereas the poorest 116 countries contribute less than 17 percent of the budget yet control more than 63 percent of the vote (see fig. 14.5). Because the UN budgetary decisions must be approved by a two-thirds General Assembly vote, the poor Third World nations that contribute less than 20 percent to the budget can determine the organization's financial decisions. Al-

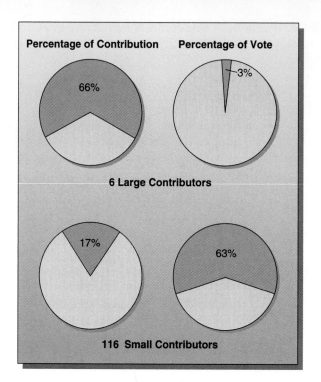

FIGURE 14.5
Relationship between Regular UN Budget Assessments and Voting Strength in General Assembly, 1997
Source: Based on assessments from UN Secretariat, "Status of Contributions as of 30 May 1997," pp. 5-9.

though a number of UN-related institutions, such as the International Monetary Fund and the World Bank, function on the basis of weighted voting, the governance of many specialized agencies is based on a similar discrepancy between financial contributions and decision-making influence. Partly because of this, the United States, supported by a number of industrial states, began calling for institutional reforms.

To put pressure on the UN system, the United States began in the early 1980s to reduce or halt voluntary contributions to UN agencies that were pursuing policies that it did not support. For example, the United States refused to pay its $1 million assessment for the UN Deep Seabed Authority, an agency created by the Third UN Convention on the Law of the Sea to promote deep seabed mining. Moreover, after unsuccessfully seeking to alter its policies, the United States withdrew from the UN Education, Scientific, and Cultural Organization (UNESCO) in 1983. Tensions between the United States and the UN increased in 1985 with the passage of the Kassebaum-Solomon Amendment, which required the U.S. government to reduce its payments of assessed obligations until the UN adopted reforms to increase institutional efficiency. Although the UN carried out a number of modest reforms, the U.S. government continued to delay or withhold part of its obligations. By 1996, the UN debt had mushroomed to more than $2.8 billion, resulting in a major institutional crisis. Of the total debt—$1.7 billion for peacekeeping operations and $1.1 billion for the regular budget—the United States owed the largest amount ($1.5 billion), followed by Russia ($401 million) and Ukraine ($245 million).[19] Only 10 of the UN's 185 member-states were debt-free in 1996. Because of the financial crisis facing the United Nations, the 1997 regular budget was the first no-growth budget in the organization's history.

Other Organs

The *Economic and Social Council (ECOSOC)* promotes economic and social development globally but especially in the developing nations. The agency directs research on human welfare and makes policy recommendations. In addition, it oversees and coordinates numerous specialized agencies involved in economic and social development, such as regional economic commissions, specialized functional commissions, and other related UN bodies. Because nearly three-fourths of all UN expenditures relate directly or indirectly to economic and social programs, ECOSOC is an influential organ of the UN. ECOSOC decision making is carried out by a council of fifty-four members, elected by the General Assembly for three-year terms, with one-third of the terms expiring each year.

The *Secretariat* represents the bureaucracy or civil service of the United Nations. As of 1996, it employed close to 14,200 persons, one-third of them working at its headquarters in New York City. The organization is headed by the secretary-general, who is appointed by the Security Council and elected by the General Assembly for a five-year term and normally renewed for a second term. Since 1946 the position has been held by six officials, including Dag Hammarskjöld of Sweden (1953–1961), Kurt Waldheim of Austria (1972–1981), and Javier Perez de Cuellar of Peru (1982–1991). Boutros Boutros-Ghali of Egypt, who served only one term (from 1992–1996), was replaced by Kofi Annan of Ghana after the United States vetoed a second term for Mr. Boutros-Ghali.

The *International Court of Justice,* examined in the previous chapter, serves as the United Nation's judiciary, issuing advisory opinions (interpretations of the UN Charter) as well as binding judgments in contentious cases.

Finally, the *Trusteeship Council,* the smallest and least-important UN organ, was established to administer non-self-governing lands designated as trust territories. From 1957 to 1975 ten trust territories became independent states, leaving only the Territory of the Pacific Islands (sometimes referred to as Micronesia). In November 1994, the major powers suspended the Council's operations after Palau became an independent state.

In addition to these major organizations, the UN system also involves many other programs and specialized agencies. Some of these are directly under the supervision of the General Assembly or the Economic and Social Council, whereas others function independently in an affiliated capacity (see table 14.3).

THE ROLE OF THE UNITED NATIONS IN GLOBAL SOCIETY

In assessing the UN, it is important to recognize what the organization is not. It is not a supranational governmental organization with independent goals and interests. Nor is it a legal institution that develops and implements programs and policies it considers beneficial for global society. The UN does not transcend world politics. Rather, it is an organization based on the interests and wills of its sovereign member-states. When the UN takes action, it does so because its members have agreed to a shared objective.

The UN was not created to modify the sovereign power of states but to promote transnational cooperation. Its aim is to channel state interests and to facilitate international problem solving. Its success or failure thus ultimately depends on the level of cooperation and coordination that states voluntarily achieve. Trygve Lie, the first secretary-general, realistically captured the organization's potential: "The United Nations is no stronger than the collective will of the nations that support it. Of itself it can do nothing. It is a machinery through which the nations can cooperate. It can be used and developed . . . or it can be discarded and broken."[20] Although Lie made this assessment in 1946, it is no less valid in 1997.

The UN and Social Welfare

Although the UN was created primarily as an instrument of world order, most UN activities and programs have focused on nonpolitical concerns. Historically, the

TABLE 14.3   Major UN-Affiliated IGOs

I. **UN Programs   (directly supervised by the UN)**

UNRWA	United Nations Relief and Work Agency for Palestine Refugees in the Near East
UNHCR	Office of the United Nations High Commissioner for Refugees
INSTRAW	International Research and Training Institute for the Advancement of Women
UNIFEM	United Nations Development Fund for Women
UNCHS	United Nations Centre for Human Settlements (Habitat)
UNCTAD	United Nations Conference on Trade and Development
UNDP	United Nations Development Programme
UNU	United Nations University
ITC	International Trade Center
UNFPA	United Nations Population Fund
UNEP	United Nations Environment Program
UNITAR	United Nations Institute for Training and Research
UNDCP	United Nations International Drug Control Program
UNICEF	United Nations Children's Fund
WFC	World Food Council
WFP	World Food Program

II. **Specialized Agencies and Other Autonomous Organizations within the UN**

IAEA	International Atomic Energy Agency
ITU	International Telecommunication Union
UPU	Universal Postal Union
ICAO	International Civil Aviation Organization
FAO	Food and Agriculture Organization of the United Nations
WHO	World Health Organization
UNESCO	United Nations Educational, Scientific, and Cultural Organization
IBRD	International Bank for Reconstruction and Development (World Bank)
IDA	International Development Association
IFC	International Finance Corporation
IMF	International Monetary Fund
WTO	World Trade Organization
IFAD	International Fund for Agricultural Development
ILO	International Labor Organization
IMO	International Maritime Organization
WIPO	World Intellectual Property Organization
WMO	World Meteorological Organization

III. **Other UN Bodies**

Functional Commissions

Regional Commissions

Expert Bodies

Seasonal and Standing Committees

bulk of UN expenditures (assessed and voluntary) have been devoted to social, economic, scientific, and educational programs. Moreover, most UN employees serve in the general and specialized agencies designed to improve human welfare and strengthen socioeconomic interdependence, with only a small number concerned with political and military matters. Of the estimated one billion pages of studies and reports the UN publishes annually, the bulk is devoted to social and economic analysis. In light of the past emphasis on socioeconomic affairs, it is commonly assumed that the greatest successes of the UN have been in the nonpolitical realms. Jeane Kirkpatrick, who served as U.S. ambassador to the UN in the Reagan administration, once observed that the UN comprised two elements: "the political UN General Assembly which doesn't work, and the technical agencies which do."[21]

Some of the most important nonpolitical functions of the UN and its affiliated agencies include: economic growth and development, disease control, education, child protection, health care, refugee assistance, and global resource management. Following are some UN-affiliated programs and organizations focusing on social and economic issues:

World Health Organization (WHO)—a Geneva-based program designed to improve medical care in the world and to eradicate diseases; its successes include the eradication of smallpox

Food and Agriculture Organization (FAO)—a Rome-based organization that seeks to develop better farming techniques and to improve food supply and distribution

United Nations Conference on Trade and Development (UNCTAD)—a Geneva-based organization that meets every four years to discuss economic relations between the rich and poor nations

United Nations Children's Fund (UNICEF)—this New York City-based institution supports humanitarian projects for children, including programs in health, education, and nutrition

United Nations High Commission for Refugees (UNHCR)—coordinates voluntary contributions and programs for refugees; Palestinian refugees are cared for by a separate organization—the United Nations Relief and Works Agency for Palestine Refugees in the Near East (UNRWA)

Economic Commission for Latin America (ECLA)—this Santiago-based commission carries out research on Latin American economies to encourage their economic expansion

Although specialized organizations such as these have had varying levels of success in promoting economic and social welfare, they have played an important role in raising global awareness of human needs in the developing nations. Indeed, during the Cold War, the promotion of social and economic development was undoubtedly the chief concern of the United Nations and its subsidiary agencies. Moreover, the development of specialized agencies has, as noted at the outset of this chapter, helped to foster functional interdependence by encouraging analysis and action in areas of common global concern. Examples of recent major functional initiatives include such conferences as: the 1992 Earth Summit in Rio de Janeiro, Brazil; the 1993 World Conference on Human Rights in Vienna; the 1994 Population Conference in Cairo, Egypt (see case 14.1); the 1995 Social Summit in Copenhagen; and the 1995 International Conference on Women in Beijing. Although the UN was originally designed chiefly as a peacekeeping, world-order organization, its primary activity throughout much of its history has been the promotion of human well-being.

CASE STUDY

Case 14.1 The 1994 Cairo Population Conference: Debating Body Politics

In September 1994, some 20,000 representatives from more than 150 states and hundreds of NGOs gathered in Cairo, Egypt for the United Nations Conference on Population and Development. This was the third in a series of decennial international UN-sponsored conferences on population. The first was convened in 1974 in Budapest, and the second was held in Mexico City. The first conference was noteworthy because it helped to draw attention to the population explosion and to popularize the notion that, in the absence of a reversal of population growth, global economic, social, and ecological catastrophe would result. The 1984 conference was significant because, under the banner of "population and development," it brought together the developed countries' concern about population growth with the developing nations' concern about economic development. "Development is the best contraceptive" became a commonly accepted Third World slogan and the underlying premise not only for the Mexico City gathering but for its subsequent work as well.

Building on the previous two international gatherings, the 1994 conference sought to emphasize the need for decreased fertility through increased education, the "empowerment of women," and the encouragement of family planning. What was especially new about the conference agenda was the emphasis on Western conceptions of individual autonomy, human choice, and sexuality, involving an extension of human rights conceptions to such notions as "reproductive rights" and "abortion rights." Because some of the conference themes represented a direct challenge to Christian, Muslim, and traditional cultural norms, the conference proceedings were highly contentious. Fundamentally, the debate pitted modern, Western interests, which sought to legitimize individualistic and permissive perspectives about sexuality and family life, against traditional, religious forces, which emphasized moral obligations in human sexuality and reaffirmed the sanctity of human life. The Vatican, led by Pope John Paul II, strongly objected to the secular assumptions underlying the conference proceedings and in particular, to the legitimacy of abortion as an instrument of family planning.[22]

After nine days of intense discussion, the Cairo conference delegates adopted a 113-page action program calling for increasing the annual funding for population stabilization initiatives from $5 billion to $17 billion by the turn of the century. The aim of the increased expenditures is to help stabilize the world's population at about 7.2 billion in 2015. Although the Cairo action program reemphasizes the goal of family planning, it also goes beyond traditional population programs by encouraging women to take increased control over their lives, by assuring gender equality, and by emphasizing reproductive health care.[23]

The UN and Conflict Resolution

Peacekeeping and Peacemaking

In promoting international peace and preventing war, the UN utilizes two different strategies: peacekeeping and peacemaking. As noted before, peacekeeping involves the introduction of UN forces into areas of conflict in which the disputing parties have achieved a cease-fire. Peacemaking, by contrast, involves the imposition of order in an area of conflict in which the warring parties continue to resort to violence to achieve desired goals.

From 1948 to 1995, the United Nations sponsored thirty-five multilateral peacekeeping operations in conflicts that threatened international peace. These conflicts included domestic disputes over the establishment of legitimate political authorities (such as El Salvador, Namibia, Nicaragua, and Western Sahara); ethnic, religious, and domestic disputes (such as the ethnic strife in Bosnia, Cyprus, and Rwanda); and regional interstate disputes (such as the Arab-Israeli conflict and the Iran-Iraq war). To promote international peace, UN peacekeeping forces have done the following:

1. Maintained cease-fires in areas of conflict, including the India-Pakistan dispute over Kashmir and Jammu (1949–present), the Greek-Turkish dispute in Cyprus (1964–present), and the Iran-Iraq border dispute (1989–1991)

2. Maintained domestic order while supervising elections in such countries as Cambodia (1991–1993), Nicaragua (1989–1991) and Namibia (1989–1990)

3. Supervised the demilitarization of areas of conflict, such as Angola (1989–1991), El Salvador (1991-1996), Haiti (1993–1997), and Nicaragua (1989–1991)

4. Guided the transition of former colonies to political independence, including Congo (1960–1964) and Namibia (1989–1990)

5. Maintained observer missions in areas of potential conflict, including West New Guinea (1962–1963), Georgia (1993–present), Liberia (1992–present), Rwanda (1994–1996), and Tajikistan (1994–present)

Although the context has varied among these disputes, the primary goal of each observer mission or peacekeeping operation has been to prevent war. In effect, the UN has sought to use its symbolic authority to inhibit violence.

In the organization's early years, peacekeeping operations were limited principally to observer missions. The Truce Supervision Organization (UNTSO), established in 1948 to keep peace among Israel, Jordan, Lebanon, and Syria, is one example. As of 1995, UNTSO continued to function in the Middle East with nearly 300 observers from seventeen countries. A more comprehensive approach, known as **preventive diplomacy,** led the UN to extend its peacekeeping activities. Developed by Secretary-General Dag Hammarskjöld, this peacekeeping strategy attempted to deploy military forces to keep adversaries apart and to keep major powers from becoming embroiled in regional conflicts. It was, in effect, a strategy of international containment.

The doctrine was first applied in 1956 during the Suez War, when Hammarskjöld dispatched a multinational force of some 6,000 soldiers to Egypt. Significantly, the UN Emergency Force (UNEF) comprised soldiers from more than twenty countries, but none from the Soviet Union or the United States, nor from France or Britain, the two European powers directly involved in the conflict. Four years later, the secretary-general once again used preventive diplomacy to contain an explosive civil war in the Congo (Zaire). Immediately after Belgium granted its former colony independence, major fighting broke out among competing tribal factions. To forestall the entry of Belgium and other major powers into conflict, Hammarskjöld established the *Operation de Nations Unies—Congo* (ONUC), the largest (16,000 soldiers) and most expensive ($120 million) UN peacekeeping operation during the Cold War era.

Other important UN peacekeeping operations during the 1970s and 1980s include:

UNEF II—UN Emergency Force, 1973–1979: an operation, designed in accordance with the Egyptian-Israeli Peace Treaty of 1979, to keep peace and order in Sinai and Gaza Strip

UNDOF—UN Disengagement Observer Force, 1974–present: a UN force of 1,330 designed to maintain a cease-fire between Syria and Israel

UNIFIL—UN Interim Force in Lebanon, 1978–present: a 5,876-member UN force from ten countries designed to maintain order along the Lebanon-Israel border;

ONUCA—UN Observer Group in Central America, 1989–1991: 1010-member UN force sent to temporarily monitor a cease-fire between the Sandinista forces and Nicaraguan rebels and to supervise the demobilization of the Nicaraguan Resistance

UNTAG—UN Transition Assistance Group, 1989–1990: a nine-month operation involving 6,700 UN personnel (4,300 soldiers, 1,500 police, and 900 civilians) for the purpose of maintaining a cease-fire in Namibia and assisting in elections and the transition to full political independence

Preventive diplomacy
A United Nations strategy of keeping local disputes from escalating by introducing multinational peacekeeping forces. During the Cold War this strategy was utilized to limit superpower involvement in local and regional conflicts.

Ernest Haas has examined the UN's conflict-resolution record during the Cold War and has concluded that it has been more successful than many observers had thought. Although his study confirmed that the UN's overall effectiveness in maintaining international order and preventing conflict declined from the 1950s to the mid-1980s, Haas concluded that it simply was not true that "the UN has lost all relevance with respect to conflict management." According to him, of the 319 international disputes during the 1945–1984 period, 43 percent (137) were referred to the United Nations, 27 percent (86) were referred to regional organizations (e.g., the Organization of American States and the Organization of African Unity), and 30 percent (96) were not referred to any organization.[24] As fig. 14.6 suggests, of the disputes assigned to the UN, 25 percent were resolved, 34 percent were isolated, 37 percent resulted in the halting of hostilities, and 54 percent led to a reduction of tensions. (The outcomes for regional organizations were largely the same.)

The United Nations has been much better at peacekeeping than at peacemaking. This is due, in great measure, to the fact that peacekeeping is a more modest form of conflict resolution. Whereas peacemaking through collective security requires the multinational use of power to punish aggressors, peacekeeping attempts only to prevent the escalation of conflict. Rather than resolving disputes, peacekeeping initiatives are designed solely to prevent the expansion of conflict by isolating combatants and easing the underlying tensions.

Post–Cold War Peacekeeping

With the end of the Cold War, UN peacekeeping and peacemaking responsibilities have greatly increased. From 1988 to 1994, the UN was called upon to mount thirteen new peacekeeping operations. Some of these have contributed to conflict resolution (see table 14.4), whereas others, such as Bosnia, Cambodia, and Haiti, have brought temporary stability without leading to a permanent peace settlement. Two major UN operations that illustrate ambiguous outcomes are the peacekeeping operations in the former Yugoslavia and Cambodia.

In late 1991 the UN Security Council authorized the creation of the *UN Protection Force (UNPROFOR),* a 20,000-member peacekeeping force to halt civil strife in the former Yugoslavia. After Croatia and Slovenia declared independence from the Serbian-controlled central government in 1991, a bitter civil war broke out be-

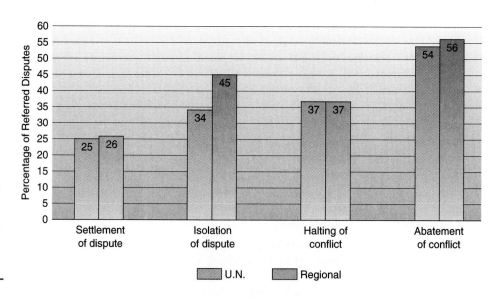

FIGURE 14.6
Performance of Conflict Management Tasks by the United Nations and Regional Organizations, 1945–1984

TABLE 14.4 UN Participation in Settling Regional Disputes, 1988-1994

Conflict	Source	Settlement Year	United Nations Role
Afghanistan	Soviet invasion, 1979	1988	Gorbachev announces withdrawal of Soviet troops; UN personnel monitor troop disengagement
Iran-Iraq	Iraq attacks Iran, 1980	1988	Iran accepts UN cease-fire resolution; UN military observers supervise disengagement
Cambodia	Vietnam occupies Cambodia, 1978	1989	UN supports Vietnam-Cambodia negotiations, resulting in a disengagement accord
Nicaragua	Civil war, 1981-1987	1989	Central American states establish a regional peace accord, calling for elections and demilitarization; UN observers monitor demobilization
Angola	Civil war, 1975-1988	1989	Peace talks between United States, Angola, Cuba, and South Africa result in 1989 accord calling for withdrawal of Cuban forces and elections in Namibia; UN peacekeeping force supervises cease-fire, elections, and transition to independence
Iraq-Kuwait	Iraq invades Kuwait, 1990	1991	Security Council passes thirteen resolutions condemning Iraq and authorizing sanctions, including force
El Salvador	Civil war, 1980-1991	1992	UN peace talks between the guerrillas and the government result in a peace accord
Guatemala	Civil war 1960-1994	1994	UN monitors compliance with cease-fire, ending a thirty-four-year civil conflict

tween Croatian and Serbian forces. And when Bosnia-Herzegovina announced its independence in mid-1992, the war became even more brutal as ethnic, religious, and political rivalries intensified the fighting. Because of Serbia's continued aggression against Bosnia and Croatia, the General Assembly voted in mid-1992 to expel the Serbian government from Yugoslavia's UN seat. Although the introduction of UN peacekeeping forces into Croatia and Bosnia helped to contain fighting among warring factions, the brutal civil war continued to take a heavy toll in casualties and human suffering from sickness, hunger, and displacement. By the end of 1993, the war had resulted in more than 200,000 deaths and at least one million refugees. In December 1995, UNPROFOR's peacekeeping responsibilities were transferred to a NATO Stabilization Force (SFOR) after a complex peace agreement was negotiated between the political leaders of the three major warring factions. (See case 14.2; see also case 1.2.) Although the principal objective of SFOR was to keep civic order, the NATO force assumed some peacemaking responsibilities, including the capture of indicted war criminals.

The second major post–Cold War UN peacekeeping operation was *UN Transitional Authority in Cambodia (UNTAC),* the largest and most expensive peacekeeping operation in the UN's history. (See case 14.3.) After the warring parties achieved a cease-fire in 1991, the Security Council authorized a major transitional force to assist Cambodia in disarming the antagonists and in helping to establish the processes and institutions of civic society. The eighteen-month transitional operation, which cost more than $3 billion, was considered successful while UNTAC was underway in Cambodia, but it began to unravel soon thereafter. By 1997, the UN peace initiative had begun to collapse in the face of continuing factionalism, corruption, and the lack of communal solidarity.

CASE STUDY

Case 14.2 The Bosnian Peace Accord

After nearly four years of bitter fighting, the three warring parties in the Bosnia-Herzegovina civil war agreed in October 1995 to a cease-fire, paving the way for international peace negotiations. Subsequently, political leaders of the three rival Balkan states (Croatia, Serbia, and Bosnia) gathered at Wright-Patterson Air Force Base, in Dayton, Ohio for intense negotiations. After twenty-one days of difficult bargaining, the three leaders signed the *Bosnia Peace Accord* (known simply as the Dayton Accord). The agreement, signed in November 1995, provides the following:

- Bosnia is to remain a single country divided into two entities—a Muslim-Croat federation, covering about 51 percent of the land, and a Serb republic (known as Republika Srpska), with 49 percent of the land.
- Each entity is to have its own government, with an elected president and elected parliament.
- Ultimate governmental authority within Bosnia is to reside in a central government, composed of a collective presidency and a national parliament.
- The Sarajevo central government is to be responsible for foreign and economic policy, citizenship, immigration, and other related issues.
- Refugees have the right to return home.
- Persons indicted on charges of genocide by the international war crimes tribunal in The Hague are barred from holding office.
- A major (35,000–60,000 troops) NATO stabilization force (SFOR) is responsible for implementing the agreement.[25]

Although it is impossible to know whether this agreement will result in a permanent peace settlement, the establishment of stable preconditions, as called for by the accord, proceeded much more slowly than had been originally expected. As a result, in early 1997 the Clinton administration extended the U.S. commitment of its 10,000-member NATO force. President Clinton originally promised Congress that U.S. forces would be withdrawn from Bosnia after one year, but because of the continuing need for substantial military forces in supervising the accord's implementation, he determined to delay their withdrawal.

As called for by the Dayton Accord, Bosnian elections were held in 1996, resulting in the establishment of governmental structures for the two Bosnian state entities. The Bosnian central government, however, has remained weak and largely ineffective, and the subnational governments of the Muslim-Croat federation and the Serb republic have been plagued with corruption and bitter internal strife. Moreover some political leaders associated with the Bosnian war, most notably Radovan Karadzic, the former head of Bosnian Serbs, have remained influential, even though they are not officially in government. Although the Dayton peace plan calls for prosecution of some seventy indicted war criminals, SFOR has been reluctant to capture Karadzic and other indicted officials, lest such attempts lead to the resumption of fighting. In mid-1997, however, NATO forces carried out a successful raid, leading to the capture of one indicted criminal and the killing of another.

Despite SFOR's success in holding and monitoring elections in 1996 and in 1997, SFOR had been relatively ineffective in reducing mistrust among the major ethnopolitical groups and in facilitating the repatriation of refugees to their home communities. As a result, peace is likely to continue in Bosnia only so long as an effective external force continues to monitor and implement the Dayton Accord.

Because of the failure of UN peacekeeping missions to resolve completely major post–Cold War conflicts, such as the Bosnian and Somalian disputes, a growing number of officials have expressed disillusionment with UN peacekeeping operations. This disillusionment is misplaced, however, because the UN operations were being asked to "keep" peace in environments in which none had existed beforehand. What was needed in many regions of conflict was peacemaking, not peacekeeping. The perceived failure of UN peacekeeping operations was thus based on the fact that UN forces were introduced in environments to carry out tasks for which such forces were ill-equipped.

Case 14.3 | UN Peacemaking in Cambodia

Cambodia, a small poor country of slightly less than 9 million people, is located between two larger, more powerful states—Vietnam and Thailand. Its history and evolution have been closely tied to the geopolitical developments of the Southeast Asian region. In 1975, the Khmer Rouge, a Maoist-inspired Communist guerrilla group, seized control of Cambodia's government. During the next four years, the Khmer Rouge, under the leadership of Pol Pot, carried out one of the most brutal genocides of modern times, killing more than one million persons, or more than 15 percent of Cambodia's population. As a result of the genocide, Vietnam invaded Cambodia, forcing the Khmer Rouge from power. The Vietnamese-installed puppet regime governed Cambodia until 1989, when Vietnam withdrew its troops.

When Vietnam withdrew its forces from Cambodia, it left the Hanoi-supported regime of Hun Sen in control of the government. Vietnam's withdrawal, however, precipitated fighting among competing guerrilla groups, especially among the Khmer Rouge, the anti-Vietnam forces of Prince Norodom Sihanouk (Cambodia's head of government during the 1950s and 1960s) and the pro-Vietnamese forces of Hun Sen. To help resolve the conflict, the United Nations, with the support of China, the United States, and the USSR, sponsored peace talks beginning in early 1989. After numerous delays and failures, the major warring parties, under the prodding of the major powers, developed a peace accord in 1991. The Paris Peace Agreement, signed in Paris in October 1991, provided that:

- The warring parties would maintain a cease-fire.
- The UN would assume administrative oversight of the state during a transitional process.
- A UN peacekeeping force would maintain order and would carry out the demobilization of existing guerrilla factions and government military forces.
- The UN would oversee the repatriation of some 350,000 refugees from camps along the Thai border.
- The UN would supervise elections to establish a constitutional assembly charged with drafting a new constitution.[26]

To ensure impartiality, Cambodia's government during the transitional phase was to consist of three parts: first, existing governmental structures (under the leadership of Hun Sen) would continue to func-

tion, but under UN supervision; second, the 22,000-member UN peacekeeping operation (UNTAC) would assume major police and military control of the state; and third, a Supreme National Council, headed by Prince Sihanouk, would assume the symbolic tasks of chief of state.[27] To encourage peaceful accommodation, the Paris peace process provided that all groups, including the Khmer Rouge, could participate in forming a new regime. In addition, despite the Khmer Rouge's brutal genocide, no provision was made for punishing Pol Pot and other officials responsible for the genocide. The accord was not a means to seek justice; rather, it aimed solely at bringing about peace by disarming more than 400,000 soldiers and members of the militia, demobilizing 70 percent of them, and creating a new government based on free elections.

The May 1993 elections were won by the royalist party (known by the acronym FUNCINPEC), headed by Prince Ranariddh, the son of Sihanouk. Ranariddh won 45 percent of the vote, while the pro-Vietnamese Cambodian People's Party, headed by Hun Sen, won 38 percent of the vote. Hun Sen, who maintained significant power because of his control over police and security forces as well as over the major departments of the government, refused to give up, and threatened civil war if his party was not included in the new, provisional government. As a result, the state's Supreme National Council appointed two prime ministers—Ranariddh as first prime minister and Sen as second prime minister. The provisional government functioned satisfactorily in the first two years, establishing, among other things, a new constitution with Sihanouk as constitutional monarch. But increased friction also developed between the two leaders as they, along with other factions, competed for power. In order to counter his diminishing influence in government, Ranariddh sought to expand his ties with the Khmer Rouge and to increase his group's military forces. As a result, Sen ousted Ranariddh from power in mid-1997, forcing him into exile.

In the wake of the mini-coup, Cambodia remains a fragile regime, with significant distrust and factional antagonism continuing among the major political groups. Despite UNTAC's effort to create the social and political conditions for a stable political order, as well as to foment economic growth with the support of significant foreign aid, Cambodia remains a weak, corrupt state. Although the UN
continued

Case 14.3 | UN Peacemaking in Cambodia—*continued*

peacemaking initiative was judged a success when UNTAC completed its operations in November 1993, the dream of a stable and peaceful Cambodia remained elusive in 1997. Although UNTAC had succeeded in holding elections, it failed to disarm the warring factions and to pacify the deep political and ideological animosities among the major political groups. The political frailty of Cambodia was especially evident in 1997, when Sen carried out a mini-coup against the first prime minister. The unravelling of the UN's large and expensive Cambodian operation suggests that peacemaking is far more elusive than had been originally anticipated.

One of the features of the post–Cold War world has been the growing magnitude of human suffering from domestic political conflicts, tribal wars, and ethnic genocide. If the international community decides that such strife threatens global order and that the fighting must be halted, even against the wishes of the warring parties, then coercive peacemaking strategies will be required. The UN is not well equipped to carry out such operations because the major powers have been reluctant to transfer military resources to establish a standing military force, as called for by the UN Charter (art. 43).

If the United Nations is to contribute to future regional order, its operations must be carefully defined and properly conceived. Peacekeeping operations should be carried out only in areas in which UN forces are introduced to keep warring parties apart. But where the breakdown of order is more profound, significant military force may be required to impose order, even in opposition to some or most of the warring parties. A capable, integrated military force is unlikely to be developed from the voluntary forces of developing nations. Rather, an effective military force will require the support, coordination, and modern weapons of a major power, as was the case in the UN operation to restore order in Somalia in 1991 and democracy in Haiti in 1993.

REGIONAL AND OTHER INTERNATIONAL ORGANIZATIONS

European Union (EU)
A regional organization of 15 Western European states that promotes increased economic, social, and political unity. The EU was formerly known as the European Community (EC).

Although the UN is the most important international governmental organization, more than three hundred other IGOs exist that contribute significantly to the stability and well-being of the international community. As noted in chapter 2, these organizations perform general and specific tasks and operate at the global as well as regional levels. When the UN was established in 1945, its charter encouraged the development of regional organizations that could carry out many of its responsibilities through institutions in specific geographical areas. As a result, numerous regional organizations have been established, such as the Organization of African Unity (OAU) and the Organization of American States (OAS). By far the most successful of these is the **European Union (EU),** a fifteen-member institution created in 1950.

The European Union (EU)

The EU is important for a number of reasons. First, the organization has achieved the highest level of institutional development of any IGO, functioning not only as an international organization dependent on the collective will of states but also as a **supranational** institution with the capacity of making decisions independent of the give and take of interstate bargaining. In effect, EU decision makers have independent political authority to make decisions on behalf of the community. To be sure, no EU member-state has given up sovereignty, but as of early 1998, no international organization had achieved a more developed level of transnational authority than the EU. A second reason for EU's significance is that it represents the most explicit application of the theory of neofunctionalism, as introduced earlier in the chapter. In accordance with the theory, the EU has promoted regional integration through functional interdependence and the establishment of regional decision-making structures. According to the theory, the growing social, economic, and political integration, coupled with the development of increasingly authoritative institutions, results not only in increased socioeconomic prosperity but in greater political order.

Supranational
The capacity of an international organization to make binding decisions on member-states without their individual consent.

Origins

The foundation of the EU was laid in 1950 with a historic declaration by French Foreign Minister Robert Schuman calling on European states to begin the gradual process of European unification. The central idea of the **Schuman Plan** was to develop economic cooperation among Western European states in order to foster

Schuman Plan
The plan, set forth in 1950 by French Foreign Minister Robert Schuman, called on European states to develop increasing economic cooperation in order to foster peace within Western Europe.

MAP 14.1
The European
Union

peace and reconciliation within the region, especially between France and Germany. The plan, based on ideas of Jean Monnet, a French civil servant, called for pooling production in one "decisive target" (coal and steel) and establishing a supranational institution to guide governmental decision making in coal and steel. A year after the Schuman Plan was proposed, six European states (France, West Germany, Italy, the Netherlands, Belgium, and Luxembourg) signed a treaty establishing the European Coal and Steel Community (ECSC). In ratifying this treaty, the six European states pledged, among other things:

> to substitute for historic rivalries a fusion of their essential interests; to establish, by creating an economic community, the foundation of a wider and deeper community among peoples long divided by bloody conflicts; and to lay the bases of institutions capable of giving direction to their future common destiny.

After successfully developing economic coordination of the coal and steel industries, the six countries agreed to extend cooperation to other areas. In 1957, they signed treaties establishing the European Economic Community (EEC) and the European Atomic Energy Community (Euratom). The goal of the EEC was to create a common market by abolishing internal trade barriers and establishing a common external economic policy; the aim of Euratom was to encourage the development of peaceful uses of nuclear energy. Both organizations were modeled after the ECSC and provided their respective executive authorities with some supranational authority. In 1967 the ECSC, EEC, and Euratom merged into a single institution, the European Community (EC), thereby establishing the three institutional pillars of the European integration process.

One of the important dimensions of the European integration process has been the growth of its membership, increasing from six member-states in 1951 to fifteen states in 1995. In the early 1960s, the United Kingdom applied for EU membership, but French President Charles de Gaulle blocked its entry, perhaps fearing the diminution of French influence. In 1967 Britain reapplied for entry, and three years later Norway, Ireland, and Denmark also applied. In 1973, Britain, Ireland, and Denmark were granted membership; Norway, however, refused to join when a referendum failed to confirm the government's initiative. The EU expanded southwards with the accession of Greece in 1981 and Portugal and Spain in 1986. In January 1995, Austria, Finland, and Sweden joined the European community, while Norway again rejected membership after its citizens failed to pass an EU referendum.

A number of other European states are eager to join the EU. As of 1996, thirteen countries had made formal membership application. These countries, listed in the chronological order of their applications, are: Turkey, Cyprus, Malta, Switzerland, Hungary, Poland, Bulgaria, Estonia, Latvia, Lithuania, Romania, Slovakia, and the Czech Republic. Currently the major preoccupation of the EU is the development of increasing economic and monetary union among the existing member-states. It is unlikely, therefore, that the EU will encourage further membership expansion until some of the additional European unification initiatives are underway.

Organization

The major institutions of the European Union are the Commission, the Council of Ministers, the European Parliament, and the Court of Justice. The *Commission,* the heart of the EU, is the executive arm that monitors, guides, directs, and assesses the European unification process. Its importance lies in the fact that it initiates all new EU norms and rules. The Commission includes twenty members, one from each small state and two from the five largest states (Britain, France, Germany, Italy, and Spain), each serving a five-year term. Once appointed, Commission members agree to act only in the EU's interest and may not receive instruction from their national government. The major duties of the commission are: (1) to ensure that EU principles and rules are respected; (2) to initiate proposals for the strengthening of European unification; and (3) to implement and administer EU programs. In carrying out these duties, the Commission is supported by a civil service staff of nearly 15,000 persons, most of them located at the Commission's headquarters in Brussels. Because the EU has eleven official languages, about 20 percent of the Commission's staff are translators.

The *Council of Ministers* is the chief decision-making authority of the EU. Comprised of one representative from each EU member-state, the council is the real legislature of the European integration movement. Foreign ministers are normally the chief delegates to the council, although other government ministers participate in accordance with the agenda. For example, agricultural ministers gather when dealing with the EU's Common Agricultural Policy (CAP), whereas finance ministers meet when addressing the community's fiscal and monetary concerns. The council is assisted in its work by a general secretariat with a permanent staff of 2,000 persons.

Two or three times a year, the Council of Ministers becomes the *European Council* when the heads of government gather to address the most important issues facing the Community. These periodic high-level meetings provide an opportunity to resolve contentious issues and to establish new programs and policies. As the dominant political body, the council seeks to reconcile the interests of member-states and to maintain the collective solidarity needed to implement decisions and regulations. Voting is carried out either through unanimity or a qualified majority. Vital issues, such as membership expansion, treaty modifications, internal security, and political issues, require the consent of all states, although other issues, such as the development of common economic and social policies, are taken with a weighted voting scheme, in which member-states are apportioned different votes (from two for Luxembourg to ten for Germany, France, Italy, and the United Kingdom) according to their economic size. A qualified majority requires sixty-two of eighty-seven votes.

The *European Parliament* is an assembly of 626 members representing the interests of the people. The representatives, who are apportioned by member-states' population, are elected directly for five-year terms. Members sit according to political affiliation rather than national representation. The parliament, located in Strasbourg, France, is supported by a staff of about 2,900 civil servants. The European Parliament is a pseudo-legislative body with limited legislative powers. Unlike national parliaments, it does not appoint governments, make laws, or control the budget. These tasks are carried out primarily by the Council of Ministers. Rather, the assembly's more limited duties involve reviewing of Commission initiatives and policy recommendations, discussing and debating major issues under consideration by the Council of Ministers, and overseeing the EU budget.

The *European Court of Justice,* with its fifteen judges, is responsible for EU judicial matters. As the supreme legal authority within the EU, the Court offers binding interpretations of Community law. In addition, it offers judgments and preliminary rulings on the judicial validity of measures adopted by the Commission, the Council of Ministers, or national governments in light of EU treaties. Finally, the Court settles judicial disputes between the individuals, firms, EU institutions, and national governments.

Evolution

The development of an integrated European market was a long and difficult process. Beginning as distinct economic and political units, the original six EU states became progressively more integrated—first in the coal and steel industries (through the ECSC) and then in other areas (through the EEC). The process of economic integration has followed the path, sketched in chapter 4, proceeding through four distinct phases. To recall, these phases involve: first, a *free trade area* is established by abolishing tariffs and quotas among its members; second, a *customs union* is created in which member-states establish a common external trade policy, with common tariffs and quotas on nonmembers; the third level involves the creation of a *common market,* in which goods, services, capital, and labor move freely among community members; and finally, the *economic union* phase is achieved when member-states' fiscal and monetary policies are fully integrated and are based on a common currency.

The EU achieved the free trade area and customs union targets in the late 1960s, ahead of schedule, and with the elimination of most major barriers to the intercommunity mobility of goods, services, and capital by the early 1980s, the EU was well on its way to becoming a common market. But because of widely different domestic standards and rules governing particular commodities, agricultural produce, health, technology, education and technical training, internal security, and other related matters, significant obstacles to trade and labor mobility remained. For example, diverse national health regulations restricted plant and veterinary imports, different standards governing automobile safety and motor emissions resulted in widely different automobile prices within the EU, and the lack of mutually recognized educational systems and professional diploma programs restricted labor movement. Moreover, the quest for a common market became even more elusive in the late 1970s and early 1980s as European governments erected new non-tariff barriers and expanded the number of rules governing the movement of labor and capital.

Single European Act (SEA)
A 1985 treaty that amended European Community treaties in order to establish goals and procedures for achieving a fully unified market by the end of 1992.

To reinvigorate the unification process, the EU Commission issued a White Paper in 1985, proposing a fully integrated market by December 1992. The proposed initiative, known as *Europe 1992,* was set forth in the **Single European Act (SEA),** a treaty that amended the original treaties in order to establish goals and procedures for achieving a fully unified market by the end of 1992. The SEA proposed to achieve this by harmonizing product standards, harmonizing technical standards, establishing an open market for services such as banking, insurance, and securities, eliminating border controls, removing foreign exchange controls, and the mutual recognition of professional diplomas. In addition, the SEA expanded the Parliament's legislative role and replaced the EU Council's unanimity rule with qualified majority voting in order to facilitate decision making on nonvital economic issues. EU leaders believed that the establishment of a unified market would greatly expand the EU's wealth, increasing its GDP by 4–6 percent, lowering consumer prices by 6.1 percent, and creating 1.8 million new jobs.[28]

By the end of 1992, nearly 95 percent of the measures called for by the White Paper had been adopted by EU governments. Although one of the aims of European unification was to permit the free mobility of persons within the EU, the quest for an integrated community "without frontiers" has proved elusive. The major reason why governments have been reticent to eliminate border controls is the fear of potential threats to national security and communal well-being, whether from terrorism, organized crime, or drug trafficking. The goal of a "frontier-free" Europe, first set forth in 1985 in the *Schengen Agreement,* committed signatory states to the gradual removal of all internal customs checks and border controls so that persons could travel freely within the EU. The Schengen Agreement went into partial effect in 1995 between eight signatory states: Austria, Belgium, France, Germany, Luxembourg, the Netherlands, Portugal, and Spain. Other EU states are expected to join the Schengen "frontier-free" area after establishing appropriate border arrangements.[29]

In December 1990, EU leaders formally started the process of creating a full economic union, based on a common currency, with a more integrated and coherent foreign and defense policy. Based on the preparatory work of two task forces, European heads of state gathered a year later in Maastricht, the Netherlands, for a two-day summit to work out provisions of a **Treaty on European Union.** The Maastricht Treaty went into effect in November 1993 after all member-states had ratified it, and since then the European Community has been referred to as the European Union.

The Maastricht Treaty establishes three pillars for the European Union. The first pillar, the most important, calls for the establishment of an **Economic and Monetary Union (EMU),** based on a common currency and a central EU Bank; the second pillar calls for a **Common Foreign and Security Policy,** with procedures for joint action in foreign and security affairs; the third pillar focuses on internal affairs and social justice issues, including immigration, external border crossing, asylum policy, and border cooperation on shared concerns on such issues as terrorism, crime, and drug trafficking. Issues in the first pillar are governed by Community rules and procedures, whereas issues on the other two pillars are regulated by intergovernmental cooperation.

The quest for greater monetary integration began in 1979, when a *European Monetary System (EMS)* was established to increase coordination of member-states' monetary policies and to help stabilize currency exchange rates. The EMS is based on a monetary standard known as the *Ecu (European currency unit).* The Ecu, whose value is determined by the combined market rate of members' currencies, provides a basis for coordinating exchange rates and a means for settling monetary accounts among member-states. In 1995, an Ecu was worth about $1.30. An important element of the EMU is the *Exchange Rate Mechanism (ERM),* which requires states to limit their currency's fluctuations to a band of 15 percent of the Ecu. Originally, EU member currencies were allowed to fluctuate no more than 2.5 percent from the EU monetary norm, but because of increased currency instability in the early 1990s, this rate was increased to 15 percent. In fact, in September 1992 Britain and Italy withdrew from the ERM because of currency market pressures.

One of the most important elements of the Maastricht Treaty is the decision to establish a common currency. Because of the cost and inefficiency involved in coordinating fifteen national currencies, the treaty calls for increased monetary integration by establishing an Economic and Monetary Union no later than January 1999. The EMU will involve a fully integrated monetary system based on a new currency, the **Euro,** and backed by a European Central Bank. In order to join the EMU, states must meet demanding standards, including the following:

1. Inflation must be within 1.5 percentage points of the average rate of the three states with lowest inflation.
2. Long-term interest rates must be within 2 percentage points of the average rates of the three states with lowest interest rates.
3. The national budget must be below 3 percent of the GNP.
4. The national debt must be below 60 percent of GNP.
5. The national currency's value must have remained stable in the previous two years (no devaluation and the currency must have remained within a 2.25 percent margin of the EMS norm).[30]

The countries most likely to join the EMU in January 1999 are the following eight: Austria, Belgium, Finland, France, Germany, Ireland, Luxembourg, and the Netherlands. Britain, Denmark, and Sweden might also be eligible to participate in the new currency, but they are unlikely to join immediately because they have expressed skepticism about the nature and role of this initiative.[31]

The EU's Impact

Economically, the EU has been highly successful. It has reduced trade barriers and facilitated the movement of labor and capital across national borders, thereby increasing production efficiency and expanding the size of the consumer market.

Treaty on European Union
This accord, also known as the Maastricht Treaty, calls for increased political, economic, and military unity among EU member-states.

Economic and Monetary Union (EMU)
This proposal, which is to go into effect in 1999, calls for an integrated monetary system based on a single currency (euro) and a central EU bank.

Common Foreign and Security Policy
The EU's joint policies on foreign affairs and defense matters.

Euro
The proposed common currency of the EU, projected to be implemented in 1999.

TABLE 14.5 Comparison Between the EU, United States, and Japan, 1994

	EU	United States	Japan
Population (millions)	371	258	125
Total output, GNP (in $US billions)	7,294	6,638	4,321
*Share of world trade (percent of exports)**	19	15	10

*Excludes trade between EC countries

Sources: EU and U.S. data are from the Delegation of the European Commission, "Facts and Figures on the European Union and the United States," Washington, D.C.: Office of Press and Public Affairs, 1995; data on Japan are from CIA, *The World Factbook, 1995* (Washington, D.C.: Central Intelligence Agency, 1995).

From 1958 to 1987, intra-EU trade increased dramatically—from 37 percent of member-states' total exports to 59 percent. At the same time, the EU has maintained a strong international economic position, maintaining a 15–19 percent share of total world trade. By the 1980s, Europe had become the world's biggest trader, exceeding the United States and Japan (see table 14.5). Moreover, the EU had also become the largest economic bloc in the global economy, with a gross national product $600 billion larger than that of the United States.

Whether economic, monetary, and political integration will proceed in accordance with the Maastricht Treaty timetable is unclear in 1998. Major political and economic obstacles, including high unemployment, large governmental indebtedness, and foreign immigration, are threatening further European unification. Although the future of the EU is unknown, the economic, social, monetary, and political integration that has already been achieved is unprecedented in the modern world. Indeed, the EU represents the most significant effort to modify the world's decentralized, anarchic structures since the existing Westphalian order was established in the mid-seventeenth century.

Other IGOs

The continuing expansion of global functional interdependence is likely to result in a further increase in the number and significance of IGOs. Although political IGOs, like the Arab League and the Nonaligned Movement, are likely to continue to play an important role in global politics, specialized organizations will no doubt play an even more significant role in the future as they manage and coordinate the rapidly expanding networks of economic, social, technical, and educational interdependence. As noted in chapter 3, the growth of "globalism" has been made possible through extraordinary technological developments that have increased the speed and efficiency of communications, travel, and commerce. And because of the growing *globalization of culture* and the expanding *internationalization of production and consumption,* the world's borders are likely to become even more permeable. Thus, as states attempt to regulate and coordinate functional interactions, they will rely increasingly on existing and newly established IGOs to help carry out this shared responsibility.

To a significant degree, the extraordinary success of the EU has spawned other IGOs that seek to extend regional economic cooperation and integration in other areas. Some of the most important of these are listed in table 14.6.

Although none of these associations has approached the EU's level of institutionalization and economic and social integration, each plays an important role in

TABLE 14.6 Selected Regional Organizations, 1996

Name	Number of Members	Year Established	Purpose
Andean Group (AG)	5	1969	Promote harmonious development through economic integration
Arab Cooperation Council (ACC)	4	1989	Promote regional economic cooperation
Association of Southeast Asian Nations (ASEAN)	6	1967	Encourage economic, social, cultural cooperation
Caribbean Community and Common Market (CARICOM)	14	1973	Encourage economic integration
Council of Arab Economic Unity (CAEU)	11	1964	Foster economic integration among Arab states
*Economic Community of Central African States (CEEAC)**	10	1983	Promote regional economic cooperation and establish a Central African Common Market
Economic Community of West African States (ECOWAS)	16	1975	Promote regional economic cooperation
European Free Trade Association (EFTA)	7	1960	Promote free trade among European states not part of the EU
Latin American Integration Association (LAIA)	11	1981	Foster regional trade
South Asia Association for Regional Cooperation (SAARC)	7	1985	Encourage economic, social, and cultural cooperation
Southern African Development Coordination Conference (SADCC)	10	1980	Promote regional economic development and reduce dependence on South Africa

*Acronym from Communate Economique des Estats de l'Afrique Centrale

Source: CIA, *CIA Factbook, 1995* (Washington, D.C.: Central Intelligence Agency, 1995).

facilitating regional cooperation in particular issue areas. To the extent that these and other related organizations foster functional interdependence, they contribute to the development of a more prosperous and cohesive global community.

IN CONCLUSION

International organizations have played and continue to play an important role in the international community. In the twentieth century two major experiments in global organization have been attempted, the League of Nations in the aftermath of World War I and the United Nations following World War II, but neither organization has contributed significantly to effective international conflict resolution and the creation of global order. A major reason is that the ability of the organizations to work toward shared interests is impaired by the decentralized nature of global society. During the Cold War era, for example, the deep ideological divisions between the superpowers and their allies made cooperation within UN agencies, especially the Security Council, difficult and at times impossible. As a result, the Security Council was generally unable to effectively address international problems. Indeed, the political and ideological conflicts dividing the major powers were introduced into the forums of the UN, thereby further impeding global cooperation.

The end of the Cold War and the death of Soviet Communism provided a new possibility for UN peacekeeping. Not surprisingly, since the late 1980s, the UN has become more effective in contributing to the peace process.

The most important experiment in regional organization is the EU. Its importance lies in the fact that it directly challenges the forces of political disintegration that have swept global politics throughout most of the twentieth century, and especially the post–World War II era. Whereas nationalism has encouraged the further political division of the world, the EU represents an effort not only to halt the division of the world but also to seek to promote economic, social, and political cohesion among Western European states. Although the EU experiment is still underway, the level of economic and political integration that has been realized in Europe over the past thirty years is extraordinary, and certainly much greater than most European idealists had ever anticipated when the unification movement began. If Europe becomes a federal state, the EU experiment will represent one of the most significant political achievements of the twentieth century.

SUMMARY

1. There are six major theories of world order: world federalism, collective security, international peacemaking, international peacekeeping, third-party dispute settlement, and functionalism. The first three theories assume that power should be managed; the other three assume that power should be avoided.

2. World federalism seeks to build international community by centralizing authority in a global federal structure. Collective security, by contrast, attempts to maintain peace and stability within the existing anarchic world order by establishing an association that punishes aggression with the combined power of association members. International peacemaking involves the use of multilateral forces to impose a settlement on an ongoing military conflict.

3. International peacekeeping involves the use of multilateral peacekeeping forces to forestall direct conflict. In third-party dispute settlement, an intermediary assists the disputing parties in conflict resolution. The aim of functionalism is to promote peace and prosperity by promoting functional interdependence and avoiding politics altogether.

4. The principal IGO is the United Nations. Although its chief purpose is to promote international peace, most of its activities have been focused on social, economic, and technical concerns. These functional interests are carried out primarily through its specialized agencies.

5. The chief peacekeeping UN organ is the Security Council. The General Assembly and the secretary-general also contribute to this task indirectly. One of the major ways in which the UN seeks to keep peace is by introducing multilateral peacekeeping forces into areas of conflict. If conflict cannot be halted, power may have to be imposed on the contesting parties in order to establish order.

6. The effectiveness of the UN depends on global political dynamics. Because of the decline of Cold War rivalries, international cooperation has increased. As a result, the United Nations has become a more influential organization in global society.

7. The most important regional organization is the EU, an institution that has been extraordinarily successful in fostering regional economic integration among its fifteen members.

KEY TERMS

IGO	third-party dispute settlement	neofunctionalism	Treaty on European Union
world federalism		preventive diplomacy	Economic and Monetary Union (EMU)
collective security	good offices	European Union (EU)	
League of Nations	mediation	supranational	Common Foreign and Security Policy
peacemaking	arbitration	Schuman Plan	
peacekeeping	functionalism	Single European Act (SEA)	Euro

RECOMMENDED READINGS

Archer, Clive. *International Organizations*. London: George Allen & Unwin, 1983. A short introduction to the literature on international organization. Chapter 3 analyzes relevant literature in terms of four major perspectives: traditional, revisionist, Marxist, and Third World.

Baehr, Peter R., and Leon Gordenker. *The United Nations in the 1990s*. New York: St. Martin's Press, 1992. A succinct and current assessment of the structures and functions of the most important UN agencies.

Bennett, A. LeRoy. *International Organizations: Principles & Issues*. 5th ed. Englewood Cliffs, N.J.: Prentice-Hall, 1991. An up-to-date introductory text on international organization focusing on institutional concerns and areas of functional cooperation, including disarmament, economic development, the management of global resources, human rights, and social welfare.

Buckley, William F., Jr. *United Nations Journal: A Delegate's Odyssey*. Garden City, N.J.: Anchor Books, 1977. Buckley, an influential conservative columnist, provides a lively, informative, and witty account of United Nations politics based on his experiences as a 1972 U.S. representative to the United Nations. A penetrating assessment of the global politics of human rights.

Claude, Inis L., Jr. *Swords into Plowshares: The Problems and Progress of International Organization*. 4th ed. New York: Random House, 1973. Although dated, this study provides invaluable descriptions and critiques of the major theories of world order and penetrating

assessments of the key constitutional problems of global institutions.

Daltrop, Anne. *Politics and the European Community*. 2nd ed. London: Longman, 1986. A succinct introduction to the institutions, historical evolution, key issues, and regional and foreign impact of the EC.

Franck, Thomas M. *Nation Against Nation: What Happened to the U.N. Dream and What the U.S. Can Do About It*. New York: Oxford University Press, 1985. Franck, a former director of research of UNITAR (the UN's "think tank"), provides a penetrating critique of the work of the United Nations from a U.S. perspective. The author suggests that, although the UN has often undermined human rights and hampered conflict resolution, the organization can become more effective if the United States and its allies confront its weaknesses.

Haas, Ernest. *Why We Still Need the United Nations*. Berkeley: Institute of International Studies, University of California, 1986. A short, insightful study of the impact of the United Nations on global conflict management. Haas argues that the UN has a modest but important role to play in the global political system.

Tessitore, John, and Susan Woolfson. *A Global Agenda: Issues Before the 50th General Assembly of the United Nations*. Lanham, Md.: University Press of America, 1995. This annual publication of the United States UN Association describes major activities and concerns of the United Nations and its affiliated agencies.

RELEVANT WEB SITES

Academic Council on the United Nations System (ACUNS)	www.brown.edu/Departments/ACUNS/index.html
European Union	www.europa.eu.int
NATO	www.nato.int
United Nations	www.un.org/organs
UN Peacekeeping Operations	www.un.org/Depts/dpko/

15

North-South Conflict and Cooperation

As noted in chapter 4, two systemic disputes have dominated the global postwar system—the East-West conflict, which ended in 1990, and the North-South conflict, which continues in the late 1990s but with little impact on global politics. Chapter 5 examined the nature, evolution, and termination of the East-West dispute; this chapter examines the second conflict between the rich and poor states. An analysis of the North-South dispute is important because it, like the East-West conflict, has been a major factor in structuring international relations in the second half of this century. In contrast to the ideological superpower conflict, the North-South dispute is characterized by several features: first, it is concerned with economic resources, not with military power or political ideologies; second, it is global in character, involving nearly all of the world's countries, rather than focusing on two superpowers and their respective allies; third, it is more diffuse, with major powers playing a comparatively small role; and fourth, it is nonviolent, with military force nearly absent from the dispute.

The North-South conflict developed in the early 1960s, partly in response to two major international developments. First, during the 1960s and 1970s the number of Third World countries increased dramatically, rising from about thirty-five in the mid-1950s to nearly eighty in the mid-1970s. Virtually all of the new developing nations were former colonies, economically backward, and located in Asia and Africa. Shortly after gaining political independence, the new states sought to increase their political and economic autonomy and began making economic claims against the major industrial powers in order to foment economic expansion and thereby reduce poverty. Moreover, the new states tried to modify the structures of the international economic order to make the global system more favorable to them.

The second major development involved the rise of modern economic consciousness in the new states. The new consciousness, largely a by-product of the global spread of economic modernization, involved an increasing awareness of the poverty of developing nations, especially when compared with the wealth of modern industrial states. As modernization spread to these new lands in the 1960s, a revolution of rising expectations began to emerge in the new states. This revolution transformed Third World aspirations and expectations and led to demands for domestic economic improvements and for changes in the rules and institutions of the international economic system. In addition, developing nations began to request and demand increasing financial assistance from the rich states in order to promote national economic expansion. In response to growing Third World needs and demands, developed countries began transferring large amounts of resources to the poor countries. For example, of the total U.S. foreign economic assistance given from 1946 to 1990 (about $177 billion), more than 80 percent went to the Third World.[4]

This chapter analyzes the North-South conflict as a case study in systemic conflict management. It examines the nature of participants and the origins and nature of the dispute, and then compares distinctive features of the North's and the South's perspectives on wealth creation. It also highlights the forces that contributed to cooperation among the states of the South and of the North. The chapter then traces the evolution of the conflict, from its inception in the 1960s to its transformation in the 1980s. The chapter concludes with an assessment of why the South's influence has declined and why North-South relations have been radically transformed by growing transnational economic interdependence.

CONFLICT PARTICIPANTS

The North-South dispute is rooted in the significant economic disparity between two groups of states—the rich, industrial states in Europe and North America and the developing nations in Asia, Africa, and Latin America. The North represents those countries with developed economies, modern and integrated societies, and governments based on democratic procedures; the South, by contrast, represents countries with developing economies and significant poverty, dualistic societies with some traditional and some modern norms, and governments based on limited democratic legitimacy. Although neither the North or South has established a formal coalition, each group is represented by informal associations.

The organization that perhaps best represents the North is the **Organization for Economic Cooperation and Development (OECD),** an association of twenty-four industrial democracies designed to promote international economic cooperation and to improve assistance to the Third World. (See table 15.1.) Although they possess only one-fifth of the world's population, the OECD countries account for nearly two-thirds of the world's wealth and more than 70 percent of the world's trade. To the extent that the North has had leadership, it has been provided by the seven leading industrial states, known as the **Group of 7 (G-7),** comprised of Britain, Canada, France, Germany, Japan, Italy, and United States. The G-7 meets annually in economic summits involving the heads of government. (See chap. 12.) With the addition of Russia to this group in 1997, the G-8 is now less representative of the industrial democratic states.

The organization that best represents the South is the **Group of 77 (G-77),** an informal association of developing nations that emerged in the early 1970s to present shared Third World concerns at international forums such as the **United Nations Conference on Trade and Development (UNCTAD),** the Nonaligned Movement (NAM), and the UN General Assembly and its Economic and Social Council. More than any other international association, G-77 has been the primary voice for the developing nations' economic interests, especially their demands for transforming the international economic system. G-77 originally involved 77 countries, but by the early 1990s its membership had increased to more than 120 states.

Organization for Economic Cooperation and Development (OECD)
A Paris-based consortium of the twenty-four leading industrial economies of the world.

Group of 7 (G-7)
An alliance of the world's seven leading industrial democratic countries: Britain, Canada, France, Germany, Italy, Japan, and the United States.

Group of 77 (G-77)
An informal alliance of developing nations that emerged in the 1960s to promote Third World economic development. In the 1970s, G-77 became chiefly concerned with reforming the international economic order as a means of empowering developing nations. Originally, G-77 consisted of 77 members, but by the late 1980s the number had increased to more than 120 states.

United Nations Conference on Trade and Development (UNCTAD)
A series of conferences, begun in 1964 by the United Nations, with the aim of fostering economic development in the Third World. The program is supported by a Geneva-based secretariat.

TABLE 15.1 Participants of the North-South Conflict

The North: OECD Members				
Australia	Finland	Ireland	New Zealand	Switzerland
Austria	France*	Italy*	Norway	Turkey
Belgium	Germany*	Japan*	Portugal	United Kingdom*
Canada*	Greece	Luxembourg	Spain	United States*
Denmark	Iceland	Netherlands	Sweden	

*Members of G-7

The South: Group of 77				
The Third World				
Algeria	Cuba	Iran	Morocco	Seychelles
Antigua and Barbuda	Cyprus	Iraq	Namibia	Singapore
Argentina	Dominica	Jamaica	Nicaragua	South Africa
Bahamas	Dominican Rep.	Jordan	Oman	Sri Lanka
Bahrain	Ecuador	Kiribati	Pakistan	Suriname
Barbados	Egypt	S. Korea	Panama	Swaziland
Belize	El Salvador	Kuwait	Paraguay	Syria
Bolivia	Fiji	Lebanon	Peru	Thailand
Botswana	Gabon	Libya	Philippines	Trinidad/Tobago
Brazil	Grenada	Malaysia	Qatar	Tunisia
Brunei	Guatemala	Maldives	St. Kitts/Nevis	U. Arab Emirates
Chile	Guyana	Malta	St. Lucia	Uruguay
China	Honduras	Mauritius	St. Vincent	Venezuela
Colombia	India	Mexico	Saudi Arabia	Vietnam
Costa Rica	Indonesia	Mongolia	Senegal	
The Fourth World				
Afghanistan	Cape Verde	Guinea	Mauritania	Somalia
Angola	Central African Rep.	Guinea-Bissau	Mozambique	Sudan
Bangladesh	Chad	Haiti	Nepal	Tanzania
Benin	Comoros	Ivory Coast	Niger	Togo
Bhutan	Congo	Kenya	Nigeria	Uganda
Burkina Faso	Congo Rep.	Laos	Papua New Guinea	Vanuatu
Burma	Djibouti	Lesotho	Rwanda	Western Somoa
Burundi	Equatorial Guinea	Liberia	Sao Tome/Principe	Yemen
Cambodia	Ethiopia	Madagascar	Sierra Leone	Zambia
Cameroon	Gambia, The	Malawi	Solomon Islands	Zimbabwe
Congo	Ghana	Mali		

Sources: Based on data from U.S. Department of State, *Atlas of United States Foreign Relations* (Washington, D.C.: GPO, 1985), pp. 26, 31, and 69; 1985, GPO, World Bank, *World Bank Atlas 1996,* (Washington, D.C.: The World Bank, 1996), pp. 18–19; and UNDP, *Human Development Report, 1997* (New York: Oxford University Press, 1997).

Like the North, the South has not been a unified actor in global politics, but a highly heterogeneous group of states, deeply divided politically, economically, and ideologically. For example, some countries have established strong democratic institutions whereas others have been governed through traditional autocratic structures. Moreover, some countries have achieved high levels of economic development, while others have remained poor. Indeed, the economic disparity among the members of the South has been so great that some countries have been incapable of meeting the basic needs of their people whereas others have achieved high levels of development. In view of the large economic disparities among nations of the South, scholars have classified these countries as part of the "third" world or part of the "fourth" world (see table 15.1). The **Third World** represents the middle-income countries that have achieved some level of modernization and have the potential and capacity to provide an adequate standard of living for inhabitants; the **Fourth World** represents the low-income countries that cannot meet the basic needs of a large portion of their population. Fundamentally, the former group represents countries that have achieved economic viability, whereas the latter represents those that have not. Despite the great economic and social diversity represented by the South, the group classification has been useful, nonetheless, in conceptualizing important political dynamics between rich and poor countries throughout the 1960–1990 period.

During the Cold War the concept "second world" was used to define states aligned with the Soviet communist system. With the end of the East-West conflict and the disintegration of the Soviet Union, this classification is no longer appropriate. As a result, about twenty-five states now exist that do not easily fit into either the First or the Third World classifications. Of these states, those identifying most strongly with the First World include: the Czech Republic and the Slovak Republic (formerly Czechoslovakia); the three Baltic states of Estonia, Latvia, and Lithuania; the former Yugoslavia republics of Bosnia-Herzegovina, Croatia, and Slovenia; the Central European countries of Bulgaria, Hungary, Poland, and Romania; and Russia. States identifying with the Third World include: Albania, Macedonia, North Korea, and the former USSR republics of Armenia, Azerbaijan, Belarus, Georgia, Kazakstan, Kyrgyzstan, Moldova, Tajikistan, Turkmenistan, Ukraine, and Uzbekistan. Because these former communist countries have not been active in the North-South dispute, none are listed in table 15.1.

Third World
A classification developed in the 1960s to include all developing nations in Asia, Africa, and Latin America. This category was used to differentiate states from the First World (developed democracies) and the Second World (industrializing communist states).

Fourth World
The poorest Third World countries, incapable of meeting citizens' basic needs, especially food.

Economic development in Third World countries has commonly resulted in deeply divided societies with modern and traditional sectors existing side by side, as depicted in this photograph of Rio de Janeiro, Brazil.

THE ORIGINS AND NATURE OF THE CONFLICT

The Origins of the Conflict

In order to understand the origins of the North-South conflict, it is important to understand the historical context from which the dispute emerged. From the fifteenth century through the beginning of the twentieth century, European powers sought to extend their political and economic influence throughout the world. This process of gaining control over other territories in distant lands was called **imperialism,** and the establishment of direct control over the conquered or dominated territories was called **colonialism.**

Throughout modern history, European states pursued imperial policies for economic, political, religious, and cultural reasons. Economically, European empires sought to acquire raw materials, markets for export commodities, and a source of cheap labor. In particular, they sought to establish trade routes that would be commercially beneficial to the imperial state. Politically, major powers competed for hegemonic leadership within the European continent by extending their control over foreign territories. Indeed, during the eighteenth and nineteenth centuries a major criterion of national power was the number, size, and location of its colonial territories. Religiously, European powers sought to Christianize territories that were conquered and colonized. Although early European imperialism (e.g., Spain and Portugal) placed a high priority on official, state-supported proselytization, eighteenth- and nineteenth-century colonialism deemphasized the role of the state in propagating religion, leaving this task to missionaries. Culturally, European powers pursued imperialism in the belief that the norms and values of Western civilization were superior to those of indigenous societies. European leaders, like Cecil Rhodes, the British imperial leader who shaped the late-nineteenth century development of southern Africa, believed that Western civilization was superior to indigenous cultures and that the West had a responsibility to civilize and improve humankind.

Although major political powers (e.g., Babylonians, Assyrians, Romans, Aztecs, Incas) had historically sought to maximize the size of their empires, the rise of European imperialism in the late fifteenth century was different from previous imperial systems in that the new systems were truly global empires based upon maritime power. In 1494, Spain and Portugal, the two leading European powers at the time, signed the *Treaty of Tordesillas,* dividing the world into two spheres at an imaginary north-south line about 300 miles west of the Azores Islands in the Atlantic Ocean. Spain was given the right to territories west of the line of demarcation; Portugal was given the areas to the East. As a result, Spain established control over all of the Americas, while Portugal gained control over the eastern tip of South American (now Brazil), much of the African coastline, and territories surrounding the Indian Ocean.

In the seventeenth, eighteenth, and nineteenth centuries, Britain, France, and the Netherlands were actively involved in extending their imperial control over territories throughout the world. For example, the Dutch government, through its Dutch East India Company, established control over South Africa, Indonesia, Ceylon (Sri Lanka), and various territories in the Americas. The French, for their part, sought territories in North America and the Caribbean in the eighteenth century and then extended their influence to Africa (by establishing trading outposts in such territories as Mauritius, Madagascar, the Seychelles, and Senegal) and the Pacific (by colonizing numerous islands, such as Tahiti). The British were also interested in controlling North America, which led to a war with the French. After defeating the French in the mid-eighteenth century and consolidating their power

Imperialism
The policy of establishing political and economic control over foreign territories.

Colonialism
Establishment of direct political control over a foreign dependency.

over the North American continent, the British extended their imperial policy to Africa and Asia, gaining control over many of the territories surrounding the Indian Ocean.

During the nineteenth century European powers continued to extend their imperial control throughout the world. Beginning in the last half of the century, several other European imperial powers, including Belgium, Italy, and Germany, established colonies in Africa. It has been estimated that by the early nineteenth century European powers controlled about one-third of the world's land and that by the beginning of the twentieth century they have extended control to another third. Indeed, the British boasted at the turn of the century that the sun never set on their empire.

The colonial system disintegrated in the aftermath of World War II. Although Latin American countries had become independent from Spain and Portugal in the nineteenth century, much of Asia and Africa was still controlled by Europe in 1945. The process of postwar **decolonization** began in 1947 when the British relinquished control over India, permitting India and Pakistan to become independent states. The decolonization process greatly accelerated in the late 1950s, and during the 1960s more than forty countries achieved political independence, with three-fourths of them in Africa alone. More than a hundred developing countries from Asia, Africa, the Pacific, and the Caribbean have joined the community of nations as a result of post–World War II decolonization.

Decolonization
The process by which European powers relinquished control over dependent territories.

This brief review of European imperialism and colonialism is important because the countries comprising the South are, for the most part, descendants of the imperial and colonial policies of the North. Not surprisingly, some critics of the North have attributed the North-South gap to the very structures, policies, and values institutionalized by the colonial powers. On the other hand, others argue that, in the absence of Western colonialism, the conditions of the Third World would be far worse. They insist that the North introduced modernization that has resulted in an improved quality of life.

Regardless how European imperialism and colonialism are assessed, it is clear that they resulted in conditions that were both beneficial and harmful to the developing nations. Some of colonialism's positive contributions to the long-term well-being of indigenous peoples include: development of educational systems, introduction of modern science and health care, development of a culture that gives priority to rational decision making and planning, introduction of economic modernization that has led to increased production, and establishment of governmental structures and procedures that have contributed, however imperfectly and unevenly, to greater protection of human rights. On the other hand, colonialism has also resulted in detrimental developments. Some of these include: destruction of indigenous cultures, economic and political exploitation of indigenous peoples, development of dualistic societies deeply divided between modern and traditional sectors, establishment of territorial boundaries in disregard for tribal and communal affinities, and rapid introduction of modern values and practices, resulting in unbalanced social changes (e.g., rapid population growth, uneven demographic profiles, rapid urbanization).

In sum, imperialism and colonialism, especially as practiced in the 1850–1950 period, introduced cultural, social, economic, and political developments that contributed to significant socioeconomic inequalities within and among countries. Whether the developing nations would have achieved higher levels of national development without imperialism and colonialism is, of course, disputed. What cannot be denied, however, is that these forces played an important role in fostering global interdependence and generating substantial inequalities between the modern industrial states and the developing nations in Asia, Africa, and Latin America.

The Nature of the Conflict

The central issue of contention between the North and the South has been the inequitable distribution of wealth among states. The developing nations are poor, weak, and vulnerable, whereas the developed countries are rich, strong, and comparatively invulnerable. World Bank data confirm the large gap between the rich and poor nations. According to the World Bank, in 1994 there were 44 high-income countries with an average per capita income of more than $24,000 and 165 middle- and low-income countries with an average per capita income of about $1,100.[5] (See fig. 15.1.) To be sure, income is distributed unequally within most countries, especially within developing nations. The North-South debate, however, is not about economic policies and problems within states, but rather it is an attempt to redistribute economic resources among states.

Because of the significant economic disparities between the North and the South, it is falsely assumed that most developing nations have been unable to sustain economic growth. However, since the mid-1960s, the economies of developing nations have been growing at a faster rate than the economies of developed nations. Indeed, from 1965 to 1980, the average annual rate of economic growth was 3.7 percent for industrial, developed nations and 5.9 percent for the developing nations. Even taking into consideration the South's faster population growth, economic expansion there (3.4 percent per capita) was greater than in the North (2.8 percent per capita growth). Only in the 1980s did the developed economies grow at a slightly higher per capita rate than the developing nations (2.5 percent as opposed to 2.3 percent).[6] Most importantly, the developing nations are expected to grow much more rapidly than the developed nations in the near future. The World Bank has projected that during the 1994–2003 period, the developing nations' annual economic growth rate will be 4.8 percent, compared to 2.7 percent for the developed nations.[7]

Despite the continued economic expansion of the developing nations, the income gap between the North and the South has continued to increase. In 1968, for example, the gap between average annual per capita income in the developed and developing nations was $2,580, but by 1994 the gap had increased to more than $23,000. Moreover, although the developing nations' average per capita income was about 6 percent of the developed nations' average income in 1968, by 1994 its income share had declined to 4 percent.[8]

Notwithstanding the increasing North-South income disparities, the standard of living for most Third World peoples has risen significantly. Modern science and

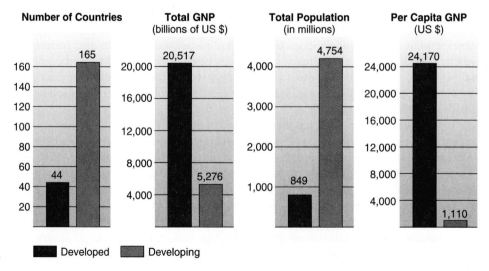

FIGURE 15.1
Developed and Developing Nations Compared, 1994
Source: *World Bank Atlas,* 1996 (Washington, D.C.: The World Bank, 1996), p. 20.

technology have resulted in great improvements in the physical quality of life for most people in developing nations, including a significant fall in infant mortality rates, a dramatic rise in life expectancy, and the rise of adult literacy. Some of the important gains in the quality of life of Third World countries are further examined in chapter 17 on the political economy of development.

Finally, it is important to stress that the large international economic inequalities among states are not rooted, as is commonly alleged, in different endowments in natural resources but in different productive capacities. Although such capacities require tangible resources, the major determinants of wealth are intangible resources, especially human resources. To be sure, the possession of resources, such as petroleum, gold, and diamonds, can enhance the economic development of countries. But the modern economic history of countries like Denmark, Japan, the Netherlands, and Singapore suggests that the bulk of modern wealth has been created by inventing, producing, and marketing goods and services with efficiency.

COMPETING PERSPECTIVES

Although the primary dispute between the North and the South has been the unequal distribution of wealth among states, the conflict between the two groups has involved other issues. As political economist Stephen Krasner has noted, the North-South conflict is about wealth and power. The Third World, he argues, wants greater influence in the world community in order to be able to bring about changes in the principles, rules, and institutions governing the world economy. Thus, even though the conflict has focused on the distribution of wealth and resources, the real conflict, Krasner believes, is over power.[9]

The intractability of the North-South conflict derives in great measure from the conflicting visions of political economy espoused by each group. The North seeks a "liberal" or market allocation of resources, in which governments play a limited role in economic life. The South, by contrast, favors "authoritative" allocation of economic resources, in which governments play an important role in producing and distributing goods and services both within and among states. These incompatible regime preferences, which are themselves the by-product of the underlying disparities in national power, make compromise and reconciliation especially difficult.

The First World Perspective

The developed nations, led by the United States, assume that international economic inequalities derive from different productive capacities. These different productive capacities are not based on tangible resources, such as oil, land, and copper, but on intangible resources, such as technology, marketing skills, and human skills. Although some states have achieved short-term wealth by acquiring resources through imperial exploitation (e.g., Spain and Portugal in the sixteenth and seventeenth centuries) or by exporting key commodities (e.g., Chilean nitrate in the late nineteenth century and Saudi Arabian oil in the 1970s and 1980s), modern wealth has been created, not acquired. Countries like Hong Kong, Japan, the Netherlands, and Switzerland, for example, have few natural resources but have been able to achieve extraordinary levels of wealth by producing quality goods and services at comparatively low costs.

The political economy advocated by the First World—sometimes referred to as the **modernization thesis**—is based on four major premises:

First, *modern wealth is created*, not taken or acquired. The North's political economy assumes that the natural condition of life is poverty and scarcity, not plenty. Although aristocratic peoples enjoyed wealth in premodern times, the basic

Modernization thesis
The belief that wealth creation is the result of increased productive efficiency, which is best achieved domestically through free enterprise and internationally through free trade.

condition of life for millennia has been poverty. Only the past 150 years have brought significant improvements in living conditions for a growing number of societies. This rise in living standards is due, according to the modernization thesis, to increased economic production.

Second, *creating wealth does not require economic exploitation.* According to modernization advocates, economic growth is a *positive-sum process,* meaning that a rise in income in one state does not involve an economic decline in another. Unlike competition for power, a *zero-sum process* in which an increase for one actor requires a commensurate decline for another, wealth creation is a dynamic process in which the rise or decline in income in one nation is not necessarily related to income changes elsewhere. Economic growth will, of course, result in income disparities because it rewards the most productive peoples, groups, and nations, but such inequalities are not the result of exploitation or unfair distribution of resources but are chiefly the result of different relative productive capabilities.

Third, *the primary determinants of job creation are human attributes,* not economic factors. Economist P. T. Bauer has noted that economic achievement historically has depended chiefly on human capabilities and attitudes combined with a society's social and political climate. "Differences in these determinants," he writes, "largely explain differences in levels of economic achievement and rates of material progress."[10]

Primary resources are, of course, important in production, but their possession does not assure economic progress. Indeed, the focus on tangible resources is basically misconceived because economic growth has little to do with the possession of resources per se. Some scholars have noted that the creation of modern wealth is not based on tangible resources, but on ideas, techniques, information, and other intangibles that encourage higher productivity through better motivation, superior organization, and more efficient marketing.[11] The validity of this conclusion is corroborated by the modern economic history of countries such as the Netherlands, Hong Kong, Japan, Singapore, Switzerland, and Taiwan—all of which have achieved impressive levels of economic development despite limited primary resources.

Fourth, *wealth is created by increasing productive efficiency, which is best realized domestically through free enterprise and internationally through free trade.* According to modernization theorists, economic resources are allocated most efficiently through market mechanisms. Authoritative, centralized economic decision making impedes economic efficiency. On the international level, the doctrine of comparative advantage (see chap. 16) suggests that national welfare increases when countries produce goods for which they have a relative productive efficiency and import goods for which they have relative economic disadvantage. Rather than weakening an economy, the North assumes that free trade provides the most efficient way for a country to determine what goods it should import and export. Because the continuing economic well-being of a society depends upon its efficiency in production, the economic status of states fluctuates. Whether a national economy grows or contracts will depend upon its ability to make and sell goods and services.

In light of the above principles, the North advocates a liberal, or free, international economic order—a system in which international organizations provide stable and efficient mechanisms for financial and monetary transfers as well as unimpeded international commerce. The Bretton Woods international economic order, established by the United States and its Western allies at the conclusion of World War II, is based on these premises. (See chap. 16.)

The Third World Perspective

The economic approach advocated by the Third World assumes that poverty and global income disparities are based on unjust international economic structures, not different productive capacities, as propounded by the First World. Unlike the North's market perspective, the South's international political economy is based on two related but distinct theories, one moderate and the other radical.

The moderate theory, known as **structuralism,** assumes that international economic problems are rooted in the perceived unfair terms of trade among states. **Dependency theory,** which was briefly examined in chapter 1 as one of the major interpretive paradigms of contemporary international relations, provides the more radical approach to the South's political economy. Dependency theory is the more extreme perspective because it assumes that Third World poverty and international exploitation derive not only from interstate commerce but from the capitalist system itself. Because both of these theories provide the theoretical basis for the South's international political economy, the major elements of each are briefly examined below.

The structural thesis was first popularized in the mid-1960s by Raul Prebisch, the first secretary general of UNCTAD. Contrary to the North's perspective, which assumes that the international economic order is relatively neutral, structuralism assumes that it is biased in favor of the industrial states that form its core. Although economic modernization increases productivity in all countries, the process of economic growth breeds different outcomes in industrial and developing nations. The heart of the argument, as Robert Gilpin has observed, is that the developing nations have experienced a deterioration in the terms of trade because of cyclical price movements and differences in demand for industrial goods and primary products. Because of the decline in prices of their commodity exports relative to the prices of the manufactured goods they import from developed countries, developing nations are able to develop economically but at a slower rate than the developed nations.[12] In short, the structures and trade patterns of the global economy exacerbate international economic inequalities.

Because of the assumed imbalance in the terms of trade, structuralists doubt that trade can alleviate the plight of the poor nations, especially if the existing domestic and international economic patterns are not significantly modified. Rather, they argue that even if the developing nations achieve significant gains from world trade, their economic position relative to the industrial states is unlikely to improve.

Dependency theory, an approach based on neo-Marxist political economy, assumes that poverty and underdevelopment are a by-product of the transnational expansion of capitalism.[13] According to the theory, the spread of world capitalism has enabled the industrial democracies to exploit the poor nations, thereby exacerbating economic inequalities and increasing poverty. Andre Gunder Frank, one of the theory's founders, argues that before capitalism reached the developing nations, the poor countries were "undeveloped." But as capitalism spread to the Third World—first through colonialism and then through MNCs—the result was uneven economic expansion and the establishment of dualistic societies in which one sector was modern and the other backward. Frank thus argues that the expansion of capitalism has had the ironic effect of promoting both wealth and poverty, development and underdevelopment. He writes: "Underdevelopment was and still is generated by the very same historical process which also generated economic development: the development of capitalism itself."[14]

In addition, the theory assumes that modern economic growth leads to increased international economic "dependence," a condition that Brazilian economist Theotonio Dos Santos defines as "a situation in which the economy of certain countries is conditioned by the development and expansion of another economy to which the former is subjected."[15] Economic dependence is considered harmful because it compromises the indigenous economic evolution of countries. Originally, all dependency was considered detrimental because it was thought to result in economic stagnation and even backwardness. But during the 1960s and 1970s a

Structuralism
An approach to Third World development that asserts that existing international economic structures are unfair to developing nations and need to be reformed.

Dependency theory
A neo-Marxist theory attributing the wealth of the industrial states and the poverty of the Third World to global capitalist structures. According to the theory, international economic structures foster income inequalities among states, thereby increasing Third World dependency.

number of developing nations achieved spectacular economic growth, in great part through the infusion of foreign capital. Although this MNC-led growth resulted in significant economic development, it also led to a decrease in national autonomy. Peter Evans terms this condition **dependent development**[16] because the economic expansion was subject to significant foreign influence. For example, after a military regime established economic stability in Brazil in the mid-1960s, major foreign enterprises launched new business ventures that resulted in high economic growth rates. But because a large portion of the new capital was foreign, the economic expansion was significantly conditioned by external interests.

The dominant perspective on international political economy in the South is based on elements of both structuralist theory and dependency theory, or what Gilpin terms "the underdevelopment position."[17] Because the South's perspective seeks to explain the wealth and poverty of nations as a function of global (political and economic) structures, it is sometimes called **World System Theory (WST).**[18] Some of the major features of this theory include the following:

First, *capitalist economic expansion results in uneven economic development.* According to WST, growth creates developed regions ("cores" or "centers") and dependent regions ("peripheries" or "satellites"), both within countries and among countries. Thus, capitalism results in uneven growth domestically, as wealth is divided between the core regions and the peripheral regions, and uneven growth internationally, as wealth is distributed between developed countries and developing countries. Although modernization may bring absolute economic improvements to states, the gains from growth will be distributed inequitably, with the industrial states gaining at the expense of the developing nations.

Second, *economic expansion is fundamentally a zero-sum process* in which a rise in income in one state inevitably results in a decline in another. World capitalism is thus an inherently exploitative process. Because the total level of wealth cannot be significantly increased, the task of governments is to ensure an equitable distribution of existing resources within and among states.

Third, *an inevitable consequence of capitalist expansion is poverty and underdevelopment.* According to WST, poverty has increased in the developing countries because the spread of modernization has encouraged uneven development *within* and *among* states. Even though foreign investment has resulted in increased economic output in developing nations, MNCs have also increased income inequalities as the economic rewards from such enterprises have been limited chiefly to its employees. Similarly, the expansion of global capitalism has resulted in increased international economic disparities.

Fourth, *the expansion of international capitalism leads to economic dependence.* As countries become more economically developed, they become more integrated with the global economy and therefore, more dependent on commercial and financial development beyond national boundaries. Increased economic dependence can be especially harmful to developing nations because it compromises national economic self-determination. In effect, developing nations can lose control over their economic life. Even where foreign resources contribute to significant economic expansion (i.e., dependent development), increased dependency can impede indigenous economic evolution. According to Gilpin, some harmful effects of such development are:

1. Overdependence upon raw materials as a source of foreign exchange
2. Maldistribution of national income, with little public concern for the social and economic needs of the masses
3. The displacement of local entrepreneurship and local technology by foreign investors, especially large MNCs
4. Introduction of capital-intensive, rather than labor-intensive, technology

Dependent development

Economic development that is conditioned and controlled by foreign actors.

World System Theory (WST)

A theory claiming that the spread of global capitalism results in uneven economic development, with the gains from development accruing disproportionately to the advanced, capital-intensive economies.

5. MNCs' distortion of the local labor market because of their unduly high wages in comparison to domestic employers[19]

In short, economic growth that is heavily tied to foreign investment and international commerce can seriously impair indigenous control over the national economy.

EVOLUTION OF THE CONFLICT

The North-South conflict has gone through four phases: (1) the era of commercial reform, (2) the rise of OPEC, (3) the call for a new international economic order, and (4) the transformation of the debate.

Development Through Commercial Reform (1964–1973)

The North-South conflict emerged in the early 1960s as developing nations pressed for greater economic assistance from Western democracies and demanded more favorable terms of trade. The first collective challenge of the South against the North took place at the first UNCTAD meeting in Geneva in 1964. Politically, UNCTAD I was important for two reasons. First, it led to the emergence of a loose Third World coalition (G-77) committed to reforming the existing rules and institutions of the world economy. Second, it created a forum in which the shared economic concerns of the Third World could be developed and articulated. At subsequent UNCTAD meetings (see table 15.2), G-77 pressed for a variety of reforms in the international economic order, including reduced trade barriers, enactment of trade preferences for Third World commodities, foreign debt relief, and stabilization of commodity prices.

Economically, UNCTAD was significant because it popularized the "structural" explanation for Third World poverty that subsequently led to a number of policy

TABLE 15.2   UN Conferences on Trade and Development, 1964–1996

Year	Place	Attendance	Major Issues
1964	Geneva, Switzerland	120 states	International commodity problems; trade and economic development
1968	New Delhi, India	121 states	Trade preferences for LDCs; world food problem; international monetary reform
1972	Santiago, Chile	131 states	International commodity problems; technology transfers; international monetary reform
1976	Nairobi, Kenya	139 states	Establishment of an integrated commodities program, including a common fund; foreign aid and debt rescheduling
1979	Manila, Philippines	144 states	International economic reform; impact of high oil prices on poor states
1983	Belgrade, Yugoslavia	150 states	Third World debt; establishment of commodity stabilization program with target price; resource development
1987	Geneva, Switzerland	160 states	Resource development; Third World debt; common fund reform
1992	Cartagena, Colombia	166 states	Multilateral economic cooperation, economic development of low-income states
1996	Midrand, South Africa	135 states	Called for the restructuring of UNCTAD, for greater Third World participation in the global market, and for job creation through small business expansion

reforms, especially in Latin America. The structural perspective, articulated in an influential document titled "Towards a New Trade Policy for Development," was overwhelmingly adopted as the South's explanation for the growing economic disparities between the rich and poor countries. The central premise of the UNCTAD report, authored by UNCTAD Secretary-General Raul Prebisch, was that the world economy was biased against the economies of the developing nations. According to the report, the international commercial system was biased because the terms of trade (the ratio of exports to imports) favored manufactured and other processed goods (the primary exports of the North) over agricultural and mineral products (the primary exports of the South).

The Third World's widespread acceptance of the structuralist thesis led many developing nations to adopt initiatives designed to alter the terms of trade and to curtail the flow of economic resources toward the North. As a result, developing nations pursued two distinct economic development strategies in the 1960s and early 1970s—national self-sufficiency and economic regionalism.

New Strategies: Self-Reliance and Regionalism

The strategy of self-reliance involves the development of greater economic autonomy in order to decrease reliance on the products and markets of the industrial democracies. Developing nations used two different approaches to achieve this goal—a modest approach focusing on **import substitution** and a more radical program of state-wide economic planning. The import-substitution approach, advocated by Prebisch at UNCTAD I,[20] sought to increase national self-sufficiency by stimulating domestic industrial production. As a result, developing nations, especially Latin American countries, began establishing commercial policies in the 1960s and 1970s that restricted industrial imports and subsidized many new business ventures.

The more radical approach, applied in countries like China, Cuba, and North Korea, involved the establishment of state-regulated economic production and distribution. Fundamentally, this approach attempted not only to regulate international commerce but also to centrally manage economic production and distribution. The result has been the establishment of state socialism.

The aim of economic regionalism, the second major Third World initiative during this era, was to stimulate regional trade in order to promote national economic expansion. Because North-South trade was assumed to be detrimental to indigenous development, developing nations were encouraged to decrease trade with the North and to increase regional commercial and financial ties. It was assumed that greater intra-South trade would encourage regional economic specialization and thereby expand productive efficiency. Trading associations that were established under this initiative include the Latin American Free Trade Association (LAFTA), the Central American Common Market, and the Andean Group.

Despite the popularity of import substitution and economic regionalism, neither strategy contributed to national economic expansion or to the reduction in North-South economic inequalities. Import substitution encouraged inefficient resource allocation, whereas increased state regulation of the economy decreased the efficiency of production, thereby further exacerbating poverty. Third World countries that relied on economic planning and state-directed enterprise uniformly failed to stimulate job creation. For example, the GNP per capita growth rate for Ethiopia, Tanzania, and Uganda, three state-directed economies, was –0.1, –0.5, and –3.1 percent during the 1965–1988 period.[21] China's economy similarly stagnated throughout the 1950s and 1960s from the burdens of excessive governmental controls. But since the 1970s, China's economy has prospered greatly because of increased protection of property rights and the introduction of market reforms and economic decentralization.

Import substitution
The policy of fostering domestic production by restricting imports and subsidizing new domestic enterprises. Throughout the 1960s and 1970s, this policy was utilized to stimulate industrial development in the LDCs.

Economic regionalism has similarly failed to promote economic development in the developing nations. Although a number of regional experiments were begun in Third World regions to encourage trade among developing nations, they have had little impact. Indeed, to date the only successful experiments in regional economic cooperation have been the European Economic Community in Western Europe and COMECON in Eastern Europe. The success of these regional associations, especially the EEC, is no doubt partly due to the geographical proximity of member-states, the member-states' high level of economic development, and the high degree of shared political and economic values. Economic associations in the Third World, by contrast, have typically involved members with different political and economic aspirations, different levels of economic development, and significant geographical barriers that impede efficient transportation. In short, the obstacles to economic cooperation are greater for developing nations than for developed states.

The Rise of OPEC (1973–1975)

Historically, developing nations have relied heavily on exports of primary products, such as coffee, tea, sugar, tin, and copper. (See table 15.3.) Because commodity prices have often fluctuated widely in response to changes in supply and demand, Third World nations have tried to stabilize prices through commodity agreements and other joint ventures. These efforts had been largely unsuccessful

TABLE 15.3 Leading Export Product of Selected Third World Countries, 1992 (As a percentage of exports)

Country	Product	Percentage
Uganda	coffee	97
Nigeria	oil	95
Kuwait	oil	90
Burundi	coffee	88
Rwanda	coffee	85
Botswana	diamonds	77
Niger	uranium	75
Ethiopia	coffee	60
Cameroon	petroleum products	56
Liberia	iron ore	61
Burma	rutile	50
Chad	cotton	48
Chile	copper	48
Mozambique	shrimp	48
Ecuador	petroleum	47
Ghana	cocoa	45
Madagascar	coffee	45
Mauritius	textiles	44
Congo (former Zaire)	copper	37

Source: Data from Central Intelligence Agency, *The World Factbook, 1991-92*, Brassey's (US), Inc., 1992, Washington, D.C., passim.

TABLE 15.4   Oil-Exporting States

OPEC		Non-OPEC
Algeria	Libya	Bahrain
Gabon	Nigeria	Canada
Indonesia	Qatar	Ecuador
Iran	Saudi Arabia	Mexico
Iraq	United Arab Emirates	Norway
Kuwait	Venezuela	Russia

Organization of Petroleum Exporting Countries (OPEC)
An international organization of major oil-producing countries in the world.

Cartel
An organization of commodity producers that seeks to control the commodity's price by regulating its supply.

until 1973. In that year, the **Organization of Petroleum Exporting Countries (OPEC)** successfully increased the price of oil nearly fourfold and dramatically increased revenues of oil-exporting nations.

The Oil Cartel

A **cartel** is an international agreement designed to regulate a commodity's supply in order to stabilize price and maximize income. To be effective, cartels require that the demand for commodities be relatively insensitive to price (i.e., the demand must be "inelastic") and that principal producers must be able to enforce collective discipline among suppliers. Few resource cartels have met these conditions. In 1973, however, oil-exporting states, led by Saudi Arabia, managed to do what no other commodity cartel had done—create excess demand over supply.

Before the 1970s, oil was controlled by seven major oil companies, five of them U.S.-based MNCs: British Petroleum, Exxon, Gulf, Mobil, Shell, Standard Oil of California, and Texaco. Collectively these companies were known as the "seven sisters." During the 1950s and 1960s, these companies provided an ample supply of inexpensive oil to industrial states, thereby contributing to global economic expansion.

OPEC was created in 1960 to give oil-producing states greater control over oil production. However, it did not begin to play a significant role until the 1970s, after the balance of economic power had begun to shift from the oil corporations to the oil states. OPEC's increased influence was rooted in the rising industrial demand for oil coupled with the shift from coal to petroleum as the major energy source.

The first display of OPEC's new role in the global community came shortly after the Yom Kippur War of October 1973. The Arab members of OPEC (see table 15.4) announced an oil embargo against the United States and the Netherlands because of their steadfast support of Israel and reduced sales to other industrial states that refused to support the Arab cause. To strengthen OPEC's ability to pressure Western European states, Arab OPEC (OAPEC) members began reducing production. Saudi Arabia, the major oil producer in the world, decreased its production by one-fourth. Coupled with the fall in the oil supply, OPEC increased its petroleum price nearly fourfold—from $2.70 per barrel in October 1973 to $10.50 per barrel six months later. After several years of oil price stability, a second oil crisis developed in the late 1970s with the fall of Shah Pahlavi's regime in Iran. Before the revolution, Iran had been a leading oil-exporting state, providing more than 5 million barrels of oil per day. The 1979 Islamic revolution, however, resulted in a virtual collapse of Iran's oil exports, causing a significant decrease in international supplies. The shortfall led OPEC to increase prices again, from $13.00 per barrel in early 1979 to more than $25.00 by the end of 1979, and to $34.00 by the end of 1981.

OPEC's Rise and Fall

OPEC's success in raising petroleum prices—first in 1973 and then in 1979—was based on several conditions. First, during the 1970s the industrial countries were heavily dependent on oil imports. Second, because the development of alternative energy supplies (e.g., coal, nuclear energy) requires time, industrial states were unable to meet short-term energy needs through other sources. Third, OPEC accounted for more than 50 percent of the world's petroleum production, which gave the cartel's Arab members significant control over oil supplies (and prices). Fourth, although OPEC was democratic in structure, several leading exporters controlled it. Indeed, Saudi Arabia, with nearly one-fourth of the world's oil reserves, served as the de facto leader of OPEC, bringing recalcitrant states into line with the implicit threat of flooding the world with its oil. Finally, OPEC was successful because of commonly shared political interest, especially among the Arab states. This commonality of purpose provided the impetus for both oil crises.

Beginning in the early 1980s, OPEC's influence declined. This decline was due largely to its loss of oil market share (from 50 percent in 1973 to about 33 percent in 1985) to centrally planned economies, especially the Soviet Union, and to new oil-exporting states, such as Britain, Mexico, and Norway. A second factor accounting for OPEC's decline was the static demand for petroleum. From the mid-1970s through the mid-1980s, total petroleum consumption remained largely the same worldwide (at roughly 55 to 60 million barrels per day), in part because of dramatically improved energy efficiencies precipitated by higher petroleum prices. After the second oil crisis, a major oil glut developed, forcing OPEC to reduce daily production from about 31 million barrels in 1979 to less than 17 million barrels in 1985. Despite the decline in production, oil prices continued to fall in the 1980s (from $34 per barrel in 1981 to less than $14 per barrel in 1986) leading to severe economic dislocations in many of the oil-exporting states. (See fig. 15.2.) Whereas OPEC countries had managed to generate a trade surplus of more than $100 billion in 1980, by 1982 OPEC was generating a trade deficit of more than $20 billion. In 1985, Saudi Arabia's balance of payments deficit alone was $20 billion.[22]

In the late 1980s OPEC regained some of its economic power as oil prices stabilized at about $22 to $23 per barrel—in great measure because of increasing oil demand fueled by global economic expansion. But despite the growth in revenues for oil-exporting states, OPEC was unable to regain economic power and political cohesion. And in August 1990, two OPEC states, Iraq and Kuwait, became involved in a war, a development that deeply injured the Pan Arabic Movement and further weakened OPEC. Indeed, Iraq's invasion of Kuwait may be regarded as evidence of the near collapse of OPEC. Even though the invasion may have been precipitated partly by a long-standing territorial dispute, the immediate reason for Iraq's military action was its need for additional revenues coupled with its desire

FIGURE 15.2
World Crude Oil Price, 1973–1994
Source: Data from Energy Information Administration, U.S. Department of Energy, "Monthly Energy Review, various issues.

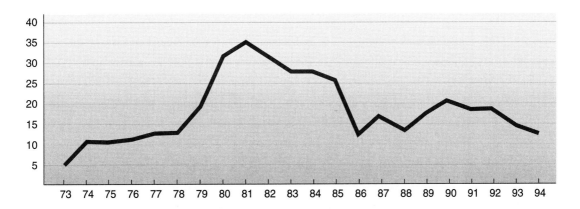

to punish Kuwait for producing petroleum above its OPEC quota. The effect of Iraq's action, however, was to further divide and weaken OPEC. As of 1998, UN sanctions remained in effect against Iraq, allowing Saddam Hussein's government limited petroleum sales to only cover essential foods and medicines.

The Call for a New International Economic Order (1975–1982)

The third phase of the North-South conflict involved a growing demand by Third World nations for radical changes in the rules and institutions of the global economy. The call for a new international economic order emerged in the mid-1970s partly in response to two developments. First, structural initiatives, such as import-substitution policies, had failed to decrease international economic inequalities and to promote Third World economic growth. Second, OPEC's early economic success had encouraged other Third World countries to explore the development of other commodity cartels.

The NIEO

New International Economic Order (NIEO)
The Third World's alternative economic system designed to give the developing countries more influence in the global economy and to help transfer economic resources from the rich to the poor countries.

The South's call for a **New International Economic Order (NIEO)** rested on the conviction that the perceived development needs of the poor nations justified changes in the international economic system. Specifically, it was based on three major premises: (1) rich nations should provide major financial and technological transfers to the poor nations; (2) rich nations should contribute to the economic expansion of developing nations in order to more effectively provide for the needs of their growing populations; and (3) the machinery of international economic relations should be modified so that the developing nations could have greater participation and influence in the global economy. Some specific elements of the NIEO include:

1. Establishing commodity agreements for Third World exports
2. Increasing economic aid from the rich to the poor nations
3. Increasing the developing nations' share of Special Drawing Rights (SDRs) of the IMF
4. Providing debt relief to the Third World, either by forgiving or postponing repayment
5. Providing preferential treatment to Third World exports
6. Facilitating transfers of appropriate technology to the developing nations
7. Ensuring the right to expropriate foreign investment without regard to international legal conventions
8. Altering decision-making procedures of the World Bank and the International Monetary Fund to ensure greater Third World influence in those institutions[23]

From an ethical perspective, the aim of the NIEO was to promote interstate justice by reducing economic disparities among states. Although the NIEO's moral appeal was rooted in the belief that the proposed reforms would help eradicate Third World poverty, in actuality the proposed changes had little to do with the personal well-being of people. Indeed, as Stephen Krasner has noted, the Third World's proposed NIEO was more about the redistribution of power than of wealth. According to Krasner, the South's proposal called for the replacement of the existing market-oriented rules and institutions with "authoritative regimes" that could allocate economic resources among states.[24] The South's desire for quasi-governmental institutions with the authority to regulate global transactions is illustrated by the South's vigorous support of the International Seabed Authority, an IGO responsible for regulating mining in the open seas.

The Failure of the NIEO

The South's call for a new international economic order resulted in few tangible reforms. The failure to alter the existing rules and institutions of the postwar liberal international economic order was due to several factors.

First, the South had a comparatively weak bargaining position. The South had, of course, achieved increasing majorities in global institutions with the growing number of developing nations, each claiming sovereign, juridical equality. Despite achieving voting majorities in numerous international economic and political organizations, these majorities did not translate into power. Even though developing nations were able to challenge the existing norms, they were unable to effectively alter the existing rules and institutions because of their vulnerability and limited power. Krasner observes that developing nations "can attack and undermine existing international regimes but they cannot destroy or replace them."[25]

A second reason for failing to implement the NIEO was the South's social, political, and economic heterogeneity. Whereas the North comprised a smaller, more homogeneous group of states sharing market economies and democratic institutions, the South represented states with widely diverse cultural, social, religious, and political norms and institutions. Undoubtedly, the most important disparity among developing nations was the large and expanding economic inequalities among countries. For example, the per capita income of the poorest states, such as Bangladesh, Chad, Ethiopia, Mozambique, and Tanzania, was less than $200 in 1988, but Argentina, Brazil, Gabon, South Korea, Trinidad and Tobago, and Venezuela all had per capita incomes of more than $2,000, or more than ten times that of the former group. And because of differing economic growth rates, income inequality increased throughout the 1970s and 1980s as some low-income countries, such as Congo, Haiti, Nicaragua, Peru, and Zambia became poorer, whereas other states, such as Botswana, Chile, China, India, and Malaysia, achieved significant economic expansion.

Third, the South failed to implement the NIEO because of the unwillingness of developing nations to give shared concerns precedence over their particular interests. Third World nations formed the NIEO initiative in order to reduce their poverty and vulnerability, but their individual political and economic interests weakened the G-77's shared efforts in confronting the North. In effect, the nationalism that facilitated the development of the Third World alliance also undermined it. According to Gilpin,

> The history of the NIEO demonstrates the fundamental dilemma of less developed countries that, in the name of nationalism, attempt to change the operation of the world market economy to improve their relative position. The dilemma is that the same nationalistic spirit frequently undermines their efforts to cooperate with one another and to form an economic alliance against the developed countries. Although the confrontation with the North and the ideological appeal of the NIEO provide a basis for political agreement, powerful and conflicting national interest greatly weaken Third World unity.[26]

In the final analysis, the failure of the South to effectively reform the international economic order was rooted in the decentralized structures of the global community itself. Reducing political and economic inequalities among states is difficult because, as political scientist Robert Tucker notes, world economic inequality is an inescapable outcome of a world system based on national sovereignty and territorial independence.[27] To affirm the right of independence is to affirm the potential of economic disparities. Such inequalities can, of course, be modified, but this requires the persistent efforts of individual states and collective institutions. As noted in chapter 4, states seek to maximize their absolute economic and political power through cooperation, but they are also concerned with relative economic and political advantages. The tension between cooperation and conflict within the South is a direct consequence of the inherent forces of ordered anarchy in the international system.

In sum, the developing nations were successful in making the NIEO one of the major issues of contention in the North-South conflict. To the South's credit, it succeeded in raising awareness about the economic disparities by repeatedly hosting meetings and conferences at which the NIEO agenda was addressed. In the end, however, it failed to reform the liberal international economic order.

Transformation of the Conflict (1982–1992)

As noted above, the early phases of the North-South conflict were concerned chiefly with the nature and impact of international commercial and monetary relations. But after unsuccessfully applying structuralist remedies and failing to reform the international economic order, the Group of 77 began shifting its concerns from structural economic issues to other global problems, such as the ownership of global resources, international environmental protection, and the promotion of environmentally sustainable economic development. To illustrate the shift in the South's worldview, we examine in the following sections two recent North-South disputes—the deep seabed and environmental protection.

The Deep Seabed

Deep seabed
The ocean floor of the high seas. The seabed is considered economically important because of its vast mineral deposits.

A conflict emerged in the mid-1970s when scientists began developing technologies that raised the potential for mining the **deep seabed.** The ocean floor is covered with large quantities of coal-like lumps, known as polymetallic nodules, that contain minerals such as copper, cobalt, nickel, and manganese. Until the 1960s there was little interest in these mineral deposits because there was no effective way to mine them. However, in the early 1970s, some industrial countries, including Germany, France, Italy, Japan, the Netherlands, Switzerland, and the United States, began developing technologies that made the mining of the deep seabed potentially feasible, if not profitable. Because these manganese nodules lie outside the territorial jurisdiction of states, deep-seabed mining raises questions about ownership: Does the seventeenth-century doctrine of the "freedom of the seas" apply to minerals on the deep seabed? Are mineral resources on the ocean floor common property, as the South contends, belonging to all nations of the international community? Or do the mineral resources belong to the countries that successfully mine them, as the North holds?

Third UN Conference on the Law of the Sea (UNCLOS III)
A series of UN-sponsored negotiating sessions from 1973 to 1982 leading to the Third UN Law of the Sea Treaty—the most comprehensive legal convention on maritime law.

The forum for carrying out this dispute was the **Third United Nations Conference on the Law of the Sea (UNCLOS III),** which met in periodic sessions from 1973 until 1982. In the protracted UNCLOS sessions, the South argued that the mineral resources on the ocean floor were part of the "common heritage of mankind," and therefore, could be used by individual states only with the consent of the international community. Reflecting the structuralist worldview, the South advocated the creation of a transnational mining authority that would regulate the use of the deep seabed and distribute profits from mining ventures in a just and equitable manner among all of the world's states. Because deep-seabed minerals were assumed to belong to all of humankind, the aim of the proposed mining IGO was to transfer economic resources from industrial states capable of deep-sea mining to the developing nations.

By contrast, the North, led by the United States, opposed the establishment of a centralized mining authority for both economic and political reasons. Economically, it opposed the creation of supranational institutions qualifying the economic right of states to explore and mine the open seas. Because some U.S. companies had developed technological innovations that might make deep-seabed mining feasible, the United States, along with several other industrial states, opposed the delimitation of the historic right of the "freedom of the seas" doctrine. Politically, the North opposed the creation of international organizations that might qualify sovereignty and shift power to the South.

During the long and difficult UNCLOS III negotiations, the South succeeded in gaining widespread support for the proposed seabed-mining regime. By claiming that global welfare must take precedence over states' rights, the developing nations succeeded in gaining broad international support for their cause and were not only successful in incorporating the deep-seabed issue into the final UNCLOS accord—the Third UN Convention on the Law of the Sea—but in securing signatures from more than 150 states.[28] Although the treaty covers all major areas of maritime law (such as territorial waters, economic zones, international straits, and the continental shelf), the provisions covering the deep seabed, which take up nearly 20 percent of the treaty's 320 articles, represent a radical departure in the historic norms governing the international law of the sea. Some of the treaty's key deep-seabed provisions include:

1. Affirmation of the *"common heritage" principle* and declaration that the deep seabed belongs to all of humankind;

2. Establishment of an *International Seabed Authority (ISA),* comprised of an assembly representing all countries and a thirty-six-member executive council, to supervise and regulate the exploitation of the deep seabed;

3. Creation of an intergovernmental mining company ("the Enterprise") responsible for mining as well as transporting, processing, and marketing minerals recovered from the deep seabed. Because only industrial states have the technological, financial, and managerial skills required for such a business venture, the company will be wholly dependent on the North for initial capitalization.

Although the South won a temporary victory at UNCLOS III, the North's resistance to transnational regulation of deep-seabed mining subsequently forced the international community to amend the original treaty. As a result, in the early 1990s the original treaty was amended in order to increase market incentives for ocean mining and to reduce the obligations for redistributing wealth through the deep-seabed mining regime. Under the amended provisions, mining companies would no longer have to pay $1 million a year to explore for minerals on the ocean floor, and developed nations would not be obligated to transfer mining technology to poor countries.[29] UNCLOS III entered into force in November 1993 after sixty states had ratified the treaty. As of January 1995, it had been ratified or accepted as binding by seventy-two states.[30]

Environmental Protection

Modern economic development has resulted in spectacular improvements in living standards throughout the world. As noted more fully in chapter 19, the expansion of industrialization has also led to unintended harmful environmental consequences, including depletion of natural resources, deforestation, and air and water pollution. Although most ecological destruction is caused by industrial developments within a state's territorial boundaries, the spread of industrialization has also brought about increasing transboundary air and water pollution as waste and chemicals are transported from the state of origin to neighboring states.

The burning of fossil fuels—the major source of energy for the modern economy—is one of the principal sources of air pollution. Although indispensable for generating heat and electricity, the combustion of fuels results in many harmful gasses and particulates that contribute to global warming by trapping the sun's radiation. It also contributes to the depletion of the atmosphere's ozone layer, which is indispensable in protecting human life from the sun's harmful ultraviolet rays. The discharge of pollutants into streams and rivers also damages the world's environment by contaminating international waterways and oceans. In addition, industrialization has resulted in the destruction of forests, especially the tropical rain forest. Deforestation not only destroys species of flora and fauna, but it also adversely affects global weather patterns.

In response to growing ecological awareness in the 1970s and 1980s, the North began to develop technologies for reducing pollution within countries as well as to devise strategies for controlling transboundary pollution. Subsequently, developing countries began to express similar concerns about environmental protection as pollution became an increasing problem within their urban, industrial centers. Whereas the North's approach to global environmental protection emphasized each states' responsibility for pollution within its borders, the South's approach was radically different, focusing on the responsibility of the major industrial states for global pollution. As a result, the South began to demand that the rich, industrial states not only contribute a disproportionate share to the establishment of sustainable economic development but also contribute to the cleanup of Third World pollution.

From the South's perspective, the North had to take responsibility for transnational environmental protection because most of the earth's air and water pollution was brought about by the industrial states. Moreover, because the rich states had already achieved a high standard of living and had developed environmentally safe technologies, they had both the financial and technological resources to assist the poor nations in implementing sustainable economic development strategies. The North's perspective, by contrast, assumed that each country had to be responsible for implementing policies that were conducive to long-term national and global development.

These different perspectives were graphically illustrated at the historic **United Nations Conference on Environment and Development (UNCED),** or *Earth Summit,* held in Rio de Janeiro (Brazil) in 1992. (See case 19.3.) At the Rio summit, the South pressed the North for increased economic transfers to help sustain ecologically sound economic expansion. Specifically, the South called on the North, and especially the G-7 states, to increase their annual economic assistance to 0.7 percent of their individual GNP by the year 2000. It also called on developed states to decrease emissions of global warming gasses, to share biotechnology necessary to preserve species, and to cooperate in research projects, such as the discovery of pharmaceuticals from rain forest flora and fauna. The North, for its part, wanted the South to limit population growth, to protect the tropical rain forest from further destruction, and to promote economic development conducive to the earth's environment.

The summit produced no clear victory for either the North or the South. Although the South had hoped that the North would commit 0.7 percent of its GNP to Third World development, the industrial states refused to make any explicit aid commitments. The South did receive a pledge of about $6 billion in new money to implement *"Agenda 21,"* the UNCED strategy devised for protecting the earth.[31] In addition, although industrial states supported the *Climate Treaty*—a multilateral accord designed to reduce gas emissions contributing to global warming—they did so without specific time tables. The North, for its part, had wanted an agreement protecting the South's tropical rain forest, but developing nations refused to accept such an accord because they believed that it would limit national sovereignty.

THE DECLINE OF THE SOUTH

Throughout the 1980s the South lost much of its global influence and credibility. Three factors contributed to the South's decline. First, OPEC-led increases in petroleum prices had a devastating impact on poor, oil-importing states. Second, a growing number of developing nations experienced significant economic expansion through export-driven strategies, thereby discrediting the structuralist and statist-oriented economic ideologies prevalent in much of the Third World. Third, the increasing disparities in economic performance among developing states called into question the validity of the South as a coherent international actor.

OPEC's Third World Impact

Although OPEC had a salutary impact on the few economies of the oil-exporting states, it had a harmful impact on the South as a whole. The second oil crisis of 1979–1980 had an especially devastating impact on the developing nations because it triggered a global recession that reduced demand for their commodity exports. However, the most harmful effect of the 1973 and 1979 petroleum price hikes was not economic but political. Third World ideology had viewed the South's poverty as a function of the North's wealth. Because the primary beneficiaries of the oil crises were not the Northern industrial states but the Third World oil-exporting countries, the South's doctrinal and political cohesion was seriously damaged as oil-consuming developing nations became aware that international economic problems were not solely the result of the North-South conflict but of growing inequalities among Third World nations themselves.

The failure of the oil-exporting Third World states to provide significant economic assistance to the poorer developing nations exacerbated tensions with the South. Gilpin observes that, "OPEC members have been unwilling to put their power and wealth at the service of other Third World states. . . . They have used their newly gained economic power to support their own nationalist interests and have invested most of their financial surplus in Western markets."[32] In short, even though OPEC may have temporarily strengthened the South with the transfer of economic resources from the North to the South's petroleum-exporting states, OPEC's success also increased economic inequalities within the South, thereby undermining the group's solidarity.

The Loss of Faith in Structuralism

The second factor contributing to the decline of the South was the growing skepticism about its structuralist ideology of development. To a significant degree, the loss of faith in dependency theory and structuralism was due to the failure of statist economic strategies to promote adequate job creation, especially when compared with the relative success of market-oriented economic strategies. In general, countries that followed statist and inward-oriented economic policies tended to have lower rates of job creation in the 1970s and 1980s than countries that followed global market-oriented strategies (see chap. 17). The developing nations that popularized the market-oriented strategies were the so-called **newly industrializing countries (NICs),** including Brazil, Chile, Hong Kong, Malaysia, Singapore, South Korea, and Taiwan. As a result of their success, other emerging Third World economies in Africa and Latin America began instituting market-oriented economic strategies. For example, in the early 1990s both Argentina and Mexico embarked on a vigorous program of selling state-owned businesses, whereas Zaire and Zambia announced the adoption of market-oriented economic strategies.

In the final analysis, the loss of faith in statist and socialist strategies was due to the collapse of communism in Eastern Europe and the former Soviet Union. To a great extent the USSR had helped to promote and sustain the idea of socialism by providing political and financial assistance to developing nations that were applying statist strategies. After Soviet officials began declaring the bankruptcy of

Newly industrializing countries (NICs)
A group of Third World countries, including Hong Kong, Malaysia, Singapore, South Korea, and Taiwan, that have achieved impressive economic growth through export-oriented strategies.

state socialism, Eastern European nations and former Soviet republics began decentralizing and privatizing their economies, encouraging foreign direct investment, and promoting increased participation in the global economy. And as of 1997, nearly all former communist states were experimenting with market-oriented reforms, although some (e.g., Czech Republic, Estonia, and Poland) had been far more successful in such efforts than others (e.g., Belarus, Tajikistan, and Turkmenistan).[33]

In short, as a result of the relative success of market-oriented economic strategies in many developing nations, coupled with the reform policies adopted in Eastern Europe, Russia, and other former Soviet republics, the South's commitment to WST had almost vanished by the early 1990s.

The Growth of Economic Inequalities

The third factor contributing to the South's decreased cohesion and influence was the expanding income disparities among developing nations. Regionally, the areas that had the highest rates of economic growth during the 1970s and 1980s were East Asia and the Middle East/North Africa. From 1968 to 1988, these regions had an average annual growth rate of 7.7 percent and 6.3 percent. During the same period, by contrast, Sub-Saharan Africa and South Asia grew by 3.2 percent and 4.4 percent, respectively.[34] More recently, the economic growth of South Asia and Latin America have increased significantly, whereas the Middle East/North Africa region has declined. During the 1994–2003 period, the World Bank estimates that economic growth in East Asia will continue to outpace other regions, increasing at an estimated 7.6 percent annually.[35]

Although North-South income gaps continued to rise during the 1970s and 1980s, many developing nations achieved extraordinary increases in national economic growth during this period. Despite the South's rhetoric about the unfairness of the international economic structures, the rapid economic development achieved by a growing number of Third World countries was realized not through isolation but through participation in the global economy. International trade, rather than the structuralist agenda advocated by the South, was responsible for the extraordinary economic expansion of Third World countries like Botswana, Chile, Malaysia, and Thailand. As figure 15.3 suggests, the economies of developing nations grew at varying rates, further increasing income disparities within the South. Some nations, especially the NICs, prospered greatly, while others experienced absolute economic declines. Regrettably, some of the LDCs with the highest rates of economic decline were low-income countries with high population growth rates, further compounding the problem of poverty.

But for the vast majority of peoples in the developing nations, especially those in Asia and Latin America, living standards continued to improve because of their nations' further improvement in national productive capabilities. The significant improvement in living conditions in Asia and Latin America is due to the increased productive capabilities of Third World nations. This improved productive capacity is clearly evident in the growing importance of manufactured exports in the South. Even though only 5 percent of the developing economies' exports were manufactured products in 1955, by 1993 manufactured goods accounted for nearly 60 percent of their exports. Moreover, during this period of time the Third World's share of global manufactured exports increased from 5 percent in 1955 to 22 percent in 1993.[36] During the 1994–2003 period the South is expected to grow annually at nearly 5 percent, compared with a rate of 2.7 in the North. If Third World economies continue to pursue liberal economic policies that further increase productive efficiency, the share of global economic output will continue to shift from the North to the South. Indeed, if current projects hold, China, India, and Indonesia could rank among the top five economies in the world by the year 2020.[37]

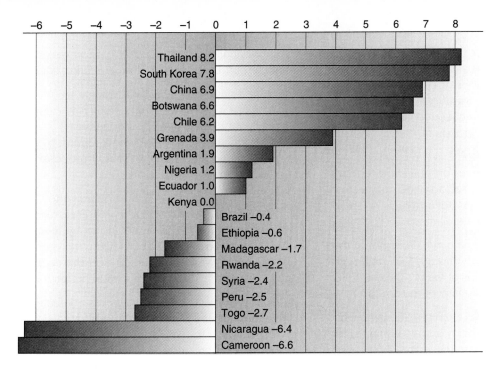

FIGURE 15.3
Average Annual Economic Growth Rate of Selected States, 1985–1994 (in percentages)
Source: Data from *World Bank Atlas,* 1996 (Washington, D.C.: The World Bank, 1996), pp. 18–19.

In the final analysis, the declining significance of the North-South conflict is due to the South's loss of political influence. Although numerous factors contributed to this development, the declining role of the South was greatly influenced by the rise in economic and social disparities among developing nations and the loss of credibility of the Third World's structuralist ideology. Unlike the high level of cohesion exhibited in the early UNCTAD meetings, the South has become a larger but more heterogeneous global actor, with growing economic inequalities among its members. Thus, although tensions between the developed and developing nations continue to be articulated in global forums, the North-South conflict had all but dissipated by the early 1990s.

IN CONCLUSION

Like the East-West conflict, the North-South conflict has been a major systemic dispute in the international community during the second half of this century. Although less significant than the Cold War, the North-South dispute has been a principal source of tension between the modern industrial states and the poor developing nations. Even though the death of this systemic conflict has not been officially announced, the political and intellectual debate has all but ended. This is due to a number of developments, including the South's growing economic diversity, the reduced global influence of the structuralist ideology, and the increasing political influence of market-based economic strategies. Still, even though the South is a smaller, less coherent actor now than in the late 1970s and the dependency theory has lost most of its mythic appeal, the issues that gave rise to the North-South dispute persist. In particular, the abysmal poverty in low-income countries has not been resolved, nor have international economic inequalities among states been reduced. Thus, although the North-South conflict has vanished, the challenge of how to alleviate Third World poverty (a topic explored in chap. 17) and reduce global inequalities will continue to challenge political leaders.

SUMMARY

1. The North-South conflict is a major systemic dispute between the rich, industrial states and the developing nations of Asia, Africa, and Latin America. To a significant degree, this conflict is based on economic inequalities between these two groups of states.

2. The North-South dispute is rooted in conflicting perspectives on political economy. The North has espoused a liberal perspective, whereas the South has advocated a structuralist perspective.

3. The North-South dispute, which began in the early 1960s, has gone through four stages: an era of reform, the rise of OPEC, the call for the NIEO, and the demise of the South.

4. In the first phase, developing nations sought to decrease their poverty and economic vulnerability by promoting strategies of regionalism and import substitution.

5. In the second phase, OPEC countries increased the price of petroleum fourfold, thereby demonstrating the power of economic cartels. The power of OPEC decreased substantially in the early 1980s, however, in great part because of its loss of market share.

6. In the third phase, the South sought to decrease its economic vulnerability by calling for major changes in the international economic order. Despite broad support from the developing nations, the NIEO proposal resulted in few reforms.

7. During the 1980s—the fourth phase—the North-South debate began to address issues less directly related to international trade and finance. Two conflicts symbolizing this shift in orientation were the conflicts over the deep seabed and global environmental protection.

8. By the late 1980s, the North-South conflict had all but ended. To a significant degree, this was due to the South's loss of influence because of declining Third World cohesion. Two factors that contributed significantly to the South's decreasing role in global politics were the destructive impact of OPEC oil increases on poor nations and the growing economic inequalities among the developing nations.

KEY TERMS

Organization for Economic Cooperation and Development (OECD)

Group of 7 (G-7)

Group of 77 (G-77)

United Nations Conference on Trade and Development (UNCTAD)

Third World

Fourth World

imperialism

colonialism

decolonization

modernization thesis

structuralism

dependency theory

dependent development

World System Theory (WST)

import substitution

Organization of Petroleum Exporting Countries (OPEC)

cartel

New International Economic Order (NIEO)

deep seabed

Third UN Conference on the Law of the Sea (UNCLOS III)

United Nations Conference on Environment and Development (UNCED)

newly industrializing countries (NICs)

RECOMMENDED READINGS

Brandt, Willy et al. *North-South: A Programme for Survival.* Report of the Independent Commission on International Development Issues. Cambridge: MIT Press, 1980. A comprehensive examination of economic issues that divide the developed and developing nations, with numerous proposed recommendations.

Gilpin, Robert. *The Political Economy of International Relations.* Princeton: Princeton University Press, 1987. Chapter 2 of this important study explores competing economic ideologies relevant to the North-South conflict. Chapter 7 examines the issue of economic dependence and the problem of Third World development.

Kaplan, Robert D. *The Ends of the Earth: A Journey at the Dawn of the 21st Century.* New York: Random House, 1996. Kaplan, a noted journalist, describes the social, economic, and political dynamics of some eighteen Asian and African countries, suggesting that demographic and environmental pressures are resulting in social decay, economic decline, and political disorder in many developing nations. Kaplan's assessment may be overly pessimistic, but his account is essential reading for anyone concerned with Third World development.

Krasner, Stephen D. *Structural Conflict: The Third World against Global Liberalism.* Berkeley: University of California Press, 1985. A study of North-South relations, focusing on regimes dealing with international financial institutions, MNCs, international transport, and ocean resources. A major thesis of this study is that the North-South debate is fundamentally about power, with the South seeking to alter the liberal rules and institutions established by the North at the end of World War II.

Nyerere, Julius et al. *The Challenge to the South.* Report of the South Commission. New York: Oxford University Press, 1990. A critical analysis of the nature of North-South economic relations during the 1980s from the perspective of the South.

Schwartz, Herman M. *States Versus Markets: History, Geography, and the Development of the International Political Economy.* New York: St. Martin's Press, 1994. An interpretive, theoretical account of the rise and evolution of the global system of political economy, from the fifteenth century to the contemporary world. Schwartz examines the interplay between market forces, which involve a continuing relocation of economic activities in response to increased productive efficiency, and states, which seek to regulate those forces in order to modify market redistribution.

Singer, Max, and Aaron Wildavsky, *The Real World Order: Zones of Peace, Zones of Turmoil.* Chatham, N.J.: Chatham House, 1993. In this stimulating and provocative study, Singer and Wildavsky divide the world into democratic zones of peace and nondemocratic zones of conflict. International relations among developed democratic states are likely to be harmonious where conflicts will be settled without force. Relations among poor, undemocratic Third World states, by contrast, will involve significant domestic instability and transnational conflict.

Spero, Joan Edelman, and Jeffrey A. Hart. *The Politics of International Economic Relations.* 5th ed. New York: St. Martin's Press, 1997. A readable introductory study of international political economy. After examining key elements of the existing Western economic order, the study addresses issues in the North-South economic conflict, focusing on international finance, trade, MNCs, and the oil cartel.

RELEVANT WEB SITES

Fletcher School of Law and Diplomacy Database Trade and Commercial Relations — www.TUFTS.EDU/fletcher/multilaterals.html

Organization for Economic Cooperation and Development — www.oecd.org/

United Nations Children's Fund (UNICEF) — www.unicef.org/statis/

United Nations Conference on Trade and Development — www.unicc.org/unctad/

16 International Economic Relations

Transformations in the real world have made economics and politics more relevant to one another than in the past and have forced the recognition that our theoretical understanding of their interactions has always been inadequate, oversimplified, and arbitrarily limited by disciplinary boundaries.[1]

Robert Gilpin, *international political economist*

. . .industrial policy and trade policy are becoming more important than defense and foreign policy.[2]

Susan Strange, *international political economist*

The international scene is still primarily occupied by states and blocs of states that extract revenues, regulate economic as well as other activities for various purposes, pay out benefits, offer services, provide infrastructures, and—of increasing importance—finance or otherwise sponsor the development of new technologies and new products.[3]

Edward Luttwak, *international relations scholar*

A brief reading of the daily news suggests that economics is an integral part of IR. Newspapers, radio, and television regularly report on developments such as international trade disputes, the relative decline or rise of the economic potential of states, important changes in the international monetary system, significant actions taken by major international economic institutions, the contribution of foreign aid in alleviating Third World poverty, and the role of global economic institutions in fostering free enterprise in former communist states.

The priority of international economic relations in global society is due partly to the extraordinary growth of international economy in the last half of the twentieth century. As a result of the expansion of transnational economic networks, economic production and consumption have become global in nature. For example, a significant portion of the goods and services used in Wheaton, Illinois (where the author lives), are imported from foreign countries or are manufactured domestically from components made in foreign states. Moreover, a portion of the goods and services produced in Wheaton are exported. In effect, the economic welfare in Wheaton, as in other towns and cities of the United States or other developed countries, has become increasingly dependent upon a global economy.

The importance of global economic relations is also due to the priority of national wealth in contemporary world politics. The relative economic potential of states is significant for at least two major reasons. First, because people desire rising standards of living, a government's ongoing legitimacy will depend partly on its capacity to meet citizens' rising economic expectations. Second, national wealth is a main component of power. As noted earlier, the ability of a state to pursue its national interests in global society is directly related to its national economic capabilities. Given the importance of wealth in world politics, some of the major interstate conflicts involve economic disputes over issues such as trade, foreign investment, ownership of natural resources, and foreign debt repayment.

This chapter examines the interrelationship of economics and politics in the contemporary international community. First, it analyzes the nature of international political economy and three different approaches that have influenced states' international economic policies—liberalism, mercantilism, and dependency theory. Second, the chapter examines the major rationale for international trade and then describes major instruments of trade policy as well as some of the justifications for applying such tools. Third, the chapter examines the major features of the dominant twentieth-century systems of international trade, focusing on the significant reductions in trade barriers achieved through the General Agreement on Tariffs and Trade (GATT). Finally, the chapter examines the nature of the global monetary system, calling attention to the role of exchange rate markets, the nature of different monetary exchange systems, and the important role of international institutions in coordinating financial transactions.

THE NATURE OF INTERNATIONAL POLITICAL ECONOMY

International Political Economy (IPE) concerns the interaction of politics and economics, power and wealth, in the international community. Although wealth and power have been closely related in international affairs, scholars and public officials have tended to separate economics from politics. In the sixteenth and seventeenth centuries, for example, mercantilists separated commerce from state building and assumed that the former should serve the aims of the latter. In the eighteenth century, Adam Smith reinforced the separation of economics and politics with his *laissez-faire* doctrine, which assumed that government should keep its "hands off" of the economy in order to maximize productive efficiency. Later, nineteenth-century British economists developed the notion that expanding international commerce would lead not only to prosperity, but to world peace. In the modern age, advocates of the "interdependence" school of world politics have reinforced the division of politics and economics by dividing IR into the "low" politics of transnational economic and social relations and the "high" politics of national security. Similarly, disciples of political realism have diminished the role of economics, assuming that the overriding problem in world politics is the quest for national security. By defining world politics in largely political and military terms, they have neglected economic elements of vital importance to the understanding of contemporary world politics.

IPE can be defined in a variety of ways, each emphasizing different dimensions or aspects of political and economic phenomena. Three major definitional emphases include (1) goals and purposes, (2) organizational principles, and (3) spheres of interaction.

Defined in terms of purposes, IPE is the "reciprocal and dynamic interaction in international relations of the pursuit of wealth and the pursuit of power."[4] Such an approach focuses on the aims and methods by which states maximize welfare and political influence. Although the quest for wealth is a top state priority, states normally give precedence to national security over economic welfare—a truth corroborated by the fact that governments normally devote more money to national defense than to any other budgetary item. According to realists, because states give greater priority to the problem of security than to the problem of national economic welfare, the "high" politics of national security is more fundamental in international politics than the "low" politics of international economic and social cooperation emphasized by neoliberal and interdependence theorists.

IPE can also be defined in terms of the norms governing the creation of wealth and generation of power within the international system. This approach calls attention to the nature and role of the market, which seeks to break down interstate barriers, and to the nature and role of the state, which seeks to regulate and control all activity within its territorial boundaries. In particular, it explores the inherent tensions between the market and the state in international relations.

International Political Economy (IPE)
An area of international relations that emphasizes the interrelationship of political and economic phenomena in global society.

Whereas the market seeks to avoid control and expand its sphere of action, the state seeks to promote loyalty and exclusivity within defined boundaries. Robert Gilpin writes: "the logic of the market is to locate economic activities where they are most productive and profitable; the logic of the state is to capture and control the process of economic growth and capital accumulation."[5]

Finally, IPE can be defined in terms of spheres of interaction between political and economic phenomena. Three major dimensions of IPE are:

1. Domestic economics—international politics
2. Domestic politics—international economics
3. International politics—international economics

The first sphere (1) focuses on the interaction between domestic economic life and global politics. It calls attention to the impact of domestic economic conditions on foreign policy and to the effect of international political dynamics on the domestic economic environment. The second sphere (2) focuses on the interrelationship of domestic political conditions and international economic relations. The third sphere (3) focuses on the interaction of international politics and international economics. Fundamentally, then, *IPE is concerned with the politics of international economic relations and with the economic dimensions of international politics.*

INTERNATIONAL POLITICAL ECONOMY: THREE APPROACHES

Robert Gilpin, a leading IPE scholar, argues that three major IPE traditions have influenced twentieth-century international relations. These three approaches are: liberalism, mercantilism, and dependency theory.[6] Of these approaches to political economy, liberalism has been the most influential in the last half of the twentieth century, providing the intellectual foundation for the international economic policies and institutions established by the major industrial powers in the aftermath of World War II. The least influential doctrine has been mercantilism. Although few states have publicly espoused this approach in the post–World War II era, mercantilism remains marginally important because states periodically increase governmental regulations of international economic relations in the hope of increasing relative wealth. During the Cold War, dependency theory was influential in communist countries and in many Third World nations, but with the demise of the Soviet Union, this perspective has lost much of its former influence. In the following sections we examine the nature and contemporary role of each of these approaches.

Liberalism

Liberalism
The ideology that calls for limited government rooted in consent in order to assure maximum protection of individual rights and human freedoms. In international economic relations, liberalism is associated with free trade.

The origins of economic **liberalism** are associated with the rise of capitalism in Great Britain in the late eighteenth century. In his landmark book *The Wealth of Nations,* published in 1776, Adam Smith argued that the most effective way to foster national economic prosperity and promote individual welfare is through a market economy, a system in which people freely buy and sell goods and services to satisfy human needs and wants. According to Smith, the best economic system is one in which government keeps its hands off of domestic and international economic activities. Voluntary economic exchange should be practiced domestically through *free enterprise* and internationally through *free trade.*

According to liberalism, people create markets, money, and economic institutions in order to facilitate economic exchange. Such developments are not the result of human planning but are the natural by-product of individual behaviors. And because economic behavior is highly predictable, liberalism assumes that markets are stable, especially in the long run. Market stability is based on the so-called "law of demand," which holds that people will buy more of a good as its relative price falls and less as it rises, and that individuals will buy more goods and services as their relative income increases and less as it falls. According to the liberal perspective, the pursuit of economic self-interest encourages productive efficiency, stimulates job creation, and promotes market stability. Moreover, liberalism assumes that government should not interfere with free economic exchange unless there is a severe "market failure" that causes a shortage of important public goods.

Liberalism's rationale for free trade is based on Smith's theory and its subsequent development by other political economists. In particular, it is based on the theory of comparative advantage of the nineteenth-century English economist David Ricardo and its subsequent refinement by two twentieth-century Swedish economists, Eli Heckscher and Bertil Ohlin, whose work resulted in the so-called *Heckscher-Ohlin theory.* Some key elements of the Smith-Ricardo-Heckscher-Ohlin liberal perspective on international trade are examined next.

According to Smith, countries possess different productive capabilities. In order to increase economic efficiency, Smith argued that countries should specialize in producing those goods in which they had an *absolute advantage* and trade these commodities for goods produced by other countries. David Ricardo developed Smith's theory by showing that international trade would be economically beneficial even if a country had an absolute advantage in all of its commodities, meaning it could produce all goods cheaper than foreign countries. In his 1817 book *Principles of Political Economy,* Ricardo developed the theory of **comparative advantage,** which has served as the cornerstone of liberal trade theory. According to Ricardo, countries possess different productive endowments (e.g., natural resources, labor, technology, management) that lead to different relative production capabilities. In order to maximize national economic output, countries should specialize in producing commodities in which they have a comparative advantage and import those goods that other countries can produce more efficiently. Although a nation might, in theory, be able to produce all necessary products for itself, Ricardo showed that national economic welfare is maximized when countries produce goods in which they have a relative advantage and buy goods that they produce less efficiently.

In the 1930s Eli Heckscher and Bertil Ohlin refined Ricardo's theory by arguing that national comparative advantages were based not only on different productive efficiencies but also on national factor endowments (i.e., resources such as land, labor, and capital). Because the quality and quantity of resources differ among countries, different factor endowments lead to different relative costs. As a result, the Heckscher-Ohlin theory posits that countries will produce and sell goods and services that utilize factors that are abundant and import those commodities that require scarce factors.[7]

The Smith-Ricardo-Heckscher-Ohlin theory of international trade does not assert that all states will necessarily improve their *relative* economic welfare from unrestricted trade. Rather, it asserts only that trade provides potential *absolute* benefits for all states. Moreover, the doctrine does not assert that states will benefit equally from trade. Rather, it maintains that all states have the potential to gain absolutely, even when the relative benefits are different. In short, the argument for free trade, as Gilpin notes, is not based on grounds of equity but on increased efficiency and the maximization of world wealth.[8]

Of the three economic perspectives, liberalism has been the most influential in the last half of the twentieth century. Throughout the postwar decades the liberal doctrine has dominated global economic relations. This has been due in great part to the commitment to such a system by the major powers, especially the United States. Following World War II, the major democratic states established a liberal

Comparative advantage
The doctrine that national economic welfare is maximized when countries produce goods and services in which they are comparatively efficient.

international economic order designed to reduce barriers to international trade and to facilitate efficient international financial transactions. Later in the chapter we examine elements of this postwar economic order.

Mercantilism

Mercantilism
The economic doctrine that international trade should be regulated by the state in order to maximize national income.

The doctrine of economic nationalism known as **mercantilism** first emerged in the late sixteenth and early seventeenth centuries with the rise of the nation-sate. As rulers of the emerging nation-states began to consolidate their power, they established increasing state control over foreign trade, believing that regulated commerce would maximize national income. Fundamentally, mercantilism holds that national economic welfare is maximized in the global economy when a state achieves greater economic wealth relative to other states. Relative economic gains are normally realized when states achieve a trade surplus—that is, by exporting more goods and services than the country imports. By doing so, a state accumulates wealth and economic power, which can then be translated into international influence. Although the doctrine of mercantilism has evolved from its early conceptualization and implementation, the doctrine's key premise, that national economic policy can be manipulated for national advantage, has remained unchanged.

Mercantilism's belief in international economic conflict is based on two assumptions. First, it assumes that trade is a *zero-sum game,* in which one country's gains result in a commensurate loss for another. Liberalism, by contrast, assumes that trade is a *positive-sum game,* in which all actors can benefit, even if some benefit more than others. Second, mercantilism gives priority to *relative* economic gains, whereas liberalism stresses *absolute* gains, regardless of economic changes in other countries. Because global politics is rooted in anarchy, mercantilists believe that states must pursue wealth and power in terms of the capabilities of other states. Because a state's trade surplus is possible only when another state runs a trade deficit, it is impossible for all nations to achieve trade surpluses. When states pursue relative gains, one state's economic gains can only be achieved by another's relative decline. Not surprisingly, the quest for relative gains fosters international conflict.

Mercantilism is the antithesis of liberalism. Whereas liberalism assumes that the interests of peoples, firms, and states are fundamentally complementary, mercantilism assumes that states' interests are basically competitive and conflictual. Moreover, whereas liberalism assumes national economic expansion is best undertaken without government direction, mercantilism assumes states should manage their international economic relations to ensure the greatest national wealth.

Although liberalism has been the prevailing international economic doctrine in the twentieth century, mercantilism has regained some of its influence in modern times. During the 1980s, a new, more sophisticated mercantilism became more popular with the growing economic success of state-directed free enterprise. This phenomenon, called **neo-mercantilism** by scholars and euphemistically "*organized free trade*" by the French and "*managed trade*" by North Americans, has been defined as "trade policy whereby a state seeks to maintain a balance-of-trade surplus and to promote domestic production and employment by reducing imports, stimulating home production and promoting exports."[9] The new mercantilism is practiced through a variety of economic policies to encourage exports and limit imports. Like traditional mercantilism, the fundamental aim of managed trade is to increase national output by merging industrial policy and trade policy.

Neo-mercantilism
The policy whereby a state seeks to manage international trade by promoting export-oriented production in order to assure a trade surplus.

The growing influence of state-managed international economic policies stems in great measure from the extraordinary economic success of Japan and the Pacific rim *newly industrialized countries (NICs),* especially Hong Kong, Singapore, South Korea, and Taiwan. East Asian economies have not followed the English political economy of *laissez faire*. Rather, they have pursued a neo-mercantilist strategy based on the belief that the management of trade can, under the right circumstances, increase a nation's wealth.[10] For example, Japan, a country with significant nontariff barriers, increased its share of global exports during the 1980s from about 6 percent to 10 percent, with significant increases in several manufacturing areas (see fig. 16.1). Moreover, from 1965 to 1986 the East Asian NICs increased their global share of manufacturers from 1.5 percent to 8.5 percent by implementing a managed trade policy.[11] Partly in response to the rising economic impact of Pacific-rim countries, Western industrial states have enacted a growing number of nontariff trade barriers to control expanding imports that threaten key domestic industries. At the same time, East Asian economies, especially Japan, have also established a variety of export controls and restraints to avert more significant trade retaliatory action by the United States and other developed countries (see case 16.1).

In the 1980s a number of influential economists developed a new theory of international trade known as **strategic trade theory**.[17] Although this new theory shares with neo-mercantilism a willingness to manage trade in order to maximize a nation's wealth, its major focus is not on general international commerce but on the economics of highly technical industries, such as aerospace, advanced electronics, and telecommunications. Unlike liberal trade theory, which assumes that domestic and international competition will foster efficiency and expand productivity, strategic theory assumes that some technical, capital-intensive industries are fundamentally *oligopolistic* (in which few firms control the production of particular goods) and are therefore not compatible with free trade. The development of oligopolistic markets is due to the fact that product development costs are so high in some industries, such as semiconductors and aerospace, that only a limited number of firms can expect to succeed in the global economy. Because of the high levels of specialization and capital that are required in developing such goods as a commercial aircraft, a fighter jet, a new type of satellite, or a different type of computer software, the new theory suggests that companies that first succeed in such industries accrue significant advantages over would-be competitors. These "first-mover" advantages are based not so much on factor endowments or specialization but on the fact that they were initially successful.[18] From the perspective of strategic trade theory, because only a limited number of companies can successfully build commercial aircraft and computer software, the economic dominance of such companies as Boeing in passenger jets and Microsoft in computer software, is due to the fact that both companies were first in establishing a dominant position

Strategic trade theory
A theory that posits that a nation can improve its international competitiveness when the government provides subsidies to selective industries.

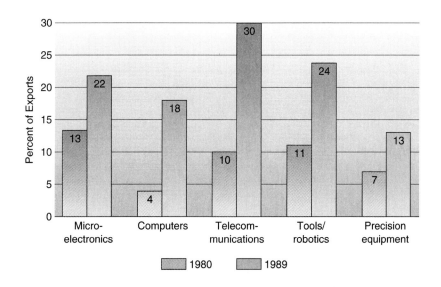

FIGURE 16.1
Japan's Shares of Global Exports of Selected Industries, 1980 and 1989 (in percent)
Source: Data from *Handbook of Economic Statistics,* 1990, Central Intelligence Agency, CIA 1990 Washington, D.C.

CASE STUDY

Case 16.1 The U.S.-Japan Automobile War

From 1986 to 1996, the average annual U.S. trade deficit with Japan was more than $50 billion, with nearly half of this accounted for by vehicles and vehicle parts. When U.S. government officials first began expressing concern in the early 1980s over Japan's growing share of the American automobile market, Japan's government responded by imposing *voluntary export restraints (VERs)*, thereby limiting the number of vehicles exported to the United States. Subsequently, the major Japanese car manufacturers—Honda, Nissan, and Toyota—began assembling vehicles in the United States. Despite these and other initiatives, the U.S.-Japan automobile trade deficit not only continued, but increased further, so that by the early 1990s it exceeded $30 billion annually.[12] As a result, in 1995 the Clinton administration threatened Japan with major trade penalties if it did not modify its domestic economic policies that unfairly restricted imports.

Competing Theories

To a significant degree, the tensions over international trade between the United States and Japan have been rooted in different conceptions of political economy. The different theories are based on alternative approaches to economic production and different visions of the goals of economic life. From the perspective of Western *liberalism*, the basic purpose of economics is to maximize consumer welfare through efficient production and distribution of goods and services. This can be most effectively realized through free enterprise domestically and free trade internationally.[13] Japanese and other East Asian leaders, by contrast, have assumed that because international economic relations are competitive and conflictual, the market will not necessarily assure national economic prosperity. As a result, the East Asian model assumes that governments play an indispensable role in defining and implementing long-term national economic objectives. Because East Asian leaders have assumed that managed domestic production and strategic trade policy can best foster national wealth and power and promote the relative economic well-being of a country, they have pursued a *neo-mercantilist strategy* that involves close cooperation between the public and private sectors.

The Conflict

From the U.S. perspective, three major issues were impeding fair automobile trade with Japan. First, American automobile manufacturers did not have adequate access to the Japanese market, in great part because of the limited number of "quality dealerships" carrying foreign automobiles. Second, the U.S. government contended that Japan deliberately refused to use foreign parts in manufacturing cars in Japan, preferring to use parts made by companies with deep ties to the major auto makers. U.S. officials argued that if American parts were good enough to be used in Japanese autos made in the United States, such parts should also be good enough for cars built in Japan. And third, U.S. officials complained that Japan's highly regulated auto inspection and repair system relied almost exclusively on Japan-made parts. According to U.S. officials, the dependence on domestic parts was due to the fact that repairs were done in shops closely tied to Japanese auto makers. Japan disputed these conclusions, arguing that the imbalance in trade was due to consumer preferences, not to governmental collusion with Japanese industries, as U.S. officials had alleged.[14]

After nearly two years of unsuccessful negotiations, the U.S. government announced in May 1995 that it was imposing a 100 percent tariff on thirteen Japanese-made luxury car models, including Honda Acura, Nissan Infiniti, and Toyota Lexus. Because these models accounted for $5.9 billion in sales in the United States in 1994, the tariffs represented a major threat to Japanese exports. In imposing the tariffs, administration officials said that the sanctions would be rescinded if an agreement could be reached within six weeks.[15]

Resolution

On June 28, 1995, just hours before the trade sanctions were to go into effect, the United States and Japan reached an agreement involving mutual compromises. According to the accord, the Japanese government agreed to encourage existing dealers to sell more imported automobiles. In addition, Japanese manufacturing companies pledged to increase their use of U.S.-made parts through 1998 by using an additional $6.75 billion in U.S. manufactured parts in U.S.-based Japanese car plants and by using about $2 billion more in U.S. parts in Japanese-based car plants. Finally, Japan agreed to modify its auto inspection system in order to allow greater flexibility in using foreign-made parts.[16]

in these highly specialized industries. The costly nature of technology-intensive industries is illustrated by the fact that Boeing spent about $5 billion in developing its new 777 passenger aircraft, requiring it to sell at least 200 of its new airplanes simply to recoup its research and development (R & D) expenditures.

One implication of strategic trade theory is that governments can contribute to national competitiveness by supporting potentially successful companies in oligopolistic industries. Although strategic trade theorists stress the role of innovation, entrepreneurship, and luck in giving a "first-mover" advantages, they also call attention to the role of government aid in getting an industry underway. Boeing, after all, did receive significant financial support when it was building its first successful passenger jet (707). In sum, strategic trade theory provides some support for seeking to manage international commercial relations.

Dependency Theory

The perspective known as the **dependency theory** is rooted in Marxist analysis. Classical nineteenth-century Marxism assumed that the fundamental evils within and among states were due to capitalist economic exploitation. As explained by Karl Marx, capitalism was not only an evil system because of the poverty and powerlessness that it perpetuated, but also an irrational system that would ultimately collapse because of its inherent contradictions. But instead of vanishing, as Marx predicted, capitalism has become the dominant economic system.

The rise of dependency theory in the postwar decades derives from efforts to apply Marxist analysis to contemporary international economic problems. Although the expansion of free enterprise has resulted in large gains in economic production, capitalist expansion has also increased domestic and international economic inequalities. According to dependency theory, the growing income gaps between the rich and poor nations are the result of economic exploitation perpetrated by capitalism. Indeed, Third World poverty is allegedly rooted in the global capitalist structures that foster an unjust distribution of goods and services.

According to this economic perspective, the international economic order is conflictual. Because these international economic disparities exacerbate interstate tensions, dependency theorists assume that the expansion of capitalism has intensified international conflicts unnecessarily. In their view, as firms and states compete for wealth under a capitalist system, global conflict will increase both in scope and intensity, especially between the industrial and developing nations.

The dependency theory suggests that exchange between developed and undeveloped states is unfair because, contrary to the liberal perspective, the gains from trade are distributed inequitably. The world capitalist system not only perpetuates inequalities, but also accentuates them through a system of capital accumulation. The growth of economic inequalities does not mean, however, that capitalism perpetuates economic backwardness. On the contrary, countries may follow a pattern of "dependent development," in which economic expansion is influenced, if not regulated, by foreign economic forces. Such economic growth, however, is harmful because it does not allow domestic authorities to direct and regulate national economic expansion.[19]

The dependency theory has had limited impact on post–World War II global economic relations, especially when compared with the enormous influence of liberalism. During the first half of the Cold War era, the theory achieved popularity in the Third World, in part because Soviet communism was a highly influential global ideology, but also because it offered a simple explanation and solution to the problem of expanding international economic inequalities. As noted in chapter 15, the dominant collective demands of the Third World during this era were based on structuralist arguments rooted in Marxist analysis and derived more particularly

Dependency theory
A neo-Marxist theory attributing the wealth of the industrial states and the poverty of the Third World to global capitalist structures. According to the theory, international economic structures foster income inequalities among states, thereby increasing Third World dependency.

TABLE 16.1   Comparison of Three IPE Approaches

	Liberalism	Mercantilism	Dependency Theory
Nature of Economic Relations	Harmonious	Conflictual	Conflictual
Nature of Actors	Business firms	States	MNCs, social classes, and states
Goal of Economic Activity	Maximize total welfare	Maximize national gains	Minimize international inequalities maximize gains for working class
Type of International Economic Gains	Absolute	Relative	Relative
Role of Government	Hands-off	State regulation	Regulation by states and IGOs
Economic Strategy Activity	Free trade	Managed trade	Managed international economic relations

from dependency theory. But by the early 1980s, the dependency theory had begun to lose its international influence. A major reason for this was that a growing number of Third World countries were achieving significant economic growth through market economic policies, including increased privatization, government deregulation, and greater openness to the global economy. In effect, improvements in living conditions had come through liberal economic policies rather than through restructuring of the international economy, as prescribed by the dependency theory. Most importantly, the end of the Cold War and the Soviet Union's repudiation of communism greatly weakened Marxism and dependency theory. When the former Soviet republics began privatizing their economies in the early 1990s and subsequently began increasing their participation in the global international economic order, dependency theory's credibility diminished even further.

The three different IPE approaches are summarized in table 16.1.

THE POLITICAL ECONOMY OF INTERNATIONAL TRADE

International trade involves the buying (*importing*) and selling (*exporting*) of commodities across national boundaries. At a simplistic level, states export surplus goods and services and import commodities and services that are not produced efficiently in the domestic economy. The difference between the value of exports and the value of imports is called the **balance of trade.** When the value of imports exceeds the value of exports, countries have a **trade deficit;** and when exports are greater than imports, states have a **trade surplus.**

Rationale for Trade

Countries carry out international trade for two reasons—necessity and economic development. Trade becomes a necessity when countries do not have all necessary natural resources and commodities to satisfy domestic demand. Japan, for example, is highly dependent upon petroleum imports, whereas Kuwait and Saudi Arabia use their petroleum exports to buy food and industrial products. Although states can minimize foreign dependence by pursuing economic self-sufficiency (*autarky*), such a policy reduces economic efficiency, leads to slower rates of economic growth, and results in a lower standard of living. As a result, few countries have pursued even limited autarky.

Although countries vary in their level of foreign economic dependency, no country can satisfy the domestic demand for all natural resources and processed

Balance of trade
The difference in value between a country's exports and imports.

Trade deficit
When the value of imports exceeds the value of exports.

Trade surplus
When the value of exports is greater than the value of imports.

The bulk of international trade, which has increased dramatically in the last half of this century, is carried out through shipping.

goods. The United States, for example, is highly dependent on foreign countries for many minerals, including bauxite, chromium, cobalt, manganese, nickel, and titanium. Moreover, even though the United States is a major producer of petroleum, it still imports nearly 50 percent of its oil consumption.

Figure 16.2, which lists the proportion of the gross domestic product (GDP) related to trade, provides a measure of the degree to which national economies are dependent on international trade. The data also indicate the level of countries' economic vulnerability to international economic forces. Countries with a high proportion of the national economy accounted for by trade are potentially more vulnerable to changes in the world economy than those with a relatively low trade sector. Of course, what is significant is not the ratio of trade to the GDP but rather the structure of imports and exports. A state that is highly dependent on the export or import of a limited number of commodities, particularly minerals and other vital primary resources, will be especially vulnerable to changes in the foreign supply and demand for such goods. Many Latin American countries, which are highly dependent on the export of one or two agricultural or mineral products, are especially sensitive to changes in the price and demand for their exports. Similarly, most industrial states are highly dependent on petroleum imports and are therefore vulnerable to changes in its price and supply.

The second and more important reason for international trade is the potential for increased national economic output. As noted above, classical economics

FIGURE 16.2
Exports as a Percentage of Gross Domestic Product, 1965, 1980 and 1995
Source: World Bank, *World Development Report,* 1997 (New York: Oxford University Press, 1996), pp. 238–39; data for 1965 is from World Bank, *World Development Report,*1991 (New York: Oxford University Press, 1991), pp. 220–21.

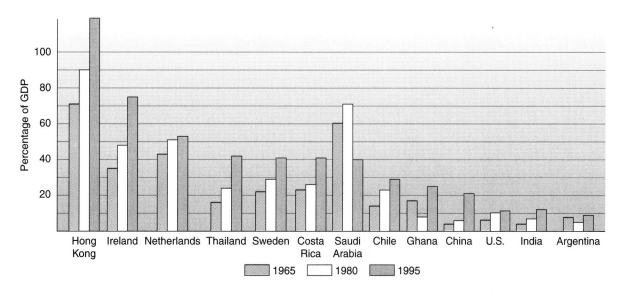

(liberalism) assumes that international trade fosters economic development by increasing productive efficiency. Because the global economy provides a larger market for selling goods and services than a national economy, international trade increases the efficiency of production through specialization and economies of scale. In light of liberalism's claims about increased productive efficiency through international trade, it is not surprising that countries that have pursued an "outward-oriented" economic strategy have achieved higher rates of economic expansion than countries pursuing an "inward-oriented" strategy.[20] The gains from an export-oriented policy have been especially evident in such East Asian countries as Hong Kong, Malaysia, Singapore, South Korea, and Taiwan, because each of these national economies has grown at an average annual rate in excess of 5 percent throughout the 1970s and 1980s. The significant growth and transformation of Chile's economy during the 1980s was similarly realized through liberal economic strategies involving increased free enterprise domestically along with greater openness to the global economy. Because of Chile's successful economic growth, most other Latin American countries, especially Mexico and Argentina, have instituted similar economic reforms. Perhaps the most significant illustration of the gains from international trade has been China, a communist state that formerly pursued economic autarky, but one that has pursued an increasingly liberal political economy since the 1970s. In response to its economic reforms, China's international trade has exploded, rising from 4 percent of GDP in 1965 to 24 percent in 1994, while the country's annual economic growth rate averaged 10.2 percent in the 1980s and nearly 13 percent during the 1990–1994 period.[21]

Instruments of Trade Policy

If countries developed international economic policies simply to maximize their national economic welfare, the analysis of international economic relations would be a relatively simple task. But trade policies are shaped not only by economic realities but also by political realities. As a result, it is important to explore the political economy of the international community in order to assess how domestic and international political factors influence domestic and international economic behavior. This is especially the case in international trade, because countries have historically used tariff and nontariff barriers to maximize national income and to influence the behavior of other states. Thus, although public officials have commonly espoused the ideal of free trade, in practice they have imposed a variety of barriers and restrictions in order to pursue specific political and economic interests. For example, the United States, a country that has officially espoused the doctrine of free trade, maintains a large number of trade barriers to protect particular sectors of the national economy. One study estimates that during the 1980s U.S. tariffs alone cost consumers about $32 billion per year.[22]

Governments use a variety of policy tools to influence international trade. Typically they are classified as tariff and nontariff barriers, the latter including such instruments as quotas, export controls, local requirements, bureaucratic controls, and subsidies. Because trade barriers increase the cost of imported goods and services, they reduce their demand. The major trade policy instruments are described next.

Tariff
A tax imposed on imported goods.

1. **Tariff:** This is a tax levied on an imported product. The tax may be levied as a fixed charge for each unit, or it may involve a percentage assessment of the market value of a product. In addition to restricting trade, tariffs are imposed to raise revenue for the national government. Because tariffs are much easier to impose than income taxes, they have been an especially popular source of government revenue in the Third World.

2. **Import quota:** This is a limitation on the quantity of a good that may be imported during a specified period of time. Quotas are imposed directly by establishing a numerical limit or indirectly by requiring import licenses for particular commodities. The first type of quota is illustrated by the U.S. sugar quota, which limits the total annual imported sugar to 2.5 million tons; the second type is illustrated by the U.S. government requirement for cheese licenses, thereby regulating the quantity of cheese imported from Europe.

3. **Export controls:** These regulations restrict the export of goods and services. The most extreme type of export control is an *embargo,* which involves a total ban on the export of particular commodities. The more common export control is the *voluntary export restraint (VER),* which is an export quota imposed by the exporting country, frequently at the request of the importing country's government. For example, since the early 1980s, Japan has limited the number of automobiles that could be exported to the United States, and Hong Kong has imposed restrictions on clothing exports.

4. **Local content requirements:** These regulations specify a particular fraction of domestically produced goods or services that must utilize local suppliers. For example, the U.S. government has insisted that Japanese automobile companies in the United States use at least 75 percent component parts manufactured domestically. And as noted earlier in the Japan-U.S. automobile case, the United States has also demanded that Japanese car manufacturers use more U.S.-made parts in Japan (see case 16.1).

5. **Bureaucratic controls:** Governments frequently impose a wide variety of administrative controls (bureaucratic red-tape), which can impede trade. An example of this nontariff barrier was the 1982 decision by the French government to require all imported videocassette recorders (VCRs) to pass through the village of Poitiers, a small town hundreds of miles inland from France's northern coastline. This requirement was designed to delay and ultimately reduce the number of imported Japanese VCRs and to dampen the growing demand for other Japanese electronic consumer goods. The resulting delays significantly reduced imported VCRs until a VER agreement was negotiated with Japan.

6. **Subsidies:** A subsidy involves government financial support to domestic producers. Such support may involve government funding of research, low-interest loans, cash grants, or even direct equity participation in a firm. The European Union, for example, provides substantial cash payments to its farmers, whereas the governments of Great Britain, France, Germany, and Spain provide substantial subsidies to Airbus Industrie, a consortium of four European aircraft companies and the second largest airplane manufacturer in the world.

Import quota
Placing quantitative limits on specific commodities imported from abroad. The quota may target particular foreign states or may apply to all commodity-exporting countries.

Export controls
Regulations that restrict the export of goods and services.

Local content requirements
The specification of domestic participation in the production of goods and services by foreign firms. States impose such requirements in order to ensure that a given level of domestic services are used in production.

Bureaucratic controls
Administrative regulations used by governments to limit international trade.

Subsidies
Government financial support to domestic producers in order to facilitate their international competitiveness.

All governments seek, in differing degrees, to influence international trade. They do so for a variety of reasons, including the maximization of national income, the protection of particular sectors of the economy, the promotion of consumer welfare, and national security. However, the tools that governments use to influence international trade vary considerably. The easiest trade barriers to identify are tariffs and quotas. Estimating the economic impact of local content requirements, bureaucratic controls, and subsidies can be difficult and result in significant international conflict.

Arguments for Trade Barriers

If free trade improves national economic conditions, as the liberal theory of international trade suggests, why have states historically restrained the transnational movement of goods and services by imposing tariff and nontariff barriers? Following are several reasons—some political and some economic:

1. **Protect undeveloped industries:** States use trade barriers to protect new firms, sometimes called *"infant industries."* Defenders of protectionist measures argue that new industries are unable to compete with well-established firms based on refined technologies and significant specialization. The aim of such trade barriers is to provide a "cushion" until the new industries are established and can effectively compete with foreign production.

2. **Protect jobs:** Governments also impose trade barriers in order to protect existing industries from foreign competition. Because the productive capacities of states are always changing, increasingly efficient industries of some states will, in the absence of trade barriers, threaten the viability of less efficient industries. In the United States, for example, the domestic shoe and clothing industries have declined significantly since the early 1970s as foreign states have developed the capacity to produce similar goods at much lower costs. Because of the increasing comparative advantage of foreign imports, the size of the labor force in U.S. clothing and shoe industries have all declined. Even though labor organizations have sought protection from inexpensive imports through the imposition of trade restrictions, U.S. trade policy has, at least until the early 1990s, avoided such a strategy. Instead, it has encouraged foreign exporters to restrict their exports to the United States.

3. **Retaliation:** States also impose barriers to compensate for domestic economic subsidies. When governments provide direct and indirect economic assistance in producing and marketing goods and services, other states may perceive their economies unjustly threatened by unfair competition and seek relief through tariff and nontariff trade barriers. For example, because of major European Union agricultural subsidies, the U.S. government maintains a variety of trade barriers against agricultural exports from EU member-states.

4. **National security:** According to the national security argument, a country should be relatively self-sufficient in materials, components, and industries considered essential in military security. Following this rationale, many governments protect vital domestic industries, such as defense-related firms or politically sensitive enterprises considered essential. For example, the U.S. government provides subsidies to shipbuilding industries in order to protect domestic firms from foreign competition. By requiring that naval ships be built in domestic shipyards, and by requiring that all direct shipping between its ports must be carried out by U.S.-built vessels, the United States protects its maritime industry from more efficient foreign firms. Similarly, because of the important role of advanced electronics in military weapons, the U.S. government has provided a significant annual subsidy (about $100 million) to Sematech, a consortium of fourteen domestic semiconductor companies.

5. **Strategic trade theory:** As noted before, the new trade theory of the 1980s calls attention to the oligopolistic nature of some highly specialized, capital-intensive industries. Because of the limited number of firms that can be supported worldwide, significant advantages accrue to firms that establish themselves successfully early in the development of a new industry. In light of this perspective, some theorists argue that governments can contribute to a country's competitiveness by providing R & D support to promising firms in newly emerging industries and subsidies to firms that are seeking to compete in industries in which other firms have already achieved "first-mover" advantages. The potential role of subsidies is illustrated by the dramatic growth of Airbus in the commercial aircraft industry. Although Boeing has remained the dominant commercial aircraft firm in the world, the European conglomerate Airbus has

increased its share of the market from 5 percent in 1975 to more than 30 percent in 1990. Airbus's rising share of the aircraft market was due, according to some observers, to the $13.5 billion subsidy it had received from the governments of Great Britain, France, Germany, and Spain.[23]

The most fundamental reason why economic protectionism flourishes is due, of course, to the decentralized nature of the world economy. Despite the increasing economic interdependence within global society, states are driven by national interests. If states simply sought to improve their economic output absolutely, there would be little incentive to restrict trade. But states are concerned not solely with net improvements in national output but, most importantly, with relative increases.[24] Although all states have the potential for increasing gross domestic output, not all states can improve their economic output relatively. Thus, if five states improve their relative economic standing in the world, five other states must decrease their relative economic welfare.

The dilemma of international economic policy is how to promote global economic growth while simultaneously reconciling national goals of improved relative income. Trade offers the potential of absolute improvements in income, but whether or not a country improves its relative standing will depend not only on its productive capabilities, but also on the economic performance of other states as well. Because states seek to improve their relative economic power, international economic relations are a major source of interstate conflict.

An economic phenomenon that greatly weakens the capacity of states to regulate trade began developing in the 1970s and accelerating in the 1980s. Known as the **internationalization of production,** this development involves the growing use of specialized components from different foreign countries in manufacturing modern goods. For example, computers, VCRs, motors, automobiles, and agricultural machinery all use parts built in different countries, either by firms owned by a single multinational corporation or by several different firms. The automobile industry illustrates this growing global interdependence in production. An American-built car, for example, may use a starter motor from Mexico, ignition parts from Britain, electronic components from Japan, motor parts from Germany, tires from France, and glass from Canada. As a result, the label "made in the USA" no longer means that a product is built with U.S.-made components. Rather, it refers chiefly to the location of the plant assembling the goods.

Internationalization of production
The process of manufacturing goods by using components from a variety of different countries.

As the production cycle becomes more globally interdependent, identifying the economic contribution of each relevant country becomes increasingly difficult. A Japanese car (e.g., Mazda) assembled in the United States, for example, may have more American components than either a European-built automobile (such as a Ford Escort) or a U.S. firm-imported Japanese car (e.g., Dodge Colt). As a result, the nationality of the firm or the location of assembly are no longer useful in determining the nationality of a product.

THE SYSTEM OF INTERNATIONAL TRADE

In the aftermath of World War II, the major democratic powers, led by the United States, established an international economic order designed to facilitate international trade and promote efficient monetary transactions. This economic order—known as the **Bretton Woods system**[25]—involved three major institutions:

1. The General Agreement on Tariffs and Trade (GATT)[26]
2. The International Monetary Fund (IMF)
3. The International Bank for Reconstruction and Development (IBRD), or World Bank

Bretton Woods system
The rules and institutions of the liberal global economic system established at the end of World War II.

The purpose of GATT was to foster freer international commerce by reducing trade barriers. The aim of the IMF was to facilitate international economic transactions by assuring an adequate source of international reserves and by regulating the interrelationship of foreign currencies. Finally, the IBRD was created to provide capital for the reconstruction of Europe and to foster the economic growth of other nations. Although the international economic order has of course undergone a number of significant modifications since it was established nearly fifty years ago, the institutions and liberal procedures created in the late 1940s continue to function largely as they were designed. In the following sections we examine the nature and evolution of GATT, and the role of the IMF in facilitating international financial transactions. In chapter 17 we examine the role of the World Bank in facilitating Third World development.

GATT and Trade Liberalization

GATT
An organization that facilitated the liberalization of international trade from the late 1940s to 1995, when it was replaced by the World Trade Organization (WTO).

MFN principle
According to this norm, international trade preferences granted to one state must be granted to all others.

The most important rules governing international trade in the postwar decades have been established by the *General Agreement on Tariffs and Trade* (**GATT**). Since its creation in 1947, this Geneva-based multilateral institution, which has grown from 19 members to 123 in 1996,[27] has contributed significantly to the reduction of tariff and nontariff barriers to trade. GATT's most basic working norm—the "most-favored-nation" **(MFN) principle**—calls on states to carry out trade policies on a reciprocal and nondiscriminatory basis. This means that when a GATT member-state accords a trade preference, it is obligated to give that same preference to all member-states.

GATT has been successful in bringing about major reductions in tariff and nontariff trade barriers. The liberalization of international trade has been undertaken through a number of negotiations, known as *"rounds"* (see table 16.2). The two most successful of these have been the Kennedy and Uruguay Rounds, which resulted in tariff reductions on most exports of 35 to 40 percent each. As a result of the GATT's significant reductions in trade barriers, international trade has increased greatly in the last half of this century, rising from $94 billion in 1955 to more than $4 trillion in 1994 (see table 16.3). Indeed, since the 1980s, the growth rate of global trade has been much greater than the growth rate of the world's total economic output.

Despite the considerable success of GATT during the early postwar period, protectionism began to reemerge in the early 1980s, thereby threatening continued trade liberalization. Four developments contributed to the reemergence of protectionist pressures: first, the extraordinary increases in petroleum prices; second, the increasing instability of the international monetary system (caused in part by the shift from fixed to flexible exchange rates); third, the extraordinary growth in exports of industrial commodities from Japan and the newly industrializing countries (NICs); and fourth, the continuation of preferential trade policies by the European Economic Community. Moreover, the global economic slow-down in the early 1980s further threatened trade liberalization. As governments adjusted to increasing international competition and slower growth rates, governments had to face growing domestic protectionist pressures from constituencies threatened by job displacement and unemployment.

This growing protectionism was evident in the United States in the late 1980s and early 1990s as the government sought to respond to large and persistent trade deficits. Beginning in 1980 with a trade deficit of more than $25 billion, the U.S. trade imbalance increased to $160 billion in 1987. The trade deficit then declined to $74 billion in 1991 before rising again to a record $183 billion in 1995. A principal reason for this large trade imbalance has been the major deficits with Japan, accounting for 30 to 50 percent of the total (see fig. 16.3).

TABLE 16.2 GATT Multilateral Negotiations (Rounds), 1947-1993

Rounds	Year	Name	Participating States	U.S. Tariff Reduction* (average cut in all duties, in percent)
First	1947	Geneva	23	33.2
Second	1949	Annency (France)	13	21.1
Third	1950-1951	Torquay (Britain)	38	1.9
Fourth	1955-1956	Geneva	26	3.0
Fifth	1960-1961	Dillon Round	26	3.5
Sixth	1964-1967	Kennedy Round	62	36.0
Seventh	1973-1979	Tokyo Round	99	29.6
Eighth	1986-1993	Uruguay Round	125	40.0

*Estimates for U.S. tariff reductions in the first seven rounds are from Steven Husted and Michael Melvin, *International Economics* (New York: Harper & Row, 1990), p. 232; the estimate for the eighth round is from *The New York Times*, December 15, 1993, pp. 1 and C18; the number of participating states is from *Economic Report of the President* (Washington, D.C.: Government Printing Office, 1995), p. 205.

TABLE 16.3 Exports as a Percentage of World Total, 1955-1995

Group	1955	1965	1975	1985	1989*	1995**
U.S.	17	15	12	11	12	13
EU	30	39	34	31	39	36
Japan	2	4	6	9	9	10
OPEC	6	5	13	7	5	5
Developing	18	18	11	21	23***	25
Communist	11	12	10	12	7***	—
Other	15	11	14	7	5	11
Total	100	100	100	100	100	100
Value of Exports (in $ billions)	$94	$188	$878	$1,997	$2902	$4300

Sources: *Economic Report of the President, 1986* (Washington, D.C.: Government Printing Office, 1986), p. 374;

*World Bank, *World Development Report 1991* (New York: Oxford University Press, 1991), pp. 230-31.

**Central Intelligence Agency, *The World Factbook 1996* (Washington, D.C.: C.I.A., 1995), passim.

***International Monetary Fund, *World Economic Survey 1992* (Washington, D.C.: IMF, 1992), p. 50.

Notwithstanding growing international commercial tensions, the major powers persisted in further reducing trade barriers. During the **Uruguay Round** (1986–1993) the hundred participating states sought to extend trade liberalization to agriculture, services, and intellectual property (patents, copyrights, trademarks). Because these areas were complex and politically sensitive, the negotiations were intense and protracted. In 1992 trade conflict came to a head over agriculture, precipitating an intense dispute between the European Community and the United States that threatened not only the trade talks but also the collapse of GATT itself. Fortunately the so-called "chablis war" (see case 16.2) was averted, and consensus between the major industrial economies was achieved on agricultural trade liberalization, thereby paving the way for the Uruguay Accord.

The Uruguay Round was especially significant for two reasons. First, it extended GATT rules to intellectual property (e.g., patents, copyrights, and

Uruguay Round
The eighth series of trade negotiations sponsored by GATT. This set of talks resulted in significant trade liberalization in agriculture, services, and intellectual property, and in the creation of the WTO.

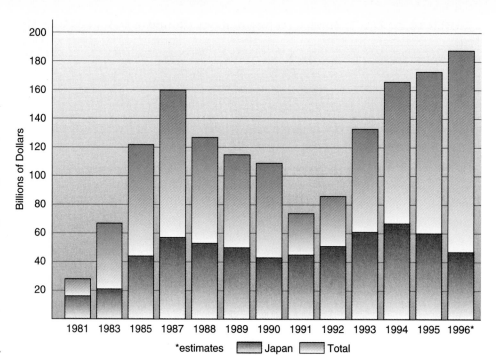

FIGURE 16.3
United States Trade Deficit, 1981–1996 (billions of dollars)
Source: Data for 1981–1985 from *Economic Report of the President*, February 1991 (Washington, D.C.: Government Printing Office, 1991), p. 405; data for 1987–1996 are from *Economic Report of the President*, February 1997 (Washington, D.C.: U.S. Government Printing Office, 1997), p. 417.

World Trade Organization (WTO)
An IGO that monitors implementation of trade agreements and resolves disputes among its members.

trademarks) and to agricultural products. Until July 1, 1995, when the Uruguay Agreement went into effect, GATT norms had applied only to industrial goods. Because of the new trade accord, about one-fourth of the world's total annual trade (more than $1 trillion) that was formerly excluded from GATT coverage is now governed by GATT rules. As a result of the further reduction in trade barriers, it has been estimated that the Uruguay trade liberalization will increase global income by $235 billion.[30] Second, the Uruguay Agreement is important because it created a more powerful trade-enforcement institution, the **World Trade Organization (WTO).** The WTO, an umbrella organization that now oversees GATT and two new sister institutions covering services and intellectual property, is responsible for monitoring implementation of the Uruguay Accord and for settling trade disputes among member-states. Although it is still too soon to know how effective the new organization will be in policing the international trading system, WTO rules give the new organization far more authority in settling trade disputes than the less formal GATT structure.[31] As of July 1996, fifty-four trade disputes had been brought to the WTO for arbitration. Of these, thirty-three were launched by the developed states, with the United States initiating the largest (eighteen) number of complaints. The developing nations were responsible for initiating twenty-one trade complaints. As of 1997, the WTO had 132 members, with another 29 states, including China and Russia, having observer status.

One of the most effective approaches to trade liberalization has been at the regional level. Neighboring states in Africa, Asia, Europe, North and South America, and the Pacific Basin have established a variety of regional organizations, including common markets and free trade associations, aimed at fostering economic expansion through trade liberalization. To date, the most successful of these experiments has been the European Union (EU). As noted in chapter 14, after creating a common market among its members, the EU has moved toward the establishment of full economic union among its fifteen member-states by seeking to create a single European currency, as well as common defense policies and foreign policies.

NAFTA
A 1993 accord that reduces trade barriers among Canada, Mexico, and the United States.

Another important regional economic development has been the establishment of the North American Free Trade Agreement (NAFTA). Created in 1994, **NAFTA** is

Case 16.2 The Chablis War: Conflict over Agricultural Trade

A major aim of the Uruguay Round of GATT negotiations was the reduction of agricultural trade barriers. From 1986 to 1992 the United States and Europe had tried to reach an agreement on agricultural trade, but despite repeated efforts, had failed to achieve a compromise. Fundamentally, the conflict boiled down to differences over the scope and rate of trade liberalization. The United States, a major exporter of grain and other agricultural products, pressed for radical reductions in tariff and non-tariff agricultural barriers. By contrast, the European Community (EC), which heavily supports agriculture through its Common Agriculture Policy, opposed major reductions in agricultural subsidies and other protective policies, even though they cause excessive and inefficient production. The EC's steadfast commitment to agriculture was due, in great measure, to the political influence of farmers, especially in France, and to the emotional reluctance of European governments to allow domestic and international markets to allocate agricultural resources.

After considering many different compromise initiatives during the six years of GATT negotiations, Europe and the United States remained deadlocked. In a nutshell, the United States wanted the EC to reduce the tonnage of subsidized grain exports by 24 percent over six years, whereas the Europeans insisted that they could not go above 18 percent. Shortly before the 1992 U.S. presidential election, U.S. negotiators presented a last-ditch proposal that called for a 22 percent reduction in agricultural subsidies but figured in a more stringent way. Although the EC responded favorably at first, after a week of governmental consultations, it subsequently refused to accept the American proposal. The trade talks had collapsed.[28]

One of the major obstacles in resolving the agricultural trade dispute was the problem of oilseed production. Because the EC was providing indirect subsidies for soybeans, rapeseed (used to make canola oil) and other seeds used in animal feed, the U.S. government had charged that the EC was discriminating against the American soybean industry. Although two GATT panels had ruled in favor of the United States, the EC refused to change its policies, using its veto to block the American claim.

As a result of Europe's unwillingness to abide by GATT rulings and its intransigence to compromise on reductions in grain subsidies, the United States announced that it would impose 200 percent punitive taxes on selected European exports if the EC did not comply with the proposed subsidy reductions. The principal European export selected for this punitive tax was white wine—a product chosen because France, the major European opponent of agricultural trade liberalization, was the leading exporter of white wine to the United States.[29] Although the American threat risked a potential trade war, the aim of the American action was to pressure the EC to accept the 22 percent compromise.

The threat worked. Two weeks later, the EC announced that it would accept the negotiated cutbacks in agricultural trade subsidies, thereby allowing the Uruguay Round to proceed to other issues.

a trade accord among Canada, Mexico, and the United States that seeks to increase regional economic output through trade liberalization. The accord calls for the removal over ten years of all restrictions on manufacturing trade and most cross-border investment barriers. In addition, tariffs and quotas on agricultural goods are to be eliminated within fifteen years. Because some American political leaders claimed that NAFTA would lead to job losses in the United States, the adoption of NAFTA by the U.S. government was a highly contentious political issue. NAFTA critics, led by business leaders and 1992 and 1996 U.S. presidential candidate Ross Perot, argued that the accord would lead to massive job migration to Mexico and harmful environmental consequences. By contrast, NAFTA advocates argued that greater trade with Canada and Mexico would increase American economic efficiency, foster domestic economic expansion, and improve living standards in all three countries, especially in Mexico. As of 1997, the effects of NAFTA in the United States have been hardly perceptible, calling into question the predictions of both its critics and supporters. At the same time, some studies suggest that the preferential treatment now being given Mexican exports has been harmful to

developing economies in the region, especially Caribbean countries. A study by the World Bank, for example, has estimated that Caribbean nations lost 123,000 jobs to Mexico during the first two years of NAFTA because of diversion of foreign investment and trade. According to this study, the Caribbean apparel industry has been especially damaged, with the forced closure of some 150 clothing manufacturing plants in 1995 and 1996 alone.[32]

THE GLOBAL MONETARY SYSTEM

One requirement for efficient trade among states is a flexible and stable international monetary system. Just as money is the major means of domestic exchange, so money is the major instrument of international trade. But even though each country has a government-regulated currency, the world economy has neither a common currency nor a governmental institution with the authority to regulate international monetary affairs.

The Nature and Role of Foreign Exchange

Foreign exchange
The accumulation of foreign currencies with which to purchase imports and meet other external financial obligations.

If a state is to effectively meet its foreign financial obligations, it will have to acquire **foreign exchange**—that is, foreign currencies with which to pay for imports and cover other financial obligations. The principal means by which states generate foreign exchange is by accumulating financial reserves through trade. These surplus funds can therefore be exchanged for foreign currencies to buy foreign goods and services. The aim of an effective international monetary system is to facilitate efficient currency convertibility.

Because each country has its own money, states acquire needed foreign currencies by trading currencies in foreign exchange markets. Because the U.S. economy is the largest, the U.S. dollar is the major international currency, accounting for more than 60 percent of world currency reserves. It has been estimated that 80 percent of all trading in foreign exchange markets involves four currencies: the U.S. dollar (41%), the German mark (20%), the Japanese yen (12%), and the British pound (7%).[33] Most foreign exchange trading is carried out in the world's principal financial centers—namely, London, New York, Tokyo, Zurich, Frankfurt, Paris, Hong Kong, with London accounting for nearly a third of all currency exchange.

Because of significant growth in international trade and a dramatic expansion of the international capital market (e.g., transborder banking, foreign stocks and bonds), the demand for foreign exchange has increased dramatically in recent years. Whereas the average daily foreign exchange trade increased modestly during the late 1970s and early 1980s, rising from a daily average of $15 billion in 1973 to $60 billion in early 1983, during the 1990s the expansion of foreign exchange trade has been extraordinary, rising to an average daily foreign exchange trade of more than $1.3 trillion, more than twenty times the 1983 level![34] Thus, although international financial assets (stocks and bonds) have increased to two and a half times the level of the gross domestic product of the developed industrial states, the volume of currency trading has increased by more than six times.

Given the political and economic significance of money, governments determine the extent to which they will allow their currencies to be freely exchanged. The system of *free convertibility* means that a government places no restrictions on the exchange of its currency. Because most governments maintain some controls over the conversion of money, free convertibility is the exception rather than the rule in the contemporary world. Moreover, governments seek, in different degrees, to establish control over the relative value of their currency. Fundamentally, countries choose among three different systems:

1. **Fixed exchange rates:** In this system—sometimes called a "pegged" system— a government seeks to maintain a fixed rate of exchange with another major currency, such as the U.S. dollar. Until 1973, the United States maintained a fixed exchange rate, promising to convert $35 for 1 ounce of gold. Maintaining fixed exchange rates is difficult, because a government must maintain a strong economy, follow sound fiscal and monetary policies, and maintain significant reserves. Because economic stability is essential to attract foreign investment and to promote long-term economic expansion, governments desire to maintain fixed exchange rates but must frequently settle for a system that allows for some flexibility.

2. **Managed exchange rates:** This system—also known as the *managed or dirty "float"*—allows the exchange rate to be set by market forces and the state. Typically, governments establish a band in which a currency can be exchanged. When market forces push the currency outside of the approved exchange zone, governments intervene and buy (or sell) their own currency with accumulated monetary reserves.

3. **Flexible exchange rates:** In this system, a currency's value is determined by *"floating"*—that is, allowing international market forces of demand and supply to establish the value of money. The relative value of a currency is thus determined much like the value of a stock or bond in the New York Stock Exchange. Because the value of a currency will depend greatly on the confidence of investors, bankers, and traders in the long-term viability of an economy, a state pursuing sound economic policies will tend to have a stronger currency than a state that is politically and economically unstable and unable to meet its financial obligations.

Fixed exchange rates
A currency exchange rate established and maintained by government or other actors.

Managed exchange rates
States manage the exchange rate of their national currency by establishing a band in which the currency can be traded.

Flexible exchange rates
A currency exchange rate determined largely by the market forces of demand and supply.

Most states maintain either fixed or managed exchange rates. Less than 20 percent of the world's countries maintain completely flexible exchange rates, with most of these being developed economies. Before the establishment of the European Union in 1992, Western European states maintained relatively flexible exchange rates, but because the move toward the creation of an *Economic and Monetary Union (EMU),* the EU has established stricter measures for coordinating member-states' currency fluctuations. Many developing countries typically peg their money to another major currency (such as the U.S. dollar or the French franc) or to a composite of foreign currencies. This provides poor states with a relatively stable monetary system that facilitates the financing of international trade, especially because the payment of commonly imported resources and commodities (such as petroleum, wheat, corn, machinery) must generally be made in dollars or some other major currency.

Regardless of what exchange rate system a state adopts, the long-term stability of a currency will depend ultimately on the perceived relative value of money. The perceptions of investors and foreign exchange traders will depend, in turn, on their confidence in the fundamental stability of a political regime and the long-term prospects for business enterprise. Moreover, if a government does not pursue sound fiscal and monetary policies, people will lose confidence in the country's economy, resulting in a declining demand for the country's currency (see case 16.3). Even if a government maintains a fixed or managed system, the loss of confidence in a country's economy will inevitably result in a loss of confidence in its money, leading to a discrepancy between the official exchange rate and the unofficial exchange rate. If the difference between the two rates is large, an illegal exchange of currencies, or *black market,* will result.

Figure 16.4 illustrates the shifting values of major currencies during the 1970–1994 period. In 1997, one U.S. dollar equaled .59 British pounds, 1.5 German marks, 1.7 Dutch guilders, 1.3 Swiss francs, and 116 Japanese yen. Large short-term currency fluctuations can be triggered by many factors, including war, domestic political turmoil, major public policy developments, and currency speculation. Over the long term, however, the value of a currency is likely to depend upon fundamental economic and political conditions associated with economic growth. These include a stable political order, a political economy that protects property rights, a culture conducive to private investment and creative enterprise, and public policies that foster economic development—namely, limited expansion of the money supply, low inflation rates, limited governmental regulation of economic life, and balance of payments equilibrium.

A country's domestic accounting system with the world economy is known as the **balance of payments** (see issue 16.1). The balance of payments provides the financial record of a state's transnational financial flows (outflows and inflows), and is therefore a good indicator of a state's overall economic health and more specifically, of its ability to buy and sell goods and services, to invest in foreign countries, and to provide capital to other countries. Ideally, a country should maintain equilibrium in its balance of payments, with a state's revenues equaling or exceeding its financial obligations. When a state's international income account

Balance of payments
A summary of a country's international financial transactions. A surplus indicates that assets exceeded liabilities in a given period of time; a deficit signifies the opposite.

FIGURE 16.4
Exchange Rates of Selected States, 1980-1994 (index relative to the U.S. dollar)
Source: Data from *Statistical Abstract of the United States,* 1995, 115th ed. (Washington, D.C.: U.S. Department of Commerce, 1995), p. 879. *Formerly West Germany

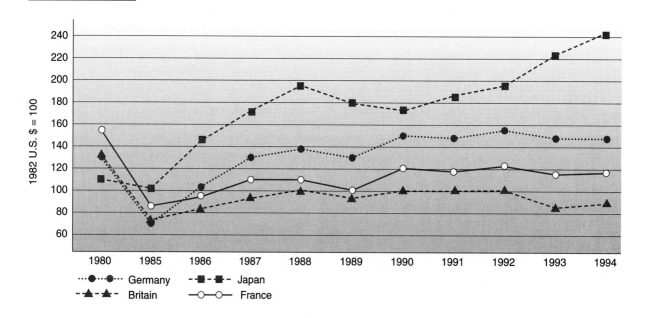

Case 16.3 Exchange Rates and the Collapse of the Mexican Peso

Since the 1980s, Mexico, as many other Third World countries, has maintained a managed exchange rate, allowing its currency (the peso) to fluctuate within an established band. Although Mexico's managed exchange-rate system allowed for a small daily depreciation in the peso, the established ceiling of about 3.5 pesos to the dollar was being increasingly threatened in the early 1990s by a decline in confidence in Mexico's economy and political system. As a result, foreign investors and speculators began selling pesos, forcing the government to use its financial reserves to defend the pegged exchange rate. During the first ten months of 1994, Mexico depleted its international reserves by more than $20 billion, falling from $28 billion in February to close to $6 billion in November.[35]

Because of continuing international monetary pressures, the Mexican government devalued its currency in December 1994 by 14 percent, allowing the peso-dollar exchange rate to increase from 3.5 to 4. Mexican officials hoped that this action would restore international confidence in the peso by expanding exports and cutting imports and thereby reducing the trade deficit. But rather than restoring monetary confidence, the government's action unleashed further speculation, forcing it to allow the peso to float freely. This later action led to an immediate further decline of 35 percent in the peso's value (to 6.3 pesos to the dollar). Only when international financial institutions, led by the United States, provided $50 billion in loan guarantees in late January 1995 did speculation on the peso ease significantly. Although foreign guarantees contributed to the stabilization of the peso's value, Mexico has maintained a flexible exchange rate since the 1994 monetary crisis. In the immediate aftermath of the crisis the exchange rate was about 5.4 pesos to the dollar; later in 1995, the rate stabilized at about 6.5 pesos to the dollar. As of October 1996 the exchange rate was 7.4 pesos to the dollar.

The 1994 monetary crisis had a profound impact on Mexican economic life. Although devaluation resulted in immediate increases in consumer prices, the imposition of governmental austerity measures—necessary in order to receive foreign loan guarantees—also resulted in significant economic hardships. The austerity measures were imposed in order to reduce governmental deficits, encourage savings and investment, and thereby encourage confidence in the Mexican economy. In response to these and other actions, Mexico's economy contracted dramatically, resulting in an overall loss in the standard of living of about 20 percent.[36] At the same time, the devaluation had an immediate salutary impact on international trade by increasing exports and reducing imports. In response to the peso's devaluation, Mexico's exports soared 31 percent in the aftermath of the crisis, while imports declined by 9 percent, resulting in a 1995 trade surplus of $7.4 billion.[37]

The Mexican monetary crisis of 1994 illustrates how international forces can profoundly affect the domestic economic life of a nation. When countries become integrated into the global economy, they gain access to foreign capital and commercial markets. But participation in the global economy also results in a loss of autonomy and control over national economic life, as the Mexican case so vividly illustrates.

(credits) is greater than its financial obligations (debits), the government has a *balance of payments surplus*. When the reverse occurs, a *balance of payments deficit* results. Modest, short-term balance of payments deficits or surpluses are not a problem. But persistent deficits are harmful, especially if the country is small and poor, because such imbalance will lead to a loss of confidence in an economy and its currency.

When countries purchase foreign commodities, they need foreign exchange, which can only be generated through exports. Thus, when states maintain a balance of payments surplus, they acquire reserves necessary for purchasing foreign goods and services. But when states run a balance of payments deficit, they generate insufficient reserves, and must seek additional revenues through loans, grants, and other financial flows if the demand for imports is to be met.

Issues in International Relations

Issue 16.1 The Balance of Payments

The balance of payments—the accounting system for recording a country's international financial activities—involves two types of transactions. The first, represented by the *current account,* includes exports and imports of merchandise and services, investment income and dividend payments, and foreign aid and other governmental transfers. The summary of all economic transactions in the merchandise and service account yields the *balance of trade.* The second type of financial transaction in the balance of payments is the *capital account,* a summary of all short-term and

long-term foreign investment inflows and outflows. A country's *official reserves* represent the foreign currencies, gold, and other financial assets that its central bank accumulates.

The balance of payments and the level of reserves are significant because investors' confidence in the value of a country's currency is influenced partly by the degree to which a country maintains an equilibrium in its current and capital accounts as well as the relative size of the financial reserves.

The Bretton Woods Monetary System

If international trade is to be carried out efficiently, there needs to be widely accepted rules governing international financial transactions. Benjamin Cohen, a leading political economist, argues that an efficient and stable international monetary system must provide three elements: *liquidity, adjustment,* and *confidence.*[38] To assure liquidity, a system must provide an adequate supply of international money (reserves) to finance trade and facilitate balance of payments adjustments among states. To assist adjustment, the system must provide an accepted means to resolve temporary national payments imbalances. And finally, the system along with the international reserve currency must enjoy the confidence of other states.

Given the absence of world government, the creation and maintenance of an international monetary system has depended on the voluntary cooperation of major powers. During the late nineteenth and early twentieth centuries, for example, the international monetary system was based on gold. Under the so-called *gold standard,* states pegged their currencies to gold, promising to redeem their currency for a particular quantity of gold. The system collapsed with the outbreak of World War I, when European powers moved to protect their gold stockpiles and ceased to back up their currencies with it. After a period of significant international monetary confusion, a new international monetary system was created toward the end of World War II. This arrangement, known as the **Bretton Woods monetary system,** was established by the Allied powers to facilitate international financial transactions, to foster global monetary stability, and to inhibit harmful, competitive monetary policies, such as those prevalent during the interwar period.

The system operated in accordance with four rules:

1. Exchange rates were to be fixed, allowing only for small shifts.
2. States could alter their exchange rate when fundamental balance of payments disequilibria developed, provided international consent was given beforehand.
3. A pool of international reserves would be created to assist states during periods of temporary balance of payments disequilibria.
4. The U.S. dollar would serve as the major currency of international exchange, with confidence in this currency assured by the United States' guarantee of convertibility of dollars into gold at $35.00 an ounce.

To implement these rules, the major powers established an international financial institution, the International Monetary Fund (**IMF**), to foster international fi-

Bretton Woods monetary system
The international monetary system, established in the aftermath of World War II, provides rules and institutions that facilitate the international convertibility of currencies and assist states facing significant financial crises.

IMF
A UN specialized agency that promotes international financial cooperation, exchange rate stability, and the availability of sufficient foreign exchange to facilitate efficient international trade.

nancial coordination. In particular, the IMF was to monitor and coordinate exchange rates and ensure international liquidity for carrying out transnational economic transactions. To assure an adequate pool of international reserves, an IMF reserve fund was created from member-states' contributions, which were to be assigned on the basis of countries' relative economic capabilities. The major powers' quotas, which determine their voting power in IMF decision making, were as follows in 1995: United States—17 percent, Japan—7 percent, United Kingdom—5 percent, Germany—5 percent, France—5 percent, and Canada—3 percent.[39] Three-fourths of each state's quota contributions are paid in the member-state's own currency and one-fourth in gold. In 1993, the IMF pool of international reserves was estimated at nearly $187 billion.

States are allowed to borrow from the IMF in order to settle international debts, up to 125 percent of their quota. As a precondition for loans, the IMF ordinarily insists on domestic austerity measures that will help correct the balance of payments disequilibria. Because IMF loans are normally associated with stringent financial requirements, developing nations often resent the economic demands of the IMF, especially when reduction in public expenditures leads to domestic strife, as was the case in Caracas, Venezuela, in March 1989 following the government's imposition of austerity measures.

Because the dollar was the key reserve currency under the Bretton Woods system, the increasing need for international reserves could only be satisfied through continued U.S. balance of payments deficits. In 1960 economist Robert Triffin pointed out that the dollar-exchange standard was fundamentally flawed because the availability of dollars could only be achieved through increasing U.S. indebtedness, a condition that would ultimately undermine confidence in the dollar.[40] By the late 1960s this is exactly what happened. As Western European economies gained strength relative to the U.S. economy, their currencies became undervalued relative to the dollar, thereby further exacerbating the U.S. balance of payments disequilibria. As a result of declining confidence in the dollar, foreigners converted their dollar holdings into gold.

In 1971 the U.S. balance of payments deficit soared to more than $10 billion, more than doubling what it had been at any time in the previous five years. To rectify this imbalance between the U.S. economy and that of other industrial states, President Richard Nixon imposed a number of radical economic changes on August 15, 1971. Specifically, Nixon stopped the convertibility of the dollar into gold and imposed a surcharge on U.S. imports from Europe and Japan until the dollar was devalued (decreased in value in relation to other currencies). Although Nixon's actions strengthened the American economy, ending the dollar's convertibility destroyed a key pillar of the Bretton Woods system. And when the IMF adopted a more flexible system of exchange rates in March 1973, it in effect brought the Bretton Woods system to an end.

The Post–Bretton Woods Monetary System

Since the demise of the Bretton Woods system, no orderly monetary system has replaced it. The post–Bretton Woods regime is essentially a "nonsystem" based on a mixture of exchange rates. The basis for this regime was laid at the IMF meeting in Kingston, Jamaica, in 1976. At the Jamaica conference, IMF member-states made the following decisions:

1. Floating exchange rates were legalized.
2. The role of gold in international reserves was reduced.
3. IMF quotas—that amount of money members contribute to the IMF—were increased, especially for OPEC members.

4. Economic aid to the Third World was increased.

5. The establishment of a currency's international value became the sole responsibility of each state.

According to one leading scholar, the actions taken at the Jamaica meeting represented the triumph of domestic autonomy over international rules.[41]

Although the post–Bretton Woods system does not provide the financial stability of the former dollar-gold system, the current norms have the advantage of greater flexibility in responding to the balance of payments disequilibria. Theoretically, under the new regime, a significant balance of payments deficit should result in less confidence in a state's national currency, and this should, in turn, lead to a currency's loss of value—either through the behavior of foreign exchange markets or through deliberate governmental action in lowering the value of a currency through *devaluation*. The decline in the currency's relative value should make exports more competitive, thereby contributing to the reestablishment of a balanced foreign trade account.

But the system has not worked this way, at least for the United States. As figure 16.3 suggested earlier, the U.S. trade position shifted dramatically during the 1980s, moving from a modest surplus in the late 1970s to a soaring deficit of close to $160 billion in 1987, and to more than $180 billion in 1995. As noted before, the perpetuation of a trade deficit normally leads to the weakening of a state's currency, but this has not happened to the dollar, in part because of heavy foreign (especially Japanese) investment in U.S. securities, and also because of the continuing confidence in the long-term prosperity and stability of the U.S. economy. As a result, foreign governments along with foreign exchange traders have maintained a high demand for dollars.

In order to cope with the expanding global trade, international reserves have increased greatly, rising from an estimated $129 billion in 1971 to more than $1.1 trillion in 1993. Most of these reserves are in the form of foreign currencies, with gold providing nearly one-third of the total. To meet the growing demand for international liquidity, the IMF established in 1969 a new reserve asset known as Special Drawing Rights (**SDRs**). The SDRs are a form of international "paper gold" assigned to IMF members in proportion to their institutional quotas in order to meet "paper" obligations among central banks of IMF member-states. Unlike gold, dollars, and other international currencies, SDRs are not used for meeting commercial and other financial obligations but only for settling accounts among central banks. As of 1993, total SDRs were valued at about $21.4 billion, or roughly 2 percent of the world's total international reserves.

Despite international pressures on the U.S. economy, the dollar remains the major international currency, accounting for more than 60 percent of total foreign exchange reserves. The German mark and the Japanese yen, by contrast, account for only 16 and 7 percent of the world's foreign exchange reserves, respectively.[42] The major reason for the dollar's preeminence is that the U.S. economy is still the strongest in the world. Two economists have written that the United States "remains in a class by itself in terms of international monetary relations by virtue of its immense economic size."[43]

SDRs
A supplemental source of international reserves created to facilitate international financial transactions. SDRs are assigned in proportion to state's institutional quotas.

THE TRANSFORMATION OF THE GLOBAL ECONOMY

One of the most important developments since the 1970s has been the dramatic expansion of the global economy. We noted earlier in this chapter that international trade, which increased to more than $4 trillion in 1994, has been rising at a much faster rate than global economic output. We also noted that foreign ex-

led to significant disparities in income, allowing the rich states to gain at the expense of the poor states.

Second, the structural approach assumes that economic expansion is a *zero-sum game* in which the rise in national income in one state comes largely at the expense of another. Because the wealth of the world is fixed, an increase in income by one country must necessarily result in a relative decline in the wealth of other countries. Thus, exploitation by the rich and powerful states is an inevitable consequence of wealth creation.

Third, the structural theory assumes that the capitalist world economy breeds economic inequalities within and among states by rewarding groups and nations that increase productive efficiency relative to other groups and nations. The increase of domestic inequalities is assumed to be a direct effect of free enterprise, whereas global inequalities are assumed to be a result of a liberal international economic order based on the free movement of commodities, capital, and money. To be sure, states can moderate domestic social and economic inequalities, as Western European states have done, through progressive social and economic policies. Similarly, the governments of industrial states have sought to moderate global inequalities by providing official economic assistance to LDCs and by encouraging the transfer of private capital. Although structuralists recognize that free enterprise is conducive to job creation, they believe that the social and economic costs of increased inequalities are unnecessarily high and harmful to the social fabric of human communities.

Finally, structural dependence assumes that the global capitalistic economy promotes economic dependence among the weak, developing nations. Economic dependence is developed by global business firms and sustained with the support of governments in the rich, capitalistic societies and with the support of business elites in the developing nations. According to this theory, dependence is harmful to nations because it impedes the development of indigenous political and economic structures.

Economic Strategies and Third World Poverty

Fundamentally, there are two different paths available to promote Third World development. As suggested in table 17.5, these paths are rooted in the two competing economic perspectives outlined earlier. The first path emphasizes job creation through free enterprise and the maintenance of a liberal international economic order that facilitates world trade. This path assumes that a rise in the standard of living is a direct by-product of a rise in economic output through increased productive efficiency. The second path emphasizes redistribution of existing resources, increased national economic autonomy, and reform of international economic structures.

As noted in chapter 15, the structuralist perspective dominated the political economy of most Third World countries during the 1960–1985 period. Countless developing nations pursued this policy in the belief that state regulation would facilitate national economic expansion and also limit domestic inequalities and protect the national economy from unfair foreign competition. But by the late 1980s, the structuralist perspective had lost much of its influence, and by the mid-1990s few developing nations remained publicly committed to illiberal, inward-looking economic strategies. Three factors contributed to the dramatic decline of structuralism's influence: (1) the collapse of communism; (2) the abysmal failure of economies pursuing a structuralist strategy; and (3) the extraordinary economic success of countries pursuing an export-oriented strategy. Because we have previously (in chap. 5) called attention to the significant influence of the collapse of

TABLE 17.5 Comparison of Economic Strategies

Theory	Strategy	Policy
Modernization	Economic growth Job creation	Encourage economic innovation Increase savings and investment rate Promote free enterprise domestically Encourage free trade internationally
Structural Dependence	Self-sufficiency	Curtail trade Limit foreign investment Increase controls over MNCs Provide debt relief
	Transform global economic order	Increase economic assistance to Third World Increase Third World influence in international economic institutions

Soviet communism and the dramatic shift in former Soviet-dominated countries toward more liberal economic policies, here we will briefly examine the impact of the second and third factors.

In *Preparing for the Twenty-First Century,* historian Paul Kennedy classifies developing nations as "winners" and "losers" on the basis of their recent economic performance. In his view, the clear winners are the East Asian newly industrializing countries (NICs), especially the "Gang of Four"—Hong Kong, Singapore, Taiwan, and South Korea. The biggest losers are the Sub-Saharan African countries. In 1965, for example, the East Asian NICs accounted for 1.5 percent of world manufacturers, while Sub-Saharan Africa accounted for 0.4 percent; two decades later the East Asian share had risen to 8.5 percent, while the Sub-Saharan Africa's share had declined to 0.2 percent.[26] Kennedy argues that several factors account for the NICs economic success: an effective national educational system, a high level of national savings, a stable government, public policies conducive to economic growth, and an emphasis on exports.[27]

The experience of the NICs and other Third World states suggests that free enterprise and unrestricted trade are more likely to improve living conditions than statist domestic economic policies or strategies of economic self-sufficiency. Countries that have pursued the latter strategies, such as Argentina, Cuba, Ethiopia, Ghana, and Tanzania, have experienced negligible economic growth. By contrast, countries that have pursued liberal international economic policies, such as Botswana, Hong Kong, Malaysia, South Korea, and Singapore, have experienced much higher rates of economic expansion. Perhaps the most dramatic example of the economic gains from a market-friendly strategy is China. During the heyday of Chinese Communism in the 1950s and 1960s, the nation experienced limited growth, with most development involving state industrial enterprises. But with the establishment of greater economic decentralization and increasing participation in the global economy, China's economy has grown at nearly 10 percent annually since 1985.

Because Third World poverty is chiefly a consequence of low productive capacities, the strategies promoting national economic self-sufficiency and curtailing international commerce are unlikely to promote economic growth. Indeed, the lack of international economic competition can lead to low growth and the protection of inefficient firms. Developing nations are, of course, highly dependent on the changing economic conditions of the international system. But, as Gilpin has noted, the developing nations' high level of dependency is not the cause of poverty and economic underdevelopment; rather, their weak and inefficient economies are themselves the source of dependency.[28] Thus, the challenge in Third World development is not to reduce dependence, but to promote job creation. Only with increased productivity will states be able to reduce their economic vulnerability and provide sustained job creation to meet the ever-rising needs of poor countries. Currently, the labor force in the Third World is estimated at 1.7 billion, but it will increase to more than 3.1 billion by 2025. This implies a need to create nearly 38–40 million new jobs every year during the next three decades.[29]

Because of continuing technological innovation, productivity has become increasingly efficient. Additionally, the continuing diffusion of modern capital and technology has caused the pace of economic growth to quicken, thereby increasing economic output in limited periods of time. It has been estimated that although Britain needed fifty-eight years to double per capita income after industrialization was introduced in the late eighteenth century, the United States needed forty-seven years (from 1829) and Japan needed thirty-four years (from 1885) to double per capita income. South Korea, by contrast, doubled its 1966 income in only eleven years, whereas China increased its national income in even less time.[30] Thus, in light of the quickening pace of economic growth, developing nations now have the potential to raise living standards in relatively brief periods of time. Whether or not countries are able to achieve high rates of sustained growth will depend in great measure on the public policies adopted by their governments.

PROMOTING SUSTAINABLE DEVELOPMENT

A significant number of scholars and public officials agree that if the quality of human life is to be improved in the LDCs, three developments must occur. First, economies must continue to expand, creating jobs for growing populations and increasing personal income in order to raise living standards. Second, countries must pursue strategies that foster **sustainable economic development.** Sustainable growth—defined as economic growth that assures enhanced living conditions for future generations—seeks to protect the ecosystem and to encourage the use of renewable resources by limiting the unnecessary depletion of natural resources. Third, governments should seek to redress significant income inequalities through domestic and international resource transfers. Our focus here is on the first challenge of job creation, because improved living conditions are impossible without economic growth. The imperative of protecting the environment, a concern given prominence at the 1992 Earth Summit (in Rio de Janeiro), will be examined in chapter 19.

Sustainable economic development
Economic growth that ensures the protection of the environment for future generations.

Although economists hold numerous theories about the causes of economic development, a widespread consensus exists about its essential requirements. Some of the most important required conditions for economic expansion include: access to investment capital, low inflation, technological innovation, an educated and skilled labor pool, adequate infrastructure, a stable political order, and a culture conducive to enterprise. Most importantly, modern economic scholarship suggests that governmental policies play a crucial role in fostering or impairing growth. Recent studies show that countries that have pursued broadly free-market policies—in particular, trade liberalization, secure property rights, and comparatively limited government expenditures—have grown faster than countries pursuing illiberal policies involving significant government controls and large public expenditures.[31]

Investment is essential if an economy is to grow. Even though domestic economic resources typically provide the foundation of a country's economic expansion, foreign resources can significantly expand the pool of investment capital. The principal sources of foreign capital are: (1) foreign direct investment, (2) foreign portfolio (indirect) investment, (3) bank loans, and (4) official development assistance.

Foreign Direct Investment

Foreign direct investment (FDI)
Direct ownership of business assets in a foreign country.

Foreign portfolio investment (FPI)
Ownership of foreign securities, such as stocks and bonds, thereby giving owners indirect control over business assets in a foreign country.

Fundamentally, foreign investment is carried out either directly or indirectly. **Foreign direct investment (FDI)** occurs when a business firm invests directly in a new or existing enterprise in a foreign country. FDI may take place when a firm establishes a new business in a foreign land, when it purchases controlling influence in a foreign business, or when it gains an interest (generally at least 10 percent) in a foreign business entity. Foreign indirect investment—known as **foreign portfolio investment (FPI)**—involves the purchase of foreign securities, such as stocks, bonds, and other financial assets, none of which involve direct control over an investment. Unlike FDI, FPI is a passive financial transaction. Because FPI is more closely associated with investment banking and commercial lending than with FDI, we examine this important source of foreign capital in the section on international lending later in this chapter.

Since the 1970s, the nature and role of FDI in the global economy has changed greatly. First, the growth rate of FDI has increased significantly, rising from an average annual outflow of $34 billion in the late 1970s to $350 billion in 1996 (see table 17.6). As a result of this extraordinary growth, the *total stock of FDI,* the total accumulated value of foreign-owned assets, increased nearly sixfold during the 1980–1996 period, rising from $518 billion to more than $3.2 trillion.[32] To a significant degree, the dramatic growth in FDI in recent years has been due to the widespread adoption of market-based reforms. Such reforms, which have involved increased privatization domestically and greater free trade internationally, have been implemented throughout Asia, Africa, and Latin America as well as countries formerly dominated by the Soviet Union.

A second major trend in FDI pertains to changes in the source, or outflows, of FDI. During the 1950s and 1960s, more than half of all FDI originated in the United States. Even as late as the late 1970s, about 47 percent of FDI outflows were from the United States. But during the 1980s this pattern changed significantly, with the U.S. FDI share falling to 11 percent in 1990 before rising again to about 20 percent during the 1992–1994 period. Japan's FDI share, by contrast, increased significantly during the 1980s, rising from 4 percent in 1980 to near 20 percent in 1990.[33] Other major foreign investment states include Canada, France, Germany, and the Netherlands. Of the total 1994 FDI stock in foreign countries, each major industrial country's share was as follows: the United States, 25.6 percent; the United Kingdom, 11.8 percent; Japan, 11.6 percent; Germany, 8.6 percent; the Netherlands, 6.1 percent; and Canada, 4.4 percent.[34]

A third major foreign investment development deals with the recipients, or inflows, of FDI. Because foreign investment capital moves to countries that offer the greatest long-term return on investment capital, it is not surprising that, throughout most of the Cold War era, the largest share of FDI went to the developed countries themselves. The largest recipient of FDI inflows was the United States, which in the mid-1980s received about 37 percent of total FDI inflows. During the early 1990s, the U.S. share declined to about 20 percent, whereas the Third World's FDI share increased. During the mid-1980s the LDCs were receiving about 16 percent of all FDI (about $20 billion annually), but by 1994 their share had risen to 37 percent ($84 billion). The largest beneficiary of this growth has been China, which in 1994 received $33.8 billion in FDI, or roughly 40 percent of all Third World in-

TABLE 17.6 Annual World FDI Inflows and Outflows, 1981–1996 (in billions of dollars)

	1981–1985* (annual average)	1986–1990* (annual average)	1991	1992	1993	1994	1995	1996
INFLOWS								
Central/Eastern Europe	—	—	2	4	6	6	14	12
Developing Countries	13	25	42	50	73	90	96	128
Developed Countries	37	130	115	120	139	142	206	208
TOTAL	50	155	159	174	218	239	317	350
OUTFLOWS								
Developing Countries	1	6	8	22	34	41	47	51
Developed Countries	47	163	190	180	205	210	291	295
TOTAL	48	169	199	201	239	251	339	347

Source: United Nations, *World Investment Report 1997* (New York: United Nations, 1997), pp. 303–12.* Data for 1981–1985 and 1986–1990 are from the *World Investment Report 1994.*

Rapid urbanization in Third World countries has resulted in massive slums, such as those in the Philippines.

flows. Other LDC economies that were major beneficiaries of FDI are listed in figure 17.4.

Most foreign investment in the Third World is made by large **multinational corporations (MNCs).** MNCs, sometimes called transnational corporations (TNCs), are firms owned by nationals of two or more states that carry out business enterprise in two or more countries. Because these MNCs are influential economic actors, they create political tensions and economic conflicts wherever they go, but especially in poor countries. On the one hand, MNCs provide investment income, technology, and a market for exports, thereby promoting more efficient production; on the other hand, they frequently threaten traditional cultures, foster economic inequality, and weaken existing social structures.

One major criticism of MNCs is that they decrease national autonomy. Peter Evans argues, for example, that although MNCs can help promote economic growth, they do so by increasing foreign dependence, a phenomenon he terms "dependent development."[35] Another criticism of MNCs is that they exacerbate income inequalities. The expansion of some domestic and international economic inequalities is, of course, inevitable because economic growth is itself associated with the rise of inequalities, especially in the early stages of development. However, as economist Simon Kuznets has shown, the growth of inequalities is only

Multinational corporations (MNCs)
Business enterprises that have productive or marketing activities in two or more states.

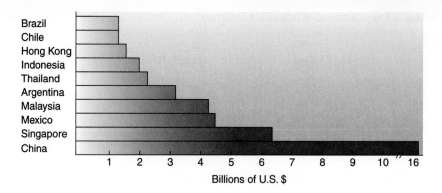

FIGURE 17.4
Average Annual FDI Received in Leading Emerging Economies, 1990–1994
Source: United Nations, *World Investment Report,* 1995 (New York: United Nations, 1995), pp. 392–95.

temporary, and as a society reaches higher levels of modernization, income becomes more equitably distributed. In effect, the process of economic growth involves a rise and fall in economic inequality.[36] To the extent that MNCs invest in developing nations that are themselves undergoing significant transformations, they are likely to contribute to modernization's short-term economic inequalities. But the long-term effect of foreign investment is likely to contribute to improvements in living conditions and ultimately, to a more egalitarian distribution of income.

Although numerous critics, especially dependency theorists, have suggested that MNCs have been detrimental to the less-developed countries (LDCs), Robert Gilpin argues that the available evidence does not support their claims. "On the whole," he writes, "the record of the multinationals in the developing countries is a favorable one." He points out that FDI can both help and harm them, but whether it results in domestic economic expansion will be determined by the country itself, because "the major determinants of economic development lie within the LDCs themselves."[37]

International Loans

International loans also play a key role in facilitating economic growth. Although multilateral financial institutions (e.g., the Inter-American Development Bank, World Bank) are an important source of capital for the developing nations, international private banks are the principal source of cross-border lending. Private international banks typically provide two types of services—commercial lending and investment banking. *Commercial banks* typically collect cash from individuals and firms in order to make *debt loans* to individuals, businesses, or governments. Debt loans require that a borrower repay a portion of the loan (principal plus interest) at specified intervals. Examples of international commercial banks include Citicorp, Chase Manhattan Bank, Credit Lyonnais, and Mitsubishi Bank.

Investment banks, by contrast, offer *equity loans* to business firms either by directly bringing together investors and borrowers (typically corporate firms) or indirectly by issuing and selling stocks and bonds. Because U.S. law prohibits commercial banks from providing investment services domestically, such loans are arranged by brokerage firms, such as Smith Barney, J. P. Morgan, Merrill Lynch, Salomon Brothers, and Morgan Stanley. By issuing and selling securities, investment firms make possible *foreign portfolio investment (FPI),* providing investment capital to business enterprises. In return for the investment, bondholders received a fixed return on their capital, while stockholders receive part ownership in a firm. Business firms honor shareholders equity claims by paying periodic dividends that rise and fall in response to their profitability.

As the pool of global capital has expanded, the role of investment banks has increased significantly because they have expanded their ability to transfer capital among countries. Because FPI provides a vital source of investment capital for

LDCs, it is likely that it will increase in importance as Third World countries seek to acquire additional capital in response to increased privatization and market reforms. During the early 1990s, FPI in the Third World increased dramatically, replacing commercial lending as the major source of foreign capital in many developing nations. Although bank loans accounted for 77 percent of all foreign capital flowing into the LDCs in 1981, by 1993 portfolio investment accounted for 74 percent of such flows, overshadowing both commercial lending and FDI.[38] FDI will of course continue to play a central role in the global economy. But in view of FDI's higher risks and greater potential political conflicts with host governments, FPI is likely to grow much more rapidly in the future than FDI.

The second type of lending institution is multilateral financial institutions, such as the IMF and the World Bank. Like private investment banks, these institutions raise a significant portion of their capital in the international market, but they are also partly financed and regulated by the governments of major industrial powers. Although their level of lending is much smaller than that of commercial and investment banks, multilateral institutions play an indispensable role in the economic development of Third World countries by providing loans at concessionary rates and by encouraging governments to establish sound fiscal and monetary policies. They perform this latter task by making loans conditional on the establishment of sound financial reforms.

The International Bank for Reconstruction and Development (IBRD), or **World Bank,** was established in the aftermath of World War II as part of the original Bretton Woods system. The IBRD is owned by the more than 150 states that have contributed to its capital stock, which in 1993 totaled $166 billion. To finance its loans, the World Bank borrows money from the international capital markets, using its existing capital to provide concessionary lending to poor countries. In its early years, the IBRD provided loans for the rebuilding of European economies. Once this was accomplished, the World Bank turned its attention to the development of the Third World.

World Bank
Originally established to help finance post-World War II reconstruction of Europe, this IGO now serves as the principal source of multilateral lending for developing nations.

The World Bank makes loans to governments only, and its charter requires that all loans must be for "productive purposes" that are likely to foster economic expansion. As a result, IBRD makes loans for particular projects, such as infrastructure development, but it does not provide financial help to alleviate a trade deficit or a balance of payments problem. During the 1990–1994 period, new World Bank lending averaged $15.8 billion per year.[39] Although lending by the World Bank and other international financial institutions remains essential to many poor developing nations, the relative significance of public international financial transfers has decreased since the 1980s. In 1993, for example, net private capital flows (e.g., FDI, indirect or portfolio investment, commercial loans) were many times larger than public capital flows to the developing nations.[40]

To more effectively meet the financial needs of developing nations, the World Bank established three subsidiary institutions. The first, the *International Development Association (IDA),* provides concessionary loans to the poorest developing nations. Borrowers typically have fifty years to repay the loan, and the interest rate is generally less than 1 percent a year. About 40 percent of all World Bank lending is channeled through the IDA. The second institution, the *International Finance Corporation (IFC),* fosters private sector development in Third World nations. The IFC functions much like an investment bank, facilitating and supplementing equity loans for commercial developments. The third World Bank affiliate is the *Multilateral Investment Guarantee Agency (MIGA),* established in 1988 to encourage FDI in low-income countries by providing insurance against noncommercial risks. The aim of MIGA is to provide protection against political risks in developing nations.

The **global capital market,** which can be defined as the institution by which investors make available cross-border loans to firms and governments, has increased dramatically in both size and the level of integration. For example, in 1980 total

Global capital market
The transnational institution that facilitates cross-border lending by firms and governments.

international commercial lending was estimated at $324 billion, but by 1991 it had increased more than twentyfold (to $7.5 trillion) and by 1993 by nearly fortyfold (to $12.5 trillion). Similarly, from 1980 to 1990, cross-border equities (stocks and bonds) transactions increased at a compound rate of 28 percent annually, rising from $120 billion to $1.4 trillion.[41] As a result of these and other global financial developments, a truly transnational capital market has emerged in the modern world.

The dramatic growth of cross-border financial flows is due to several developments. First, the growth of the global capital market is a direct by-product of the increasing demand for foreign investment capital. Second, it is due to increasing economic deregulation, a development that has spawned a thirst for investment capital for which economic transition is being implemented. Third, the growth in the global capital market is due to modern information technology, which provides an efficient and nearly instantaneous means by which to carry out cross-border financial transactions. Because of advances in international data processing and global communications, the international capital market involving stocks, bonds, foreign exchange, and other financial services, is an efficient, ongoing operation.

Much of the growth of foreign indebtedness during the 1970s and 1980s occurred in the Third World, with nearly 40 percent accounted for by Latin American countries. According to one estimate, Third World debt in 1970 was estimated at $100 billion,[42] but by 1992 it had risen to $1.4 trillion (see fig. 17.5). The major Third World debtor states in 1992 were: Argentina ($46 billion), Brazil ($82 billion), China ($46 billion), Egypt ($34 billion), India ($61 billion), Indonesia ($45 billion), Mexico ($76 billion), and Venezuela ($25 billion). Given the scope of sudden indebtedness, one U.S. newsweekly observed wryly that "never in history have so many nations owed so much money with so little promise of repayment."[43]

In comparison with foreign investment, commercial loans have the advantage of allowing Third World states to control the use of capital. But this increased control comes at a price. First, the borrowing nation must pay interest on the loan; and second, the government must bear the risk of possible failure. If a foreign firm fails, for example, the government is deprived of tax revenues but does not lose any capital. On the other hand, if indigenous institutions are not successful, they must still meet their foreign debt obligations. As the 1980s Third World experience demonstrates, loans can be risky for the borrowing states because if the capital is not used productively, or if international economic conditions impede the development of the export sector, countries will be unable to fulfill foreign debt obligations. This is, of course, what happened in the early 1980s when the Third World debt crisis first arose (see case 17.1).

FIGURE 17.5
Foreign Debt of Third World Nations, 1982–94 (in billions of U.S. dollars)
Source: International Monetary Fund, *World Economic Outlook, May 1991,* (Washington, D.C.: IMF, 1991), p. 193. Data for 1982 is from IMF, *World Economic Outlook, May 1990,* (Washington, D.C.: IMF, 1990), p. 185.

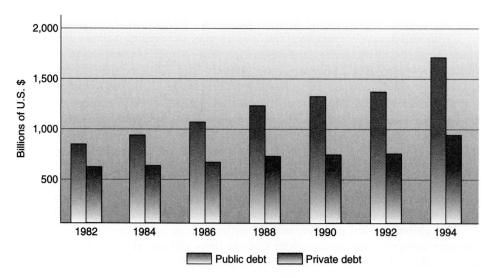

Case 17.1 The Third World Debt Crisis

The **Third World debt crisis** that developed in the early 1980s was rooted in an exorbitant level of debt and a declining capacity to fulfill loan obligations. Because loan obligations were rising faster than export revenues, Third World **debt-service ratios** (the relationship of debt-service payments, including interest and principal, to export revenues) increased significantly. From 1980 to 1986, for example, the average ratio for indebted developing countries increased from 16 percent to more than 22 percent, and for some severely indebted countries in Latin America the ratios rose to more than 35 percent.[44]

Two major global developments contributed to the severity of the crisis. First, an international economic recession in the early 1980s reduced global demand, resulting in major declines in export earnings. Second, interest rates increased dramatically during this recessionary period, in great part because much of the Third World's foreign debt was based on variable interest rates. Indeed, most of the rise in Third World indebtedness in the late 1970s and early 1980s was from the compounding of inflated interest rates, rather than from the original principal. But external sources were not the only contributing factors to the debt crisis. Many foreign loans were not used productively. Instead of investing the capital in productive ventures, a large portion of the foreign resources was used for increased consumption or simply transferred to foreign banks. One international bank estimated that by 1982 about $87 billion of Mexican, Brazilian, and Argentine capital had been deposited in foreign bank accounts.[45] Another source estimated that nearly 70 percent of Argentina's foreign loan had been invested abroad.[46]

When the debt crisis first emerged, developed countries responded by treating it as a temporary liquidity imbalance that could be resolved through domestic austerity programs, rescheduling of debt payments, and the provision of new loans. But this strategy did not work well. In 1985 U.S. Secretary of the Treasury James Baker outlined the so-called **Baker plan,** which called for increased economic austerity, a further rise in commercial and multilateral lending coupled with the implementation of market-oriented reforms. This strategy was also largely ineffective because commercial banks, fearing additional losses, refused to grant further loans to highly indebted states, even though debtor governments were unwilling or unable to institute significant privatization reforms. Most importantly, the imposition of austerity reforms demanded by the International Monetary Fund decreased investment confidence and reduced economic growth to a near standstill, thereby exacerbating capital outflows.

In 1989 Treasury Secretary Nicholas Brady, Baker's successor, unveiled a new, more radical debt strategy. Unlike the Baker plan, which emphasized debt rescheduling, the **Brady plan** sought to stimulate economic growth through debt reduction. The aim of the Brady plan was to reduce the foreign debt of the fifteen major Third World debtor states by about 20 percent (roughly $20 billion). According to the plan, the IMF, the World Bank, and leading economic powers would support *debt-forgiveness*, provided LDC-debtor states encouraged increased privatization and maintained monetary stability. For states meeting these conditions, the IMF and the World Bank would make available funds to facilitate debt reduction by guaranteeing the sale or conversion of part of the foreign debt at deeply discounted prices. As a result of the Brady initiative, a number of debtor states, including Argentina, Brazil, and Mexico, signed debt accords that reduced their foreign commercial debt.

By the early 1990s the foreign debt crisis had greatly eased for most middle-income states. This was due partly to agreements signed under the Brady plan but also due to the fall of interest rates, the growing productive efficiency of economies, and the rising demand for Third World exports. By 1996, however, the situation for the poorest debtor states had not improved. Indeed, national economic conditions deteriorated for some of them. The most serious threats to human dignity were in the highly indebted states, most of which were in Africa, that had debts ranging from 200 to 2,300 percent of annual export earnings. Some of these countries included Burundi, Congo, Haiti, Ivory Coast, Mali, Mozambique, Nicaragua, Rwanda, and Uganda. Because of worsening human conditions in these countries, the World Bank and the IMF were exploring ways to forgive up to 67 percent of poor, highly indebted countries.[47] As of 1997 no debt-relief plan had been implemented for these poor nations.

Moreover, even if countries invest capital wisely, increased participation in the global economy will inevitably increase countries' vulnerability to the forces of global financial markets. Thus, when investors and speculators began losing confidence in the financial policies and economic structures of South and East Asian countries in 1997, the currencies and stock markets of many countries, including Indonesia, Malaysia, Singapore, South Korea, and Thailand, experienced declines of 20 to 40 percent. These dramatic economic shifts reverberated throughout the world, including the economies of the industrial states, whose stock markets briefly declined 3–6 percent. Brazil, an emerging economy increasingly dependent on foreign capital, was especially damaged, with a stock market decline of more than 20 percent.

Foreign Aid

Official development assistance (ODA)
The loans and grants that governments give bilaterally and multilaterally to developing nations in order to foster economic expansion.

Foreign economic assistance, generally called **official development assistance (ODA),** involves bilateral and multilateral loans and grants to LDCs in order to assist their economic growth. It has been estimated that developed nations gave more than $1.1 trillion (1988 constant dollars) in ODA during the Cold War era.[48] Although most of this aid was transferred bilaterally, about $370 billion was provided through multilateral financial organizations. Historically, ODA has been given to encourage economic development. In the immediate aftermath of World War II, foreign aid was used for the reconstruction of Europe, but beginning in the mid-1950s, aid was given chiefly to Third World nations, with the poorest LDCs receiving the largest amount of ODA. In 1990, for example, low-income countries received more than 60 percent ($29 billion) of all economic aid, an amount representing 2.8 percent of their GNP.[49]

When compared with other cross-border financial transfers, ODA was the largest source of foreign capital during the Cold War, slightly exceeding FDI. But beginning in the early 1980s foreign investment became an increasingly important source of capital, displacing ODA as the chief source of external capital in the mid-1980s. (See fig. 17.6.) Since 1990, commercial lending and other private cross-border financial transfers have become the largest source of international financial transfers.

Historically, the largest donor of foreign aid has been the United States, providing more than $233 billion in net ODA during the Cold War era.[50] Even as late as 1985 the United States provided about one-third of all ODA, but since the late 1980s, the U.S. share of ODA has declined to less than one-fourth. In 1988, Japan

FIGURE 17.6
Foreign Aid and Direct Foreign Investment to Developing Countries (in billions of current U.S. dollars)

Source: Data from David Halloran Lumsdaine, *Moral Vision in International Politics: The Foreign Aid Regime, 1949-1989* (Princeton: Princeton University Press, 1993), p. 35.

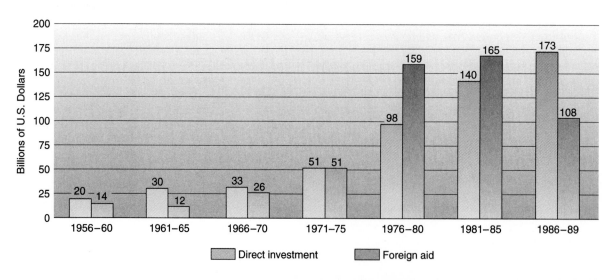

CHAPTER 17: PROMOTING THIRD WORLD DEVELOPMENT

promised to give developing nations $50 billion over a five-year period. As a result of this commitment, Japan became the largest foreign aid donor, providing nearly $9 billion in 1989 alone.[51] As of 1993, it remained the top donor, giving $11.3 billion compared to $9.7 billion for the United States.[52]

Why do states provide foreign economic assistance? One reason is political. Because foreign aid is a tool of statecraft, it can be used to influence and reward regimes and to promote friendly relations. During the 1950s and 1960s, for example, the most common justification for U.S. foreign aid to developing nations was that it helped establish preconditions for democracy, thereby combating the spread of communism. Because poverty and backwardness were thought to be the breeding grounds for revolutionary communism, economic growth was viewed as an important precondition for establishing representative democracy.

A second reason why states provide aid is to promote economic development in the poor nations. According to the economic rationale, aid is given both because it increases the living standards of citizens in the receiving state and also because it is in the long-term economic interest of donor-states. Although the immediate aim of economic assistance is to stimulate economic expansion in the receiving state, aid is also given because the prosperity of developing nations encourages new markets for the donor's exports. In effect, this view assumes that what is good for the poor states is also good for rich states, and vice versa. This view, widely accepted among Western political leaders during the Cold War, was set forth in the influential Brandt Commission Report, which investigated the strengthening of North-South relations in the late 1970s.[53]

Moral values provide a third justification for giving aid. As noted in chapter 7, moral norms are an important element in the development and implementation of foreign policy. According to the moral argument, countries with bountiful resources have a moral obligation to assist countries that are poor and destitute, regardless of the causes and sources of their poverty. The case for aid is not based on the existence of significant income disparities within or among countries, but rather, is rooted in human needs themselves. While in office, Secretary of State Cyrus Vance (1977–1979) articulated this rationale as follows:

> One reason this nation has a foreign aid program is that we believe we have a humanitarian and moral obligation to help alleviate poverty and promote more equitable economic growth in the developing world. We cannot be indifferent when half a billion people are hungry and malnourished, when 700 million adults are illiterate, and when one and a half billion people do not have minimal health care. As a free people who have achieved one of the highest standards of living in the world, we cannot fail to respond to such staggering statistics and the individual lives they encompass.[54]

In an important study of foreign aid, David Lumsdaine found that moral values were in fact a major determinant of Western ODA. He suggests that the major rationale for giving aid was donor-states' humanitarian concerns, not their political or economic interests as has been alleged by some critics of foreign aid.[55] For Lumsdaine, the origins and growth of ODA during the Cold War era can only be explained by the moral and humanitarian concerns of donor-states.

Despite the great needs of the low-income countries, some scholars and public officials oppose official aid.[56] Aid critics argue that ODA, among other things, encourages economic waste, strengthens corrupt regimes, overpoliticizes the economic development process, and results in inefficient and at times counterproductive investments. Most importantly, some authors, including British economist P.T. Bauer, argue that official aid to Third World nations tends to harm the productive capacities of nations by reinforcing existing inefficient practices and policies.[57] The problems and failures of official aid are nowhere better illustrated than in Sub-Saharan Africa. During the 1970s the West poured in some $22.5 billion in aid, most of it geared to agriculture, yet by the mid-1980s African agricultural production had not only failed to increase but had actually declined. Indeed, by the mid-1980s, the West was pouring in more than $7 billion annually into Africa in order to prevent starvation.[58]

Economic assistance can contribute to job creation only if the financial resources are channeled into productive investments. To minimize fraud, waste, and political corruption, governments are channeling development aid increasingly through nongovernmental institutions and nonprofit development associations, seeking to bypass the host government as much as possible. In addition, development strategies are placing greater emphasis on the development of human qualities instead of the transfer of tangible resources.

In the final analysis, an LDC will be able to carry out sustainable development only if it achieves significant economic growth. And such growth will be possible only when countries establish the preconditions for successful business enterprise. External financial resources—whether from FDI, FPI, bank loans, or ODA—can of course play an important role in expanding the pool of investment capital. But such resources are not sufficient. Countries themselves must establish values, practices, and institutions that support and sustain an environment conducive to economic growth. At a minimum, they must institute cultural, social, political, and economic norms and conditions that are associated with what economists have termed "competitiveness" (see issue 17.2). Some of these prerequisites include:

culture	emphasis on material improvements; future-oriented; rational decision making; entrepreneurship is valued; high level of honesty and frugality; planning and savings
society	education and training are given priority; high level of literacy and skills; science and technology are emphasized; high level of trust and cooperation; a modern infrastructure that facilitates efficient communications and transportation of goods and services
politics	a stable political order; a limited government that protects civil rights; effective prevention and prosecution of crime; limited corruption
economics	a stable monetary system; protection of property rights; limited governmental interference in economic life; full participation in the global economy

In addition to growth, sustainable development requires that special measures be undertaken to protect the ecosystem for future generations. Moreover, it may also require governmental intervention to limit significant income inequalities within society as well as to provide assistance to peoples suffering from poverty. Although ecological and social policies are important, they will only be possible if a nation achieves sufficient economic expansion to make possible increased living standards. The challenge, in sum, is to foster economic growth.

In Conclusion

Although most Third World countries have achieved significant social and economic modernization in the past two to three decades, a large portion of the world's population continues to suffer from disease, malnutrition, hunger, and lack of shelter. Although many factors have contributed to these conditions, a fundamental reason for the continuing, and in some cases worsening, poverty of many Third World regions is the failure of job creation to keep pace with population growth. And because modernization often results in significant human and structural discontinuities, poverty is often a by-product of economic expansion as well.

Issue 17.2 National Economic Competitiveness

Beginning in the late 1980s, the World Economic Forum (WEF) and the International Institute for Management Development (IMD), two Swiss-based organizations concerned with economic development, began publishing an annual "World Competitiveness Report." *Competitiveness* can be defined as the "ability of a nation to achieve economic growth and a rising standard of living, even while exposed to international trade and capital flows."[59] The WEF/IMD report ranks leading industrial countries in terms of their international economic competitiveness. In response to criticisms of the report's rankings, the WEF modified its methodology for measuring competitiveness. In 1996 the WEF therefore issued a report separate from the one prepared by the IMD, and not surprisingly, its rankings differ slightly (see table 17.7). It is significant that of the top twenty countries in the WEF ranking, seven are Third World countries.

Economists differ about the significance of the competitiveness of nations. For example, Paul Krugman, an influential American economist, has argued that competitiveness is unimportant in international economic relations because countries, unlike firms, do not compete in the same way. When business cor-

porations compete, he suggests, one firm's gain is the other's loss. But because international trade is not a zero-sum game, when countries compete internationally, they all win. As a result, Krugman claims that excessive concern with national competitiveness can distort economic priorities and encourage unwise (protectionistic) international economic policies.[60] However, other political economists, especially those identified with the neo-mercantilist strategy (see previous chapter), claim that states inevitably engage in economic competition as they seek to maximize national income. The relative economic success (competitiveness) of countries in the global economy will depend upon their relative capabilities to maximize growth with full employment and thereby increase the standard of living for its inhabitants.

From a perspective of political economy, measures of economic competitiveness can highlight the relative abilities of a nation to successfully participate in the global economy. Although such measures are not comparable to the competitiveness of a business firm, the WEF and IMD rankings are useful in providing rough measures of countries' comparative economic potential.

TABLE 17.7 Rankings of National Economies, 1996

Country	WEF	IMD	Country	WEF	IMD
Singapore	1	2	Denmark	11	5
Hong Kong	2	3	Australia	12	21
New Zealand	3	11	Japan	13	4
United States	4	1	Thailand	14	30
Luxembourg	5	8	Britain	15	19
Switzerland	6	9	Finland	16	15
Norway	7	6	Netherlands	17	7
Canada	8	12	Chile	18	13
Taiwan	9	18	Austria	19	16
Malaysia	10	23	South Korea	20	27

Source: *The Economist,* June 1, 1996, p. 76.

Thus, poverty is a problem not only in low-income countries but also in many middle-income countries.

In light of the enormous human needs in the Third World, developed nations can contribute to human dignity by providing material aid to relieve hunger and disease in the poorest LDCs and by assisting in the process of job creation. Although many of the poorest nations need significant humanitarian aid to meet immediate human needs, the major long-term challenge in the low-income countries is to promote and facilitate economic expansion that results in job creation in the regions of greatest poverty. Developed countries can help improve the social and economic welfare of people suffering from poverty by providing technical, material, and educational assistance that encourages job creation.

SUMMARY

1. Poverty remains one of the major problems of the contemporary international system. Despite significant economic growth during the Cold War era, a significant portion of the Third World's population continues to suffer from severe poverty.

2. One factor contributing to Third World poverty is the high rate of population growth. Many of the poorest nations have the highest rates of population expansion.

3. Two basic strategies have been advocated to reduce poverty. The first assumes that the most effective way of caring for human needs is to redistribute resources within states and within the international system. The other strategy assumes that only continuing economic expansion can solve the needs and wants of a growing population.

4. Countries that have relied on state-directed economic strategies of economic growth and limited international trade have been less successful in promoting economic expansion than those with market-oriented economic strategies.

5. Economic growth requires investment. The most important sources of investment capital are FDI, FPI, bank loans, and ODA. Because of increasing foreign demand for capital and because of increasing integration of global telecommunications, a large, dynamic capital market has emerged that greatly facilitates global financial transactions.

KEY TERMS

less-developed countries (LDCs)

purchasing power parity (PPP)

human development index (HDI)

demographic transition theory

modernization theory

structural dependence

sustainable economic development

foreign direct investment (FDI)

foreign portfolio investment (FPI)

multinational corporations (MNCs)

World Bank

global capital market

Third World debt crisis

debt-service ratio

Baker plan

Brady plan

official development assistance (ODA)

RECOMMENDED READINGS

Cassen, Robert, and associates. *Does Aid Work?* New York: Oxford University Press, 1986. This study, commissioned by eighteen governments, surveys the theoretical and empirical literature on economic aid, explores the impact of aid through seven case studies, and then offers a number of recommendations for strengthening the impact of aid.

Donnelly, Jack. *Universal Human Rights in Theory and Practice.* Ithaca: Cornell University Press, 1989. An incisive examination of the nature of human rights in light of competing cultural traditions and historical contingency. The study explores trade-offs between human rights and development as well as problems involved in the international defense of basic rights.

Kennedy, Paul. *Preparing for the Twenty-First Century.* New York: Basic Books, 1993. Kennedy explores how transnational forces in a modern world of increasing interdependence, instant communications, expanding threats to the environment, and exploding population are likely to affect developed and developing nations in the future. Especially noteworthy are Kennedy's comparison of China and India (chapter 9) and Third World winners and losers (chapter 10). An informative, provocative study.

Lairson, Thomas D., and David Skidmore. *International Political Economy: The Struggle for Power and Wealth,* 2nd ed. New York: Harcourt Brace, 1997. A superior introduction to international political economy. More than half of the book's chapters focus on the Third World, with special attention given to trade, foreign aid, FDI, and commercial lending.

Lumsdaine, David Halloran. *Moral Vision in International Politics: The Foreign Aid Regime, 1949–1989.* Princeton: Princeton University Press, 1993. A comprehensive analysis of postwar economic assistance, focusing on sources, recipients, purposes, and the historical evolution of the aid regime. The study claims that morality played a decisive role in contributing to aid transfers.

Packenham, Robert H. *Liberal America and the Third World: Political Development Ideas in Foreign Aid and Social Science.* Princeton: Princeton University Press, 1973. Although dated, this study remains a penetrating description and assessment of the ideas that inspired early postwar U.S. foreign economic aid.

Seligson, Mitchell A., ed. *The Gap Between Rich and Poor: Contending Perspectives on the Political Economy of Development.* Boulder: Westview Press, 1984. An invaluable collection of theoretical and empirical studies on the economic inequalities between rich and poor countries.

Singer, Max. *Passage to a Human World.* Indianapolis: Hudson Institute, 1987. Singer argues that the extension of economic modernization to developing nations will result in improved living conditions worldwide and eventually lead to reductions in global economic inequalities. A highly optimistic view of the future.

Wilber, Charles K., and Kenneth P. Jameson, eds. *The Political Economy of Development and Underdevelopment,* 5th ed. New York: McGraw-Hill, 1992. A collection of theoretical, historical, and topical studies relating to the process of economic development in the Third World.

World Bank. *World Development Report 1992: The Challenge of Development.* New York: Oxford University Press, 1992. A detailed and penetrating assessment of the prospects for social and economic development in the Third World, richly illuminated by tables and graphs. Statistical appendices provide an invaluable source on socioeconomic data in the developing nations. More recent editions of this annual report provide more recent social and economic data.

RELEVANT WEB SITES

Humanitarian relief site	www.reliefweb.int
Institute of Development Studies (IDS) See databases	www.ids.ac.uk/dbases.html
International Affairs Network (IAN) Economic development resources	www.pitt.edu/~ian/resource/develop.htm
International Institute for Sustainable Development (IISD)	http://iisdil.iisd.ca/

International Relations and Security Network (ISN)
    See the following subjects:
        Development
        Economics and Trade
	www.isn.ethz.ch/

Socioeconomic Data and Applications Center (SEDAC)	http://sedac.ciesin.org/
United Nations Development Programme (UNDP)	www.undp.org
U.S. Agency for International Development (AID)	www.info.usaid.gov/
World Bank See: Topics on development	www.worldbank.org/html/extdr/thematic.htm

18 Controlling Weapons Proliferation

Disarmament, no less than the armaments race, is a reflection of the power relations among nations concerned. . . . As the armaments race aggravates the struggle for power through the fear it generates and the burdens it imposes, so disarmament contributes to the improvement of the political situation by lessening political tensions and by creating confidence in the purposes of the respective nations.[1]

Hans J. Morgenthau, *international relations theorist*

Two paths lie before us. One leads to death, the other to life.[2]

Jonathan Schell, *author*

The major military danger now facing the United States is not a particular country but rather a trend: nuclear proliferation.[3]

Michael Mandelbaum, *IR scholar*

The time when we can say goodbye to nuclear weapons is still far distant. . . . Until that time comes, we must live with our weapons as responsibly and as quietly as we can.[4]

Freeman Dyson, *noted U.S. physicist*

In 1994 the total number of persons participating in the armed forces of all states was 23.5 million, representing approximately 4.2 soldiers for every 1,000 persons. Moreover, governments spent in that year more than $840 billion on military defense (roughly $142 for every human being) to train and sustain these military personnel, as well as to develop, produce, or purchase weapons. This amount represented 3.0 percent of the world's total 1994 economic output (GNP) and more than 10 percent of all central government expenditures.[5] Military defense was thus the largest single governmental expenditure—higher than health, education, or social programs.

As noted in earlier chapters, because each state is ultimately responsible for defending its territory and for promoting its national interests, governments maximize their military power by maintaining large and well-equipped military forces. This quest for national security often results in competition in military capabilities among two or more states, resulting in the growth of armed forces and the modernization of weapons. Although military defense is a legitimate governmental expenditure, the quest for security can also result in excessive defense allocations and the misuse of public funds. In addition, the growth and modernization of the armed forces can encourage arms races that ultimately reduce national security. In chapter 3 we noted that, because of the security dilemma, increases in military forces might result in less national security. An increase in military forces by one state could lead to reciprocal increases by others, thereby negating potential benefits from original defense expenditures. Thus, if the quest for national security is not to result in senseless arms races among states, governments need to cooperate in managing military resources.

This chapter explores the problem posed by the expansion of armed forces and the continuing modernization of weaponry. It also explores how governments have tried, individually and collectively, to regulate the proliferation of arms. More specifically, this chapter (1) examines the impact of weapons proliferation on global politics; (2) describes the threat posed by weapons of mass destruction; (3) compares the major strategies for managing military weaponry—namely, disarmament and arms control; and (4) describes and assesses major disarmament and arms control initiatives, focusing on nuclear weapons accords.

THE NATURE OF THE PROBLEM

The growth and modernization of armaments poses three types of problems. First, continued weapons modernization can result in greater destruction in wartime. Second, continued arms proliferation can exacerbate political tensions and increase the possibility of war. Finally, the continued expansion of military weaponry can lead to a misallocation of scarce public resources. Each of these factors is briefly examined in this chapter.

Increased Destructiveness

The history of modern warfare illustrates graphically the growing lethality of weaponry. Originally warfare was carried out at close range through swords, knives, and mechanical instruments. By the thirteenth and fourteenth centuries firearms were being developed and refined, which further increased the lethality of warfare, although casualties were chiefly the result of direct physical killing. By the eighteenth century, muskets had become more accurate, gunpowder had become more efficient, and artillery had become more powerful. As a result, a typical battle would have resulted in more than two-fifths casualties from musket fire, two-fifths casualties from field artillery, and less than one-fifth casualties from swords and bayonets.[6] By the nineteenth century rifles had become the chief armament of military forces. In the American Civil War, for example, of the 622,000 soldiers who died in battle, the largest share were killed by rifle bullets, whereas only a small percentage were killed by artillery shells or swords and bayonets.[7]

Two military developments revolutionized warfare in the early twentieth century—the development of the machine gun and the development of trench warfare. The enormous loss of life in World War I (about 20 million persons) was due largely to artillery bombardment of trenches coupled with the use of machine guns. The most extraordinary technological development in the history of armaments has been the invention and application of nuclear physics to military weapons. As noted in chapter 10, nuclear and thermonuclear arms are so destructive that they provide the potential for destroying a significant portion of the earth.

Destruction in Tel Aviv, Israel, from an Iraqi Scud missile attack carried out during the 1991 Persian Gulf War.

Arms Proliferation

Vertical proliferation
An increase in the number and capability of military weapons within existing states. Refers especially to nuclear armaments.

Horizontal proliferation
The spread of modern type of weapons to more states. Refers especially to nuclear armaments.

Weapons proliferation can be of two sorts. **Vertical proliferation** involves a numerical increase, or qualitative improvement, in the military capabilities of individual states. The growth in a country's military armaments, such as an increase in the number of tanks or jet aircraft or the development of new types of bombs or missiles, represents this type of proliferation. For example, the Cold War superpower nuclear arms race, which resulted in a dramatic increase in the nuclear arsenals of the Soviet Union and the United States, illustrates vertical weapons proliferation. **Horizontal proliferation,** by contrast, involves the spread of modern weapons to new states. Such proliferation entails a growth in the number of states possessing particular types of modern weapons, such as intermediate-range ballistic missiles or chemical or biological weapons. For example, the expansion in the number of states with nuclear capabilities and ballistic missiles represents horizontal proliferation.

Weapons proliferation is a problem in the international community because it can exacerbate global instability and even stimulate war. Because the interrelationship between weapons, international political disputes, and war is complex and ambiguous, scholars and statesmen have historically held a wide variety of perspectives on this subject. Three "ideal-type" perspectives are depicted in figure 18.1.

The *realist perspective*—rooted in the priority of power—assumes that the perceived insecurity of states leads governments to acquire more powerful military armaments and larger military forces. The fundamental cause of international conflict is not arms races but rather political disputes among states. Hans Morgenthau has noted that "Men do not fight because they have arms. They have arms because they deem it necessary to fight."[8] The explanatory power of this approach is clearly evident in the dramatic decline in the superpowers' and their allies' military expenditures in the post–Cold War era. U.S. military expenditures declined from $365 billion in 1986 to $288 billion in 1994, while Warsaw Pact countries' expenditures declined from a peak of $450 billion in 1988 to $112 billion in 1994, a 75 percent reduction.[9] The end of the political conflict between the East and the West had thus reduced global ideological conflict and national insecurity, permitting states to carry out deep cuts in military forces.

Unlike the realist approach, the *idealist perspective* assumes that armaments themselves are the source of the problem. Specifically, this perspective assumes that the proliferation of arms breeds suspicions and increases political tensions that, if unresolved, can lead to war. Arms races among neighboring states or nations involved in political and economic conflicts can thus greatly exacerbate political tensions.

FIGURE 18.1
Comparative Perspectives on Politics, Arms, and War

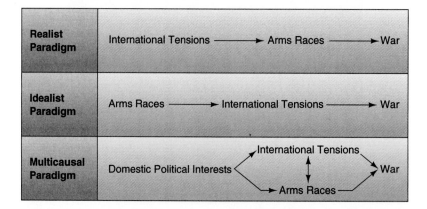

The *multicausal perspective* emphasizes the interrelated nature of politics, arms, and war, incorporating both realist and idealist perspectives. According to this view, weapons acquisitions arise not only in response to arms proliferation of adversaries and political tensions in global society, but also in response to domestic political demands. As a result, war, arms races, international tensions, and domestic political influences all interact with each other, thereby contributing to the rise or decline of arms races, interstate tensions, and war.

Regardless of which approach is used in assessing weapons and global conflict, it is clear that weapons modernization and proliferation can threaten the peace and stability of the world. Although arms races may provide short-term benefits to some states, they also may result in counterproductive outcomes to individual states and to the international system itself. Thus, in seeking to prevent and limit international violence, the challenge in global society is to collectively manage armaments and establish stable political conditions within and among states.

Misuse of Scarce Resources

Military weapons are costly and can deprive states of scarce financial resources that could be used in meeting domestic human needs. For example, a study of the U.S. nuclear weapons program during the 1940–1995 period estimates that the total cost of the program was more than $4 trillion.[10] Of course, major wars are far more costly. A 1948 estimate of the military, economic, and commercial cost of the two world wars translates into about $22 trillion in mid-1990's currency.

Arms races among states competing for regional or global influence can be especially costly. The political tensions and insecurity in the Middle East, for example, has led many of the region's major countries, including Jordan, Kuwait, Iraq, Israel, and Saudi Arabia, to devote a large percentage of national resources to military security. Indeed, since the early 1980s, the Middle East has remained the region with the largest level of arms imports (accounting for more than 40 percent of the world's total) and the highest burden of military expenditures to economic output (accounting for 15–18 percent of GNP during the 1984–1992 period).[11]

The impact of arms races was especially evident in the U.S.-USSR military competition during the Cold War. For example, in the late 1970s the Soviet Union began deploying intermediate-range nuclear ballistic missiles (SS-20) in Europe. NATO regarded the unilateral introduction of such missiles as unacceptable because it altered the fundamental balance of power in Europe. As a result, NATO officials devised a "double-track" policy calling for the elimination of the new Soviet class of missiles, and, in the event that production and deployment were not halted, they threatened to deploy a similar type of ballistic missile. Thus, when the Soviet Union failed to heed NATO's demand, the United States began deploying modern intermediate-range (cruise and Pershing II) ballistic missiles in West Germany and Britain in 1983. Four years later, both superpowers signed the Intermediate Nuclear Forces Treaty calling for the elimination of all intermediate-range nuclear missiles. In effect, the costly U.S. development and deployment of these forces achieved one objective—the elimination of Soviet weapons.

Finally, the misuse of scarce public funds is especially evident in the global arms trade. Although the end of the Cold War has greatly contributed to a decline in total weapons imports from a high of $83 billion in 1984 to $22 billion a decade later (see fig. 18.2), developing nations continue to demand modern, sophisticated armaments from developed countries. In 1990, for example, the developing nations purchased foreign arms worth $37 billion, or about 70 percent of the total arms imports.[12] The largest share of these weapons went to the Middle East (52 percent) and East Asia (17 percent). Figure 18.3 identifies the major arms importers during the 1970s and 1980s.

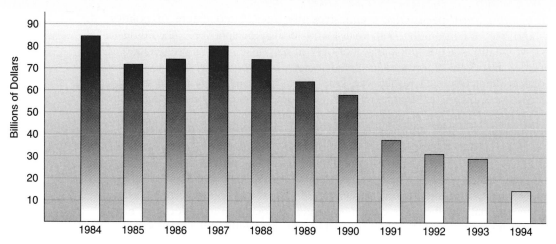

FIGURE 18.2
Total World Arms
Exports, 1984–94
Source: U.S. Arms Control
and Disarmament Agency,
World Military Expendi-
tures and Arms Transfers,
1995 (Washington, D.C.:
ACDA, 1996), p. 103

THE THREAT OF UNCONVENTIONAL WEAPONS

There are two types of unconventional armaments: chemical/biological and nuclear/thermonuclear. Although chemical/biological weapons can be extraordinarily dangerous, they are less destructive than nuclear/thermonuclear weapons. As a result, chemical/biological weapons are often viewed as an intermediate category of arms between conventional and nuclear.

Chemical and Biological Weapons (CBW)

Chemical weapons (CW)
Weapons that use chemical agents to injure and kill.

Biological weapons (BW)
Weapons that disperse lethal microorganisms in order to spread diseases and epidemics.

Chemical weapons (CW) use inert chemicals (e.g., nerve agents, mustard gas, and toxins) to injure or kill. **Biological weapons (BW),** by contrast, use microorganisms (e.g., viruses and bacteria) to cause disease and death in human, animal, and plant life. Even though both CW and BW are extraordinarily lethal, BW are considered much more dangerous to society and morally unacceptable because of the lack of control over the effects of such weapons. Because microorganisms can multiply indefinitely, once the anthrax, cholera, or typhus germs have been disseminated, for example, controlling the epidemic is extraordinarily difficult.

Germ warfare and chemical gas agents have been around since the early twentieth century. And although there has been no documented use of biological weapons in wartime, this is not the case for chemical arms. During World War I chemical weapons were used extensively and caused great destruction among sol-

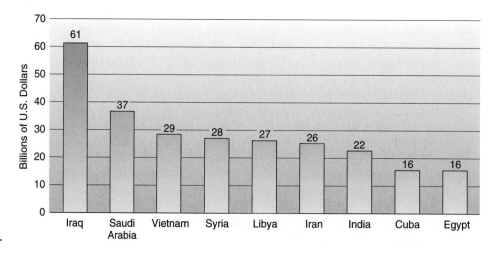

FIGURE 18.3
Leading Arms
Importers,
1969–1988
(billions of dollars,
cumulative)
Source: Data from Ruth
Leger Sivard, *World Mili-*
tary and Social Expendi-
tures, 1991. (Washington,
D.C.: World Priorities,
1991).

diers and civilians. Hitler had significant stockpiles of CW but did not use them, perhaps because he feared that the Allies would have responded in kind. And during the Iran-Iraq war, Iraq allegedly used CW on numerous occasions. According to an Iranian published report, during the war Iraq carried out 242 CW attacks, resulting in 44,000 casualties.[13] And in the late 1980s, Iraq began using CW against civilian populations, such as the Kurds in the northern area of Iran. The most destructive of these civilian attacks was carried out in March 1988 against the village of Halabja, resulting in some 3,000 to 5,000 victims.[14] During the 1990 Persian Gulf War, extensive preparations were taken by U.S. military forces to cope with the possibility of Iraqi chemical attacks. Because Iraq had acquired short-range SCUD ballistic missiles capable of delivering chemical agents, Israel, fearing CW attack, disseminated gas masks to all civilians before the start of the war. Although Iraq carried out many SCUD missile attacks against Israel and Saudi Arabia during the war, none involved chemical weapons.

In 1989, the U.S. Arms Control and Disarmament Agency estimated that some twenty states had a CW capability. At the time, however, only two states—the Soviet Union and the United States—had publicly admitted having a CW capability. In 1987 France announced that it would develop a CW capacity, and it was widely believed that by the early 1990s it had developed a small arsenal of CW bombs. And even though Iraq is alleged to have used chemical weapons in its war with Iran in the 1980s, Iraq had never officially declared its CW capability. But in the aftermath of the Gulf War, allied forces and UN inspectors confirmed that Iraq had acquired a significant arsenal of CW. Moreover, arms control officials have also classified China and Iran as CW states. Other countries suspected of having CW are listed in table 18.1.

Because chemical weapons are viewed as the "poor man's atom bomb," some Third World governments have been eager to acquire CW capability in the belief that such weapons would enhance national prestige and military power. Because of the relative ease of acquiring the necessary elements for developing such weapons, as well as the difficulty in detecting and monitoring CW facilities, horizontal proliferation of CW, especially to unstable developing nations, is a major contemporary global concern.

Because biological weapons are prohibited by international law, no country has declared its capacity to build and deploy BWs. Still, a number of countries,

TABLE 18.1   Confirmed and Probable Chemical Weapons States, 1997

Confirmed CW States		
France	Iran	Iraq
India	Russia	United States
Probable CW States		
Belarus	Bulgaria	China
Croatia	Czech Republic	Egypt
Hungary	Indonesia	Israel
Libya	North Korea	Pakistan
Romania	Serbia	Slovak Republic
Slovenia	South Africa	South Korea
Syria	Ukraine	Vietnam

Source: Author's estimate based on the Arms Control and Disarmament Agency, *World Military Expenditures and Arms Transfers, 1989* (Washington, D.C.: ACDA, 1989), p. 21 and news reports.

including China, Libya, Iran, Iraq, Syria, and Russia, are known to possess BW capability.[15] Perhaps the most recent blatant disregard for the international prohibition against BW was by Iraq during the Persian Gulf conflict of 1990, when some 200 bombs and warheads were loaded with several toxic agents, including botulin, the most poisonous substance known. It has been estimated that inhalation of a minute trace causes death in 80 percent of victims within three days.[16] Although arms control officials had assumed that Iraq had the capability to build BW munitions, not until 1995 were Western sources able to conclusively prove that Iraq had developed a significant BW arsenal.[17]

Nuclear Arms

The most powerful weapons ever developed are the atomic and hydrogen bombs. Because of their enormous destructive potential, nuclear arms cannot be easily encompassed by traditional modes of strategic thinking. Because they are instruments of mass destruction, they pose a radical challenge to international politics in general and foreign policy in particular. For the first time in history, government officials have the capacity not only to influence foreign affairs, but also to threaten the world itself.

The continued development of nuclear arsenals has posed two types of challenges to global society. The first involves minimizing the risk of war between nuclear powers; the second involves the limitation of horizontal nuclear proliferation, especially to unstable Third World states. During the Cold War the challenge of minimizing the possibility of nuclear war focused chiefly on the United States and Soviet Union. Because they were engaged in an intense ideological and political contest, and because they possessed more than 90 percent of the world's nuclear destructive power, scholars assumed that the risk of nuclear war, whether intentional or accidental, would be related to this global conflict.[18] Moreover, because each superpower possessed close to 25,000 nuclear weapons, the principal challenge faced by American and Soviet statesmen was to minimize the risks of nuclear war. Thus, the challenge of arms control was not necessarily to reduce or eliminate weapons, but to limit the incentives for their use. Now that the Soviet Union has collapsed and the Cold War has ended, the risk of major war between the nuclear powers has greatly receded.

The major challenge in the post–Cold War era is nuclear proliferation. The disintegration of the Soviet Union resulted in four potential nuclear powers—Belarus, Kazakstan, Russia, and Ukraine. Although all nuclear weapons formerly stationed in Belarus, Kazakstan, and Ukraine have been transferred to Russia, the disintegration of the second largest nuclear power has greatly increased the danger of nuclear proliferation, particularly in the transfer of nuclear technology and weapons-grade nuclear fuels to nonnuclear states. Because of major economic dislocations within Russia and other former Soviet republics, the scientific personnel and resources of the nuclear arms program of the former Soviet Union are increasingly vulnerable. Although Russian officials have sought to establish increasing control over the nuclear industry, the knowledge and technology of the former Soviet defense establishment will remain potentially vulnerable to foreign bribes, blackmail, and extortion. The potential danger of proliferation was amply demonstrated in August 1994, when German authorities seized 363 grams of plutonium from a commercial aircraft arriving in Munich from Moscow. In addition, six months later police in Prague seized 2.7 kilograms of weapons-grade enriched uranium, arresting a Czech, a Russian, and a Belarussian with ties to the nuclear industry.[19]

Charles Krauthammer has suggested that the primary source of instability in the post–Cold War world will come from Third World countries that possess weapons of mass destruction and missiles to deliver them. The states most likely to acquire modern, highly destructive weapons are what Krauthammer calls "weapon states"—aggressive, nondemocratic, resource-rich states like Iraq, Iran, Libya, and Syria. Krauthammer argues that "the proliferation of weapons of mass destruction and their means of delivery will constitute the greatest single threat to world security for the rest of our lives."[20] Although none of these four "weapon states" has developed nuclear arms, the first three are viewed as prospective nuclear states. Indeed, until the 1991 Iraq-Kuwait war, Western governments had thought that Iraq was four to five years away from developing a nuclear capability. But in the aftermath of the war, UN inspection teams discovered a much more advanced nuclear weapons program. In fact, to the surprise of most arms control experts, the UN teams confirmed that Iraq had developed a number of small-scale methods for developing weapons-grade nuclear fuel.

As of 1998, the world had five declared nuclear weapons states—China, France, Great Britain, Russia, and the United States. Five other states are believed to have acquired the technology and the fissionable material necessary for the construction of nuclear weapons. These five states are:

India: First tested a nuclear device in 1974 and then, the the surprise of most Western leaders, carried out five underground tests in mid-1998; one of the explosions was a hydrogen bomb; estimated to have the capability to build twenty to fifty nuclear bombs.

Israel: Thought to have obtained nuclear capabilities in the late 1960s or early 1970s; estimated to have capabilities for deploying fifty to a hundred atomic bombs; has reportedly developed tactical nuclear weapons based on the hydrogen-bomb principle.

South Africa: Thought to have obtained the capability to build nuclear bombs in the early 1980s; in 1993 it announced that it had built and then dismantled six nuclear weapons.

Pakistan: In response to India's nuclear tests, it carried out five underground tests in mid-1998; estimated to have the fissionable material for five to ten atomic bombs.[21]

North Korea: Although not officially confirmed, some observers suggested in the mid-1990s that it may have acquired the nuclear fuel to build four to five crude atomic bombs.

TABLE 18.2 Current and Prospective Nuclear States, 1996

Declared Nuclear Weapons States	Undeclared Nuclear Weapons States	Prospective Nuclear Weapons States	Renunciation of Nuclear Weapons Program
United States	India	Iran	Argentina
Russia*	Israel	North Korea**	Brazil
France	Pakistan		Iraq***
Great Britain			South Africa****
China			

*At the time of the Soviet Union's dissolution, nuclear weapons were deployed in four republics—Belarus, Kazakstan, Russia, and Ukraine. As of 1997, all strategic nuclear weapons had been transferred to Russia and destroyed or placed under Russian command.

**Unofficial reports in mid-1994 suggested that North Korea had built, or was close to building, several nuclear bombs.

***Iraq's nuclear weapons program was damaged greatly by Allied bombing in the 1991 Persian Gulf War. UN inspection teams have confirmed that Iraq was much closer to building a crude nuclear bomb than Western intelligence had originally estimated.

****In 1993 South Africa announced that it had built nuclear arms and subsequently dismantled them.

In addition to these five "probable" nuclear states, Argentina, Brazil, Iran, Iraq, Libya, and Taiwan have had active nuclear energy programs and are thought to be eager to acquire nuclear arms. As a result of the growth of populist, democratic sentiments in Latin America, both the Argentine and Brazilian governments declared in 1990 that they were not embarked on a nuclear weapons acquisition program. Iraq, which until 1991 was close to becoming a nuclear power, is no longer considered a "prospective" nuclear club member, because its nuclear program was heavily damaged in the 1991 Persian Gulf War and has subsequently been under careful UN scrutiny. In sum, although it is impossible to verify the nuclear status of these and other states, it is widely assumed that, as of 1998, the "nuclear club" has less than ten members. (See table 18.2.)

MANAGING WEAPONS PROLIFERATION

Disarmament Versus Arms Control

Disarmament
Bilateral and multilateral accords that reduce and eliminate military weapons in order to decrease the probability of war.

Arms control
Bilateral and multilateral accords designed to reduce the risk and destructiveness of war by regulating the number and type of military armaments. During the Cold War arms control referred chiefly to the management of nuclear arms.

Two alternative approaches exist for managing weapons proliferation: **disarmament** and **arms control.** The disarmament approach assumes that the best way to promote world order is through the reduction and possible elimination of the instruments of war. Idealistic in vision, disarmament assumes that the promotion of peace is best achieved by reducing and banning armaments, believing that the elimination of military weapons will facilitate international peace.

Arms control, by contrast, assumes that the quest for international peace cannot be achieved simply by reducing and eliminating weapons. Unlike disarmament, arms control seeks to strengthen deterrence and to reduce the risk of accidental or deliberate use of major weapons, especially unconventional arms. According to arms control, the possibility of war is not directly related to the numbers or sophistication of countries' weapons arsenals. Indeed, war is not assumed to be inevitable. Arms races do not lead inexorably to war. Because international order, like war, is a result of human choices, bilateral and multilateral strategies of conventional and nuclear arms control can influence the prospect for global order. The road to peace and international stability is thus partly determined by the nature and scope of weapons modernization and proliferation.

Arms control initiatives are generally guided by three objectives: first, they seek to reduce the risk of war; second, they seek to reduce the consequences of war in the event that deterrence fails; and third, they seek to reduce the size and costs of military forces. Of these objectives, the first is the most important. Moreover, what makes the quest for arms control difficult is that these goals are not al-

Superpower summits have played a key role in postwar diplomacy. Here Russian President Boris Yeltsin and U.S. President Bill Clinton meet in January 1994 in Moscow to sign an agreement to stop aiming long-range nuclear missiles at each other.

ways complementary. Indeed, the pursuit of one of these goals may often come at the expense of another. For example, the effort to reduce the risk of nuclear attack by developing a less vulnerable sea-based missile may be costly and contrary to the aim of cost reduction. At the same time, the failure to pursue the second and third goals may bring about developments that make peacekeeping more difficult in the long run. Arms control is therefore a difficult and often ambiguous quest, requiring diplomatic sensitivity and great moral courage.

The distinction between disarmament and arms control applies chiefly to nuclear arms. The reason for this is that the avoidance of war is a much more important goal for nuclear armaments than for conventional ones. In disarmament, the aim is to reduce the prospect for war, but it seeks to achieve this goal by reductions in the lethality and cost of weaponry. With nuclear arms, by contrast, the overriding objective is the avoidance of war altogether, even if increased expenditures or further vertical proliferation is involved.

Historically, war had been used as a means of settling interstate disputes. Conventional military force provided a means by which states could try to prevent, halt, or punish aggression. But whereas conventional weapons provide usable force to compel an enemy state, modern nuclear arms do not provide usable force. Because of their enormous, indiscriminate destructive potential, the primary usefulness of nuclear arms has been in deterring major aggression. Once it became clear that the "balance of terror" could not provide stable security indefinitely, the United States and the Soviet Union began exploring how these instruments of mass destruction could be managed to minimize potential nuclear conflict, especially the accidental use of such weapons. The challenge of arms control has thus been to manage the development and deployment of new strategic weapons systems without increasing the risk of nuclear conflict.

During the Cold War, the arms control perspective dominated the national security policy of the superpowers. But with the end of the Cold War, the disarmament perspective has gained adherents among scholars and government officials. One arms control theorist, for example, has recently suggested that, in view of the disintegration of the Soviet Union, the major powers should eliminate ballistic missiles altogether.[22] The post–Cold War era demands, he believes, prohibition of nuclear arms, not simply their regulation.

Conventional Arms Disarmament

Since the beginning of the nineteenth century, there have been a growing number of initiatives to reduce conventional armaments and control military expenditures. A few of these have been successful; most have not. Undoubtedly the most successful nineteenth-century disarmament accord is the **Rush-Bagot Agreement.** The accord, originally signed in 1817 between the United States and Britain, provides for naval disarmament in the Great Lakes. The aim was to limit the United States and Britain (later Canada) to three patrol ships of equal size and military capacity. The accord, which was modified in the early 1940s to permit Canada to construct naval vessels in the Great Lakes during World War II, still remains in force.

A second example of successful disarmament is the 1922 **Washington Naval Treaty.** The accord involved the five major powers of the world—United States, Britain, Japan, France, and Italy—and called on these states to reduce their capital ships (i.e., battleships and aircraft carriers). The method for carrying out disarmament was to maintain the original ratio of naval power. This ratio was established as five for the United States and Britain, three for Japan, and 1.67 for France and Italy. Although of modest scope, the naval accord helped to reduce the number of battleships and to stabilize naval power among the major powers. However, because the agreement did not cover other ships, such as cruisers, destroyers, and

Rush-Bagot Agreement
An early nineteenth-century accord between the U.S. and Britain that provided for naval disarmament in the Great Lakes.

Washington Naval Treaty
A 1922 treaty between Britain, France, Italy, Japan, and the U.S. calling for reductions in the largest types of military ships.

submarines, the agreement tended to divert shipbuilding into unregulated areas rather than halt it.

A third illustration of successful disarmament is the 1990 **Conventional Forces Europe (CFE) Treaty**—an accord between NATO and the Warsaw Pact. The agreement places equal ceilings on NATO and Soviet-bloc states in five major conventional weapons categories—tanks, armored vehicles, artillery, helicopters, and combat aircraft. Because both NATO and the Warsaw Pact had weapons arsenals higher than the treaty's limits, both military alliances were required to carry out significant arms reductions. For example, Soviet-bloc states were required to reduce tanks and artillery pieces from an estimated 60,000 and 61,000 respectively, to 20,000 each by 1994. Because the arms accord was the result of more than twenty years of arms negotiations between the United States and the Soviet Union, the signing of the treaty in 1990 was hailed as a major breakthrough in East-West disarmament.

Since then, the treaty has been overtaken by subsequent events of even greater military and political magnitude, including the end of the Cold War, the dissolution of the Warsaw Pact, and the disintegration of the Soviet Union. Although CFE signatory states have agreed that the treaty should continue to influence European security affairs, some states, led by Russia and other former Soviet republics, have called for an adaptation of the CFE Treaty in light of the major political and military changes in the European landscape since the accord was signed in 1990. As a result member-states agreed at the 1996 *Organization for Security and Cooperation in Europe (OSCE) Summit* to begin negotiations on potential modifications in the CFE Accord. Some of the major issues being considered for treaty adaptation include: (1) replacing the existing treaty structure, based on the East-West divisions, with a more current structure; (2) adjustments in the geographic distribution of forces in order to inhibit destabilizing concentration of military forces; and (3) strengthening verification procedures. Despite the significant changes in European security affairs, and the potential modifications in the original accord, the CFE Treaty remains an important agreement, providing enhanced political security to Europe.

The Rush-Bagot Accord is sometimes cited as an example of the important role that disarmament plays in promoting peace. The historical record does not support this view, however. Throughout the early- and mid-nineteenth century, a number of violations occurred as British naval vessels were brought in to protect disputed territorial claims. It was not until Canada and the United States informally resolved their territorial disputes toward the latter part of the nineteenth century that the Rush-Bagot provisions were regularly implemented. Morgenthau has noted that the reason for the accord's triumph lies in successful political accommodation between the two countries. The lack of power competition that might lead to an armed quest for each other's territory constitutes, in Morgenthau's view, "the political precondition for the permanent success of naval disarmament on the Great Lakes."[23] Because of a high level of cooperation between Canada and the United States, the U.S.-Canadian border remains the longest unarmed frontier in the world.

Most efforts at comprehensive disarmament have had little effect on global politics. In 1899 and 1907, for example, two international peace conferences were held in The Hague to promote pacific settlement of disputes and to encourage global disarmament. Unfortunately, neither gathering was able to move beyond innocuous rhetoric about the control of military expenditures and the limitation of the size of military forces. The Hague Peace Conferences, however, contributed to the peace process in several ways, including the codification of rules of war and the promotion of global participation in peaceful conflict resolution.

When the League of Nations was established at the end of World War I, the new organization was charged with the responsibility of reducing "national armaments to the lowest point consistent with national safety" (art. 8 of the League Charter). The League's Council was given the responsibility to initiate disarmament programs and, after struggling for more than a decade with this issue, convened a World Disarmament Conference in 1932. Although this meeting met intermittently for more than two years, it was unable to reach agreement on any disarmament proposal.

Since its creation in 1945, the United Nations has also tried to promote disarmament initiatives, but with limited success. Originally the major responsibility for developing disarmament proposals was given to the UN Disarmament Commission. The commission was established in 1952 by the General Assembly and was gradually enlarged to include all UN members. In time, however, the major responsibility for promoting disarmament initiatives was transferred to a smaller, more specialized committee, known as the Conference on Disarmament. Comprised of forty countries, the conference holds regular sessions at its headquarters in Geneva. To promote greater concern for and awareness about disarmament, the General Assembly has sponsored special sessions concerned solely with the reduction of global armaments.

Some of the most successful disarmament measures have been specific conventions banning particular weapons systems. For example, some armaments that were considered inhumane have been banned—such as exploding bullets, which were banned in 1863, and fragmenting (so-called dumdum) bullets, which were prohibited by the Hague Convention of 1899. Recently, more than 120 states signed the **Land Mine Treaty** banning antipersonnel mines. UN officials estimate that some 110 million mines contaminate the land of sixty-four countries, killing or injuring more than 20,000 civilians annually. (See table 18.3.) Notwithstanding the danger posed by such weapons, some countries—especially those involved in domestic or regional strife—continue to rely heavily on such weapons. Indeed, although 100,000 mines are typically cleared each year, another 2–5 million more have been deployed in zones of conflict,[24] thereby increasing the threat to tens of millions of persons. The aim of the new treaty is to reduce the killing and suffering from antipersonnel mines by banning their production, use, stockpiling, or transfer. Interestingly, even though the United States supports the goals of the land

Land Mine Treaty
An international treaty, signed in 1997, that bans antipersonnel land mines.

TABLE 18.3   Deployment of Land Mines by Country, 1995

Country	Total Land Mines	Average Land Mines per Square Mile
Egypt	23,000,000	59
Iran	16,000,000	25
Angola	15,000,000	31
Afghanistan	10,000,000	40
Cambodia	10,000,000	142
China	10,000,000	3
Iraq	10,000,000	60
Bosnia-Herzegovina	3,000,000	152
Croatia	2,000,000	92
Mozambique	2,000,000	7
Eritrea	1,000,000	28
Somalia	1,000,000	4

Source: *New York Times,* October 8, 1995, p. E3.

mine convention, it refused to sign the accord because of its continuing use of mines in protecting its forces in South Korea.[25]

Chemical/Biological Weapons (CBW) Disarmament

As a result of the mass killing caused by chemical gases in World War I, major powers sponsored a conference in 1925 resulting in the first significant convention on chemical weapons. The **1925 Geneva Protocol,** eventually signed by more than 110 states, prohibits the use of chemical weapons, but it does not halt its production and stockpiling. As a result, numerous countries have developed a capability to build and deploy chemical weapons.

It has been estimated that the United States, Russia, and China possess nearly 90 percent of existing CW stockpiles. Because of increased concerns with the potential instability of its chemical weapons, the United States passed legislation in 1985 requiring the destruction of its CW stockpiles by the year 2004. Moreover, as a result of easing of East-West political relations in the late 1980s, the United States and the Soviet Union concluded a major CW accord calling for the reduction of CW stockpiles to a maximum of 5,000 tons by the year 2002. Although no major power has publicly declared the size of its CW arsenal, it was estimated that the U.S. arsenal in the late 1980s was close to 30,000 tons and that the Soviet arsenal was slightly larger than that.[26]

At the same time, the international community, encouraged by the major powers, sponsored a major disarmament conference in Paris in 1989 on the total banning of CW. As a result of this major diplomatic initiative, 130 countries signed the **Chemical Weapons Convention (CWC)** calling for the complete elimination of chemical weapons by 2007. The CWC became effective in April 1997 after seventy-five states, including the United States, had ratified it. As noted earlier, the CWC bans the development, production, acquisition, stockpiling, transfer, and use of chemical weapons. In addition, the CWC prohibits signatory states from helping any other country to do any of the above. To ensure compliance with its provisions, the CWC provides for the establishment of an organization (the Organization for the Prohibition of Chemical Weapons) to conduct routine and unannounced inspections of companies using chemicals covered by the treaty.

As a result of efforts by the UN Conference on Disarmament to ban BW, the conference adopted the **Biological Weapons Convention (BWC)** in 1972. The BWC is significant because it bans BW altogether, prohibiting the development, production, stockpiling, and use of biological and toxin weapons. As of 1995, 135 states had become party to the BW convention.

Cold War Nuclear Weapons Disarmament

Because of the danger posed by nuclear weapons, the most important arms control and disarmament initiatives during the Cold War were those concerned with nuclear arsenals. In the following sections we examine the most important bilateral and multilateral nuclear accords. First we address those that have been based on the disarmament approach; then we examine those that have been based on the assumptions of arm control.

Three different disarmament strategies were used in seeking to reduce the level of nuclear arms—freezing growth, reductions, and abolition.

Freezing Growth

The **nuclear freeze** initiative, the least radical expression of disarmament, sought to halt the arms race altogether by stopping further development and production

---

1925 Geneva Protocol
A convention that prohibits the use of chemical weapons.

Chemical Weapons Convention (CWC)
An international treaty requiring the complete elimination of chemical weapons.

Biological Weapons Convention (BWC)
An international treaty that prohibits the development, production, and use of biological weapons.

Nuclear freeze
A U.S. initiative to halt the nuclear arms race by stopping the testing, production, and deployment of nuclear arms.

of nuclear weapons. Until the late 1970s, antinuclear forces had concentrated their efforts on achieving a comprehensive ban of nuclear tests. But in 1982 a joint resolution was introduced into the U.S. Congress calling on the United States and the Soviet Union to achieve a mutual and verifiable freeze on the "testing, production, and future deployment of nuclear warheads, missiles, and other delivery systems."[27] Because of its simplicity, the freeze initiative gained immediate widespread support, not only in the United States but in Western Europe as well. Unlike the complex arms control proposals popularized in the 1970s, the freeze initiative provided a simple formula for a complex problem—the way to peace is to halt the arms race.

Despite the popularity of the freeze proposal, arms control experts criticized it. One problem they pointed out was the proposal's focus on numbers and its disregard for stability. According to some strategists, a sound arms control strategy involved eliminating weapons systems that were destabilizing and adopting strategies that reduced the risk of nuclear conflict. Another criticism was that the proposal was unverifiable. Even though experts admitted that the deployment of new warheads and missiles could be verified, many thought that the testing and production of new weapons could be concealed. Finally, the freeze proposal was criticized for only halting the development of nuclear weapons and not reducing existing arsenals.

Reductions

The second type of nuclear disarmament was the call for significant cuts in existing strategic arsenals. Underlying the reductions option was the belief that lower levels of nuclear weapons between the superpowers would contribute to international peace and stability. One of the early expressions of this option was articulated by diplomat George Kennan when he accepted the Albert Einstein Peace Prize in May 1981. In his speech he proposed a "bold and sweeping departure" involving an across the board 50 percent reduction in nuclear arsenals.[28] A year later President Reagan inaugurated the *Strategic Arms Reduction Talks (START)* with the aim of reducing ballistic missile warheads to about 5,000 for each superpower—or roughly one-half of the number they possessed at that time. After nine years of difficult and often painstaking negotiations, the first START Accord was signed in July 1991 by Presidents Mikhail Gorbachev and George Bush. In contrast to the original Reagan proposal calling for a 50 percent reduction in strategic weapons, the START I Accord called for a 30 percent reduction in strategic warheads.

The notion of deep cuts, like the freeze initiative, was simple and attractive. Several justifications were given for major reductions: First, deep cuts would decrease the total destructive nuclear potential of states and thereby decrease the possibility of a "nuclear holocaust"; second, deep reductions would decrease the economic waste involved in maintaining redundant weapons; and third, major reductions would model peaceful and constructive behavior.

At the same time, the "deep cuts" strategy raised significant issues. Thomas Schelling, for example, questioned the importance of reductions as a way of promoting peace, especially because nuclear strategists had been unable to identify an optimal weapons level.[29] Critics of deep cuts also pointed out that a lower number of warheads, although potentially desirable, was less important than how the strategic arsenal was distributed. They claimed that such reductions could contribute to strategic instability because of the increased vulnerability of land-based nuclear forces. This situation might occur because of the incentive to eliminate older, less accurate single-warhead ICBMs and to keep the newer, more accurate hydra-headed MIRVed missiles. If this were to happen, the ratio of warheads to potential targets would increase, thereby weakening deterrence.

Abolition

Abolition—the complete elimination of nuclear warheads—was the most radical option available for regulating superpower nuclear weapons. Because it was impossible to eliminate knowledge of nuclear physics, nuclear abolition did not call for the destruction of nuclear technology but only for the elimination of weapons. In *The Abolition,* Jonathan Schell proposed a policy in which deterrence would be based on the capacity to build bombs, not on the bombs themselves. This capacity—which Schell defined as *"weaponless deterrence"*—provided the delayed capability to punish a nuclear aggressor without requiring the maintenance of nuclear bombs. Schell believed that a world with 50,000 nuclear weapons was a dangerous place and assumed that, if nuclear arms were eliminated, the world would be safer. Even if a superpower conflict were to develop under such a regime, the conflict would be much less destructive than in an international environment with thousands of strategic nuclear weapons.

Unlike the other two disarmament options, abolition was never seriously considered by the superpowers. The closest they came to adopting such a proposal was at the October 1986 summit meeting in Reykjavik, Iceland. At the meeting, Soviet leader Mikhail Gorbachev proposed cutting strategic nuclear weapons in half and President Reagan responded by suggesting their complete elimination over a period of ten years. But the proposed elimination of strategic nuclear missiles was scuttled when President Reagan refused to halt the U.S. Strategic Defense Initiative.

Cold War Nuclear Arms Control

The key elements of arms control were developed in the late 1950s and early 1960s after both superpowers acquired significant nuclear arsenals. Although the U.S. nuclear monopoly in the late 1940s led to an enhancement of American military power, the Soviet Union's acquisition of such weapons in the early 1950s tended to cancel whatever advantages the United States had possessed early on. Once the United States lost its nuclear monopoly, a chief challenge in global politics was to ensure stable superpower relations and to avoid a major military confrontation that might lead to nuclear conflict. The fundamental challenge, therefore, was to manage superpower strategic capabilities, and this became the central mission of arms control during the Cold War era.

Principles

Stable deterrence
A condition where nuclear aggression is unthinkable because of the certainty of unacceptable retaliation.

The central premise of Cold War arms control was the need to reduce the risk of nuclear war. According to nuclear strategists, the most effective way of maintaining peace and preventing nuclear conflict was through the promotion of stable superpower relationships and, more particularly, through **stable deterrence**—a condition for which no adversary could perceive an advantage in resorting to nuclear aggression. Three conditions were considered necessary for such stability: (1) population and industrial targets of an adversary state had to be vulnerable; (2) strategic nuclear forces had to be relatively invulnerable to a surprise attack; and (3) strategic forces had to be capable of carrying out assured destruction. Although the scope of retaliation was not unimportant, the emphasis was on the capacity of carrying out unacceptable punishment, not the magnitude of destruction.[30]

Because of the need for stability in superpower nuclear relations, both the soviet Union and the United States were especially concerned with technological developments that might weaken deterrence. Developments that could potentially reduce strategic stability included improvements in submarine detection (making the sea-based strategic missiles vulnerable and thereby decreasing the capacity to retaliate credibly), expansion of a civil defense program (decreasing the vulnerability of industrial and population centers), and deployment of a strategic defense system. Although paradoxical, strategic defense coupled with strategic offense was viewed as less stable than a purely offensive nuclear capability. In this connection Charles Krauthammer noted that "weapons aimed at people lessen the risk of war; weapons aimed at weapons, increase it."[31]

Agreements

From the late 1950s through the late 1980s, the United States and the former Soviet Union concluded numerous arms control agreements. In addition, a number of multilateral accords were developed to minimize further weapons proliferation. Fundamentally, four types of nuclear accords were signed: (1) those regulating nuclear testing; (2) those reducing the risk of superpower nuclear conflict by improving communication links and control over their weapons; (3) those preventing horizontal proliferation or prohibiting nuclear arms in particular geographical regions; and (4) those limiting the further proliferation of the superpowers' arsenals. Table 18.4 lists the principal accords in the first three categories.

In addition to the Limited Test Ban and Nonproliferation Treaties, the most important Cold War arms control agreements were those that placed limits on the superpowers' nuclear arsenals. The five most important accords limiting vertical proliferation were: the Antiballistic Missile Treaty (ABM) of 1972, the Strategic Arms Limitations Talks (SALT) Agreement of 1972, the SALT II Treaty of 1979, the

TABLE 18.4   Major Cold War Arms Control Agreements, 1960–1990

Year	Agreement	No. of States*	Provisions
Nuclear Testing Limits			
1963	Limited Test Ban	M	Bans nuclear weapons testing in the atmosphere, space or underwater
1974	Threshold Test Ban	B	Limits underground testing of weapons with a yield of 150 kt or less
Reduction of Nuclear War Risks			
1963	"Hot-Line" Accord	B	U.S. and USSR establish a direct teletype link for use during a crisis
1971	Nuclear Accidents Accord	B	U.S. and USSR establish measures for reducing risk of accidental or unintended use of nuclear weapons
1973	Prevention of Nuclear War Accord	B	U.S. and USSR establish measures to reduce the risk of nuclear war
1984	"Hot-Line" Modernization	B	Further improves U.S.-USSR communications links for use in a crisis
1987	Crisis Centers	B	Establishes communication centers in Moscow and Washington
Prevention of Nuclear Proliferation			
1959	Antarctic Treaty	M	Bans military activity in the Antarctic
1967	Outer Space Treaty	M	Prohibits military activity in outer space
1967	Treaty of Tlatelolco	M	Prohibits nuclear weapons in Latin America
1968	Nonproliferation Treaty	M	Prohibits acquisition of nuclear arms by nonnuclear powers
1971	Seabed Treaty	M	Prohibits placing nuclear weapons on the ocean subsoil beyond territorial waters (12 miles)

*M—multilateral; B—bilateral

Intermediate Nuclear Forces (INF) Treaty of 1987, and the Strategic Arms Reductions Talks (START) Treaty of 1991. Because of the significance of these agreements, we briefly examine each one in the following sections.

Limited Test Ban Treaty
A 1963 U.S.-USSR treaty, subsequently ratified by many other states, banning atmospheric nuclear tests.

Limited Test Ban Treaty The **Limited Test Ban Treaty,** adopted in 1963, bans nuclear testing in the atmosphere, outer space, and underwater. Only small, underground tests are permitted. Although more than 120 states have ratified the treaty, it has been important primarily to existing nuclear states, especially the superpowers, which from 1945 to 1996, accounted for some 1,745 nuclear explosions, or more than 85 percent of the total. The treaty does not eliminate nuclear testing but simply seeks to regulate its scope and location. Nor does the agreement seek to regulate the frequency of the tests. Indeed, whereas the superpowers carried out 529 nuclear tests before the signing of this accord (i.e., from 1945 to 1963), in the two decades following the adoption of the test ban accord (1964 to 1985) the superpowers carried out 874 tests, or nearly a third more than when there was no treaty.[32] Thus, the test ban accord represents a modest accord in regulating a specific aspect of the arms race. In the words of Michael Mandelbaum, it was a "preface" to arms control.[33]

NPT
This 1968 treaty seeks to curb horizontal proliferation of nuclear weapons.

Nonproliferation Treaty (NPT) The **NPT,** signed in 1968 and put into effect in 1970, attempts to limit the spread of nuclear arms to other states. It prohibits nuclear states from transferring nuclear resources and technology to nonnuclear states; moreover, nonnuclear states are prohibited from developing or acquiring nuclear arms. The accord also requires that nonnuclear states accept international safeguards, implemented by the *International Atomic Energy Agency (IAEA),* in order to inhibit the diversion of nuclear energy from peaceful uses to the construction of nuclear explosives. Although all declared nuclear powers, including Belarus, Kazakstan, and Ukraine, had signed the NPT, a number of major potential nuclear powers, including Brazil, India, Israel, and Pakistan, had not signed the treaty as of 1995.

According to provisions in the original accord, signatory states were required to review the treaty twenty-five years after it had become effective in 1970. As a result, officials from 170 states gathered at the United Nations headquarters in New York in mid-1995 to determine whether to modify, extend, or terminate the treaty. After significant lobbying by the major powers, especially the United States, representatives from the signatory states agreed by acclamation to extend the NPT permanently and without conditions. By making the NPT a permanent international accord, the international community has accepted the unequal distribution of nuclear weapons, affirming that only the five declared nuclear states (Britain, China, France, Russia, and the United States) are entitled to possess nuclear arms.

A major criticism of the NPT is that it discriminates against nonnuclear states because it limits states without nuclear arms but not existing nuclear powers. By freezing the number of eligible members of the "nuclear club," it favors states that already have nuclear capabilities. In effect, the NPT controls horizontal proliferation without controlling vertical proliferation. Not surprisingly, the renewal of the NPT was bitterly opposed by some states, which viewed the inegalitarian character of the accord as unfair.

Controlling proliferation can also be carried out apart from the NPT regime. For example, in 1991 both Argentina and Brazil, which at the time had not signed the treaty, concluded an important bilateral accord that achieved many of NPT's objectives, including a pledge not to build nuclear weapons and comprehensive inspections of each other's nuclear facilities under the supervision of the Vienna-based IAEA.[34] In addition, countries may unilaterally renounce nuclear arms. For example, in 1993 South African President F.W. de Klerk disclosed that his country had built nuclear bombs but that it was renouncing nuclear arms altogether. De Klerk indicated that all nuclear devices would be dismantled and that IAEA inspections would be encouraged.[35] This extraordinary development is significant because it represented the first time that a nuclear power voluntarily gave up its nuclear status. The decision by the new governments of Belarus, Kazakstan, and Ukraine to sign NPT and to transfer their nuclear arsenals to Russia is a major step in limiting nuclear proliferation.

ABM Treaty   The **Antiballistic Missile (ABM) Treaty** of 1972 is a formal agreement between the United States and the USSR that restricts strategic defense—missiles designed to destroy incoming strategic nuclear weapons. In the late 1960s the United States began developing an antiballistic missile (Safeguard) designed to protect land-based strategic missiles from a sudden nuclear attack. By the early 1970s the Soviet Union was also developing a similar weapons system. The aim of the ABM Treaty was to limit antiballistic missiles that could be deployed by the United States and the USSR. According to the original treaty, each superpower was limited to two ABM sites, and later this number was reduced to one. The single American ABM site was located in Fargo, North Dakota, but it was subsequently closed. As of 1995 Russia still maintained an operational ABM site near Moscow.

Antiballistic Missile (ABM) Treaty
This 1972 U.S.-USSR treaty limited the superpowers' ballistic missile defense to two ABM sites.

SALT Accords   Beginning in 1969, the superpowers carried out three years of arms control negotiations, known as the **Strategic Arms Limitations Talks (SALT),** that resulted in the 1972 Interim Agreement on Strategic Offensive Arms, commonly denoted as the SALT I Accord. The five-year agreement froze the number of fixed land-based (ICBM) and sea-based (SLBM) ballistic missiles that were in operation or under construction in 1972. Each nation was permitted to expand its number of SLBMs (up to 710 for the United States and 950 for the USSR), but only if an equal number of ICBMs were dismantled. Although the Soviet Union was allowed 600 more launchers than the United States, the Soviet superiority in missiles (2,358 for the USSR and 1,720 for the United States) was counterbalanced by a larger U.S. strategic bomber fleet and by a greater number of individual nuclear warheads.

Strategic Arms Limitations Talks (SALT)
The U.S.-USSR arms control negotiations carried out during the 1970s. The negotiations resulted in a 1972 interim accord (SALT I) and a 1979 comprehensive treaty (SALT II).

The second SALT agreement, a product of nearly seven years of negotiation, was signed by President Carter and President Brezhnev on June 18, 1979, in Vienna. SALT II, like the earlier SALT I Interim Agreement, sought to limit but not reduce the number of strategic weapons. Because of the Soviet intervention in Afghanistan in 1979, the Carter administration withdrew the SALT II Treaty from the Senate and it was never ratified. Later, the U.S. government announced that it would abide by the provisions of the accord as long as the Soviet Union did so as well.

The SALT II Accord had three parts—(1) a treaty that limited the number of offensive nuclear weapons, (2) a protocol that temporarily limited the deployment of new types of strategic weapons, and (3) a statement of principles and guidelines for future negotiations. Unlike SALT I, the SALT II Accord provided for equal limits on both superpowers' nuclear arsenals. These limits included ceilings on the total number of: (1) nuclear warheads, (2) strategic delivery vehicles (bombers and ballistic missiles), and (3) ballistic missiles with multiple warheads. Because neither the United States nor the USSR had deployed the maximum number of land-based missiles with multiple warheads, the agreement did not limit strategic weapons per se. Rather, the accord sought to channel the arms race by regulating the distribution of particular weapons systems.

The INF Treaty   The **Intermediate Nuclear Forces (INF) Treaty** of 1987 is a bilateral U.S.-Soviet accord calling for the elimination of all medium-range missiles (those with a range of 300 miles to 3,400 miles) over a three-year period. At the

Intermediate Nuclear Forces (INF) Treaty
A 1987 U.S.-USSR treaty that eliminated intermediate-range nuclear ballistic missiles.

time the treaty became effective in June 1988, it was estimated that the Soviet Union would have to destroy 1,836 missiles and that the United States would have to scrap 867 missiles.

In 1977, the Soviet Union began deploying a mobile, three-warhead intermediate missile (the SS-20), placing Western European societies under a new military and political threat. To counter this Soviet action, NATO agreed in 1979 to deploy in Europe comparable intermediate nuclear forces if the Soviet Union did not halt further deployment of SS-20s. When the Soviet Union failed to halt deployment of its new type of nuclear weapons, the United States began deploying ground-based cruise missiles (highly accurate, low-flying missiles) and Pershing II ballistic missiles in 1983, as called for by the 1979 NATO decision. By 1987 the United States had deployed nearly two-thirds of a total deployment of 689 Pershing II and cruise missiles.

The INF accord is one of the most important arms control agreements of the Cold War era for a number of reasons. First, the agreement eliminated an entire class of strategic nuclear weapons. Whereas SALT I and SALT II sought to regulate the number of missiles and warheads, the INF Treaty scrapped a category of destabilizing weapons. As such, the treaty is a form of disarmament rather than of arms control. Second, the agreement was important because it was based on the principle of parity. Unlike SALT I, which provided for inequalities in the number of missiles, the INF Treaty required asymmetric reductions in order to achieve parity. Third, the accord increased regional nuclear stability. With the introduction of highly accurate intermediate ballistic missiles, the amount of time for assessing and responding to enemy threats decreased significantly (to about ten minutes), thereby increasing strategic instability. The elimination of these accurate ballistic missiles thus decreased the possibility of a major surprise nuclear attack. Fourth, the treaty was the first superpower arms control agreement that provided for comprehensive verification, including on-site inspection. Finally, the accord represented an important internal political victory for NATO. The treaty would not have been possible had the Western European nations been unable to demonstrate political resolve in deploying intermediate nuclear forces in the face of formidable denuclearization campaigns. But in each of the countries scheduled for missile deployments governments committed to NATO's 1979 policy were voted into power, thus demonstrating cohesion and resolve.

Strategic Arms Reductions Talks (START I) Treaty
The U.S.-USSR arms control negotiations carried out in the 1980s by the Reagan and Bush administrations. The negotiations resulted in two major strategic weapons reduction treaties—START I in 1991 and START II in 1993.

START I The first **Strategic Arms Reductions Talks (START I) Treaty,** signed by Mikhail Gorbachev and George Bush at the July 1991 Moscow Summit, calls for major reductions in existing strategic nuclear arsenals. The landmark treaty, which involved nearly nine years of negotiations, seeks to reduce the superpowers' most destabilizing weapons—land-based ballistic missiles. Since the USSR's dissolution in December 1991, treaty obligations have been transferred to the Commonwealth of Independent States (CIS) and in particular to Russia, the largest and most influential former Soviet republic.

According to one estimate, the CIS's strategic nuclear delivery vehicles (ballistic missiles and bombers) and warheads are expected to decline by about 37 percent (from 2,526 to 1,600) and 33 percent (from 10,741 to 7,160), respectively. The U.S. arsenal of vehicles and warheads, by contrast, is expected to decline by 14 percent (from 1,855 to 1,600) and 19 percent (from 11,714 to 9,480), respectively.[36] A key provision of the treaty calls for a ceiling of 1,600 strategic delivery vehicles for each state, requiring the elimination of about 250 vehicles for the United States and about 900 vehicles for the CIS. In addition, the treaty calls for a 50 percent reduction in CIS's heavy land-based ballistic missiles (SS-18s), the most destabilizing elements of the triad. Finally, START I, like the INF Treaty, involves comprehensive verification based on on-site inspection.

Post–Cold War Arms Control

Following the abortive August 1991 coup against the government of Mikhail Gorbachev, the United States became increasingly concerned about the weakening authority of the Soviet government and the potential loss of control over nuclear arms, especially tactical weapons. Because of improving U.S.-Soviet political ties and the growing concerns over potential weakening of control over the Soviet nuclear arsenal, President Bush ordered further unilateral reductions in the American arsenal on September 28, 1991. The order, designed to encourage Soviet cuts, called for: (1) the elimination of all tactical nuclear weapons (about 1,740 artillery shells and 1,250 short-range missiles), except bombs dropped from airplanes; (2) the withdrawal of all nuclear cruise missiles and bombs from naval ships, attack submarines, and land-based naval bases; (3) the removal of all strategic bombers from a high-alert status; and (4) the halting of development and deployment of mobile ICBMs.[37]

As expected, the Soviet government responded shortly thereafter with comparable reductions. Specifically, President Gorbachev called for, among other things, the elimination of all land-based tactical nuclear arms (about 4,670 artillery and short-range missiles) and the removal of nuclear arms from all ships, attack submarines, and land-based naval aircraft (about 3,400 tactical warheads).[38] Because the Soviet Union had an estimated 14,000 tactical nuclear arms in 1991, the reduction and centralization of control over these weapons represented an important step in maintaining superpower military stability.

Although the Bush-Gorbachev initiatives on tactical nuclear arms were hailed throughout the world when they were first announced, their significance became especially apparent in December 1991, when the Soviet state ceased to exist. Thus, by the time the Soviet Union began to dissolve at the end of 1991, the centralization of control over tactical nuclear weapons was well underway. By mid-1992, it was estimated that all tactical weapons in the former Soviet republics had been consolidated in Russia.[39]

START II and START III In his State of the Union address of January 1992, President Bush offered to reduce strategic weapons even beyond the START I ceilings. According to his proposal, the United States would reduce the number of its SLBM warheads by one-third if Russia, Ukraine, and Kazakstan eliminated all of their heavy MIRVed ICBMs. In effect, the Bush proposal called for reductions in

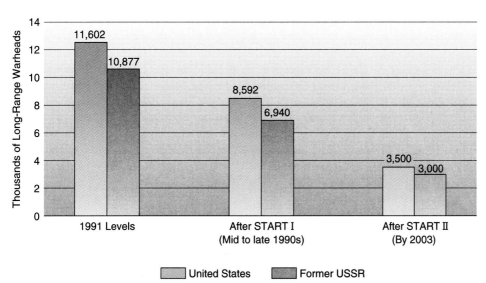

FIGURE 18.4
START II Accord, 1993
Source: Data from *The New York Times*, June 17, 1992, p. 7 and December 30, 1992, p. 7.

strategic warheads and bombs to nearly 60 percent of existing arsenals (about 4,700 for the United States and about 4,400 for the CIS). Subsequently, Boris Yeltsin, who had replaced Mikhail Gorbachev as Russian president in December 1991, called for even larger weapons cuts. He proposed that each side reduce its strategic arsenals to about 2,500 warheads.

Based on these initiatives, presidents Bush and Yeltsin signed a preliminary START II agreement in June 1992 (at the first U.S.-Russia summit in Washington, D.C.), establishing a framework for further strategic weapons reductions from those already approved by the START I Treaty. The two major powers continued negotiations in the latter half of 1992 and culminated their work in early 1993 with a **START II Treaty.** The accord calls for the elimination of all ICBMs with multiple warheads and the reduction of the total number of nuclear warheads to 3,500 for the United States and 3,000 for Russia. The terms of the agreement are to be implemented by 2003, although the reductions may be achieved faster if the United States provides economic and technical assistance in the dismantling of Russia's nuclear arsenal.[40] The U.S. Senate ratified START II in January 1997, but as of 1998 Russia's parliament (Duma) had not ratified the treaty. The Russian opposition to START II is based on a number of factors, including Russian opposition to the expansion of NATO and the unwillingness to divert scarce economic resources to the destruction of existing weapons and the dismantling of existing missile silos. Most importantly, the Russians have claimed that START II will leave them at a disadvantage in land-based missiles, without the development of a new type of single-warhead ballistic missile.[41]

The United States has encouraged Russia to ratify START II, with the understanding that both countries would move expeditiously toward a START III agreement that would limit the strategic nuclear arsenals of both major powers to a maximum of 2,000–2,500 weapons for each side. The lower limits would be especially advantageous to Russia, because it could achieve complete parity with the United States without developing a new type of ICBM. At the 1997 U.S.-Russia Summit in Helsinki, both Presidents Yeltsin and Clinton agreed to pursue further reductions in strategic weapons after Russia ratifies START II.[42]

Comprehensive Test Ban Treaty Since the end of the Cold War, the major nuclear powers, led by the United States, have sought to establish a comprehensive ban on all nuclear weapons testing. By 1993, both Russia and the United States had halted nuclear testing, and by 1996, Britain, China, and France had also agreed to a testing moratorium. Beginning in 1995 the Geneva-based Disarmament Conference held ongoing negotiations over the adoption of a comprehensive ban on nuclear testing, but after failing to adopt an accord in Geneva, the major powers shifted the debate to the UN General Assembly. In September 1996, that body, by a vote of 158 to 3, formally adopted the **Comprehensive Test Ban Treaty (CTBT).** In order for the CTBT to become international law, it needs to be ratified by all (44) countries possessing nuclear reactors. India, one of the nuclear states that must ratify the accord if it is to become effective, has vigorously opposed the CTBT, however, because it believes that the treaty should require, by a specified future date, the complete elimination of nuclear armaments. At the time of the CTBT's signing, India announced that so long as the treaty failed to require complete nuclear disarmament, it would seek to prevent the treaty from entering into force.[43]

START II Treaty
A 1993 treaty that greatly reduces the strategic arsenals of the United States and Russia.

Comprehensive Test Ban Treaty (CTBT)
A 1996 treaty that calls for a complete halt to all nuclear weapons testing.

In Conclusion

The effort to control weapons proliferation, especially nuclear armaments, became a dominant global issue during the 1970s and 1980s. The heightened public concern with arms control and disarmament was due in great measure to the growing concern over nuclear weapons proliferation coupled with a shift toward more discriminating, war-fighting nuclear strategies. As a result, the United States and the Soviet Union devoted significant energies to the development of bilateral arms control agreements.

Controlling weapons proliferation and modernization is important in developing a more peaceful and just international political system and in easing international political tensions. However, even though arms control and disarmament can contribute to a more peaceful and secure world, they cannot serve as the chief instruments of conflict resolution and the promotion of international security, because as Hans Morgenthau has noted, the basic source of international conflict is politics, not armaments. As a result, the pursuit of international harmony in global society requires that political tensions be eased, if not resolved, before states can effectively reduce their weapons. Morgenthau writes:

> . . . a mutually satisfactory settlement of the power contest is a precondition for disarmament. Once the nations concerned have agreed upon a mutually satisfactory distribution of power among themselves, they can then afford to reduce and limit their armaments. Disarmament, in turn, will contribute greatly to the general pacification. For the degree to which the nations are able to settle the issue of disarmament will be the measure of the political understanding they were able to achieve.[44]

The truth has been vividly illustrated by the significant arms control agreements that the United States and Soviet republics have been able to achieve since the easing of East-West tensions in the late 1980s and the end of the Cold War in 1990.

SUMMARY

1. Weapons proliferation and modernization can be harmful because they increase the potential destruction of war, exacerbate political tensions, and result in a misuse of governmental resources.

2. The major threat to the well-being of global society arises from the spread of unconventional arms—chemical, biological, and nuclear weapons. Although weapons proliferation among leading powers is problematic, the major threat to global stability arises from the potential horizontal proliferation of these weapons to unstable Third World nations.

3. There are two basic ways of responding to weapons proliferation—disarmament and arms control. The first seeks to control the military threat by reducing, if not eliminating, weapons. The second seeks to regulate weapons in order to reduce the risk of war.

4. In the past two centuries numerous efforts have been made to reduce conventional and unconventional weapons. But with few exceptions, conventional disarmament

measures have been relatively ineffective. By contrast, arms control and disarmament measures covering unconventional arms have been more important and more effective.

5. The major aims of nuclear arms control are the avoidance of war, the reduction of the consequences of major war, and the reduction of the cost of strategic arsenals. The overriding objective is the first, and this is best achieved through strategic stability.

6. During the Cold War, the superpowers achieved many significant arms control agreements. The most important were the Limited Test Ban Treaty, the NPT, the ABM Treaty, SALT I and SALT II, the INF Treaty, and START I. Since the end of the Cold War, the major arms control achievements are the indefinite extention of the NPT, the establishment of the CTBT, and START II.

7. Although the post–Cold War era has encouraged further reductions in nuclear weapons, the disintegration of the Soviet Union has increased the dangers of nuclear proliferation.

KEY TERMS

vertical proliferation
horizontal proliferation
chemical weapons (CW)
biological weapons (BW)
disarmament
arms control
Rush-Bagot Agreement
Washington Naval Treaty

Conventional Forces
  Europe (CFE) Treaty
Land Mine Treaty
1925 Geneva Protocol
Chemical Weapons
  Convention (CWC)
Biological Weapons
  Convention (BWC)

nuclear freeze
stable deterrence
Limited Test Ban Treaty
NPT
Antiballistic Missile (ABM)
  Treaty
Strategic Arms Limitations
  Talks (SALT)

Intermediate Nuclear
  Forces (INF) Treaty
Strategic Arms Reductions
  Talks (START I) Treaty
START II Treaty
Comprehensive Test Ban
  Treaty (CTBT)

RECOMMENDED READINGS

Caldwell, Dan. *The Dynamics of Domestic Politics and Arms Control: The SALT II Treaty Ratification Debate.* Columbia: University of South Carolina Press, 1991. This authoritative study examines the role of domestic political factors—including public opinion, interest groups, the executive branch of government, and the Congress—in the ratification debates of the SALT II Treaty.

Clausen, Peter A. *Nonproliferation and the National Interest: America's Response to the Spread of Nuclear Weapons.* New York: Harper Collins, 1993. A study of the evolution of U.S. policy toward nuclear proliferation—from the early postwar era through the end of the Cold War. This lucid and informative analysis identifies key principles and lessons from the historical record.

Lamb, Christopher J. *How to Think About Arms Control, Disarmament, and Defense.* Englewood Cliffs, N.J.: Prentice-Hall, 1988. A clear, well-organized introduction to the history, theory, and practice of arms control and disarmament. An especially useful study for the beginning student because of its nontechnical orientation.

Mayers, Teena Karsa. *Understanding Weapons and Arms Control: A Guide to the Issues,* 4th ed., rev. McLean, Va.: Brassey's (U.S.) 1991. A brief historical guide to U.S. strategic arms control. Graphics and tables are exceptionally useful.

Sivard, Ruth Leger. *World Military and Social Expenditures, 1996,* 16th ed. Washington, D.C.: World Priorities, 1996. An invaluable data source on global trends on war casualties, military expenditures, social welfare, international ecology, and arms control.

Sagan, Scott D. *The Limits of Safety: Organizations, Accidents, and Nuclear Weapons.* Princeton, N.J.: Princeton University Press, 1993. Using organization theory, Sagan examines a number of serious accidents and near-accidents with the U.S. nuclear forces during the 1960s and 1970s. Based on his analysis, he argues that nuclear arms involve a high level of danger, not so much because of their enormous power but because strategic systems are complex. A path-breaking study.

Sagan, Scott D., and Kenneth N. Waltz. *The Spread of Nuclear Weapons: A Debate.* New York: W. W. Norton, 1995. Two leading scholars use different approaches to explain the potential dangers of nuclear proliferation. Waltz, using neorealism, argues that the dangers of nuclear proliferation have been greatly exaggerated; by contrast, Sagan, using organization theory, argues that the proliferation of nuclear weapons is likely to destabilize global politics.

Smoke, Richard. *National Security and the Nuclear Dilemma: An Introduction to the American Experience,* 2nd ed. New York: Random House, 1987. A lucid, jargon-free introduction to the issues and debates surrounding the role of nuclear arms in U.S. national security policy during the Cold War. Arms control is a major theme of the study.

Spector, Lennard S., and Mark G. McDonough with Evan S. Medeiros. *Tracking Nuclear Proliferation: A Guide in Maps and Charts, 1995.* Washington, D.C.: Carnegie Endowment for International Peace, 1995. A current assessment of the ambitions and capabilities of potential nuclear weapons states. An informative guidebook.

RELEVANT WEB SITES

Arms Control Association

Canadian Forces College
  War, Peace and Security Guide

Fletcher School of Law and Diplomacy Database

International Affairs Network (IAN)

International Committee of the Red Cross (ICRC)
  Data on land mines

www.armscontrol.org/

www.cfcsc.dnd.ca/links/peace/disarm.html

www.TUFTS.EDU/fletcher/multilaterals.html

www.pitt.edu/~ian/resource/prolif.htm

www.icrc.ch/unicc/icrcnews

International Institute for Strategic Studies (IISS)   www.isn.ethz.ch/iiss/

National Security Archive   www.seas.gwu.edu/nsarchive
   Nuclear Non-Proliferation Database

Stockholm International Peace Research   www.sipri.se/
   Institute (SIPRI)

U.S. Arms Control and Disarmament   www.acda.gov
   Agency (ACDA)

World Military Expenditures and Arms   www.acda.gov/wmeat95/
   Transfers (ACDA)

19 The Management of Global Resources

On April 26, 1986, a nuclear power plant in Chernobyl, Ukraine, had a meltdown, leading to radioactive fallout equivalent to ten Hiroshima bombs. The Soviet government estimated that radioactive contamination had permanently poisoned an area the size of the Netherlands, resulting in the displacement of some 200,000 persons from Belarus and Ukraine. Although the major costs of the malfunction at Chernobyl were borne by the Soviet Union, other European countries were affected as well. For example, the governments of Finland and Norway banned the commercial sale of reindeer because of excessively high levels of radiation in the meat. Moreover, because of fears about potential long-term health hazards, the European Economic Community banned all fresh produce from nations within 1,000 kilometers of the accident, thereby barring agricultural exports from Eastern Europe. One group of scientists estimated that the total direct and indirect costs of the accident were about $15 billion.[3]

Historically, the protection of the environment has been regarded chiefly as a domestic political concern. But as the Chernobyl incident suggests, ecological disasters can have significant transnational consequences. Moreover, it has become increasingly evident to scholars and political leaders alike that continued global industrialization involves environmental costs, including threats to the diversity of biological life, depletion of natural resources, and the introduction of chemical pollutants into the atmosphere and water streams. If states are to effectively conserve natural resources, protect endangered species, and limit transboundary pollution, they need to cooperate with other states in establishing global environmental regimes that protect and preserve global resources and biological life. The following incidents illustrate the growing transnational character of ecological problems:

1. On March 19, 1978, the Amoco *Cadiz*, an American supertanker, ran aground off the coast of France, spilling more than 67 million gallons of petroleum. Much of this oil drifted toward the French coastline, covering some 200 miles of Brittany's shore. Subsequently, the Amoco Corporation paid more than $400 million in reparations to the French

government. Eleven years later (March 1989) the Exxon *Valdez* ran aground in Prince William Sound, Alaska, spilling 10.8 million gallons of oil. Although the quantity of oil discharged by the *Valdez* was much less than in the earlier incident, the ecological destruction of Prince William Sound was much greater.

2. On December 3, 1984, a Union Carbide insecticide plant in Bhopal, India, malfunctioned and led to a leak of highly toxic gases. The white lethal fumes quickly spread to the nearby town of Bhopal, killing more than 2,100 persons. Five years later, the U.S. corporation agreed to pay $470 million to the Indian government, which was to distribute the funds to those who had suffered personal loss from the disaster.

3. On November 1, 1986, a fire in a chemical plant in Sweizerhalle, Switzerland (near Basel), resulted in the accidental washing of some thirty tons of deadly chemicals into the Rhine River. The herbicides and pesticides that were carried into the Rhine turned the river water red and killed tens of thousands of fish and eels. Because the Rhine is a major source of water for four countries (France, Germany, the Netherlands, and Switzerland), the spillage of chemicals had major international repercussions.

4. From 1979 to 1989, the number of elephants in Africa declined precipitously (from 1.3 million to 625,000)[4] because of illegal poaching. In an effort to preserve this endangered species, the international community (through the Convention on the International Trade in Endangered Species) banned all exports and imports of ivory in 1989.

5. Because of growing industrialization, acid rain—rain contaminated by air pollutants—has been destroying significant parts of European forests, especially in Germany, the Czech Republic, and Poland. One study estimates that acid rain annually destroys 118 million cubic meters of wood worth about $27 billion in Western and Eastern Europe, including the European regions of Russia and of other former Soviet republics.[5] In order to reduce acid rain, European countries signed a convention to promote cooperation in lowering acid rain.

6. Although dolphins are not an endangered species, annually tens of thousands of them are killed unnecessarily by fishermen because they get trapped in tuna nets and drown. In an effort to limit the slaughter of dolphins, the U.S. government enacted the Marine Mammal Protection Act of 1972 that limits U.S. fisherman to killing 20,500 dolphins annually. In 1988, a congressional amendment directed the U.S. Department of Commerce to ban tuna imports from countries that had a higher level of dolphins killed. When this congressional provision was applied to Mexico and four other states in 1990, they complained and took their case to the Geneva-based General Agreement on Tariffs and Trade organization. Subsequently, a three-member GATT panel ruled that the United States could not restrict imports in this manner because the dolphins were killed in international waters and the U.S. government had no authority to extend its laws to another sovereign state.[6]

As these illustrations suggest, developments in one country can have significant environmental effects in other countries. In view of the growing transnational threats to the earth's environment and its diverse biological life, this chapter explores some of the major global ecological problems and then examines significant international environmental initiatives to conserve resources, protect endangered species, and limit pollution. In the first part of this chapter, the challenge of developing a global strategy to manage and conserve global resources is examined by employing the tragedy of the commons analogy and by contrasting two influential environmental perspectives. In the second part, I describe several transnational ecological initiatives that have resulted in the emergence of important environmental regimes in areas such as the atmosphere, land, water and marine resources, biodiversity, and waste disposal. A major aim of this chapter is to describe and assess international initiatives in managing global resources.

DEVELOPING A GLOBAL PERSPECTIVE

As noted earlier, in domestic society the promotion of the common good, including the protection and preservation of a country's environment, is ultimately the responsibility of each national government. Whether or not states are farsighted in preserving and protecting their environment from harmful consequences of economic modernization is ultimately determined by the policies of each national government. From a global perspective, however, whether or not the global common good is promoted and protected depends on the voluntary actions of a large number of member-states. The United Nations and its various specialized agencies—such as the International Maritime Organization, the UN Environment Program, and the UN Conference on Environment and Development—can of course facilitate international functional coordination and cooperation, but the extent to which shared economic and ecological interests are protected and advanced is ultimately dependent on the behaviors of individual governments.

One of the reasons why countries find it difficult to cooperate in protecting global resources and promoting shared ecological concerns is that governments regularly face overwhelming pressure to meet immediate national goals and to postpone or even disregard long-term issues, especially those that are multilateral in character. Moreover, because economic growth and environmental protection are often in conflict, governments must make difficult trade-offs between facilitating immediate economic expansion and the long-term protection of global resources. Thus, governments may desire a clean atmosphere and ample water resources but may be unwilling to sacrifice the limited national interests for the common good.

Tragedy of the Commons Analogy

Tragedy of the commons
A metaphor used to explain the danger of unregulated use of public goods. The tragedy occurs when the commons' collective interests are overwhelmed by individual short-term claims.

Carrying capacity
The maximum long-term economic capacity of a given territory.

The dangers in pursuing a foreign policy guided by parochial interests are illustrated in the **tragedy of the commons** analogy. The analogy, first articulated in 1833 by English political economist William Foster Lloyd and popularized in the mid-twentieth century by scientist Garrett Hardin,[7] illustrates the dilemma of reconciling immediate national interest with the long-term global common good. According to the analogy, villagers raise livestock on private plots and also on a common pasture. Whereas grazing on private land is carefully controlled by each owner, the use of the communal land is unregulated. As a result, the pasture on private plots is better maintained than the village green and results in much healthier animals.

The problem posed by the commons is this: How many animals should each villager allow to graze in the commons? Because the pasture can only sustain a limited number of animals (this is the commons' **carrying capacity**), the challenge for the farmers is to maximize their individual well-being without destroying the communal property. If each villager defines his interests in light of the common good, he will place only a limited number of animals in the commons to avoid overgrazing. If the villagers, however, seek to maximize their immediate self-interest and disregard other villagers' shared interests, as well as their own long-term individual welfare, the communal property will be overgrazed, resulting in the deterioration of the pasture and the eventual destruction of the commons.

According to Hardin, when property is collectively owned, few incentives exist to promote the long-term common good. For example, when a villager adds an animal to the common pasture, it results in an individual farmer's immediate gain, even though its long-term cost (the declining productivity of the pasture) is distributed to all villagers. As a result, the incentives of pursuing individual interests are stronger than those of pursuing the collective good through self-sacrifice.

Hardin applied the tragedy of the commons metaphor to the population explosion, leading him to conclude that countries with rapidly growing populations were overcrowding the earth. Because population growth in the developing nations was outstripping the ability of the world to feed its people, the Third World's population explosion posed challenges similar to those of the expanding animal population in the village green. If tragedy was to be avoided, Hardin reasoned that states needed to abandon the "freedom to breed."

The tragedy of the commons analogy has important implications for global society.[8] If the earth is regarded as a "global commons," in which states share such resources as the ocean, the atmosphere, and the deep seabed, then states should—for reasons of morality as well as self-interest—cooperate in protecting the collective goods. The overuse or misuse of common resources can lead to their deterioration and even destruction. The challenge, then, is for states to cooperate in managing and protecting the global environment, especially those collective goods like the atmosphere and the oceans.

Competing Perspectives

Natural and social scientists differ greatly on the severity of the ecological, social, and economic problems facing global society. Fundamentally, two different perspectives are articulated by scholars and policy advocates—one pessimistic and the other optimistic. These different perspectives are not rooted in facts themselves but in the underlying values and assumptions that individuals use in assessing reality.

Economist Thomas Sowell has observed that modern social and political thought is based in significant measure on different worldviews or visions. According to him, most social, political, and economic theories since the seventeenth century have been based on one of two major worldviews—a "constrained vision" or an "unconstrained" one.[9] These different visions explain in great part, in Sowell's view, why John Locke, Adam Smith, Thomas Malthus, Karl Marx, and other social thinkers held such divergent theories about how to constitute social, political, and economic life.

Similarly, the different approaches of environmental pessimists and optimists reflect profoundly different worldviews toward the planet earth. In particular they reflect different assumptions about the nature of persons, the extent that social progress is possible, the ability to promote human welfare through science and technology, and the availability of natural resources. Because these differing orientations profoundly influence perceptions about global reality, key features of each of these approaches are sketched on the following pages.

Ecopessimism

The perspective of **ecopessimism** assumes that continued modernization and economic expansion will not necessarily result in a more desirable world. Because resources are finite, and because modernization produces many harmful by-products, global economic expansion must be carefully regulated in order to reduce the harmful effects of industrialization and to control the use of scarce resources.

Ever since Thomas Malthus predicted in the late eighteenth century the earth's declining capacity to feed itself, social critics have been issuing dire warnings about the fate of the earth. As the world has become more complex and interdependent,

Ecopessimism
A pessimistic perspective about the long-term effects of continued modernization and economic expansion.

these warnings have multiplied and the predictions have become more ominous. In 1968 Paul Ehrlich published *The Population Bomb,* a study that helped revive the pessimistic Malthusian thesis about the growing imbalance between population and food. According to Ehrlich, because the world's resources were finite, the continued population explosion in the developing nations would inevitably lead to hunger and disease and ultimately to global catastrophe. In 1990, Ehrlich and his wife Anne published a follow-up study titled *The Population Explosion* that repeated the pessimistic warnings articulated earlier. But whereas the world's population was 3.5 billion in 1968, by 1990 it had increased to more than 5.3 billion, thereby greatly exacerbating social and economic problems in rapidly growing poor countries. Because of the extraordinary population growth on the earth, the Ehrlichs suggested that the population "bomb" had exploded, making overpopulation the major global environmental problem.[10]

The most influential postwar report crystallizing the ecopessimistic perspective was a 1972 study titled *The Limits to Growth.*[11] The report, sponsored by a group of businessmen and academicians collectively known as the Club of Rome, was prepared by a group of computer scientists at the Massachusetts Institute of Technology. Using computer simulations, the study predicted that if the world's population continued to rise exponentially and the consumption of nonrenewable resources continued at existing rates the world economy would inevitably collapse. If disaster is to be avoided, population growth must be reduced, resource conservation must be strengthened, and pollution control must be combined with limited economic expansion. Although the report was criticized for exaggerating population growth rates, consumption patterns, and industrial pollution, the study received much publicity and contributed to the popularization of the ecopessimistic approach in North America and Western Europe.

In 1980, two U.S. government agencies—the Council on Environmental Quality and the Department of State—issued a comprehensive but less pessimistic study titled *The Global 2000 Report to the President.* Commissioned by President Jimmy Carter, the report predicted continued population expansion, further depletion of natural resources, deforestation, growing air and water pollution, and increasing extinction of species. The report stated:

> If present trends continue, the world in 2000 will be more crowded, more polluted, less stable ecologically, and more vulnerable to disruption than the world we live in now. Serious stresses involving population, resources, and environment are clearly visible ahead. Despite greater material output, the world's people will be poorer in many ways than they are today.[12]

The report did not seek to predict the future. Rather, it called attention to long-term developments if social, economic, ecological, and technological patterns continued unchanged. Although less deterministic and less pessimistic than the Club of Rome report, this study was nonetheless rooted in the ecopessimistic worldview.

Undoubtedly, the most influential organization in propagating concerns about the global environment has been the United Nations. Since the early 1970s, it has become the principal organ for calling attention to global problems and for fostering international cooperation. In 1972 it officially recognized environmental protection as a key global issue by sponsoring the first international conference on the environment. The Global Conference on the Human Environment, convened in Stockholm, addressed a number of ecological issues and set forth a number of principles in the so-called *Stockholm Declaration* to promote environmentally sound economic expansion. One of the most important elements of the declaration is Principle No. 21, which reads:

> States have, in accordance with the Charter of the United Nations and the principles of international law, the sovereign right to exploit their own resources pursuant to their

own environmental policies, and *the responsibility to ensure that activities within their jurisdiction or control do not cause damage to the environment of other States or areas beyond the limits of national jurisdiction.*[13] (emphasis mine)

Another important action taken at the Stockholm conference was the creation of the **United Nations Environment Program (UNEP)** in order to monitor global environmental issues and promote ecological coordination.

In June 1992—twenty years after the first international conference on the environment—the UN sponsored a follow-up global meeting in Rio de Janeiro. This conference, popularly dubbed the **Earth Summit,** is generally considered the most important event in contemporary global environmental politics. The summit, which some ecologists had billed as the "last chance to save the planet," resulted in a number of important agreements (see case 19.1). Most significantly, it generated a significant amount of publicity and increased global awareness about the need to manage global resources and protect the earth's environment.

Ecooptimism

The perspective of **ecooptimism** places great confidence in the ability of humans to use modern science and technology to further improve global living standards. Like ecopessimists, ecooptimists believe that industrialization and modernization bring about many undesirable by-products, including excessive urbanization, traffic congestion, air and water pollution, environmental degradation, and resource depletion. Economists define these social and economic costs as *externalities* because they are not normally included in the pricing of goods and services or in the assessment of economic growth. Whereas the ecopessimists are skeptical about the reduction or elimination of these harmful by-products, ecooptimists believe that the unwanted effects of industrialization can be moderated, if not eliminated. In effect, they believe that the scientific method that helped create global improvements in health and living standards can also contribute to further improvements in the world's environment.

Ecooptimists point to successful efforts in replenishing forests, purifying lakes and rivers, and reducing air pollutants from industrial firms. For example, during the 1960s and 1970s the quality of water in Lake Erie and Lake Michigan improved greatly because of the imposition of stringent water pollution regulations. Although fishing had almost ceased in these lakes by the mid-1960s because of excessive chemical pollutants, by the mid-1980s the quality of water had improved dramatically and fishing began to thrive again. Similarly, European governments have cooperated in reducing pollutants dumped into the Rhine river. As a result, the quality of water has greatly improved, resulting in a growth in the variety of fish life, which increased from fewer than twenty-five species in 1980 to more than a hundred species in 1986.[16] The governments of a number of industrial countries have also imposed increasingly stringent air pollution regulations, resulting in significant reductions in air pollutants.

The ecooptimist perspective is illustrated in Max Singer's *Passage to a Human World,* a study about future economic life in the world.[17] According to Singer, the world was originally poor, and as countries began to adopt the modern tools of science and technology, wealth expanded. Currently great disparities in national income exist because of different productive capacities. But as economic modernization spreads to the poor nations—a process that he calls "the passage"—the capacity of wealth creation will increase and lead to continuing improvements in living conditions, ultimately narrowing income inequalities between rich and poor states. According to Singer, the major threats to human beings in the past were to their bodies in the form of famine, plague, pestilence, and war. Singer believes that in the modern world being established, war will be the only remaining major physical threat to humankind. In addition, people will have to fear the harmful

United Nations Environment Program (UNEP)
This IGO seeks to monitor global ecological issues and promote international environmental protection.

Earth Summit
A 1992 UN-sponsored conference that called attention to global environmental protection and to economic growth that was environmentally safe.

Ecooptimism
An optimistic perspective about the long-term effects of continued modernization and economic expansion.

Case 19.1 Global Environmental Politics: The Case of the Earth Summit

The 1992 Earth Summit, formally called the **UN Conference on Environment and Development (UNCED),** is the largest international conference ever held. More than 25,000 persons—including 172 official governmental delegations, 115 heads of state, and more than 15,000 representatives from thousands of environmental NGOS—participated in the two-week Rio de Janeiro conference. The basis of the summit was laid in 1983, when the World Commission on Environment and Development warned that current consumption and development patterns were not conducive to sustainable development. The aim of the conference was thus to seek to develop norms and guidelines that were conducive to both economic growth and environmental protection.

The central issue at the Earth Summit was how to foster economic growth that was consistent with environmental conservation. The major fault line on sustainable development was between the rich, industrial countries (North) and the emerging Third World nations (South). Officials from the North and South agreed that managing global resources was important, that the global environmental commons needed to be protected, and that economic development strategies should be sustainable over the long term. But the North and South held significantly different perspectives on who was chiefly responsible for environmental decay and what types of strate-

gies should be pursued. The North assumed that all countries, whether developed or developing, should institute conservation measures and should pursue only sustainable growth policies. For example, the industrial states, concerned that tropical deforestation was potentially harmful to the earth's atmosphere, believed that tropical countries should more effectively protect the rain forest. By contrast, the South emphasized the sovereignty norm, arguing that the use of domestic resources was solely a prerogative of individual states. In addition, the South argued that the major burden for protecting the global commons should fall on the North, because the industrial states were responsible for most of the earth's pollution. Finally, the South demanded that the North provide significant economic aid to help protect the global environment and to facilitate the South's implementation of sustainable development strategies.

The summit resulted in the signing of two conventions: the Climate Treaty, which, as noted earlier, seeks to reduce greenhouse gas emissions, and the Biodiversity Treaty, which seeks to protect endangered species. In addition, participating states agreed by consensus to three nonbinding documents:

1. *Declaration on Environment and Development,* listing twenty-seven principles for guiding national environmental conservation strategies

effects of wealth, power, knowledge, and freedom—qualities that are desirable in themselves but can weaken character if not used properly. Singer does not examine the ecological and environmental problems produced by economic growth; rather, his ecooptimistic message is that people will use increasing knowledge to maintain and improve living conditions.

Another example of ecooptimism is Julian Simon's population studies that challenge the widespread belief that population growth is harmful to the world. In *The Ultimate Resource,* Simon argues that population growth, far from being a source of poverty and social underdevelopment, is a key resource for promoting economic expansion.[18] Simon directly challenges the central themes of Paul Ehrlich's studies that popularized the notion that population growth is a major obstacle to Third World development. Rather than viewing population growth as a barrier to improvements in living standards, as is typically the case, Simon regards people as a rich resource for promoting economic growth and improving the quality of life for all. Whereas some ecopessimists like Lester Brown, head of the Worldwatch Institute, believe that the carrying capacity of global society is about 6 billion persons, Simon believes that there are no fixed limits on the world's ability to feed itself and to meet its basic human needs.

2. *Statement on Forest Principles,* listing recommendations on sustainable forestry
3. *Agenda 21,* an 800-page blueprint for promoting environmentally sustainable economic development[14]

In addition, although industrial states agreed to increase foreign aid to the South to assist implementation of environmental protection programs, only Japan made a fixed pledge, promising to increase its annual foreign aid from $1 billion to a five-year average of $1.45 billion.[15]

The impact of the Rio summit on the earth's environment has been, at best, mixed. As noted in table 19.1, with the exception of North America and Europe, environmental conditions have continued to deteriorate in other geographical regions, especially Latin America and Asia.

TABLE 19.1   A Report Card on the Global Environment, 1992–1997

Problems	North America	Latin America	Africa	Europe & Former USSR	West Asia	East Asia
Land Degradation	-	+	+	0	+	+
Deforestation	0	+	+	0	+	+
Biodiversity Loss	0	+	+	0	+	+
Water Scarcity	0	+	+	0	+	+
Marine Degradation	0	+	0	+	+	+
Air Pollution	0	+	0	0	0	+
Waste Disposal	0	+	0	0	+	+

+ = increasing   0 = relatively stable   – = decreasing

Source: William K. Stevens, "Environmental Problems: A Report Card," *New York Times,* June 17, 1997, p. B14.

In 1984, Simon and Herman Kahn authored *The Resourceful Earth,* a study challenging the pessimistic conclusions of the *Global 2000* report. To highlight their differences with the *Global 2000* study, Simon and Kahn use the *Global 2000* summary statement with their substitutions italicized.

> If present trends continue, the world in 2000 will be *less crowded* (though more populated), *less polluted, more stable ecologically,* and *less vulnerable to resource-supply disruption* than the world we live in now. Stresses involving population, resources, and environment *will be less in the future than now.* . . . The world's people will be *richer* in most ways than they are today. . . . The outlook for food and other necessities of life will be *better* . . . life for most people on earth will be *less precarious* economically than it is now.[19]

Simon and Kahn do not deny the existence of major global problems (e.g., hunger, malnutrition, pollution, and disease), but they differ with ecopessimists in their assessment of global problems and in the degree to which those problems can be moderated and resolved.

The competing perspectives that have been examined in this chapter (see table 19.2) are significant because they influence the analysis and policy debates about global environmental protection. Because such paradigms help to structure

TABLE 19.2 Comparison of Ecooptimist and Ecopessimist Perspectives

Approach	Resource Availability	Population Growth	Economic Development	Environmental Protection
Ecopessimism	Limited, continued depletion	Barrier to economic expansion	Favor managed growth	Public regulation
Ecooptimism	Unlimited, continual renewal	An asset to economic expansion	Favor unlimited growth	Private voluntary cooperation

the conceptualization of global ecology, they profoundly influence the development of international environmental regimes. Although scholars have developed other approaches to the management of the global commons, these two alternative perspectives define ideal-type ecological visions along a continuum, with most analysts and political leaders subscribing to positions in between these extremes.

DEVELOPING GLOBAL ENVIRONMENTAL REGIMES

Developing international environmental cooperation is a challenging, daunting task. As with all politics, the development of global environmental regimes involves a significant level of conflict. Three major sources of environmental conflict include: (1) the competing national interests of states, especially when governments reconcile short-term economic interests with long-term interests in sustainable development; (2) governmental and nongovernmental group politics based on conflicting political ideologies and competing economic interests; and (3) alternative perspectives on the nature, severity, causes, and potential solutions of perceived global environmental problems. In effect, global cooperation requires the development of consensus, involving reconciliation among states' individual and group interests.

This section examines a variety of environmental concerns and some of the major international ecological initiatives designed to protect the global commons. Because the most basic natural resources are air, water, and land, our analysis focuses on the impact of economic development on these basic resources. Even though modern economic expansion has greatly improved living standards worldwide, it has also resulted in increased air, water, and soil pollution. Some of these unwanted and unintended environmental problems are national in scope, but many of them are transboundary problems. Some of the most important contemporary transnational environmental problems involve acid rain, ozone depletion, ocean pollution, and the destruction of animal and plant species.

The Atmosphere

One of the major harmful by-products of economic modernization is the pollutants that are discharged into the atmosphere. Some of the major concentrations of air pollution are in industrial and urban centers (see table 19.3), especially major cities in the Third World. It has been estimated that breathing the air of Bombay is equivalent to smoking ten cigarettes a day. Hungary estimates that one of every seventeen deaths can be attributed to air pollution. In Santiago, Chile, air pollution is so harmful during the winter months that driving is rationed, and children are frequently urged to stay indoors.

Fossil fuels (petroleum, coal, and natural gas), a major source of air pollution, provide about 88 percent of the world's energy, whereas hydroelectric installations

TABLE 19.3 Air Pollution in Selected Cities, 1989–1994

City	Sulfur Dioxide (average micrograms)	Particulates* (average micrograms)
Bangkok	1,224	171
Tehran	140	263
Shenyang	132	357
Warsaw	125	n.a.
Beijing	89	363
Tokyo	70	50
Shanghai	69	225
Zagreb	39	72
New York	38	62
Sao Paulo	37	36
Frankfurt	23	37

* Suspended particulate matter.

Source: Data from World Resources Institute et al., *World Resources, 1996–97* (New York: Oxford University Press, 1996), p. 154.

and nuclear power plants provide only 7 percent and 5 percent, respectively.[20] When fossil fuels are burned, they result in a number of harmful by-products, including carbon dioxide, methane, nitrous oxide, and sulfur dioxide. Although developing nations use comparatively low levels of energy, many of them have extremely high levels of air pollution because of heavy use of coal for generating electricity. In order to reduce harmful gas emissions from coal-burning, industrial states have developed pollution control equipment that greatly decreases sulfur oxides and particulates. As a result, industrial states, including Canada, Germany, Japan, and the United States have greatly reduced their sulfur dioxide emissions.[21] Additionally, many industrial states have shifted towards alternative energy sources. For example, in the 1980s, Britain abandoned coal subsidies, thereby encouraging the shift toward natural gas, a cleaner energy source. Other industrial states have increased their reliance on nuclear power, which in the mid-1990s supplied 75 percent of the electricity in France, 50 percent in Sweden, 30 percent in Germany, and 20 percent in the United States.[22]

The automobile is a principal source of air pollution in modern societies. A single tank of gasoline, for example, produces 300–400 pounds of carbon dioxide, the gas most responsible for global warming, and large quantities of ozone, the principal ingredient in urban smog. Other harmful pollutants resulting from engine combustion include nitrogen dioxide, carbon monoxide, lead, and toxic hydrocarbons. Beginning in the late 1960s the United States began imposing increasingly stringent pollution controls on new automobiles, resulting in significant reductions in harmful gas emissions. Subsequently many industrial countries, along with some emerging economies, have imposed pollution controls on new vehicles.

Global Warming

One of the harmful consequences of air pollution is the phenomenon of global warming. Although the earth's temperature is a result of a delicate balance among physical conditions, energy phenomena, and chemical processes, the chemical composition of each planet's atmosphere is of critical importance. The difference in temperatures between Mars (where people would freeze), Venus (where people would burn), and the earth, for example, is due to the widely different chemical compositions of each planet.

Scientists have become increasingly convinced that air pollution has harmful consequences on the earth's climate. Because man-made gases (chiefly carbon dioxide along with methane and nitrous oxide) trap solar radiation—much like the glass of a plant-breeder's hothouse—the rise in some types of air pollution can influence climate change. The so-called **greenhouse effect** occurs because water vapors and man-made gases allow more of the sun's heat to be absorbed by the earth than is released back into space. It is estimated that electrical power plants, cars and trucks, and households and business enterprises each produce roughly one-third of total man-made greenhouse gases.[23]

Although scientists differ as to the nature, causes, and extent of the greenhouse effect, little doubt exists that the earth has increased its temperature slightly in the past century. Although the global average temperature in the 1890s was about 58.2 degrees Fahrenheit, by the late 1980s it had climbed to 59.4 degrees. Interestingly, six of the seven warmest years since 1850 took place in the 1980s, and 1990 was the warmest since scientists began measuring the earth's temperature.[24] An international body of scientists convened by the UN—the so-called Intergovernmental Panel on Climate Change—has predicted that if humans continue to generate greenhouse gases at the present rate, the earth's mean temperature will rise by 1.8 to 6.3 degrees Fahrenheit by the end of the next century.[25]

Although it is impossible to predict the impact of a temperature shift of this magnitude, it is clear that some regions will benefit from climate change whereas others will lose. For example, as northern temperate regions become warmer, the climates could become more conducive to agricultural production, with grain production increasing in such countries as Canada and Russia. By contrast, regions closer to the equator could become less productive because of insufficient rainfall or excessive heat. As a result, agricultural production could decline in southern states of the United States and in countries such as Argentina and the Ukraine. One of the most serious effects of global warming is likely to be the rise in the level of the ocean because of thermal expansion of sea water. Studies have found that a 6 degree temperature increase would result in the sea rising about 3 feet[26]— a development that would destroy low-lying islands like the Seychelles and the Maldives and create a new category of international refugees known as "ecological refugees." Moreover, if the oceans were to rise 3 feet, some 72 million people would be left homeless in China, 11 million in Bangladesh, and 8 million in Egypt.[27]

It has been estimated that the burning of fossil fuels generates more than 70 percent of all electricity, energy, and heat in industrial states. Because such states have the highest levels of energy consumption, they are responsible for the bulk of the world's air pollution. In the early 1990s, total carbon dioxide emissions were estimated at 26.4 billion metric tons, of which 84 percent were from the developed nations. As of the mid-1990s, the major air-polluting countries in the world were the United States, the European Union, China, Russia, and Japan. They were responsible, respectively, for 22, 13, 12, 9, and 5 percent of the world's global emissions of carbon dioxide.[28] Even though per capita energy consumption varies significantly among states, the growth in energy consumption has stabilized in some developed nations but is rising rapidly in some emerging economies (see fig. 19.1).

Several international efforts have been made to reduce the industrial states' greenhouse gas emissions. At the Second World Climate Conference, held in Geneva in November 1990, 135 states adopted a declaration calling for a reduction in greenhouse gases and for the development of an international convention on climate change. The latter goal was realized at the 1992 Earth Summit (see case

Greenhouse effect
Because of increasing industrial pollution, especially from carbon dioxide, heat is trapped by these "greenhouse" gases, thereby raising the earth's temperature.

Climate Treaty
A binding convention, signed at the 1992 Earth Summit in Rio de Janeiro, that seeks to counter global warming by calling on states to reduce emissions of carbon dioxide, methane, and other "greenhouse" gases.

Ozone depletion
The loss of the atmosphere's ozone layer because of the release of ozone-destroying chlorofluorocarbons (CFCs). The ozone layer is important because it protects the earth from the sun's ultraviolet rays.

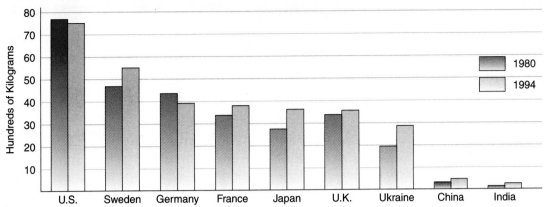

FIGURE 19.1
Annual Per Capita Energy Consumption, 1980 and 1994 (hundreds of kilograms of oil equivalent)
Source: World Bank, *World Development Report 1997: The State in a Changing World* (New York: Oxford University Press, 1997), pp. 228–29.

19.1) with the signing of the *UN Framework Convention on Climate Change,* commonly called the **Climate Treaty.** This accord—which by 1997 had been ratified by 166 countries, including the United States—established general guidelines for curbing greenhouse emissions.[29] According to the accord, signatory states agreed to seek the stabilization of greenhouse gas emissions at a level that would prevent "dangerous anthropogenic interference with the climate system." In particular, the developed countries agreed to reduce greenhouse emissions to the 1990 level by the year 2000. However, because the treaty imposed no specific national obligations on emissions reductions, most developed countries have failed to curb greenhouse gas emissions. Indeed, only two countries—Britain and Germany—are expected to realize the goal of reducing emissions to the 1990 target at the turn of the century. Most industrial states are expected to increase their emissions by 5–15 percent over the target, with U.S. emissions expected to exceed the 1990 level by 13 percent.

In view of the growing scientific consensus that man-made gases are harmful to the earth's climate, and in view of the failure of the Climate Treaty to reduce greenhouse gas emissions, the United Nations sponsored a major conference in Kyoto, Japan in 1997 to strengthen the climate regime. The politics of the Kyoto Summit is briefly examined in case 19.2.

Ozone Depletion

Another major effect of air pollution is **ozone depletion.** Ozone is an important ingredient in the atmosphere because it is the only gas in the atmosphere that

FIGURE 19.2
Leading States of Carbon Dioxide Emissions, 1992 (million metric tons of carbon dioxide equivalents)
Source: Data from World Resources Institute et al., *World Resources, 1996–97* (New York: Oxford University Press, 1996, p. 316.

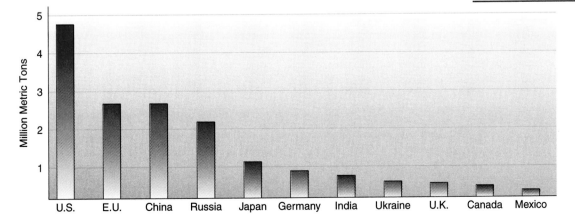

Case 19.2 The Kyoto Summit: The Politics of Global Warming

In December 1997 some 5,000 representatives from 150 countries met in Kyoto, Japan, to develop a more effective climate convention than the one approved at the Rio Summit in 1992. The challenge in Kyoto was to develop more realistic goals and to establish binding obligations on signatory states. The 1992 Climate Treaty had called on states to stabilize greenhouse gas emissions at the 1990 level but, as noted, virtually all states had continued to increase their gas emissions. Because the UN Intergovernmental Panel on Climate Change had concluded in 1995 that continued greenhouse emissions would be detrimental to the earth's climate, the aim of the Kyoto Summit was to develop an authoritative global warming regime—one that would stabilize greenhouse emissions by establishing binding national targets.

Stabilizing total gas emissions presents an extraordinary challenge for a number of reasons. First, the world's population continues to increase rapidly, with the largest growth occurring in the poorest countries. It is estimated that the world's population will expand from 6 billion in 1997 to more than 10 billion by 2050. Second, because people in developing nations continue to demand an increasing standard of living, and because economic growth is impossible without increasing energy consumption, a rise in living conditions in most Third World nations is unlikely without significant increases in greenhouse gas emissions. As a result, greenhouse emissions are expected to rise significantly in the developing nations—increasing from roughly 20 percent of total world emissions to more than 50 percent by the year 2025.[30] Because energy use is likely to rise rapidly in emerging economies, one scholar estimates that the stabilization of world greenhouse emissions during the 1995–2005 period would require that industrial states reduce their emissions by 35 percent.[31]

As noted earlier, most greenhouse gas emissions have been produced by industrial states. As a result, developing nations believe that they should be freed from restrictions until they are able to achieve an adequate standard of living for their people. According to them, industrial states should bear the major responsibility for reducing emissions in the short run. China and India, for example, have been especially vigorous in their opposition to binding greenhouse targets because each has substantial coal deposits. Thus, the central international political dilemma in seeking to manage climate change through the reduction of total world greenhouse gases is how to define and allocate emissions targets. Should the developing nations be held to a lower standard than industrial states? Should they be exempted from emissions requirements until their peoples achieve an adequate standard of living? How should targets be allocated among the industrial states?

After intense negotiations at the Kyoto conference, states agreed to emissions reductions on the developed countries but not on developing nations. The treaty—the so-called **Kyoto Protocol**—requires that industrial countries reduce their greenhouse gas emissions by about 5 percent below the 1990 level by the period 2008–2012. To achieve this target, the accord requires that the European Union reduce its emissions by 8 percent, the United States by 7 percent, and Japan by 6 percent. Because this goal represents a cut of roughly 30 percent in what emissions would be otherwise, achieving this goal will involve radical reductions in the national use of fossil fuels in industrialized states. Although no specific binding targets are established for the developing nations, they are encouraged to set voluntary reduction targets. An important, though contentious, element of the Kyoto Protocol is the provision of trading *"emissions rights."* According to this concept, nations that are unable to meet their emissions targets can buy the excess "quota" from countries that have lower emissions standards than is required.

Fearing that the North would be called on to bear the major burden for reducing greenhouse gas emissions, the U.S. Senate overwhelmingly passed a resolution before the Kyoto conference requiring that any climate treaty had to involve developing nations as well. As a result, President Clinton, although announcing his support for the accord, indicated that he would not submit the Kyoto treaty for Senate ratification until the developing nations had agreed to participate.

protects the earth from the sun's harmful ultraviolet rays. Ozone is a type of oxygen in which the molecules have three atoms instead of the normal two. Because of this, ozone can absorb the sun's rays and thereby protect human beings from solar radiation. Ultraviolet rays are detrimental because they can cause blindness and skin cancer, including the deadly melanoma, and can weaken the body's immune system that helps fight diseases. The two major ozone-depleting chemicals are halons and chlorofluorocarbons (CFCs). The most widely used CFC is the refrigerant Freon, accounting for 35 percent of the CFCs used globally. Other major CFSc include foam, cleaning agents, and aerosol sprays. The most widespread use of halons is in fire-fighting equipment.

Soon after an ozone hole over the Antarctic was confirmed in 1985, governments began to take seriously the problem of ozone depletion. In 1987 diplomats from twenty-four industrial countries gathered in Montreal at a UN-sponsored conference on the status of the ozone. At the end of the meeting diplomats signed the *Montreal Protocol on Substances That Deplete the Ozone Layer*—commonly denoted simply as the **Montreal Protocol.** This agreement, which went into effect in 1989, requires states to reduce the production of CFCs by one-half by the year 2000. Soon after the protocol went into effect, additional studies revealed that the threat to the ozone was far more serious than had been originally thought. As a result, the Montreal Protocol was amended in June 1990 to require a complete halt to CFC production by the end of the century. In January 1992 the National Aeronautics and Space Administration (NASA) announced that they had discovered extraordinarily high levels of ozone-depleting chemicals in the Northern Hemisphere and warned that a large ozone hole could develop in the populated regions of North America and Europe. The U.S. government promptly called for an accelerated phaseout of CFCs.

The reduction and eventual elimination of ozone-depleting chemicals can only be successful if states cooperate internationally. Most industrial states have either eliminated or have significantly reduced the production of aerosol products. The most difficult remaining challenge involves the development of alternative systems of refrigeration and the development of tighter controls over CFCs in existing refrigerators and air conditioners. Because CFCs are a major source of ozone depletion, the DuPont Corporation has decided to halt its $750-million production of Freon and to develop a CFC-free alternative. Many industrial states have already taken CFC-reduction measures, including the use of machines for recycling CFCs from refrigerators and home and car air conditioners. But if the reduction of ozone-depleting chemicals is to succeed, the transitional countries of Central Europe and the developing nations in Asia, Africa, and Latin America will have to cooperate as well. Currently, China and India, whose combined population accounts for about 35 percent of the world's population, contribute only about 3 percent of total ozone-depleting chemicals. But in view of the growing demand for refrigeration in those countries, control over CFC production is essential. At first both China and India refused to sign the Montreal Protocol because of the emerging demand for refrigeration among their citizens. But after receiving a pledge of financial aid from developed countries to assist in switching to CFC-free technologies, both countries signed the Protocol.

Acid Rain

A final major air pollution problem is **acid rain**—rain contaminated with chemical pollutants, especially sulfur dioxide and nitrogen oxide. When these and other chemicals are released into the atmosphere and then deposited through precipitation in distant places, they can have a highly destructive effect on vegetation and animal life. The harmful effect of acid rain was first recognized in Scandinavia, where the increasing acidic (pH) content of its lakes had destroyed aquatic life in

Montreal Protocol
An agreement, signed in Montreal in 1987, calling on signatory states to limit the production and use of ozone-depleting CFCs in order to protect the earth from the sun's harmful ultraviolet rays.

Acid rain
Precipitation contaminated with industrial pollutants, especially sulphur dioxide and nitrogen oxide.

thousands of small lakes in Finland, Norway, and Sweden. More recently scientists have recognized that acid rain destroys trees and other vegetation. Because the principal sources of chemical pollutants are the industrial states, the major areas suffering from acid rain are the northeast industrial corridor of North America and the northwestern part of Europe. Britain, the Netherlands, and West Germany are major victims of acid rain. In 1982, 8 percent of West Germany's forests were dying or in decline from acid rain; by 1988 that figure had increased to 52 percent.[32] It has been estimated that 50 million hectares of European forests, representing 35 percent of the total, have been damaged by acid rain and air pollution.

The most important international cooperation on acid rain has been among European states. As a result of their initiative, officials from industrial nations met in Geneva in 1979 and signed the *Convention on Long-Range Transboundary Air Pollution*. The convention established a framework for scientific cooperation and consultation, including an executive body that meets annually to review progress in moderating air pollution. Because of growing awareness of the dangers of transboundary air pollution, industrial countries have subsequently developed four other treaties based on the Geneva Convention framework. These four conventions involve reductions in sulfur emissions (1985), nitrogen oxide emissions (1988), emissions of volatile organic compounds (1991), and the further reduction of sulfur emissions (1994).

Acid rain is also a special problem between bordering states, such as Canada and the United States, and Russia and Finland. In 1986, for example, Canadian Prime Minister Brian Mulroney designated acid rain as his top priority for the 1986 U.S.-Canadian summit. According to Canadian government officials, because of the northeastern wind currents, air pollution from U.S. industries is carried to Canada where it is deposited on forests and lakes. As a result of growing Canadian pressure, the U.S. government has attempted to allocate increasing funds to assist in industrial antipollution programs. Finland has also publicly condemned the high level of chemical pollutants carried from Russia to its territory. To help reduce air pollution, the Finnish government has provided Russia with nearly a $1-billion loan to establish antipollution technology in industrial plants near the Finnish border in order to reduce sulfur dioxide emissions. Norway, too, has accused the United Kingdom of being a major source of the acid rain along its southern coast. Because of wind currents, air pollution from the British Isles' coal power plants is carried to southern Norway, where it contaminates the water streams and destroys the forests.

Land

A thin layer of topsoil provides food for 5.8 billion people and some 4 billion domesticated animals. But overuse, misuse, or neglect of the land threatens the earth's soil. Some of the principal causes of land degradation are overgrazing, overcultivation, and waterlogging and salting of irrigated lands. Overgrazing results from allowing too many animals to graze on rangelands, leading to destruction of plant life and the eventual erosion of topsoil from the ravages of wind and water. In effect, overgrazing occurs when the soil's carrying capacity is exceeded. Overcultivation results from the overuse or misuse of agricultural land by failing to fertilize, rotate crops, or allow the earth to regenerate. Finally, irrigated lands can become waterlogged when there is insufficient drainage and the land is allowed to become an unproductive "wet desert." Moreover, in hot, dry areas the irrigation of land can result in the salinization of land, because the rapid evaporation of water leaves a damaging residue of salt. UNEP has estimated that some 100 million acres of irrigated lands suffer from salinization.[33]

International environmental concerns on land use have focused on two major problem areas: destruction of agricultural lands (known as desertification) and the destruction of forests (known as deforestation). **Desertification** is the process by which land becomes like a desert, completely unusable for productive purposes. This process, which annually claims an estimated 15 million acres worldwide (about the size of West Virginia), occurs because of unfavorable atmospheric conditions but also because of human neglect or land misuse. In 1977 the UN sponsored a conference to address desertification in Africa, where it is most acute. Although the African representatives accepted a Plan of Action to Combat Desertification, the UNEP found that virtually none of the twenty-eight recommended measures had been implemented seven years later. Indeed, UNEP concluded in 1984 that the problem of desertification had become more severe and that some 11 billion acres—35 percent of the world's land surface—were now threatened.[34] As a result of growing international concern, especially among developing nations, approximately a hundred states signed the *1994 UN Convention to Combat Desertification*—a treaty that seeks to combat desertification and to mitigate the effects of drought, especially in Africa, by encouraging national action programs with the support of the international community.

Deforestation, the second major global land issue, involves the destruction of the earth's virgin forests. Three factors contribute to deforestation: first, forests are cleared to permanently convert land for agricultural use; second, virgin forests are cut down for the economic value of timber; and third, forests are used to meet the local demand for fuelwood, fodder, and other forest products. Deforestation is especially acute when it involves the tropical forests. Although tropical rain forests comprise only 6 percent of the earth's land, they play a disproportionate role in influencing the biosphere. Because the continuous warm, tropical climate fosters continuous growth, the rain forests provide a powerful ecosystem, storing and absorbing billions of tons of water from the atmosphere and generating large volumes of clouds that influence weather cycles not only in the tropics but globally. Moreover, because trees absorb carbon dioxide from the atmosphere during photosynthesis (a plant's respiratory cycle), tropical rain forests serve as large carbon-holding dumps. Rain forests thus contribute greatly to the reduction of carbon from the atmosphere. When forests are burned, they release large amounts of carbon dioxide into the atmosphere, greatly increasing greenhouse gases. It has been estimated that tropical deforestation contributes from 7 to 31 percent of the total carbon dioxide released each year. Moreover, the destruction of Amazonian forests has been estimated to contribute as much as 20 percent of the carbon emitted each year into the atmosphere and to account for as much as 11 percent of all global warming gases.[35] The destruction of tropical rain forests therefore has significant implications, extending far beyond state borders.

As a result of deforestation, the tropical rain forest has been estimated at 55 percent of its original size. Moreover, annual destruction of the rain forest has been estimated at 1 percent of the total, or an area roughly the size of the Netherlands and Switzerland combined.[36] Because Latin America holds more than half (57 percent) of the world's rain forest, the largest amount of deforestation is in this region. Of the 20 million hectares of tropical forests destroyed annually, about 12 million are in Latin America, slightly less than 4 million are in Africa, and slightly more than 4 million are in Asia (see fig. 19.3). Brazil, which contains 30 percent of the earth's remaining tropical forests, destroys some 9 million hectares annually.[37] To help control deforestation, more than fifty countries signed the *1983 International Tropical Timber Agreement*. This accord provides a framework for cooperation between timber producers and consumers and encourages the establishment of national policies aimed at sustainable utilization of tropical forests. In 1994 this accord was supplemented by a more comprehensive agreement that seeks to ensure that by the year 2000 all exports of tropical timber originate from sustainable forests. The 1983 accord will expire when sufficient states have ratified the 1994 International Tropical Timber Agreement.

Desertification
The process by which potentially productive land is transformed into arid, desert-like territory, unfit for productive uses.

Deforestation
The indiscriminate destruction of the earth's virgin forests to achieve rapid economic expansion. The loss of forests, especially those in the tropics, has been highly destructive to the environment.

FIGURE 19.3
Annual
Deforestation in
Three Regions (in
thousands of
hectares;
percentages
indicate the area of
each region
deforested
annually)
Source: Data from World
Resources Institute, *World
Resources,* 1990–1991
(New York: Oxford Univer-
sity Press, 1990), p. 43.

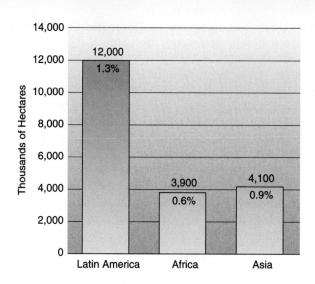

Water and Marine Resources

Water, one of the most pervasive elements on the earth, is estimated at 1.41 billion cubic kilometers—or enough to cover the earth's surface 3,000 meters deep. Of this amount only 2 percent is usable fresh water; the remainder is ocean saltwater. Although total water supplies in the world are sufficient to meet current demand, fresh water is unevenly and irregularly distributed, with some regions of the world suffering from growing water scarcities. Because of continuing population growth, increasing human demand for fresh water, and global climatic changes that make water supply and demand more uncertain, some regions are experiencing growing water scarcities. It has been estimated that by the year 2050 about 4.4 billion of the earth's population of 10 billion will suffer from chronic water shortages.[38]

Because fresh water is a vital resource for human life, some scholars argue that water and water-supply systems are likely to be an important source of future international conflict.[39] Such conflict will be especially likely in areas in which water is scarce and in which access to water is considered a matter of national security. According to one scholar, countries that are highly vulnerable to water scarcities are likely to "fight for access to water, use water as a tool and weapon in battle, and target the water facilities of enemies."[40] During the 1991 Persian Gulf War, for example, both sides targeted water-supply systems; for example, withdrawing Iraqi forces destroyed most of Kuwait's desalination plants.

Because rivers are the principal source of fresh water, and because rivers often serve numerous countries, the distribution of water has historically created friction among states. The River Jordan, for example, provides a significant portion of the water consumed by Israel, Jordan, and Syria. And because each state seeks increasing water supplies, the distribution of water is likely to be a continuing source of international conflict in the Middle East. Tensions are also likely between Iraq, Syria, and Turkey over water use from the Tigris and Euphrates Rivers, both of which originate in eastern Turkey. Although the Tigris runs directly into Iraq and into the Persian Gulf, the Euphrates flows through Syria before arriving in Iraq. Turkey is presently completing the Ataturk Dam along the Euphrates River, which will greatly increase its hydroelectric power and irrigation capabilities. To the extent that this project reduces water for Syria or Iraq, it is likely to contribute to regional tensions.

Undoubtedly, the most important waterway in the Middle East is the Nile River, which originates in Ethiopia (Blue Nile) and Uganda (White Nile). The river serves nine countries, providing Egypt with almost all of its water needs. Because

Egypt is the last country along the river's long course, the availability of water depends greatly upon other countries' willingness to share water with Egypt. Given the increasing demand for water in the countries surrounding the Nile, it is not surprising that UN Secretary-General Boutros Boutros-Ghali, Egypt's former foreign minister, has observed that "the next war in our region will be over the water of the Nile, not politics."[41] Other potential conflicts over water supplies focus on the Okavango River in Angola, Namibia, and Botswana and the Ganges River in India and Bangladesh.

One of the major obstacles to potable water is the introduction of pollutants into the water ecosystem. Because water is regularly replenished, the introduction of chemical pollution into the water cycle can severely harm the capacity of nature to replenish water sources. The discharge of human wastes, chemical fertilizers, industrial wastes, DDT, fossil fuel pollutants, and other contaminants into water streams is ecologically destructive and especially damaging to lakes and rivers that supply fresh water. As developed countries have become more aware of the harmful impact of water pollution, significant efforts have been made to reduce chemical pollutants into water streams. But much more needs to be done, especially in the newly industrializing countries.

Historically, the oceans have been viewed as a shared, collective good. Although the principle of the "freedom of the seas" dates to ancient times, the doctrine did not become fully developed until the seventeenth century with the publication of *Mare Liberum* (open seas) by Dutch jurist Hugo Grotius. Because the sea is a shared good, like the "village common" noted earlier in this chapter, its protection and preservation is dependent on the wise collective management of all states. Case 19.3 briefly describes some of the measures that the international community has enacted to regulate the open seas.

Biodiversity

Biologists estimate that the earth has more than 10 million species, of which 1.4 million have been identified. Of the known species, nearly 750,000 are insects, some 250,000 are flowering plants, and some 4,000 are mammal species.[42] Scientists refer to this large variety of animal and plant life as **biodiversity.**[43] Because of a decline in genetic diversity and the destruction of diverse ecosystems that sustain animal and plant life, a growing number of scientists believe that more stringent conservation measures are needed.

Biodiversity
The large variety of animal and plant species on earth.

One of the earliest marine conservation measures was the adoption in 1946 of the *International Convention for the Regulation of Whaling.* The treaty, which established an International Whaling Commission (IWC), called for the setting of

Case 19.3 | The Management of Ocean Waters

Fundamentally, three types of ocean waters exist—the territorial sea, exclusive economic zones, and the high seas. The *territorial sea*, the ocean adjacent to the territorial state, extends up to 12 nautical miles (NM) from the coast and is under the exclusive control of the coastal state. Before entering the territorial sea, ships need to get permission from the territorial state. Until the late 1970s states claimed a wide variety of territorial waters, ranging from 3 NM to more than 20, with the norm being about 6. As a result of the **Third UN Convention on the Law of the Sea (UNCLOS III),** adopted in 1982 and put into effect in 1993, the maximum territorial limit was established at 12 NM. One of the effects of the extension of territorial waters was the potential impairment of channels and straits of less than 24 NM. As a result, UNCLOS III reaffirmed the historic right of *innocent passage*, which gives ships the right to travel through a state's territorial waters as long as it is carried out peacefully, and the right

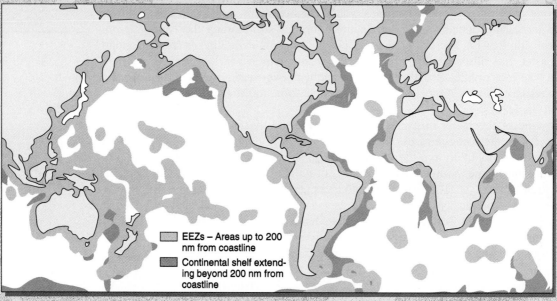

EEZs – Areas up to 200 nm from coastline

Continental shelf extending beyond 200 nm from coastline

MAP 19.1
The Management of Ocean Waters.

fishing quotas and the regulation of whaling seasons. Despite its aim, the IWC was ineffective in limiting whaling. Indeed, more whales were killed annually after the IWC was established than before the creation of the regime. As a result of continued depletion of whales, the IWC, led by the United States and with the support of a growing number of nonwhaling states, adopted a whaling moratorium in 1987. This moratorium was further strengthened in 1994, when the IWC instituted a long-term ban on whaling in waters surrounding the Antarctica (below the 40 degrees south latitude). Despite the IWC ban, a number of countries—most noticeably, Japan, Norway, and Iceland—have continued to carry out "scientific" whaling.[44]

Another important collective effort to manage global marine resources is the *1958 Convention on Fishing and Conservation of Living Resources of the High Seas.* This treaty, which went into effect in 1966, seeks to protect species from overfishing in the ocean. Subsequently, other regional and international accords have been

to use *international straits*—narrow passageways joining two bodies of international water. Because the world has more than 120 straits of 24 miles or less, the right of passage through such straits was considered essential in maintaining efficient shipping.

The *high seas* are the ocean waters that extend beyond the territorial sea. In these waters each state has an equal right to use the ocean, whether for fishing, transportation, or other purposes. A complex body of international law governs the high seas, and ships are responsible for abiding by these rules and principles. In addition, ships are under the jurisdiction of the *flag state,* the country in which a ship is registered and denoted by the nationality of the flag flown in the open seas.

The **exclusive economic zone (EEZ),** a concept that became accepted with UNCLOS III, gives the territorial state exclusive economic control over a zone up to 200 NM from its coastline. According to the 1982 treaty, the coastal state has sole control over the EEZ and can therefore regulate all fishing, mining, and other economic activity in those waters. Because the division between the territorial sea and the high seas is normally at 12 NM, the EEZ involves an additional 188 NM of high seas. Ships can move freely in these waters, requiring the territorial state's consent only when undertaking economic activity. Although the creation of EEZs represents a major delimitation of the high seas, it is ironically contributing to improved management of marine resources.

One of the most important and innovative developments of UNCLOS III is the claim that resources in the high seas are a "common heritage" and belong to all of humankind. Whereas the historic doctrine of "freedom of the seas" had asserted that ocean resources in the open seas were free until appropriated, the **common heritage principle** asserts that the mineral resources in the high seas belong to all nations. Because the ocean floor is covered with manganese nodules and small amounts of copper, nickel, and cobalt, access to the deep seabed is potentially of major economic importance if efficient and cost-effective technologies can be devised to mine the floor.

In order to give force to this new principle, UNCLOS III established an *International Seabed Authority (ISA)* to regulate deep-sea-mining operations and to distribute revenues from mining business ventures. As originally conceived, mining of the deep seabed was to be carried out by a supranational mining company using technologies developed by industrial countries. But because developed countries, led by the United States, opposed such an initiative, UNCLOS III was amended in 1993. According to the revised treaty, private mining companies can carry out deep-sea-mining exploration without paying annual dues, and industrial countries are not obligated to transfer mining technologies to the developing nations. As now conceived, the ISA is to be a regulative institution over the deep seabed, not a multinational organization charged with mining, processing, and marketing of ocean minerals. Notwithstanding the significant North-South debate over deep-sea mining, as of 1997 no industrial country had found an economically feasible way to carry out mining in the high seas.

developed to regulate specific fish species. These initiatives include the establishment of organizations such as the International Pacific Halibut Commission and the Inter-American Tuna Commission and the development of regional fishing regimes. During the late 1970s and early 1980s, for example, northern European countries temporarily banned the fishing of herring in the North Sea because its stock had become unduly depleted.

But continued overfishing poses a major threat to the global marine commons. The open seas remain the major source of fish for human consumption, providing seven times the amount of fish caught in inland freshwaters. From 1950 to 1988, the total marine catch quintupled, rising from 17.6 to 84 million metric tons,[45] leading some scientists to conclude that fishing levels had reached the sea's carrying capacity and that failure to regulate fishing would endanger species and threaten the future productivity of the seas. Thus, continuing efforts to monitor and regulate fishing are important in protecting marine species and providing sustainable marine resources. One of the most important developments in managing marine life has resulted from the creation of EEZs, in which more than 90 percent of the ocean's fish are caught. With the establishment of these zones, the responsibility for regulating fishing in the waters surrounding countries has been placed in the hands of territorial states.

Another noteworthy international initiative for protecting endangered species is the **Convention on the International Trade in Endangered Species of Wild Flora and Fauna (CITES).** The CITES seeks to protect threatened species, especially exotic wildlife, from overexploitation by regulating the international trade of endangered animal and plant species. This is done by requiring export and import permits or by complete trade bans, such as the CITES 1989 ban of ivory. It is estimated that the value of the annual international trade of exotic wildlife, much of it illegal, is about $5 billion.[46] A related biodiversity initiative is the *1971 Convention on Wetlands,* which encourages states to protect soggy wildlands, including mangroves, freshwater marshes, peatlands, flood plains, and deltas. Wetlands are important ecosystems, providing a habitat to waterfowl and other wildlife.

To date, the most comprehensive initiative to protect biological life is the **Convention on Biological Diversity,** generally referred to as the Biodiversity Treaty. This 1992 treaty, which was signed by more than 160 states at the Earth Summit and which was subsequently ratified by 161 countries, seeks to protect the habitats of endangered species by encouraging states to pursue conservation programs and strategies that sustain biological diversity. The United States, which originally opposed the treaty because it believed that the accord threatened patents in the emerging biotechnology industry, became party to the convention in 1993 after Bill Clinton became president.

Convention on the International Trade in Endangered Species of Wild Flora and Fauna (CITES)
This 1973 multilateral accord seeks to regulate the export, transit, and importation of endangered animal and plant species.

Convention on Biological Diversity
This 1992 treaty seeks to protect the habitats of endangered species by encouraging states to pursue conservation measures.

Waste Disposal

One of the major effects of industrial development is the generation of hazardous wastes, including chemical sludge, incinerator ash, organic solvents, pesticides, and radioactive wastes. It is estimated that 90 percent of the world's toxic wastes are generated by the developed countries. Although most of this waste is disposed of domestically through incineration and landfills, hazardous waste is also exported to other countries. It is estimated that of the total hazardous waste traded internationally, about 20 percent is accounted for by the developing nations.[47] Because many developing nations lack the technology or administrative capacity to dispose of toxic wastes safely, the international trade of hazardous wastes has generated significant tension between developed and developing nations.

Because of numerous reports of illegal transboundary shipments of toxic wastes, the United Nations Environment Program began addressing this issue in the early 1980s. In 1985, a UNEP working group issued a series of guidelines and principles for managing the disposal of industrial wastes in an environmentally safe manner. Because these norms were nonbinding, UNEP sought to strengthen controls on hazardous waste trade. UNEP's initiatives resulted in an important treaty—the *1989 Basel Convention on the Control of Transboundary Movements of Hazardous Wastes and Their Disposal*—to further reduce transnational movements of toxic wastes and to assist the developing nations in safely disposing of the wastes they generate. Although the treaty affirmed the right of states to unilaterally ban the importation of hazardous wastes, it also allowed for transboundary movement of such wastes, provided importing states could dispose of the waste in an "environmentally sound" manner and the receiving government had consented to such trade. Subsequently, some developing nations began demanding a complete ban to the international trade of toxic wastes, believing that only a complete halt in the transboundary movement of waste could effectively protect their countries' environments. As a result of persistent lobbying by African countries, the Basel Convention's signatory states adopted in 1994 a complete prohibition of waste trade, in effect reversing the aim of the original regime.[48]

The dumping of wastes into the sea is also a major environmental threat to the global commons. Because the bulk of ocean pollution comes from industrial and human wastes disposed directly and indirectly by states, the most important actions that can be taken to improve the quality of ocean waters lie with coastal states and countries sharing common river systems. It has been estimated that more than 2.1 million tons of liquid chemical waste is poured into the North Sea alone each year.[49] Protection of ocean waters thus requires the control of the type and quantity of wastes dumped into coastal waters. Although no major global treaty has been developed to control ocean waste disposal by states, a number of regions—including the Northeast Atlantic, the Baltic, the Mediterranean, the Persian Gulf, and the Southeast Pacific—have developed general accords that seek to limit land-based ocean pollution.

The international community has been more effective in developing binding agreements on the waste disposal in the open seas. One of the first treaties to limit pollution by ships was the *International Convention for the Prevention of Pollution of the Sea by Oil* (London, 1954). This accord, which regulated marine oil pollution within 50 miles of coastal states, was replaced in 1973 by the more comprehensive *International Convention for the Prevention of Pollution from Ships* (also known as the MARPOL Convention). This treaty limits oil discharges at sea, establishes minimum distances from land for discharging wastes, and establishes protective zones in which discharges are prohibited altogether. Another treaty that regulates ocean dumping is the *Convention on the Prevention of Marine Pollution by Dumping of Wastes and Other Matter* (London, 1972). This accord prohibits ocean dumping of selected toxic wastes, and requires permits for the disposal of other matter.

In sum, the international community has developed a large number of conventions (some of these are listed in table 19.4) that contribute to environmental protection of the global commons. As with all emerging regimes, the development of authoritative norms and the establishment of effective enforcement of rules has

TABLE 19.4   Selected Global Environmental Conventions

Atmosphere	Convention on Long-Range Transboundary Air Pollution (1979) Montreal Protocol on Substances That Deplete the Ozone Layer (1987) UN Framework Convention on Climate Change (1992) Kyoto Protocol (1997)
Land	International Convention to Combat Desertification (1994) International Tropical Timber Agreement (1994)
Ocean	Convention of Fishing and Conservation of Living Resources of the High Seas (1958) Third UN Convention on the Law of the Sea (1982)
Biodiversity	Convention on Wetlands of International Importance Especially as Waterfowl Habitat (1971) Convention on the International Trade in Endangered Species of Wild Flora and Fauna-CITES (1973) Convention on Biological Diversity (1992)
Waste Disposal	London Convention on the Prevention of Marine Pollution (1972) International Convention for the Prevention of Pollution from Ships—MARPOL (1973) Basel Convention on the Control of Transboundary Movements of Hazardous Wastes and their Disposal (1989)

been a major challenge. Despite modest achievements in establishing authoritative conservation norms, international cooperation has resulted in an increasing number of international environmental treaties, increasing from less than 10 in 1950 to more than 130 in 1990.[50]

IN CONCLUSION

Although scholars differ on the nature and severity of the world's existing ecological problems, there is widespread agreement that governments need to cooperate in managing global resources and in preserving the world's environment. To a significant degree, this growing conviction is rooted in the belief of **ecological interdependence**—that is, the conviction that the quality of the earth's environment is dependent on the collective behavior of all countries. Clearly, air and water pollution and other harmful environmental developments can be passed along from one state to another, thereby contributing not only to ecological destruction in neighboring states, but more importantly, threatening the quality of life for the entire world.

Because economic development normally creates harmful by-products on the environment, developed states are increasingly regulating business enterprise and modifying technology to reduce pollution and limit other harmful consequences to the environment. The developing nations, while also aware of the detrimental ecological effects of modernization, are pressing for rapid economic expansion in order to improve living conditions. They are therefore less eager to impose environmental restrictions that might limit business enterprise. Because of different national perspectives on the world's environment, the allocation of responsibility for protecting the global commons will continue to be a source of conflict among states, especially between the developed and developing countries.

Ecological interdependence
The belief that global environmental protection requires the shared participation of many states.

SUMMARY

1. Managing the earth's natural resources and protecting its environment requires a global perspective. Because states share many natural resources, such as air, water, and land, the stewardship of these collective goods requires international cooperation.

2. The tragedy of the commons provides an apt metaphor for protecting the world's environment. According to the commons analogy, the misuse and overuse of the earth's shared resources can result in ecological destruction. Because no central governing authorities exist in the international system, the protection of the earth's collective resources can be realized only through the individual and shared actions of member-states.

3. Scholars and public officials hold widely different perceptions about the nature and extent of the world's ecological problems and the means by which they can be ameliorated. Ecopessimists are critical of unregulated economic growth and strongly support global environmental protection initiatives. Ecooptimists, by contrast, assume that despite some of the harmful by-products of industrialization, economic growth can continue to improve living conditions.

4. One of the major harmful effects of modernization is air pollution, caused in great part by the burning of fossil fuels. The major international problems resulting from the contamination of the atmosphere are global warming, ozone depletion, and acid rain.

5. Significant parts of the earth's soil are being destroyed, especially in the Third World. Two major types of land depletion are desertification and deforestation. The first involves the destruction of agricultural land and the second the destruction of virgin forests. Because rain forests greatly influence the world's climate, tropical deforestation is an especially important global issue.

6. Given the expanding demand for fresh water, water scarcity is likely to be an increasing source of international conflict. Moreover, the continued contamination of rivers and coastal waters threatens not only ecosystems but also marine life. The creation of EEZs has significantly expanded the state's responsibility over coastal waters, thereby increasing the potential for managing marine life.

7. There is increasing evidence that continuing economic development and industrialization are threatening ecosystems and genetic diversity, and endangering species. As a result, states have signed numerous conventions to protect animal and plant life and the earth's environment that sustains such life.

8. Because economic growth involves the generation of hazardous wastes, countries need to develop environmentally safe strategies and technologies for the disposal of such wastes. Because some industrial wastes have been exported, the international community has sought to regulate, and more recently to ban, such trade.

KEY TERMS

tragedy of the commons

carrying capacity

ecopessimism

United Nations Environment Program (UNEP)

Earth Summit

UN Conference on Environment and Development (UNCED)

ecooptimism

greenhouse effect

Climate Treaty

Kyoto Protocol

ozone depletion

Montreal Protocol

acid rain

desertification

deforestation

Third UN Convention on the Law of the Sea (UNCLOS III)

exclusive economic zone (EEZ)

common heritage principle

biodiversity

Convention on the International Trade in Endangered Species of Wild Flora and Fauna (CITES)

Convention on Biological Diversity

ecological interdependence

RECOMMENDED READINGS

Benedick, Richard Elliot. *Ozone Diplomacy: New Directions in Safeguarding the Planet.* Cambridge: Harvard University Press, 1991. A lucid, comprehensive case study of how the world first became aware of the ecological threat posed by ozone depletion and then developed a treaty to respond to the threat. Benedick, the chief U.S. negotiator for the Montreal Protocol on ozone depletion, provides an insightful account of ecological diplomacy.

Brown, Lester R., fwrd by. *World Watch Reader on Global and Environmental Issues.* New York: W.W. Norton, 1991. An informative and readable collection of essays covering some of the major concerns in the management of global ecology.

Brundtland Commission. *Our Common Future.* New York: Oxford University Press, 1987. The UN-created World Commission on Environment and Development presents its conclusions in this report. The study calls for increased international cooperation in promoting ecologically responsible economic development.

The Global 2000 Report to the President: Entering the Twenty-First Century. A Report Prepared by the Council on Environmental Quality and the Department of State. New York: Penguin Books, 1982. This comprehensive study offers a somewhat pessimistic view of the future of the world. It argues that apart from effective collective actions, global ecological, economic, and social conditions are likely to deteriorate.

Lynn-Jones, Sean M., and Steven E. Miller, eds. *Global Dangers: Changing Dimensions of International Security.* Cambridge: MIT Press, 1995. These essays, previously published in the journal *International Security,* examine changing conceptions of international security. Several path-breaking articles analyze the impact of ecological issues on national security.

Miller, Marian A.L. *The Third World in Global Environmental Politics.* Boulder: Lynne Rienner Publishers, 1995. An informative overview of the North-South politics of environmental protection. The study provides three illuminating case studies on regime formation: ozone depletion, hazardous waste disposal, and biodiversity.

Pirages, Dennis. *Global Technopolitics: The International Politics of Technology & Resources.* Pacific Grove, Calif.: Brooks/Cole, 1989. This short study examines the growing functional interdependence of states, addressing such global issues as energy, hunger, environmental protection, natural resources, and technology transfers.

Porter, Gareth, and Janet Welsh Brown. *Global Environmental Politics,* 2nd ed. Boulder, Co.: Westview Press, 1996. Because of its clarity, succinctness, and comprehensive coverage, students will find this study an exceptionally useful introduction to global environmental politics.

Simon, Julian L., and Herman Kahan, eds. *The Resourceful Earth: A Response to Global 2000*. Oxford: Basic Blackwell, 1984. Contrary to the Global 2000 report, this study presents an optimistic view of future economic, ecological, and social conditions of the earth.

Susskind, Lawrence E. *Environmental Diplomacy: Negotiating More Effective Global Agreements*. New York: Oxford University Press, 1994. Presents a framework for developing a more effective global environmental regime. After examining key issues and problems in fostering global sustainable economic development, Susskind offers recommendations for strengthening environmental diplomacy.

Vogler, John. *The Global Commons: A Regime Analysis*. New York: John Wiley & Sons, 1996. This study examines international regimes that have been established to foster global cooperation and governance in four areas of common interest—the oceans, the Antarctica, outer space, and the atmosphere. According to Vogler, regime effectiveness is not based on hegemonic leadership but on the perception of mutual concern.

World Resources Institute et al. *World Resources, 1996–1997*. New York: Oxford University Press, 1996. An invaluable source of data on international economic, environmental, and social issues.

RELEVANT WEB SITES

Consortium for International Earth Science Information	www.ciesin.org
Environmental Treaties and Resources Indicators (ENTRI)	http://sedac.ciesin.org/ridb/texts-menu.html
Fletcher School of Law and Diplomacy Database Flora and Fauna; Biodiversity; Environment	www.TUFTS.EDU/fletcher/multilaterals.html
UN Conference on Environment and Development	www.ciesin.org/datasets/unced/unced.html
UN Environment Program (UNEP)	www.unep.org
U.S. Environmental Protection Agency (EPA) Data on global warming	www.epa.gov/globalwarming/index.text.html
U.S. Global Change Research Information Office	www.gcrio.org/
World Resources Institute	www.wri.org/wri/wr-96-97

EPILOGUE

Epilogue

Prospects for Future Cooperation

What will the international community look like at the turn of the century? In A.D. 2020? In light of the abrupt end of the Cold War and the disintegration of the Soviet Union—developments largely unanticipated by IR scholars—it would be foolish to attempt to predict the future of global politics. But based on major themes developed throughout this text, it is possible to outline some possible alternative scenarios. The purpose of this epilogue is to sketch possible IR futures for the first part of the twenty-first century.

OPTIMIST VERSUS PESSIMIST VISIONS

As noted in chapter 19, social scientists often hold different worldviews ("visions") that account for radically different perceptions about present and possible future social, political, and economic conditions. Based on Thomas Sowell's "constrained" and "unconstrained" worldviews,[5] models of the future world can be identified from two fundamentally different perspectives, one optimistic and the other pessimistic. Because the two visions represent extremes along a continuum, future social reality is unlikely to be represented by either worldview. Rather, the future global order will undoubtedly involve both cooperation and conflict, development and decay, integration and fragmentation, and therefore reflect both perspectives.

The optimistic vision assumes that political, economic, and social conditions will continue to improve domestically and internationally. The world will become more stable, living standards will improve in most Third World countries, democracy will become more prevalent, human rights abuses will decline, and the growth of international cooperation will increase the prospects for peace and decrease the potential for war. In effect, global society will become more humane, stable, and just.

The pessimistic vision, by contrast, assumes that, despite increasing interdependence and continuing economic expansion, the international community will remain conflictual, unstable, and unjust. More specifically,

Although the earthly ideal of Socialism-Communism has collapsed, the problems it purported to solve remain: the brazen use of social advantage and the inordinate power of money, which often direct the very course of events. And if the global lesson of the 20th century does not serve as a healing inoculation, then the vast red whirlwind may repeat itself in entirety.[1]

Aleksandr I. Solzhenitzyn, *noted Russian author*

Another form of competition has been emerging that could be just as stark, and just as pervasive as was the rivalry between democracy and totalitarianism at the height of the Cold War: It is the contest between forces of integration and fragmentation in the contemporary international environment.[2]

John Lewis Gaddis, *noted historian*

The passing of Marxism-Leninism first from China and then from the Soviet Union will mean its death as a living ideology of world historical significance. . . . And the death of this ideology means the growing "Common Marketization" of international relations, and the diminution of the likelihood of large-scale conflict between states.[3]

Francis Fukuyama, *international relations theorist*

domestic and international economic inequalities will increase, ethnic and religious nationalism will foster political fragmentation within and among states, dictatorial regimes will continue abusing human rights, international economic conflict will increase as industrial powers compete for scarce resources, and weapons of mass destruction will proliferate, making the world a more dangerous environment.

In chapter 1, four major paradigms of global politics were presented—realism, idealism, interdependence, and dependency. Based on the opposing worldviews sketched here, and using the four paradigms from chapter 1, we sketch eight alternative futures.

REALISM

From a realist perspective, the twenty-first century international system will remain largely unchanged. Despite increasing influence of nonstate actors, the nation-state will continue as the major actor in global society. By A.D. 2020, the number of states will rise by more than twenty-five, bringing total UN membership close to 210. The United Nations will continue to play a modest but important role in international conflict resolution and global peacekeeping. And although the military dimension of power will decline in significance in the twenty-first century, military force will remain the ultimate instrument of conflict resolution. Economically, North America, Europe, and the Pacific rim states will continue as the three centers of economic power. Even though the United States will remain the preeminent economic power in the world, its economic capabilities will continue to decline relative to China, the EU, Japan, and leading Asian and Latin American NICs.

1. Optimist-Realist Scenario

The *optimist-realist scenario* assumes that the state-centric global system will remain stable and peaceful. Although conflicts will inevitably arise in the decentralized, anarchic system, future global disputes will tend to be based less on politics and ideology and more on social, economic, and environmental issues. Moreover, the increasing destructiveness of modern armaments will ironically reduce the propensity for war. The major powers of the global system—Western Europe, Japan, and the United States—will serve as a collective hegemon in providing political and economic stability and in fostering democratic structures and further institutionalizing a liberal international economic order. As a consequence of the spread of democracy, the prospects for international peace will increase and compliance with international human rights will become widespread. And as a result of the spread of market economies, the standard of living will greatly increase, significantly decreasing infant mortality, disease, and increasing longevity in the developing nations. Moreover, the development and application of new ecological technologies will make environmental protection more feasible.

2. Pessimist-Realist Scenario

According to the *pessimist-realist scenario,* the future international system will be characterized by more frequent and more intense political and economic conflict. Factors that will contribute to the expansion of domestic and international disputes include the rise in religious and ethnic nationalism, growing claims of national self-determination by political minorities, and increasing international economic competition coupled with a growing protectionist demand in developed states. In addition, the structure of global society will become more multipolar as power becomes more dispersed. Not only will some NICs become relatively stronger economically, but several oil-exporting states will become regional security threats with the acquisition of modern armaments, including weapons of mass destruction and sophisticated delivery systems. The number of states with nuclear weapons capabilities will increase to more than fifteen, making the international system less stable. Moreover, the proliferation of conflict will lead to growing demands for UN peacekeeping missions, but these will be largely ineffective in containing intense nationalistic and ethnic disputes. Finally, the rise of ethnic conflict will displace tens of millions of persons, creating a major humanitarian crisis that will be aggravated by the increasingly restrictive asylum policies of industrial states.

IDEALISM

The idealist perspective assumes that international law, global organizations, and world public opinion will play an increasingly important role in the future world order. Even though the nation-state will continue as the principal actor in global society, governments will increasingly coordinate their foreign policies through the UN and its specialized agencies as well as through regional institutions. The continuing spread of democracy will foster international cooperation, decrease the prospects of interstate warfare, and improve compliance with international human rights norms. Moreover, the further institutionalization of market-based economic systems will greatly expand world economic output. The spread of modern technologies and global communications networks, coupled with adoption of market reforms by former socialist and communist regimes, will increase global economic integration. Additionally, because of the continuing growth in the number of states and the further diffusion of power within the international community, IGOs, especially the UN and regional organizations, will play an increasingly important role in facilitating global cooperation and fostering international conflict resolution.

3. Optimist-Idealist Scenario

The *optimist-idealist scenario* assumes that the rising number and expanding authority of IGOs will lead to greater international stability and justice. The growing global stability will be due in part to the major powers' commitment to democracy and capitalism. By A.D. 2020 more than three-fourths of the world's countries will be classified as democratic or partly democratic, including all permanent members of the Security Council. Because public opinion will be the basis of domestic politics in most middle- and high-income states, world public opinion will also become more influential in international relations. As a result, interstate war will become increasingly rare, with most violent conflict occurring in low-income Third World states. In addition, the international economic order, strongly backed by the major industrial powers, will continue to foster monetary stability and liberal trade patterns and provide a structure by which stable and well-governed developing nations can greatly expand income through trade. At the same time, IGOs and NGOs will play an increasingly important role in protecting the global environment and in promoting sustainable economic development. Finally, the increasing influence of IGOs will foster stronger global loyalties, thereby reducing the impact of nationalism.

4. Pessimist-Idealist Scenario

The *pessimist-idealist scenario* assumes that, in spite of the growing influence of global organizations, international law, and world public opinion, international relations will become increasingly conflictual and unstable. The forces of nationalism and political fragmentation will prove more potent than the integrative forces of global institutionalism. Ethnic and national claims will be a major barrier to the consolidation of regional and global organizations. To cite two examples, (1) the European Union will not become a federal state (the United States of Europe) as originally anticipated; and (2) the International Seabed Authority, established by UNCLOS III to regulate the mining of the ocean's deep-seabed resources, will be bypassed altogether by the major industrial states. Moreover, although governments will continue professing commitments to sustainable economic development and to the preservation of nonrenewable resources, they will carry out policies and practices that exacerbate global pollution and global warming, and threaten the environment. In short, in spite of stronger, more institutionalized global structures, the claims of ethnic and religious minorities, the domestic demands for national economic growth, and the increased claims of national self-determination will result in a more unstable and conflictual international system.

INTERDEPENDENCE

Acording to this paradigm, the world will become increasingly interdependent—economically, socially, politically, scientifically, informationally, and environmentally. The growth of economic integration and instant telecommunications, made possible by the far-reaching revolution in information technology, will not only expand the rate and scope of global transactions but will weaken national loyalties and strengthen global affinities. As a result, state sovereignty will decline and the role of nation-states in global society will become less important, as IGOs and NGOs exert increasing influence on global politics. Because of greater permeability of territorial boundaries, states will have less control of international transactions and the protection from foreign developments. Even though states will continue as major international actors, they will lose some of their ability to determine behavioral outcomes, both domestically and internationally. At the same time, international forces, including economic modernization, global culture, and world communications, will exert more influence over IR than the nationalistic claims of ethnic and religious groups or the security policies of major powers. In effect, the dynamics of "McWorld" will be more important than the forces of "Jihad."[6]

5. Optimist-Interdependency Scenario

The *optimist-interdependency scenario* assumes that transnationalism will foster global harmony, international order, human rights, and world justice. Even though regional, national, and local loyalties will persist, transnationalism will strengthen global, cosmopolitan affinities. The growth of functional cooperation and the increasing economic and social interdependence of the international community will reduce patriotic and nationalistic claims and foster global political consciousness. In some progressive countries in Western Europe individuals will begin flying the flags of IGOs like the UN and the EU. In addition, governments, prodded by NGOs, will establish policies and programs that protect the environment and foster sustainable economic development. In effect, growing interdependence will encourage shared values and interests, foster increasing commitments to the common good, and decrease international antagonisms, thereby reducing the prospect of war.

6. Pessimist-Interdependency Scenario

The *pessimist-interdependency scenario* assumes that increasing global integration will not necessarily result in a stable and peaceful world. Indeed, the rise of nonstate actors and global information flows will lead to a decline in governmental authority and further reduce the capacity of states to control domestic and international events. For example, the dissemination of Western cultural values (e.g., materialism, secularism, and modern pop culture) is likely to continue to undermine the traditional cultural values and mores of developing nations, thereby fostering frustration and unhappiness rather than enhancing human dignity. Moreover, rather than promoting economic expansion and enhancing human rights, interdependence will continue to weaken civic bonds and undermine governmental authority, resulting in the breakdown of communal institutions and the rise of crime and lawlessness. In addition to fostering cultural decay and a weakening of governmental authority, interdependence will facilitate the transnational movement of crime and disease (such as AIDS) and encourage further ecological degradation by the unwise exploitation of natural resources.

Dependency

According to this paradigm, international relations are influenced decisively by the economic structures and processes in global society. In particular, the dependency approach claims that global capitalism fosters unjust economic disparities among states. As a result of the further institutionalization of a liberal international economic order and the spread of market economies in the post–Cold War world, the effects of global capitalism will increase further in the world, especially among the former communist states and emerging developing nations. Although increased integration of the world economy will lead to a rise in global productivity, increased international trade, an expansion in transnational production, and greater foreign investment and cross-border financial transactions, such developments will also result in greater domestic and international economic inequalities, with poverty remaining a major problem in many developing nations. Thus, rather than resolving the North-South conflict, the spread of capitalism will further increase divisions within the developing nations. The political strife within and among Third World nations will be due less to poverty itself, however, than to the perceptions of relative deprivation, reinforced through global informational networks.

7. Optimist-Dependency Scenario

The *optimist-dependency scenario* assumes that, despite growing economic disparities within and among states, the standard of living for most Third World citizens will improve dramatically in the first two decades of the twenty-first century. The growing economic prosperity of the Third World will be led by such NICs as Argentina, Brazil, Chile, Indonesia, Mexico, and South Korea. These emerging industrial powers, along with some twenty-five other prospering Third World nations, will become major industrial exporters, capably competing in the international economy. Moreover, because many Asian and Latin American countries' economies will grow significantly, the number of low-income countries in the Third World will greatly decline. Even though the South comprised some 110 countries in the 1970s, fewer than 60 of these countries will be classified as poor by the early part of the twenty-first century. Finally, to the extent that economic inequalities contribute to political strife, the effects of global economic disparities will be chiefly domestic, not international.

8. Pessimist-Dependency Scenario

The *pessimist-dependency scenario* assumes that global capitalist structures will continue to threaten indigenous cultures, increase poverty, foster environmental pollution, and perpetuate unjust exploitation of human and natural resources. The expansion of global capitalist structures, held in check during the Cold War by the Soviet Union, will threaten human dignity and impoverish millions in both developed and developing nations. In the former countries, economic growth will foster materialism, consumerism, and cultural degradation; in the latter, economic growth will provide benefits to a small elite, but increase poverty among the masses. Partly because of the population explosion and the nature of economic development, capitalist expansion in many Third World countries will lower living conditions for the bulk of the population. Because of increasing poverty, many developing nations will become more unstable and less democratic and the tensions between high-income and low-income states will rise significantly, even as many poor countries experience increased domestic strife as a result of growing social and economic frustration among the masses. The growing demands for better living standards among Third World peoples will result not only in domestic conflicts but will foster regional and global wars as states compete for scarce resources.

IN CONCLUSION

The nature of IR in A.D. 2020 is unlikely to be defined by any one of these eight scenarios; rather, it will probably reflect elements from several of them. What that future will be like is, of course, impossible to predict. But students who know modern history and understand the core concepts and theories presented in this text will be better prepared to grasp ongoing changes in the international community and to help influence the evolution of future international relations.

Basic Principles of International Relations

Actors

1. The international community is comprised of sovereign nation-states. Although states are the principal actors in the international system, nonstate actors are also important in global politics. The most significant of these include international governmental organizations (IGOs), nongovernmental organizations (NGOs), multinational corporations, and transnational movements.

2. States, like individuals, have rights and duties. Two important rights are political independence and territorial integrity; two important duties are the obligation to respect states' political sovereignty (nonintervention) and to resolve disputes peacefully.

3. The growth of transnational interactions in areas such as communications, popular culture, economic production and consumption, finance, science and technology, and environmental concerns has resulted in a significant decline in state autonomy. Because of the growing impact of functional interdependence, governmental sovereignty has decreased in the last half of the twentieth century.

International Community

4. Because no central authority exists in global society, the security of states is ultimately in the hands of each government. The international community is thus an anarchic (self-help) system.

5. Anarchy does not mean that there is no order in global society; rather, it means that global order is achieved by the cooperative efforts of states, not by the institution of a central power.

6. Global politics is characterized by cooperation and conflict. Cooperation occurs when states pursue common interests harmoniously; conflict results when states pursue mutually exclusive goals.

7. Scholars hold differing perceptions of the nature and causes of political conflict and cooperation within global society. International

conflicts are sometimes viewed as a result of different interpretations of facts (empirical knowledge); sometimes conflicts are interpreted differently because scholars apply different concepts, theories, and paradigms (conceptual knowledge). The application of different theories and normative assumptions about the nature of persons and politics frequently results in significantly different interpretations of world politics.

8. Although there are a wide variety of schools and perspectives about IR, Western scholars tend to identify with either idealism or realism. Idealists hold optimistic assumptions about human nature and tend to view politics chiefly as a cooperative enterprise; realists, by contrast, hold pessimistic assumptions about human nature and tend to view politics as a conflictual, competitive process.

Power

9. The ability of states to pursue vital national interests in global society is dependent, in great part, on power—that is, the ability to determine outcomes. Although power is based on numerous factors, tangible resources (such as wealth and military force) and intangible resources (such as national morale and structure of government) are especially important in determining the relative capabilities of states.

10. Although states pursue a variety of interests in the international community (e.g., wealth, preservation and promotion of cultural traditions, promotion of global structures conducive to world trade), the most fundamental national interest is security. Because there is no central authority, states rely ultimately on national power to ensure survival, political independence, and territorial integrity.

11. Most tensions and conflicts among states are resolved through peaceful negotiation. When states are unable to resolve their disputes peacefully, however, they frequently resort to military force. Because coercive power is the ultimate instrument of national power, miliary force is generally the most important element of national power.

12. Order in global society is achieved by managing power. The two most common strategies of power management in global society are balance of power and centralization of power. These two strategies are implemented either directly (formally) through international organizations or indirectly (informally) through the individual actions of states.

Foreign Policy

13. States pursue a wide variety of interests in global society. The most fundamental wants of states are defined by the concept of national interest.

14. Foreign policy is the means by which states pursue national goals beyond territorial boundaries. To be successful, foreign policy objectives must be carefully prioritized, defined in light of other states' interests, and implemented with adequate resources.

15. Statecraft involves the deliberate and organized actions of governments in promoting national interests in global society. Although states use a variety of policy instruments to pursue foreign policy goals, four types of statecraft dominate contemporary world affairs: diplomacy (peaceful negotiation), propaganda, economic sanctions, and military force.

International Cooperation

16. International relations are determined by the actions of individuals, the policies of states, and the structures and processes of global society. The analysis of international relations must therefore focus on developments at three levels: (a) the nature and role of individuals, especially national political leaders; (b) the decisions of governments, with special emphasis on the nature and role of domestic politics; and (c) the nature and role of the international system itself.

17. In promoting shared transnational interests, states have developed international regimes (i.e., norms, decision-making patterns, and institutions) in specific issue-areas, such as environmental protection, human rights, international trade, and disarmament.

18. To facilitate international cooperation, states have established formal rules governing international behaviors. These rules, known as international law, cover most areas of international relations, including diplomatic representation, territorial jurisdiction, maritime boundaries, human rights, and war. Although no central authority exists to enforce international law, there is widespread compliance with its rules.

19. IGOs have also been established to facilitate conflict resolution and to promote transnational cooperation. Although states remain sovereign, IGOs foster global order by channeling and influencing the behaviors of state and nonstate actors. NGOs also play an important role in fostering transnational cooperation.

International Conflict

20. States are frequently unable to resolve international disputes. When conflicts involve vital interests, states often resort to military force. War is thus the ultimate instrument of conflict resolution in global society.

21. Although the frequency of war has greatly declined in recent centuries, the destructiveness of war has increased dramatically, largely because of the growing lethality of modern weapons. Moreover, with the dramatic rise in the number of new states in the post–World War II era, the proportion of intranational wars has greatly increased relative to international wars. Many of these domestic wars are due to conflicts over ideology, increased demands for self-determination by ethnonationalist groups, and conflict over domestic governance.

22. Although democracies and nondemocracies are equally prone to war, democracies do not go to war against other democracies. This empirical conclusion has resulted in the so-called democratic peace thesis (DPT). According to the DPT, democracies are prone to peace toward other democracies because of (a) the significant influence of liberal ideology on the goals and motives of free societies and (b) the structural constraints imposed by democratic institutions.

International Political Economy

23. International political economy (IPE) concerns the interaction of politics and economics, power and wealth, in the international community. Because of increasing globalization, IPE is of growing importance in the analysis of IR.

24. The growth of international economic interdependence has been greatly facilitated by the establishment of a liberal international economic order in the aftermath of World War II. This liberal system has involved three institutions: a trading system (GATT and, since 1994, WTO), a global banking system to foster economic growth and development (the World Bank), and an international financial organization (IMF) to assure the efficient processing of international financial transactions.

International Ethics

25. International politics, like domestic politics, rests on ethics—that is, moral judgments about the justice and injustice, rightness and wrongness of governmental decisions. Although the role of ethical judgment is more limited in global society than in domestic society, global politics is not an amoral realm dictated solely by necessity. On the contrary, international affairs allow decision makers a wide range of moral choice.

26. Although the international community is characterized by a heterogeneity of cultures and moral traditions, there is, nonetheless, significant consensus about fundamental moral values about states and human beings.

27. Using normative analysis, foreign policies can be assessed ethically. Such assessment should be carried out using a tri-partite framework that judges the morality of a policy in terms of its goals, means, and results.

Notes

Chapter 1

1. Raymond Aron, *Peace and War: A Theory of International Relations* (New York: Praeger, 1968), p. 7.

2. William Pfaff, *The Wrath of Nations: Civilization and the Furies of Nationalism* (New York: Simon & Schuster, 1993) p. 238.

3. Kenneth Waltz, *Theory of International Politics* (Reading, Mass.: Addison-Wesley, 1979), pp. 88–116.

4. Domestic communities differ greatly in their level of political, social, economic, and cultural homogeneity. Some states, such as Denmark and Norway, are highly consensual; others, such as Bosnia-Herzegovina, Nigeria, Russia, and South Africa, are highly heterogeneous linguistically, religiously, socially, and politically.

5. John Foster Dulles, "Institutionalizing Peace," *The Department of State Bulletin* 43 (May 7, 1956), p. 740.

6. As noted in chap. 13, however, states may accept the World Court's compulsory jurisdiction by explicitly endorsing Article 36 of its Statute, commonly known as the "optional clause." Slightly less than one-third of the United Nations members have endorsed this clause, although most of them with reservations.

7. Donald Kagan, *On the Origins of War and the Preservation of Peace* (New York: Doubleday, 1995), p. 55.

8. Thucydides, *History of the Peloponnesian War,* trans. Rex Warner (London: Penguin, 1972), p. 23. Donald Kagan argues that the Peloponnesian War, contrary to Thucydides' claims, was not inevitable. See Donald Kagan, *The Outbreak of the Peloponnesian War* (Ithaca: Cornell University Press, 1969).

9. Quoted in Samuel P. Huntington, *The Clash of Civilizations and the Remaking of World Order* (New York: Simon & Schuster, 1996), p. 29.

10. John Lewis Gaddis, "Toward the Post–Cold War World," *Foreign Affairs* 70 (spring 1991), p. 101.

11. This three-dimensional analysis is based on the three key "images" or factors that Kenneth Waltz uses in his classic study of war. See Kenneth Waltz, *Man, The State and War: A Theoretical Analysis* (New York: Columbia University Press, 1959).

12. For a superior journalistic account of the disintegration of Yugoslavia, see Misha Glenny, *The Fall of Yugoslavia: The Third Balkan War* (New York: Penguin Books, 1996). For an insightful account of the role of cultural, religious, and historic forces influencing Balkan ethnonationalism, see Robert D. Kaplan, *Balkan Ghosts: A Journey Through History* (New York: Vintage Books, 1994).

13. Warren Zimmermann, "Origins of a Catastrophe," *Foreign Affairs* 74 (March/April 1995), pp. 4 and 7.

14. Warren Zimmermann, "The Captive Mind," *The New York Review of Books* (February 2, 1995), p. 3.

15. Hans J. Morgenthau, *Politics Among Nations: The Struggle for Power and Peace,* 5th ed., rev. (New York: Random House, 1978) p. 5.

16. Ibid., p. 12.

17. Edward Hallett Carr, *The Twenty Years' Crisis, 1919–1939: An Introduction to the Study of International Relations* (New York: Harper & Row, 1964) pp. 46–54.

18. For an examination of the distinctives of the neorealist perspective, see Kenneth Waltz, "The Origins of War in Neorealist Theory," in Robert I. Rotberg and Theodore K. Rabb, eds., *The Origin and Prevention of Major Wars* (Cambridge: Cambridge University Press, 1988), pp. 39–52. See also Robert O. Keohane, ed., *Neorealism and Its Critics* (New York: Columbia University Press, 1986).

19. For a review of key features of neoliberalism, see Joseph M. Grieco, "Anarchy and the Limits of Cooperation: A Realist Critique of the Newest Liberal Institutionalism," *International Organization* 42 (summer 1988), pp. 600–624; J. Grieco, *Cooperation Among Nations: Europe, America, and Non-Tariff Barriers to Trade* (Ithaca: Cornell University Press, 1990), especially chaps. 1 and 2; Joseph S. Nye, Jr., "Neorealism and Neoliberalism," *World Politics* 40 (January 1988), pp. 235–51.

20. Robert O. Keohane and Joseph S. Nye, *Power and Interdependence: World Politics in Transition* (Boston: Little, Brown, 1977), pp. 23–25.

21. Graham T. Allison, *Essence of Decision—Explaining the Cuban Missile Crisis* (Boston: Little, Brown, 1971), pp. 245–51.

22. John J. Mearsheimer, "The False Promise of International Institutions," *International Security* 19 (winter 1994/95), p. 40.

23. There is a growing literature on a postmodern perspective on international relations. See, for example, Richard K. Ashley, "The Poverty of Neorealism," *International Organization* 38 (spring 1984), pp. 225–86; Alexander Wendt, "The Agent-Structure in the World Polity," *International Organization* 48 (spring 1992), pp. 391–425; and Wendt, "Collective Identity Formation and the International State," *American Political Science Review* 88 (June 1994), pp. 384–96.

24. Quoted in Robert Gilpin, *The Political Economy of International Relations* (Princeton: Princeton University Press, 1987), p. 71.

25. For a comprehensive survey of the literature on gender and IR, see Craig N. Murphy, "Seeing Women, Recognizing Gender, Recasting International Relations," *International Organization* 50 (summer 1996), pp. 513–38.

26. J. Ann Tickner, *Gender in International Relations: Feminist Perspectives on Achieving Global Security* (New York: Columbia University Press, 1992), p. 7.

27. Joshua S. Goldstein, *International Relations,* 2nd ed. (New York: HarperCollins, 1996), pp. 108–16 and 123–25.

28. Tickner, pp. 5–9.

29. Ibid., p. 130.

30. For an excellent analysis of dependency theory, see Robert A. Packenham, *The Dependency Movement: Scholarship and Politics*

in Development Studies (Cambridge: Harvard University Press, 1992). Packenham argues that dependency theory is fundamentally about socialism versus capitalism, rather than about autonomy versus dependence.

31. See, for example, Peter Evans, *Dependent Development: The Alliance of Multinational, State, and Local Capital in Brazil* Princeton: Princeton University Press, 1979).

Chapter 2

1. Quoted in "With all her Faults, She is My Country Still," *The Economist* (December 22, 1990), p. 43.

2. Kalevi J. Holsti, *The State, War, and the State of War* (Cambridge: Cambridge University Press, 1996), p. 195.

3. Quoted in Attar Chand, *Jawaharlal Nehru and his Social Philosophy* (Delhi: Amar Prakashan, 1989), p. 101.

4. Paul Kennedy, *Preparing for the Twenty-First Century* (New York: Random House, 1993), p. 134.

5. For a historical overview of the rise of the nation-state, see Charles Tilly, *Coercion, Capital and European States, A.D. 990–1990* (Oxford: Basil Blackwell, 1990), chap. 1.

6. Barry Buzan, *People, States, and Fear: An Agenda for International Security Studies in the Post–Cold War Era.* (Boulder, Colo.: Lynne Reinner, Publishers, 1991), chap. 2.

7. Excerpts from Jean Bodin, *Six Books on the State,* in William Ebenstein, *Great Political Thinkers: Plato to the Present,* 4th ed. (Hinsdale, IL: Dryden, 1969), pp. 354–55.

8. Hedley Bull, *The Anarchical Society* (London: Macmillan, 1977), p. 8.

9. Walker Connor, *Ethnonationalism: The Quest for Understanding* (Princeton, N.J.: Princeton University Press, 1994), p. 80.

10. Karl W. Deutsch, *Politics and Government: How People Decide Their Fate,* 3rd ed. (Boston: Houghton Mifflin, 1980), p. 120.

11. John Stuart Mill, "Representative Government," in Robert Maynard Hutchins, ed., *Great Books of the Western World,* vol. 43 (Chicago: Encyclopedia Britannica, 1952), p. 424.

12. Hans Kohn, *Nationalism: Its Meaning and History,* rev. ed. (New York: Van Nostrand, 1965), p. 10. For a more current discussion of nationalism, see Ernst B. Haas, "What Is Nationalism," *International Organization* 40 (summer 1986), pp. 707–44.

13. Alain Touraine, *Return of the Actor: Social Theory in Postindustrial Society,* trans. Myrna Godzich (Minneapolis: University of Minnesota Press, 1988), pp. 81–82.

14. Holsti, *The State, War, and the State of War,* pp. 84–90.

15. Robert Jackson, *Quasi States: Sovereignty, International Relations, and the Third World* (Cambridge: Cambridge University Press, 1990). See also I. William Zartman, ed., *Collapsed States: The Disintegration and Restoration of Legitimate Authority* (Boulder, Colo.: Lynn Reinner, 1994).

16. Benjamin R. Barber, *Jihad vs. McWorld: How Globalism and Tribalism Are Reshaping the World* (New York: Ballantine Books, 1996), p. 232.

17. Walker Connor, "Nation-Building or Nation-Destroying," *World Politics* 24 (April 1972), p. 424.

18. Michael Ignatieff, *Blood and Belonging: Journeys into the New Nationalism* (New York: Farrar, Straus and Giroux, 1993), p. 5.

19. Barber, *Jihad vs. McWorld,* p. 166.

20. Ibid., p. 10.

21. Kohn, *Nationalism,* p. 9.

22. Walker Connor, "Beyond Reason: The Nature of the Ethnonational Bond," *Ethnic and Racial Studies* 16 (July 1993), pp. 376–77.

23. Colin Williams, "Conceived in Bondage—Called unto Liberty: Reflections on Nationalism," *Progress in Human Geography* 9 (September 1985), p. 338.

24. Roman Szporluk, "The National Question," in Timothy J. Colton and Robert Legvold, eds., *After the Soviet Union: From Empire to Nations* (New York: W.W. Norton, 1992), p. 89.

25. For an assessment of Poland's Solidarity Movement, see Touraine, *Return of the Actor,* and Timothy Garton Ash, *The Uses of Adversity: Essays on the Fate of Central Europe* (New York: Vintage Books, 1990).

26. For an illuminating assessment of Czechoslovakia's "velvet revolution" of December 1989, see Theodore Draper, "A New History of the Velvet Revolution," *The New York Review of Books* 40 (January 14, 1993), pp. 14–20.

27. Ignatieff, *Blood and Belonging,* p. 6.

28. Ibid., p. 5.

29. For recent analyses of the origins of World War I, see James Joll, *The Origins of the First World War* (New York: Longman, 1984); Marc Trachtenberg, *History and Strategy* (Princeton: Princeton University Press, 1991), chap. 2; and Samuel R. Williamson, "The Origin of World War I" in Robert Rotberg and Theodore Rabb, eds., *The Origin and Prevention of Major Wars* (New York: Cambridge University Press, 1989), pp. 225–48.

30. Quoted in Daniel Patrick Moynihan, *Pandaemonium: Ethnicity in International Politics* (New York: Oxford University Press, 1993), p. 149.

31. For an analysis of the international legal problems created by the conflict between self-determination and state sovereignty, see Moynihan, *Pandaemonium,* chaps. 2 and 4.

32. An exception to this practice is the European Union, which has all but eliminated border controls among the citizens of its fifteen member-states.

33. For an assessment of refugee migrations in the post–Cold War international system, see Doris Meissner, "Managing Migrations," *Foreign Policy* 86 (spring 1992), pp. 66–83.

34. Union of International Associations, ed., *Yearbook of International Organizations 1990/91, Volume 1,* 27th ed. (Munich: K.G. Sauer, 1990), p. 1659.

35. Ibid., p. 1660.

36. Raymond Vernon, *Sovereignty at Bay* (New York: Basic Books, 1971).

37. Stephen D. Krasner, *Structural Conflict: The Third World Against Global Liberalism* (Berkeley: University of California Press, 1985), p. 188.

38. See, for example, Michael Novak, *The Spirit of Democratic Capitalism* (New York: Simon & Schuster, 1982).

39. Douglas Johnston, "Looking Ahead: Toward a New Paradigm," in Douglas Johnston and Cynthia Sampson, eds., *Religion: The Missing Dimension of Statecraft* (New York: Oxford University Press, 1994), pp. 332–33.

40. Edward Luttwak, "The Missing Dimension," in Johnston and Sampson, *Religion: The Missing Dimension of Statecraft,* p. 10.

41. Barry Rubin, "Religion and International Affairs," in Johnston and Sampson, *Religion: The Missing Dimension of Statecraft,* p. 33.

42. For an analysis of the Vatican's foreign policy, see J. Bryan Hehir, "Papal Foreign Policy," *Foreign Policy* 78 (spring 1990), pp. 26–48; and Eric O. Hanson, *The Catholic Church in World Politics* (Princeton: Princeton University Press, 1987).

43. The emphasis of political leaders in international relations is commonly associated with the so-called "great-leader" approach to history, which seeks to explain domestic and international affairs in terms of the actions of key decision makers. See chap. 7.

Chapter 3

1. Kenneth Waltz, *Theory of International Politics* (Reading, Penn.: Wesley, 1979), p. 112.

2. John le Carré, "The Shame of the West," *New York Times* (December 14, 1994), p. 17.

3. Stephen D. Krasner, "Compromising Westphalia," *International Security* 20 (winter 1995/96), pp. 150–51.

4. The comparison of the different versions of international society is based on Hedley Bull, *The Anarchical Society: A Study in Order in World Politics* (New York: Columbia University Press, 1977), pp. 24–27.

5. Joseph S. Nye, Jr., "What New World Order?" *Foreign Affairs* 71 (spring 1992), p. 89.

6. Paul Kennedy, *Preparing for the Twenty-First Century* (New York: Random House, 1993), p. 134.

7. Daniel Philpott, "Sovereignty: An Introduction and Brief History," *Journal of International Affairs* 48 (winter 1995), p. 360.

8. One of the earliest and most forceful expressions of this idea is the *Calvo doctrine,* a principle prohibiting states from intervening in foreign states in order to assure protection of their citizens living overseas equal to that at home. According to Carlos Calvo, a nineteenth-century Argentine diplomat and jurist, because states were sovereign and equal, a foreign government could not intervene to protect its nationals, so long as the treatment of aliens was no different from that of its own citizens. To grant this intervention, according to Calvo, would imply a legal inequality of states.

9. Robert W. Tucker, *The Inequality of Nations* (New York: Basic Books, 1977), p. 3.

10. Until the Soviet Union disintegrated in 1991, the major nuclear powers included United States, Soviet Union, China, France, and Great Britain; but since 1991, thee other countries now possess former USSR strategic weapons—Belarus, Kazakstan, and Ukraine. Moreover two other countries—India and Israel—are generally considered to have such weapons as well, although North Korea and Pakistan are thought to have acquired the technology and weapons-grade material necessary for building nuclear weapons. In 1993 South Africa announced that it had developed nuclear weapons but that it had dismantled them.

11. World Bank, *From Plan to Market: World Development Report 1996* (New York: Oxford University Press, 1996), pp. 188–89.

12. Roger Masters, "World Politics as a Primitive Political System," *World Politics* XVI (July 1964), pp. 594–619.

13. Raymond Aron, *Peace and War: A Theory of International Relations* (New York: Praeger, 1968), pp. 5–8 and 16.

14. Waltz, *Theory of International Politics,* p. 118.

15. U.S. Arms Control and Disarmament Agency, *World Military Expenditures and Arms Transfers, 1995* (Washington, D.C.: Government Printing Office, 1996), p. 53.

16. See, for example, Barry Buzan, *People, States, and Fear: An Agenda for International Security Studies in the Post–Cold War Era* (Boulder: Lynne Reinner Publishers, 1991).

17. Waltz, *Theory of International Politics,* pp. 111–16.

18. John Rawls, "Two Concepts of Rules," *Philosophical Review* 64 (1955), pp. 3–32.

19. Quoted in Daniel Patrick Moynihan, *Pandaemonium: Ethnicity in International Politics* (New York: Oxford University Press, 1993), p. 151.

20. Ibid., p. 150.

21. Michael Mandelbaum, "The Reluctance to Intervene," *Foreign Policy* 95 (summer 1994), p. 8.

22. Dorothy Jones, *Code of Peace: Ethics and Security in the World of Warlord States* (Chicago: University of Chicago Press, 1992), pp. xii and 163–64.

23. Michael Walzer, *Just and Unjust Wars: A Moral Argument with Historical Illustrations* (New York: Basic Books, 1977), p. 61–63.

24. See Paul Kennedy, *Preparing for the Twenty-First Century* (New York: Random House, 1993), chap. 7. For an assessment of the order and stability of the post–Cold War era, see Lawrence Freedman, "Order and Disorder in the New World," *Foreign Affairs* 71,1 (1991/92), pp. 20–37.

25. Krasner, "Compromising Westphalia," pp. 115–18.

26. Kalevi Holsti, "War, Peace, and the State of the State," *International Political Science Review* 16 (October 1955), pp. 319–39.

27. Benjamin R. Barber, "Jihad vs. McWorld," *The Atlantic Monthly* 269 (March 1992), p. 53.

28. James N. Rosenau, *Turbulence in World Politics: A Theory of Change and Continuity* (Princeton: Princeton University Press, 1990), pp. 339 and 440.

29. Barber, "Jihad vs. McWorld," p. 58.

30. "A Survey of the World Economy," *The Economist* (October 7, 1995), p. 10.

31. Robert Jervis, "The Future of World Politics," *International Security* 16 (winter 1991/92), pp. 50–51.

32. Quoted in Moynihan, *Pandaemonium,* p. 61.

33. For an insightful essay on how states cooperate in an anarchic system, see Robert Jervis, "Cooperation Under the Security Dilemma," *World Politics* 30 (January 1978), pp. 167–86. For a more recent and comprehensive study, see Arthur A. Stein, *Why Nations Cooperate* (Ithaca: Cornell University Press, 1990).

34. Kenneth N. Waltz, *Man, the State and War* (New York: Columbia University Press, 1965), pp. 167–68.

35. For an excellent introduction to the historical dimensions of the conflict between the Arab and Jewish people, see David K. Shipler, *Arab and Jew: Wounded Spirits in a Promised Land* (New York: Penguin, 1986).

36. Two useful introductory studies of the Arab-Israeli conflict are Alvin Z. Rubenstein, ed., *The Arab-Israeli Conflict: Perspectives,* 2nd ed. (New York: HarperCollins, 1991); and Charles D. Smith, *Palestine and the Arab-Israeli Conflict* (New York: St. Martin's Press, 1988).

37. Harold H. Saunders, *The Other Walls: The Politics of the Arab-Israeli Peace Process* (Washington, D.C.: American Enterprise Institute, 1985), p. 7.

38. The most thorough account of the Camp David negotiations is William B. Quandt, *Camp David: Peacemaking and Politics* (Washington, D.C.: Brookings Institution, 1986).

Chapter 4

1. Klaus Knorr, *The Power of Nations: The Political Economy of International Relations* (New York: Basic Books, 1975), p. 3.

2. Kenneth Oye, "Explaining Cooperation Under Anarchy: Hypotheses and Strategies," *World Politics* 38 (October 1985), p. 1.

3. Kenneth Waltz, *Theory of International Politics* (Reading, Mass.: Addison-Wesley, 1979), p. 176.

4. Joseph M. Grieco, *Cooperation Among Nations: Europe, America, and Non-Tariff Barriers to Trade* (Ithaca: Cornell University Press, 1990), p. 22. For an examination of different perspectives on the nature and conceptualization of international cooperation, see Kenneth A. Oye, ed., *Cooperation Under Anarchy* (Princeton: Princeton University Press, 1986).

5. Helen Milner, "International Theories of Cooperation Among Nations: Strengths and Weaknesses," *World Politics* 44 (April 1992), pp. 469–70. See also Arthur A. Stein, *Why Nations Cooperate* (Ithaca: Cornell University Press, 1990).

6. Robert Keohane defines cooperation more restrictively, arguing that it involves the deliberate promotion of common goals through negotiation. Whereas harmony refers to the common interests automatically pursued by individuals and organizations, cooperation is the deliberate effort to reconcile conflicting interests. For Keohane, therefore, Axelrod's voluntary cooperation is not cooperation but harmony. For a discussion of these concepts, see Robert O. Keohane, *After Hegemony: Cooperation and Discord in the World Political Economy* (Princeton: Princeton University Press, 1984), pp. 51–57.

7. See Robert Axelrod, *The Evolution of Cooperation* (New York: Basic Books, 1984).

8. For a description and explanation of different variations of this theory see: Robert Gilpin, *War and Change in World Politics* (Cambridge: Cambridge University Press, 1981) and *The Political Economy of International Relations* (Princeton: Princeton University Press, 1987); Robert O. Keohane, "The Theory of Hegemonic Stability and Changes in International Economic Regimes, 1967–1977," in Ole R. Holsti, Randolph Siverson, and Alexander L. George, eds., *Change in the International System* (Boulder: Westview Press, 1980); and Duncan Snidal, "The Limits of Hegemonic Stability Theory," *International Organization* 39 (autumn 1985), pp. 579–614.

9. See, for example, Lisa L. Martin, "Institutions and Cooperation," *International Security* 16 (spring 1992), pp. 143–77.

10. Joseph M. Grieco, "Anarchy and the Limits of Cooperation: A Realist Critique of the Newest Liberal Institutionalism," in Charles W. Kegley, Jr., ed., *Controversies in International Relations Theory: Realism and the Neoliberal Challenge* (New York: St. Martin's Press, 1995), pp. 156–58.

11. Ibid., p. 161.

12. See Oran Young, "International Regimes: Problems of Concept Formation," *World Politics* 32 (April 1980), pp. 331–56. For a comprehensive account of the regime concept, see Stephen Krasner, ed., *International Regimes* (Ithaca: Cornell University Press, 1983).

13. Stephen D. Krasner, "Structural Causes and Regime Consequences: Regimes as Intervening Variables," *International Organization* 36 (spring 1982), p. 186.

14. J. Martin Rochester, "The Rise and Fall of International Organization as a Field of Study," *International Organization* 40 (autumn 1986), p. 798.

15. Arthur Stein, "Coordination and Collaboration: Regimes in an Anarchic World." *International Organization* 36 (spring 1982), p. 299.

16. Keohane, *After Hegemony,* p. 89.

17. Oran R. Young, *International Cooperation: Building Regimes and Natural Resources and the Environment* (Ithaca: Cornell University Press, 1989), pp. 200–202. For two cases of how regimes develop and evolve, see Ethan A. Nadelmann, "Global Prohibition Regimes," *International Organization* 44 (autumn 1990), pp. 479–526; and Peter Haas, "Do Regimes Matter? Epistemic Communities and Mediterranean Pollution Control," *International Organization* 43 (summer 1989), pp. 377–403.

18. See Peter Haas, "Introduction: Epistemic Communities and International Policy Coordination," *International Organization* 46 (winter 1992), pp. 1–35.

19. Peter Haas, "Banning Chlorofluorocarbons: Epistemic Community Efforts to Protect Stratospheric Ozone," *International Organization* 46 (winter 1992), pp. 187–224.

20. William J. Drake and Kalypso Nicolaidis, "Ideas, Interests, and Institutionalization: Trade in Services and the Uruguay Round," *International Organization* 46 (winter 1992), pp. 37–100.

21. For an assessment of the political development concept, as applied to states, see Samuel P. Huntington, "The Goals of Development," in Myron Weiner and Samuel P. Huntington, eds., *Understanding Political Development* (Boston: Little, Brown, 1987), pp. 3–32.

22. Raymond W. Mack and Richard C. Snyder, "The Analysis of Social Conflict—Toward an Overview and Synthesis," in Clagett G. Smith, ed., *Conflict Resolution: Contributions of the Behavioral Sciences* (Notre Dame: University of Notre Dame, 1971), pp. 8–9.

23. Ted Robert Gurr, "Peoples Against States: Ethnopolitical Conflict and the Changing World System." *International Studies Quarterly* 38 (September 1994), p. 354.

24. Stephen D. Krasner, *Structural Conflict: The Third World Against Global Liberalism* (Berkeley: University of California Press, 1985), pp. 14–18.

25. Ibid., chap. 3.

26. Samuel P. Huntington, "The Clash of Civilizations?" *Foreign Affairs* 72 (summer 1993), pp. 22–49. For a more complete development of this argument, see Samuel P. Huntington, *The Clash of Civilizations and the Remaking of World Order* (New York: Simon & Schuster, 1996). For a critique of Huntington's thesis, see "Comments," *Foreign Affairs* 72 (September/October 1993), pp. 2–26 and Samuel Huntington, "If Not Civilizations, What?" *Foreign Affairs* 72 (November/December 1993), pp. 186–94.

27. Ibid., "The Clash," p. 22.

28. Ibid, pp. 39–41.

29. Stephen M. Walt, "Building up New Bogeymen," *Foreign Policy* 106 (spring 1997), p. 187.

30. Foud Ajami, "The Summoning," *Foreign Affairs* 72 (September/October 1993), p. 9.

31. Ibid., p. 5.

32. Ronald Steel, "Paradigm Regained," *The New Republic* (December 30, 1996), p. 25.

33. James Kurth, "The Real Clash," *The National Interest* (fall 1994), pp. 14–15.

34. Kalevi J. Holsti, *Peace and War: Armed Conflicts and International Order, 1648–1989* (Cambridge: Cambridge University Press, 1991), pp. 279–82.

35. Ibid., p. 283.

36. See Lewis Coser, *The Functions of Social Conflict* (New York: Free Press, 1956), pp. 121–37.

37. Joseph S. Nye, Jr., "Nuclear Learning and US-Soviet Security Regimes," *International Organization* 41 (summer 1987), pp. 371–402.

38. Quoted in John G. Stoessinger, *Henry Kissinger: The Anguish of Power* (New York: W.W. Norton, 1976), p. 14.

39. K.J. Holsti, *International Politics: A Framework for Analysis,* 6th ed. (Englewood Cliffs, N.J.: Prentice-Hall, 1992), pp. 359–63.

40. Don Oberdorfer, "The War No One Saw Coming," *The Washington Post National Weekly Edition* (March 18–24, 1991), p. 7.

41. "The Road to War," *Newsweek* (January 28, 1991), p. 56.

42. *New York Times* (March 25, 1991), p. 1.

43. *New York Times* (February 11, 1991), p. 7.

44. *New York Times* (August 11, 1990), pp. 1 and 4.

45. *New York Times* (September 9, 1990), p. 10.

Chapter 5

1. George F. Kennan, [Mr. X], "The Sources of Soviet Conduct," in James M. McCormick, ed., *A Reader in American Foreign Policy* (Itasca, Ill.: F.E. Peacock, 1986), p. 71.

2. Richard Nixon, *Beyond Peace* (New York: Random House, 1994), p. 33.

3. William G. Hyland, *The Cold War Is Over* (New York: Times Books, 1990), p. 1.

4. John L. Gaddis, *The Long Peace: Inquiries into the History of the Cold War* (New York: Oxford University Press, 1987), p. 245.

5. Ibid.

6. See especially John J. Mearsheimer, "Back to the Future," *International Security* 15 (summer 1990), pp. 5–56. A condensed version of the same article appeared as "Why We Will Soon Miss the Cold War." *The Atlantic Monthly* (August 1990), pp. 35–50.

7. John G. Stoessinger, *Nations in Darkness: China, Russia, and America,* 5th ed. (New York: McGraw-Hill, 1990), p. 283.

8. Ibid., pp. 286–87.

9. Karl W. Ryavec, *United States-Soviet Relations* (New York: Longman, 1989), p. 40.

10. Winston S. Churchill, *Triumph and Tragedy* (Boston: Houghton Mifflin, 1953), pp. 227–28.

11. Examples of "traditional" explanations of the Cold War include: A.W. DePorte, *Europe Between the Super-Powers: The Enduring Balance* (New Haven: Yale University Press, 1979); Herbert Feis, *Churchill, Roosevelt, Stalin: The War They Waged and the Peace They Sought* (Princeton: Princeton University Press, 1957); Louis J. Halle, *The Cold War As History* (New York: Harper & Row, 1967); and William H. McNeill, *America, Britain, and Russia* (London: Oxford University Press, 1953).

12. Leading "revisionist" accounts include: William Appleman Williams, *The Tragedy of American Diplomacy* (New York: Dell, 1962); Gar Alperovitz, *Atomic Diplomacy: Hiroshima and Potsdam, The Use of the Atomic Bomb and the American Confrontation with Soviet Power* (London: Secker and Warburg, 1966); and Gabriel Kolko, *The Politics of War: The World and United States Foreign Policy, 1943–1945* (New York: Random House, 1968).

13. Examples of important "moderate" interpretations of the Cold War include: John Lewis Gaddis, *The United States and the Origins of the Cold War, 1941–47* (New York: Columbia University Press, 1972) and *Russia, the Soviet Union, and the United States: An Interpretive History* (New York: Alfred A. Knopf, 1978); and Walter LaFeber, *America, Russia, and the Cold War, 1945–50,* 6th ed. (New York: McGraw-Hill, 1990).

14. Gaddis, *The Long Peace,* p. 47.

15. Robert J. Art, "America's Foreign Policy," in Roy C. Macridis, ed., *Foreign Policy in World Politics,* 7th ed. (Englewood Cliffs, N.J.: Prentice Hall, 1989), p. 138.

16. *New York Times* (February 26, 1991), p. 1.

17. *New York Times* (Thursday, September 1, 1994), p. 3.

18. See, for example, John Lewis Gaddis, "International Relations Theory and the End of the Cold War," *International Security* 17 (winter 1992/93), pp. 5–58.

19. See, for example, Peter Rutland, "Sovietology: Notes for a Post-Mortem," *The National Interest* (spring 1991), pp. 109–22. See also other articles in the same issue on the end of the Soviet Union.

20. For an assessment of this perspective, see Daniel Deudney and G. John Ikenberry, "Who Won the Cold War?" *Foreign Policy* 87 (summer 1992), pp. 123–38.

21. Ben J. Wattenberg, "Neo-Manifest Destinarianism," *The National Interest* 21 (fall 1990), p. 51.

22. *New York Times* (October 28, 1992), p. 21.

23. Daniel Deudney and G. John Ikenberry, "The International Sources of Soviet Change," *International Security* 16 (winter 1991/92), p. 80.

24. Hyland, *The Cold War Is Over,* p. 200.

25. John Lewis Gaddis, "Coping with Victory," *The Atlantic Monthly* (May 1990), p. 60.

26. Robert Conquest, "Academe and the Soviet Myth," *The National Interest* (spring 1993), p. 87.

27. Raymond L. Garthoff, "Why Did the Cold War Arise, and Why Did It End?" in Michael J. Hogan, ed., *The End of the Cold War: Its Meaning and Implications* (New York: Cambridge University Press, 1992), p. 129.

28. Jack F. Matlock, Jr., *Autopsy on an Empire: The American Ambassador's Account of the Collapse of the Soviet Union* (New York: Random House, 1995), pp. 668–69.

29. Richard Ned Lebow and Janice Gross Stein, *We All Lost the Cold War* (Princeton: Princeton University Press, 1994), p. 371.

30. Arthur Schlesinger, Jr., "Some Lessons from the Cold War," in Hogan, *The End of the Cold War,* pp. 61–62.

31. John Lewis Gaddis, *The United States and the End of the Cold War* (New York: Oxford University Press, 1992), chap. 10.

32. Robert Heilbroner, "The Triumph of Capitalism," *The New Yorker* (January 23, 1989), p. 98.

33. Adrian Karatnyckz et al, *Freedom in the World: The Annual Survey of Political Rights & Civil Liberties, 1996–1997* (New York: Freedom House, 1997), p. 4.

34. See Mearsheimer, "Back to the Future."

35. Stanley Hoffmann and Robert O. Keohane, "Back to the Future, Part II." *International Security* 15 (fall 1990), pp. 191–99. See also Bruce M. Rusett and Thomas Risse-Kapp, "Back to the Future, Part III," *International Security* 15 (winter 1990/91), pp. 216–22.

36. G. John Ikenberry, "The Myth of the Post–Cold War Chaos," *Foreign Affairs* 75 (May/June 1996), p. 79.

37. See Samuel P. Huntington, *The Clash of Civilizations and the Remaking of World Order* (New York: Simon & Schuster, 1996).

38. See Charles Krauthammer, "The Unipolar Moment," *Foreign Affairs: America and the World* 70 (1990/91). For a critique of this view, see Christopher Layne, "The Unipolar Illusion: Why New Great Powers Will Rise," *International Security* 17 (spring 1993), pp. 5–51.

Chapter 6

1. Hans J. Morgenthau, *Politics Among Nations: The Struggle for Power and Peace,* rev. 5th ed. (New York: Alfred A. Knopf, 1978), p. 29.

2. Quoted in Raymond L. Garthoff, *The Great Transition: American-Soviet Relations and the End of the Cold War* (Washington, D.C.: The Brookings Institution, 1994), p. viii.

3. Susan Strange, "What About International Relations?" in Susan Strange, ed., *Paths to International Political Economy* (London: Allen & Unwin, 1984), p. 184.

4. Kenneth N. Waltz, *Theory of International Politics* (Reading, Mass.: Addison-Wesley, 1979), pp. 194–95.

5. E.H. Carr, *The Twenty Years' Crisis, 1919–1939: An Introduction to the Study of International Relations* (New York: Harper & Row, 1964), pp. 93–94.

6. Karl W. Deutsch, *The Analysis of International Relations,* 3rd ed. (Englewood Cliffs, N.J.: Prentice-Hall, 1988), p. 20.

7. Ibid., pp. 47–48.

8. Morgenthau, *Politics Among Nations,* p. 9.

9. Ibid., p. 36.

10. Ibid., p. 9.

11. Stephen Krasner, *Structural Conflict: The Third World Against Global Liberalism* (Berkeley: University of California Press, 1985).

12. Joseph S. Nye, Jr., *Bound to Lead: The Changing Nature of American Power* (New York: Basic Books, 1990), p. 31.

13. For a comparison of these types of power, see Klaus Knorr, *The Power of Nations: The Political Economy of International Relations* (New York: Basic Books, 1975), pp. 9–14.

14. Morgenthau, *Politics Among Nations,* p. 117.

15. Paul Kennedy, *The Rise and Fall of the Great Powers* (New York: Random House, 1987), p. xxii.

16. See, for example, Samuel P. Huntington, "The U.S.—Decline or Renewal?" *Foreign Affairs* 67 (winter 1988/1989), pp. 76–96; and Joseph S. Nye, Jr., "The Misleading Metaphor of Decline," *The Atlantic Monthly* (March 1990), pp. 86–90, and *Bound to Lead*.

17. Nye, *Bound to Lead,* pp. 14–16 and 52–68.

18. U.S. Arms Control and Disarmament Agency, *World Military Expenditures and Arms Transfers, 1996* (Washington, D.C.: U.S. Government Printing Office, 1997), pp. 55–56.

19. Ibid., p. 1.

20. Ibid., p. 52

21. Ibid., p. 11.

22. U.S. Arms Control and Disarmament Agency, *World Military Expenditures and Arms Transfers, 1990* (Washington, D.C.: U.S. Government Printing Office, 1991), p. 75.

23. Morgenthau, *Politics Among Nations,* p. 146.

24. Nye, *Bound to Lead,* p. 175.

25. For a discussion of newer conceptions of national security see, for example, Jessica Tuchman Mathews, "Redefining Security,"

Foreign Affairs 68 (spring 1989), pp. 162–77; and Theodore C. Sorensen, "Rethinking National Security," *Foreign Affairs* 69 (summer 1990), pp. 1–18.

26. Nye, *Bound to Lead,* pp. 188–89.

27. Quoted in James E. Dougherty and Robert L. Pfaltzgraff, Jr., *Contending Theories of International Relations: A Comprehensive Survey,* 3rd ed. (New York: Harper & Row, 1990), p. 30.

28. Ibid., pp. 32–33.

29. Waltz, *Theory of International Politics,* p. 166.

30. This is similar to the achievement of the common economic good under a market economy. According to Adam Smith, the father of modern capitalism, the general welfare was not achieved by a general public plan but was realized through collective actions of persons, each pursuing his or her self-interest. Because the totality of individual economic actions in society would produce economic order, Smith argued that capitalism was guided by an "invisible hand."

31. A.F.K. Organski, *World Politics,* 2nd ed. (New York: Alfred A. Knopf, 1968), p. 294.

32. Morgenthau, *Politics Among Nations,* pp. 210–28.

33. Dougherty and Pfaltzgraff, *Contending Theories of International Relations,* pp. 31–32.

34. Charles Krauthammer, "The Unipolar Moment," *Foreign Affairs* 70 (1990/91), pp. 23–33.

35. See Robert O. Keohane, "The Theory of Hegemonic Stability and Changes in International Economic Regimes, 1967–1977," in Ole R. Holsti, Randolph M. Siverson, and Alexander L. George, eds., *Change in the International System* (Boulder, Colo.: Westview Press, 1980); Robert O. Keohane, *After Hegemony: Cooperation and Discord in the World Political Economy* (Princeton: Princeton University Press, 1984); and George Modelski, *Long Cycles in World Politics* (Seattle: University of Washington Press, 1987). For a critique of the hegemonic stability theory, see Duncan Snidal, "Limits of Hegemonic Stability Theory," *International Organization* 39 (autumn 1985), pp. 579–614; and Isabelle Grunberg, "Exploring the 'Myth' of Hegemonic Stability," *International Organization* 44 (autumn 1990), pp. 431–77.

36. Organski, *World Politics,* p. 294.

Chapter 7

1. Hans J. Morgenthau and Kenneth W. Thompson, *Politics Among Nations: The Struggle for Power and Peace,* 6th ed. (New York: Alfred A. Knopf, 1985), p. 6.

2. Dean Acheson, "Ethics in International Relations Today: Our Standard of Conduct," *Vital Speeches of the Day* 31 (February 1, 1965), p. 227.

3. Arnold Wolfers, *Discord and Collaboration: Essays on International Politics* (Baltimore: The Johns Hopkins University Press, 1962), p. 58.

4. Arthur Schlesinger, Jr., "The Amorality of Foreign Affairs," *Harper's Magazine* (April 1971), p. 72.

5. Thucydides, *History of the Peloponnesian War,* trans. Rex Warner (London: Penguin, 1972), p. 121.

6. Edward Hallett Carr, *The Twenty Years' Crisis, 1919–1939: An Introduction to the Study of International Relations* (New York: Harper & Row, 1964), p. 93.

7. John Rawls, *A Theory of Justice* (Cambridge: Harvard University Press, 1971), p. 15.

8. Lord Moulton of Bank, "Law and Manners," quoted in Rushworth M. Kidder, *How Good People Make Tough Choices* (New York: William Morrow and Co., 1995), p. 67.

9. Lea Brilmayer, *American Hegemony: Political Morality in a One-Superpower World* (New Haven: Yale University Press, 1994), p. 25.

10. Max Weber, *Politics As a Vocation* (Philadelphia: Fortress Press, 1965), pp. 46–49.

11. For an excellent discussion of these two contrasting traditions, see Terry Nardin and David R. Mapel, eds., *Traditions of International Ethics* (Cambridge: Cambridge University Press, 1992).

12. Adapted from Joseph S. Nye, Jr., *Nuclear Ethics* (New York: Free Press, 1986), p. 18.

13. The classification of international political morality is from Charles R. Beitz, "Bounded Morality: Justice and the State in World Politics," *International Organization* 33 (summer 1979), pp. 406–10.

14. See, for example, Kenneth Thompson, *The Moral Issue in Statecraft* (Baton Rouge: Louisiana State University Press, 1966).

15. Morgenthau and Thompson, *Politics Among Nations,* p. 12.

16. Beitz, "Bounded Morality," p. 408.

17. For example, some political theorists have emphasized obligations to political community, whereas others have stressed individual rights. Moreover, some thinkers have tried to illuminate foundational principles by which to justify governmental decisions, and others sought to have defined justice in terms of desirable outcomes.

18. Stanley Hoffmann, *Duties Beyond Borders: On the Limits and Possibilities of Ethical International Relations* (Syracuse: Syracuse University Press, 1981), pp. 164–65.

19. Michael Walzer, *Just and Unjust Wars: A Moral Argument with Historical Illustrations* (New York: Basic Book, 1977), pp. 20–108.

20. *The New Republic* (December 28, 1992), p. 12.

21. *Newsweek* (December 14, 1992), p. 31.

22. R.J. Vincent, "The Idea of Rights in International Ethics," in Nardin and Mapel, eds., *Traditions of International Ethics,* p. 267.

23. Jack Donnelly, *International Human Rights* (Boulder, Colo.: Westview Press, 1993), p. 24.

24. *Newsweek* (April 18, 1994), p. 22.

25. For a review of Lee Kuan Yew's views about human rights and governance, see Fareed Zakaria, "Culture Is Destiny: A Conversation with Lee Kuan Yew," *Foreign Affairs* 73 (March/April 1994), pp. 109–26.

26. Kishore Mahbubani, "The United States: 'Go East, Young Man'," *The Washington Quarterly* 17 (spring 1994), p. 11.

27. Before the Vienna conference, meetings were held in each major geographical region of the world to develop preparatory documents that expressed regional perspectives and concerns. Asian and Pacific delegates met in Bangkok, for example, and issued a declaration that emphasized the need for cultural contextualization of rights. In a direct challenge to the Western conception of human rights, the Bangkok Declaration declared that rights must be defined and interpreted in the context of "national and regional particularities and various historical, cultural and religious backgrounds."

28. In view of the different perspectives on human rights represented by regional groups, delegates decided that the conference proceedings would be based on "consensus"—that is, unanimity. This meant that the final declaration had to be approved by all governments or there would be no final declaration.

29. Charles J. Brown, "In the Trenches: The Battle Over Rights," *Freedom Review* (September-October, 1993), p. 9.

30. A.J.M. Milne, "Human Rights and the Diversity of Morals: A Philosophical Analysis of Rights and Obligations in the Global System," in Moorehead Wright, ed., *Rights and Obligations in North-South Relations* (New York: St. Martin's Press, 1986), p. 21.

31. Michael Walzer, *Thick and Thin: Moral Argument at Home and Abroad* (Notre Dame: University of Notre Dame Press, 1994), pp. 1–19.

32. R.J. Vincent, *Human Rights and International Relations* (Cambridge: Cambridge University Press, 1986), pp. 54–55.

33. Michael Walzer, *Just and Unjust Wars* pp. xiv–xv.

34. Ibid., p. 19.

35. For contrasting perspectives on this practice, see A.M. Rosenthal, "Female Genital Torture," *New York Times* (November 12, 1993), p. 15; and Maynard H. Merwine, "How Africa Understands Female Circumcision," *New York Times* (November 24, 1993), p. 15.

36. For a discussion of the 1996 U.S. law prohibiting genital mutilation, see *New York Times* (October 12, 1996), p. 1.

37. *New York Times* (June 14, 1996), p. 1. For a comprehensive review of this case, see *New York Times* (September 11, 1996), pp. 1, 8, and 9.

38. Schlesinger, "The Amorality of Foreign Affairs," pp. 72–74.

39. Dean Acheson, "Ethics in International Relations Today," *Vital Speeches of the Day* 31 (February 1, 1965), p. 227.

40. George F. Kennan, *Realities of American Foreign Policy* (New York: W.W. Norton, 1966), pp. 47–50.

41. Robert F. Kennedy, *Thirteen Days: A Memoir of the Cuban Missile Crisis* (New York: W.W. Norton, 1971), pp. 17 and 27.

42. Walzer, *Just and Unjust Wars*, p. 12.

43. John C. Bennett, *Foreign Policy in Christian Perspective* (New York: Charles Scribners, 1966), p. 36.

44. Henry Kissinger, "The Realities of Security," American Enterprise Institute, *Foreign Policy and Defense Review* 3, no. 6 (1982), p. 11.

45. Herbert Butterfield, *International Conflict in the Twentieth Century* (New York: Harper and Brothers, 1960), pp. 23–25.

46. Reinhold Niebuhr, *Moral Man and Immoral Society* (New York: Charles Scribners, 1960), pp. 88–89.

47. Robert McElroy, *Morality and American Foreign Policy* (Princeton: Princeton University Press, 1992), p. 86.

48. Ibid., p. 63.

49. Ibid., p. 59.

50. Ibid., p. 71

51. Ibid., p. 58.

52. Hans J. Morgenthau, *Scientific Man Versus Power Politics* (Chicago: University of Chicago Press, 1965), p. 263.

53. Hoffmann, *Duties Beyond Borders*, p. 33. Joseph Cropsey also makes this argument in "The Moral Basis of International Action" in Joseph Cropsey, ed., *Political Philosophy and the Issues of Politics* (Chicago: University of Chicago Press, 1977), p. 179.

54. Carr, *The Twenty Years' Crisis*, pp. 63–101.

55. Peter L. Berger, "Moral Judgment and Political Action," *Vital Speeches of the Day* 54 (December 1, 1987), p. 120.

56. Nye, *Nuclear Ethics*, pp. 20–26.

Chapter 8

1. Quoted in John Lewis Gaddis, *The United States and the End of the Cold War* (New York: Oxford University Press, 1992), p. 194.

2. John L. Harper, "The Dream of Democratic Peace: Americans Are Not Asleep," *Foreign Affairs* 76 (May/June 1997), p. 120.

3. Kalevi J. Holsti, *The State, War and the State of War* (Cambridge: Cambridge University Press, 1996), p. 168.

4. This action represented a dramatically altered Soviet foreign policy, because the USSR was originally responsible for installing communist regimes in Eastern European states and for keeping them in power in the postwar years. Indeed, it was Soviet military force that brutally crushed the popular uprisings in Hungary in 1956 and in Czechoslovakia in 1968.

5. For further discussion of the foreign policy concept, see Cecil V. Crabb, Jr., *American Foreign Policy in the Nuclear Age,* 4th ed. (New York: Harper & Row, 1983), pp. 15–16; and Bruce Russett and Harvey Starr, *World Politics: Menu for Choice,* 3rd ed. (New York: W.H. Freeman, 1989), pp. 124–37.

6. President of the United States, "A National Security Strategy for a New Century," The White House (May 1997).

7. See, for example, Richard Ullman, "Redefining Security," *International Security* 8 (summer 1983), pp. 129–53; and Michael T. Klare and Daniel C. Thomas, eds., *World Security: Trends and Challenges at Century's End* (New York: St. Martin's Press, 1991).

8. See Matthew Connelly and Paul Kennedy, "Must It Be the Rest Against the West?" *The Atlantic Monthly* 274 (December 1994), pp. 61–84.

9. This concept is central to the realist perspective. See Hans J. Morgenthau, *Politics Among Nations: The Struggle for Power and Peace,* 5th ed., rev. (New York: Random House, 1978), pp. 4–17. For a critical assessment of the concept see Alexander George and Robert O. Keohane, "The Concept of National Interest: Uses and Limitations," in Alexander George, ed., *Presidential Decision Making in Foreign Policy* (Boulder: Westview, 1980), pp. 217–37.

10. Thomas Robinson, "National Interests," in James N. Rosenau, ed., *International Politics and Foreign Policy: A Reader in Research and Theory* (New York: Free Press, 1969), pp. 184–85.

11. See Abraham H. Maslow, *Toward a Psychology of Being,* 2nd ed. (Princeton: Van Nostrand, 1968).

12. Kenneth Waltz, *Theory of International Politics* (Reading, Mass.: Addison-Wesley, 1979), p. 92.

13. Michael Walzer, *Just and Unjust Wars: A Moral Argument with Historical Illustrations* (New York: Basic Books, 1977), pp. 53–55 and 58–63.

14. Morgenthau, *Politics Among Nations*, p. 586.

15. Ibid., p. 5.

16. See, for example, Jessica Tuchman Mathews, "Redefining Security," *Foreign Affairs* 68 (spring 1989), pp. 162–177; Richard Ullman, "Redefining Security," *International Security* 8 (summer 1983), pp. 129–53; and Nicholas Eberstadt, "Population Change and National Security," *Foreign Affairs* 70 (summer 1991), pp. 115–31.

17. Paul Kennedy, *The Rise and Fall of the Great Powers* (New York: Random House, 1987).

18. Lloyd Jensen, *Explaining Foreign Policy* (Englewood Cliffs, N.J.: Prentice-Hall, 1982), pp. 72–74.

19. G. John Ikenberry, "The Future of International Leadership," *Political Science Quarterly* 111 (summer 1996), p. 388.

20. Henry Kissinger, "Domestic Structure and Foreign Policy," in Rosenau, ed., *International Politics and Foreign Policy,* pp. 267–73.

21. Ikenberry, "The Future of International Leadership," pp. 388–96.

22. See, for example, Alexander L. George, "The Operational Code: A Neglected Approach to the Study of Political Leaders and Decision-Making," *International Studies Quarterly* 13, 2 (1969) pp. 199–222; Ole R. Holsti, "The Belief System and National Images: A Case Study," *The Journal of Conflict Resolution* VI (September 1962), pp. 244–52; and Robert Jervis, *The Logic of Images in International Relations* (New York: Columbia University Press, 1989).

23. The classic study of misperception in foreign policy is Robert Jervis, *Perception and Misperception in International Politics* (Princeton: Princeton University Press, 1976).

24. Holsti, "The Belief System."

25. See Kennedy, *The Rise and Fall of the Great Powers,* especially chap. 1.

26. See James N. Rosenau, "Pre-Theories and Theories of Foreign Policy," in R. Barry Farrell, ed., *Approaches to Comparative and International Politics* (Evanston, Ill.: Northwestern University Press, 1966), pp. 27–92; see also James N. Rosenau, *The Scientific Study of Foreign Policy,* 2nd ed. (London: Frances Pinter, 1980).

27. A recent review of public opinion scholarship suggests, however, that public opinion has been more coherent and more influential than previously thought. Indeed, one scholar found that the impact of public opinion on U.S. foreign policy has been increasing in recent decades. See Ole R. Holsti, "Public Opinion and Foreign Policy: Challenges to the Almond-Lippmann Consensus," *International Studies Quarterly* 36 (December 1992), pp. 439–66.

28. It is important to note that Americans are not well informed about foreign affairs, with Western Europeans and Canadians being far

more knowledgeable about global issues. *Time* (March 28, 1994), p. 22.

29. John E. Rielly, "The Public Mood at Mid-Decade," *Foreign Policy* 98 (spring 1995), p. 78.

30. For an overview of the core elements of NAFTA, see *New York Times* (November 11, 1993), p. 8.

31. *New York Times* (November 17, 1993), p. 11.

32. For an overview of the domestic politics of NAFTA, see Howard J. Wiarda, *Democracy and Its Discontents: Development, Interdependence, and U.S. Policy in Latin America* (Lanham, Md.: Rowman & Littlefield, 1995), pp. 143–71.

33. *New York Times* (November 16, 1993), pp. 1 and 11.

34. *New York Times* (November 19, 1993), p. 26.

35. *New York Times* (November 11, 1997), pp. 1 and 8.

36. Alexis de Tocqueville, *Democracy in America,* vol. I (New York: Alfred A. Knopf, 1945), pp. 234–35.

37. Walter Lippmann, *The Public Philosophy* (New York: Mentor Books, 1955), pp. 23–24.

38. For a discussion of the impact of the media on foreign policy decision making, see Johanna Neuman, "The Media's Impact on International Affairs, Then and Now," *The National Interest* 16 (winter 1995/1996), pp. 109–23.

39. This effect is associated with the Cable News Network, a 24-hour television news channel that broadcasts throughout the world.

40. Reported in John Newhouse, *Cold Dawn: The Story of SALT* (New York: Holt, Rinehart and Winston, 1973), p. 6.

41. Immanuel Kant, "Perpetual Peace," in Peter Gay, ed., *The Enlightenment* (New York: Simon & Schuster, 1974), p. 790.

42. Quincy Wright, *A Study of War,* abridged ed. (Chicago: University of Chicago Press, 1964), p. 163.

43. R.J. Rummel, "The Politics of Cold Blood," *Society* 27 (November/December 1989), p. 38.

44. Jack Levy, "Domestic Politics and War," *Journal of Interdisciplinary History* 18 (spring 1988), p. 662.

45. Christopher Layne, "Kant or Cant: The Myth of the Democratic Peace," *International Security* 19 (fall 1994), p. 8.

46. Bruce Russett, *Grasping the Democratic Peace: Principles for a Post–Cold War World* (Princeton: Princeton University Press, 1993), p. 119.

47. Bruce Russett, *Controlling the Sword: The Democratic Governance of National Security* (Cambridge: Harvard University Press, 1990), p. 45.

48. Levy, "Domestic Politics and War," p. 661.

49. Russett, *Controlling the Sword,* p. 45.

50. See, for example, Michael E. Brown, Sean M. Lynn-Jones, and Steven E. Miller, eds., *Debating the Democratic Peace* (Cambridge: MIT Press, 1996); and James Lee Ray, *Democracy and International Conflict: An Evaluation of the Democratic Peace Proposition* (Columbia: University of South Carolina Press, 1995).

51. Quoted in "The Politics of Peace," *The Economist* (April 1, 1995), p. 17.

52. Ibid.

53. Alfred T. Mahan, *The Influence of Sea Power upon History, 1660–1783* (Boston: Little, Brown, 1941).

54. Sir Halford Mackinder, *Democratic Ideals and Reality* (New York: Henry A. Holt, 1919).

55. Nicholas J. Spykman, *The Geography of Peace* (New York: Harcourt, Brace, 1942), p. 43.

56. See, for example, Patrick O'Sullivan, *Geopolitics* (New York: St. Martin's Press, 1986); Colin S. Gray, *The Geopolitics of the Nuclear Era: Heartland, Rimlands and the Technological Revolution* (New York: Crane, Russak, 1977); and Zbigniew Brzezinski, *The Grand Chessboard: American Primacy and Its Geostrategic Imperatives* (New York Basic Books, 1997).

57. S.E. Finer, *Comparative Government* (Harmondsworth, England: Penguin Books, 1970), p. 136.

58. Morgenthau, *Politics Among Nations,* chap. 15.

59. Robert F. Kennedy, *Thirteen Days: A Memoir of the Cuban Missile Crisis* (New York: W. W. Norton, 1971), p. 27.

Chapter 9

1. Quoted in Richard Ned Lebow and Janice Gross, *We All Lost the Cold War* (Princeton: Princeton University Press, 1994), p. 291.

2. Graham T. Allison, *Essence of Decision: Explaining the Cuban Missile Crisis* (Boston: Little, Brown, 1971), p. 145.

3. Susan Strange, "The Defective State," *Daedalus* (spring 1995), p. 56.

4. Quoted in Elie Abel, *The Missile Crisis* (New York: Bantam, 1966), p. 134.

5. These models are based on Graham Allison's seminal study of decision making during the Cuban missile crisis. These two models emphasize the role of organizational dynamics in decision making and the role of bureaucratic politics. See Allison, *Essence of Decision.*

6. Ibid., p. 68.

7. For an examination of the role of perceptions and misperceptions in foreign affairs, see Robert Jervis, *Perception and Misperception in International Politics* (Princeton: Princeton University Press, 1976); and Robert Mandel, "Psychological Approaches to International Relations," in Margaret G. Hermann, ed., *Political Psychology* (San Francisco: Jossey-Bass, 1986).

8. Allison, *Essence of Decision,* p. 67. For a more comprehensive account of the role of bureaucracies in foreign policy, see Morton H. Halperin and Arnold Kanter, "The Bureaucratic Perspective," in Morton H. Halperin and Arnold Kanter, *Readings in Foreign Policy: A Bureaucratic Perspective* (Boston: Little, Brown, 1973). For a critique of the bureaucratic approach, see Robert J. Art, "Bureaucratic Politics and American Foreign Policy," *Policy Sciences* 4 (1973), pp. 467–90.

9. Roger Fisher, *Conflict for Beginners* (New York: Harper & Row, 1969), pp. 182–89.

10. See Herbert Simon, *Models of Man* (New York: Wiley, 1957); and *Models of Bounded Rationality* (Cambridge: MIT Press, 1982).

11. For a discussion of this theory, see Jack S. Levy, "An Introduction to Prospect Theory," *Political Psychology* 13 (June 1992), pp. 171–86. See also Janice Gross Stein and Louis W. Pauly, *Choosing to Cooperate: How States Avoid Loss* (Baltimore: The Johns Hopkins University Press, 1993); and Barbara Farnham, ed., *Avoiding Losses/Taking Risks: Prospect Theory and International Conflict* (Ann Arbor: University of Michigan Press, 1994).

12. See Irving Janis, *Groupthink,* 2nd ed. (Boston: Houghton Mifflin, 1982).

13. David Braybrooke and Charles E. Lindblom, *A Strategy of Decision: Policy Evaluation as a Social Process* (New York: Free Press, 1963), pp. 61–79.

14. See Charles F. Hermann, "Some Issues in the Study of International Crisis," in Charles F. Hermann, ed., *International Crises* (New York: Free Press, 1972), pp. 3–17. See also Jonathan M. Roberts, *Decision-Making during International Crisis* (New York: St. Martin's Press, 1988); and Irving L. Janis, *Crucial Decisions: Leadership in Policymaking and Crisis Management* (New York: The Free Press, 1989).

15. Revelations by Soviet officials during the 1980s have made plain that the initiative for placing intermediate ballistic missiles in Cuba did not come from Cuban leader Fidel Castro but from Party Chairman Khrushchev. He advanced the idea in early spring 1962 among key officials in the Soviet government and then sent one of his aids to Cuba in late May to confer with Castro.

16. J. Anthony Lukas, "Class Reunion: Kennedy's Men Relive the Cuban Missile Crisis," *New York Times Magazine* (August 30, 1987), p. 58.

17. McGeorge Bundy, *Danger and Survival: Choices about the Bomb in the First Fifty Years* (New York: Random House, 1988), p. 443.

18. Ibid., p. 164.

19. Ibid., pp. 432–33.

20. Castro was so unhappy with Khrushchev's unilateral decision to withdraw the missiles that Cuban soldiers surrounded the missile bases on October 28 and remained there for three days!

21. Raymond Garthoff, *Reflections on the Cuban Missile Crisis* (Washington, D.C.: Brookings Institution, 1987), pp. 61–83.

22. Raymond Garthoff, "Cuban Missile Crisis: The Soviet Story," *Foreign Policy* 72 (fall 1988), p. 77.

23. Raymond L. Garthoff, "Cuba: Even Dicier Than We Knew," *Newsweek,* October 26, 1987, p. 34.

24. Garthoff, "Cuban Missile Crisis," p. 67.

25. Robert Kennedy, *Thirteen Days: A Memoir of the Cuban Missile Crisis* (New York: W.W. Norton, 1971), pp. 89–90.

26. For an excellent short account of the representatives and positions of each of these groups, see James G. Blight, Joseph S. Nye, Jr. and David A. Welch, "The Cuban Missile Crisis Revisited," *Foreign Affairs* 66 (fall 1987), pp. 170–88.

27. Kennedy, *Thirteen Days,* p. 102.

28. For an excellent discussion of this concept, see David A. Baldwin, *Economic Statecraft* (Princeton: Princeton University Press, 1985), pp. 8–12.

29. For a general discussion of different types of influence, see Robert A. Dahl, *Modern Political Analysis,* 5th ed. (Englewood Cliffs: Prentice Hall, 1991), pp. 39–48.

30. Fisher, *Conflict for Beginners,* pp. 27–59.

31. David Halloran Lumsdaine, *Moral Vision in International Politics: The Foreign Aid Regime, 1949–1989* (Princeton: Princeton University Press, 1993), p. 34.

32. National Association of Manufacturers, "A Catalog of New U.S. Unilateral Economic Sanctions for Foreign Policy Purposes, 1993–96," (Washington, D.C.: National Association of Manufacturers, 1997), pp. 1–4.

33. *New York Times* (April 20, 1997), p. E5.

34. Donald L. Losman, *International Economic Sanctions: The Cases of Cuba, Israel and Rhodesia* (Albuquerque: University of New Mexico, 1979), pp. 1 and 124.

35. Gary C. Hufbauer, Jeffrey J. Schott, and Kimberly Ann Elliott, *Economic Sanctions Reconsidered: History and Current Policy,* 2nd ed. (Washington, D.C.: Institute for International Economics, 1990), pp. 49–73.

36. Ibid.

37. Charles Kindleberger, *Power and Money: The Economics of International Politics and the Politics of International Economics* (New York: Basic Books, 1970), p. 97.

38. Margaret P. Doxey, *Economic Sanctions and International Enforcement* (New York: Oxford University Press, 1971), p. 139.

39. Baldwin, *Economic Statecraft,* p. 57.

40. For an excellent critique of why economic sanctions are ineffective in bringing about behavioral change, see Robert A. Pape, "Why Economic Sanctions Do Not Work," *International Security* 22 (fall 1997), pp. 90–136.

41. Some scholars argue that the popularity of economic sanctions is rooted in the belief that they are useful instruments of punishment. See Kim Richard Nossal, "International Sanctions as International Punishment," *International Organization* 43 (spring 1989), pp. 301–22.

42. Jennifer Davis, "Sanctions and Apartheid: The Economic Challenge to Discrimination," in David Cortright and George A. Lopez, eds., *Economic Sanctions: Panacea or Peacebuilding in a Post–Cold War World?* (Boulder, Colo.: Westview Press, 1995), p. 178.

43. Thomas W. Hazlett, "Did Sanctions Matter?" *New York Times* (July 22, 1991), p. 11.

44. Quoted in Richard E. Sincere, Jr., *The Politics of Sentiment: Churches and Foreign Investment in South Africa* (Washington, D.C.: Ethics and Public Policy Center, 1984), p. v.

45. Drew Christiansen and Gerard F. Powers, "Economic Sanctions and the Just-War Doctrine," in Cortright and Lopez, eds., *Economic Sanctions,* p. 102.

46. For an insightful conceptual and historical overview of the role of force in international affairs, see Gordon A. Craig and Alexander L. George, *Force and Statecraft: Diplomatic Problems of Our Time,* 3rd ed. (New York: Oxford University Press, 1995), pp. 153–257.

47. I am indebted to Donald P. Snow for these distinctions. See his *National Security: Enduring Problems in a Changing Defense Environment,* 2nd ed. (New York: St. Martin's Press, 1991), pp. 233–34.

48. Craig and George, *Force and Statecraft,* p. 191.

49. Ibid., p. 197.

50. Amos A. Jordan, William J. Taylor, Jr., and Lawrence J. Korb, *American National Security: Policy and Process,* 3rd ed. (Baltimore: The Johns Hopkins University Press, 1989), p. 130.

51. Roberta Wohlstetter, *Pearl Harbor: Warning and Decision* (Stanford: Stanford University Press, 1962), p. 387.

Chapter 10

1. Laurence Martin, "Is Military Force Losing Its Utility?" in John F. Reichart and Steven R. Sturm, eds., *American Defense Policy,* 5th ed. (Baltimore: Johns Hopkins University Press, 1982), p. 40.

2. Quoted in Seyom Brown, *The Causes and Prevention of War* (New York: St. Martin's Press, 1987), p. 57.

3. Quoted in Christopher J. Lamb, *How to Think About Arms Control, Disarmament, and Defense* (Englewood Cliffs, N.J.: Prentice-Hall, 1988), p. 63.

4. Robert J. Art, "To What Ends Military Power?" *International Security,* 4 (spring 1980), p. 10.

5. For an analysis of the legitimacy of preemptive attack, and in particular of Israel's preemptive attack on Egypt, Jordan, and Syria, see Michael Walzer, *Just and Unjust Wars: A Moral Argument with Historical Illustrations* (New York: Basic Books, 1977), chap. 5.

6. See Barry M. Blechman and Stephen S. Kaplan, *Force Without War: U.S. Armed Forces as a Political Instrument* (Washington, D.C.: Brookings Institution, 1978).

7. For a discussion of this category of force, see Loren B. Thompson, *Low-Intensity Conflict: The Pattern of Warfare in the Modern World* (Lexington, Mass.: Lexington Books, 1989), pp. 1–25.

8. For a brief but illuminating analysis of the role of deterrence and coercive diplomacy in international relations, see Gordon A. Craig and Alexander L. George, *Force and Statecraft: Diplomatic Problems of Our Time,* 3rd ed. (New York: Oxford University Press, 1995), pp. 180–94 and 196–211.

9. Blechman and Kaplan, *Force Without War,* pp. 16–46.

10. Ibid., pp. 517–34.

11. Henry A. Kissinger, *American Foreign Policy,* exp. ed. (New York: W.W. Norton, 1974), p. 102.

12. Mao Tse-tung, *On Guerrilla Warfare,* trans. Samuel B. Griffiths (New York: Holt, Rinehart and Winston, 1961), p. 103.

13. Quoted in Gary G. Sick, "The Political Underpinnings of Terrorism," in Charles W. Kegley, Jr., ed., *International Terrorism: Characteristics, Causes, Controls* (New York: St. Martin's Press, 1990), p. 53.

14. Wars frequently involve intentional killing of noncombatants, such as the Allied bombing of Dresden and Tokyo during World War II and the shelling of Sarajevo and other Bosnian urban centers by Serb miliary forces during the 1992–1995 Balkans War.

15. Brian Jenkins, *International Terrorism: A New Mode of Conflict* (Los Angeles: Crescent Publications, 1975), p. 3.

16. Michael Walzer, *Just and Unjust Wars: A Moral Argument with Historical Illustrations* (New York: Basic Books, 1977), p. 197.

17. *The New York Times* (February 16, 1986), p. 10.

18. Charles W. Kegley, Jr., "Introduction," in Kegley, *International Terrorism*, p. 4.

19. Ibid., p. 14.

20. Michael Mandelbaum, "The Reluctance to Intervene," *Foreign Policy* 95 (summer 1994), p. 8.

21. Dorothy Jones, *Code of Peace: Ethics and Security in the World of Warlord States* (Chicago: University of Chicago Press, 1992), pp. xii and 163–64.

22. See Walzer, *Just and Unjust Wars*, pp. 82–85.

23. See John Stuart Mill, "A Few Words on Non-Intervention," *Dissertations and Discussions* (Boston: William V. Spencer, 1968).

24. Walzer, *Just and Unjust Wars*, p. 89.

25. Mandelbaum, "The Reluctance to Intervene," p. 14.

26. Walzer, *Just and Unjust Wars*, pp. 90–108.

27. Lloyd Cutler, "The Right to Intervene," *Foreign Affairs* 64 (fall 1985), pp. 96–112. See also Stephen J. Solarz, "When to Intervene," *Foreign Policy* 63 (summer 1986), pp. 20–39.

28. Quoted in Cutler, "The Right to Intervene," p. 97.

29. Charles Krauthammer, "When to Intervene," *The New Republic* (May 6, 1985), p. 11.

30. See "The Decision to Assist Grenada," U.S. Department of State, Bureau of Public Affairs (January 24, 1984). In this statement Langhorne Motley, the assistant secretary of state for Inter-American Affairs, explains to the House Armed Services Committee why the United States intervened in Grenada.

31. Terry Nardin and Kathleen D. Pritchard, "Ethics and Intervention: The United States in Grenada, 1983," *Case Studies in Ethics and International Affairs*, no. 2 (New York: Carnegie Council on Ethics and International Affairs, 1990), p. 16.

32. Ibid., p. 7.

33. Alberto R. Coll, "Why Grenada Was Important," *Naval War College Review* 40 (summer 1987), pp. 4–13.

34. For an excellent theoretical critique of the U.S. intervention in Grenada, see Michael W. Doyle, *Ways of War and Peace* (New York: W. W. Norton, 1997), pp. 402–20.

35. Jack Donnelly, "Human Rights, Humanitarian Intervention and American Foreign Policy: Law, Morality and Politics," *Journal of International Affairs* (winter 1984), p. 313.

36. Bernard Brodie, *The Absolute Weapon* (New York: Harcourt Brace, 1946), p. 52.

37. Thomas C. Schelling, *Arms and Influence* (New York: Yale University Press, 1966), p. 34.

38. Ibid., p. 20.

39. In the early 1970s both the United States and the Soviet Union developed antiballistic missile (ABM) systems to defend military targets. Because of their dubious effectiveness and significant cost, the superpowers signed the ABM Treaty (1972), limiting each country to two ABM sites (later reduced to one). In the 1980s, the United States sought to develop a comprehensive nuclear defensive system (known as SDI), but despite extraordinary efforts, little progress was made in developing such a system.

40. The number of warheads is greater than the number of launchers because some ballistic missiles can carry more than one warhead. In the early 1970s the superpowers begin deploying missiles with *multiple independently-targeted reentry vehicles (MIRVs)*—that is, warheads that were capable of being targeted separately from the main missile itself.

41. William E. Burrows, "Ballistic Missile Defense: The Illusion of Security," *Foreign Affairs* 62 (spring 1984), p. 844.

42. McGeorge Bundy, George F. Kennan, Robert S. McNamara, and Gerard Smith, "The President's Choice: Star Wars or Arms Control," *Foreign Affairs* 63 (winter 1984/85), p. 265.

43. Brodie, *The Absolute Weapon*, p. 46.

44. Robert S. McNamara, "The Military Role of Nuclear Weapons: Perceptions and Misperceptions," *Foreign Affairs* 62 (fall 1983), p. 79.

45. Robert Jervis, *The Nuclear Revolution: Statecraft and the Prospect of Armageddon* (Ithaca: Cornell University Press, 1989).

46. The concept of firebreak, which is used by firefighters, denotes the area cleared of all combustible material in order to halt a forest fire.

47. The notion of nuclear deterrence is extraordinarily complex. It has spawned different theories and strategies, resulting in a large literature. A useful historical overview of the changing nature of U.S. strategic policy is Lawrence Freedman, *The Evolution of Nuclear Strategy* (New York: St. Martin's Press, 1981). A more recent collection of articles on the same topic is Philip Bobbitt, Lawrence Freedman, and Gregory Treverton, eds., *U.S. Nuclear Strategy: A Reader* (New York: New York University Press, 1989).

48. Henry Kissinger, *The Necessity for Choice: Prospects of American Foreign Policy* (Garden City, N.Y.: Doubleday, 1962), p. 12.

49. Editorial, *The New York Times* (January 19, 1986).

50. Barry N. Blechman and Stephen S. Kaplan, *Force Without War: U.S. Armed Forces as Political Instrument* (Washington, D.C.: Brookings Institution, 1978), pp. 47–49.

51. See, for example, John Mueller, "The Essential Irrelevance of Nuclear Weapons: Stability in the Postwar World," *International Security* 13 (fall 1988), pp. 55–79.

52. Jonathan Schell, *The Fate of the Earth* (New York: Avon Books, 1982).

53. For a critique of this view, see John A. Vasquez, "The Deterrence Myth: Nuclear Weapons and the Prevention of Nuclear War" in Charles W. Kegley, Jr., ed., *The Long Postwar Peace: Contending Explanations and Projections* (New York: HarperCollins, 1991), pp. 205–223. See also Mueller, "The Essential Irrelevance of Nuclear Weapons."

54. Quoted in Jervis, *The Nuclear Revolution*, p. 24.

55. Thomas Schelling, "What Went Wrong with Arms Control," *Foreign Affairs* 64 (winter 1985/86), p. 233.

56. John Mearsheimer, "Why We Will Soon Miss the Cold War," *The Atlantic Monthly* (August 1990), p. 37.

57. Maxwell Taylor, "The Legitimate Claims of National Security," *Foreign Affairs* 52 (April 1974), p. 582.

58. McGeorge Bundy, *Danger and Survival: Choices about the Bomb in the First Fifty Years* (New York: Random House, 1988), p. 446.

59. Marc Trachtenberg, "The Influence of Nuclear Weapons in the Cuban Missile Crisis," *International Security* 10 (summer 1985), pp. 155–56.

60. Mearsheimer, "Why We Will Soon Miss the Cold War," p. 37.

61. Bundy, *Danger and Survival*, pp. 593–94.

62. Goodpaster Committee, "The Declining Utility of Nuclear Weapons," *The Washington Quarterly* 20 (summer 1997), pp. 93–94.

63. International Generals and Admirals, "Statement on Nuclear Weapons," *The Washington Quarterly* 20 (summer 1997), p. 126.

64. See *New York Times* (December 8, 1997), p. 3.

65. Graham T. Allison, Owen R. Cote Jr., Richard A. Falkenrath, and Steven E. Miller, "Avoiding Nuclear Anarchy," *The Washington Quarterly* 20 (summer 1997), p. 191.

66. Goodpaster Committee, "The Declining Utility of Nuclear Weapons."

Chapter 11

1. Donald Kagan, *On the Origins of War and the Preservation of Peace* (New York: Doubleday, 1995), p. 566.

2. Martin van Creveld, *The Transformation of War* (New York: Free Press, 1991), p. 2.

3. Kalevi J. Holsti, *The State, War, and the State of War* (Cambridge: Cambridge University Press, 1996), p. 206.

4. John Mueller, *Retreat from Doomsday: The Obsolescence of Major War* (New York: Basic Books, 1989), p. 240.

5. John Keegan, *A History of Warfare* (New York: Vintage Books, 1993), p. 56.

6. Carl von Clausewitz, *On War*, trans. Michael Howard and Peter Paret (Princeton: Princeton University Press, 1976), p. 87.

7. Ibid., p. 101.

8. Quincy Wright, *A Study of War* (Chicago: University of Chicago Press, 1942), p. 651.

9. Geoffrey Blainey, *The Causes of War* (New York: Free Press, 1973), p. 3.

10. Melvin Small and J. David Singer, "Patterns in International Warfare, 1816–1980," in Melvin Small and J. David Singer, eds., *International War: An Anthology and Study Guide* (Homewood, Ill.: Dorsey Press, 1985), p. 14.

11. Jack Levy, "Historical Trends in Great Power War, 1495–1975," *International Studies Quarterly* 26 (June 1982), pp. 278–300.

12. Francis A. Beer, *Peace Against War: The Ecology of International Violence* (San Francisco: W.H. Freeman, 1981), pp. 42–49.

13. David Rieff, "An Age of Genocide," *The New Republic* (January 29, 1996), p. 34.

14. John Keegan, *A History of Warfare* (New York: Vintage Books, 1993), p. 373.

15. Wright, *A Study of War,* p. 656.

16. Ruth Leger Sivard, *World Military and Social Expenditures, 1986,* 11th ed. (Washington, D.C.: World Priorities, 1986), p. 26.

17. *New York Times* (February 3, 1992), p. 6.

18. Holsti, *The State, War, and the State of War*, p. 29.

19. *New York Times* (June 16, 1982), p. 1.

20. Lawrence Freedman, *Britain and the Falklands War* (New York: Basil Blackwell, 1988), pp. 116–17.

21. Josua Hammer, "Meet the New Kuwait," *Newsweek* (March 10, 1997), p. 40.

22. *New York Times* (August 10, 1988), pp. 1 and 6.

23. Gary Sick, "Moral Choice and the Iran-Iraq Conflict," *Ethics and International Affairs* 3 (1989), pp. 120–21.

24. For an analysis of the war operations itself, see David Segal, "The Iran-Iraq War: A Military Analysis," *Foreign Affairs* 67 (summer 1988), pp. 946–55.

25. Holsti, *The State, War, and the State of War,* p. 37.

26. Ibid., p. 22.

27. Ibid., p. 15.

28. Gérard Prunier, *The Rwanda Crisis: History of a Genocide* (New York: Columbia University Press, 1995), pp. 159–92.

29. The ineffectiveness of UNAMIR after the genocide began was also due to the fact that the original mission was limited to being an observer force. Even after evidence became available that a major genocide was underway, the UN Security Council refused to increase the size of UNAMIR or to expand its mandate.

30. David Rieff, "The Age of Genocide," *The New Republic* (January 26, 1996), p. 31.

31. James Fenton, "A Short History of Anti-Hamitism," *New York Review of Books* (February 15, 1996), p. 9.

32. Kenneth Waltz, *Man, The State and War* (New York: Columbia University Press, 1965).

33. Sigmund Freud, "Why War?" in William Ebenstein, *Great Political Thinkers: Plato to the Present,* 4th ed. (Hinsdale: Dryden Press, 1969), pp. 857–60.

34. Konrad Lorenz, *On Aggression,* trans. Marjorie Kerr Wilson (New York: Bantam Books, 1967). For a more sophisticated and recent application of the evolutionary biological approach to war, see R. Paul Shaw and Yuwa Wong, *Genetic Seeds of Warfare: Evolution, Nationalism, and Patriotism* (Boston: Unwin, Hyman, 1989), especially chaps. 1–5.

35. Reinhold Niebuhr, *The Nature and Destiny of Man,* vol. I (New York: Charles Scribners, 1964), pp. 280–89.

36. Erich Remarque, *All Quiet on the Western Front* (Greenwich, Conn.: Fawcett Publications, 1967), p. 126.

37. Jack S. Levy, "Misperception and the Causes of War: Theoretical Linkages and Analytical Problems," *World Politics* 36 (October 1983), pp. 82–91.

38. John G. Stoessinger, *Why Nations Go to War* (New York: St. Martin's Press, 1974), p. 227.

39. Ole R. Holsti, "Perceptions and Actions in the 1914 Crisis," in J. David Singer, ed., *Quantitative International Politics* (New York: Free Press, 1968), pp. 123–58.

40. Ole R. Holsti, Richard A. Brody, and Robert C. North, "Measuring Affect and Action in International Reaction Models: Empirical Materials from the 1962 Cuban Crisis," in James N. Rosenau, ed., *International Politics and Foreign Policy,* rev. ed. (New York: Free Press, 1969), pp. 679–96.

41. See Jack Snyder, *The Ideology of the Offensive: Military Decisionmaking and the Disasters of 1914* (Ithaca: Cornell University Press, 1984).

42. Richard Ned Lebow, *Nuclear Crisis Management: A Dangerous Illusion* (Ithaca: Cornell University Press, 1987), especially, pp. 23–28.

43. Bruce Bueno de Mesquita, "Risk, Power Distributions, and the Likelihood of War," *International Studies Quarterly* 25 (December 1981), p. 541. See also Bruce Bueno de Mesquita and David Lalman, "Reason and War," *American Political Science Review* 80 (December 1986), pp. 1113–29.

44. Bruce Bueno de Mesquita, *The War Trap* (New Haven: Yale University Press, 1981), p. 129.

45. Richard Barnet, *Roots of War* (Baltimore: Penguin Books, 1973), p. 337.

46. R. J. Rummel, "The Politics of Cold Blood," *Society* 27 (November/December 1989), p. 33. See also Michael W. Doyle, "Kant, Liberal Legacies, and Foreign Affairs, Part 2," *Philosophy & Public Affairs* 12 (fall 1983), pp. 232–53.

47. Rummel, "The Politics of Cold Blood," p. 33.

48. John Lewis Gaddis, "International Relations Theory and the End of the Cold War," *International Security* 17 (winter 1992/93), p. 24.

49. John A. Vasquez, "The Steps to War: Toward a Scientific Explanation of Correlates of War Findings," *World Politics* 40 (October 1987), p. 119.

50. See Randolph Siverson and Joel King, "Alliances and the Expansion of War," in J. David Singer and Michael D. Wallace, eds., *To Augur Well: Early Warning Indicators in World Politics* (Beverly Hills, Calif.: Sage Publications, 1979), pp. 37–49.

51. Michael D. Wallace, "Arms Races and Escalation: Some New Evidence," *Journal of Conflict Resolution* 23 (March 1979), pp. 3–16.

52. Vasquez, "The Steps to War," p. 143.

53. Karl Deutsch and J. David Singer, for example, argue that multipolar systems are more stable because they offer less opportunity for intense, long-term conflicts to develop. Moreover, because such systems encourage the development of cross-cutting cleavages, they tend to dissipate tensions more effectively than bipolar systems. See Karl W. Deutsch and J. David Singer, "Multipolar Power Systems and International Stability," *World Politics* 16 (April 1964), pp. 390–406. Kenneth Waltz, by contrast, argues that bipolarity is more stable in part because states need to concentrate resources on only two poles and also because the frequency of bipolar interactions inhibits unexpected developments. See Kenneth N. Waltz, "International Structure,

National Force and the Balance of Power," *Journal of International Affairs* 21 (1967), pp. 220–28.

54. J. David Singer, Stuart A. Bremer, and John Stuckey, "Capability Distribution, Uncertainty, and Major Power War, 1820–1965," in Bruce M. Russett, ed., *Peace, War, and Numbers* (Beverly Hills, Calif.: Sage, 1972), pp. 19–48.

55. See Robert O. Keohane, "The Theory of Hegemonic Stability and Changes in International Economic Regimes, 1967–1977," in Ole R. Holsti, Randolph Siverson, and Alexander L. George, eds., *Change in the International System* (Boulder, Colo.: Westview Press, 1980); and Robert O. Keohane, *After Hegemony: Cooperation and Discord in the World Political Economy* (Princeton: Princeton University Press, 1984).

56. A.F.K. Organski and Jacek Kugler argue that the origins of the Franco-Prussian War, the Russo-Japanese War, and the two world wars began from preventive motives. See A.F.K. Organski and Jacek Kugler, *The War Ledger* (Chicago: University of Chicago Press, 1980), chaps. 1 and 2.

57. Ibid.

58. George Modelski, *Long Cycles in World Politics* (Seattle: University of Washington Press, 1987); see also Joshua S. Goldstein, *Long Cycles in War and Economic Growth* (New Haven: Yale University Press, 1988).

59. Graham T. Allison, "What Fuels the Arms Race?" in John F. Reichart and Steven R. Sturm, eds., *American Defense Policy,* 5th ed. (Baltimore: Johns Hopkins University Press, 1982), pp. 463–80.

60. James E. Dougherty and Robert L. Pfaltzgraff, Jr., *Contending Theories of International Relations: A Comprehensive Survey,* 3rd ed. (New York: Harper & Row, 1990), p. 342.

61. Thucydides, *The Peloponnesian War,* trans. Rex Warner (New York: Penguin Books, 1982), p. 408.

62. Michael Walzer, *Just and Unjust Wars: A Moral Argument with Historical Illustrations* (New York: Basic Books, 1977), pp. 58–63.

63. The moral debate on the Gulf War precipitated a large number of articles and books. Two informative anthologies are: James Turner Johnson and George Weigel, eds., *Just War and the Gulf War* (Washington, D.C.: Ethics and Public Policy Center, 1991); and David E. DeCosse, ed., *But Was It Just?: Reflections on the Morality of the Persian Gulf War* (New York: Doubleday, 1992).

64. James Turner Johnson, "The Just War Tradition and the American Military," in Johnson and Weigel, *Just War and the Gulf War,* p. 22.

65. Michael Walzer, "Perplexed," *The New Republic* (January 28, 1991), p. 14.

66. Robert W. Tucker, "Justice and the War," *The National Interest* (fall 1991), pp. 111–12. For a critique of Tucker's argument, see "An Exchange: Justice and the Gulf War," *The National Interest* (winter 1991/92), pp. 103–7.

Chapter 12

1. Quoted in Harold Nicolson, *Diplomacy,* 3rd ed. (New York: Oxford University Press, 1973), p. 21.

2. Henry Kissinger, *Diplomacy* (New York: Simon & Schuster, 1994), pp. 27–28.

3. Abba Eban, "Interest and Conscience in Diplomacy," *Society* (March/April 1986), p. 22.

4. *New York Times* (February 5, 1995), p. 1.

5. *New York Times* (February 27, 1995), p. 1. See also *New York Times* (February 27, 1995), p. C1.

6. Elmer Plischke, "Diplomacy—Search for Its Meaning," in Elmer Plischke, ed., *Modern Diplomacy—The Art and the Artisans* (Washington, D.C.: American Enterprise Institute, 1979), p. 33.

7. Nicolson, *Diplomacy,* pp. 4–5.

8. Ibid., p. 52.

9. Harold H. Saunders, *The Other Walls* (Washington, D.C.: American Enterprises Institute, 1985), p. 23.

10. Quoted in Adam Watson, *Diplomacy—The Dialogue Between States* (New York: McGraw-Hill, 1983), p. 225.

11. Nicholson, *Diplomacy,* pp. 55–67.

12. For an assessment of postwar superpower summits, see Gordon R. Weihmiller, *U.S.-Soviet Summits: An Account of East-West Diplomacy at the Top, 1955–1985* (Lanham, Md.: University Press of America, 1986).

13. James Schlesinger, "Reykjavik and Revelations: A Turn of the Tide?" *Foreign Affairs* 65 (spring 1987), pp. 429–31.

14. "A New Social Contract," *UN Chronicle* (June 1995), p. 58.

15. "Symbolic Gains Temper Social Summit Losses," *U.N. Observer & International Report* (April 1995), p. 14.

16. Saunders, *The Other Walls,* pp. 22–37.

17. Ibid., p. 24.

18. The participation of non-PLO officials was facilitated by two Gulf War developments: first, because the PLO had supported Iraq throughout the war, it had lost significant global influence in the wake of Iraq's total military defeat; and second, Arab states, deeply grateful to the United States and other Western states for their military liberation of Kuwait, strongly encouraged Palestinian leaders from the occupied territories to participate in the talks.

19. For an analysis and assessment of international conflict resolution through improved communication, see John W. Burton, *Conflict: Resolution and Prevention* (New York: St. Martin's Press, 1990).

20. Hans J. Morgenthau, *Politics Among Nations: The Struggle for Power and peace,* 5th ed. rev. (New York: Alfred A. Knopf, 1978), pp. 543–50.

21. Ibid., pp. 5–6.

22. Robert Kennedy, *Thirteen Days: A Memoir of the Cuban Missile Crisis* (New York: W.W. Norton, 1971), pp. 102–5.

23. Morgenthau, *Politics Among Nations,* pp. 555–58.

24. Roger Fisher, *International Conflict for Beginners* (New York: Harper & Row, 1969), p. 75.

25. Ibid., pp. 90–95.

26. The Contadora Group, established in 1983 in the small island of Contadora off the coast of Panama, is comprised of Colombia, Panama, Mexico, and Venezuela.

27. William B. Quandt, *Camp David: Peacemaking and Politics* (Washington, D.C.: Brookings Institution, 1986), pp. 257–58.

28. See, for example, James L. Garrett, "The Beagle Channel Dispute: Confrontation and Negotiation in the Southern Cone," *Journal of Interamerican Studies and World Affairs* 27 (fall 1985), pp. 81–109.

29. Thomas Princen, *Intermediaries in International Conflict* (Princeton: Princeton University Press, 1992), pp. 155–58.

30. Garrett, pp. 101–2. The major provisions of the Treaty are: (1) the PLN islands belong to Chile; (2) the boundary line between Argentina and Chile does not extend due east from the PLN islands, but south toward Cape Horn, beginning just east of Nueva Island; and (3) Argentina has exclusive maritime jurisdiction in the area north and east of the boundary zone, Chile has exclusive jurisdiction in the area south and west of the boundary line. In effect, the accord is a compromise between land and maritime rights, Chile receiving title to territory (the PLN islands) and Argentina receiving maritime rights (over Atlantic Ocean waters).

31. For a brief overview of the important role of the two Israeli academics in bringing about the Oslo peace talks, see Clyde Haberman, "How the Secret Oslo Connection Led to the Israeli-PLO Pact," *New York Times* (September 5, 1993), pp. 1 and 10.

32. Amos Elon, "The Peacemakers," *The New Yorker* 69 (December 20, 1993), p. 81.

33. David Mankovsky, *Making Peace with the PLO: The Rabin Government's Road to the Oslo Accord* (Boulder, Colo.: Westview Press, 1996), p. 22.

34. Quoted in Elon, "The Peacemakers," p. 77.

35. Ibid., p. 82.

36. Mankovsky, *Making Peace with the PLO,* p. 64.

Chapter 13

1. Robert H. Bork, "The Limits of International Law," *The National Interest* (winter 1989/90), p. 9.
2. Dorothy V. Jones, *Code of Peace: Ethics and Security in the World of Warlord States* (Chicago: University of Chicago Press, 1991), p. xi.
3. Quoted in Gerhard von Glahn, *Law Among Nations: An Introduction to Public International Law,* 6th ed. rev. (New York: Macmillan, 1992), p. 4.
4. Daniel Moynihan, *Loyalties* (New York: Harcourt Brace Jovanovich, 1984), p. 83.
5. George F. Will, "The Perils of Legality," *Newsweek* (February 27, 1984), p. 84.
6. Michael Akehurst, *A Modern Introduction to International Law,* 6th ed. (London: Unwin, Hyman, 1987), p. 24.
7. von Glahn, *Law Among Nations,* p. 16.
8. For a discussion of regimes, see Stephen D. Krasner, ed., *International Regimes* (Ithaca: Cornell University Press, 1983); and Oran Young, *International Cooperation: Building Regimes and Natural Resources and the Environment* (Ithaca: Cornell University Press, 1989).
9. Peter H. F. Bekker, "The 1995 Judicial Activity of the International Court of Justice," *The American Journal of International Law* 90 (April 1996), pp. 328–30.
10. Akehurst, *A Modern Introduction to International Law,* pp. 2–4.
11. E. H. Carr, *The Twenty Years' Crisis, 1919–1939: An Introduction to the Study of International Relations* (New York: Harper & Row, 1964), pp. 177–80.
12. Ibid., p. 199.
13. von Glahn, *Law Among Nations,* p. 882.
14. *New York Times* (May 6, 1996), p. 1.
15. Therese Raphael, "The War Crimes Tribunal Has Clout . . . ," *Wall Street Journal* (April 2, 1996), p. 15.
16. *New York Times* (June 18, 1996), p. 1.
17. Roger Fisher, *International Conflict for Beginners* (New York: Harper & Row, 1969), pp. 151–77.
18. Louis Henkin, *How Nations Behave: Law and Foreign Policy,* 2nd ed. (New York: Columbia University Press, 1978), p. 28.
19. Hedley Bull, *The Anarchical Society: A Study of Order in World Politics* (New York: Columbia University Press, 1977), p. 137.
20. Karl W. Deutsch, *Politics and Government: How People Decide Their Fate,* 3rd ed. (New York: Houghton Mifflin, 1980), pp. 15–18.
21. J. L. Brierly, *The Law of Nations: An Introduction to the International Law of Peace,* 6th ed. (Oxford: Clarendon Press, 1954), p. 56.
22. Bull, *The Anarchical Society,* p. 139.
23. See James Madison Federalist No. 10 in Alexander Hamilton, James Madison, and John Jay, *The Federalist Papers* (New York: New American Library, 1961), p. 78.
24. Robert M. Hutchins, "World Government for Now," in Robert A. Goldwin, ed., *Readings in World Politics,* 2nd ed. (New York: Oxford University, 1970), p. 523.
25. Carr, *Twenty Years' Crisis,* p. 180.
26. Gordon A. Craig and Alexander F. George, *Force and Statecraft* (New York: Oxford University Press, 1995), pp. 291–92.

Chapter 14

1. Quoted in William Hyland, *Mortal Rivals: Superpower Relations from Nixon to Reagan* (New York: Random House, 1987), p. 260.
2. Hans J. Morgenthau, *Politics Among Nations: The Struggle for Power and Peace,* 4th ed. (New York: Alfred A. Knopf, 1967), p. 438.

3. Michael Mandelbaum, "The Reluctance to Intervene," *Foreign Policy* 95 (summer 1994).
4. Inis L. Claude, Jr., *Swords into Plowshares: The Problems and Progress of International Organization,* 4th ed. (New York: Random House, 1971), p. 216.
5. Ibid., p. 422.
6. *New York Times* (November 12, 1995), p. 8.
7. Claude, *Swords into Plowshares,* p. 219.
8. Ibid., chap. 17.
9. David Mitrany, *A Working Peace System* (Chicago: Quadrangle Books, 1966), p. 28.
10. See Ernest B. Haas, *Beyond the Nation-State: Functionalism and International Organization* (Stanford: Stanford University Press, 1964).
11. Because of political demands by Greece, Macedonia is provisionally called "the Former Yugoslav Republic of Macedonia" in the UN.
12. Inis L. Claude, Jr., *The Changing United Nations* (New York: Random House, 1967), p. xvii.
13. Theodore A. Couloumbis and James H. Wolfe, *Introduction to International Relations: Power and Justice,* 4th ed. (Englewood Cliffs, N.J.: Prentice-Hall, 1990), p. 288.
14. *New York Times* (January 6, 1995), p. 3.
15. *New York Times* (February 2, 1996), p. 1.
16. Gordon A. Craig and Alexander F. George, *Force and Statecraft,* 3rd ed. (New York: Oxford University Press, 1995), p. 288.
17. Robert E. Riggs and Jack C. Plano, *The United Nations: International Organization and World Politics* (Chicago: Dorsey Press, 1988), p. 77.
18. Ibid., p. 86.
19. "Cash Crunch Continues as Debt Nears $3 Billion," *UN Chronicle* 33 (June 1996), pp. 67–68.
20. Quoted in Andrew W. Cordier and Wilder Foote, eds., *The Public Papers of the Secretaries-General of the United Nations,* vol. I (New York: Columbia University Press, 1969), p. 55.
21. Quoted in Richard S. Williamson, "The United Nations: Some Parts Work," *Orbis* 32 (spring 1988), p. 188.
22. For a critical assessment of the Cairo conference, see George Weigel, "What Really Happened at Cairo," *First Things* (February 1995), pp. 24–31.
23. *New York Times* (September 14, 1994), p. 2.
24. Ernst B. Haas, *Why We Still Need the United Nations* (Berkeley: Institute of International Studies, University of California, Berkeley, 1986), p. 9.
25. *New York Times* (November 22, 1995), pp. 1 and 6. See also *Washington Post National Weekly* (December 25–31, 1995), pp. 6–11.
26. *New York Times* (October 24, 1991), pp. 1 and 6.
27. Stan Sesser, "Report from Cambodia," *The New Yorker* (May 18, 1992), p. 46.
28. *Christian Science Monitor* (June 27, 1988), p. 1.
29. Pascal Fontaine, *Europe in Ten Points* (Brussels: Office for Official Publications of the European Communities, 1995), p. 17.
30. Ibid., p. 26.
31. *New York Times* (December 14, 1996), pp. 25–26.

Chapter 15

1. Stephen D. Krasner, *Structural Conflict: The Third World Against Global Liberalism* (Berkeley: University of California Press, 1985), p. 267.
2. Max Singer and Aaron Wildavsky, *The Real World Order: Zones of Peace, Zones of Turmoil* (Chatham, N.J.: Chatham House, 1993), p. 3.

3. "Survey: The Global Economy," *The Economist* (October 1, 1994), p. 3.

4. Agency for International Development, *U.S. Overseas Loans and Grants and Assistance from International Organizations, July 1, 1945–September 30, 1990* (Washington, D.C., Agency for International Development, 1991), p. 4 and passim.

5. World Bank, *World Bank Atlas, 1989* (Washington, D.C.: World Bank, 1989), p. 10.

6. World Bank, *World Development Report 1990* (New York: Oxford University Press, 1990), p. 16.

7. "Survey: The Global Economy," *The Economist* (October 1, 1994), p. 1.

8. World Bank, *World Tables, 1989–1990 Edition* (Baltimore: Johns Hopkins University Press, 1990), pp. 2–5.

9. Krasner, *Structural Conflict,* chap. 3.

10. P.T. Bauer, "Western Guilt and Third World Poverty," *Commentary* (January 1976), p. 22.

11. Max Singer and Paul Bracken, "Don't Blame the U.S.," *New York Times Magazine* (November 7, 1976), p. 34.

12. Robert Gilpin, *The Political Economy of International Relations* (Princeton: Princeton University Press, 1987), pp. 276–77.

13. For a discussion of Third World development from a dependency theory perspective, see Ronald Chilcote, *Theories of Development and Underdevelopment* (Boulder, Colo.: Westview Press, 1984).

14. Andre Gunder Frank, "The Development of Underdevelopment" in Robert I. Rhodes, ed., *Imperialism and Underdevelopment* (New York: Monthly Review Press, 1970), p. 9.

15. Theotonio Dos Santos, "The Structure of Dependence" in K.T. Fann and Donald Hodges, eds., *Readings in U.S. Imperialism* (Boston: Porter Sargent, 1971), p. 226.

16. See Peter Evans, *Dependent Development: The Alliance of Multinational, State, and Local Capital in Brazil* (Princeton: Princeton University Press, 1979).

17. Gilpin, *The Political Economy of International Relations,* pp. 273–74.

18. For brief overview of WST see Herman M. Schwartz, *States Versus Markets: History, Geography, and the Development of the International Political Economy* (New York: St. Martin's Press, 1994), pp. 46–48. For a fuller account of the theory, see Immanuel Wallerstein, "The Rise and Future Demise of the World Capitalist System: Concepts for Comparative Analysis," *Comparative Studies in Society and History* 16 (September 1974), pp. 387–415.

19. Gilpin, *The Political Economy of International Relations,* p. 286.

20. Ibid., p. 275.

21. World Bank, *Development Report 1990,* p. 178.

22. David H. Blake and Robert S. Walters, *The Politics of Global Economic Relations,* 3rd ed. (Englewood Cliffs, N.J.: Prentice-Hall, 1987), pp. 187–88.

23. For a description and assessment of the NIEO, see Gilpin, *The Political Economy of International Relations,* pp. 298–301.

24. Krasner, *Structural Conflict,* pp. 14–18 and passim.

25. Ibid., p. 314.

26. Gilpin, *The Political Economy of International Relations,* p. 300.

27. Robert W. Tucker, *The Inequality of Nations* (New York: Basic Books, 1977), pp. 3–6.

28. Gerhard von Glahn, *Law Among Nations: An Introduction to Public International Law,* 6th ed. (New York: Macmillan Publishing Co., 1992), p. 485.

29. *New York Times* (July 1, 1994), pp. 1 and 2.

30. "Law of the Sea: Sea Law Convention Enters Into Force," *UN Chronicle* (March 1995), p. 8.

31. *The Washington Post* (June 15, 1992), p. 13.

32. Gilpin, *The Political Economy of International Relations,* p. 300.

33. For an excellent description and assessment of the reform policies pursued by the former Soviet-bloc countries during the 1990–1995 period, see World Bank, *World Development Report 1996* (New York: Oxford University Press, 1996), which is devoted to the economic transition from planned economies to market economies.

34. The World Bank, *World Tables, 1989–90 edition* (Baltimore: Johns Hopkins University Press, 1990), pp. 6–9 and 18–21.

35. "Survey, The Global Economy," *The Economist* (October 1, 1994), p. 1.

36. Ibid., p. 2.

37. Ibid.

Chapter 16

1. Robert Gilpin, *The Political Economy of International Relations* (Princeton: Princeton University Press, 1987), p. 3.

2. Susan Strange, "The Defective State," *Daedalus* 124 (spring 1995), p. 56.

3. Edward N. Luttwak, "From Geopolitics to Geo-Economics," *National Interest* 20 (summer 1990), p. 18.

4. Robert Gilpin, *U.S. Power and the Multinational Corporation: The Political Economy of Foreign Direct Investment* (New York: Basic Books, 1975), p. 43.

5. Gilpin, *The Political Economy,* p. 11.

6. Ibid., pp. 25–64.

7. In an important empirical test of this theory, Wassily Leontief, a Noble Prize economist, found that, contrary to the Heckscher-Ohlin theory, the United States's imports were more capital-intensive that its exports. Because the United States had a large supply of capital, Leontief had expected that U.S. exports would be based chiefly on capital. Because the results did not confirm the theory, his findings have been called the Leontief paradox.

8. Gilpin, *The Political Economy,* p. 179.

9. David H. Blake and Robert S. Walters, *The Politics of Global Economic Relations,* 4th ed. (Englewood Cliffs, N.J.: Prentice-Hall, 1992), p. 20.

10. James Fallows, *Looking at the Sun: The Rise of the New East Asian Economic and Political System* (New York: Vintage Books, 1995), pp. 179–94.

11. Paul Kennedy, *Preparing for the Twenty-First Century* (New York: Random House, 1993), p. 195.

12. *New York Times* (May 7, 1995), pp. 1 and 6.

13. Fallows, *Looking at the Sun,* pp. 208–9.

14. *New York Times* (May 7, 1995), p. 6. See also, *New York Times* (June 29, 1995), pp. 1 and C4.

15. *New York Times* (May 17, 1995), p. 1.

16. *Wall Street Journal* (June 29, 1995), p. A8.

17. For a general description of the key elements of strategic trade theory, see E. Helpman and Paul Krugman, *Market Structure and Foreign Trade: Increasing Returns, Imperfect Competition, and the International Economy* (Boston: MIT Press, 1985). See also Paul Krugman, "Does the New Trade Theory Require a New Trade Policy?" *World Economy* 15, no. 4 (1992), pp. 423–41. For a general critique of the theory, see David J. Richardson, "The Political Economy of Strategic Trade Policy," review essay, *International Organization* 44, no. 1 (1990), pp. 107–33.

18. M.B. Lieberman and D.B. Montgomery, "First-Mover Advantages," *Strategic Management Journal* 9 (summer 1988), pp. 41–58.

19. See Peter Evans, *Dependent Development: The Alliance of Multinational, State, and Local Capital in Brazil* (Princeton: Princeton University Press, 1979).

20. "The Gains from Trade," *The Economist* (September 23, 1989), pp. 25–26.

21. World Bank, *World Development Report, 1996* (New York: Oxford University Press, 1996), p. 208.

22. Gary C. Hufbauer and Kimberly Ann Elliott, *Measuring the Costs of Protectionism in the United States* (Washington, D.C.: Institute for International Economics, 1993).

23. "Airbus and Boeing: The Jumbo War," *The Economist* (June 15, 1991), pp. 65–66.

24. For an illuminating argument why relative standing is important in international relations, see Samuel P. Huntington, "Why International Primacy Matters," *International Security* 17 (spring 1993), pp. 68–83.

25. The name "Bretton Woods system" comes from an international planning conference, attended by delegates from forty-four countries, held in Bretton Woods, New Hampshire, in 1944. At the meeting the fundamental elements of the postwar liberal international economic order were worked out.

26. Originally, the Bretton Woods plan called for the establishment of the International Trade Organization (ITO), with GATT functioning within the structure of that organization. Because the ITO treaty was never ratified, GATT functioned as the principal trade institution in the global economy.

27. *The Economist* (August 3, 1996), pp. 17–18.

28. *New York Times* (November 23, 1992), p. C3.

29. *New York Times* (November 21, 1992), pp. 1 and 20.

30. *New York Times* (April 16, 1994), pp. 1 and 25.

31. Under GATT, a member could veto the verdict of a panel set up to rule on a quarrel, even if it was a party to the dispute. But under the WTO, panel decisions can be overturned only by consensus.

32. *New York Times* (January 30, 1997), p. 1.

33. *Washington Post National Weekly* (June 19–25, 1995), p. 20.

34. *The Economist* (March 16, 1996), p. 75.

35. Thomas D. Rojas, "Mexico's Dysfunctional Neoliberalism," *North-South Focus: Mexico,* no. 1 (1995), p. 6.

36. *New York Times* (September 25, 1996), p. 19.

37. *New York Times* (February 9, 1996), p. 18.

38. Benjamin J. Cohen, *Organizing the World's Money: The Political Economy of International Monetary Relations* (New York: Basic Books, 1977), p. 28.

39. Ricky W. Griffin and Michael W. Pustay, *International Business: A Managerial Perspective* (New York: Addison-Wesley, 1996), p. 123.

40. Robert Triffin, *Gold and the Dollar Crisis: The Future of Convertibility* (New Haven: Yale University Press, 1960).

41. Gilpin, *The Political Economy,* p. 141.

42. Ibid., p. 85.

43. Ibid.

44. Ibid.

45. "A Survey of the World Economy," *The Economist* (October 7, 1995), p. 10.

46. George Soros, "The Capitalist Threat," *The Atlantic Monthly* (February 1997), pp. 45–58.

47. William Greider, *One World, Ready or Not* (New York: Simon & Schuster, 1997).

48. *The Economist* (October 7, 1995), p. 4.

49. *New York Times* (February 13, 1997), p. 17.

Chapter 17

1. Miguel de Cervantes, *Don Quixote,* part II, chapter XX, trans. Samuel Putnam (New York: Viking Press, 1949), p. 641.

2. World Bank, *World Development Report 1990* (New York: Oxford University Press, 1990), p. 1.

3. World Bank, *World Development Report 1997* (New York: Oxford University Press, 1997), p. 214.

4. Ibid., pp. 194–95 and 208–9.

5. According to economist Simon Kuznets, although the process of economic growth generates income inequalities, the shift from economic backwardness to economic modernity results in a more egalitarian distribution of national income. See Simon Kuznets, *Economic Growth of Nations* (Cambridge: Harvard University Press, 1971).

6. Reuben P. Mendez, *International Public Finance: A New Perspective on Global Relations* (New York: Oxford University Press, 1992), p. 96.

7. Robert S. McNamara, *One Hundred Countries, Two Billion People* (New York: Praeger, 1973), pp. 6–8.

8. United Nations Development Programme, *Human Development Report 1994* (New York: Oxford University Press, 1994), p. 135.

9. For a discussion of the HDI, see United Nations Development Programme, *Human Development Report 1994* (New York: Oxford University Press, 1994), chap. 5.

10. United Nations Development Programme, *Human Development Report 1995* (New York: Oxford University Press, 1995), pp. 11–12.

11. For a short analysis of the impact of population growth on global politics, see Michael S. Teitelbaum, "The Population Threat," *Foreign Affairs* 71 (winter 1992/93), pp. 63–78.

12. The "carrying capacity" metaphor is based on the tragedy of the commons analogy. See the discussion of this in chap. 19.

13. "Two Billion People Discover the Joys of the Market," *The Economist* (December 21, 1985), p. 66.

14. United Nations, *World Population Monitoring 1993* (New York: United Nations, 1995), pp. 43–45.

15. World Bank, *World Development Report 1991* (New York: Oxford University Press, 1991), pp. 256–57.

16. World Bank, *World Development Report 1997* (New York: Oxford University Press, 1997), pp. 224–25.

17. Estimate based on data from World Bank, *World Development Report 1996* (New York: Oxford University Press, 1996), pp. 194 and 204.

18. United Nations, *World Population Monitoring, 1993* (New York: United Nations, 1996), p. 179.

19. *World Development Report 1996,* p. 194.

20. See, for example, Myron Weiner, "Security, Stability, and International Migration," *International Security* 17 (winter 1992/93), pp. 91–126; and Thomas F. Homer-Dixon, "On the Threshold: Environmental Changes as Causes of Acute Conflict," *International Security* 16 (fall 1991), pp. 76–116.

21. Robert Kaplan, "The Coming Anarchy," *The Atlantic Monthly* (February 1994), pp. 44–76.

22. Thomas F. Homer-Dixon, "Environmental Scarcities and Violent Conflict," *International Security* 19 (summer 1994), pp. 5–40.

23. Matthew Connelly and Paul Kennedy, "Must It Be the Rest Against the West?" *The Atlantic Monthly* (December 1994), pp. 76 and 79.

24. *New York Times* (April 4, 1994), p. B5.

25. See Thomas Sowell, *A Conflict of Visions* (New York: William Morrow, 1987).

26. Kennedy, *Preparing for the Twenty-First Century* (New York: Random House, 1993), p. 195.

27. Ibid., pp. 197–99.

28. Robert Gilpin, *The Political Economy of International Relations* (Princeton: Princeton University Press, 1987), p. 304.

29. Kennedy, *Preparing for the Twenty-First Century,* p. 27.

30. *The Economist* (October 12, 1991), p. 4.

31. For a succinct summary of recent research on economic growth, see "Economic Growth: The Poor and the Rich," *The Economist* (May 25, 1996), pp. 23–25.

32. United Nations, *World Investment Report, 1997* (New York: United Nations, 1997), p. 319.

33. United Nations, *World Investment Report, 1995* (New York: United Nations, 1995), p. 401.

34. Ibid., p. 407.

35. Peter Evans, *Dependent Development: The Alliance of Multinational, State and Local Capital in Brazil* (Princeton: Princeton University Press, 1979), especially chap. 1.

36. See Simon Kuznets, *Economic Growth of Nations* (Cambridge: Harvard University Press, 1971).

37. Gilpin, *The Political Economy of International Relations,* pp. 248 and 290.

38. Thomas D. Lairson and David Skidmore, *International Political Economy: The Struggle for Power and Wealth* (New York: Harcourt, Brace, 1997), p. 355.

39. United Nations, *World Economic and Social Survey, 1995* (New York: United Nations, 1995), p. 334.

40. *The Economist* (July 23, 1944), p. 73.

41. "Fear of Finance: Survey of the World Economy," *The Economist* (September 19, 1992), pp. 5–7.

42. *Christian Science Monitor* (January 12, 1989), p. 9.

43. *Time* (January 10, 1984), p. 42.

44. *New York Times* (August 2, 1987), p. E2.

45. Quoted in *New York Times* (January 15, 1989), p. E5.

46. *Washington Post National Weekly Edition* (December 19–25, 1988), p. 24.

47. *New York Times* (March 16, 1996), pp. B17 and 18.

48. David Halloran Lumsdaine, *Moral Vision in International Politics: The Foreign Aid Regime, 1949–1989* (Princeton: Princeton University Press, 1993), p. 34.

49. Agency for International Development, *U.S. Overseas Loans and Grants and Assistance from International Organizations: Obligations and Loan Authorizations, July 1, 1945–September 30, 1990* (Washington, D.C.: A.I.D., 1990), p. 4.

50. Ibid., pp. 4, 7, 35, 69, and 147.

51. *Newsweek* (February 6, 1989), pp. 36 and 40.

52. World Bank, *World Development Report 1995* (New York: Oxford University Press, 1995), p. 196.

53. Report of the Independent Commission on International Development Issues, *North-South: A Programme for Survival* (Cambridge: MIT Press, 1980). The optimistic views on North-South relations found in this report are slightly at odds with a similar study issued a decade later by a group of LDC political leaders, known as the South Commission. The report, chaired by Julius Nyerere (of Tanzania) is titled *The Challenge to the South: The Report of the South Commission* (New York: Oxford University Press, 1990).

54. Cyrus Vance, "Foreign Assistance and U.S. Policy," *Department of State Bulletin* (June 1978), p. 14.

55. Lumsdaine, *Moral Vision in International Politics,* p. 3.

56. For a useful collection of studies assessing the impact of economic aid, see Robert Cassen and Associates, *Does Aid Work?* (Oxford: Clarendon Press, 1986).

57. For a penetrating critique of foreign aid, see P.T. Bauer, *Equality, the Third World and Economic Delusion* (Cambridge: Harvard University Press, 1981), especially chap. 5. See also P.T. Bauer, *Reality and Rhetoric: Studies in the Economics of Development* (Cambridge: Harvard University Press, 1984); and Nick Eberstadt, "The Perversion of Foreign Aid," *Commentary* (June 1985), pp. 19–33.

58. Jack Shepherd, "When Foreign Aid Fails," *The Atlantic Monthly* (April 1985), p. 43.

59. Lairson and Skidmore, *International Political Economy: #38,* p. 167.

60. Paul Krugman, "Competitiveness: A Dangerous Obsession," *Foreign Affairs* (March/April 1994), pp. 28–44. For responses to this argument, see *Foreign Affairs* (July/August 1994), pp. 186–202.

Chapter 18

1. Hans J. Morgenthau, *Politics Among Nations: The Struggle for Power and Peace,* 5th ed., rev. (New York: Alfred A. Knopf, 1978), pp. 413–14.

2. Jonathan Schell, *The Fate of the Earth* (New York: Avon Books, 1982), p. 231.

3. Michael Mandelbaum, "Lessons on the Next Nuclear War," *Foreign Affairs* (March/April 1995), p. 22.

4. Freeman Dyson, "The Race is Over," *The New York Review of Books* (March 6, 1997), p. 4.

5. U.S. Arms Control and Disarmament Agency, *World Military Expenditures and Arms Transfers, 1995* (Washington, D.C.: U.S. Government Printing Office, 1996), passim.

6. Gwynne Dyer, *War* (Homewood, Ill.: Dorsey Press, 1985), p. 63.

7. Ibid., p. 78.

8. Morgenthau, *Politics Among Nations,* p. 410.

9. ACDA, *World Military Expenditures,* pp. 60 and 99.

10. "Costing a Bomb," *The Economist* (January 4, 1997), p. 30.

11. ACDA, *World Military Expenditures,* p. 26.

12. Ibid., pp. 103–6.

13. Stockholm International Peace Research Institute, *SIPRI Yearbook 1989: World Armaments and Disarmament* (Oxford: Oxford University Press, 1989), p. 100.

14. Ibid.

15. U.S. Arms Control and Disarmament Agency, *Threat Control Through Arms Control: Annual Report to Congress* (Washington, D.C.: ACDA, 1995), pp. 66–68.

16. *New York Times* (August 16, 1995), pp. 1 and 3.

17. "Plagues in the Making," *Newsweek* (October 9, 1995), pp. 50–51.

18. For a discussion of the risks of nuclear war, see Harvard Study Group, *Living with Nuclear Weapons* (Cambridge: Harvard University Press, 1983), pp. 47–68. See also Graham T. Allison, Albert Carnesale, and Joseph S. Nye, Jr., eds., *Hawks, Doves and Owls: An Agenda for Avoiding Nuclear War* (New York: W.W. Norton, 1985), p. 10.

19. John F. Sopko, "The Changing Proliferation Threat," *Foreign Policy* (winter 1996/97), pp. 4–5.

20. Charles Krauthammer, "The Unipolar Moment," *Foreign Affairs* 70, no. 1 (1990/91), pp. 30–32.

21. Leonard S. Spector, *Nuclear Ambitions: The Spread of Nuclear Weapons, 1989–1990* (Boulder, Colo.: Westview Press, 1990), p. 6.

22. Alton Frye, "Zero Ballistic Missiles," *Foreign Policy* 88 (fall 1992), pp. 3–20.

23. Morgenthau, *Politics Among Nations,* p. 400.

24. *New York Times* (October 8, 1995), p. E3.

25. *New York Times* (September 18, 1997), pp. 1 and 8.

26. Teena Karsa Mayers, *Understanding Weapons and Arms Control: A Guide to the Issues,* 4th ed., rev. (New York: Brassey's [US], 1991), pp. 84–85.

27. For a description and assessment of the nuclear freeze proposal, see Edward M. Kennedy and Mark O. Hatfield, *Freeze! How You Can Help Prevent Nuclear War* (New York: Bantam Books, 1982). For a more analytical overview, see Randall Forsberg, "A Bilateral Nuclear-Weapon Freeze," *Scientific American* 247 (November 1982), pp. 52–61.

28. George F. Kennan, "A Modest Proposal," *New York Review of Books* 25 (July 16, 1981), pp. 14+.

29. Thomas Schelling, "What Went Wrong with Arms Control," *Foreign Affairs* 64 (winter 1985/86), pp. 219–33.

30. For a short analysis of strategic stability, see Jerome H. Kahan, *Security in the Nuclear Age* (Washington, D.C.: Brookings Institution, 1975), pp. 272–82 and 330–37. See also McGeorge Bundy, "Maintaining Stable Deterrence," *International Security* 3 (winter 1978/79), pp. 5–16.

31. Charles Krauthammer, "How to Prevent Nuclear War," *The New Republic* (April 28, 1982), p. 15.

32. Estimates based on data from *New York Times* (March 23, 1986), p. E3.

33. Michael Mandelbaum, *The Nuclear Question: The United States and Nuclear Weapons, 1946–1976* (Cambridge: Cambridge University Press, 1979), p. 186.

34. Eugene Robinson, "Brazil and Argentina Step Back from the Nuclear Brink," *The Washington Post National Weekly Edition* (February 3–9, 1992), pp. 16–17.

35. For an assessment of South Africa's nuclear status, see J.W. de Villiers, Roger Jardine, and Mitchell Reiss, "Why South Africa Gave Up the Bomb," *Foreign Affairs* (72 (November/December 1993), pp. 98–109.

36. *Time* (August 5, 1991), p. 22.

37. *New York Times* (September 29, 1991), p. 1.

38. *New York Times* (October 6, 1991), p. 1.

39. *New York Times* (February 7, 1992), p. 6.

40. *New York Times* (December 30, 1991), p. 7.

41. According to Edward Rowny, START II allows each party to have 500 single-warhead ICBMs. Because Russia is permitted 350 SS-25 single-warhead missiles and 105 modified single-warhead SS-19 ICBMs, this total of 455 ICBMs leaves Russia 45 missiles short of the 500 limit. To bridge this gap, Russia has been developing a new mobile, single-warhead missile (known as the SS-X-27). See Edward L. Rowny, "A New START with Russia," *The Wall Street Journal* (December 11, 1996), p. 15.

42. Bill Powell, "A Summit, But Not of Equals," *Time* (March 31, 1997), p. 32.

43. *New York Times* (September 11, 1996), p. 3.

44. Morgenthau, *Politics Among Nations,* p. 413.

Chapter 19

1. David A. Wirth, "Climate Chaos," *Foreign Policy* 74 (spring 1989), p. 10.

2. Gareth Porter and Janet Welsh Brown, *Global Environmental Politics,* 2nd ed. (Boulder, Colo.: Westview Press, 1996), p. 147.

3. Lynn R. Anspaugh, Robert J. Catlin, and Marvin Goldman, "The Global Impact of the Chernobyl Reactor Accident," *Science* 242 (December 16, 1988), p. 1518.

4. World Resources Institute, *World Resources, 1990–1991* (New York: Oxford University Press, 1990), p. 135.

5. William Bown, "Europe's Forests Fall to Acid Rain," *New Scientist* (August 11, 1990), p. 17.

6. In January 1992, a U.S. federal district judge disregarded the GATT ruling and barred about half of the 266,000 metric tons of tuna imported annually. See *New York Times* (January 19, 1992), sec. 4, p. 5.

7. See Garrett Hardin, "Living in a Lifeboat," *Bioscience* 24 (October 1974), pp. 561–68; and "The Tragedy of the Commons," *Science* 162 (December 13, 1968), pp. 1243–48.

8. See Per Magnus Wijkman, "Managing the Global Commons," *International Organization* 36 (summer 1982), pp. 511–36.

9. According to Thomas Sowell, the "constrained vision" is based on pessimistic assumptions about human nature, affirms decentralization of government authority, and supports the development of governmental institutions that protect human creativity and initiative. The "unconstrained vision," by contrast, is based on optimistic assumptions about human nature, has great faith in the role of government in promoting the common good, and believes in the positive role of government in carrying out social progress. For a comprehensive examination of these competing visions, see Thomas Sowell, *A Conflict of Visions* (New York: William Morrow and Co., 1987).

10. See Paul R. Ehrlich and Anne H. Ehrlich, *The Population Explosion* (New York: Simon & Schuster, 1990).

11. Dennis L. Meadows et al., *The Limits to Growth: A Report for the Club of Rome's Project on the Predicament of Mankind,* 2nd ed. (New York: Universe Books, 1974). For a critique of this report, see H.S.D. Cole et al., eds., *Models of Doom: A Critique of the Limits to Growth* (New York: Universe Books, 1975).

12. *The Global 2000 Report to the President: Entering the Twenty-First Century.* A Report Prepared by the Council on Environmental Quality and the Department of State (New York: Penguin Books, 1982), p. 1.

13. Taken from Lars Bjorkbom, "Resolution of Environmental Problems: The Use of Diplomacy," in John E. Carroll, ed., *International Environmental Diplomacy: The Management and Resolution of Transfrontier Environmental Problems* (Cambridge: Cambridge University Press, 1988), p. 126.

14. *New York Times* (June 15, 1992), p. 5.

15. *New York Times* (June 14, 1992), p. 6.

16. *Time* (November 24, 1986), pp. 36–37.

17. Max Singer, *Passage to a Human World: The Dynamics of Creating Global Wealth* (New Brunswick, N.J.: Transaction Publishers, 1989).

18. Julian L. Simon, *The Ultimate Resource* (Princeton: Princeton University Press, 1981). See also his *The Economic Consequences of Economic Growth* (Princeton: Princeton University Press, 1986) and *Population Matters* (New Brunswick, N.J.: Transaction Books, 1990).

19. Julian L. Simon and Herman Kahan, eds., *The Resourceful Earth: A Response to Global 2000* (Oxford: Basil Blackwell, 1984), pp. 1–2.

20. *World Resources, 1990–1991,* pp. 142–43.

21. World Resources Institute, *World Resources, 1996–97* (New York: Oxford University Press, 1996), p. 331.

22. *New York Times* (December 4, 1997), pp. 1 and 8.

23. *New York Times* (June 22, 1997), p. D14.

24. Christopher Flavin, "The Heat is On," in Lester R. Brown, fwrd. by, *The World Watch Reader on Global Environmental Issues* (New York: W.W. Norton & Co., 1991), p. 80.

25. *New York Times* (June 22, 1997), p. D14.

26. Flavin, "The Heat Is On," p. 83.

27. *New York Times* (February 17, 1992), p. 3.

28. *World Resources, 1996–97,* p. 15.

29. *New York Times* (June 13, 1992), pp. 1 and 4.

30. Sharon Begley, "Too Much Hot Air," *Newsweek* (October 20, 1997), p. 50.

31. Robert Repeto and Jonathan Lash, "Planetary Roulette: Gambling with the Climate," *Foreign Policy* 108 (fall 1997), p. 87.

32. "Planet at the Crossroads," *National Parks* (March/April 1990), p. 43.

33. Sandra Postel, "Restoring Degraded Land," in Lester R. Brown, frwd. by, *The World Watch Reader on Global Environmental Issues* (New York: W.W. Norton & Co., 1991), p. 29.

34. Ibid., p. 27.

35. Christopher C. Joyner, "Deforestation in Amazonia: Policies, Politics, and Global Implications," *International Studies* 16 (winter 1991), p. 24.

36. Daniel J. Kevles, "Some Like It Hot," *The New York Review of Books* (March 26, 1992), p. 31.

37. *World Resources, 1990–1991,* p. 42.

38. *Wall Street Journal* (December 4, 1997), p. 17.

39. See, for example, Peter H. Gleick, "Water and Conflict: Fresh Water Resources and International Security," *International Security* 18 (summer 1993), pp. 79–112; and Thomas F. Homer-Dixon, "Environmental Scarcities and Violent Conflict: Evidence and Cases," *International Security* 19 (summer 1994), pp. 5–40.

40. Gleick, "Water and Conflict," p. 95.

41. Postel, "Restoring Degraded Land," p. 128. See also Joyce R. Starr, "Water Wars," *Foreign Policy* 82 (spring 1991), pp. 17–36.

42. Raynor Cannastra Associates, ed., *A Global Agenda* (Washington, D.C.: Edison Electric Institute, 1992), p. 26.

43. Technically, biodiversity refers to three types of diversity: genetic, species, and ecosystem. Genetic diversity refers to the variety of genes within a species; species diversity refers to the variety of species within a region; and ecosystem diversity refers to the number and distribution of ecosystems. See Marian A. L. Miller, *The Third World in Global Environmental Politics* (Boulder, Colo.: Lynne Rienner, 1995), p. 109.

44. Gareth Porter and Janet Welsh Brown, *Global Environmental Politics*, 2nd ed. (Boulder, Colo.: Westview Press, 1996), pp. 78–80.

45. *World Resources, 1990–1991*, p. 180.

46. Ibid., p. 81.

47. Miller, *The Third World in Global Environmental Politics*, p. 88.

48. Porter and Brown, *Global Environmental Politics*, p. 87.

49. Ibid., p. 48.

50. Nazli Choucri, *Global Accord: Environmental Challenges and International Responses* (Cambridge: MIT Press, 1993), p. 493.

Epilogue

1. Aleksandr I. Solzhenitzyn, "To Tame Savage Capitalism," *New York Times* (November 28, 1993), p. E11.

2. John Lewis Gaddis, *The United States and the End of the Cold War* (New York: Oxford University Press, 1992), p. 196.

3. Francis Fukuyama, "The End of History?" *The National Interest* 16 (summer 1989), p. 18.

4. Quoted in Bruce Russett, *Grasping the Democratic Peace: Principles for a Post–Cold War World* (Princeton: Princeton University Press, 1993), pp. 128–29.

5. See Thomas Sowell, *A Conflict of Visions* (New York: William Morrow and Co., 1987).

6. See the discussion of globalism and tribalism in chap. 3.

Photo Credits

Chapter 1

p.13(both): AP/Wide World Photos

Chapter 2

p.37, p.46: AP/Wide World Photos

Chapter 3

p.54: Bettmann Archive;
p.72: AP/Wide World Photos

Chapter 4

p.96: AP/Wide World Photos

Chapter 5

p.107, p.120: Reuters/Bettmann

Chapter 6

p.131: Reuters/Bettmann

Chapter 7

p.158: Reuters/Bettmann

Chapter 8

p.185: Reuters/Bettmann

Chapter 9

p.209: UPI/Bettmann

Chapter 10

p.232, p.238: AP/Wide World Photos

Chapter 11

p.257: AP/Wide World Photos,
p.263: © 1994 Gilles Peress/Magnum Photos, Inc.

Chapter 12

p.287: AP/Wide World Photos

Chapter 13

p.315: AP/Wide World Photos

Chapter 14

p.335: UPI/Bettmann

Chapter 15

p.363: AP/Wide World Photos

Chapter 16

p.395: © Margot Granitsas/The Image Works
p.404: AP/Wide World Photos

Chapter 17

p.429: AP/Wide World Photos

Chapter 18

p.441: Reuters/Bettmann,
p.448: AP/Wide World Photos

Chapter 19

p.481: AP/Wide World Photos

Photo Research by LouAnn Wilson

Glossary

A

absolute gains An increase in the capabilities of one actor without regard to other actors.

absolute poverty A condition of subhuman existence.

acid rain Precipitation contaminated with industrial pollutants, especially sulphur dioxide and nitrogen oxide.

actual power An actor's actual capability to determine other actors' behavior in light of its effective utilization of tangible and intangible resources.

adjudication The resolution of disputes through legal principles and procedures.

advisory opinion A nonbinding legal opinion by the International Court of Justice, provided for UN organizations and other specialized agencies.

anarchy A community without government or institutions that can resolve conflict and impose order.

Anti-Ballistic Missile (ABM) Treaty This 1972 U.S.-USSR treaty limited the superpowers' ballistic missile defense to two ABM sites.

apartheid The policy of racial segregation implemented in South Africa from 1948 to 1990.

appeasement A policy designed to avoid conflict by giving in to an aggressor's demands.

Arab League An organization of Arab countries that promotes common cultural, economic, political, and religious interests.

arbitration The settlement of a dispute through a binding third-party judgment.

arbitration tribunal An international court that settles disputes by issuing a binding judgment.

arms control Bilateral and multilateral accords designed to reduce the risk and destructiveness of war by regulating the number and type of military armaments. During the Cold War, arms control referred chiefly to the management of nuclear arms.

autarky National economic self-sufficiency.

authority The capacity to command obedience through voluntary, noncoercive means.

B

Baker Plan A 1985 plan to provide increased bilateral and multilateral lending to deeply indebted Third World countries that carried out austerity measures and market reforms.

balance of payments A summary of a country's international financial transactions. A surplus indicates that assets exceeded liabilities in a given period of time; a deficit signifies the opposite.

balance of power The principle that peace and global stability are best achieved and maintained through a fundamental equilibrium of power among major actors.

balance of terror A concept that describes a condition of mutual nuclear deterrence, in which states have the ability to carry out unacceptable nuclear retaliation after suffering a surprise nuclear attack.

balance of trade The difference in value between a country's exports and imports.

Balfour Declaration A British policy, announced in 1917 by Foreign Secretary Arthur Balfour, that legitimized the return of Jews to Palestine.

Beagle Channel Treaty This 1984 treaty, negotiated by the Vatican, ended a territorial dispute between Argentina and Chile.

behavioralism An approach to political analysis that emphasizes empirical investigation utilizing a scientific methodology.

belief system A collection of core values, beliefs, and images that make up an individual's worldview.

biodiversity The large variety of animal and plant species on earth.

biological weapons Weapons that disperse lethal microorganisms in order to spread diseases and epidemics.

Biological Weapons Convention A 1972 convention that prohibits the development, production, and use of biological weapons.

bipolar system A system in which states are grouped around two major power centers.

bluff A threat not backed by capability and/or resolve.

bounded rationality A theory suggesting that decision makers frequently fulfill minimal conditions, rather than optimize utility, because they rely on simplified worldviews based on limited or "bounded" perspectives.

boycott The refusal of a country to import goods and services from another country.

Brady Plan A late 1980s plan that sought to resolve the Third World's debt crisis through market reforms, prioritization, and debt forgiveness.

Bretton Woods Monetary System The international monetary system, established in the aftermath of World War II, provided rules and institutions to facilitate the convertibility of currencies and to assist states facing significant monetary crises.

Bretton Woods System The rules and institutions of the liberal global economic system established at the end of the World War II.

Brezhnev Doctrine The doctrine, articulated in 1968 by President Leonid Brezhnev, that the Soviet Union had the right to intervene in Eastern-bloc states in order to preserve communist government.

bureaucratic bargaining model The analysis of policy making that stresses bargaining among different relevant governmental actors.

bureaucratic controls Administrative regulations used by governments to limit international trade.

C

Camp David Accords   The 1978 accords established the basis for the 1979 Egypt-Israel Peace Treaty.

carrying capacity   The maximum long-term economic capacity of a given territory.

cartel   An organization of commodity producers that seeks to control the commodity's price by regulating its supply.

chargé d'affaires   The senior diplomat authorized to act on behalf of the ambassador during his/her absence.

chemical weapons   Weapons that use chemical agents to injure and kill.

Chemical Weapons Convention (CWC)   An international treaty requiring the complete elimination of chemical weapons.

classical wars   An interstate war fought by military forces of two or more states in order to resolve political disputes.

Climate Treaty   A binding convention, signed at the 1992 Earth Summit in Rio de Janeiro, that seeks to counter global warming by calling on states to reduce emissions of carbon dioxide, methane, and other "greenhouse" gases.

CNN effect   The impact of televised political events on public opinion.

coercive diplomacy   The threat or use of limited force to persuade an actor to comply with a state's foreign policy demands.

cognitive dissonance   Psychological conflict between existing beliefs and newly acquired information.

coherent states   A country characterized by a close fusion of nation and state.

Cold War   The forty-five-year ideological conflict between the Soviet Union and its allies and the United States and its allies.

collective security   A theory of world order, first applied by the League of Nations, that seeks to deter aggression by promising collective retaliation against any community member committing aggression.

colonialism   Establishment of direct political control over a foreign dependency.

command theory of law   The view that law exists only when it is backed by force.

commodity agreement   An agreement to stabilize prices of raw materials by regulating the supply of a commodity. Agreements also establish buffer stocks in order to increase a commodity's supply when production falls.

Common Foreign and Security Policy   The European Union's joint policies on foreign affairs and defense matters.

common heritage principle   The notion that natural resources located beyond the territorial control of states belong to all of humankind. The principle was developed to justify a global claim on minerals in the deep seabed.

Commonwealth of Independent States (CIS)   An organization that seeks to promote economic, political, and military cooperation among eleven of the fifteen former Soviet republics.

communism   The Marxist-Leninist ideology assumes that the state should regulate the production and distribution of goods and services.

communitarian justice   Justice focusing on equitable and fair relations among states.

communitarianism   A tradition that assumes that states are morally legitimate and subject to widely accepted legal and moral norms.

comparative advantage   The doctrine by which national economic welfare is maximized when countries produce goods and services in which they are comparatively efficient.

compellent power   The use of force or threat of force to persuade an adversary to stop some unwanted action or to fulfill a desired action.

Comprehensive Test Ban (CTB) Treaty   A 1996 treaty that calls for a complete halt to all nuclear weapons testing.

compromise   The resolution of conflict through mutual accommodation.

conceptual knowledge   Knowledge based on concepts—that is, abstract ideas that correspond to observable phenomena.

Conference on Security and Cooperation in Europe (CSCE)   A structure, begun in 1975 with the Helsinki Act, that promoted European East-West cooperation in economic, social, political, and related areas.

conflict   A real or perceived incompatibility between two or more actors.

conflict avoidance   The effort to disregard political conflicts in the hope that neglecting them will facilitate their resolution.

conflict management   An approach that seeks to manage social and political conflict by seeking to reduce the harmful effects of conflict while also protecting the constructive, creative role of conflict.

consequentialism   An ethical tradition that assumes that actions should be judged by their consequences.

constitutive norms   The rules that define which actors can join a system.

containment   The U.S. Cold War strategy designed to limit Soviet expansionism.

content analysis   An approach that examines the belief systems and worldviews of statesmen by analyzing the content of their communications, giving particular attention to the nature and frequency of key words.

contentious cases   ICJ cases dealing with legal disputes between two or more states.

Convention on Biological Diversity   This 1992 treaty seeks to protect the habitats of endangered species by encouraging states to pursue conservation measures.

Convention on the International Trade in Endangered Species (CITES)   This 1973 multilateral accord seeks to regulate the export, transit, and importation of endangered animal and plant species.

Conventional Forces in Europe (CFE) Treaty   This 1990 accord between NATO and Warsaw Pact countries established limits on five categories of conventional arms.

cosmopolitanism   An ethical tradition that assumes that persons, not states, are morally significant in global society. Humanitarian intervention is thus morally permissible.

cosmopolitan justice   Justice focusing on equitable and fair relations among persons.

Council for Mutual Economic Assistance (COMECON)   A Cold War organization that sought to promote economic cooperation among Soviet-bloc states.

counterforce strategy   A strategy that calls for discrimination in the targeting of strategic nuclear arms. Under this strategy, the chief targets are an enemy's military and political forces.

counterintelligence   A government's effort to protect the secrecy of its operations from foreign intelligence agents.

countervalue strategy   The targeting of strategic nuclear arms on cities and industrial centers of an enemy society without effort to discriminate between combatants and noncombatants.

crisis   A situation involving a threat to a country's vital interests, limited time constraints, the potential use of force, and the involvement of a government's top leadership.

crisis decision making   Decision making during an international crisis.

cruise missile   An accurate, subsonic missile, capable of delivering conventional or nuclear warheads up to a distance of 1,500 miles. To evade detection, the missile flies near the surface of the earth.

D

debt crisis *See* Third World debt crisis.

debt-service ratio The relationship of debt-service payments (including interest and principal) to export revenues.

decolonization The process by which European powers relinquished control over dependent territories.

deep seabed The ocean floor of the high seas. The seabed is considered economically important because of its vast mineral deposits.

defensive power The ability to repel an attack and limit destruction from aggression.

deforestation The indiscriminate destruction of the earth's virgin forests to achieve rapid economic expansion.

Delian League This defensive alliance of some 200 Greek city-states was established by Athens during the fifth century B.C. in order to deter Persian aggression.

democracy A system of limited government based on free, periodic, and competitive elections.

democratic peace thesis (DPT) This theory attributes the absence of war among democratic states to the ideals and values of constitutional regimes and to democratic structures.

demographic transition theory A theory that attributes changes in birth and death rates to increasing modernization.

dependency theory A neo-Marxist theory attributing the wealth of the industrial states and the poverty of the Third World to global capitalist structures. According to the theory, international economic structures foster income inequalities among states, thereby increasing Third World dependency.

dependent development Economic development that is conditioned and controlled by foreign actors.

desertification The process by which potentially productive land is transformed into arid, desertlike territory, unfit for productive uses.

detente The policy of relaxing tensions through accommodation.

deterrence The use of explicit or implicit threats of coercion in order to inhibit unwanted behavior.

deterrent power The capacity to inhibit action through the credible threat of punishment.

diplomacy The process by which states and other international actors pursue peaceful international relations, reconciling competing and conflicting interests through negotiation.

diplomatic asylum The granting of temporary asylum within a foreign embassy to a political refugee wanted by the host government.

diplomatic policy The political dimension of foreign policy.

diplomatic precedence A tradition that the seniority of diplomats in a particular state is determined on the basis of continuous service in the host state.

disarmament Bilateral and multilateral accords that reduce and eliminate military weapons in order to decrease the probability of war.

discrimination norm A just war principle that prohibits direct attack on noncombatants.

distributive (substantive) justice An approach to justice requiring a fair or equitable distribution of good and resources.

doctrine of cultural relativism The belief that, because the world is comprised of many different cultures, each with its own moral norms, there is no universal, binding international morality.

E

Earth Summit A 1992 UN-sponsored conference that called attention to global environmental protection and to economic development that was environmentally safe.

ecological interdependence The belief that global environmental protection requires the shared participation of many states.

economic integration The process of building an economic community by breaking down barriers that impede the mobility of goods, services, capital, and labor.

economic refugees Displaced persons seeking improved living conditions in a foreign country.

economic sanctions Actions that impose economic hardship on a target state in order to influence its behavior. Economic sanctions may also involve positive rewards.

economic statecraft The economic instruments used by governments in order to influence the behaviors of state and nonstate actors.

economic summits Annual face-to-face diplomacy among the heads of state of the major industrial powers that focus on global economic concerns.

ecooptimism An optimistic perspective about the long-term effects of continued modernization and economic expansion.

ecopessimism A pessimistic perspective about the long-term effects of continued modernization and economic expansion.

Egypt-Israel Peace Treaty The 1979 treaty that established peace between Egypt and Israel by returning the Sinai to Egypt.

embargo The refusal of one country to export goods to another country.

emigration The right of persons to leave their country of habitation.

empirical Objective, observable phenomena.

empirical knowledge Knowledge based on concepts—that is, abstract ideas that correspond to observable phenomena.

epistemic community A global network of knowledge-based professionals in such scientific and technological areas as trade, arms control, biotechnology, and environmental protection.

ethics The critical analysis of moral values and their application.

euro The proposed common currency of the EU, projected to be implemented in 1999.

European Court of Justice (ECJ) The regional court of the European Union.

European Monetary Union (EMU) This proposal, which is to go into effect in January 1999, calls for an integrated monetary system among EU members based on a single currency (euro) and a central EU bank.

European Union (EU) A regional organization of fifteen Western European states that promotes increased economic, social, scientific, and political unity. The EU was formerly known as the European Community (EC).

exclusive economic zone (EEZ) According to the 1982 Third Law of the Sea Treaty, territorial states have exclusive economic control over ocean waters extending up to 200 NM from the coastline.

expected utility of war theory A theory that attributes the outbreak of war to decision makers' estimated gains. According to the theory, the higher the expected gains (utility) from war, the greater the likelihood that leaders will resort to war.

export controls Regulations that restrict the export of goods and services.

export quota A quantitative limit on the export of particular commodities.

extended deterrence The use of threats, especially nuclear ones, to deter aggression against one's allies.

extralegal sanctions Enforcement procedures based on norms other than law.

F

failed state A state that has lost its ability to perform the rudimentary tasks of governing.

famine relief Humanitarian assistance given to peoples suffering from extreme food shortages.

firebreak The psychological barrier between conventional and nuclear weapons.

first-strike capability The ability to destroy the bulk of a nation's strategic nuclear weapons in a surprise attack.

First World The developed, industrial democracies of the world.

fixed exchange rate A currency exchange rate established and maintained by government or other actors.

flexible exchange rate A currency exchange rate determined largely by the market forces of demand and supply.

flexible response This U.S. deterrence strategy, developed in the 1960s, required the maintenance of military capabilities sufficient to respond in kind to an attack of any intensity or duration.

force The application of military power in order to punish or compel.

foreign direct investment (FDI) Direct ownership of business assets in a foreign county.

foreign exchange The accumulation of foreign currencies with which to purchase imports and meet other external financial obligations.

foreign policy The actions of governmental officials designed to promote national interests beyond a country's territorial boundaries.

foreign portfolio investment (FPI) Ownership of foreign securities, such as stocks and bonds, thereby giving owners indirect control over business assets in a foreign country.

Fourth World The poorest Third World countries, incapable of meeting citizens' basic needs, especially food.

free trade International trade without tariff or nontariff barriers.

free trade area A group of countries committed to the removal of trade barriers among themselves, but pursuing independent external trade policies.

functionalism A theory emphasizing socioeconomic cooperation as the basis of community building. According to this approach, cooperation in technical, nonpolitical areas can eventually lead to cooperation in other, more difficult areas.

G

GATT Round A series of negotiations designed to reduce tariff and nontariff trade barriers. Eight major trade negotiations have taken place, the latest (the Uruguay Round) lasting from 1986 to 1993.

General Agreement on Tariffs and Trade (GATT) An organization that facilitated the liberalization of international trade from the late 1940s to 1995, when it was replaced by the World Trade Organization (WTO).

General Assembly The parliament of the United Nations, in which each member-state has one vote.

geopolitics The field that examines the interrelationship of geography, national power, and foreign policy.

glasnost The USSR policy of increased openness, developed and pursued by Soviet leader Mikhail Gorbachev in the late 1980s.

global capital market The transnational institution that facilitates cross-border lending by firms and governments.

global warming The gradual rise in the earth's temperature, much of it attributed to greenhouse emissions that trap the earth's heat.

globalism The growing role of transnational interactions among peoples, groups, states, and other actors.

good offices The use of a third party to facilitate communication between two or more disputing actors.

greenhouse effect Because of increasing industrial pollution, especially from carbon dioxide, heat is trapped by these "greenhouse" gases, thereby raising the earth's temperature.

Group of 77 (G-77) An informal alliance of developing nations that emerged in the 1960s to promote Third World economic development. In the 1970s, G-77 became chiefly concerned with reforming the international economic order as a means of empowering developing nations. Originally, G-77 consisted of 77 members, but by the late 1980s the number had increased to more than 120 states.

Group of Seven (G-7) An alliance of the world's seven leading industrial democratic countries: Britain, Canada, France, Germany, Italy, Japan, and the United States with the addition of Russia in 1997, the G-7 became the G-8.

groupthink The tendency of groups to encourage conformity of thought and thereby impair open, creative deliberation.

guerrilla war An unconventional war involving irregular forces using "hit-and-run" tactics.

Gulf of Tonkin Resolution A congressional resolution authorizing the president to take whatever military actions considered necessary to protect U.S. military forces in Vietnam.

H

Hague Peace Conferences (1899 and 1907) These conferences are important because they codified the rules of war and established peaceful methods of conflict resolution. Most existing states participated in these two diplomatic meetings.

hard power The ability to influence the behavior of international actors through coercive threats or positive inducements.

hegemon A dominant state that uses its military and economic power to establish global rules and institutions in accord with its interests.

hegemonic stability theory The belief that international peace and economic prosperity are a by-product of a hegemonically imposed structure.

Helsinki Act (1975) A 1975 accord among NATO and Warsaw Pact member-states, as well as thirteen nonaligned states, that sought increased East-West cooperation.

high politics The global politics concerned with national security and international peacekeeping.

high seas The ocean waters beyond the sovereign control of states.

horizontal proliferation The spread of modern types of weapons to more states. Refers especially to nuclear weapons.

Human Development Index (HDI) A UN-developed indice based on life expectancy, literacy, and per capita income. A high coefficient represents a high level of development.

human rights The fundamental political, civil, socioeconomic, and cultural rights of human beings.

humanitarian intervention Foreign intervention justified on humanitarian grounds.

I

idealism This optimistic approach to politics assumes that law, institutions, and morality can contribute to the development of peaceful, just international relations.

ideology A simplified political belief-system that inspires and guides governmental decision making.

immigration The process by which persons seek permanent residence in a foreign country.

imperialism The policy of establishing political and economic control over foreign territories.

import quota Placing quantitative limits on specific commodities imported from abroad. The quota may target particular foreign states or may apply to all commodity-exporting countries.

import substitution The policy of fostering domestic production by restricting imports and subsidizing new domestic enterprises. Throughout the 1960s and 1970s, this policy was utilized to stimulate industrial development in the LDCs.

incremental decision making Routine, piecemeal decision making by relevant bureaucratic and governmental agencies.

influence   The ability of an actor to alter the preferences and behavior of another actor.

intelligence   Evaluated data on the goals, capabilities, and likely actions of foreign actors. Most intelligence is gathered and processed secretly.

interdependence   An approach to politics that emphasizes the growing influence of transnational socioeconomic cooperation and the role of nonstate actors.

Intermediate Nuclear Forces (INF) Treaty   A 1987 U.S.-USSR treaty that eliminated intermediate-range nuclear ballistic missiles.

International Bank for Reconstruction and Development (IBRD)   *See* World Bank.

International Court of Justice (ICJ)   This fifteen-member world court, a formal UN organ, is the highest institution charged with adjudicating international law. It is located in The Hague, Netherlands.

international criminal court   A court established to deal with specific wartime crimes (e.g., Nuremburg Tribunal, The Hague War Crimes Tribunal).

international crisis   An unexpected short-term international conflict involving vital interests of states.

international economic policy   The international economic dimension of foreign policy.

international governmental organization (IGO)   An international organization whose members are states.

international justice   This approach to international relations emphasizes justice among states. State boundaries are morally significant.

international law   The customs, rules, and principles that states accept as binding in their mutual relations.

International Monetary Fund (IMF)   A UN specialized agency that promotes international financial cooperation, exchange rate stability, and the availability of sufficient foreign exchange to facilitate efficient international trade.

international nongovernmental organizations (NGOs)   Multi-national nongovernmental groups that influence international affairs.

international political economy (IPE)   An area of international relations that emphasizes the interrelationship of political and economic phenomena in global society.

international regime   The rules, principles, and decision-making procedures governing international behavior in a given issue-area.

international relations (IR)   The totality of transnational interactions among state and nonstate actors. As a field of study, IR is concerned with the analysis of the politics of global society.

International Seabed Authority (ISA)   An international organization, established by the Third Law of the Sea Treaty, that seeks to regulate the mining of the deep seabed.

international war   Armed conflicts between two or more states.

internationalism   A view of the international community that incorporates both the realities of power and sovereignty and the idealistic claims of transnational moral and legal obligations.

internationalization of production   The process of manufacturing goods by using components from a variety of different countries.

intervention   The direct or indirect interference of one state in the sovereign affairs of another state.

intifada   A 1987–1993 Palestinian uprising that challenged Israel's continued occupation of the West Bank and Gaza.

intranational war   An internal military conflict between two or more domestic political groups, or between the state and a particular segment of society.

inviolability of diplomats and embassies   Diplomatic personnel and embassies are immune from the governmental jurisdiction of the host state.

irredentist war   A war that results from a foreign states's claim on a people and territory of another state.

Israel-PLO Accords (1993 and 1995)   Based on the principle of land for peace, two major treaties that provide for increasing Palestinian self-government over Gaza and the West Bank.

Israel-PLO Declaration of Principles   A 1993 framework that provides for peace between Israel and the PLO and for increasing PLO authority in Gaza and selected areas of the West Bank.

Israel-Jordan Peace Accord   This 1994 treaty formally ended the state of war between Israel and Jordan and established a basis for increased bilateral cooperation.

J

jus ad bellum   Just war principles utilized in deciding whether or not to go to war.

jus in bello   Just war principles relevant to the use of violence in war.

just war doctrine   A body of moral principles, developed from ancient secular and religious sources, that establishes a framework for judging the justice of going to war and the justice in war.

justiciable   Disputes that are legal in character and subject to settlement by a court.

K

Kellogg-Briand Pact   A 1928 treaty that attempted to outlaw war as a policy instrument.

Kyoto Protocol   This 1997 treaty requires that industrial countries reduce greenhouse gas emissions in order to limit global warming.

L

Land Mine Treaty   An international treaty, signed in 1997, that bans antipersonnel land mines.

League of Nations   An international organization established at the end of World War I as part of the Treaty of Versailles. The League functioned until 1945, when it was replaced by the United Nations.

legal sanctions   Enforcement procedures based on international law and implemented by states and international governmental organizations.

legalist paradigm   The international legal framework that specifies basic rights and duties of states.

less-developed country (LDC)   A poor, Third World country.

levels of analysis   A tri-partite framework that explains international affairs by focusing on the role of decision makers, the attributes of states, and the structures of the international system.

liberalism   The ideology that calls for limited government rooted in consent in order to assure maximum protection of individual rights and human freedoms. In international economic relations, liberalism is associated with free trade.

Limited Test Ban Treaty   A 1963 U.S.-USSR treaty, subsequently ratified by many other states, banning atmospheric nuclear tests.

local content requirements   Regulations that specify the degree of domestic participation in the production of goods and services, imposed to ensure that a given level of domestic resources are used by foreign firms.

long-cycle theory   A theory that seeks to explain the evolution of international affairs by emphasizing the rise and fall of the major powers. In particular, the theory claims that power shifts in the leading state (hegemon) play a crucial role in fomenting international disorder. *See* hegemonic stability theory.

long peace   The 45-year Cold War era that resulted in one of the longest periods of international peace among major powers.

low-intensity conflict (LIC)   Conflicts carried out with limited military coercion.

low politics   The politics involving the promotion of socioeconomic welfare.

M

Maastricht Treaty   This accord, signed in Maastricht, Netherlands, in 1991, sets forth the process for increased economic and political union among EC member-states.

Madrid talks   The 1991 Arab-Israeli negotiations, initiated by the United States and the USSR, that resulted in the renewal of the Middle East peace process.

managed exchange rates   States manage the exchange rate of their national currency by establishing a range or "band" in which the currency can be traded.

managed trade   A strategy designed to influence a country's balance of trade.

Marshall Plan   A 1947 plan, set forth by U.S. Secretary of State George Marshall, committing the United States to assist Western Europe's post–World War II economic recovery.

massive retaliation   The 1950s U.S. strategic policy that sought to inhibit Soviet aggression by threatening major nuclear retaliation.

mediation   The process by which a third-party facilitates conflict resolution by guiding discussions and offering nonbinding solutions.

mercantilism   The economic doctrine that international trade should be regulated by the state in order to maximize national income.

meta-power   The ability to make, sustain and reform the fundamental rules and institutions of the international system.

military-industrial complex   A concept that calls attention to the convergence of interests between the armed forces, major weapons industries, and government agencies responsible for national security.

military statecraft   The use of military force in order to maximize a state's national interests.

misperception   Distortions of reality caused by factors such as human biases, personal values, and ideological presuppositions.

modernization theory   The belief that wealth creation is the result of increased productive efficiency, which is best achieved domestically through free enterprise and internationally through free trade.

monopoly capitalism   The Marxist-Leninist belief that capital would become increasingly concentrated in the hands of a small number of industrial and financial elites.

Montreal Protocol   An agreement, signed in Montreal in 1987, calling on signatory states to limit the production and use of ozone-depleting CFCs in order to protect the earth from the sun's harmful ultraviolet rays.

moral absolutism   This approach to ethics (also known as deontogical ethics) insists on strict adherence to moral rules, regardless of consequences.

moral skepticism   The belief that moral principles do not apply directly to international relations.

moralism   The simplistic use of moral stereotypes to complex foreign policy issues.

morality   Values of right and wrong, good and bad.

most favored nation (MFN)   According to this principle, international trade preferences granted to one state must be granted to all others.

multilateral diplomacy   Diplomatic discussions and negotiations among three or more nations, such as the G-8 or specialized UN-sponsored conferences.

multinational corporation (MNC)   A business enterprise that has productive or marketing activities in two or more states.

multinational state   A state comprising two or more nations.

multipolar system   An international system based on three or more centers of power.

multistate nation   A nation whose people are in two or more states.

mutual assured destruction (MAD)   A condition in which nuclear powers have the ability to carry out unacceptable destruction after surviving a nuclear attack.

N

nation   A people sharing a common culture, language, history, and desire for political self-rule.

national goals   The specific objectives pursued by states.

national interest   A concept denoting the basic corporate interests of a nation-state.

national security policy   The dimension of foreign policy concerned with a state's territorial security and political independence.

national strategy   The design and implementation of foreign policy based on a state's interests and capabilities and in terms of the interests and capabilities of other states. *See* statecraft.

nationalism   The exclusive attachment and political commitment to one's nation, leading to demands for political self-determination and the consolidation of modern nation-states.

naval quarantine   A peacetime maritime blockade, utilized by the United States in the Cuban missile crisis.

negotiation   The bargaining process designed to achieve a mutually acceptable settlement.

neofunctionalism   A peacekeeping approach based on the promotion of functional interdependence and the creation of international organizations.

neoliberal institutionalism   The belief that international organizations and other nonstate actors can contribute significantly to international cooperation.

neomercantilism   The policy by which a state seeks to manage international trade by promoting export-oriented production in order to assure a trade surplus.

neorealism   A leading IR approach that assumes that the anarchic structure of global society leads states to focus on security and relative gains.

New International Economic Order (NIEO)   The Third World's alternative economic system designed to give the developing countries more influence in the global economy and to help transfer economic resources from the rich to the poor countries.

newly industrialized countries (NICs)   A group of Third World countries, including Hong Kong, Malaysia, Singapore, South Korea, and Taiwan, that have achieved impressive economic growth through export-oriented strategies.

1925 Geneva Protocol   A convention that prohibits the use of chemical weapons.

Nixon Doctrine   A 1969 promise that the United States would support countries threatened by aggression, provided indigenous forces assumed primary responsibility for defense.

Nonaligned Movement (NAM)   A movement, formally begun in 1961, to encourage Third World to remain independent from the East-West ideological conflict.

nonalignment   A posture of independence and nonattachment toward competing state rivalries, especially the East-West conflict during the Cold War era.

nonintervention   This core principle of international law prohibits the direct or indirect interference in the domestic affairs of foreign states.

Nonproliferation Treaty (NPT)   This 1968 treaty seeks to curb horizontal proliferation of nuclear weapons.

nontariff barriers   A restriction on trade other than an import or export tariff, such as an embargo or a quota.

normative   Prescriptive, value-based norms.

normative politics An approach to politics that emphasizes the moral purposes of government, such as the promotion of social justice and the defense of human rights.

North American Free Trade Association (NAFTA) A 1993 accord that reduces trade barriers among Canada, Mexico, and the United States.

North Atlantic Treaty Organization (NATO) A military alliance of Western European and North American states established in 1949 to provide collective defense. Throughout the Cold War, NATO's chief aim was to deter Soviet aggression in Europe.

nuclear freeze A Cold War initiative that called on the superpowers to stop testing, producing, and deploying nuclear arms.

nuclear weapons Bombs of mass destruction utilizing nuclear fission (the splitting of atoms) or nuclear fusion (the joining of two hydrogen nuclei).

nuclear winter The anticipated climactic conditions following a major nuclear war. Because a nuclear war would greatly increase atmospheric dust and fallout and thereby impede the sun's rays, some scientists believe that the earth's temperature could fall dramatically, resulting in a "nuclear winter."

O

official development assistance (ODA) The loans and grants that governments give bilaterally and multilaterally to developing nations in order to foster economic expansion.

optional clause In accordance with Article 36 of the ICJ Statute, states may give the world court compulsory jurisdiction beforehand in certain types of disputes.

Organization for Economic Cooperation and Development (OECD) A Paris-based consortium of the twenty-four leading industrial economies of the world.

Organization of Petroleum Exporting Countries (OPEC) An international organization of major oil-producing countries in the world.

organization-process model A decision-making approach that emphasizes the role of standard operating procedures and established behavior patterns within complex bureaucratic and governmental agencies.

Oslo connection Refers to Norway's role in bringing together Israeli and Palestinian officials in 1993 and thereby facilitating the mutual recognition of antagonists.

ozone depletion The loss of the atmosphere's ozone layer because of the release of ozone-destroying chlorofluorocarbons (CFCs). The ozone layer is important because it protects the earth from the sun's ultraviolet rays.

P

pacifism A tradition that prohibits the use of violence to settle conflicts.

pacta sunt servanda A basic principle of international law stipulating that states must fulfill treaty obligations.

paradigm An intellectual framework, such as dependency theory or political realism, that structures analysis.

Paris Peace Treaty (1973) This peace accord, signed by the United States, South Vietnam, North Vietnam, and the National Liberation Front, ended the Vietnam War, thereby bringing to an end the long and costly U.S. involvement in Southeast Asia.

parochial conflicts International disputes between two or more states over specific territorial, political, economic, or other related issues.

peacekeeping The introduction of multilateral forces in an area of conflict (after the belligerents have accepted a cease-fire) in order to keep parties apart and thereby prevent a resumption of hostilities.

peacemaking The introduction of multilateral forces into regions of conflict in order to obtain a truce between warring parties.

Peloponnesian War A twenty-five-year war during the fifth century B.C. between two major Greek city-states—Athens and Sparta.

perestroika Economic reform policies established by Soviet President Mikhail Gorbachev in the late 1980s, resulting in some economic decentralization.

persona grata A diplomat who is considered acceptable by the host state.

PLN islands Three islands (Picton, Lennox, and Nueva) in the Beagle Channel along the southern tip of South America.

political integration The process by which political decision making is centralized and consolidated in authoritative supranational institutions.

political refugee A person who has fled his/her homeland because of a well-founded fear of persecution.

positive-sum game Interactions in which all actors can achieve gains.

post-Westphalian system The emerging post-Cold War international relations system. The new system of rules and institutions is characterized by, among other things, decreasing state sovereignty, increasing influence of nonstate actors, and the declining role of military force.

postmodern war Intranational conflicts fought over the nature of existing political authority.

postmodernism An intellectual tradition that emphasizes the subjective nature of knowledge. According to postmodern scholars, because knowledge is determined by prevailing ideas, and because concepts and theories are themselves a human creation, knowledge of reality requires careful interpretation and "deconstruction" of oral and written communications.

potential power The anticipated capacity of a state to determine outcomes based on its tangible and intangible resources. Whether power becomes actualized will be determined partly by an actor's relative effectiveness in utilizing resources.

power The capacity to determine outcomes.

power transition theory A theory that suggests that war becomes more likely as power differentials decrease among leading states.

preferential trade An agreement allowing selected types of exports preferential treatment in order to foster LDC economic development.

prestige power National power based on modern weaponry, symbols, and reputation.

preventive diplomacy A United Nations strategy of keeping local disputes from escalating by introducing multinational peacekeeping forces. During the Cold War this strategy was utilized to limit superpower involvement in local and regional conflicts.

preventive war A preemptive war that seeks to avoid a more serious future military conflict.

primary products Minerals, agricultural products, and other raw materials.

principle of discrimination The just war norm that only combatants can be directly targeted in war.

principle of nonintervention A basic norm of the international system that prohibits a state from interfering in the domestic affairs of another.

principled realism A realist perspective that incorporates and applies moral norms.

procedural justice An approach to justice requiring strict, consistent, and impartial adherence to rules and procedures.

propaganda The deliberate attempt to influence the attitudes and opinions of a target population through systematic dissemination of information.

proportionality norm The just war norm that violence inflicted in war must be proportional to the ends of war.

prospect theory This theory suggests that, because humans are more concerned with minimizing losses than with maximizing gains, policy makers are more risk-prone in seeking gains and less risk-prone with respect to potential losses.

protectionism   The use of tariff and nontariff trade barriers to protect domestic industries from foreign competition.

proxy war   A war conducted through surrogate regimes. During the Cold War, the superpowers carried out a number of these conflicts in Asia, Africa, and Latin America.

prudence   The virtue of selecting and implementing policies in light of alternative moral actions.

purchasing power parity (PPP)   An index that measures the relative purchasing power of different countries' currencies.

Q

quasi-state   A politically and economically weak state, incapable of providing the rudimentary functions of government without external support.

R

ratification   The official acceptance of a treaty.

rational actor model   A theory that emphasizes the coherence of state actors and the rationality of their foreign policy decisions.

Reagan Doctrine   The U.S. policy of supporting weak democratic states from communist revolutionaries and of assisting anticommunist insurgencies seeking to overthrow communist regimes.

realism   A political approach that emphasizes the conflictual nature of global politics, the priority of national security, a pessimistic assessment of human nature, and a consequentialist moral perspective.

rebus sic stantibus   A principle of international law providing that treaties lose their validity when the original conditions change.

refugee   A person who flees his or her country of origin because of fear of persecution, discrimination, or political oppression. A refugee is a displaced person without a political home.

regime   *See* international regime.

regional court   International courts of regional organizations that adjudicate disputes among member-states.

regulative norms   The rules that define how actors should behave within a system.

relative gains   An increase in one actor's capabilities relative to the capabilities of other actors.

reprisal   A hostile, illegal act that is rendered legal when carried out in response to a prior illegal act.

retortion   A hostile, legal act carried out in retaliation for a foreign state's prior hostile action.

routine foreign policy making   Slow, incremental, bureaucratic decision making using standard operating procedures (SOPs).

Rush-Bagot Agreement   An 1817 accord between the United States and Britain that provided for naval disarmament in the Great Lakes.

S

sanctions   Measures designed to enforce compliance with binding rules.

Schuman plan   The 1950 plan developed by French Foreign Minister Robert Schuman, called on European states to develop increasing economic cooperation in order to foster peace within Western Europe.

second-strike capability   The ability to carry out nuclear retaliation after sustaining nuclear aggression.

Secretary-General   The chief administrative officer of the United Nations.

Security Council   The chief peacekeeping organ of the United Nations. Although its members come from fifteen countries, the Council's authority is rooted in its five permanent members (Britain, China, France, Russia, and the United States), who have the power to veto any unwanted action.

security dilemma   The dilemma created when states seek to enhance national security by increasing military capabilities. Because security is relational, a rise in one state's capabilities will normally result in a perceived loss of security of other states, leading them to increase their military capabilities.

self-determination   The claim, first popularized in the twentieth century by President Woodrow Wilson and subsequently enshrined in the United Nations system, that people have a right to political self-rule.

self-help   A system in which each actor is ultimately responsible for its own welfare and security.

separatist war   A conflict precipitated by a group's demand for political secession from a state.

Single European Act (SEA)   A 1985 treaty that amended European Community treaties in order to establish goals and procedures for achieving a fully unified market by the end of 1992.

Six-Day War   The 1967 Arab-Israeli war that gave Israel control over the Golan Heights, the Gaza Strip, and the West Bank.

soft power   The ability to influence international affairs through cooptive strategies involving political ideals, cultural values, and economic and social norms.

Solidarity   A union-based political movement led by Lech Walesa that challenged the communist government in Poland throughout the 1980s. After winning the country's first democratic elections, Solidarity assumed power in 1989.

sovereignty   Supreme authority to make binding decisions within states; from an international perspective, state sovereignty implies states' legal equality and political independence.

Special Drawing Rights (SDRs)   A supplemental source of international reserves created to facilitate international financial transactions. SDRs are assigned in proportion to state's institutional quotas.

sphere of influence   A region in which a dominant power has major influence.

stable deterrence   A condition where nuclear aggression is considered unthinkable because of the certainty of unacceptable retaliation.

START I   A 1991 treaty between the United States and the Soviet Union to reduce the number of strategic nuclear weapons by about 25 percent.

START II   A 1993 treaty that further reduces the strategic nuclear arsenals of the United States and Russia.

state   A political community with people, territory, and sovereign government.

state-sponsored terrorism   Terrorism, frequently carried out in a foreign country, that is supported or directed by a government.

statecraft   The actions undertaken by government officials toward foreign state and nonstate actors in order to maximize national interests. Similar to national strategy.

Strategic Arms Limitation Talks (SALT)   The U.S.-USSR arms control negotiations carried out during the 1970s. The negotiations resulted in a 1972 interim accord (SALT I) and a 1979 comprehensive treaty (SALT II).

Strategic Arms Reduction Talks (START)   The U.S.-USSR arms control negotiations carried out in the 1980s by the Reagan and Bush administrations. The negotiations resulted in two major strategic weapons reduction treaties—START I in 1991 and START II in 1993.

Strategic Defense Initiative (SDI)   A plan, initiated by President Ronald Reagan, to develop a ballistic missile defense system using space-based lasers.

strategic nuclear weapons   Long-range nuclear arms, delivered by bombers, ICBMs, and SLBMs, designed to protect a state's territorial integrity and political independence.

strategic trade theory   A theory that posits that a nation can improve its international competitiveness when the government provides subsidies to selective industries.

strong state   A coherent and stable nation-state with authoritative governmental institutions.

structural dependence   An approach that attributes the poverty and inequalities in the international system to the rules and institutions of the existing international economic order.

structuralism   This perspective assumes that existing international economic structures impair the economic development of Third World nations. In order to foster a more just global economic system, this approach advocates a reform of the international economic order.

subsidies   Government financial support to domestic producers in order to facilitate their international competitiveness.

summit   Face-to-face negotiations among leaders of major states.

superpower   A major nuclear power. After the United States and the Soviet Union acquired a credible retaliatory capacity in the 1960s, both states were classified as superpowers.

superpower summits   The face-to-face diplomacy between the heads of the two Cold War superpowers, the United States and the Soviet Union.

supranational authority   The capacity of an international organization to make binding decisions on member-states without their individual consent.

sustainable economic development   Economic growth that ensures the protection of the environment for future generations.

systemic conflicts   International disputes that involve a large number of states, such as the East-West conflict or the North-South dispute.

T

tactical nuclear weapons   Short-range nuclear weapons designed for battlefield use.

tariffs   A tax imposed on imported goods.

terms of trade   The ratio of the value of exports to the value of imports.

territorial sea   The waters surrounding a territorial state that are under its exclusive jurisdiction.

terrorism   The use of indiscriminate violence for political ends. Terrorists target civilians in order to foster fear within society.

Tet offensive   A major 1968 military offensive by communist forces against the regime of South Vietnam.

theater terminal defense   An antimissile defense system that seeks to protect specific areas, especially those with potential political and military targets.

theoretical knowledge   Knowledge based on explanatory or causal theories.

third-party conflict resolution   An approach to dispute resolution involving an external party. Common third-party procedures include conciliation, mediation, arbitration, and adjudication.

Third World   A classification developed in the 1960s to include all developing nations in Asia, Africa, and Latin America. This category was used to differentiate states from the First World (developed democracies) and the Second World (industrializing communist states).

Third World debt crisis   The Third World financial crisis that developed in the early 1980s when many LDCs could not meet their foreign debt obligations.

total war   An international dispute involving unlimited use of force to achieve the complete defeat of the enemy.

trade balance   *See* balance of trade.

trade deficit   When the value of imports exceeds the value of exports.

trade surplus   When the value of exports is greater than the value of imports.

tragedy of the commons   A metaphor used to explain the danger of unregulated use of public goods. The tragedy occurs when the commons' collective interests are overwhelmed by individual short-term claims.

transnational relations   Cross-border interactions among nonstate actors.

Treaty of Rome (1957)   This treaty established the European Economic Community.

Treaty of Westphalia   This mid-seventeenth-century treaty, ending thirty years of religious wars among European states, is significant because it affirmed the notion of state sovereignty, thereby establishing the foundation of the modern state-based global order.

Treaty on European Union   This accord, also known as the Maastricht Treaty, calls for increased political, economic, and military unity among EC member-states.

triad   The three elements of the superpowers' strategic nuclear arsenal: intercontinental ballistic missiles (ICBMs), submarine-launched ballistic missiles (SLBMs), and bombers.

tribalism   The demand for increasing political autonomy by tribal, ethnic, religious and political groups.

Truman Doctrine   A policy, set forth by President Harry Truman in 1947, committing the United States to support peoples threatened by communist aggression.

U

UNCLOS III   The third UN conference on the Law of the Sea culminated in a historic 1982 convention that greatly expands maritime law.

unipolar system   An international system in which one major power dominates global politics.

United Nations   An international organization established in 1945 to promote global peace, economic prosperity, and social welfare. The UN replaced the League of Nations.

United Nations Conference on Environment and Development (UNCED)   This 1992 Rio de Janeiro Conference, known as the Earth Summit, sought to establish guidelines for protecting the environment while also fostering economic growth.

United Nations Conference on the Law of the Sea (UNCLOS)   A series of UN-sponsored negotiating sessions from 1973 to 1982 leading to the Third UN Law of the Sea Treaty—the most comprehensive legal convention on maritime law.

United Nations Conference on Trade and Development (UNCTAD)   A series of conferences, begun in 1964 by the United Nations, with the aim of fostering economic development in the Third World. The program is supported by a Geneva-based secretariat.

United Nations Environment Programme (UNEP)   This IGO seeks to monitor global ecological issues and promote international protection of the environment.

Uniting for Peace Resolution   As a result of this resolution, adopted by the General Assembly in 1950, UN peacekeeping operations were legitimized in the Korean War.

Universal Declaration of Human Rights   This human rights statement, adopted by the UN General Assembly in 1948, is generally regarded as the international charter of human rights.

Uruguay Round   The eighth series of trade negotiations sponsored by GATT. This set of talks resulted in significant trade liberalization in agriculture, services, and intellectual property and in the creation of the WTO.

V

vertical proliferation An increase in the number and capability of military weapons within existing states. Refers especially to nuclear armaments.

veto The right to prohibit an action. In the Security Council, the five permanent members have this right because their unanimous consent is required on all substantive actions. A veto, or negative vote, by any one of them halts the Council's actions.

Vienna Declaration of Human Rights A comprehensive, post-Cold War statement on international human rights. The declaration, adopted in 1993 in Vienna, emphasizes social, economic, and cultural rights and de-emphasizes civil-political rights commonly associated with liberal democracies.

Vietcong Marxist guerrillas that fought against the regime of South Vietnam with the financial, military, and strategic support of North Vietnam.

voluntary habits of compliance Voluntary compliance based on habit and self-interest.

W

war Resort to armed violence in order to resolve international disputes.

Warsaw Pact A Cold War military alliance of communist states in Central and Eastern Europe. This organization was created by the Soviet Union in 1955 and disbanded shortly before the USSR disintegrated in 1991.

Washington Naval Treaty A 1922 treaty between Britain, France, Italy, Japan, and the United States calling for reductions in the largest types of military ships.

weak state A divided and unstable nation state ruled by a weak government. A regime with limited legitimacy.

West Bank This territory, located between Israel and the Jordan River, has been occupied by Israel since the 1967 war. As a result of the 1993 and 1995 Israel-PLO accords, Palestinians now govern Gaza, Jericho, and numerous other regions in the West Bank.

Westphalian system The anarchic nation-state system established with the 1648 Treaty of Westphalia.

World Bank This institution, formally known as the International Bank for Reconstruction and Development (IBRD), was originally established to help finance the post–World War II reconstruction of Europe, but since the 1950s it has served as the principal source of multilateral lending for developing nations.

world federalism This world order approach assumes that international peace and global stability are best realized by the establishment of an international federal union of states.

world justice An approach to global justice that assumes that persons, not states, are morally significant in the international community. As a result, this approach makes the protection and defense of human rights morally imperative.

World System Theory (WST) A theory claiming that the spread of global capitalism results in uneven economic development, with the gains from development accruing disproportionately to the advanced, capital-intensive economies.

World Trade Organization (WTO) An IGO that monitors implementation of trade agreements and resolves disputes among its members.

Y

Yalta Conference A 1945 summit meeting between Franklin D. Roosevelt, Winston Churchill, and Joseph Stalin to design policies and structures governing the post–World War II system.

Yom Kippur War This 1973 Arab-Israeli war began with a surprise attack by Egyptian and Syrian forces on a Jewish holy day (Yom Kippur).

Z

zero-sum game A set of interactions in which one actor's gains result in a commensurate loss of another. War, like chess, is a zero-sum activity.

Zionism An international Jewish movement committed to establishing and maintaining a homeland in Palestine.

INDEX

Index

A

absolute poverty, 416
Abu Alaa, 202, 301
Acheson, Dean, 148, 163
acid rain, 465, 477
actual power, 132
adjudication, 91
advisory ICJ cases, 314
Afghanistan, 29, 37, 41, 89, 103, 187,
    214, 218, 231, 238, 347
Africa, 26, 35, 261, 335, 361, 402, 480
African National Congress (ANC), 43, 44
Agency for International Development
    (AID), 290
Agenda 21, 380, 471
Aidid, Mohammed Farah, 158
air pollution. *See* pollution, air
Ajami, Fouad, 88
Akehurst, Michael, 309, 314
Albania, 29, 90, 363
Allende, Salvador, 235, 322
Alliance for Progress, 165
alliances
    and war, 10, 269
Allison, Graham, 17, 200, 272
ambassador, 289-291
American Friends Service Committee, 46
Amoco *Cadiz,* 464
anarchy
    in the international community,
      56, 57
Andean Group (AG), 357, 372
Andorra, 334
Angola, 103, 114, 187, 347
Annan, Kofi, 341
Antarctic conservation regime, 82
Anti-Ballistic Missile Treaty (ABM), 113,
    284, 455, 457
apartheid, 47, 170, 214, 218
appeasement, 90
Aquinas, St. Thomas, 265
Arab Cooperation Council (ACC), 357
Arab-Israeli dispute, 51, 68-72, 236,
    295, 344
Arab League, 289
Arafat, Yassir, 48, 71

arbitral tribunal, 318-319, 320
arbitration, 91, 318, 320, 332
Argentina, 89, 196, 226, 256-257, 381,
    396, 424, 432, 433,
    447, 456
Arias, Oscar, 297
Aristide, Jean-Bertrand, 37, 200
Aristotle, 152
Armenia, 35, 66, 231, 363
arms control, 386, 391-398
    list of agreements on, 393
arms proliferation, 442-443
arms races, 118, 269, 271-272, 443
Aron, Raymond, 1, 57
Art, Robert, 110, 226
Asia, 26, 35, 335, 361, 402, 480
Association of Southeast Asian Nations
    (ASEAN), 357
assured destruction. *See* mutual assured
    destruction
Ataturk Dam, 480
Athens, 8
Augustine, Saint, 14-15, 265
Austin, John, 308
Australia, 135, 314, 437
Austria, 130, 181, 282, 352, 354,
    355, 437
autarky, 394
authoritarian decision making, 189-192
authority, 128
Axelrod, Robert, 78
Azerbaijan, 35, 66, 363

B

Baker, James, 293, 433, 490
Baker Plan, 433
balance of payments, 406, 407, 408
balance of power, 141, 206, 269
    practice of, 142-143
    techniques of, 142
    theory of, 142
balance of trade, 394, 408
Baldwin, David, 217
Balfour Declaration, 68
Balkans, 35
Baltic republics, 26, 51, 115

Bangladesh (East Pakistan), 238
Barber, Benjamin, 30, 32
Barnet, Richard, 268
Basel Convention on the Control of
    Transboundary
    Wastes, 484
Basques, 43, 232
Bauer, P. T., 368, 435
Bay of Pigs invasion, 208
Beagle Channel, 297, 299
    conflict over, 299-300
Beer, Francis, 254
Begin, Menachem, 293, 298
Beitz, Charles, 153, 154
Belarus, 334, 363, 382, 456, 457
Belgium, 31, 352, 354, 355, 365
belief system, 183, 186
Bell, Daniel, 66
Bennett, John C., 165
Bentham, Jeremy, 151, 216
Berger, Peter, 169
Berlin blockade, 231
Berlin wall, 115
Biafrans, 35
Bible, 156, 464
biodiversity, 481
Biodiversity Treaty, 470, 484
biological weapons (BW), 444, 445-446
Biological Weapons Convention, 452
black market, 406
blacklists, 214
boat people, 37
Bodin, Jean, 27
Bolshevik Revolution, 102
Bork, Robert, 305
Bosnia-Herzegovina, 27, 29, 89, 66, 182,
    231, 331, 337, 344, 347,
    363, 451
Bosnian Peace Accord. *See* Dayton
    Accords
Bosnian War, 12-14, 51, 77, 253
Botswana, 382, 426
bounded rationality
    theory of, 204
Boutros-Ghali, Boutros, 481
bovine spongiform encephalopathy
    (BSE), 3

D

d'Azeglio, Massimo, 25
Dante, 16, 52, 282
Dayton Accords, 13, 287, 297, 318, 348
de Klerk, F. W., 48, 139, 140, 456
debt-forgiveness, 433
decision making, 283
    authoritarian *versus* participatory,
        189-193
    models of, 201-205
    routine *versus* crisis, 205-207
decolonization, 365
deep seabed, 378
Defense Condition (DefCon), 211
Defense Intelligence Agency (DIA), 222
defensive power, 226
deforestation, 479-480
deGaulle, Charles, 139, 352
Delian League, 8
democratic peace thesis (DPT), 193,
        194-195, 268
demographic profiles, 423
demographic transition theory, 405-407
Denmark, 31, 352, 437
dependency theory, 369-370
    approach to IR, 19-21
    features of, 393
    and Third World political economy,
        369-370
dependent development, 21, 370
desertification, 479
detente, 112-113
deterrence, 92, 210, 211, 218, 226,
        229, 244
deterrent power, 226, 246
Deudny, Daniel, 119
Deutsch, Karl, 28, 129, 322
Dien Bien Phu, 111
diplomacy
    agents of, 289
    definition of, 280-281
    evolution of, 281-283
    functions of, 291-292
    principles for effectiveness in,
        295-297
    role of third parties in, 297-302
diplomatic accreditation, 289-291
diplomatic asylum, 291
diplomatic immunity, 291
diplomatic inviolability, 291
diplomatic policy, 176
diplomatic precedence, 282
disarmament, 338
    conventional, 449-452
    nuclear, 452-454
discrete force, 240
discrimination norm, 275. *See also* just
        war theory
disinvestment, 219
divestment, 219
Dobrynin, Anatoly, 210
doctrines
    Brezhnev, 112
    containment, 108

Nixon, 112
    Reagan, 114
    Truman, 108-109
dolphins, 465
Dominican Republic, 235
Donnelly, Jack, 239
Dos Santos, Theotonio, 369
Dougherty, James, 142, 272
Doxey, Margaret, 217
Dulles, John Foster, 5, 217
Dumbarton Oaks Conference, 334
Dutch East India Company, 364
Dyson, Freeman, 440

E

Earth Summit, 287, 343, 427, 469. *See
        also* United Nations
        Conference on
        Environment and
        Development (UNCED)
East Germany, 115, 182, 206
Eastern Europe, 106, 108, 115-116, 173
East-West conflict. *See* Cold War
Eban, Abba, 279, 305
ecological interdependence, 486
Economic Commission on Latin America
        (ECLA), 343
Economic Community of West African
        States (ECOWAS), 357
economic competitiveness, 437
economic development, 436
    as a factor of power, 134-135
    by groups of states, 417
    prerequisites for, 436
economic growth
    importance of, 425-536
    rates of selected states, 383
    strategies for, 427-436
economic inequalities, 366-367,
        382-383
economic integration, 83
    stages of, 83-84
economic refugees, 37
economic sanctions, 213-218
    impact of, 216-218
    imposed by the U.S., 214-215
    nature of, 212
    toward Haiti, 200-201
    toward Nicaragua, 217
    toward Panama, 217
    toward South Africa, 219-220
    types of, 214
economic statecraft, 213
economic summits, 284, 286
economic union, 84, 354
ecooptimism, 469-472
ecopessimism, 467-469
Ecuador, 310, 312
Egypt, 69-71, 95, 236, 432, 481
Egypt-Israel Peace Treaty, 196, 298
Ehrlich, Paul, 468
Eisenhower, Dwight, 193, 285
El Salvador, 103, 228, 231, 316, 332, 344,
        345, 347

embargo, 397. *See also* trade embargo
embassy organization, 290
emigration, 36
emmission rights, 476
environmental protection, 81, 379-380
    of the atmosphere, 472-478
    of biodiversity, 481-484
    conventions on, 485
    of land, 478-479
    perspectives on, 467-472
    record of, 471
    of water and marine resources, 480
epistemic communities, 83
Eritrea, 334
Estonia, 115, 117, 334, 352, 363, 382
ethical analysis, 150-151
ethical traditions, 151-154
ethics, 149, 153
    and war, 272-276
Ethiopia, 114, 330, 372, 426
ethnic cleansing, 51
ethnic conflict, 87
ethnonationalism, 34, 86, 123
ethnopolitical groups, 65
Euphrates River, 480
Euro, 355 .
European Atomic Energy Community
        (Euratom), 352, 353
European Coal and Steel Community
        (ECSC), 352, 353
European Council, 353, 354
European Court of Human Rights, 317
European Court of Justice, 317-318, 332
European Free Trade Association
        (EFTA), 357
European Parliament, 353, 354
European Union (EU), 40, 80, 84, 333,
        350-356, 373, 402, 474
    economic and monetary union (EMU)
        of, 355, 405
    economic relations of, 403
    evolution of, 353
    global impact of, 355-356
    organization of, 352-353
    origins of, 351-352
Evans, Peter, 370
exchange rates, 406
exclusive economic zone (EEZ), 80, 305,
        310, 483
expected utility of war theory, 266-267
export controls, 397
exports
    as percentage of GDP, 395
    as percentage of world total, 401
    of primary products, 373
expropriation, 214
Exxon *Valdez,* 465

F

failed state, 30, 261
Falkland Islands (Islas Malvinas), 34, 222
    war, 89, 226, 253, 256-257
famine relief, 166

multinational corporations (MNCs), 21,
    41-43, 429-430
    compared with GDP of states, 42
multinational state, 31
multistate nation, 32
Munich Conference, 178, 270
Muslim fundamentalism, 45, 74, 81,
    105, 279
mutual assured destruction (MAD), 242
mutual assured security (MAS), 242
Mutual Balanced Force Reductions
    (MBFR), 116

N

Nagasaki, 150
Namibia, 26, 338, 344, 345
Nasser, Gamal Abdel, 69
nation
    characteristics of, 28-29
national goals, 175
national intelligence estimates, 222
national interest, 175
    classification of, 179
    definition of, 179
    hierarchy of, 180-183
    types of, 179
national morale, 139
national security, 66-67, 440
National Security Agency (NSA), 222
national security policy, 175
    of the U.S., 177
national strategy, 175
nationalism, 182
    characteristics of, 33
    definition of, 32
    impact of, 35-36
    types of, 33-34
    and war, 268-270
nation-states
    rise of, 25-27
    strength of, 29, 30
    types of, 30-31
NATO. *See* North Atlantic Treaty
    Organization
negotiations, 78, 293-295
    and the Beagle Channel dispute,
        299-300
    and the Camp David Accords, 298
    and the Madrid Peace Talks, 71
    and the Oslo Peace Process, 301-302
Nehru, Jawaharlal, 25
neofunctionalism. *See* functionalism
neoliberal institutionalism, 18, 20
neomercantilism, 390, 392. *See also*
        managed trade
neorealism, 18
Netanyahu, Benjamin, 72
Netherlands, 130, 135, 206, 352, 354,
        364, 367, 368, 378, 437
New International Economic Order
        (NIEO), 87, 89, 376
    failure of, 377-378
    features of, 376

New Jewel Movement, 240
New Zealand, 437
newly industrialized countries (NICs),
        381, 390, 391, 426
Nicaragua, 34, 103, 206, 218, 231, 316,
        344, 345, 347
Nicaragua *versus* United States, 315, 316
Nicaraguan rebels (contras), 103, 206
Nicolson, Harold, 280, 281, 283
Niebuhr, Reinhold, 14, 152, 165,
        168, 265
Nile River, 480-481
Nixon Doctrine, 112, 113
Nixon, Richard, 48, 100, 112, 113, 178,
        184, 285, 409
Nkrumah, Kwame, 414
Nonaligned Movement (NAM), 43, 80
    list of conferences, 44
nongovernmental organizations (NGOs),
        17, 21, 40-41
nonintervention, 59, 235
nonproliferation regime, 82, 455, 456
Nonproliferation Treaty, 28, 82, 310
Noriega, Manuel, 173, 217, 218, 227, 291
North American Free Trade Agreement
        (NAFTA), 3, 85, 98,
        190-191, 206, 293,
        402-403
North Atlantic Treaty Organization
        (NATO), 39, 102, 110, 115,
        116, 197, 206, 226, 235,
        245, 271, 295, 330, 443,
        450, 458
    expansion of, 77
    involvement in Bosnia, 13-14, 348
North Korea, 32, 110, 135-136, 334, 363,
        372, 447
North, Robert, 266
North Sea, 483
North, the, 19, 361-362
North-South conflict, 87, 360, 361,
        422-423, 470-471
    competing perspectives about,
        361-363
    and environmental protection,
        379-380
    evolution of, 371-380
    nature of, 364-367
    participants in, 361-371
Norway, 31, 36, 352, 375, 437, 478
nuclear freeze, 452-453
Nuclear Nonproliferation Treaty (NPT),
        28, 310
nuclear states, 55
nuclear weapons, 239, 241-248,
        446-449
    characteristics of, 241-243
    impact of, 245-248
    reductions of, 457-460
    role of, 243-245
Nuremburg Military Tribunal, 306, 318
Nye, Joseph S., Jr., 17, 140, 169

O

Ohlin, Bertil, 389
Olympic Games, 174
optional clause. *See* international law,
        jurisdiction of
Organization for Economic Cooperation
        and Development (OECD),
        240, 361, 362
Organization for Security and
        Cooperation in Europe
        (OSCE), 450
Organization of African Unity (OAU), 39,
        346, 350
Organization of American States (OAS),
        40, 200, 235, 240, 287,
        346, 350
Organization of Petroleum Exporting
        Countries (OPEC)
    evolution of, 475-476
    impact on Third World, 381
    membership in, 374
    rise of, 373-376
organization process model, 203
Organski, A. F. K., 142, 271
Oslo Connection, 71, 297, 301-302
Ottoman Empire, 130
Outer Space Treaty, 455
Oye, Kenneth, 76
ozone depletion, 475-477

P

pacifism, 272, 273
pacta sunt servanda, 311
Pakistan, 270, 365, 447, 456
Palestine, 68
Palestinian Liberation Organization
        (PLO), 43, 44, 70, 73,
        95-96, 197, 294, 301-302
Palestinian Mandate, 68
Palestinian people, 38
Palmerston, Lord, 173
PanAm, 232, 233
Panama, 173-174, 217, 227, 291
Paquette Havana case, 311
paradigms, 14
    comparison of alternative
                approaches, 14-21
Paraguay, 292
Paris Peace Treaty (1973), 112
Paton, Alan, 219
Pax Americana, 145
Pax Britannica, 145
peace diffusion, 254
peace process, 293
peacekeeping, 329, 331-332, 337,
        344-345
peacemaking, 329, 330-331, 344-345
Pearl Harbor, 222
Peloponnesian War, 8-10, 148, 281
    lessons of, 10
People's Republic of China (PRC).
        See China

soft power, 131
Sohn, Louis, 325
Solidarity Movement, 29, 48, 140
Solzhenitzyn, Alexsandr, 489
Somalia, 337
    U.S. intervention in, 158-159
Somoza, Anastasio, Jr., 231
Sorokin, Pitirim, 254-255
South Africa, 26, 31, 85, 214, 217, 218,
        219-220, 365, 447, 456
South Asian Association for Regional
        Cooperation (SAARC), 357
South Korea, 32, 110, 135-136, 197, 334,
        381, 396, 414-415, 426,
        427, 434, 437
South, the. See Third World
Southern African Development
        Coordination Conference
        (SADCC), 357
sovereignty, 27-28, 55, 59
    decline of, 60
Soviet Union, 26, 55, 58, 116, 182, 206,
        214, 231, 247, 457-458
    breakup of, 117
    Cold War foreign policy of, 104, 114
    effects of its collapse, 120-122
Sowell, Thomas, 476, 489
Spain, 130, 314, 352, 354, 364-365, 399
Sparta, 8
Special Drawing Rights (SDRs), 81
special military operations, 229, 235
sphere of influence, 105-106
Spykman, Nicholas, 194
stable deterrence, 454
Stalin, Joseph, 105, 184, 284, 334
standard operating procedures
        (SOPs), 203
states, 27, 54
    classification of, 56
    features of, 27
    growth of, 26-27
statecraft, 207, 210-212
state-sponsored terrorism, 232, 323
Steel, Ronald, 88
Stevenson, Adlai, 208
Stockholm Declaration, 468-469
Stoessinger, John, 104
Strange, Susan, 127, 200
Strategic Arms Limitations Talks (SALT),
        113, 284, 455, 457
Strategic Arms Reductions Talks (START),
        242, 246, 453, 458-460
Strategic Defense Initiative (SDI), 66,
        169-170, 241,
        242-243, 454
strategic nuclear weapons, 239
    reductions in, 286-287
strategic trade theory, 391, 398. See also
        managed trade
Stroessner, Alfredo, 292
strong state, 29-30
structural dependence. See structuralism
structuralism, 369, 424-425, 426
submarine-launched ballistic missiles
        (SLBMs), 241, 457-460

subsidies, 397
Sudan, 34, 64, 231
Sudentenland, 270
summits, 284-287
    dangers of, 286
    types of, 284-285
Sun Tzu, 221
superpower summits, 284-285
supranational, 352
sustainable development, 427-428
Sweden, 130, 352, 355, 473
Switzerland, 32, 36, 334, 367, 368,
        378, 437
Syria, 136, 196, 232, 236, 345, 446, 480

T

tactical nuclear weapons, 239, 459
Taiwan, 32, 135-136, 269, 368, 381, 396,
        426, 437
Tajikistan, 345, 363, 382
Tamils, 35, 43, 269
Tanzania, 372, 426
tariff, 214, 396
Taylor, General Maxwell, 208
Tehran Conference, 284
territorial sea, 305-306, 313
territory
    and power, 132-133
terrorism, 231
    impact of, 233-234
    nature of, 231-233
tet offensive, 112
Thailand, 382, 434, 437
Thatcher, Margaret, 184, 195
theater terminal defense, 243
third party dispute settlement, 332
Third World, 361-362, 363
    conflict with North, 360-380
    countries of, 362
    decline of, 380-383
    economic perspective of, 368-371
    foreign debt, 431-434
    quality of life in, 418
Third World poverty, 425-427
    distribution of, 417
    indices of, 415
    nature of, 19, 416-419
    reduction strategies, 423-427
Thirty Years' War, 26
Thompson, Kenneth, 152
threats, 229-230
Thucydides, 8, 10, 14, 148, 225, 272, 281
Tiananmen Square massacre, 63, 178
Tickner, J. Ann, 22
Tigris River, 480
Tocqueville, Alexis de, 189
Tokyo Military Tribunal, 306, 318
total war, 258-260
Touraine, Alain, 29
Trachtenberg, Marc, 247
trade barriers, 396-397
    arguments for, 397-399
trade deficit, 394
    of the United States, 402

trade embargo, 214
    of Cuba, 216
    of Iraq, 216
trade surplus, 394
tragedy of the commons, 466-467
transboundary pollution. See pollution
transnational relations, 62-64
treaties, 310-311
Treaty of Tlatelolco, 455
Treaty of Tordesillas, 364
Treaty of Versailles, 92
Treaty of Westphalia, 26, 53, 55
Treaty on European Union, 188,
        354-355, 356
triad, 241
Truman Doctrine, 108
Truman, Harry, 105, 150, 320
Trusteeship Council, 341
Tse-tung, Mao, 230
Tucker, Robert W., 275, 377
Tudjman, Franjo, 13
Tunisia, 314
Tupamaros, 232
Turkey, 68, 108, 130, 210, 314, 352, 480
Turkmenistan, 231, 363, 382
Tutu, Desmond, 48, 219

U

Uganda, 372
Ukraine, 334, 340, 363, 456, 457, 459
United Kingdom, 90, 105, 130, 135, 194,
        197, 226, 256-257, 282,
        299, 312, 314, 352, 355,
        364-365, 375, 399, 409,
        427, 437, 447, 449, 460, 478
United Nations, 65, 144, 287, 450
    affiliated IGOs, 342
    assessments, 339
    budgetary problems of, 339-340
    budgets, 336
    Charter of, 28, 36, 58, 80, 157, 235,
        236, 261, 274, 317,
        324, 331, 334, 336, 337
    creation of, 334
    and disarmament, 451
    Economic and Social Council
        (ECOSOC), 340-341
    finances, 339-340
    General Assembly, 58, 336, 337,
        338-340, 347
    membership, 334-335
    organization, 336-341
    peacekeeping operations,
        337-338, 345
        in Bosnia, 346-347
        in Cambodia, 347, 349-350
        in Somalia, 158-159
    purposes of, 335-336
    Secretariat, 341
    Secretary-General, 341
    Security Council, 28, 200, 219, 262,
        331, 336, 337-338
    Resolutions on the Persian Gulf
        crisis, 94-97